Ireland

M. Guillot/MICHELIN

"Were such scenery lying upon English shores
it would be a world's wonder. If it were on the
Mediterranean or the Baltic, English travellers would
flock to it. Why not come to see it in Ireland ?"

William Makepeace Thackeray

Travel Publications

38 Clarendon Road – WATFORD Herts WD1 1SX - U.K.
☎ (01923) 415 000
www.michelin-travel.com
TheGreenGuide-uk@uk.michelin.com

Manufacture française des pneumatiques Michelin
Société en commandite par actions au capital de 2 000 000 000 de francs
Place des Carmes-Déchaux – 63 Clermont-Ferrand (France)
R.C.S. Clermont-Fd B 855 200 507

© Michelin et Cie, Propriétaires-éditeurs, 2000
Dépôt légal mai 2000 – ISBN 2-06-000023-8 – ISSN 0763-1383
Printed in France

Typesetting: Nord Compo, Villeneuve d'Ascq
Printing and binding : IFC, St-Germain du Puy

Cover design: Carré Noir, Paris 17ᵉ arr.

THE GREEN GUIDE:
The Spirit of Discovery

*The exhilaration of new horizons,
the fun of seeing the world,
the excitement of discovery: this
is what we seek to share with you.
To help you make the most of your
travel experience, we offer first-hand
knowledge and turn a discerning eye
on places to visit.
This wealth of information gives
you the expertise to plan your own
enriching adventure. With THE
GREEN GUIDE showing you the way,
you can explore new destinations
with confidence or rediscover old
ones.
Leisure time spent with THE GREEN
GUIDE is also a time for refreshing
your spirit and enjoying yourself.
So turn the page and open a window
on the world. Join THE GREEN
GUIDE in the spirit of discovery.*

Contents

Temple Finghin, Clonmacnoise

Dan Foley's Pub, Anascaul

Statue of Turlough O'Carolan, Mohill

SLIDEFILE, Dublin

Postbox near Skull, Co Cork

Pratt/Pres/DIAF

Maps
and Plans

COMPANION PUBLICATIONS

A map reference to the appropriate Michelin map is given for each chapter in the Sights section of this guide.

Michelin map 923 – Ireland:

Scale 1: 400 000 – 1cm = 4km – 1in: 6.30 miles - covers the Republic of Ireland and Northern Ireland, and the network of motorways and major roads. It provides information on shipping routes, distances in miles and kilometres, town plans of Dublin and Belfast, services, sporting and tourist attractions and an index of places; the key and text are printed in four languages.

Michelin Tourist and Motoring Atlas Great Britain & Ireland:

Scale 1: 300 000 – 1cm = 3km – 1in: 4.75 miles (based on 1: 400 000) - covers the whole of the United Kingdom and the Republic of Ireland, the national networks of motorways and major roads. It provides information on route planning, shipping routes, distances in miles and kilometres, over 60 town plans, services and sporting and tourist attractions and an index of places; the key and text are printed in six languages.

Michelin map 986 – Great Britain and Ireland:

Scale 1: 1 000 000 – 1cm = 10km – 1inch: 15.8 miles - covers the whole of the United Kingdom and the Republic of Ireland, the national networks of motorways and major roads. It provides information on shipping routes, distances in miles and kilometres, a list of Unitary Authorities for Wales and Scotland; the key and text are printed in four languages.

Internet:

Users can access personalised route plans, Michelin mapping on line, addresses of hotels and restaurants listed in The Red Guides and practical and tourist information through the internet:

www.michelin-travel.com

LIST OF MAPS AND PLANS

Town plans

Republic of Ireland

Northern Ireland

Plans of monuments

Republic of Ireland

Northern Ireland

Local maps

Republic of Ireland

Northern Ireland

Using this Guide

- The summary maps on pages 12–23 are designed to assist at the planning stage: the **Map of Principal Sights** identifies the major attractions according to their star ratings; the **Map of Touring Programmes** outlines regional motoring itineraries; the **Map of Activities** shows a range of leisure and sporting activities and several categories of places to stay.

- The **Practical Information** section provides useful travel advice, addresses, services, information on recreational facilities, a calendar of events and bibliography.

- It is worth reading the **Introduction** before setting out as it gives background information on history, the arts and traditional culture.

- The main natural and cultural attractions are presented in alphabetical order in the **Sights** section; excursions are attached to many of the town chapters. Place names often have two versions – the English and the Irish; the official version has been adopted in this guide.

- The clock symbol ⊘ placed after the name of a sight refers to the Admission times and charges chapter.

- This guide is designed to be used in conjunction with the Michelin road **Map 923** (Ireland), **Map 986** (Great Britain and Ireland) and the Michelin **Atlas Great Britain and Ireland**. Cross references appear under the chapter headings.

- For a selection of hotels and restaurants, consult the **Northern Ireland and Republic of Ireland** sections in the **Michelin Red Guide Great Britain and Ireland**, which also contains town plans.

- To find a particular place or historic figure or event or practical information, consult the **Index**.

- We greatly appreciate comments and suggestions from our readers. Contact us at

Michelin Travel Publications,
38 Clarendon Road, Watford WD1 1SX, UK
Tel 01923 415 000
Fax 01923 415 250
thegreenguide-uk@uk.michelin.com
www.michelin-travel.com

Crown Liquor Saloon, Belfast

Key

★★★ **Worth a journey**

★★ **Worth a detour**

★ **Interesting**

Tourism

⊙	Admission Times and Charges listed at the end of the guide	►►	Visit if time permits
●	Sightseeing route with departure point indicated	AZ B	Map co-ordinates locating sights
🛉🛉🛉🛉	Ecclesiastical building	🛈	Tourist information
	Synagogue – Mosque	⚞ ⋰	Historic house, castle – Ruins
	Building (with main entrance)	⌣ ☼	Dam – Factory or power station
■	Statue, small building	☆ ⌓	Fort – Cave
ⱡ	Wayside cross	⛏	Prehistoric site
◎	Fountain	▼ 𝗪	Viewing table – View
●■►	Fortified walls – Tower – Gate	▲	Miscellaneous sight

Recreation

🐎	Racecourse	🏃	Waymarked footpath
⛸	Skating rink	♦	Outdoor leisure park/centre
≋	Outdoor, indoor swimming pool		Theme/Amusement park
⛵	Marina, moorings		Wildlife/Safari park, zoo
🏠	Mountain refuge hut	✤	Gardens, park, arboretum
	Overhead cable-car		
🚂	Tourist or steam railway		Aviary, bird sanctuary

Additional symbols

	Motorway (unclassified)	✉ ⊙	Post office – Telephone centre
❶ ❶	Junction: complete, limited	✉	Covered market
	Pedestrian street	·ˣ·	Barracks
	Unsuitable for traffic, street subject to restrictions	△	Swing bridge
	Steps – Footpath	⌣ ✗	Quarry – Mine
🚆 🚌	Railway – Coach station	B F	Ferry (river and lake crossings)
	Funicular – Rack-railway		Ferry services: Passengers and cars
	Tram – Metro, Underground	⟶	Foot passengers only
Bert (R.)...	Main shopping street	③	Access route number common to MICHELIN maps and town plans

Abbreviations and special symbols

C	County council offices	U	University
H	Town hall		
J	Law courts	M3	Motorway
M	Museum	A2	Primary route
POL.	Police		Forest, Country Park, National Park
T	Theatre		

Principal Sights

Worth a journey ★★★
Worth a detour ★★
Interesting ★

The names of towns or sights described
in the guide appear in black on the maps.
See the index for the page number.

De	in Deutsch
En	in English
Es	en Español
Fr	en Français
It	in Italiano
Ne	in het Nederlands
Po	em Português

0	20	40 miles
0	30	60 km

NORTH CHANNEL

Scotland
De / En
Es / Fr
It / Ne

JURA

ISLAY

Port Ellen

KINTYRE

Campbeltown

Carrick-a-rede Bridge

MURLOUGH BAY

Glenoe Waterfall

Ulster Folk and
Transport Museum

Bangor

GIANT'S CAUSEWAY

Dunluce

Rathlin I

Ballycastle

Cushendall

Glendun

ANTRIM GLENS

Glenariff

Larne

A2

Carrickfergus

BELFAST

Antrim

M2

M22

A26

Lough Neagh

Ardboe

Portrush

Portstewart

Downhill

Coleraine

Gortmore

Roe
Valley

Londonderry

A2

Bann

Glenshane Pass

Springhill

Wellbrook Mill

NORTHERN IRELAND

Ulster History
Park

Beaghmore

Parkanaur

A5

Malin Head

Lag Sand Dunes

Moville

Gap of Mamore

Inishowen
Peninsula

Magilligan
Strand

Grianán
of Aileach

Mourne

Sperrin Mountains

Rosguill
Peninsula

Horn Head

Doe

Knockalla

R 245

R 246

Rathmelton

Letterkenny

Gweebarra Estuary

The Rosses

Glenveagh
National Park

Donegal Glens

N 56

Ulster-American
Folk Park

Castle Archdale

White I

Tully

Janus Figure

Lough Erne

CLIFFS
OF MAGHO

OCEAN

ATLANTIC

Donegal Coast

Naran

R 263

Glencolumbkille

Trabane Strand

Cliffs of Bunglass

Glengesh Pass

Rossnowlagh Strand

Donegal

Creevykeel

Céide Fields

Downpatrick Head

Broad Haven

Touring Programmes

Leinster : 430 miles - 690 km
(10 days including 2 days in Dublin)

Munster : 720 miles - 1160 km
(10 days including 1 day in Cork)

Connaught : 530 miles - 850 km
(9 days)

Ulster : 790 miles - 1270 km
(16 days including 1 day in Belfast)

Northern Ireland : 530 miles - 850 km
(13 days including 1 day in Belfast)

Overnight Stop

Ring of Beara ★ Name under which a route is described
See the index for the page number

0   20   40 miles
0   30   60 km

Jaunting Cars at Muckross

Practical Information

Planning your Trip

Tourist Information – For information, brochures, maps and assistance in planning a trip to Ireland apply to –

– **Irish Tourist Board** (Bord Fáilte) – www.ireland.travel.ie
Baggot Street Bridge, Dublin 2. ☎ 01850 230 330; Fax 066 979 2035 (callers within Republic of Ireland only)
53 Castle Street, Belfast BT1 1GH. ☎ 028 9032 7888; Fax 028 9024 0201;
44 Foyle Street, Londonderry. ☎/Fax 028 7136 9501; – *For addresses abroad see below.*
– **Northern Ireland Tourist Board** (NITB) – www.discovernorthernireland.com
St Anne Court, 59 North Street, Belfast BT1 1NB. ☎ 028 9024 6609; Fax 028 240 960; infog@nitb.com; – *For addresses abroad see below.*
– The Republic of Ireland government – www.irlgov.ie
– The *Irish Times* newspaper – www.ireland.com

Tourist Information Centres – The addresses and telephone numbers of the Tourist Information Centres to be found in most large towns and many tourist resorts in Ireland are printed in the Admission Times and Charges; some are open only during the summer months. The centres can supply town plans, timetables and information on sightseeing, local entertainment and sports facilities. Many have bureau de change facilities.

Climate – The best time of year to visit Ireland is in the summer; the sunniest months are May and June, the warmest are July and August. The southeast enjoys the most sun and the east coast is drier than the west.

Time – In winter standard time throughout Ireland is Greenwich Mean Time (GMT). In summer (mid March to October) clocks are advanced by one hour to give British Summer Time (BST), which is the same as Central European Time.
Time may be expressed according to the 24-hour clock or the 12-hour clock:

12.00	12 midday	19.00	7pm
13.00	1pm	20.00	8pm
14.00	2pm	21.00	9pm
15.00	3pm	22.00	10pm
16.00	4pm	23.00	11pm
17.00	5pm	24.00	12 midnight
18.00	6pm		

Public and Bank Holidays – On such holidays shops, museums and other monuments may be closed or may vary their times of admission.
In the Republic of Ireland national museums and art galleries are usually closed on Mondays. In addition to the usual school holidays at Christmas and in the spring and summer, there are mid-term breaks at Hallowe'en and around St Patrick's Day (17 March).

> 1 January
> 17 March (St Patrick's Day) (Republic only)
> Monday nearest 17 March (Northern Ireland only)
> Good Friday (Republic only)
> Easter Monday
> Monday nearest 1 May (Northern Ireland only)
> Last Monday in May (Northern Ireland only)
> First Monday in June (Republic only)
> 12 July (Northern Ireland only)
> First Monday in August (Republic only)
> Last Monday in August (Northern Ireland only)
> Last Monday in October (Republic only)
> 25 December
> 26 December (St Stephen's Day/Boxing Day)

Passport – Visitors entering Ireland must be in possession of a valid national passport (except British nationals). In case of loss or theft report to the appropriate embassy and the local police.

Visa – Visitors who require an **entry visa** for the Republic of Ireland or Northern Ireland should apply at least three weeks in advance to the Irish Embassy *(see below)* or the United Kingdom Embassy.
The booklets *Your Trip Abroad* (US$1.25) and *Safe Trip Abroad* (US$1.50), published by the US Government Printing Office, provide useful information for US nationals on visa requirements, customs regulations, medical care etc for international travel; available by telephone ☎ 1-202-512-1800 and via the Internet on website www.access.gpo.gov

Medical Treatment – Visitors from EU countries should apply to their own National Social Security Offices for **Form E111** (not obligatory for UK nationals; proof of identity only necessary) which entitles them to medical treatment under an EU Reciprocal Medical Treatment arrangement, provided treatment is sought from a doctor in Ireland whose name is on the Health Board Panel of Doctors (list available from the local health board). Nationals of non-EU countries should take out comprehensive insurance.

Customs Regulations – Tax-free allowances for various commodities are governed by EU legislation. Details of these allowances are available at most ports of entry to Ireland and the UK, and from customs authorities. It is against the law to bring into the United Kingdom drugs, firearms and ammunition, obscene material featuring children, counterfeit merchandise, unlicensed livestock (birds or animals), anything related to endangered species (furs, ivory, horn, leather) and certain plants (potatoes, bulbs, seeds, trees).
The booklet *Know before you go*, containing useful information for US nationals returning to the US after travelling abroad, is published by the US Customs Service (whose offices are listed in the phone book in the Federal Government section under the US Department of the Treasury) and can be obtained by consulting website www.customs.ustreas.gov

    Customs and Excise, Dublin Airport, ☏ 01 844 5538.

    HM Customs and Excise, Dorset House, Stamford Street, London SE1 9PY. ☏ 020 7620 1313 (HQ); 020 7928 3344 (switchboard); 020 7202 4227 (Advice Centre).

Domestic Animals – No animals, pets or other, may be brought into the Republic of Ireland, except from the United Kingdom. Domestic animals (dogs, cats) with vaccination documents are allowed into the United Kingdom.

Tourism for the Disabled – Some of the sights described in this guide are accessible to disabled people *(see Admission times and charges at the end of the guide)*. The **Michelin Red Guide Great Britain and Ireland** indicates hotels with facilities suitable for disabled people. Information on tourism, accommodation, transport and activity centres is available from several organisations:

    Irish Wheelchair Association, Blackheath Drive, Clontarf, Dublin 3, ☏ 01 818 6400; Fax 01 833 3873; info@iwa.ie; www.iwa.ie

    Comhairle, 44 North Great George's Street, Dublin 1, ☏ 01 874 7503; Fax 01 764 7490.

    Disability Action, Portside Business Park, 189 Airport Road West, Belfast BT3 9AD, ☏ 028 9049 1011; Fax 028 9029 7881; Text phone 028 9029 7882; hq@disabilityaction. org; www.disabilityaction.org

Irish Tourist Board – The offices of the **Irish Tourist Board** (Bord Fáilte) situated in certain countries are listed here below.

Australia – 5th Level, 36 Carrington Street, Sydney, NSW 2000. ☏ 029 299 6177, 02 275 0171; Fax 029 299 6323.

Belgium – Avenue Louise 327, 1050 Brussels. ☏ 02 6432 121; Fax 02 6429 051.

Canada – Callers from Canada should telephone the New York office on ☏ 1800 223 6470.

Denmark – Klostergarden, Amagertorv 29,3, 1160 København K. ☏ 33 15 80 45; Fax 33 93 63 90.

Finland – Irlannin Matkailutoimisto, Embassy of Ireland, Erottajankatu 7A, 00130 Helsinki. ☏ 09 60 89 66; Fax 09 64 60 22.

France – 33 rue de Miromesnil, 75008 Paris. ☏/Fax 01 70 20 00 20.

Germany – Untermainanlage 7, D-60329 Frankfurt/Main. ☏ 069 92 31 85 50; Fax 069 92 31 85 88.

Japan – Ireland House 5F, 2-10-7 Kojimachi, Chiyodi-ku, Tokyo 102. ☏ 03 52 75 16 11; Fax 03 52 75 16 23.

Netherlands – Spuistraat 104, 1012 VA Amsterdam. ☏ 020 62 23 101; Fax 020 62 08 089.

Norway – Drammensveien 126A, PB 295 Skøyen, 0212 Oslo. ☏ 22 56 33 10; Fax 22 12 20 70.

Spain – Paseo de la Castellana 46.3, 28046 Madrid. ☏ 91 57 71 787; Fax 91 57 76 934.

Sweden – Sibyliegatan 49, PO Box5292, 10246 Stockholm. ☏ 08 66 28 510; Fax 08 66 17 595.

United Kingdom – All Ireland Information Desk, **Britain Visitor Centre**, 1 Regent Street, London SW1Y 4XT (personal callers and written enquiries only). ☏ 020 8846 9000 (British Tourist Authority).
150 New-Bond Street, London WIY 0AQ *(no callers)*. ☏ 020 7493 3201; Fax 020 7493 9065.

United States – 345 Park Avenue, New York, NY 10154. ☏ 212 418 0800; ☏ 1800 223 6470 (information line); Fax 212 379 9052.

Northern Ireland Tourist Board – The offices of the **Northern Ireland Tourist Board** (NITB) situated in the following countries are listed below.

Ireland – 16 Nassau Street, Dublin 2. ☎ 01 679 1977; Fax 01 679 1863.

Europe – Fur Fremdenverkehr, Westendstr 16-22, D-60325, Frankfurt, Germany. ☎ 069 23 45 04; Fax 069 23 34 80.

North America – 551 5th Avenue, Suite 701, New York, NY 10176. ☎ 212 922-0101; Fax 212 922-0099.

United Kingdom – All Ireland Information Desk, **Britain Visitor Centre**, 1 Regent Street, London SW1Y 4XT (personal callers and written enquiries only. ☎ 020 8846 9000 (British Tourist Authority).
24 Haymarket, London SW1Y 4DG. ☎ 08701 555 250 (info line); Fax 020 7766 9929.

Regional Tourism Organizations –

Cork/Kerry Tourism – Grand Parade, Cork. ☎ 021 427 3251; Fax 021 427 3504; user@cktourism.ie

Dublin Tourism – *See p 169.*

Ireland West Tourism – Aras Fáilte, Victoria Place, Eyre Square, Galway. ☎ 091 563 081; Fax 091 565 201; user@irelandwest.ie

Midlands East Tourism – Market House, Mullingar, Co Westmeath. ☎ 044 48650; Fax 044 40413; midlandseasttourismm@tinet.ie; www.midlandseastireland.travel.ie

North West Tourism – Aras Reddan, Temple Street, Sligo. ☎ 071 61201; Fax 071 60360; irelandnorthwest@tinet.ie; www.ireland-northwest.trave.ie

South East Tourism – 41 TheQuay, Waterford. ☎ 051 875 823; Fax 051 877 388.

Shannon Development – Arthur's Quay, Limerick, Co Limerick. ☎ 061 317 522; Fax 061 317 939.

Foreign Embassies and Consulates –

Australia – Fitzwilton House (2nd floor), Wilton Terrace, Dublin 2. ☎ 01 676 1517, Fax 01 678 5185; austremb.dublin@dfatgov.au; www.ausatralianembassy.ie

Canada – Canada House, 65 St Stephen's Green, Dublin 2. ☎ 01 478 1988, Fax 01 478 1285; cndembsy@iol.ie

New Zealand – 37 Leeson Park, Dublin 6. ☎ 01 660 4233, Fax 01 660 4228; nzconsul@indigo.ie

United Kingdom – 29 Merrion Road, Ballsbridge, Dublin 4. ☎ 01 205 3700, Fax 01 205 3885; bembassy@internet-ireland.ie; visas@dulin.mail.fco.gov.uk; www.britishembassy.ie
USA – 42 Elgin Road, Ballsbridge, Dublin 4. ☎ 01 668 8777, Fax 01 668 9946; www.usembassy.ie

Irish Embassies Abroad –

Australia – Lever 30, 400 York Street, Sydney, NSW 2000, Australia. ☎ 02 9231 6999.

Australia – 20 Arkana Street, Yarralumla, Canberra, ACT 2600, Australia. ☎ 02 733 022; Fax 02 733 741.

Belgium – 89/93 Rue Froissart, B-1040 Brussels. ☎ (02) 23 05 337; Fax (02) 23 05 360.

Canada – Suite 1105, 130 Albert Street, Ottawa, Ontario KIP 5G4. ☎ 613 233 6281; Fax 613 233 5835.

Denmark – Østbanegade 21, I TH.DK-2100 Copenhagen. ☎ 031 42 32 23; Fax 035 43 18 58.

Finland – Erottajankatu 7A, 00130 Helsinki. ☎ (09) 646 0 06; Fax (09) 646 022.

France – 12 Avenue Foch, 75116 Paris. ☎ 01 44 17 67 00; Fax 01 44 17 67 60.

Germany – Godesberger Allee 119, 53175 Bonn. ☎ (0228) 95 92 90; Fax (0228) 37 35 00.

Japan – Ireland House 5F, 2-10-7 Kojimachi, Chiyoda-Ku, Tokyo 102. ☎ (03) 32 63 06 95; Fax (03) 32 65 22 75.

Netherlands – Dr Kuyperstraat 9, 2514-BA The Hague. ☎ (070) 3630993, 363 0994; Fax (070) 361 7604.

Portugal – Rua da Imprensa, a Estrela 1-4, 1200 Lisbon. ☎ (01) 39 29 440; Fax (01) 39 77 363.

Spain – Ireland House, Paseo de la Castellana 46-4, 28046 Madrid. ☎ (091) 57 63 500; Fax (091) 43 51 677.

Sweden – Ostermalmsgatan 97, PO Box 10326, 100 55, Stockholm. ☎ 08 66 18 005; Fax 08 66 01 353.

United Kingdom – 17 Grosvenor Place, London SW1X 7HR. ☎ 020 7235 2171; Fax 020 7245 6961.

United States – 2234 Massachusetts Avenue NW, Washington DC 20008. ☎ 202 462 3939, 462 3940; Fax 202 232 5993.

Getting there

By Air – Many international airlines operate flights to the international airports in Ireland – Dublin, Shannon, Knock and Belfast. There are also flights from the UK to the regional airports and a shuttle service from Heathrow to Belfast. All airports are linked by bus to the neighbouring towns.

Information, brochures and timetables are available from the airlines and from travel agents. Fly-Drive schemes are operated by most airlines.

Aer Lingus – www.aerlingus.ie
☏ 0645 737 747 (from within the UK)
40–41 Upper O'Connell Street, Dublin 1
13 St Stephen's Green, Dublin 2
Jury's Hotel, Ballsbridge
12 Upper George's Street, Dun Laoghaire

Ryanair – www.ryanair.com
☏ 0541 569 569
☏ 00 353 94 67222 (Knock International Airport, Co Mayo)

British Airways – www.britishairways.com
Reservations ☏ 0845 77 333 77
UK sales office ☏ 00 44 141 222 2345 (from outside the UK)
UK sales office ☏ 0345 222 111 (from within the UK)
Reservations Dublin ☏ 1800 626 747 (Open daily 6am-10.15pm (5.15pm Sat; 2.15pm Sun)

British Regional Air – Book through British Airways

British Midland – www.britishmidland.com
☏ 0345 554 554 (reservations)
☏ 00 44 1332 854 854 (from outside the UK)
☏ 0870 607 0555

British European – www.british-european.com
☏ 08705 676 676 (to Dublin, Cork, Shannon and Belfast from London City, London Gatwick and London Stansted)

Manx Airlines – www.manx-airlines.com
☏ 08457 256 256; Fax 0151 448 0599 (Liverpool); Fax 01624 826 151 (Isle of Man) (to Dublin from Manchester and the Isle of Man)

Easyjet – www.easyjet.com
☏ 0870 600 0000 (London-Belfast)

By Sea – Details of passenger ferry and car ferry services to Ireland from the United Kingdom and France can be obtained from travel agencies or from the main carriers. Information about ferries to the offshore islands is given in the Admission times and charges *(at the end of the guide)*.

Brittany Ferries – www.brittany-ferries.com
The Brittany Centre, Wharf Road, Portsmouth, Hants PO2 8RU. ☏ 0990 360 360 (from within UK); Fax 01705 873 237;
Millbay Docks, Plymouth, Devon. PL1 3^{E}W ☏ 0990 360 360;
Tourist House, 42 Grand Parade, Cork ☏ 021 4277 801; Fax 021 4277 262.

Irish Ferries – www.irishferries.ie
2-4 Merrion Row, Dublin 2; ☏ 00 353 1 638 3333 (reservations).
Ferryport, Alexandra Road, Dublin 1, ☏ 01 855 2222 (Head Office);
Rosslare Harbour ☏ 00 353 53 33158
Bridge Street, Cork ☏ 00 353 21 455 1995
Reliance House, Water Street, Liverpool L2 8TP ☏ 0990 17 17 17 (reservations - from within UK).

Stena Line – www.stenaline.co.uk
Charter House, Park Street, Ashford, Kent TN 24 8^{E}X ☏ 0990 70 70 70; Fax 01233 202 231
Passenger Terminal, Corry Road, Belfast BT3 9SS ☏ 028 9074 8748 (Stranraer–Belfast; Liverpool-Belfast)
Ferry Terminal, Dún Laoghaire, Co Dublin ☏ 00 353 1204 7777 (Holyhead–Dublin, Holyhead-Dún Laoghaire, Fishguard–Rosslare)

P&O – www.poirishsea.com
Larne Harbour, Larne BT40 1AQ ☏ 0870 242 4777 (Cairnryan–Larne); Fax 028 2887 2195

Seacat – www.steam-packet.com
Seacat Terminal, Donegal Quay, Belfast BT1 3AL ☏ 0990 523 523; Fax 028 9031 4918 (Troon Belfast, Heysham-Belfast; Liverpool-Dublin)

Swansea Cork Ferries – www.swansea-cork.ie
Harbour Office, Kings Dock, Swansea SA1 1SF; ☏ 01792 456 116; Fax 01792 644 356; scf@iol.ie

By Rail – Irish Rail Service (Iarnród Éireann), Northern Ireland Railways and British Rail operate train services between the major cities in Ireland and the United Kingdom.

Irish Rail – www.irishrail.ie; www.cie.ie; www.cietours.ie (coach tours and fly drive in Ireland, Britain and Europe); www.railtours.ie (day excursions by rail)

Irish Rail Mobility Impaired Liaison Officer ☎ 01 703 2634

Travel Centre, 35 Lower Abbey Street, Dublin 1, ☎ 01 836 6222; ☎ 1850 366 222 (info line); ☎ 01 703 3592 (Customer Services); Fax 01 703 4690

Connolly Station, Dublin 1, ☎ 01 703 2613 (Inter-City Customer Services); 01 836 3333 (enquiries), Fax 01 836 4760.

Heuston Station, Dublin 8, ☎ 01 677 1871 (enquiries), Fax 01 677 1350.

Pearse Station, Westland Road, Dublin 2, ☎ 01 703 3592 (Suburban Rail Customer Services); 01 703 3634 (booking office).

Talking timetables: 01 854 299 Dublin to Ballina
                                      01 8054 200 / 021 504 544 Dublin to Cork
                                      01 8054 211 / 061 41 33 55Dublin to Limerick
                                      01 8054 222 Dublin to Galway
                                      01 8054 233 Dublin to Waterford
                                      01 8054 255 Dublin to Sligo
                                      01 8054 266 Dublin to Killarney and Tralee
                                      01 8054 277 Dublin to Belfast
                                      01 8054 244 Dublin to Westport
                                      01 8054 288 Dublin to Wexford and Rosslare

Dublin Area Rapid Transit (DART) – *See p 170.*

Northern Ireland Rail, www.translink.co.uk

Central Station, Belfast BT1 3PB, ☎ 028 9089 9400; 028 9089 9411 (enquiries); Fax 028 9035 4090l feedback@translink.co.uk

Concessionary Fares – Special Rover, Explorer and Emerald Card tickets are available, which enable passengers to travel throughout Ireland, by rail only or by rail and bus; price according to the duration of the ticket.

Student Travelsave, enabling students with an International Student Card to obtain 50% reduction on Irish Rail and 30% reduction on Bus Éireann, available from **USIT**, 19–21 Aston Quay, Dublin, ☎ 01 679 8833; Fax 01 602 1617; www.usitnow.ie

Eurorail Pass, **Flexipass** and **Saver Pass** are options available in the US for travel in Europe and must be purchased in the US, ☎ 212 308 3103; ☎ 1-800-4ᴱURAIL, 1-888-BRITRAIL and 1-888-EUROSTAR (automated lines for callers within the US only); www.raileurope.com/us

By Coach – **Bus Éireann**, **Ulsterbus** and **National Express** operate a regular coach service via the car ferry ports at Rosslare, Dublin Ferryport and Larne between the major Irish towns and the major cities in the UK and on the Continent.

Bus Éireann – www.buseireann.ie

Store Street, Dublin 1. ☎ 01 836 6111, 01 830 2222; Fax 01 873 4534.

Dublin Bus – www.dublinbus.ie (*see also p 170*)

Ulsterbus – www.translink.co.uk

Europa Bus Centre, Glengall Street, Belfast BT12 5AH. ☎ 028 9033 3000 (enquiries), 028 9032 0011 (bus station)

Eurolines – www.eurolines.com

Store Street, Dublin 1. ☎ 01 836 6111 (Bus Eireann)

52 Grosvenor Gardens, London SW1W OAU. ☎ 020 7730 8235; 0990 143 219 (in London), 0990 808080 (outside London)

National Express – www.gobycoach.com

Birmingham; ☎ 08705 808 080 (National call centre); ☎ 0121 625 1122; Fax 0121 456 1397 (Head Office)

Concessionary Fares – Special Rambler, Rover, Explorer and Emerald Card tickets are available, which enable passengers to travel throughout Ireland, by rail only or by rail and bus; price according to the duration of the ticket – *see also above By Rail.*

Motoring in Ireland

Documents – Nationals of EU countries require a valid national driving licence; nationals of non-EU countries require an **international driving licence**. This is obtainable in the US for US$10 from the National Auto Club, Touring Department, 188 The Embarcadero, Suite 300, San Francisco CA 94105 or from the local branch of the American Automobile Association for US$12 (non-members), US$6 (basic members), free (plus member). ☎ 800 222 4537.

For the vehicle it is necessary to have the **registration papers** (log-book) and a **nationality plate** of the approved size.

Insurance – Insurance cover is compulsory. Although no longer a legal requirement, the International Insurance Certificate (Green Card) is the most effective proof of insurance cover and is internationally recognised by the police and other authorities.

Certain motoring organisations in Ireland and the UK run accident insurance and breakdown service schemes for members. Members of the American Automobile Club should obtain the brochure *Offices to serve you abroad.*

Automobile Association (AA) – www.theaa.co.uk
23 Suffolk Street, Dublin 2, ☎ 01 283 3555
Fanum House, Basing View, Basingstoke, Hants, RG21 4EA,
☎ 0990 448 866 (switchboard), 0800 444 999 (joining & membership renewal)

Royal Automobile Club (RAC) – www.rac.co.uk
New Mount House, 22–24 Lower Mount Street, Dublin 2, ☎ 01 676 0113.
RAC House, 1 Forest Road, Feltham, TW13 7RR.
☎ 020 8917 2500 (Head Office), 0906 834 7333 (travel information); ☎ 0990 722 722 (Customer Services); Fax 020 8917 2525

Europ-Assistance – www.europ-assistance.com
IDA Business Park Athlumney, Navan, Co Meath. ☎ 046 77333; 046 74396
Sussex House, Perrymount Road, Haywards Heath, West Sussex, RH16 1DN,
☎ 01444 442 442 (Customer Services); Fax 01444 441 527; marketing@-europassistance.co.uk

Highway Code – The **minimum driving age** is 16 years old in the Republic of Ireland and 17 in Northern Ireland. Traffic drives on the **left**. Traffic on main roads and on roundabouts has priority.

Seat belts – The driver and front-seat passenger must wear seat belts. Rear-seat belts must be worn where they are fitted; children under 12 must travel in the rear seats.

Lights – Full or dipped headlights should be switched on in poor visibility and at night; use sidelights only when the vehicle is stationary in an area without street lighting.

Breakdown – It is obligatory to carry a red warning triangle or to have hazard warning lights to use in the case of a breakdown or accident.

Penalties – Drivers suspected of **speeding** or **driving while under the influence of alcohol** are liable to prosecution. Parking offences in the Republic may attract an on-the-spot fine.

Speed limits			
	Republic of Ireland	30mph/48kph	in built-up areas
		60mph/96kph	on country roads
		70mph/112kph	on motorways
	Northern Ireland:	30mph/48kph	in built-up areas
		60mph/96kph	on country roads
		70mph/112kph	on dual carriageways and motorways

Parking regulations – There are multi-storey car parks in towns, parking meters, disc systems and paying parking zones; in the last case, tickets must be obtained from the ticket machines (small change necessary) and displayed inside the windscreen; failure to display may result in a fine.

In Northern Ireland city centre parking may be restricted. Illegal parking is liable to fines and also in certain cases to the vehicle being clamped or towed away. The usual restrictions are as follows:

Double red line = no stopping at any time (freeway)
Double yellow line = no parking at any time
Single yellow line = no parking for set periods as indicated on panel
Dotted yellow line = parking limited to certain times only.

Petrol/Gas – In many service stations dual-pumps are the rule; **unleaded pumps** are identified by green pump handles or a green stripe.

Tolls – The only toll roads are the Dublin East-Link (65p), which spans the Liffey estuary, and the West-Link (80p), which runs north–south on the western edge of the city. ☎ 01 668 2888 (East-Link); 01 820 2000 (West-Link).

Route Planning – Michelin Map 923 Ireland and the Michelin Atlas Great Britain and Ireland show the major roads (N or A) and many of the minor roads (R/L or B).

Car Rental – There are car rental agencies at airports, railway stations and in all large towns throughout Ireland. European cars usually have manual transmission but automatic cars are available on request. An **international driving licence** is required for non-EU nationals. Many companies do not hire to drivers under 21 or 25.

Before crossing the border between the Republic and Northern Ireland it is important to check that the insurance cover extends to the other country. It is cheaper to return a hire car to its pick-up point than to leave it elsewhere.

Places to Stay

The Touring Programmes Map *(see p 15)* and the Activities Map *(see p 17)* indicate places to stay overnight and seaside resorts.

The **Michelin Red Guide Great Britain and Ireland** provides a selection of hotels, guesthouses and restaurants.

The Irish Tourist Board (Bord Fáilte) publishes several useful booklets:

Be Our Guest Guide, which gives a comprehensive listing of all approved hotels and guesthouses in Ireland;

Ireland's Blue Book of country houses and restaurants;

The Hidden Ireland, listing accommodation in private heritage houses;

Friendly Homes of Ireland, listing family homes and small hotels.

The Northern Irish Tourist Board (NITB) publishes

Where to stay (£3.99).

Accommodation Booking Service – A booking service is operated by Irish Regional Tourism Organisations and by Tourist Information Centres; a small fee is charged for the service and a proportion of the price is paid direct to the booking service and the balance to the proprietor.

Gulliver Call Centre ☎ 0800 783 5740; 00 800 6686 6866

Guesthouses – The properties vary from modern purpose-built premises to Georgian and Victorian houses.

Irish Guesthouse Owners' Association, Kathleen's Country House, Killarney, Co Kerry ☎ 064 32810; Fax 064 32340

Staying in an Irish Home – This option provides the opportunity to share in Irish family life.

Town and Country Homes Association, Belleek Road, Ballyshannon, Co Donegal ☎ 072 22222; Fax 072 22207; tchal@iol.ie; www.commerce.ie/towns_ and_country

Farmhouse Holidays – A booklet is available from the umbrella organisation.

Irish Farm Holidays, 2 Michael Street, Limerick, Co Limerick, ☎ 061 400 700, 400 707; Fax 061 400 771.

Self-Catering Holiday Homes – Information about accommodation to rent is available from Dublin Tourism and the NITB *(addresses above)* and the organising body.

Irish Cottages and Holiday Homes Association, 4 Whitefriars, Aungier Street, Dublin 2 ☎ 01 475 1932; Fax 01 475 5321; margaret@irishwelcometours.ie; www.ichh.ie

Low-Budget Accommodation – Simple accommodation is available in hostels (single, twin and 4/6-bedded rooms) at the following addresses:

Kinlay House, 2–12 Lord Edward Street, **Dublin 2**, ☎ 01 679 6644, Fax 01 679 7437; kinlay-dublin@usitworld.com (also in Cork and Galway)

Avalon House, 55 Aungier Street, Dublin, ☎ 01 475 0001; Fax 01 475 0303; info@avalon-house.ie; www.avalon-house.ie

Harding Hotel, Fishamble Street, Temple Bar, **Dublin 2**, ☎ 01 679 6500, Fax 01 679 6504 (also hostels in Cork and Galway)

Independent Holiday Hostels Ireland, 57 Lower Gardiner Street, Dublin 1 ☎ 01 836 4700; Fax 0 836 4710

Accommodation in **universities** (single rooms and self-catering apartments) is available during the vacations:

Usit Accommodation Centres, c/o UCD Village, Belfield, Dublin 4, ☎ 01 706 1071, Fax 01 269 1129; accommodation@usitworld.com; www.iol.ie/usitaccm

MUSA – Marketing University Summer Accommodation, Plassey Campus Centre, University of Limerick ☎ 061 202360; Fax 061 330316.

c/o Accommodation Office, Trinity College, Dublin 2, ☎ 01 608 1177, Fax 01 671 1267; reservations@tcd.ie; www.tcd.ie/accommodation

Youth Hostels – There are 50 **youth hostels** in the Republic and six in Northern Ireland. Package holidays are available comprising youth hostel vouchers, rail and bus pass or hostel vouchers, return rail fare and cycle hire:

An Oige, 61 Mountjoy Street, Dublin 7, ☎ 01 830 4555, Fax 01 830 5808; mailbox@anoige.ie; www.irelandyha.org

Hostelling International Northern Ireland, 22 Donegal Road, Belfast BT12 5JN, ☎ 028 9032 4733, Fax 028 9043 9699; info@hini.org.uk; www.hini.org.uk

Horse-drawn caravans, Co Kerry

Camping – Ireland has many officially graded caravan and camping parks with modern facilities and a variety of additional sports facilities.

A brochure *Where to Stay* (£3.99), published by the NITB, lists camping and caravan parks in Northern Ireland only.

A brochure (IR£2), which covers the whole country, is available from:

Irish Caravan & Camping Council, PO Box 4443, Dublin 2; Fax 098 28237 (to request brochures); info@camping-ireland.ie; www.camping-ireland.ie

Horse-Drawn Caravans – The caravan provides accommodation as well as a leisurely way of exploring the Irish country roads:

Slattery's Horse-drawn Caravans, 1 Russell Street, Tralee, Co Kerry; ☎ 066 26277; Fax 066 25981.

Mayo Horsedrawn Caravan Holidays Ltd, Belcarra, Castlebar ☎ 094 32054.

Cruising – *Cruising Ireland*, published by the Irish Tourist Board, provides information on hiring cruisers on rivers, lakes and canals, holiday cruises and short pleasure cruises on the Shannon, barge or waterbus cruises and cruising restaurants. It is recommended that boat operators be members of the Irish Boat Rental Association (IBRA).

The Inland Waterways Association publishes a guide to the *Grand Canal*. Details of annual waterway rallies and festivals are also available from Tourist Information Centres.

Skelan Lock, Shannon–Erne Waterway

The main waterways for cruising are the River Shannon, the Shannon–Erne Waterway and Lough Erne; canal barges are more suited to the River Barrow, the Grand Canal and the River Shannon. Short day-time canal or river trips are mentioned in the appropriate chapters.

Irish Boat Rental Association, 2 Granville Road, Blackrock, Co Dublin Fax 01 289 7430.

Sailing Holidays in Ireland, c/o Trident Hotel Marina, Kinsale, Co Cork; ☎ 021 772 067; Fax 021 774 170 – for yacht charter.

Activity Holidays – The Irish Tourist Board provides information on a range of holidays on the following themes – cruising, horse racing, cycling, golf, walking, gardens, cookery and summer schools of many kinds such as learning the Irish language.

Services

Currency – The currency is the *punt* (IR£1 = 100 pence) in the Republic of Ireland and Sterling (£1 = 100 pence) in Northern Ireland.
In the Republic the euro can be used for non-cash transactions; Irish pound notes and coins will remain in circulation until 1 Jan 2002.
There is no limit on the amount of currency visitors can import into the Republic of Ireland; as there is a limit on the amount that may be exported in Irish currency and in foreign bank notes, non-residents are advised to complete a currency declaration form on arrival.

Banking – Banks are open Mondays to Fridays (except public holidays), 10am–12.30pm and 1.30–3pm (3.30pm in Northern Ireland).
Exchange facilities outside these hours are available at Belfast, Dublin, Shannon, Connaught and Cork Airports, in some tourist information centres, travel agencies and hotels.
Some form of identification is necessary when cashing travellers' cheques or Eurocheques in banks. Commission charges vary; hotels usually charge more than banks.

Credit Cards – The major credit cards – American Express, Visa/Barclaycard (Carte Bleue), Eurocard (Mastercard/Access) and Diners Club – are widely accepted in shops, hotels, restaurants and petrol stations.

Post – Irish postage stamps must be used in the Republic, British stamps in Northern Ireland; they are available from Post Offices and some shops (newsagents, tobacconists etc).
In the Republic post offices are open Mondays to Saturdays, 8am–5pm or 5.30pm; they are closed on Sundays and public holidays and for 1hr 15min at lunchtime; sub-post offices usually close at 1pm one day a week. In Northern Ireland post offices are open Mondays to Fridays, 9am–5.30pm, and Saturdays, 9am–12.30pm; sub-post offices close at 1pm on Wednesdays.

Telephone – In an **emergency** phone **999** – fire, police, ambulance, lifeboats, coastal, mountain and cave rescue.
Mobile telephones can be brought into Ireland.
The telephone service in the Republic of Ireland is organised by Eircom – www.eircom.ie
Pre-paid callcards for internal and international calls from public phones are available from post offices and some shops (newsagents, tobacconists etc). Card phones are cheaper than pay phones.
It is usually more expensive to make a long-distance telephone call from a hotel than from a telephone box.
To make an **international call** dial 00 followed by the country code, followed by the area code (without the initial 0), followed by the subscriber's number. The codes for direct dialling to other countries are printed at the front of telephone directories and in code books.

00 61	Australia
00 1	Canada
00 353	Republic of Ireland
00 64	New Zealand
00 44	United Kingdom (including Northern Ireland)
00 1	United States of America

When dialling from the Republic to Northern Ireland, dial 080 followed by the subscriber's number.

Electricity – The electric current is 230 volts AC (50 hertz); 3-pin flat or 2-pin round wall sockets are standard.

Shopping and Crafts

Opening Times – Shops in the major cities are open Mondays to Saturdays, 9am–5.30pm (8pm Thursdays). Elsewhere there is all-day or early closing on Mondays or Wednesdays or Thursdays. Some shops may open later and may close for an hour at lunchtime.

Craft Shops and Studios – Ireland produces not only certain articles which have an international reputation, such as **Waterford Crystal** or **Donegal Tweed**, but also many less well-known hand-made articles created by small enterprises.

Manufacturers of textiles, glass and porcelain usually offer a tour of the factory and have showrooms and shops on the premises; their goods are often available in department stores or specialist shops in the major towns.

Some craft workers, such as weavers in Donegal, are grouped in certain regions. Others congregate in the special **craft villages**, set up by the Government, such as those in Dingle, Donegal town, Blennerville near Tralee or Roundstone in Connemara. The **Kilkenny Design Centre**, set up in the early 1960s, infused new life into domestic and industrial design in Ireland.

Some Folk Museums and Folk Villages organise demonstrations of obsolete crafts.

The *Linen Homelands Tour* visits the **Irish Linen Centre** as well as various linen manufacturers in and around Lisburn *(see p 346)*.

Glass – The most famous and oldest glass factory in Ireland is in **Waterford**, but since its revival in 1951 several smaller enterprises have started to produce hand-blown lead crystal which is cut, engraved or undecorated – Cavan Crystal, Galway Crystal, Grange Crystal, Sligo Crystal, Tipperary Crystal, Tyrone Crystal. Most have factory shops where first- and second-quality pieces can be bought and many offer a guided tour of the workshops.

Knitwear – The thick cream-coloured (undyed) knitwear associated with the Aran Islands is the best known of Irish knitwear and is on sale throughout the country. Ireland produces a great variety of other knitted garments in a variety of textures and colours, particularly thick sweaters to keep out the wind and rain, using the traditional stitches – basket, blackberry, blanket, cable, diamond, moss, plait, trellis and zigzag.

Lace – In the 19C there were many lace-making centres in Ireland but few have survived. In most the skill was fostered by the nuns; the lacemakers of Clones and Carrickmacross have now formed themselves into cooperatives. Kenmare needlepoint lace is the most difficult to make; Clones is a crochet lace but the other centres produce "mixed lace" on a base of machine-made cotton net.

Irish Linen Centre

Linen hand-loom

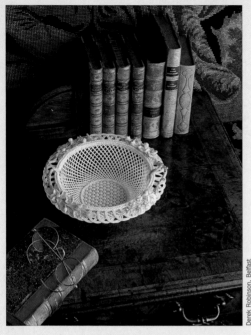
Belleek pottery

Linen – The demand for bed linen, table linen and tea towels keeps some 20 Irish linen houses in business. The popularity of linen as an apparel fabric has revived in recent years, since blending with synthetic or other natural fibres has reduced its tendency to crease. It is now used by top fashion designers all over the world who appreciate its sheen and texture, its durability and versatility – it is cool in summer and a good insulator in winter; it dyes well in bright clear colours.

Metalwork – Throughout the country, and especially in the craft villages, artists are working in gold, silver, bronze, pewter and enamel to produce dishes and plaques, necklaces, pendants and earrings; the traditional Claddagh rings *(see p 204)* worked in gold show a heart with two clasped hands.

Porcelain and Pottery – The largest porcelain factory is the one at **Belleek** which produces fine translucent Parian ware and specialises in woven basket pieces and naturalistic flower decoration. Similar wares are produced by Donegal Irish Parian china. The Irish Dresden factory *(see p 233)* preserves and develops the tradition of delicate ornamental porcelain figures which originated in Germany. There are many studio potteries in Ireland producing hand-turned articles, such as those in Connemara and the Stephen Pearce Pottery in Shanagarry.

Tweed – The term was first recognised late in the 19C to describe the hand-woven woollen cloth produced in Co Donegal. Donegal tweed is still the most well-known and is now produced, mostly on power looms, by four firms, in Ardara, Donegal Town, Downies and Kilcar. Three of these companies also employ out-workers using hand looms and most have diversified into the production of knitwear and ready-made garments or into weaving other natural fibres – linen, cotton and silk. The original tweeds were made from natural undyed wool – grey, brown or cream; as coloured wool was produced only in small quantities it was introduced as speckles when the wool was carded. The dyes used were obtained from plants, lichens, turf, soot and minerals.

Avoca Weavers *(see p 291)* were founded in 1723 and the Kerry Woollen Mills *(see p 226)* also date from the 18C. Foxford *(see p 239)* and Blarney *(see p 152)* were started in the 19C.

Woodwork – There are a number of craftsmen producing hand-turned articles such as bowls, lamp stands and ornaments; the unique pieces are the graceful and delightful carvings produced by artists from skeletal pieces of **bogwood**. Some wood-turners produce musical instruments such as pipes and drums *(bodhráns)*.

Bogwood

The extensive peat bogs of the Midlands – on the banks of the Shannon south and west of Longford and Athlone, as well as those in the north of Co Mayo – are being exploited by **Bord na Mona**, principally to generate electricity; narrow-gauge railway tracks carry wagons loaded with peat to the processing plant.

The tree roots uncovered by the great peat-harvesting machines are turned into beautiful and fascinating bogwood sculptures by Michael Casey, whose studio is at Barley Harbour on the east bank of Lough Ree. Several of his works stand in the attractive village of **Newtown Cashel**, which clusters round its green beside the church (1833).

Entertainment

Cultural Festivals – Ireland hosts a number of literary and musical festivals in honour of individual artists or groups of artists *(see p 37)*. Many are accompanied by bands and parades, horse races and regattas according to the region.

Theatres – Ireland has a lively theatrical scene with theatres in many provincial towns as well as Belfast and Dublin.

In Dublin modern and classic plays are performed at the **Abbey Theatre** and the **Gate Theatre**.

The traditional seasonal festivals and rural way of life are evoked in music, song, dance and mime in the performances of the **National Folk Theatre of Ireland** in Tralee *(see page 273)*, which draw on the local Gaelic tradition. Productions in the Irish language are put on by the Irish Theatre **(Taibhearc na Gaillimhe)** in Galway *(see page 204)*, which is a state-sponsored body.

Music – The **Wexford Festival Opera** *(late October)* has an international reputation and attracts a large cosmopolitan audience. At **Castle Ward Opera** *(June; see p 273)* the occasion is enhanced by the beauty of the venue, the grounds of a Georgian country house. Concerts of **chamber music** *(summer)* are given by Irish and international musicians in some of the great Irish houses; details available from the National Concert Hall in Dublin.

In Dublin the **National Concert Hall** (Earlsfort Terrace) has a regular programme of classical and modern orchestral music. Smaller venues offering more specialised music, such as jazz, blues etc, are to be found in Temple Bar *(see p 181)*.

In Belfast the **Waterfront Hall** offers a varied programme of events.

Traditional Music – In recent years traditional music has grown in importance. This sort of music is played at sessions in pubs, at a gathering known as a *céile* and at the weekly and monthly sessions held in the local branches of the national **cultural organisation** – Comhaltas Ceoltóirí Éireann, Cultúrlann na hÉireann, 32 Belgrave Square, Monkstown, Co Dublin, ✆ 01 280 0295. Information also available from Tourist Information Centres.

The most popular instruments are the violin – called the fiddle by traditional musicians – the flute, the goatskin drum *(bodhrán)* and the free-reed instruments such as the accordion, melodeon and concertina; and also more recently the guitar and banjo.

The harp is now rarely played but there are two harp festivals in Keadew *(July–Aug)* and Nobber *(October)*.

The Secretary, O'Carolan Harp Festival Keadew, Co Roscommon ✆ 078 47204; Fax 078 47511; ✆ 046 52115 or 52272.

Dancing – The most popular form of dance is "set dancing", which dates from the 18C and is, for the most part, an adaptation of military dances to existing tunes such as jigs, reels, hornpipes and polkas. Individual old-style *(sean-nós)* dancing is also a feature of Irish traditional music.

Evening Entertainment – Evening entertainment in the form of various combinations of dinner and music is provided at several venues – Knappogue Castle *(see p 200)*; Bunratty Castle *(see p 244)*; Dunguaire Castle *(see p 106)*; Killarney Manor *(see p 226)*;

Traditional dancing - group of three

Tracing Ancestors

The organisations listed below can assist in tracing Irish ancestors; some charge fees.

Republic of Ireland

Co Cavan   **Cavan Genealogical Centre**, Tourist Information Office, Farnham Street, Cavan, Co Cavan; ☎ 049 61094.

Co Clare   **Clare Heritage Centre**, Corrofin, Co Clare – ♿ Open mid Mar–Oct, daily, 10am–6pm; otherwise, Mon–Fri, 9am–5pm. £2. ☎ 065 37955. Parking. Tearoom. – Extensive genealogical records making it possible to trace people who emigrated from Clare in the last century; in the aftermath of the Great Famine between 1851 and 1871 at least 100 000 people left the region.

Co Cork   **Cork Archives Institute**, Cork, Co Cork – Copious material consisting of family and private papers, some of potential genealogical interest, and chiefly of historical records relating to business, local government and trade union activities.

Co Donegal   **Donegal Genealogical Centre**, Lifford Old Courthouse, Main Square, Lifford, Co Donegal.

Rathmelton Family History Research Centre, Rathmelton, Co Donegal – Open all year, Mon–Fri, 9am–4.30pm, ☎ 074 38124 (Caretaker).

Co Dublin   **National Library of Ireland**, Kildare Street, Dublin 2; ☎ 01 661 8811 – No postal queries.

General Register Office, Births, Deaths and Marriages, Joyce House, 8-11 Lombard Street East, Dublin 2; ☎ 01 671 1000.

Hibernian Research Co Ltd, P O Box 3097, Dublin 6; ☎ 01 496 6522 (24hr), Fax 01 497 3011.

National Archives, Bishop Street, Dublin 8; ☎ 01 478 3711.

Co Leitrim   **Leitrim Heritage Centre**, County Library, Ballinamore, Co Leitrim – Open Mon–Fri, 10am–1pm and 2–5pm. ☎ 078 44012; Fax 078 44425.

Co Limerick   **Irish Palatine Heritage Centre**, Rathkeale, Co Limerick – Genealogical service for tracing Palatine ancestors.

Co Monaghan   **Roslea Heritage Centre**, Monaghan Road, Roslea, Monaghan – Open Apr–Sept, Mon–Fri, 9am–5pm, weekends by appointment; Oct–Mar, Mon–Fri, 9am–5pm. £1, 50p (child), ☎ 013657 51750.

Co Offaly and Co Laois   **Offaly and Laois Historical and Archeological Society**, Tullamore, Co Offaly – Open Mon–Fri, 9am–1pm and 2–4pm. **Public Reading Room:** Open 10am–4pm.

Co Roscommon   **Roscommon County Heritage Centre**, Strokestown, Co Roscommon – Genealogical research service.

Co Tipperary   **Genealogical Service**, Old Gaol, Tipperary; Clans Office, James Street, Tipperary.

Brú Ború Cultural Centre, Cashel, Co Tipperary – Genealogy and Celtic Studies Centre.

North Tipperary Genealogical Service, Nenagh District Heritage Centre, Nenagh, Co Tipperary – Open daily except bank holidays, 10am–4pm; closed at lunchtime, ☎ 067 33850; Fax 067 33586.

Roscrea Heritage Centre, Damer House, Roscrea, Co Tipperary – Computerised genealogical service.

Co Waterford   **Genealogy Office**, St Patrick's Church, Jenkin's Lane, Waterford.

Co Westmeath   **Dún na Sí (Fairy Fort)**, Moate, Co Westmeath – Genealogy Research Centre for Co Westmeath.

Co Wicklow   **Genealogical Research Unit**, Wicklow County Heritage Centre, Wicklow, Co Wicklow.

Clan Gatherings

There are 243 Irish clans which hold annual **clan gatherings** on ancestral sites; information available from Clans of Ireland, Dr Margaret Tierney, Grange Clare, Kilmeague, Neath, Co Kildare.

Northern Ireland

Co Armagh   **Genealogical Research Centre**, St Patrick's Trian, Armagh.

Armagh Ancestry, 42 English Street, Armagh, BT61 7BA – Open all year, Mon–Sat, ☎ 01861 527 808; Fax 01861 528 329.

Co Tyrone   **Genealogical Research Centre**, Heritage World, Main Street, Dungannon, Co Tyrone – Extensive computerised archives enabling people to discover the path to their Irish roots.

Sport and Leisure

Ireland is naturally well-endowed to provide many different physical environments for outdoor **sports and leisure activities**. The long and indented coastline provides facilities for deep-sea fishing, angling, sailing, wind-surfing, scuba-diving and bathing. The many inland lakes and waterways attract anglers and are good for cruising, canoeing and water-skiing. For golfers there are both inland and links courses. The magnificent mountain ranges which fringe the Atlantic coast from north to south provide exhilarating locations for walking, rambling, orienteering and mountaineering. Hunting and horse racing are concentrated in the flatter, agricultural counties of the south and midlands; pony trekking is country-wide.

Information on all the activities listed below is available from the Irish Tourist Board (Bord Fáilte) and the Northern Irish Tourist Board (NITB).

Leisure

Dúchas – The Irish Heritage Service is the State body responsible for the protection and conservation of the natural and built heritage.
A **Yearly Ticket/Heritage Card** (£15; reductions available), offering unlimited admission to all Dúchas sites, is available at most properties or by phone *(see below)*.

Dúchas Education and Visitor Services, 6 Ely Place Upper, Dublin 2 ☎ 01 647 2453; Fax 01 661 6764' LoCall 1890 474 847 (Ireland only); ☎ 01 647 2461 or CALLSVE 1850 600 601 (yearly ticket by credit card); info@heritageireland.ie; www.heritageireland.ie

Heritage Towns – Some 25 towns have been designated Heritage Towns because of their architecture and history or particular character, which is illustrated in the Heritage Centre.

Historic Monuments – In Northern Ireland many historic monuments are the responsibility of the Department of the Environment.

Environment and Heritage Service: Built Heritage, Department of the Environment, 5-33 Hill Street, Belfast BT1 2LA ☎ 028 9054 3034; Fax 028 9054 3111.

National Trust – The Trust owns over 200 historic house and gardens and 49 industrial monuments and mills in England, Wales, Scotland and Northern Ireland. Members in Great Britain may use their membership cards to visit NT properties in Northern Ireland. Annual membership (£30), offering unlimited admission to all NT sites, is available at most sites or shops or from The National Trust, Freepost MB 1438, Bromley, Kent BR1 3BR.

Head Office in Northern Ireland, Rowallane House, Saintfield, Ballynahinch, Co Down BT24 7LH, ☎ 01238 510 721; Fax 01238 511 242; www.nationaltrust.org.uk

Nature Reserves – Ireland has four **national parks** – Glenveagh, Connemara, Wicklow Mountains and Killarney – in the Republic, many **forest parks** and **country parks** managed for public use and recreation, and numerous **nature reserves** (wildfowl sanctuaries, peat bogs and sand dunes) on both sides of the border:

The Wildlife Service (Dúchas), 6 Upper Ely Place, Dublin 2 ☎ 01 647 3000; Fax 662 1767; www.heritageireland.ie

Birdwatch Ireland, Ruttledge House, 8 Longford Place, Monkstown, Co Dublin ☎ 01 280 4322; Fax 01 284 4407; bird@indigo.ie; www.birdwatchireland.ie

Irish Peatland Conservation Council, Capel Chambers, 119 Capel Street, Dublin 1, ☎/Fax 01 872 2397; ipcc@indigo.ie; www.ipcc.ie

Royal Society for Protection of Birds, Belvoir Park Forest, Belfast BT8 4QT ☎ 028 9049 1547; Fax 028 9049 1669

Environment & Heritage Service, Natural Heritage, Commonwealth House, 35 Castle Street, Belfast BT1 1GH ☎ 028 9025 1477; Fax 028 9045 6660; www.ehsni.gov.uk

Scenic Routes – Scenic routes for cars are indicated by signs *(Slí)* erected by the local Tourist Boards.

Steam Railways – There are a few tourist railways in Ireland and occasional excursions by steam trains on the national network.

Railway Preservation Society, Ashgrove House, Kill Avenue, Dun Laoghaire, Co Dublin ☎ 01 280 9147; David461@iol.ie

Railway Preservation Society, P O Box 6238, Whitehall Dublin 9, ☎/Fax 01 837 4533

Sport

Various bodies provide a general umbrella for other specialist organisations.

Irish Sports Council – Frederick Buildings, South Frederick Street, Dublin 2 ☎ 01 662 1444; Fax 01 679 9291;

AFAS – Association for Adventure Sports, House of Sport, Longmile Road, Dublin 12 ☎ 01 450 9845, 1633; Fax 01 450 2805;

Sports Council for Northern Ireland, House of Sport, 2A Upper Malone Road, Belfast BT9 5LA ☎ 028 9038 1222; Fax 028 9068 2757; info@sportscouncil-ni.org.uk; www.sportni.org

Canoeing – Two organisations can provide useful information.

Irish Canoe Union ☎ 01 450 9838, 1633; Fax 01 450 2805; 01 460 4795; icu@iol.ie *See also AFAS above.*

National Mountain and Whitewater Centre, Tiglin, Devil's Glen, Ashford, Co Wicklow ☎ 040 40169; Fax 0404 40701; mail@tiglin.com; www.tiglin.com

Cycling – *Cycling*, a brochure published by the Irish Tourist Board, suggests several routes. Airlines, ferry companies and the rail network will transport accompanied bicycles. Facilities for cycle hire exist throughout Ireland; a list of shops hiring cycles in Northern Ireland is available from the NITB.

Irish Cycling Federation, Kelly Roche Hous, 619 North Circular Road, Dublin 1 ☎ 01 855 1522/3; Fax 01 855 1771.

Raleigh Rent-a-Bike Division, Raleigh Ireland Limited, PO Box 3520, Raleigh House, Kylemore Road, Dublin 10 ☎ 01 626 1333; Fax 01 626 1770; raleigh@iol.ie; http/ireland.iol.ie/raleigh/
See also Rambling below.

Fishing – The Irish Tourist Board publishes three brochures on *Game Angling*, *Sea Angling* and *Coarse Fishing*, which provide information on the seasons, fisheries, price of licences and permits, dates of festivals and accommodation. Detailed information is available from the Fisheries Board:

Central Fisheries Board, Mobhi Boreen, Glasnevin, Dublin 9 ☎ 01 837 9206; Fax 836 0060; info@cfb.ie

Game fishing permits and licences in Northern Ireland are available from local tackle shops and from the fishery authorities:

Fisheries Conservancy Board for Northern Ireland, 1 Mahon Road, Portadown, BT62 3EE ☎ 028 3833 4666; Fax 028 3833 8912; www.fcbni.org

Gliding – Paragliding and hang-gliding are both organised by the same body:

Irish Hang-Gliding and Paragliding Association – ☎ 087 243 6554 (hang-gliding) and ☎ 086 258 5978 (para-gliding). *See also AFAS above.*

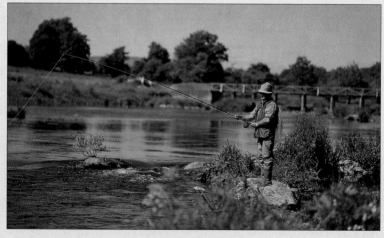

Slide File, Dublin

Castleconnell, Co Limerick

Golf in Co Kerry

Golf – The Irish Tourist Board publishes *Golfing*, a brochure identifying a selection of golf courses, both links and parkland. The NITB publishes a leaflet listing the 80 golf courses in Northern Ireland.

Golfing Union of Ireland, 81 Eglinton Road, Dublin 4 ☎ 01 269 4111; Fax 01 269 5368; gui@iol.ie; www.gui.ie

Greyhound Racing – There are 18 race tracks for this popular evening entertainment: Ballyskeagh, Cork, Dublin, Dundalk, Dungannon, Enniscorthy, Galway, Kilkenny, Lifford, Limerick, Londonderry, Longford, Mullingar, Newbridge, Thurles, Tralee, Waterford and Youghal.

Bord na gCon, Irish Greyhound Board, 104 Henry Street, Limerick ☎ 061 316 788; Fax 061 316 739.

Horse Racing – Racecourses are common in almost every part of Ireland. The most well known in the Dublin area are The Curragh, Punchestown, Leopardstown and Fairyhouse.

The particularly popular festivals are **Fairyhouse** *(Easter)*, **Killarney** *(May)*, **Curragh** *(June)*, **Killarney** *(July)*, **Galway**, **Tramore** and **Tralee** *(August)*, **Galway** and **Listowel** *(September)* and **Leopardstown** and **Limerick** *(December)*.

Irish Horseracing Authority, Leopardstown Racecourse, Foxrock, Dublin 18 ☎ 01 289 2888; Fax 01 289 8412; info@irishracing.iha.ie; www.iha.ie/iharace

Hunting – *Equestrian Holidays*, published by the Irish Tourist Board, lists all the hunts (fox hunting, stag hunting and harriers) in the Republic of Ireland.

Irish Masters of Foxhounds Association, Thornton, Dunlavin, Co Kildare ☎/Fax 045 401 294.

Mountaineering – Information on mountaineering, rock climbing and orienteering is available from the following organisations:

Mountaineering Council of Ireland, ☎ 01 450 7376; Fax 01 450 2805. *See also AFAS above.*

National Mountain and Whitewater Centre, Tiglin, Devil's Glen, Ashford, Co Wicklow ☎ 040 40169; Fax 0404 40701; mail@tiglin.com; www.tiglin.com

Tollymore Mountain Centre, Bryansford, Newcastle ☎ 028 4372 2158; Fax 028 4372 6155; admin@tollymoremc.com; www.tollymoremc.com

Sports Council for Northern Ireland – *See above.*

Parachuting – Information is available from the major association and from two clubs:

Parachute Association of Ireland – ☎ 1850 260 600. *See also AFAS above.*

Rambling – *Walking Ireland* gives details of the **national waymarked ways** in the Republic of Ireland; detailed information sheets for individual long-distance walks are available. Waymarked ways are for walking only and are unsuitable for horses and mountain bikes; large groups are also undesirable; dogs should not be brought on ways which cross farmland; any dog seen chasing domestic animals is likely to be shot.

Irish Sports Council – *See above.*

Sports Council for Northern Ireland – *See above.*

National Hunt Racing

Walking/Cycling Ireland, PO Box 5520, Ballsbridge, Dublin 4 ☎ 01 668 8278; Fax 01 660 5566; wci@kerna.ie; http://kerna.ie/wci/

East–West Mapping – www.homepage.tinet.ie/~eastwest
Ballyredmond, Clonegal, Enniscorthy, Co Wexford ☎/Fax 054 77835; eastwest@tinet.ie

Riding and Pony Trekking – *Equestrian Holidays*, published by the Irish Tourist Board, provides information on trail riding, based trails, residential centres, horse riding holidays based on hotels.

Equestrian Holidays Ireland, c/o Clonshire Equestrian Centre, Adare, Co Limerick ☎ 061 396 770; Fax 061 396 726.

Sailing – There are sailing marinas all round the coast of Ireland and on the inland lakes. *Sailing Ireland*, published by the Irish Tourist Board, gives information on **yacht chartering** and **offshore racing**, which attracts international teams. All yacht clubs are linked to the Irish Sailing Association:

Irish Sailing Association, 3 Park Road, Dun Laoghaire, Co Dublin ☎ 01 280 0239; Fax 01 280 7558; info@sailing.ie; isa@iol.ie; www.sailing.ie www.sailing.orgisa/ Visitor Information (for moorings) ☎ 020 7493 3201.

Shooting – Permits and walk-up shooting are available on application to the Forestry Service in Northern Ireland:

District Forest Office, The Grange, Castlewellan Forst Park, Castlewellan BT31 9DU ☎ 028 4377 2257.

District Forest Office, Inishkeen House, Killyhevlin, Enniskillen BT74 4EJ ☎ 028 6634 3123.

Sub Aqua Diving – Ireland has a beautiful underwater coastline, particularly on the west coast where the Gulf Stream brings an abundant marine life in the clear Atlantic waters.

Irish Underwater Council, 78A Patrick Street, Dún Laoghaire, Co Dublin ☎ 01 284 4601; Fax 01 284 4602; scubairl@indigo.ie; www.indigo.ie/scuba-irl

Sceilig Aquatics, Caherdaniel, Co Kerry ☎ /Fax 066 947 5277; info@activity-ireland; activity-ireland.com

Surfing – The best conditions are to be found on the northwest and the mid-west coasts; good conditions prevail on the north, the southwest and the south coast; the east coast is reasonable only during a storm or strong southerly winds. Surfboards are available for hire.

Irish Wind Surfing Association, c/o Moss Veterinary, Naas, Co Kildare ☎ 087 584 589; Fax 045 879 791.

Irish Surf Association, Easkey House, Easkey, Co Sligo ☎ 096 49428; Fax 096 49020.

Walking – *See Rambling above.*

Water Skiing – Information available from

Irish Water Ski Federation, Knocknacree Road, Mount Salus, Dalkey, Co Dublin ☎ 01 450 2122; Fax 01 450 2138; dbk@advance.iol.ie

Windsurfing – Some of the most popular places for windsurfing or sailboarding or boardsailing are in northwest Ireland on the coast of Co Mayo at **Easky**, where the Tiki Cold Water Classic was held in 1997, and on the coast of Co Donegal at **Bundoran**, where the European championships attract many nationalities.

Irish Sailing Association – *See Sailing above.*

Oysterhaven Boardsailing Centre, Kinsale, Co Cork ☎ 0214 770 738; Fax 0214 477 0776; info@oysterhaven.com; www.oysterhaven.com

Calendar of Events

August bank holiday weekend
Keadew .... O'Carolan Harp Festival – performance of his works, music, song and dancing, many open-air events *(see p 381)*

Early August
Dublin .... Dublin Horse Show – international equestrian event with team jumping competitions held at the Royal Dublin Society ground in Ballsbridge
Stradbally .... Steam engine rally
Clogher Valley .... William Carleton Summer School

Mid August
Killorglin .... Puck Fair – Three days and nights of revelry centred on a billy goat enthroned in a chair, one of the three great fairs of Ireland
Glenties .... Fiddle Festival and Summer School – master classes in fiddle playing

2nd weekend in August
Kinvarra .... Gathering of the boats – Galway hookers' regatta

August
Armagh .... All-Ireland Intermediate Road Bowls Finals – an ancient game, played only in Co Armagh and Co Cork, in which competitors used to throw cannonballs
Ballycastle .... Oul' Lammas Fair – oldest traditional Irish fair

Mid August
Clifden .... Connemara Pony Show

2nd last week in August
Kilbeggan .... Steam rally

Late August
Tralee .... Rose of Tralee Festival – bands, parades, dancing and horse racing

2nd week in September
Dublin .... All Ireland Hurling Finals at Croke Park
Clarinbridge .... Oyster Festival – Ladies International Oyster-opening
Map 923 – F8 Competition, oyster tasting, music, dance

Slide File, Dublin

Marching Band, Inishowen, Co Donegal

38

Dublin......................... All Ireland Gaelic Football Finals at Croke Park

Dromore Map 923 – N 4 Horse Fair

Galway......................... International Oyster Festival – World Oyster-opening Championships, held in the pubs, oyster tasting, music, song and dance

Listowel........................ Horse racing

Waterford..................... Waterford International Festival of Light Opera

Kinsale .... Gourmet Festival

Ballinasloe .... Great October Fair, one of the three great fairs of Ireland
Map 923 – H 8   – for buying and selling horses

Larne............................ Mounthill Fair – horse fair dating from the 17C

Nobber .... O'Carolan Harp and Cultural Festival – harp and instrumental workshops and competitions, traditional Irish concerts, step and set dancing, traditional festival Mass in Irish

Wexford........................ Opera Festival

Belfast.......................... Belfast Festival at Queen's – music from classical to folk and jazz, together with drama, ballet and cinema

Londonderry .... Foyle Film Festival
and Belfast

Further Reading

Titles which are out of print may be obtained through public libraries in the United Kingdom.

Art

The Architecture of Ireland from the Earliest Times to 1880 by Maurice Craig (Batsford 1982)

Irish Art and Architecture by Peter Harbison, Homan Potterton, Jeanne Sheehy (Thames & Hudson 1978)

The Irish Country House by Peter Somerville-Large (Sinclair-Stevenson 1995)

A Guide to Irish Country Houses by Mark Bence-Jones (1988)

The Painters of Ireland by Anne Crookshank and the Knight of Glin (1978/9)

Exploring the Book of Kells by George Otto Simms (1988)

History

Brendan the Navigator by George Otto Simms (O'Brien Press)

The Celts edited by Joseph Raftery (The Mercier Press, Dublin 1988)

An Introduction to Celtic Christianity by James P Mackey (T & T Clark, Ltd, Edinburgh 1989)

Ancient Ireland by Jacqueline O'Brien and Peter Harbison

Ireland in Early Medieval Europe edited by Dorothy Whitelock, Rosamund McKitterick, David Dumville (Cambridge University Press 1982)

The Peoples of Ireland by Liam de Paor (Hutchinson 1986)

Huguenot Settlements in Ireland by Gl Lee(Longman Green & Co 1936)

The Oxford History of Ireland by RF Foster – ISBN 0-19-285271

The Making of Modern Ireland 1603–1923 by JC Beckett (Faber & Faber 1966)

Citizen Lord by Stella Tillyard (Chatto & Windus) – ISBN 0-7011-6538-3

The Great Hunger by Cecil Woodham-Smith (Penguin Books 1988)

The Identity of Ulster by Ian Adamson (Pretani Press 1982)

Twilight of the Ascendancy by Mark Bence-Jones (1987)

Geography

Geology and Scenery in Ireland by JB Whittow (Penguin Books 1974)

The Book of the Irish Countryside edited by Frank Mitchell (Blackstaff Press 1987)

Reading the Irish Landscape by Frank Mitchell

The Shannon Floodlands – A Natural History by Stephen Heeny (Tir Eolas – Newtownlynch, Kinvara, Co Galway 1993) – ISBN 1-873821-026

Mythology

A Guide to Irish Mythology by Daragh Smyth (Irish Academic Press)

Fairy and Folk Tales of Ireland by WB Yeats (Colin Smythe 1973)

Novels

Castle Rackrent by Maria Edgeworth (1800)

The Macdermots of Ballycloran, The Kellys and the O'Kellys, Castle Richmond and *The Landleaguers* by Anthony Trollope (1847, 1848, 1860, 1883)

Experiences of an Irish RM by E Somerville and M Ross (1899)

The Playboy of the Western World by JM Synge (1907)

A Portrait of the Artist as a Young Man by James Joyce (1916, 1960)

Ulysses by James Joyce (1922)

The Last September by Elizabeth Bowen (1929)

Troubles by JG Farrell (Fontana 1970) – ISBN 0-000-654046-5

Good Behaviour by Molly Keane (1981, 1988)

Hungry Hill by Daphne du Maurier (1983)

Autobiography

Twenty Years A-Growing by Maurice O'Sullivan (1953, 1992)

Wheels within Wheels by Dervla Murphy (1981)

Woodbrook by David Thomson (1988)

Angela's Ashes by Frank McCourt (1997)

Recipes

Simply Delicious Recipes by Darina Allen (1989, 1992)

The Irish Food Guide by Sally and John McKenna (Anna Livia, Dublin)

World Heritage List

In 1972 the United Nations Educational, Scientific and Cultural Organization (UNESCO) adopted a Convention for the preservation of cultural and natural sites. To date, more than 150 States Parties have signed this international agreement, which has listed over 500 sites "of outstanding universal value" on the World Heritage List. Each year a committee of representatives from 21 countries, assisted by technical organizations (ICOMOS – International Council on Monuments and Sites; IUCN – International Union for Conservation of Nature and Natural Resources; ICCROM – International Centre for the Study of the Preservation and Restoration of Cultural Property, the Rome Centre), evaluates the proposals for new sites to be included on the list, which grows longer as new nominations are accepted and more countries sign the Convention. To be considered, a site must be nominated by the country in which it is located.

The protected cultural heritage may be monuments (buildings, sculptures, archeological structures etc) with unique historical, artistic or scientific features; groups of buildings (such as religious communities, ancient cities); or sites (human settlements, examples of exceptional landscapes, cultural landscapes) which are the combined works of man and nature of exceptional beauty. Natural sites may be a testimony to the stages of the earth's geological history or to the development of human cultures and creative genius or represent significant ongoing ecological processes, contain superlative natural phenomena or provide a habitat for threatened species.

Signatories of the Convention pledge to co-operate to preserve and protect these sites around the world as a common heritage to be shared by all humanity.

Some of the most well-known places which the World Heritage Committee has inscribed include: Australia's Great Barrier Reef (1981), the Canadian Rocky Mountain Parks (1984), The Great Wall of China (1987), the Statue of Liberty (1984), the Kremlin (1990), Mont-Saint-Michel and its Bay (Great Britain and Ireland, 1979), Durham Castle and Cathedral (1986).

UNESCO World Heritage sites included in this guide are:

Boyne Valley

Skellig Michael

Giant's Causeway

Mannin Bay, Co Galway

Introduction

Landscape

Ireland could not be known as "the Emerald Isle" without its mild damp climate, which is caused by presence of the Gulf Stream, and a high incidence of rainfall, particularly on the west coast, which is exposed to the Atlantic Ocean. The high humidity produces lush growth and favours the formation of extensive bogs which cover 15 per cent of the land mass. Ireland is a predominantly agricultural country with few mineral deposits and little heavy industry.

The island is almost encircled by mountain chains and highland masses, which rise round the periphery and are breached only by the major river estuaries and on the east coast between Dublin and Dundalk, where the large central lowland extends to the Irish Sea. The most dramatic mountain scenery and the highest peaks and are to be found on the west coast, particularly in Co Kerry.

Glacial Features – During the Ice Age (1.5 million to 10 000 years ago) the upper layers of sediments were largely eroded and the action of the glaciers created many troughs, corries and lakes, some impounded by moraines. Ice sheets also left unconsolidated deposits of clay, sand and gravel.

Long winding ridges of sandy gravel deposited by retreating glaciers are known as eskers; their steep sides are usually uncultivated. Eskers generally occur in chains running east–west and provide the firm ground on either bank at the major Shannon crossings – Athlone, Shannonbridge and Banagher.

Ice sheets also moulded swarms of **drumlins**, low egg-shaped mounds with or without a core of solid rock. They are most clearly visible where they are partially submerged in Clew Bay, Lough Erne and Strangford Lough. In the drumlin country which extends from the Ards Peninsula to Donegal Bay the crests are often capped by a church or a farm; the villages and pasture descend their slopes to the reedy undrained pastures in the intervening depressions.

Rivers and Lakes – The rivers (16 530mi/26 600km) are of two types. Those that rise on the seaward side of the mountains are short and steep and drain straight into the sea. Those that drain inland form slow-moving lowland streams, lined by water meadows (callows) and punctuated by lakes where their course meets a depression; the lack of significant gradient and the gentle character of the flanking terrain mean that these rivers do not create well-defined valleys but frequently widen out into lakes as if in flood. The major examples are Lough Neagh on the **Bann**, Lough Erne on the **Erne** and Lough Allen, Lough Ree and Lough Derg on the **Shannon**, the longest and most famous river in Ireland. Several Irish rivers exhibit a different peculiarity; they have eroded their courses through rather than round rocky upland. Instead of flowing west out of Lough Derg at Scarriff the Shannon makes its way south through the Killaloe Gap. Both the **Barrow** and the **Nore** describe a lazy meander through fertile farmlands and water meadows in their upper reaches, but then force a passage through the granite of the Leinster Chain at Graiguenamanagh and Inistioge, where they descend into steep-sided wooded valleys. The **Slaney** does not veer southwest to join the Barrow but flows southeast through a gap in the mountains at Bunclody. The rivers of south Cork – **Blackwater**, **Lee** and **Bandon** – flow on parallel west–east courses before turning sharply south through several rock ridges to the sea.

In other places rivers have been forced to change course by glacial deposits. The Liffey adopted its northerly course when the sand and gravel of The Curragh, deposited at the end of the Ice Age, obstructed its original western course to the Barrow. The Bush in Co Antrim was similarly diverted west at Armoy.

Many Irish rivers, particularly in the south, end in drowned river valleys, where the sea water penetrates several miles inland. Waterford Harbour, a drowned river estuary, is shared by the Suir, the Barrow and the Nore, which are known as the Three Sisters. Three river estuaries are true ice-eroded **fjords** – Killary Harbour, Lough Swilly and Carlingford Lough.

The many lakes in Ireland (357 000 acres/144 585ha) vary in size from a reedy pool to an inland sea. They are mostly concentrated in the west and north, particularly in the belt of drumlin country. A unique Irish feature is the **turlough** (turlach), a dry lake which floods intermittently according to fluctuations in the water table.

Reservoirs have been created in the Wicklow and Mourne Mountains to supply water to Dublin and Belfast respectively.

Caves – The edges of limestone country often favour the formation of caves. Rainwater, which is slightly acid, together with peaty streams, slowly dissolves the porous limestone, forming underground chambers and passages which are gradually enlarged by complex underground river courses. The five caves open to visitors – Ailwee, Crag, Dunmore, Marble Arch, Michelstown – present impressive and beautiful examples of stalactites, stalagmites and other concretions.

Peat Bogs – The ecology, conservation and exploitation of peat bogs is explained at the Peatland World at Lullymore and at Peatlands Park in Co Armagh. Some raised bogland (eg Clara Bog northwest of Tullamore) is being conserved so that botanists can study the habitat. Peatlands can be dangerous; it is unwise to visit them alone or to walk on a bog as some of the pools are very deep.

Peat is an excellent preservative medium and has yielded some interesting archaeological material, particularly sections of **bog road** or **marsh track**, which were formed by
laying cut branches in the surface of the bog *(see p 248)*. Butter packed in wooden
churns, **bog butter**, keeps well in peat for a few hundred years, eventually turning into
a sort of cream cheese. **Bogwood** is the trunks or stumps of pine trees which grew on
the bogs between 2500 BC and 2000 BC, during a decrease in rainfall, and died when
the rainfall increased.

Peat is formed in water-logged basins by the accumulation of dead plants incompletely
decomposed. The growth of micro-organisms which break down plant material is
inhibited by the acidity of the water, which is due to the presence of bog mosses
(sphagnum species). **Blanket bog** occurs where the average rainfall is over
47in/1 200mm pa (at least 235 days); it is dependent on high rainfall and humidity
and is usually found in mountainous areas, particularly on the western seaboard. The
bog is composed of dead grasses and sedges (depth from 6ft/2m to 20ft/6m) but
very little bog moss. **Raised bog**, which is more suitable for industrial exploitation, occurs
where average rainfall is 31–35in/800–900mm pa; it grows above the local ground
water and covers most of the central plain. The bog is mostly composed of bog moss
(up to 39ft/12m in depth), which forms a dome; the surface is covered by bog plants.
Owing to the shortage of timber, **hand-cut peat** has been the chief source of fuel for
many centuries; most people have turbary rights on a local bog where they cut the
sods by hand. First an area is drained, then the top layer containing live plants is
deposited on a previously cut surface to encourage regeneration. The turfs are cut
with a slane *(sleán)*, a narrow spade with a side blade set at a right angle, and laid
on a spreadground to dry. The sods are turned as each side dries and then loosely
stacked into footings. When thoroughly dry the sods are stacked into clamps near the
house. In a fine summer a family can harvest enough fuel for several years.

Turf cutting in Connemara

Since 1946 Bord na Móna (Peat Development Authority) has developed the machinery
and techniques for **mechanical peat harvesting**. The raised bogs of Ireland are expected to
produce 300 million tonnes of peat before they are exhausted. After the type and
extent of turf has been assessed, the bog is drained for five to seven years, levelled
with a slight slope to the nearest drain, and then a light railway is laid on the surface
to carry away the harvested peat. **Moss peat**, which is suitable for **horticulture** as it is
less dense and retains both air and water, comes from just under the surface. It is
harvested between June and December. **Sod peat**, used for **fuel**, is harvested by a
machine which mixes together the peat from different levels to produce a consistent
texture. **Milled peat** is scraped off the surface of the bog in fine weather and made into
briquettes for the domestic hearth or burned in power stations.

Woodland – Originally Ireland was densely covered in trees, particularly forests of
sessile oak. Clearance for agriculture began in the Stone Age. In the 17C and 18C
much of what remained was cut down for building and smelting and by the British
army to deny refuge to the rebellious Irish. Remnants of the native Irish oakwoods
are to be found by the Upper Lake in Killarney, at Abbeyleix and at Coolattin at the
southern end of the Wicklow Mountains.

The native species of tree in Ireland, which spread from southern Europe after the Ice
Age, include the hawthorn, considered sacred, and the ash, which is used for making
hurley sticks.

45

The **Irish Yew**, its branches pointing upwards, is a deviation from the bushy common yew. All Irish yews are cuttings from the original tree which was found and propagated at Florence Court in 1767. They are most commonly found in graveyards but are also used to good effect in formal gardens.

In the 18C many landowners planted their demesnes with both native and exotic species; in 1735 the Dublin Society began to offer premiums for artificial planting. Among the species introduced at this time are the eucalyptus, magnolia, tree rhododendron and eucryphia, horse and sweet chestnut, beech and copper beech, Scots pine, Chilean pine (monkey puzzle tree) and Cedar of Lebanon, which was planted singly near the house so that its silhouette could be admired.

Pitcher plant (*Sarracena purpurea*)

Strawberry (*Arbutus unedo*)

Bog cotton (*Eriophorum angustifolium*)

Bog heather (*Xalluma vulgarris*)

A Giannomi / Y Gladu / G Hofer / R Konig / G Laurent / C Nardin / P Petit / L Tarnaud / JACANA

46

Many of the former private estates are now **Forest Parks** in public ownership. As estate incomes dwindled in the late 19C and early 20C many woods were felled for timber; by 1920 only 0.5 per cent of the land was forested. The present policy of re-afforestation, promoted by the forestry training centre *(see p 296)*, aims to increase the area of land covered by forest from about 8 per cent to 24 per cent, to make Ireland self-sufficient in timber and use poor land profitably; trees are particularly suitable for drumlin soils. The best species have proved to be conifers but the planting of broad-leaf deciduous trees, particularly on cut-away bog land, is increasing.

Irish Yew *(Taxus baccata)*

Gorse *(Ulex europaeus)*

Sessile oak *(Quercus petraea)*

Fuchsia *(Fuchsia)*

Water lily *(Nymphea alba)*

Gardens

When protected from the wind in Ireland, plants will grow quickly and to a considerable height owing to the Gulf Stream and the high annual rainfall. Most are designed to take advantage of natural features but a few formal 17C gardens have survived *(see p 292)*. The Palladian mansions of the 18C were designed to be surrounded by greensward; flowers and vegetables were grown in walled gardens at some distance from the house. Shrubs and flowerbeds close to the house were introduced by the Victorians, who also created tennis courts and bowling greens; many of the 19C alterations were paid for with the proceeds from the compulsory sale of land under the Land Acts.

Mount Stewart Garden

Flora – The mild climate and heavy rainfall encourage lush plant growth. Palm trees and bamboo are an unexpected sight. On the shores of the Upper Lake in Killarney the strawberry tree grows up to 30ft/9m. The Mediterranean Heath, an erica which grows to over 6ft/2m, is found in the sheltered valley east of Corraun in Co Mayo. In spring the yellow flowers of the gorse (also known as whin and furze) brighten the landscape. Later in the year fuchsias and rhododendrons grow wild in the hedgerows. In the Burren a profusion of calcium-loving plants attracts the botanists; Arctic, Alpine and Mediterranean plants thrive in Connemara.

Fauna – There are no snakes in Ireland; according to tradition they were annihilated by St Patrick.
Skeletons of the Giant Irish Deer are on display in the Dublin and Belfast Museums but the animal itself is now extinct. The fallow deer *(see pp 250 and 335)* was introduced by the Normans; some of the present herds are confined in parks but most are wild. The only remaining native red deer are in Killarney; those elsewhere are re-introductions and in Co Wicklow they are mostly hybridised with the local Sika, a type introduced in the 19C.
Badgers are common and stoats (sometimes called weasels in Ireland) are widespread. The rarest mammal is the pine marten, which is found predominantly in Co Sligo and Co Clare. Red squirrels are found in coniferous forests; the grey has now spread from Co Longford where it was introduced in 1911.
The waterways provide a habitat for numerous otters and for the mink, which has thrived in the wild since the 1960s. Both the common seal and the grey, which is more numerous, are found along the coasts.

Agriculture – Since prehistoric times Ireland has raised cattle and sheep. Exports of dairy products (including a variety of cheeses), bacon, stout and whiskeys make a significant contribution to the economy. Ireland has 95 per cent of the best grassland in the European Union. As early as 1894 the Irish Agricultural Organisation Society was established by Horace Plunkett to raise dairy produce to compete with New Zealand and Denmark. Subsidies under the Common Agricultural Policy of the European Union have raised farming incomes since 1972 but may be reduced when funds are redirected to eastern European countries.

The **Golden Vale** in Co Tipperary contains prime farmland used for raising beef and dairy cattle and for growing barley, wheat and sugar beet, much of which is for cattle feed. The best grazing and fattening **pasture** in Ireland is found in the lowland along the east coast. Good **sheep pasture** is found on the bare limestone of the Plains of Galway and in Donegal, where the wool is turned into tweed and carpets. Owing to high sunshine duration and a light well-drained soil with a high calcareous content, central Wexford provides good **arable land**, particularly for malting barley. The best **grain-growing land** is situated in the Ards Peninsula where the farms are comparatively large.

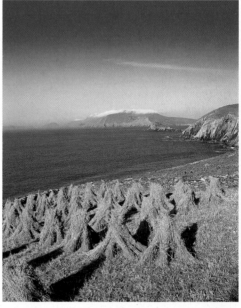

Slea Head, Dingle

Slide File

Two-thirds of Ireland's **fruit trees** grow in the Garden of Ulster in Co Armagh (25sq mi/65m²); strawberries are the speciality of Enniscorthy in Co Wexford.

Horse breeding – Until early this century Ireland supplied the best cavalry and carriage horses in the British Isles; horse breeding, particularly blood stock, is still an important activity, in which 12 000 (5%) of the agricultural labour force is employed. The headquarters of the business is The Curragh near Kildare.

Subsistence farming – This form of farming is still practised in the Gaeltacht *(see p 292)* in such places as Connemara and the Rosses in Co Donegal, where the hay is turned by hand and the cottages are built in clusters *(clachans)* in the traditional Irish way. Transhumance, known in Ireland as **booleying** (from *buaile* meaning a high milking pasture), whereby the cattle were taken up to summer pasture in the mountains, persisted in some regions until the 19C. The system of land holding known as **rundale** or **runrig** survived in the western parts of the country until the Great Famine (1845–49). Land held in common was portioned out among tenants so that all received a share of both good and poorer land; as there were no fences and one man could have strips of land scattered over up to 40 different fields, the system led to frequent disputes and the holdings were subdivided in families until each division was too small to support a man, wife and children.

Fishing – Ireland has always relied on fishing for some of its livelihood; in the Middle Ages there was considerable trade in salt fish with the Continent. In the 20 years from 1963 to 1983 Irish commercial fishlandings increased sevenfold. There are five main fishing ports in the Republic – Killybegs, Rossaveel, Castletownbere, Dunmore East and Arklow – and three in Northern Ireland – Portavogie, Ardglass and Kilkeel. Fish farming of shellfish and fin-fish such as salmon is a growing industry in the bays and estuaries.

The mostly unpolluted lakes and rivers provide many miles of **freshwater angling**. The habitat of the salmon and the trout is found in the coastal estuaries and mountain streams. The extensive coastline provides many opportunities for **sea angling** both from the shore and by boat.

Mining – Ireland has few mineral deposits and mining activity fluctuates from year to year as these deposits are exhausted or cease to be profitable. The Tara Mine in Co Meath is the largest lead and zinc mine in Europe. Coal and barytes are mined in Tipperary and slate is extracted at Portroe near Nenagh and from an underground quarry on Valencia Island.

Power – In the past in most areas **mills** and other machinery were turned by water power, except in drumlin country and Co Wexford where such power was unavailable and windmills were built.

In the 20C various hydro-electric schemes were built to produce power: in 1929 at Ardnacrushna, on the steep fall on the **Shannon** between Limerick and Killaloe, which until 1949 supplied electricity to the whole country; from 1948 to 1952 on the **Erne** at Assaroe upstream from Ballyshannon, on the **Liffey** forming the Poulaphouca Reservoir and in the **Lee** valley west of Cork. The Turlough Hill Electricity Generating Station in the Wicklow Gap, which is the only installation of its kind in Ireland, works on the pumped storage principle; to generate electricity water is pumped between two adjacent interconnecting lakes.

Since 1993, 14 per cent of the country's electricity has been provided by eight peat-burning power stations – five burn milled peat and three burn sod peat.

The wind farm at Bellacorrick in Co Mayo is to be supplemented by one in Co Kerry but another 20 are required.

Transport – Before railways and modern roads the easiest method of transport was by water. The earliest boats were cots, fashioned from hollowed-out tree trunks and used on inland waters, or curraghs like the *Brendan (see p 200)* which will ride a rough sea; St Patrick and the Celtic monks travelled great distances in such craft.

Formerly in the country districts goods were carried in shoulder creels, in donkey pan-niers, in sledges with wooden runners (slipes) or in carts drawn by donkeys or horses. Various types of slide cars and block-wheel cars are still in use today for transporting items through difficult or rough terrain. Donkeys are still used in the west of Ireland. In an outside cart the passengers sit back to back facing the roadside; in an inside cart they sit face to face. Horse-drawn **jaunting cars** can be hired in some tourist resorts, particularly Killarney and Dublin.

51

Flax and Linen

The pale blue fields of flax in flower are no longer a regular feature of the summer landscape but Ireland still manufactures **linen** products with linen imported mainly from Belgium.

A sandy soil is best for the cultivation of flax to produce a good linen thread; if the plant is grown for linseed, a heavy soil is better.

The process of turning flax into linen cloth uses a number of specialised terms. **Retting** means steeping bundles of cut flax upright in water for two to three weeks until the hard outer sheath has rotted; the bundles are then removed from the flax dam (also known as a lint dam), a stinking job, and dried. The bundles are then passed between rollers, also known as breakers, to break up the outer sheath, and twisted into a **strick** by the **strickerman** and placed in a **strick box**. **Scutching** means holding a **strick** over a bar in the path of a wheel with five wooden blades revolving at speed to remove the outer sheath; this process is then repeated by a more experienced worker, a **bufferman**. **Beetling** is the process by which balks of woven linen cloth are passed under a row of heavy wooden hammers which flatten the threads to close up the weave and give the cloth a smooth sheen.

The many processes involved in the production of linen cloth can be traced in various museums *(see pp 163, 346 and 369).*

Canals – Early attempts to improve the waterways concentrated on regulating the flow of rivers and cutting **canals** to by-pass shallows. The canals which began to cover Ireland from the 1750s were built with Government funds in the hope that they would promote trade. As well as heavy goods and agricultural produce they carried passengers, who travelled in flyboats, towed by teams of galloping horses at an average of 8mph/13kph, and stayed overnight in the canal hotels. Anthony Trollope *(see p 129)* travelled by canal boat during his early years in Ireland; his novel *The Kellys and the O'Kellys* contains a good description of travelling by flyboat. With the arrival of the railways the canals went into decline but have since been restored for leisure use with several companies offering cruising holidays on canal barges on the Grand Canal and the Barrow Navigation.

Railways – The first **railway** was built in 1838 from Dublin to Dún Laoghaire (then Kingstown). The network soon spread with narrow-gauge (3ft/1m) lines in the rural areas (Cork, Clare, Leitrim, Cavan, Donegal and Antrim). In 1922 there were 3 454mi/5 555km of line of which 2 896mi/4 660km were built to Irish standard gauge (5ft 3ins/1.06m). By 1961 all the narrow-gauge lines had closed. The standard gauge network now consists of lines from Dublin to the larger provincial towns.

Road network – The latter part of the 20C has produced great improvements in the **road system** with the construction of by-passes and motorways. There were few roads in Ireland until the 18C when Alexander Nimmo constructed the roads from Killarney via Kenmare to Glengarriff, and from Galway to Clifden; in 1832 William Bald built the road on the Antrim Coast. Several road projects were carried out during the Famine and under the Congested Districts Board to provide work in the western counties. Modern road improvements are financed in part with EU funds.

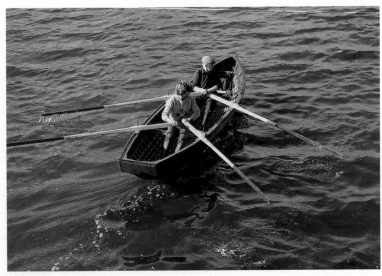

Slide File, Dublin

Traditional curraghs

Airports – There are four international **airports** in Ireland – Dublin, Shannon, Connaught/Knock and Belfast – and several domestic airports – Carrickfin in Donegal, Cork, Bantry, Belfast City, Farranfore near Killarney, Galway, Londonderry and Sligo.

Tourism – It was the construction of the railways in the 19C that stimulated tourism in Ireland. The rural tranquillity of the country, which is so attractive to the residents of the large conurbations of Europe, is being conserved and exploited. Fishing and golf continue to attract large numbers of visitors. The renovation of the canals has been put in hand as canal cruising is joining river cruising in popularity among tourists; in the late 1990s there were over 1 000 cruisers on the River Shannon. All-weather sites – an important consideration in the Irish climate – have been developed by roofing over some of the ruined buildings of historic significance and installing a sympathetic interpretation centre. All-weather leisure facilities – swimming baths etc – are a good investment both for tourism and for the local population. The development of tourism has stimulated the development of service industries and both have made great advances together. The foreign currency earned through tourism since 1989 has covered half the deficit on the balance of payments.

20C Economic Development – Although Ireland itself escaped the blight of heavy industry the country profited from the 19C industrial revolution through being part of the United Kingdom. The shipyards of Belfast and car construction developed beside textiles and agriculture (food and drink). In the years immediately following independence, the Republic of Ireland concentrated on being self-sufficient. During the Second World War (known in the Republic as the Emergency) Ireland served the Allies as a supply base and several companies converted to the manufacture of arms. After 1945 the government of the Republic adopted a policy of attracting foreign investment. Although Ireland has specialized in electronics and biotechnology, its major economic strength is in the chemical industry (fertilizers and pharmaceutical products) and in information technology (software, computers and semi-conductors). These "modern" activities constitute 75% of the total industrial output. Economic development has been assisted by various factors – the work of the Industrial Development Authority; investment in research and development and in education; the highly qualified Irish workforce, which is among the best-educated in Europe and is not extensively unionised; state intervention in various forms – European subsidies granted to the Irish government; grants made to companies which set up plants in Ireland (tax relief, repatriation of profits, installation grants, tax-free zones). Government policy tries to foster economic activity in the rural areas, particularly on the western seaboard, but 35 % of the population lives in Greater Dublin. By 1972, when Ireland joined the European Union, economic progress was well advanced and the only adverse factors were the increase in the cost of oil and the competition of the countries of South-East Asia.

Since 1993 the country has experienced another period of expansion which has enabled it to join the single European currency project in the first phase; it is one of the few countries to comply with the criteria for convergence set by the Maastricht Treaty (February 1992). Now known as the Celtic Tiger, the Republic is experiencing a period of great economic growth, with a boom in house building, and the need for immigration to fill all the vacancies.

Celtic Heritage

Some of the best sources for understanding the Celtic mind and imagination are the Celtic myths and tales. Most of the earlier stories originated in Ireland and, although many were written by Christian monks, they contain descriptions of gods and goddesses as well as of mortal heroes and heroines.

Many factors – such as emigration, the decline of the Irish language, economic prosperity and its associated social changes – have greatly affected Celtic heritage and also influenced the way in which Irish people see themselves. A great deal of older, more 'traditional', material is being rejected, while at the same time the sense of what it means to be Irish is being examined. Irish society is changing rapidly and emphasis is on the urban and technological rather than rural life. Yet aspects of Celtic influence may still be discerned in Irish language and culture.

Farmers and Herdsmen – The first references to the Celts date from the 8C BC in central Europe, where some of them crossed the Alps from Hallstatt in Austria to trade with the people of Greece. There is no written evidence from this period left by Celts themselves; accounts by Greek and Roman writers described a barbarous people. Archaeological evidence suggests, however, that the Celts were brave warriors and very fine craftsmen, hard workers who cared for the sick and elderly. They were renowned for their skills in storytelling and they passed on their epic tales orally from generation to generation. Archaeological evidence also suggests that the Celts arrived in Ireland from the continent of Europe in the early Iron Age (3C BC), although they may have begun to arrive as early as 1500 BC, and their influence endured well into the historical period.

The Celts were essentially a rural community and lived in circular homesteads where their animals were sheltered at night. They cultivated wheat and barley in clearings round the homestead and kept sheep and goats but their chief wealth lay in their

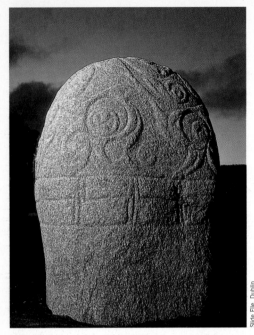

Turoe Stone

herds of cattle, which they moved in summer up to high pastures (*buaile* anglicised booley) where they built light dwellings. The Celts brought certain skills with them, among which were ale brewing, butter churning, the making of leavened bread, the use of salt, vinegar and honey to preserve food, and iron cauldrons for cooking.

Religion – The Celts seem to have acknowledged many divinities – gods of war and hunting and goddesses of fertility, harvest and healing. Among those worshipped in Ireland were Brigit and Daghdha; another was Cernunnos, god of animals, plants and forests, whose emblem was antlers. Each tribe had its own tribal god, which varied from tribe to tribe. They believed that certain goddesses lived in sacred wells and that the water goddesses had the power to cure and protect people.

They regarded not only wells, but certain springs and rivers – particularly the River Boyne – and trees as sacred. They carved images of their gods on tree-trunks. According to the Roman poet Lucan Celts let their sacred woods grow wild so that the dense branches and foliage created a dark place beneath. After a victory they sacrificed animals and sometimes human beings, in which case a criminal was the preferred victim. Assemblies, at which games and races took place, were held at ancient royal or assembly sites, such as Tara and Tullaghoge. The Celts buried their dead, sometimes cremated, with offerings of food and ornaments; they believed that after death they went to join their ancestors, the gods of the Otherworld, who were thought to live in sacred mounds, now known to be prehistoric burial mounds such as at Newgrange and Tara.

The Druids – The word "druid" is probably derived from a Celtic word meaning "extremely knowledgeable". The Celtic druids, who were of noble descent, trained for many years (12–20) and learned all their lore by heart. They committed nothing to writing and prevented others from writing and reading. They took precedence in society in many matters especially those regarding law, custom, nature and human life. They were teachers who were intimately acquainted with tribal laws. They were responsible for drafting the annual calendar and indicating certain days as lucky or unlucky. Much of their decision-making was done in secret.

A number of intricate rituals were performed through which the druids acquired their power and knowledge and their ability to "see"; visions and dreams played an important role in these events. The Irish word *draoi* occurs in early Irish literature and depicts the power of this "seer" druid personality. Druids had the power to interpret dreams, to cure illnesses and to curse people. They read omens in animal entrails or in the flight of birds, especially the raven. They were much involved in a cult of trees, particularly the oak and the hazel; the rowan tree was also of particular importance as it was on the wattles of this tree that the druids were said to sleep in order to gain their power as seers. The druids made offerings to their gods and solicited divine favours by casting valuable items such as golden goblets and weapons into the water of a lake.

The druid was a type of prophet, with mystical powers, and was given to poetry and verse. His skills included incantation and rhetoric and these qualities and powers were still associated with poets in recent times.

Certain named druids occur as dramatic characters in some of the older stories but on the whole the narratives associated with druids are from the Christian era and it is therefore no surprise that in medieval hagiography they appear in opposition to the saints, as malicious wizards, against whom prayers and fasting were deployed.

Brehon Law – In addition to their priestly role the druids had two other offices. As judges *(brithem)* they interpreted the Brehon law, the ancient law of Ireland, which provided a scale of compensation for wrongdoing, even murder, payable by the kin of the malefactor; fasting with witnesses in front of the house of a malefactor was recognised as a means of claiming redress. The code included almost every branch of modern law. It is not certain if these laws were limited in application to a particular upper social class or whether they were more widely upheld. The legal specialists preserved and to some extent developed the code. The druids taught law and their commentaries were passed from generation to generation. The Brehons were forbidden to do certain things, among them giving judgement without legality, or precedent, or security to abide by it. Certain Brehons were forbidden to judge among them one who was associated with falsehood or who had heard only one side of the case.

The Brehons were also advisors to kings and nobility. As genealogists, historians and poets *(filid)*, they recorded the history of the clan; the training for this role was conducted by Bardic schools. The *filid* were obliged to study many different texts including sagas, historical accounts, official poetry, satire, magical texts, grammatical treatises and translations.

These professions were largely hereditary in keeping with the custom at the time. The Celts were grouped in clans *(tuath)* which were divided into families *(derbfine)*. There was no primogeniture; members of three generations - uncles, brothers and nephews as well as sons of the king - were eligible to succeed to the kingship of the clan. It was the custom for sons to be fostered out with other families during their youth; this practice created another strand in the complex pattern of loyalties and was maintained well into the 19C.

Fairylore – The belief in the **Otherworld** is still an important factor in Irish tradition. This "Otherworld" may exist in a fort or in a mountain, under a lake or under the sea. Hundreds of tales and legends associated with the fairies and their world survive, as the landscape and its placenames bear witness. In Irish the fairies are called *sí* or *na daoine maithe* – the good people, or *na daoine beaga* – the little people. The fairies are said variously to be fallen angels, the ancient gods – the Tuatha Dé Danann or sometimes the community of the dead. They are believed to be a supernatural community generally invisible to mortals. They inhabit the earth, the air and water and placenames indicating fairy involvement of some kind are very common. The earthen tumuli – known as *rath* and *lios* – are often said to be fairy forts and sometimes fairy music can be heard to emanate from them. A common saying regarding people who are not giving their full attention to the matter in hand is that they are away with the fairies. Many legends are told describing how the fairies "borrowed" or "stole" a mortal to assist them in some task of their own, such as nursing a fairy child or playing music at a fairy wedding. Supernatural boats, fairy winds and stray sods – so-called because they send humans astray – are a few examples of the material of fairy legend. Fairies were also known to remove a mortal child and leave one of their own in its place; parents returning from their chores to find a sick or dying child in the cradle quickly realised that it was a "changeling".

Banshee – The Banshee *(Bean Sí)* is a solitary female spirit and when her eerie cry is heard it is a portent of death. She is said to follow certain Irish families and her cry is usually heard near the family home of the person about to die, although this cry has also been interpreted as a sign of the imminent death of someone far away. Her origins appear to lie with a goddess figure and her connection with nobility is indicated in folklore by the fact that she is frequently said to follow only those families whose surnames contain "O" or "Mac". Traditions of the banshee are still very strong in urban and in rural areas and many legends are told about her, some depicting her combing her long hair. One legend tells how a man finds her comb and brings it home. The following night he hears wailing and knocking on his window. He catches the comb in a pair of tongs and passes it out of the window. The comb is removed by the banshee and the tongs are broken or damaged; the man then understands that his hand would have met the same fate had he passed the comb with his hand.

The banshee is associated with lamenting, keening and death. The keen *(caoineadh)* was performed by women at funerals and at wakes as part of the lament for the dead. Certain, usually older, women in the community came to the house where the corpse was laid out and took it in turns to perform the keen which was usually composed *ex tempore* and sung to music with a regular refrain during the days of the wake and later at the graveyard. During the wake people also told stories, smoked clay pipes, drank whiskey and played games. The clergy disapproved of many of the wake customs and of the keen.

Dressing in Disguise – **Wrenboys** *(Dreoilíní)* are groups of people who dress up and go from house to house playing music, singing and asking for money to help "bury the wren". In former times wrenboys carried a dead wren on a staff or bush but this custom is no longer observed. The tradition is associated for the most part with the south west and takes place around Christmas time. In former times the wrenboys wore straw costumes, although today this is less so and wrenboys tend to wear other forms of disguise. The tradition of the wren is especially strong in the town of Dingle, County Kerry, where a number of groups of so-called "wrens" assemble on 26 December and march through the town, calling in at public houses, playing music and collecting money, which they spend on entertainment at the end of the day. Many of those involved in the Dingle make their own costumes from straw which they collect. Numerous other costumes are brought home by emigrants returning for Christmas. The Dingle wren is accompanied by fife and drum bands marching through the town. The custom of **Strawboys** is still in existence in certain parts of Ireland, especially in County Clare, where these entertainers in straw costumes appear either at wedding celebrations or at the public house when a honeymoon couple return home; it is deemed the leader's right to dance with the bride.

Mummers *(Cleamairí)* are associated for the most part with the eastern and north-eastern parts of Ireland. These are groups of people who go in disguise from house to house during the days before and after Christmas and perform a play involving the death and resuscitation of the hero. Many of the plays have medieval origins and may include or be followed by music.

Celtic Calendar – The Celtic year was traditionally divided according to the four quarter-days – **Imbolc** (1 February), now the feast of St Brigit; **Beltaine** (1 May) meaning bright fire, hence modern Irish *Bealtaine* (May); **Lughnasa** (1 August), named after the Celtic god Lugh, hence modern Irish *Lúnasa* (August); **Samain** (1 November), hence modern Irish *Samhain* (November). These quarterdays also marked the start of each new season and involved a great deal of celebration and ritual, especially on the eve of each new season. Some aspects of the old calendar are still observed and many new elements have been introduced over the years. **St John's Fire** is lit on the eve of the feast of St John (23 June); although formerly more widespread, the custom is now strongest in the western counties. Each community lights its own fire at a public place, such as a cross-roads; the fire is lit as night falls and the occasion is one of celebration and enjoyment. Within living memory, **Garland Sunday**, also known as Bilberry Sunday, Fraughan Sunday or Domhnach Crom Dubh was celebrated on the last Sunday of July. **Crom Dubh**, probably a version of the god Donn, is the harvest god. The harvest celebration is also closely identified with the pilgrimage to the top of Mám Éan mountain in County Galway in August. Other important days and periods in the traditional calendar include Christmas, Easter and Halloween; although they are celebrated today much as in other parts of the world, they still maintain some particularly Irish characteristics. On Christmas Eve and on other days during the twelve days of Christmas, a candle is lit and placed in the window of a house to guide and welcome the Holy Family. Many holy wells are visited on Easter Sunday and are believed to have particularly curative powers at this time. It is believed that the sun dances on Easter Sunday morning. Halloween is a time for games of divination and associated pastimes and until recently people used to leave the fire alight and go to bed early to allow their dead ancestors access to the comfort of the house.

Celtic Art – Circles formed an integral part of Celtic art; the outline of the design was marked out on the piece to be decorated with an iron compass. Other decorative motifs were S-and C-shaped curves, spirals and swirls and zig-zags, with intricate, interlaced patterns in the interstices. Similar designs, identified by archaeologists as **La Tène**, after the continental Celtic centre found at La Tène which flourished during the last five centuries BC, are found on two granite monuments – at Turoe *(see p 105)* and Castlestrange *(see p 271)* – which date from the 3C BC. They are the only two such monuments to have survived in Ireland and were probably used in religious ceremonies. They resemble the Greek *omphalos* at Delphi, a site raided by the Celts in 290 BC.

The finest Celtic pieces are designed in gold. The beauty of the torc or neckband is well attested. The goldsmith stretched the metal into long narrow strips and then twisted them around each other to make a golden rope; the torc was then shaped to fit around the warrior's neck. The Celts made personal ornaments, such as brooches for fastening clothes, horse harnesses and sword sheaths. They often decorated their goods with enamel. They favoured the colour red but also used blue, yellow and green. Many distinctive patterns on modern jewellery are of Celtic origin. A regular motif in Celtic design is the triskele, a figure with three arms or legs, symbolising earth, fire and water; it may have evolved into the three-legged straw crosses, which are part of Irish tradition.

Some early sculptures display a nude female figure with crossed legs, known as *Sheila-na-gig*, which owes much to pagan traditions. Many interpretations have been given to these carvings and it is reasonable to assume that the figure was linked to a fertility cult. Some of them are grotesque and most are to be found in or about churches. Some are found in churches which are closely associated with women or a female saint. Others are connected with holy wells and castles. These figures were most likely associated with pagan ritual in comparatively recent times. According to oral tradition, the sculptures were certainly visited and touched to facilitate childbirth. It is possible that the term *Sheila-na gig* comes from the Irish *Síle na gCíoch* meaning Sheila of the breasts and that the figures were thus named because of their disproportionate appearance.

National Museum of Ireland, Dublin

National Museum – Broche de Tara (8ᵉ S.)

Traditional Music – Music, dance and song are arguably the most vibrant and obvious aspects of traditional Irish life. Today, many public houses provide music sessions, some of which are formal, commercial and structured, while other sessions are informal and free of charge. The main instruments used in sessions are the fiddle, flute, tin whistle, accordeon, concertina, melodeon, uilleann pipes, banjo, guitar, bodhrán, keyboard and the spoons.

Schools and festivals are held throughout the year and people come from many countries and continents to learn an instrument or to learn more about aspects of Irish music. The best known of these schools is probably the **Willie Clancy Summer School**, which runs over two weekends and is held in the first half of July each year in Milltown Malbay, County Clare. Other schools and festivals take place, during the summer for the most part, and are sometimes held in memory of a local musician. Specialist classes in regional styles of instrumental playing are also held at many schools such as the fiddle classes in Glenties, County Donegal, each October.

Set-dancing originated in Ireland in the 18C; it consists of figure dances, developed by travelling dancing masters, who adapted the original French dance movements to suit Irish music. Set-dancing is very popular and can be seen in many public venues; classes are held on a regular basis in hundreds of venues. Although it could not be described as "traditional" the recent development of the Riverdance show has attracted a great deal of attention to Irish dancing.

Singing forms part of many of these festivals and at least one festival is devoted solely to this art and is held each June in Ennistymon, County Clare. Traditional singing is usually called old style *(sean-nós)* singing and is especially closely identified with singing in Irish; songs are also sung in English in this style. Traditional songs in Irish date for the most part from the last two to three hundred years although some are older and the style is certainly a good deal older still. Songs in English include recently composed songs and also many songs from the medieval ballad tradition. The style is individual, unaccompanied, free and ornate, with many regional variations. The Irish-speaking area of Rath Cairn, County Meath, hosts the Irish-language singing festival *Éigse Dharach Uí Chatháin* in October each year.

It must be remembered that song, music and dance take place on a regular, spontaneous basis in all parts of Ireland and that it is this very unpredictability which supplies much of its vibrancy and attraction. New songs and tunes are constantly being composed.

Gaeltacht – This is the name given to the parts of the country where people still speak Gaelic, the native Irish language. Most of them are in the most sparsely populated and beautiful regions of Ireland, on the west coast – Donegal, Mayo, Galway and Kerry – and in pockets in the south – near Cork, in Co Waterford and Co Meath.

The **Gaelic Summer Schools**, which were started during the 19C Gaelic revival, have become a permanent feature of the Gaeltacht, inspiring and entertaining each new generation.

The earliest known form of writing in the Irish language is in **Ogham script**. Most of the inscriptions are memorials of the dead and date from the 4C to 7C but the script continued in use until the 8C or later. The language used is Goidelic, which was introduced by Celts from the Continent, so many of the words used in Ogham were probably obsolete when they were carved in stone and it is possible that this action was seen as a form of preservation.

The script is based on the Latin alphabet and was probably adapted by poets and wise men before the Latin alphabet became more generally familiar in Christian Ireland. Ogham seems to have been quite familiar to scholars as many manuscripts contain detailed descriptions and guides relating to it. The word "'Oghma" is of uncertain origin although it is probably associated with a poetic divinity – Ogmios, the Celtic god of eloquence.

The script consists of 20 characters written as groups of a maximum of five straight lines on either side of, or horizontally or diagonally through, a central line which was usually cut into the vertical edge of a standing stone. Many of these standing stones are found in the southern districts of Ireland.

Ogham stones have been found not only in Ireland (300) but also in Scotland, Wales and on the Isle of Man.

Irish, also known as Gaelic, developed from Goidelic and was the natural language of the population until the 16C. The first documents in Irish in Latin writing date from the 7C, although a list of Irish names appeared in Ptolemy's Geography in AD 150. The decline in the use of Irish was caused by the gradual imposition of English law and administration in the 16C and the repressive clauses of the Penal Laws *(see p 63)* in the 17C. Many Irish people turned to English to achieve a position in society. This trend was accelerated by the teaching of English in the National Schools, which were set up in 1831. During and after the famine (1845–47) many Irish speakers died or emigrated; in 1835 half the population was estimated to speak Irish; in 1851 one-quarter of the population was recorded as Irish-speaking; by 1911 the number had fallen to one-eighth.

The Mythological and Historical Cycles – The stories from the four great ancient Irish cycles are arguably among the finest expressions of the Irish imagination and are still a source of artistic inspiration.

The **Mythological Cycle** tells of the heroes or gods who inhabited Ireland before the arrival of the Celts and contains the story of the Battle of Moytura, the Children of Lir and the Wooing of Etain.

The **Ulster Cycle** *(Rúraíocht)* recounts the deeds of the Red Branch Knights of Navan Fort; it includes the **Cattle Raid of Cooley** *(Táin Bó Cuailgne)*, an epic poem which describes how Queen Maeve of Connaught set out to capture the famous brown bull of Cooley and how Ferdia, the Connaught champion, was defeated by the Ulster champion, Cúchulain, which means the hound of Culann.

The **Ossianic Cycle**, also known as the **Fenian Cycle** *(Fiannaíocht)*, is set in the time of Cormac mac Airt, who is said to have reigned at Tara in the 3C, and tells about Fionn mac Cumhaill and the Fianna, whose capital was on the Hill of Allen. The Fenian tales and lore tell of the great deeds of the Fianna or Fenian warriors.

Hundreds of neolithic tombs are called Diarmuid and Gráinne's bed *(Leaba Dhiarmuid agus Ghráinne)* in the belief that these lovers from the Fenian tales slept here during their travels in Ireland.

The **Historical Cycle**, which is also known as the **Cycle of the Kings**, is probably a mixture of history and fiction. Many place-names and sites identify with characters and episodes from mythological tales.

A vast number of tales and episodes from these cycles were central to the living story-telling tradition in Ireland until very recently. In addition to their preservation in written literature, the stories were kept alive in oral form, both in Irish and in English, and formed an important part of the repertoire of the storyteller *(seanchaí)*, who was a person of great social importance.

Irish literature, from the great Cycles to current works, has been translated into many languages. Some of the best-known authors include the Connemara-born Máirtín Cadhain, former professor of Irish at Trinity College, whose novel *Cré na Cille* (1949) *(The Clay of the Graveyard)* is the best-known prose writing in recent times. The authors of the Great Blasket Island, off the coast of Co Kerry, have produced several works describing island life before the people left in the early 1950s. Modern Irish poetry, composed by Seán O Ríordéin, Máirtín O Direáin and Nuala ní Dhomhnaill among others, has appeared in a number of languages.

Gaelic Revival – The 19C saw a revival of interest in Ireland's Gaelic heritage, which was closely linked with nationalist politics. Various societies were set up to promote Irish language and culture.

The **Irish Literary Society** was founded in 1892. William Butler Yeats was joined by Edward Martyn and Lady Gregory and in 1899 the society became the **Irish Literary Theatre** (later the Irish National Theatre at the Abbey Theatre); George Moore returned to Dublin especially to take part in the new movement.

In 1893 the **Gaelic League** *(Conradh na Gaeilge)*, a non-sectarian and non-political organisation, was founded by Douglas Hyde *(see p 272)* for the "de-Anglicisation of Ireland" through the revival of Gaelic as a spoken language and a return to Irish cultural roots. It was largely an urban organisation which instituted an annual festival of native culture and campaigned sucessfully for St Patrick's Day (17 March) to be a national holiday. In 1909 Gaelic became a compulsory subject for matriculation to the National University. In 1922 the Constitution stated that Gaelic was an official language and its study

Gaelic-speaking regions

was made compulsory in primary schools. The following year it became an obligatory qualification for entry into the Civil Service of the Irish Free State. Under the Constitution of 1937 Gaelic was named as the first offical language before English.

In 1925 in order to foster the use of Gaelic the new Irish government set up a Commission to investigate conditions in the Gaelic-speaking districts; as a result of its report two organisations – **Gaeltarra Éireann** (1935) and **Údarás na Gaeltachta** (1980) – were established to develop the resources of the Gaelic-speaking regions.

With the help of Government sponsorship the **Folklore of Ireland Society**, still in existence, was founded by Douglas Hyde and other

Hurling

Hurling has been played in Ireland for over 2 000 years. It features in Irish myth, as an aristocratic, even royal, game and is mentioned favourably in early legal documents. It was banned by the Statute of Kilkenny (1367) and again by the Galway Statute (1537) but it remained popular despite fines and imprisonment. By 1600 it was again in favour with the authorities and greatly patronised by the landlords until the Rebellion in 1798. It then fell into decline until the establishment of the GAA.

Hurling is played with a curved stick, a hurl *(camán)* made from ash, and a ball *(sliothar)* made of animal hair covered in leather, on a rectangular pitch (150ydx90yd/137mx82m) by two teams, each consisting of 15 men – six backs, two midfield players, six forwards and a goalkeeper. The game lasts an hour, ie 30min each half, and is supervised by a referee, two linesmen and four umpires.

There are two goals, one at each end, consisting of two uprights held apart by a crossbar to form an H; one point is gained when the ball passes over the bar; three points when the ball goes under the bar. The ball may be lifted or struck with the *camán* on the ground or in the air; it may be juggled or carried on the *camán* or kicked or caught in the hand.

folklore scholars and enthusiasts. Further state sponsorship enabled the **Irish Theatre** *(Taibhearc na Gaillimhe)* to be launched in 1928 by Micheál Mac Liammóir and Hilton Edwards, joint founders of the Gate Theatre in Dublin.

In 1929 Queen's College Galway became a bilingual institution and a Gaelic Faculty was established.

The **Irish Folklore Commission**, founded in 1935 for the collection, preservation and publication of Irish folklore, became the Department of Irish Folklore, when its staff and holdings were transferred to University College Dublin in 1971.

In 1972 *Siamsa Tíre*, which had been set up in Tralee in 1968, became the **National Folk Theatre of Ireland**; its name derives from *siamsa*, an Irish word which describes the old Irish custom of visiting one's neighbours in the evening for entertainment. Also in 1972 the **Gaelic Radio Service** *(Radió na Gaeltachta)* was started; the Irish language television station *(Telefís na Gaeilge)* was started in October 1996.

Gaelic Athletic Association – One of the earliest societies set up in the 19C to promote Gaelic culture was the Gaelic Athletic Association *(Cumann Lúthchleas Gael)*, a largely rural movement, founded in 1884 in Thurles; the principal games fostered are hurling *(iománaíocht)*, Gaelic football *(peil)* and handball *(liathróid láimhe)*. The national GAA stadium, Croke Park in Dublin, is named after the association's first patron, Archbishop Croke (1824–1902). The history of the Association and the exploits of the hurling and football champions are excellently illustrated in the GGA Museums in Thurles and in Croke Park, Dublin.

Hurling

PLACE NAMES

Certain elements occur very frequently in Irish place names and most have a clear meaning.

Alt – cliff
Ard – high, height, hillock
Áth – ford
Bád – boat
Baile – town, townland, homestead
Bán – white, fair; grassland
Beag – little
Béal – opening, entrance, river mouth
Bealtaine – 1 May, month of May
Beann – peak, pointed hill, horn, gable
Beannchair – abounding in peaks or gables
Bearna – gap
Beith – birch tree
Bile – venerated tree
Bó – cow
Boireann – large rock, rocky district
Both – hut, tent
Bóthar – road
Buí – yellow
Bun – end, bottom
Cabhán – hollow
Caiseal – castle, circular stone fort
Caisleán – castle

Caladh – harbour, landing place, marshy
Capall – horse
Carraig – rock
Cath – battle
Cathair – circular stone fort, city
Cealtrach – old burial ground
Céide – hillock
Cill – church
Cillín – little church, children's burial ground
Cliath – a hurdle
Cloch – stone
Cluain – meadow
Cnap – knob, round little hill
Cno – hill
Coinicéar – rabbit warren
Com – mountain recess
Dairbhre – oak-grove
Dearg – red
Díseart – desert, hermitage
Doire – wooded area
Droichead – bridge
Droim – ridge, hillock

Dubh – black
Dún – fort
Eaglais – church
Eas – waterfall
Eiscir – ridge of high land
Eochaill – yew wood
Fear – man
Fearbán – strip of land
Fionn – white, fair-haired person
Fir – men
Gall – foreigner
Gorm – blue
Gort – field
Inbhear – river mouth
Inis – island
Iúr – yew tree
Lár – centre
Leithinis – peninsula
Lios – circular earthen fort, ring fort
Mór – large
Móta – moat, high mound
Muc – pig
Muirbheach – level stretch of sandy land along the seashore
Muireasc – seaside marsh meadow
Óg – young
Oileán – island
Omhna – tree, tree-trunk
Poll – hole, cave
Ráth – earthen rampart
Rinn – point of land
Sagart – priest
Sceir – sharp rock
Sean – old
Sí – bewitching, enchanting; fairy mound
Slí – route, way
Sliabh – mountain
Sruth – stream
Teach – house
Teampall – church
Tobar – well
Tóchar – causeway
Trá – beach, strand
Túr – tower
Turlach – winter lake
Uachtar – top, upper part

Christianity in Ireland

Although the majority of the population of Ireland (75 %) is Roman Catholic, most of their churches are of recent date and are built in the new centres of population or next to a ruined monastery, where the faithful heard mass in the Penal Days and where they often continue to be buried. As a result of the Reformation *(see below)* the traditional religious sites are usually occupied by the Church of Ireland, a member of the Anglican Communion. In the north the Presbyterian Church predominates. Methodism has a limited following. Huguenots, Protestants from France, settled in the south and east after the Revocation of the Edict of Nantes in 1683. In the past the Quakers, who first settled at Rosenallis in Co Laois in the 17C, played a significant social role. Christianity was probably introduced to Ireland from Roman Britain or Gaul in the 4C. Palladius, the first bishop, was appointed in 431 by Pope Celestine I but his mission met with little success; the sites of three of his churches have been identified in Wicklow.

St Patrick – The patron saint of Ireland was born on the west coast of Roman Britain where he was captured as a young man by Irish raiders. After six years of slavery near Sliabh Mis (Slemish in Co Down), he escaped to France and then returned to his birthplace. Inspired by a vision that the people of Ireland were calling him, he went to France to study, possibly at the monasteries of Lérins, Tours and Auxerre. In 432 in middle age he returned to Ireland to convert the people to Christianity. He is thought to have founded his first church at Saul and then travelled to Slane to challenge the High King and the druids of Tara. It was customary for the high-king to light a fire on the hill of Tara at Eastertime and it was forbidden for anyone else to light such a fire before this day. Patrick lit a fire before Easter at Slane and was confronted by the King Laoghaire, who pretended he would nonetheless revere Patrick; despite this, Patrick was suspicious of Laoghaire and his suspicion was later confirmed when an attempt was made to poison him.

He worked widely in Leinster, Meath and Connaught. In 444, after a visit to Rome, he founded the cathedral church of Armagh, which is still the ecclesiastical capital of Ireland. St Patrick founded many churches and created numerous bishoprics. When he died, probably at Saul in 461, the country was organised into dioceses, which coincided with the petty Irish kingdoms, each ruled by a bishop.

The biography of Patrick is to some extent uncertain and he is the subject of numerous tales and legends, according to which he banished monsters and drove the snakes out of Ireland. The "snake motif" seems to date from the 12C. Each year during the summer months pilgrimages take place to Lough Derg in County Donegal; documentary evidence from as early as the 7C affirms that Patrick had banished a monster from that lake. A cave on the island is said to be the entrance to Purgatory.

On St Patrick's day (17 March) people wear a sprig of **shamrock** *(seamróg)*, a custom which is comparatively recent, being first documented in the later part of the 17C. Popular tradition claims that, when Patrick was teaching the Irish people, he used this trefoil plant *(trifolium minus)* to illustrate the doctrine of the Holy Trinity. People used to wear coloured paper or ribbon crosses in recognition of the saint's day but in recent years commercial manufacturers have made green and gold badges showing either a shamrock or a harp. The **drowning of the shamrock** is a custom associated with the drink *pota Pádraig* (Patrick's pot). The drink is whiskey and the custom is said to have been ordained by Patrick on one occasion when he banished an evil spirit.

St Bridget – Brigit was a Celtic goddess, whose name means "the exalted person"; it is significant that the same name is given to the most popular female saint in Irish tradition and second only to St Patrick among all the saints. This Leinster saint ("Bríd"), who died c AD 524, established a convent in Kildare *(Cill Dara* in Irish meaning "the church of the oak tree") and this may have been a sacred spot in pre-Christian times. *Vitae Brigitae*, a Latin biography of Bridget, was compiled c AD 650 but contains little historical information. She is perceived to be the protectress of animals and crops, with which she is closely associated. Oral tradition holds her in equal esteem with the Virgin Mary and calls her the "Mary of the Gael". One folk legend tells that, when the Virgin Mary and the Infant Jesus were fleeing to Egypt, a band of soldiers came upon them. Bridget diverted the soldiers' attention from the fugitives by wearing a brightly coloured head-dress with candles and Mary passed by in safety. Mary rewarded Bridget by telling her that her feast-day would be one day before her own, which is on 2 February, also known as Candlemas.

The most popular legend of St Bridget is associated with her church in Kildare. She wished to build a convent but had no land; she therefore approached the local king and asked him for land. He granted her only as much land as her cloak would cover; when she spread her cloak it grew to cover a vast amount of land.

On St Bridget's day (1 February) it is customary to honour the saint by making straw or rush crosses *(Cros Bhríde)*, which have numerous regional variations in design and form. Many people place the previous year's cross under the rafters to ensure good fortune and health and to make room for the new cross. Sometimes the cross is placed in the outhouse as protection for the animals. People used to leave a piece of cloth *(Brat Bhríde)* outside the door in the belief that the saint would touch it and imbue it with curative powers. On the eve of the saint's day groups of young people, usually led by a young girl, used to travel from house to house, singing and dancing. They collected money and carried a home-made doll called a *Brídeog* (Little Bridget). These young people are known as "Biddy Boys" or *Brídeoga*.

Celtic Church – As continental Europe was overrun by barbarians, the church in Ireland developed a distinctive form of organisation based on monasticism. In the mid 6C and 7C a great many monasteries were founded and by the 8C the administration of the church had been taken over by the abbots. Although bishops continued to perform the sacramental duties and new bishops were consecrated, they were not appointed to particular sees.

Ardagh Chalice (8C)

National Museum of Ireland, Dublin

Irish Missionary Monks

In the period known as the Dark Ages, the early years of the second millennium, the monks of the Irish Celtic church travelled great distances overseas in the service of God; some were driven out by the Viking invasions. The one who went furthest was probably **Brendan** *(see p 200)* who may have reached America. **Patrick**, the patron saint of Ireland, studied in the south of France. Bangor Abbey sent out many missionary monks – **Columbanus**, who left Bangor in 590, founded monasteries in Luxeuil, Annegray and Fontaines in France before falling into disfavour; after spending some time at St Gall in Switzerland he moved to Bobbio in Italy where he founded another monastery before his death in 615; **Gall**, a disciple and companion of Columbanus, founded a church in Bregenz on Lake Constanz and gave his name to St Gall – the monastery contains a fine collection of early Irish manuscripts; **Rubha** sailed to Britain in 671 and founded Applecross in Scotland. There was a strong link with Iona in Scotland; **Columba** (**Colmcille** in Irish), who was born in Donegal *(see p 196)*, left his native country to found a monastery in Iona. In c 635 **Aidan**, an Irish clerk from Iona, moved to Lindisfarne, in the north of England. Another monk of Iona was **Adamnan**, who became 9th Abbot of Iona in 679 and died there in 704; he was born in Ireland c 628 and he wrote a life of Columba, from whose grandfather he was descended; he pursuaded the church in Northern Ireland, but not Iona, to reject the Celtic calendar and customs; in 697 his law was enacted at Birr for the protection of women, children and clergy, especially in time of war. **Dicuil** went first to Iona and thence in 800 to the court of Charlemagne in France; he wrote about grammar, astronomy and geography. **Fursey** (Fursa) went from Ireland to East Anglia but ultimately he settled in northern France, where he founded a monastery at Lagny near Paris and, after his death in 648, he became patron of the monastery of Péronne, which was founded near his tomb; another who settled in France was **Johanne Eriugena**, who lived in Laon in the second half of 9C; he was called the most important philosopher in the west between Augustine and Thomas Aquinas; **Sedulius Scottus** settled in Liège in the mid 9C but was also associated with Cologne. Several went to Germany and beyond – **Kilian** to Wurzburg in Germany *(see p 211)*; **Marianus Scottus** in the 11C to Cologne, Fulda and Mainz. Another of the same name, **Marianus Scottus** (Muiredach MacRobertaig), a member of an important Donegal family, founded the Irish monastery of St Peter in Ratisbon, where he died in 1088. **Virgil** (Fergal) left Ireland in 742 and travelled via France and Bavaria to Austria, where he became patron of Salzburg. **Donatus** fled from the Vikings in the 9C and travelled as far as Fiesole in Italy.

Some **monasteries** grew up round a hermit's retreat but many were founded by the head of a clan; members of the family entered the religious life and filled the various offices, as abbot, bishop, priest, teacher or ascetic. The manual work was done either by the monks or by the original tenants of the land, married men with families, whose elder sons usually received a clerical education in the monastery school. Most monasteries were self-sufficient communities providing their own food, clothing, books, tools and horses. Some monasteries seem to have been founded on sites which had pagan religious associations; others were set up by the main highways, often on the boundaries of a kingdom.

There were few nunneries, possibly because **women** had less access to independent land or funds. Kildare was the most famous; Monasterboice was a dual foundation for men and women; at Clonmacnoise there was a separate church for women built outside the monastic precinct.

The monastic **libraries** contained copies of the Scriptures, the early Fathers, some classical authors and some history; much early Christian scholarship was preserved in Ireland after the fall of the Roman Empire. In the scriptorium the monks made copies of existing texts or wrote their own learned works. They prepared their own materials – vellum, pens, ink and coloured pigments; their techniques are well described and illustrated at the Colmcille Heritage Centre *(see p 163)*. Important books such as the Gospels were beautifully illuminated; such **illuminated work** is on display in the Library of Trinity College in Dublin. Leather satchels were made to hold the books, which were hung from hooks to protect them from mice and damp. In their **schools** the monks taught church Latin and the study of religious texts.

Irish monks developed a strong tradition of **asceticism** with a threefold classification of martyrdom. White martyrdom meant parting from all they loved, withdrawing from society or going into exile to serve God; green was to endure labour in penitence and repentance, and red involved submission to the cross or tribulation. Ascetics seeking to contemplate the presence of God would form small monastic communities in remote places, particularly on islands. The monastic community on Great Skellig eminently fulfils this need; there was little here for the monks to do except gardening and fishing, and the island is accessible only in fine weather.

Romanisation – Following four synods held in the first half of the 12C the Irish church was gradually reorganised on the Roman pattern. Four provinces and 33 new dioceses were created, each with a bishop. Some monastic churches became cathedrals, others were used as parish churches.

Monastic orders from the continent were introduced. The Augustinians took over earlier monastic centres to be near the people. The Cistercians chose new and remote sites in accordance with their ascetic rule, which attracted many Irish monks; by 1272 there were 38 Cistercian houses in Ireland. The Franciscans settled in the towns in the 13C; in the 15C the Observants spread to the west and north.

The Irish church was further diminished by the Normans with the encouragement of King Henry II and Popes Adrian IV and Alexander III so as "to extend the bounds of the Roman Church". Under the Statute of Kilkenny (1366) Irishmen were forbidden to enter English-run monasteries, and English-speaking clergy were to be appointed to English-speaking parishes.

Reformation – In the 16C the churches in England and Ireland were declared independent of Rome; the monasteries were suppressed. Trinity College in Dublin was founded in 1591 to provide Irish priests for the established church; although Roman Catholics were admitted to degrees in 1793, membership was confined to Anglicans until 1873. The 16C reforms were only intermittently enforced in Ireland; the majority of the people remained faithful to the Roman church and many monasteries continued until suppressed by Cromwell. Early in the 17C the Plantation of Ulster with lowland Scots introduced fervent Presbyterianism.

Penal Laws – Under the repressive measures introduced after the Battle of the Boyne (1690), Roman Catholics were barred from the armed forces, law, commerce, from civic office or office under the crown, from land purchase; Roman Catholic estates could pass *in toto* to an eldest son if he converted to the established church but otherwise had to be divided among all the sons. No Roman Catholic could attend school, keep a school or go abroad to school. Education was conducted in **hedge schools**, which taught Latin, Greek, arithmetic, Irish, English, history and geography; the masters, who were paid in money or kind, were respected members of the Irish community; several were poets. All Roman Catholic bishops and regular clergy were banished from Ireland, and Roman Catholic worship was forbidden. Roman Catholic priests travelled the country in disguise and said mass out of doors in remote places or in ruined monastery churches; they used sacramental vessels which could be dismantled to avoid detection.

Denominational Freedom – Under the Catholic Relief Acts of 1791 and 1793, freedom of worship and education were granted. In 1795 **Maynooth Seminary** was established for training Roman Catholic clergy. In 1820 Edmund Rice (1762–1844), a former pupil of a hedge school, obtained papal recognition of the **Christian Brothers** *(see p 221)*, an order which established many boys' schools in Ireland. In 1831 the 18C hedge schools were replaced by the National Schools. In 1869 the Church of Ireland, a member of the Anglican Communion, was disestablished. Apart from Trinity College and two short-lived 16C colleges at Maynooth and Galway, Ireland had no medieval universities. In 1845 charters were issued to incorporate three colleges in Belfast, Cork and Galway but, owing to Roman Catholic opposition, only Queen's College in Belfast thrived. The Catholic University, founded in Dublin in 1854 with Cardinal Newman as Rector, was incorporated as University College when the National University of Ireland was founded in 1908; two years later Maynooth was also recognised as a college of the National University.

Pilgrimages and Patterns – Since the 8C, by which time Ireland was an almost entirely Christian country, the lives of the **saints** have played a major role in popular devotion and also stimulated an entire body of related legends and lore. Saints were seen to be powerful in many spheres of life on earth and in the afterlife; in many instances, they were seen as popular heroes and heroines. Some were said to have had a miraculous birth; others wielded supernatural powers and could triumph against the enemy. Saints had healing powers and even their posessions or relics could effect a cure.

Oral tradition has been profoundly influenced by biographies of saints; the lore of saints is widespread through-

Pilgrims climbing Croagh Patrick

Slide File, Dublin

out Ireland. Thousands of **holy wells**, many associated with local saints, are scattered throughout the countryside; they are said to have curative powers – of a general type or more specific – and are visited frequently, particularly on saints' days.

People still observe the feast days of local saints and the **pattern** (modern Irish *pátrún*; the word is a corruption of patron) when they make a communal visit to a holy well or other religious site under the protection of the local patron saint. Prayers are recited and rituals performed; coins, flowers and pieces of cloth are left as tokens of gratitude or hope. In many places holy wells are associated with **rag trees**, although such trees may exist independently. **Rag trees**, which are named after the hundreds of coloured pieces of cloth attached to their branches, are used to invoke divine assistance, often of a curative kind. In the past many patterns were celebrated with drinking and sometimes ended in fighting and disorder.

These days, especially along the west coast, many patterns are associated with boat racing - on St MacDara's feast day (16 July) a pattern takes place on the coast in Connemara *(see p 146)*. Many other traditional religious sites are still visited by pilgrims: Glencolumbkille on St Columba's Day (9 June); Clonmacnoise on St Kieran's Day (9 September); Croagh Patrick in July, when people climb barefoot to the summit. The most rigorous pilgrimage takes place at St Patrick's Purgatory, an island in Lough Derg (southeast of Donegal) where St Patrick spent 40 days in prayer and fasting; during the season (1 June to 15 August) pilgrims spend three days barefoot, take part in an all-night vigil and exist on one meal a day of bread and hot black tea or coffee.

Irish Diaspora

Forty million people of Irish descent live in the USA, 5 million in Canada, 5 million in Australia, unnumbered millions in Great Britain. Estimates suggest that over 60 million people in the world are of Irish origin. It is sometimes assumed that it was the Great Famine which precipitated the outflow of people but emigration has been a constant feature of Irish history.

The imposition of the Anglican Reformation in the reign of Elizabeth I caused a number to leave Munster for Spain and Portugal. The conquest of 1603 caused more departures to Spain and Brittany. Cromwell transported whole regiments, possibly 34 000 men, to Spain and Portugal, while many civilians were shipped to the West Indies where they could be sold as slaves. The Treaty of Limerick in 1691 was followed by the flight of the so-called "Wild Geese", military men who, together with their wives and children, emigrated to France, where they served in the French army until 1697; some of them moved on to Spain, where three Irish regiments were formed. The most famous name among the merchants who settled on the western coast of Europe is that of Richard Hennessy, from Cork, who started the Cognac company.

The first transatlantic emigrants were mostly Presbyterians, the Ulster-Scots (known in the USA as Scots-Irish or Scotch-Irish), descendants of lowland Scots who had settled in Ulster in the 17C. Whole families emigrated early in the 18C owing to religious disability and rising rents. The Roman Catholic Irish tended to emigrate as single young adults, both men and women.

The Scotch-Irish had an influence in America out of all proportion to their numbers, particularly in the War of Independence and in education. The heartland of Ulster settlement was in the Appalachian back country; the name hillbilly derives from King William III. Many of the settlers were involved in pushing the frontier westwards and building the American railways. Over a quarter of the Presidents of the USA are descended from Scotch-Irish settlers. This Irish-American connection is traced in detail at the Ulster-American Folk Park *(see p 370)* and Andrew Jackson Centre *(see p 328)* as well as several other family homesteads. Allied military leaders in the Second World War who were of Ulster stock include Alanbrooke, Alexander, Auchinleck, Dill and Montgomery.

Following the Napoleonic Wars emigration recommenced and during the next 25 years over a million Irishmen and women emigrated to Great Britain and the USA.

Emigration reached its peak during the Great Famine when Ireland lost 4 million people, through death and emigration; during the worst years about 1 million fled and another 2.5 million emigrated in the following decade. The great wave of 19C emigrants was largely composed of Roman Catholics from Donegal, Connaught, Munster and Leinster, counties

---

Ulster-Scots – Scotch-Irish

Theodore Roosevelt's mother, speaking of her family who came from Co Antrim, described them as "a grim stern people, strong and simple, powerful for good and evil, swayed by gusts of stormy passion, the love of freedom rooted in their very hearts' core ... relentless, revengeful, suspicious, knowing neither ruth nor pity; they were also upright, resolute and fearless, loyal to their friends and devoted to their country".

Jeanie Johnston replica built in Tralee

which until then had not seen much emigration. Many landed first in Canada but later crossed the frontier into the USA to escape from British rule. Their descendants include John Fitzgerald Kennedy, Ronald Reagan and William Jefferson Clinton.

The numbers who emigrated to Australia and New Zealand were smaller and included some who were transported to the penal colonies.

The flow of immigrants into Great Britain has waxed and waned since the Irish established colonies in Wales and Scotland in the 5C. Many, particularly those who left Ireland during the Famine in the hope of reaching America but were too weak or penniless to continue, settled in Liverpool and Glasgow. London has a flourishing Irish community, particularly north of the river. Margaret Thatcher, Prime Minister of the United Kingdom (1978–91), is descended from Catherine Sullivan, who emigrated in 1811 from Kenmare and became a washerwoman in England.

In the 18C and 19C many Irishmen, who went to work in Britain on the canals or in agriculture and the building trade, returned home for the winter. Those who went to America or Australasia seldom returned to the mother country. Despite their rural origins most Irish emigrants settled in the big cities rather than on the land of their adopted countries.

Irish emigrants in the late 20C are highly qualified young men and women seeking employment not only in English-speaking countries such as Great Britain and the USA but also throughout the countries of the European Union. In recent years emigration has declined and immigration has increased. In 1997 there was a net inflow of 15 000 people, the highest such figure since the 1970s. Many of these people are the same highly qualified former emigrants, returning to the higher standards of living and new culturally revitalised society of modern Ireland.

A project is in progress throughout Ireland to collect all information available from parish records, tombstones and other sources. Access to these computer records and assistance in tracing ancestors can be obtained through the many regional Genealogical Centres (see p 32).

There are 243 Irish clans which hold annual clan gatherings on ancestral sites.

Food and Drink

Ireland is a sociable and hospitable country where people readily gather in a bar or round a table. There are two culinary traditions: the elaborate meals served in town and country mansions, and the simple dishes of the rural and urban poor.

Although history has identified the potato (introduced at the end of the 16C) as the staple food of Ireland, the country has always produced a good range of vegetables and fruit, meat and dairy products and a wide variety of fresh- and salt-water fish; The Dublin Bay prawn and the Galway oyster have a more than local reputation. Each year in October a **gourmet festival** is organised by the many excellent restaurants in Kinsale; their high standard of *haute cuisine* can be found throughout the country, as well as the traditional fried breakfast and high tea.

Breakfast – The traditional **Irish Fry**, known in the north as an "Ulster Fry", consists of fried egg, sausage, bacon, black pudding, potato cakes, mushrooms and tomatoes; it is usually eaten at breakfast but is also served as the evening meal. Other breakfast dishes are kippers and kedgeree.

Fish – The king of the freshwater fish is the **salmon**, wild or farmed; as a main dish it is usually poached or grilled. Irish smoked salmon is traditionally cured with oak wood. Archaeologists have found evidence by the River Bann of a salmon weir and traces of salmon-smoking dating from 2000 BC.

The other most frequently served freshwater fish is **trout**, farmed or wild. **Shellfish**, such as crab, lobster, scallops, mussels and Dublin Bay prawns (also known as langoustines or scampi) are usually available near the coast, particularly in the southwest. Galway Bay oysters are plump and succulent.

The Irish fishing grounds produce Dover sole (known locally as Black sole), lemon sole, plaice, monkfish, turbot, brill, John Dory, cod, hake, haddock, mackerel and herring.

Meat – Prime **beef** is raised on the lush pastures in the east and south of Ireland; lamb comes from the uplands. **Pork** is presented in many ways: as joints and chops; as ham or bacon; as pigs' trotters *(crúibíní)*, known in English as crubeens; in white puddings; in black puddings *(drisheen)* flavoured with tansy and eaten for breakfast. The most popular game is rabbit but hare and pheasant are also served.

Traditional Dishes – These tend to be the simple dishes prepared by the poor people. There is no official recipe for **Irish stew**, which consists of neck of mutton layered in a pot with potatoes, onions and herbs. **Colcannon** is a Harvest or Hallowe'en dish of mashed potatoes, onions, parsnips and white cabbage, mixed with butter and cream. **Champ** is a simpler dish of potatoes mashed with butter to which are added chopped chives or other green vegetables such as parsley, spring onions (scallions), chopped shallots, nettles, peas, cabbage or even carrots (cooked in milk which is added to the purée). Nettles are also made into soup. To make **coddle** a forehock of bacon, pork sausages, potatoes and onions are stewed in layers. Collar and cabbage is composed of a collar of bacon, which has been boiled, coated in breadcrumbs and brown sugar and baked, served with cabbage cooked in the bacon stock.

Seaweed – Various sorts of seaweed, a highly nutritious source of vitamins and minerals, were traditionally used to thicken soups and stews. **Carrageen** is still used to make a dessert with a delicate flavour. **Dulse** is made into a sweet.

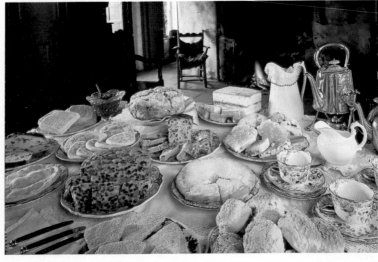

Farmhouse Cakes

Dairy Products – Irish cookery makes liberal use of butter and cream. Ice-cream is particularly popular as a dessert. In recent years many hand-made **cheeses** have appeared on the market: **Cashel Blue** (a soft, creamy, blue-veined cheese made from cow's milk in Tipperary; milder than Stilton), **Cooleeny** (a Camembert-type soft cheese from Thurles in Co Tipperary), **Milleens** (a distinctive spicy cheese from West Cork; as it matures the rind is washed with salt water), **Gubbeen** (soft surface-ripening cheese from Skull in Co Cork).

Bread – A great variety of breads and cakes is baked for breakfast and tea. The most well-known is **soda bread**, made of white or brown flour and buttermilk. **Barm Brack** is a rich fruit cake made with yeast (*báirín breac* = speckled cake).

Beverages – Stout made by **Guinness** or Murphys is the traditional thirst-quencher in Ireland but beer drinking is not uncommon. Black Velvet is a mixture of stout and champagne.

Although there are now only three **whiskey** distilleries in Ireland – Bushmills in Co Antrim, which produces the only malt, and Midleton in Co Cork, both owned by the same company, and Cooley in Dundalk – there are many different brands of whiskey. Their distinctive flavours arise from subtle variations in the production process.

/Bushmills Distillery/Pacemaker Press, Belfast

Bushmills Distillery

Whiskey or Whisky

Irish whiskey is usually but not invariably spelled with an "e" and Scottish whisky without. No certain place – Scotland or Ireland – or date is known for the invention of this spirit but it was being distilled and drunk throughout Ireland by the 16C. It flourished in the reign of Elizabeth I, who seems to have had a taste for it. Illicit whiskey *(poteen)* appeared in the 17C when the government introduced a tax on distilling (1661) and set up a department of Excisemen (Gaugers) to police the distilleries. By the end of the 17C, 2 000 stills were in operation. The most successful brands were made by the larger companies in Dublin – John Power, John Jameson, George Roe and William Jameson. They and other brands were exported all over the British Empire. Sales increased in 1872 when French brandy became scarce owing to a disease in the Cognac district of France but other factors led to a severe decline. Father Mathew, a Capuchin friar, toured Ireland in the 1840s and 1850s preaching against the evil of drink; temperance societies were set up and the consumption of alcohol dropped by over 35%. Blended whiskey, produced in Scotland, entered the market and proved very popular but the Irish distillers preferred to maintain the lightness and fuller flavour of their traditional product. When prohibition was introduced in the USA in the 1920s, the American export market was lost; the British Empire was closed off by the War of Independence. In 1966 the few surviving distilleries combined forces as the Irish Distillers Company and founded a new distillery in Midleton; in the early 1970s they took over Bushmills but were themselves taken over by Pernod-Ricard in 1989.

For a patriotic drink ask for **The Flag**, a mixture of crème de menthe, tequila and Southern Comfort representing the green, white and orange of the Republican tricolor.

Irish Coffee, a delicious creation, consists of a measure of whiskey, brown sugar and very hot black coffee mixed in a heated glass and topped with a layer of fresh cream; it is said to have been served first to passengers landing at Shannon Airport, Foynes, in the early days of transatlantic flying.

Triple distillation

The main distinction of Irish whiskey is that it is distilled three times. Since the beginning of the 20C, only barley or wheat have been used. The grain, including the husks, is milled to produce "grist" which is mixed with hot water (60°C at Midleton and 63°C at Bushmills) and stirred in a large vessel (mash tun) to release the sugars, and the liquid is then drawn off. This process is repeated twice; the liquid from the third mashing is added to the first mashing of new grist. The spent solids are known as draff. The liquid from the first and second mashing (wort) is pumped into vessels called washbacks; yeast is added which reacts with the sugars to produce a light brown liquid. When fermentation is complete the liquid is pumped to the stills, where it is distilled three times (at Cooley as at most Scottish distilleries it is distilled only twice). The spirit is matured in old sherry or Bourbon casks and then blended (vatted) for two or three days.

Music

Ireland is unusual in having a musical instrument – the harp – as its national emblem. Traditional music, song and dance are among the most vibrant aspects of Irish culture. The oldest-known form of Irish music, generally called "old style" *(sean-nós)* singing, is a highly ornate, unaccompanied, individual style associated for the most part with songs in Irish. Many of these are sung to slow airs without any regular rhythm and others are sung to faster tunes. Traditional songs in English include international ballads and native Hiberno-English songs.

Folk Musicians in a pub

The harp dominated the musical scene from the Middle Ages until it was proscribed by the English because of its nationalist allure. It was used to accompany the singing or recitation of poetry. Irish harpists, who trained for many years, were admired for their rapid fingerwork and their quick and lively technique; they enjoyed high social status. **Turlough O'Carolan** (Carolan) (1670–1738) started too late in life to reach the highest standard of skill but he was an outstanding composer, much in demand; he left over 200 tunes, which show remarkable melodic invention and are still played. The first documented mention of mouth-blown pipes in Ireland occurs in an 11C text and the earliest depiction dates from the 15C; these pipes appear to have been primarily for entertainment purposes. The particularly Irish form of pipes, the **uilleann** (elbow) **pipes**, which have regulators and drones operated by the fingers, emerged in the 18C. These pipes are renowned for the unique sound produced by highly skilled musicians and are closely identified with Irish traditional music *(see p 56)*, which in recent years has become an important industry.

18C-19C – The highly musical life of Dublin in the 18C produced two firsts: the first performance of **Handel's Messiah**, conducted by the composer himself, and the birth of **John Field** (1782–1837), an outstanding pianist who invented the Nocturne. In 1792 a great harp festival was held in Belfast. Many of the traditional tunes were written down by Edward Bunting, one of the earliest collectors of traditional tunes. Some of these were sung to words written by Thomas Moore *(The Last Rose of Summer)*. These tunes enjoyed great popularity in elegant drawing rooms as Moore's Melodies. In the 19C many Irish musicians made their name in England or abroad. Sir **Charles Villiers Stanford** (1852–1924) taught Vaughan Williams and Holst as well as making his name as a composer. **Sir Hamilton Harty** (1879–1941) was best known as the conductor of the Hallé Orchestra. **John McCormack** (1884–1945) spent most of his career as a tenor singer in the USA. Margaret Sheridan (1889–1957) was in Puccini's opinion one of the best interpreters of his work. Three 19C Irish operas – *The Bohemian Girl* by William Balfe, *Maritana* by Vincent Wallace and *The Lily of Killarney* by Benedict – achieved considerable popularity.

Contemporary Scene The **Wexford Opera Festival** was inspired by a long-established love of opera in Ireland and provides many young singers with an opportunity to start a career. The Radio Telefís Éireann Symphony Orchestra sets a standard for trained musicians. There are many Irish musicians of international stature, of whom **James Galway**, the flautist, is probably the best known.

Two significant names among modern composers are **Seán Ó'Riada** (1931–71), who wrote two settings for the Mass in Irish, and **Seoirse Bodley** (b 1933) who has evolved a system of notation for Irish slow airs and has written a setting of the Mass in English and compositions for the Irish harp.

Traditional influence on modern popular music – During the 20C traditional Irish music, which formerly had been played as the accompaniment to dancing, came to be valued in its own right. It was popularised through the recordings made by the Irish in America and the formation of *Ceoltóirí Chualann* by Seán O'Riada in the early 1960s. This group of the highest calibre of traditional musicians created a more formalised style and generated an appreciation of Irish music. Out of this group the **Chieftains** were formed and brought Irish traditional music to a worldwide audience. In the same decade in the United States the Clancy Brothers and Tommy Makem achieved the popularisation of the Irish ballad tradition. In subsequent years many traditional music groups emerged including the **Dubliners**, the **Bothy Band**, **De Dannan**, **Planxty** and **Altan**. Members of the Brennan family of the Irish-speaking region of Donegal penetrated the realm of popular music singing in both Irish and English as the group **Clannad**, while another member of the family, **Enya**, forged a highly successful international career as a solo artist.

Today traditional Irish music is no longer confined to isolated regions, as it was in the early 1900s. Now throughout the country traditional musicians come together in pubs for informal sessions. Festivals and schools such as the annual Willie Clancy Summer School in County Clare draw participants from all over the world. The phenomenon of Riverdance, created in 1994, now seen on five continents, has done for Irish dance what the Chieftains did for Irish music. Other Irish dance shows have followed, including Lord of the Dance.

During the 1950s and 1960s showbands entertained in ballrooms throughout Ireland. Musicians such as **Rory Gallagher** and **Van Morrison** began their careers in showbands before pursuing solo careers. Today showbands members such as Joe Dolan still have a considerable Irish following among the over 50s age group. Country/Irish music has a large fan base in Ireland. One of the most popular singers is Daniel O'Donnell who has been recording since the mid-1980s.

Traditional Irish music has influenced the bands of recent decades, so much so that Irish rock has often been described as "Celtic Rock". **Thin Lizzy** and **Rory Gallagher** were among the first to gain international celebrity. **Van Morrison** and **U2** still continue to maintain their positions on the international stage, entertaining new generations with their brand of Irish music. More recent international celebrities **The Cranberries**, **Sinéad O'Connor** and **The Corrs** have created a worldwide interest in "Celtic" music.

Since 1993, in the wake of similar developments in the UK, a number of Irish bands were created to appeal to the teen pop market. **Boyzone**, **B*witched** and more recently **Westlife** have had huge commercial success. Boyzone members are currently embarking on solo careers; Ronan Keating has the largest following to date.

Bands who came to the fore in the 1990s making the charts in both Ireland and the UK are Northern Ireland's Therapy? Divine Comedy and Ash. At the forefront of the Club Scene is David Holmes, a DJ turned Pop Star, who has gained a considerable reputation for his remixing and soundtrack work.

Music plays a very important role in Irish life – numerous buskers in the streets, music festivals and gigs taking place in venues large and small around the country. Bands that have not yet entered the charts have loyal fans who attend their gigs - this underground music scene was brilliantly captured in Roddy Doyle's book *The Commitments*.

Cinema

Cinema first appeared in Ireland on 20 April 1896 with a projection of a film by the Lumiére brothers in Dublin and by 1909 the *Volta* in Dublin had been opened by James Joyce himself; the seventh art began to play a major role in Irish life. In 1904 JT Jameson, a newsreel cameraman, founded the Irish Animated Company (IAC); together with the American cinema, which was anxious to please the many Irish immigrants in the States, it made cinema acceptable in Ireland and launched the local industry. In 1916 and 1917 two more companies were set up – Film Company of Ireland (FCOI) and General Film Supply (GFS).

It was not until the founding of the Free State in 1922 that Irish cinema truly flourished in Ireland. Political events supplied the first themes – the Easter Rising of 1916 in *Irish Destiny* (1926) by Isaac Eppel; other incidents in the War of Independence in *Guest of the Nation* (1935) by Denis Johnston and *The Dawn* (1936) by Tom Cooper. From the post-war era the following titles stand out – *The Rocky Road to Dublin* (1968) by Peter Lennon, *Mise Eire* (1959) by George Morrisson, *Maeve* (1981) by Pat Murphy and *The Year of the French* (1981) from the novel by Thomas Flanagan. The **Irish Film Board**, created in 1982 and relaunched in 1993, has fostered a new flowering of talent by providing funds and has enhanced the reputation of Irish films in the international field.

In the last decades of the 20C several talented directors, such as **Neil Jordan** and **Jim Sheridan**, have dealt with serious subjects – the events in Northern Ireland – as well as turning a critical eye on Irish society, a popular theme with the new generation of film-makers. Among the most successful titles are *Angel* (1982) by Neil Jordan, *Reefer* *and the Model* (1987) by Joe Comerford, *My Left Foot* (1989), *The Field* (1990), *In the Name of the Father* (1993) and *The Boxer* (1998) by Jim Sheridan (who often worked in collaboration with Daniel Day-Lewis, his favourite actor), *The Crying Game* (1992) by Neil Jordan and *The Butcher Boy* (1998) and *Michael Collins* (1996). Mention should also be made of the work of **Ken Loach** – *Hidden Agenda* (1990), *Land and Freedom* (1995) and *Carla's Song* (1997).

The category of films produced in Ireland or by film-makers of Irish descent working abroad includes *The Informer* (1935) and *The Quiet Man* (1952) by **John Ford**; the latter, the second film by the famous American director about the return to his native land of a boxer, played by John Wayne, acquired a great following. In recent years the use of Irish themes has proved successful – *The Dead* (1987) from a short story by James Joyce; *The Commitments* (1991) about the story of soul musicians in Dublin, directed by **Alan Parker**, and *The Snapper* (1993), both based on novels by Roddy Doyle; *The Van* (1996) by **Stephen Frears**; *Michael Collins* (1996) by Neil Jordan about the career of the man who played a leading role in the struggle for independence in the 1920s.

Three recent Irish TV series have earned great popularity in the UK – *Father Ted*, *The Ambassador* starring Pauline Collins and partly filmed in Ely Place in Dublin, and *Ballykissangel* (filmed in Avoca in the Wicklow Mountains).

The Irish Film Board provides loans and equity investment to independent Irish film-makers. The films listed below were produced under this policy or were filmed in Ireland or deal with Irish themes:

The Dawn (1933–34) – filmed in Killarney with a cast of 250 mainly local amateurs, who performed on Thursdays, early closing day.
Ulysses (1967) – filmed in Dublin.
Ryan's Daughter (1968) – filmed on Banna Strand and the Dingle Peninsula.
The Year of the French (1981) – filmed in and around Killala in Co Mayo.
The Lonely Passion of Judith Hearne (1987) – filmed in Blessington Street, Dublin.
My Left Foot (1989) – filmed in Bray, at Kilruddery and on Killiney Hill.
The Field (1990) – filmed near Leenane in Connemara.
December Bride (1990) – filmed in Dublin and near Strangford Lough.
The Commitments (1991) – based on a novel by Roddy Doyle.
Into the West (1992) – about children being led on an adventure by a horse.
Circle of Friends (1993) – based on a novel by Maeve Binchy.
The Snapper (1993) – filmed in Dublin.
Braveheart (1996) – filmed in Trim.
Michael Collins (1996) – filmed in Dublin and elsewhere in Ireland.

Letters

Irish men and women of letters have made a significant contribution to English litera-ture through poetry, novels and drama. Poetry was an art form practised by the Celtic bard and medieval monk but theatrical performances were unknown to Gaelic society. To the English language the Irish brought a talent for fantasy, wit and satire and Gaelic speech patterns. Four Irish writers have been awarded the Nobel Prize for Literature: William Butler Yeats in 1923, George Bernard Shaw in 1925, Samuel Beckett in 1969 and Seamus Heaney in 1995.

The Celts may not have left a written literature but their oral tradition has bequeathed a rich legacy of myth and history *(see p 57)* which inspired later generations.

The work of the monks in the scriptorium of a Celtic Church was to copy biblical and other religious texts and to write their own commentaries. They decorated their work, particularly the first capital letter of a chapter, with highly ornate Celtic patterns. Several of these **illuminated manuscripts**, of which the most famous is the Book of Kells, are displayed in the Old Library of Trinity College in Dublin.

One account from this early period is *Navigatio*, written in medieval Latin, an account of the voyage from Ireland to America made by St Brendan in the 6C *(see p 200)*.

17C – 18C

The first flowering of Anglo-Irish literature came in the late 17C and 18C when George Farquhar (1678–1707) wrote his stage works, Oliver Goldsmith (1728–74) composed poetry, novels and plays and Richard Brinsley Sheridan (1751–1816) his satirical comedies – *School for Scandal*.

The major figure of this period was **Jonathan Swift** (1667-1745) *(see also p 180)* who was born in Ireland, studied at Trinity College, Dublin, and spent many years in England before being appointed Dean of St Patrick's Cathedral in Dublin where he stayed until his death. *Gulliver's Travels* is the most famous of his satirical writings on 18C Irish society.

His friend and fellow student, **William Congreve** (1670–1729) wrote his witty costume dramas, such as *The Way of the World*, which inspired Wilde and Shaw.

After spending his early childhood among his mother's relatives in Ireland, **Laurence Sterne** (1713-68), made his name in England as an innovator among novelists with *Tristram Shandy* and *A Sentimental Journey*; he is also seen as a forerunner of the stream of consciousness technique practised by James Joyce.

Irish Themes

Several successful authors chose Irish themes for their work. Maria Edgeworth (1767–1849) achieved international fame and the admiration of Sir Walter Scott with her novels *Castle Rackrent* and *The Absentee*; William Carleton (1794–1869) wrote about rural life in County Tyrone. The theme of the novel *The Collegians* by Gerald Griffin (1803–40) was reworked by Dion Boucicault for the stage as *The Colleen Bawn* and by Benedict as an opera, *The Lily of Killarney*. **Anthony Trollope** (1815–82), who began his literary career while working for the Post Office in Ireland, wrote several novels on Irish themes. Canon Sheehan (1852–1913) was admired in Russia by Tolstoy and in the USA for his novels about rural life. Somerville and Ross, a literary partnership composed of **Edith Somerville** (1858–1949) and her cousin, Violet Florence Martin (1862–1915), whose pen-name was **Martin Ross**, produced novels about Anglo-Irish society, *The Real Charlotte* and the highly humorous *Experiences of an Irish RM*, adapted for TV in the 1980s.

19C

Many Irish writers who achieved success and fame moved to London, where they made a significant contribution to English literature and theatre. The name of the novel *Dracula* is better known than its author, **Bram Stoker** (1947-1912), who worked for several years as an Irish civil servant, writing drama reviews, before moving to London as Henry Irving's manager; only his first novel, *A Snake's Pass*, is set in Ireland. George Moore (1852–1933) described high society in Dublin *(Drama in Muslin)* and introduced the realism of Zola into the novel *(Esther Waters)*. **Oscar Wilde** (1854–1900) achieved huge success in the London theatre with his plays *(Lady Windermere's Fan, The Importance of Being Earnest)* and in society with his distinctive dress and style, before his disgrace and prison term in Reading Gaol. **George Bernard Shaw** (1856–1950) commented on the Anglo-Irish dilemma in his journalism and his play *John Bull's Other Island* and explored the contradictions of English society *(Pygmalion)*.

Irish Literary Renaissance – At this time, as part of the **Gaelic Revival** *(see p 58)*, a literary renaissance was taking place in Ireland, based to a large extent in folklore. One of its early influential figures was George Russell (1867–1935), known as AE, mystic, poet and painter, economist and journalist. The leader of this literary movement and the dominant writer of the period he old Irish myths and legends, was **William Butler Yeats** (1856–1939), who established his name as a poet and playwright and was a founder member of the Abbey Theatre. He lived for a number of years in County Sligo and he recognised the power of the native imagination in Irish oral tradition, especially in the heroic tales and in mythological material, which greatly influenced his writing. His own understanding of the occult influenced his involvement in and interpretations of Irish lore. His *Fairy and Folk Tales of the Irish Peasantry*, first published in 1888, was followed by *Irish Fairy Tales* in 1892. Here he made the distinction among folk tale, legend and myth; he was among the first writers to interpret Irish folklore. He admired Douglas Hyde because of Hyde's honest commitment to the Irish language and to native Irish lore. Yeats was part of a group of people who associated Anglo-Irish writing as part of a revival of a culture which was in danger of disappearing, to a large extent owing to social development. Another leading light in this movement was **Augusta, Lady Gregory** (1852-1932), who lived in County Galway and became friendly with Yeats. They were much influenced by one another and collected folklore together. Among her best-known works is *Visions and Beliefs in the West of Ireland* (1920), which is based on 20 years of work in this area with Yeats. The *Kiltartan History Book* (1909) contained, for the first time, accounts and descriptions of many aspects of historical lore, unchanged from the oral narration of local people. She was one of the first to publish folklore material unedited just as she had collected it. In common with Yeats, she recognised the richness of folklore among the "farmers and potato-diggers and old men" in her own district, the unbroken chain of tradition and the wealth of ballads, tales and lore which was part of the everyday life of the ordinary people around her in County Galway.

Some of the greatest successes written for the **Abbey Theatre** were the plays of **John Millington Synge** (1891–1909), *Playboy of the Western World* and *Riders to the Sea*, inspired by the Aran Islands, and *The Shadow of the Glen*, inspired by the Wicklow Mountains, where language dominates in the bleak landscape; and the pacifist plays of **Sean O'Casey** (1880–1964), *The Shadow of a Gunman*, *Juno and the Paycock* and *The Plough and the Stars*, written in the aftermath of the First World War.

National Gallery of Dublin

Literary Exiles

The narrow-mindedness of Irish society, expressed by George Moore, is also criticised in the work of **James Joyce** (1882–1941), who wrote his famous work *Ulysses* abroad, of Frank O'Connor (1903–66), who emigrated to America, and of **Samuel Beckett** (1906–89), who emigrated to Paris and wrote in French and English; with *Waiting for Godot* he was recognised as a leading figure in the Theatre of the Absurd.

20C

The early 20C produced the bleak realistic poetry of **Patrick Kavanagh** from Monaghan (1904–67 *Ploughman and Other Poems*) – whose influence can be seen in the work of John Montague (b 1929 *The Rough Field*) and Northern poet **Seamus Heaney** (b 1939 *The Death of a Naturalist*) – and of Louis MacNeice (1907–63), who was a member of Auden's circle and an early influence on Derek Mahon (b 1941 *The Hudson Letter*). Novelists included Flann O'Brien (1911–66, real name Brian O'Nolan), who wrote a famous newspaper column as Myles na Gopaleen.

James Joyce (1882–1941)
painted in 1934
by Jacques Blanche (1861–1942)

National Gallery of Ireland, Dublin

The theme of the Big House survives in the work of Elizabeth Bowen (1899–1973 *The Last September*), writing as MJ Farrell (1905–97 *The Last Puppetstown*), Aidan Higgins (b 1927 *Langrishe, Go Down*), Jennifer Johnston (b 1930 *The Illusionist*) and *Woodbrook* (1974) by David Thompson.
Influential writers include **John B Keane** (b 1928), whose work is firmly set in Co Kerry – his first play *Sive* won the all-Ireland drama festival; *The Field* was made into a film in 1990 and his best novel is *The Bodhran Makers*; also **Edna O'Brien** (b 1932 *The Country Girls*), whose frank accounts of female sexuality in the 1950s were banned in Ireland on first publication and publicly burned in her home village in Co Clare, and the highly acclaimed **John MacGahern** (b 1934 *Amongst Women*), now living in Co Leitrim. *Troubles* by JG Farrell (1935–79) brings rare humour to the grim reality of the War of Independence. **Maeve Binchy** (b 1940) writes in lighter vane about episodes in Irish family life.
Northern Irish writers Brian Moore (b 1921 *The Lonely Passion of Judith Hearne*), Patrick McCabe (b 1955 *Butcher Boy*) and Eoin MacNamee (b 1960 *Resurrection Man*) have all seen their work quickly turned into films, as have many writers from the south, including **Roddy Doyle** (b 1958 *The Commitments* and *Paddy Clarke Ha Ha Ha*, which won the Booker prize) and Colin Bateman (b 1962 *Cycle of Violence*), or from outside Ireland such as **Frank McCourt**, who won the Pulitzer Prize in 1997 with *Angela's Ashes* about his childhood in Limerick.
Among the established pillars of Irish drama are **Brian Friel** (b 1929 *Dancing at Lughnasa*, adapted as a film in 1998), Thomas Kilroy (b 1934 *The Secret Fall of Constance Wilde*), Thomas Murphy (b 1935 *Bailegangaire*) and Frank McGuinness (b 1956 *Observe the Sons of Ulster Marching towards the Somme*). Alongside them a new wave of young Irish writers is making an international impact. Encouraged by the Abbey and the Gate Theatres in Dublin, the Royal Court in London and independent theatre companies, such as Rough Magic in Dublin, the Druid Theatre Company in Galway and Red Kettle in Waterford, this new wave includes Martin McDonagh *(The Leenane Trilogy)*, Conor McPherson (b 1971 *The Weir*), Marina Carr (b 1964 *The Mai*) and Enda Walsh *(Disco Pigs)*.

Painting

When Gaelic culture waned in the 17C the chief influences on art in Ireland were English and European. A guild of painters was founded in Dublin in 1670 but there was little development until the Dublin Society's Schools were set up in 1746 to promote design in art and manufacture. The first master, Robert West (d 1770), and his assistant, James Mannin (d 1779), had trained in France. The School's most outstanding pupil was probably **Hugh Douglas Hamilton** (1739–1808), who excelled at pastel portraits; in 1778 he visited Italy and while in Rome developed as a painter in oils.
Susanna Drury (fl 1733–70), whose paintings of the Giant's Causeway are in the Ulster Museum, was a member of the Irish school of landscape painting, which emerged in the 18C. **George Barret** (c 1732–84), who moved to England in 1763, introduced the Romantic element into his landscapes. Several Irish artists travelled to Italy. Thomas Roberts (1748–78), a pupil of the Dublin Society's Schools and a brilliant landscape artist, was familiar with Dutch and French painting and exhibited several works in the style of Claude Vernet. The dominant figure of the 18C is **James Barry** (1741–1806), who produced large-scale works in the neo-Classical tradition. He travelled widely, in-

cluding in Italy, studying painting and sculpture. Joseph Peacock (c 1783 – 1837) from Dublin was famous for his outdoor fair scenes.

Among 18C visitors to Dublin were Vincent Valdré (1742–1814), who painted three panels for the ceiling of St Patrick's Hall in Dublin Castle, and Angelica Kauffmann (1741–1807), who spent seven months in Ireland in 1771 as the guest of the Viceroy, Lord Townshend.

In 1823 the **Royal Hibernian Academy** was incorporated by charter to encourage Irish artists by offering them an annual opportunity of exhibiting their works. After the Act of Union in 1800 many Irish artists moved to London: Martin Archer Shee (1769–1850), who became President of the Royal Academy in 1830, and Daniel Maclise (1806–70), a popular historical painter. Nathaniel Hone (1831–1917) spent 17 years in France painting out of doors like the painters of the Barbizon school. Roderic O'Conor (1860–1940) from Co Roscommon

Portrait of John in the Book of Kells

The Board of Trinity College, Dublin

studied in Antwerp and in France where he met Gauguin, whose influence, together with that of Van Gogh, is obvious in his work. **Sir John Lavery** (1856–1948) from Belfast studied in Paris and is known for his portraits, although he also painted scenes from the French countryside. Another artist who studied abroad is **Sarah Purser** (1848–1943), who was a prolific portrait painter and a founder of *An Túr Gloine*.

The 20C has produced several artists of note. **Jack B Yeats** (1871–1957), brother of William Butler Yeats the poet, painted his views of Irish life with bold brushstrokes in brilliant colours. **Paul Henry** (1876–1958) is known for his ability to represent the luminous quality of the light in the west of Ireland. **William Orpen** (1878–1931), who trained at the Metropolitan School of Art in Dublin and the Slade in London, became a fashionable portrait painter and an official war artist; among his Irish pupils were **Seán Keating** (1889–1977) and **Patrick Tuohy** (1894–1930). Cubism was introduced to Ireland by **Mainie Jellett** (1897–1944) and **Evie Hone** (1894–1955), who is better known for her work in stained glass.

In 1991 the National Gallery and the Hugh Lane Gallery were joined by the Irish Museum of Modern Art at Kilmainham, which is to commission works for its permanent collection and provide a stimulus for future generations.

Sculpture

Cross-slabs – The earliest stone monuments are the slabs laid flat over an individual grave but they cannot be categorised definitively as grave markers. The designs evolved from early (8C) irregularly-shaped stones marked with small crosses, through crosses inscribed in squares (8C and 9C), ringed crosses with a circle at the intersection (9C) to crosses with a circle at the intersection and semcircles at the ends of the arms (10C, 11C and 12C). Many bear the inscription OR or OROIT DO (meaning A prayer for...) followed by the name of the deceased, some of whom can be identified from the **Annals of the Four Masters** *(see p 158)*. Clonmacnoise has the largest collection of cross-slabs in the country. Some of the smaller slabs are standing monuments. Standing pillars probably followed from cross-slabs as both types have in common simple cross carvings. Coffin-shaped slabs were introduced by the Normans. Most early inscriptions are in Latin; after the 16C English was used.

High Crosses – The free-standing highly-decorated crosses are most numerous in the east of Ireland but they are also found in western and northern Britain. It is thought that high crosses are the successors to small painted or bronze-covered wooden crosses, possibly carved in stone to prevent theft by raiders, and used as a focus for kneeling congregations. They vary in height (6ft/2m–20ft/6m) and most stand on a pyramidal base; the head of the cross is usually ringed and surmounted by a finial often in the shape of a small shrine. The ring probably has a symbolic purpose.

The early carving on late 8C crosses, including some at Clonmacnoise, is mostly decorative consisting of spirals and interlacing. In the 9C and 10C, panels of figures appear illustrating stories at first from the New and then from the Old Testament; such biblical figures or scenes are rare in early Christian art. Animal scenes are often executed on the base. The Cross of Moone *(see p 108)* includes animal and biblical iconography.

The 12C crosses are a fresh batch, not a direct continuation, often lacking a ring *(see CASHEL, GLENDALOUGH)*. By this date the figure of a bishop or abbot in the Continental style predominates. The best groups of crosses are at Monasterboice, Clonmacnoise, Kells and Ahenny.

Medieval sculpture – Funeral monuments provide the largest evidence for schools or periods of sculpture, as few movable sculptures have survived. There are some exceptions – the wooden Kilcorban Madonna in Loughrea Diocesan Museum and the fine alabaster statue of the Trinity displayed in the Black Abbey in Kilkenny. The carved bestiary misericords (c 1489) in St Mary's Cathedral in Limerick are unique survivors as are the figurative stone carvings (15C; re-erected in the 20C) in the cloisters at Jerpoint. A distinctive feature of this period is the medieval box tomb found in the chancel of many churches. The lid usually bears a carved effigy of the dead man and sometimes of his wife too. The sides are decorated with figures of the Apostles and saints *(see p 108)*. In the 15C and 16C, figures and scenes from the crucifixion were carved in high relief, as on the tomb of Bishop Wellesley (c 1539) in Kildare Cathedral and the Butler effigies in St Canice's Cathedral in Kilkenny. Although predominantly religious, 17C sculpture, such as the Jacobean Segrave or Cosgrave stucco tableaux in St Audeon's Church in Dublin, widened in scope to include stone and timber carved chimneypieces; there are two fine examples of the former in the castles in Donegal and Carrick-on-Suir. On a grand scale are the Renaissance-inspired 17C tombs such as the O'Brien Monument (1600) in St Mary's Cathedral in Limerick, the Chichester Monument (c 1614) in St Nicholas' Church in Carrickfergus and the Earl of Cork's Monument (1620) in Youghal. Carvings from the Restoration period – fine wood relief and stone – survive, especially at the Kilmainham Hospital.

From the early 18C both literal and allegorical funerary monuments were popular; an early example is the monument to Sir Donat O'Brian (d 1717) by William Kidwell in Christ Church Cathedral in Dublin. Church monuments on a large scale by John Van Nost the younger (c 1712–80) can be seen in Tullamore Cathedral and Waterford Cathedral. The monumental tomb (over 23ft/7m tall) to David la Touche at Delgany in Co Wicklow by John Hickey has fine neo-Classical elements.

The spate of building in the 18C provided much work for sculptors in the secular field. The figures of **Justice** and **Mars** above the gates of Dublin Castle are the work of **Van Nost** as is a statue of George III, now in the Mansion House. **Edward Smyth** (1749–1812), who was a pupil of the Dublin Society's Schools, created the riverine heads on the keystones of the arches and the arms of Ireland on the Custom House and also worked on the Four Courts under James Gandon and on the Bank of Ireland; he had been apprenticed to Simon Vierpyl (c 1725–1810), who worked on the Marino Casino. Vierpyl's work at the Casino includes the urns flanking the external steps; the lions adjacent are the work of the English sculptor Joseph Wilton. Smyth's son John, also a fine sculptor, crafted funerary monuments at Ferns in Co Wexford and Goresbridge in Co Kilkenny.

The 19C saw the dominance of Greek Revival detailing; in St Patrick's Church in Monaghan there is a good collection of monuments, especially the monument to Lady Rossmore (c 1807) by Thomas Kirk (1781–1845). John Hogan (1800–58) is acknowledged as a most distinguished sculptor; see his fine plaster *The Drunken Faun* in the Crawford Art Galley in Cork. Two of his contemporaries, who worked on the Albert Memorial in London, were Patrick MacDowell (1799– 1870), who carved the group of Europe on the base of the monument, and John Henry Foley (1818–74), who sculpted the bronze figure of Prince Albert; Foley's best work in Dublin is the O'Connell Monument and the statues of Burke, Goldsmith and Grattan on College Green outside Trinity College in Dublin. The best work of Thomas Farrell (1827–1900) is the Cullen Memorial (1881) in the Pro-Cathedral in Dublin.

On a monumental scale is the Wellington Testimonial (c 1817) in Phoenix Park in Dublin by English architect Sir Robert Smirke; it has bronze reliefs on the base by the sculptors Joseph Robinson Kirk, Farrell and Hogan. The work of Oliver Sheppard (1864–1941) is strongly influenced by the Art Nouveau style.

The Parnell Monument in O'Connell Street in Dublin was designed by Augustus St Gaudens in 1911.

The portrait sculptor **Albert Power** (1883–1945), a resident of Dublin, was elected Associate of RHA in 1911; there are examples of his work in Cavan Cathedral, Mullingar Cathedral and in Eyre Square in Galway. More recent work of note includes the *Children of Lir* by Oisin Kelly (1916–81) in the Garden of Remembrance in Dublin. The Belfast sculptor FE McWilliam (1909–92) is well represented by a series of bronze figurative sculptures in the Ulster Museum.

Barrow - Riverine head from the Custom House, Dublin

Irish Picture Library

74

Architecture

Ecclesiastical Buildings

Romanesque (Norman)

CLONFERT CATHEDRAL, Co Galway – West door – 12C
The inner arch immediately surrounding the door is 300 years later than rest of the doorway, which consists of five rows of columns and five rows of round-headed arches framing the door, surmounted by a hood moulding containing a triangular pediment, the whole capped by a finial.

Hood moulding or tangent gable

Triangular pediment

Blind arcades with semicircular arches with a head in the top of each arch

Leaf motif on arch

Capitals

Outer pilasters decorated with **Celtic strapwork**

Scrollwork

Circular pattern

Chevrons

Diamond pattern

Finial surmounted by two flanking masks

Double rope moulding

Alternating masks and foliate triangles

Hemispheres in high relief

Circles and flowers

Maltese cross

Celtic **strapwork**

Gargoyles

Statue of **gate guard** resting on a corbel

Medieval

JERPOINT ABBEY, Co Kilkenny – 12C with 15C tower

Screen dividing nave into east end for choir monks and west end for lay brothers

Central tower over crossing with slight battering

Splayed window embrasures

Cloister garth

Cloister arcade

Refectory

Kitchen

Nave

Calefactory (warming room)

North aisle arcade

Chapter House

String course

Irish crenellations

Double lancet windows

Chancel

Transept

R. Corbel/MICHELIN

75

Gothic

ST PATRICK'S CATHEDRAL, Dublin – 13C
Construction begun in the Early English style but extensively restored in the 19C.

Tower surmounted by spire

Irish crenellations

Chancel

Flying buttress

South transept

5-light lancet window

Pinnacles

Lady Chapel / Retrochoir

Buttress

Neo-Classical

CHRIST CHURCH CATHEDRAL, Waterford – 18C

Decorated plaster vaulting

Corinthian capitals

Aisles

Aisles

Reredos with projecting pediment supported on Corinthian columns

Nave

Fluted pillars

Neo-Gothic

CHURCH OF THE MOST HOLY TRINITY (formerly Chapel Royal), Dublin Castle – 19C

Rib vaulting

Carved ceiling bosses

Carved heads in the spandrels

High relief figures over east window

Clustered columns

Perpendicular tracery (east window)

Foliate capitals

Fan vaulting

Carved wooden galleries

Military Structures

Norman

Motte and bailey

In the immediate post-invasion years, the Normans built timber castles, surmounting a natural or artificial earthern mound (motte). A outer stockaded enclosure (bailey) contained stables, storehouses etc. Later castles were built of stone.

Timber stockade

Tower

Drawbridge

Bailey

Ditch and rampart

Motte

R. Corbel/MICHELIN

77

15C-17C

DUNGUAIRE CASTLE, Co Galway – 1520 restored in the 19C
Fortified dwelling, consisting of a **tower house** surrounded by a courtyard, known as a **bawn**, enclosed by defensive wall; the main living accommodation with windows was on the upper floors.

Machicolation

Crenellations

Corner tower

Bawn wall

Small and rare transomed mullion windows

Arched entrance

Tower House

17C

CHARLES FORT, Co Cork – c 1670

Traverse

Lower battery

Parade

Sunk battery

Upper battery

Citadel

Barracks

Bastion

Bastion

Classical doorway

Causeway

Citadel

Bastion

Secular Buildings

16C

PORTUMNA CASTLE, Co Galway – 1518
Semi-fortified house, with symmetrical fenestration, approached through formal walled gardens.

Dutch gable

Decorative machicolation

String course

Crenellations

Corner flanking tower

Mannerist Classical doorcase flanked by gun loops

Transom window

Mullion window

17C

SPRINGHILL, Co Tyrone – c 1680 with 18C additions
Unfortified house with symmetrical facade and large and regular fenestration.

Gable end roof

Dormer window

Central doorway

Canted bay (on 18C extensions)

Central approach flanked by offices

Narrow windows flanking entrance

GEORGIAN URBAN HOUSING

Urban terrace houses built of red brick, with 4 storeys over basement, three bays wide, with regular fenestration, composed of sash windows with wooden glazing bars. The tall windows emphasized the importance of the first floor reception rooms.

Wrought-iron
decorative balconies

Simulated stone work

Doorcase with
pillars and fanlight

Doorcases and fanlights (1740s)

Door case capped by a lantern fan light
and flanked by pillars with Ionic capitals

Door case capped by a decorated fan light
and flanked by pillars with Ionic capitals

Door case capped by a decorative fan light
and flanked by pillars with Ionic capitals
and by side lights and door scrapers

Door case capped by a decorated
fan light and flanked by pillars with
Ionic capitals

18C

RUSSBOROUGH, Co Wicklow – 1743-56
House in the **Palladian style** consisting of a main **residential block** linked by curved or straight colonnades to two **flanking service blocks** containing the kitchens and stables.

Parapet adorned with ornamental urns

Main house

String course

Curved colonnade of Doric columns

Main entrance surmounted by a fanlight and flanked by engaged Corinthian columns supporting a triangular pediment

Monumental gateway to stable yard

Ionic pilasters decorating the service buildings

18C plasterwork

FLORENCE COURT, Co Fermanagh – 1740s

Foliate plaster cornice in high relief

Decorative plaster panels

Dado rails

Leaf and scroll frieze in high relief

Plaster panelling in simulation of raised and fielded wooden panelling

Carved stair tread ends

Open string stair case

Fluted columnar banisters

Coffered arch soffit

Swag

Lugged doorcase

Ramped hand rail

Swan neck handrail

R. Corbel/MICHELIN

81

Three-bay pedimented break front

String course on break front at level of springing of arch

Pedimented gables

Rectangular panels with swags

Quoins

Pateras (roundels) with foliated design

Blind windows

Rusticated ashlar stonework

Quoins

Rounded-headed niches

Revival styles

Medieval styles such as Gothic and Norman were revived featuring asymmetric façades and fenestration and varied rooflines.

LISMORE CASTLE, Co Waterford – 19C Neo-Gothic

Look-out turret

Hood moulding

Crenellated and corbelled parapet

String course

Corbelling

Canted bay

String course

Canted bay

Window tracery

R. Corbel/MICHELIN

Secular Architecture

Prehistoric Structures – Although the first traces of human habitation in Ireland date from c 7000 BC, the first people to leave structural evidence of their presence were Neolithic farmers, who lived in Ireland from their arrival c 4000 BC to 2000 BC. They were farmers and herdsmen and made flint tools. Traces of their huts have been found at Lough Gur *(see p 233)*.

Burial Mounds – The most visible and enduring monuments of these Neolithic people are their elaborate **Megalithic tombs**.

The most impressive are the **passage tombs** at Newgrange, Knowth and Dowth in the Boyne Valley *(see p 117)*, on Bricklieve Mountain, at Loughcrew, at Fourknocks and Knockmany. Each grave consisted of a passage leading to a chamber roofed with a flat stone or a corbelled structure, sometimes with smaller chambers off the other three sides and sometimes containing stone basins. It was covered by a circular mound of earth or stones retained by a ring of upright stones. Passage graves date from 3000–2500 BC.

The earliest Megalithic structures, **court tombs**, consisted of a long chamber divided into compartments and covered by a long mound of stones retained by a kerb of upright stones. Before the entrance was a semicircular open court flanked by standing stones as at Creevykeel *(see p 117)* and Ossian's Grave *(see p 270)*.

A third style of Megalithic tomb is known as the **portal tomb**; like Proleek *(see p 306)*, they are found mostly near the east coast of Ireland. The tomb consisted of two standing stones in front with others behind supporting a massive capstone, which was hauled into place up an earth ramp long since removed. They date from c 2000 BC.

Burial chambers which are wider at one end than the other are known as **wedge tombs**; they too were covered by mounds of stones or earth retained by standing stones near the entrance. They date from c 2000 BC.

Stone Circles – Stone circles, which date from the Bronze Age (1750–500 BC), are mostly found in the southwest of the country and are usually composed of an uneven number of stones *(see pp 196, 166, 212)*. The stone circle at Drombeg *(see p 369)* seems to have been used to determine the shortest day of the year.

R Corbel/MICHELIN

Beehive Stone Hut

Standing Stones – Single standing stones also date from the Bronze Age; their probable purpose was to mark boundaries or the site of graves. Later generations sometimes converted them into Christian monuments by inscribing them with a cross or an Ogham inscription *(see p 237)*.

Cooking Pits – Of similar antiquity is the cooking pit *(fulacht fiadh)* which was filled with water; hot stones were placed in the water to bring it to boiling-point. Experiments have been conducted in the pit (6ftx3ft/0.83mx0.91m), lined with mud and wood, found near Inishkeen and in another found at Drombeg (near Kinsale); in the latter case the water boiled within 15 minutes; in the former it took 1hr 30min to bring the water to the boil and 2hr 30min to cook half a pig.

Iron Age Dwellings – By the Iron Age, men were living in **homesteads**, approached by a causeway. A ringfort was enclosed by an earth bank *(ráth or dún)* or by a stone wall *(caiseal)* and was surrounded by a ditch. An artificial island *(crannóg)* was formed by heaping up stones in a marsh or lake. Many such dwellings were in use from the Iron Age until the 17C. There is a replica at Craggaunowen *(see p 200)*. Stone forts *(cashels)* like Dún Aonghasa *(see p 29)* and Grianán of Aileach *(see p 122)*, although restored at various periods, illustrate the type, built on a hill with massive walls and mural chambers.

R Corbel/MICHELIN

Stone Fort

Within the homestead individual huts were built of wattle and daub or of stone with a thatched roof. In the west, beehive huts *(clocháin)* were built entirely of stone using the same technique of **corbelling** inwards to form a roof that was used in the passage graves. Similar stone huts are also found in the monastery on Great Skellig and at Clochan na Carraige on the Aran Islands. They demonstrate the use of drystone construction in a treeless land.

At the centre of the homestead there was often an underground stone passage, called a **souterrain**, used for storage or refuge.

Norman Castles – The first castles built by Normans were of the **motte and bailey** type. The motte was a natural or artificial mound of earth surrounded by a ditch and usually surmounted by a wooden tower as at Clough in Co Down; the bailey was an area attached to the motte and enclosed by a paling fence. From the start of the 13C, the Normans built more solid stone donjons (keeps) which were square with corner buttresses, as at Trim, Carrickfergus and Greencastle, polygonal as at Dundrum and Athlone or round as at Nenagh; battering (a sloping face) was later added to the base; the donjon was surrounded by a stone wall of enclosure or incorporated in it. Trim, completed in 1220, has several surviving gates and barbicans and a massive keep. During the 13C entrance towers became more important and barbicans were added for additional defence. In the latter half of the 13C a new symmetrical design was developed consisting of an inner ward with four round corner towers and a combined gatehouse/donjon in the middle of one wall, as at Roscommon, which is an early example of this type called the "keepless" castle.

Tower Houses – After the Black Death (1348–50) building resumed on a more modest scale. In 1429 a £10 subsidy was offered by Edward VI for the construction of a castle or tower; the original minimum dimensions (20ftx16ftx40ft/6mx5mx12m high) were later reduced (15ftx12ftx40ft/4.5mx3.5mx12m high). Over 70% of tower houses, which were erected by native and settler alike, are south of the Dublin–Galway axis.

The most distinctive feature is their verticality, one room on each of four to five storeys. The ground floor, used as a store, was roofed with cradle vaulting formed on wicker centering; the living room, also vaulted, was often on the fourth floor where it was safer to have large windows. There was sometimes a hidden room between the vaulting and the floor above. In the 16C and 17C large windows were often opened on the upper floors. The winding or straight stair, of stone, is set either within the thickness of the walls or in a turret.

The tower defences consisted of corner loop holes, battering at the base, double-stepped merlons, known as **Irish crenellations**, and external machicolations over the corners and the entrance; the door was also defended internally by a **murder hole** in the ceiling above it. Most such towers, which were built between 1450 and 1650, were surrounded by a **bawn**, an area enclosed by a defensive wall as can still be seen at Aughnanure and Dunguaire; the largest such castles are Bunratty and Blarney. Only in the later and larger castles is decoration evident. The tower houses built in the north exhibit Scottish building styles with crow-stepped gables and corbelled turrets as at Monea.

Plantation Castles – As the country came more firmly under English control in the late 16C, more luxurious rectangular houses were built with square corner towers, as at Kanturk (c 1603), Portumna (c 1618), Glinsk (c 1620) and Ballygally (1625). Portumna has intact bawn (garden) walls, corner towers and later gatehouse. Often an existing tower house was extended by the addition of a more modern house, as at Leamaneh, Donegal and Carrick-on-Suir. These buildings show a Renaissance influence in plain and regular fenestration with large mullioned windows.

Coastal Fortifications – In the Restoration period several important towns were provided with star forts; the most complete surviving fortification is Charles Fort in Kinsale (from 1671) by William Robinson; the buildings within are mostly of 18C date. After the French invasion of Bantry Bay in 1796 and Killala in 1798, signal towers were built on the Irish coast. The building of Martello towers began in 1804 (a year earlier than in England) when the threat of a French invasion was very real; about 50 of these squat towers with very thick walls punctuate the coast from Drogheda to Cork and along the Shannon estuary. The so-called Joyce Tower in Sandycove, built of ashlar granite, is typical. Many towers had a battery attached.

Towns and Cities – Early Irish villages *(clachans)* were formed of clusters of wattle-and-daub cottages arranged in a haphazard manner. The Vikings founded a number of towns on estuaries, including Drogheda, Dublin, Waterford and Wexford. They taught the Irish to make seaworthy vessels and introduced overseas trade and coinage. Most towns of Viking origin in Ireland had a Tholsel (toll stall), where payment for rights of privilege or passage was made; the building was often an arch or gateway several storeys high. Norman settlements were mostly confined to the south and east of the country. Towns were often enclosed within town walls, parts of which have survived at Athenry, Kilmallock, Youghal, Fethard and Londonderry. The first widespread foundation of towns occurred in the late 16C and 17C during the plantations of Ulster, Munster and some parts of Leinster; they consisted of poor quality timber-framed houses, which have not survived, set out round a green or lining a street. The green was often known as "The Diamond" although rarely a true diamond shape. The name "Diamond" mostly survives in Ulster. Almshouses and similar charitable foundations were established in prosperous settlements; early survivors include Shee's Alms House (1582) in Kilkenny and the Earl of Cork's Almshouses (1613) in

Youghal. Kinsale Courthouse is an early surviving civic building; the main block is 17C with an added brick front on arches (1706). Monaghan Market House is a small but fine neo-Classical structure, the arches originally open for trade. In many Irish towns one of the most elegant buildings is the market and the courthouse, sometimes combined in one structure.

Town Planning – In the 18C and 19C many country landlords indulged in town planning, setting out wide streets as in Strokestown and Moy, tree-lined malls as in Westport, Birr and Castlebar, unusual formal street plans, such as the X-shape in Kenmare, rows of cottages built of local stone as at Glassan, northeast of Athlone, and Shillelagh in Co Wicklow or the picturesque thatched houses of Adare.

In the major towns elegant terraces of houses of Classically inspired design were built of local stone or red brick, some of which was imported from Somerset via Bristol. In 19C Dublin the materials used were grey brick from local glacial clays, local limestone and grey Wicklow granite. Although most terraces were erected piecemeal and lack a unified aesthetic, the influence of the **Wide Streets Commissioners** (in Dublin from 1758) led to distinctly Irish Georgian doorways – usually flanked by columns – and ordered fenestration. The tallest windows are on the principal floor, decreasing in size towards the roofline parapet. Some later terraces by the Wide Streets Commissioners and others were more standardised – Fitzwilliam Street and Square (south side) in Dublin, and Pery Square in Limerick. In early 19C Dublin a particular type of house, of one, two or three storeys, with basement raised up to ground level and sweeping steps to the main entrance, became very popular. Internal decoration was often of a very high standard, with Classical motifs common in chimneypieces, plasterwork and timberwork.

19C-20C – The **Gothic style** was often used in the second half of the 19C for civic buildings as well as detached houses and mansions; Trinity College Museum (completed 1857) by Deane and Woodward is a classic of the Venetian Gothic revival. The Arts and Crafts movement did not find much architectural expression in Ireland; Cavan Town Hall (1908) by William Scott is a notable exception with expressive use of planes and textures. University College Dublin in Earlsfort Terrace (1912) by RM Butler and the College of Sciences in Upper Merrion Street in Dublin (1904–13) by Sir Aston Webb exemplify the Classical revival. The young Free State restored with admirable promptness the bombed General Post Office, the Four Courts and the Custom House but the record of new design is relatively poor. The Department of Industry and Commerce in Dublin (1935–39) by Basil Boyd Barrett is an exception, steadfastly of the Monumental Style.

Among commemorative monuments are the triumphal arch, in the northeast corner of St Stephen's Green in Dublin, designed by John Howard Pentland and erected in 1906–07 to those who died in the Boer War, and the National War Memorial in Dublin (1930–40), a grand exercise in landscape building by Sir Edwin Lutyens, whose hand is also seen in the garden at Heywood (see p 99).

Vernacular Houses – The Irish countryside is full of buildings and other structures of traditional vernacular architecture – not only dwellinghouses and outhouses but also structures such as sweathouses and forges.

The small stone huts, known as sweathouses, were used to treat pleurisy and other ailments and also as a type of "sauna". A fire was lit inside and, when the interior was hot, the ashes were raked out and a layer of rushes placed on the floor to protect the feet from the heat. After spending some time in the sweathouse people went to a nearby well to wash.

The 1841 Census identified four grades of housing, of which the most modest was a windowless one-room mud cabin with a thatched roof *(bothán)*, a type of dwelling which predominated west of a line from Londonderry to Cork. Among the rural population nearly 50% lived in one-room houses and the percentage was higher in the poorest parts of the West. Such houses contained little or no furniture; more windows or rooms meant higher rents. The half door, which is to be found all over Ireland, allowed in light while keeping out animals.

The middle grades of house, single- and two-storey farmhouses, have survived in greater numbers, with glazed windows, hearths and a hierarchy of rooms for distinct social uses.

The Irish **long house**, in which all the rooms were interconnecting with the stairs at one end, was a style which lasted from the Middle Ages to the 18C; the one at Cratloe *(see p 193)* is a rare survivor.

The box-style Georgian house, often a rectory or agent's house, with symmetrical elevation, some Classical detailing such as Venetian or Wyatt windows and a fanlit and columnated doorcase, was very popular with people of more substantial means.

Simple dwellings were often destroyed during evictions or fell into decay. Some have been discovered under layers of modernisation; others, threatened with demolition, have been reconstructed or recreated in Bunratty Folk Park, Glencolmcille Folk Village, the Ulster-American Folk Park and the Ulster Folk Park near Bangor.

Although straw for thatching houses can be extremely difficult to acquire, there are many examples of thatched houses in North County Dublin, Adare in Co Limerick and the Kinvarra area of east Co Galway; many people are successfully preserving thatched -roofs and thus the art of thatching. In some regions, such as parts of county Clare, houses are roofed with local slate.

Country Houses – Between the Battle of the Boyne (1690) and the Rebellion (1798) there was a period of relative peace and prosperity for the Anglo-Irish Ascendancy during which most of the important country houses were built. While Dutch gables and red brick are attributed to the influence of William of Orange, in general English and French inspiration predominated in the late 17C. In the 18C the influence was mainly Italian sources, often distilled through England and latterly Greek-inspired architects, while in the 19C the English Gothic and Tudor revivalists were influential. Most country houses were built of local stone.

The most popular style in the 18C was the **Palladian villa** which consisted of a central residence – two or three storeys high – flanked by curved or straight colonnades ending in pavilions (usually one storey lower) which housed the kitchens or stables and farm buildings.

The major architect of the first half of the 18C was **Richard Castle** (originally Cassels) (1690–1751), a Huguenot from Hesse-Kassel, who arrived in Ireland in 1728; he knew Richard Boyle, 3rd Earl of Burlington and 4th Earl of Cork, who inherited large estates in Ireland and Yorkshire, acted as patron to William Kent and popularised the work of Palladio in England. Castle's many houses – Powerscourt, Westport, Russborough, Newbridge – tend to be very solid. He took over the practice of **Sir Edward Lovett Pearce**, who died at the age of 34 in 1733. Pearce had the major role in designing Castletown *(see p 251)*; his Houses of Parliament (from 1729), now the Bank of Ireland in Dublin, was the earliest Burlintonian public building in the British Isles.

The influence of **Robert Adam** (1728–92) arrived in Ireland in 1770, the date of the mausoleum he designed at Templepatrick. Sir William Chambers' work in Ireland is exemplified by The Casino, Marino (1769–80), a vastly expensive neo-Classical gentleman's retreat cum folly.

James Gandon (1742–1823) was brought to Ireland in 1781 by Lord Portarlington to design Emo Court *(see p 98)*. His Classical style is well illustrated by the Customs House and the Four Courts in Dublin.

The chief work of **James Wyatt** (1746–1813) was at Castle Coole but he also contributed to Slane Castle.

One of the best known of Irish architects is **Francis Johnston** (1761–1829), an exponent of both the Classical and the Gothic styles. He started his career in Armagh from 1786 to 1793 and was then sent by Richard Robinson to work under Thomas Cooley in Dublin. He was employed by the Office of Public Works, where he was responsible for Civil Buildings.

Interior Decoration – Many of the **interiors** were decorated with exuberant stuccowork executed by the Swiss-Italian **Lafranchini** brothers, one of whom executed the stairwell plasterwork at Castletown. Contemporary work of similar quality was carried out by Robert West, a Dublin stuccadore. Powerscourt House in Dublin has first-floor rooms by Michael Stapleton, one of the most skilled craftsmen in plaster in Dublin in the 18C and the principal exponent of Adam decor.

Neo-Gothic Style – The Gothic style, which made its debut in England at Strawberry Hill (1748–1792), first appeared in Ireland in the 1760s at Castle Ward and at Malahide Castle where two tall Gothic towers were added to the medieval core during restoration after a fire. At first Gothic features and intricate stuccowork vaulted ceilings were added to buildings that were basically Classical and symmetrical such as Castle Ward. In addition to the crenellations, machicolations and pointed arches, one of the key features of the Gothic style was asymmetry. In 1815 it appeared in the gate lodges built at Glin; at about the same time Tullynally Castle was converted into a vast irregular Gothic pile by – among others – Johnston and Morrison. Existing medieval castles or tower houses or Classical mansions, such as Kilkenny Castle (c 1826) by William Robertson and Dromoland Castle (1826) by George and James Pain, were enlarged and reworked in Gothic or Tudor style. Johnstown Castle and Ashford Castle are later examples of such Gothicising, which was romantic in flavour but distinctly Victorian in convenience. At Birr the surviving gatehouse was extended; Sir Joseph Paxton was responsible for the 19C additions to Lismore for the Duke of Devonshire.

Some new houses were built entirely in an antiquated style; Gosford Castle is neo-Norman; Adare Manor (1832), by the noted English Gothicist Augustus Pugin, is an unusually early example of a neo-Gothic building; Glenveagh was designed in the Irish Baronial style; for Belfast Castle, Lanyon and Lynn chose the Scottish Baronial style, which was also used for Blarney Castle House. In later years genuine defensive features were introduced in response to the Fenian threat.

Stained Glass

No medieval stained glass survives in situ in Ireland. The revival of stained glass began in the 1770s with the enamelling work of Thomas Jervais and Richard Hand, much of which was secular. Both worked extensively in England. Several foreign and Irish firms competed during the 19C for church commissions. The fashion for the neo-Gothic style of architecture in the 19C for both churches and houses created such a demand for stained glass that it declined in artistic quality towards the end of the century; good examples from this period are St Patrick's Roman Catholic Church in Dundalk, which has glass by Early of Dublin, Hardman of Birmingham and Meyer of Munich, the east window of St Patrick's Anglican Church in Monaghan by the German FS Barff, and the altar window of the Cathedral of the Assumption in Tuam by Michael O'Connor (1801–67).

A revival in Irish stained glass occurred early in the 20C with the foundation of **An Túr Gloine** (the Tower of Glass) (1903–63) at the instigation of Edward Martyn and Sarah Purser. The manager was AE Childe, who also ran the stained glass section in the Dublin Metropolitan School of Art and had been trained by the William Morris studio. Sarah Purser, who was a portrait painter, did designs for several windows including Cormac of Cashel in St Patrick's Cathedral. Another founder member was Michael Healy (d 1941) whose work can be seen in Loughrea Cathedral.

Two works by Wilhelmina Margaret Geddes from Belfast, who worked for An Túr Gloine from 1912 to 1925, can be seen in the Municipal Gallery of Modern Art in Dublin – *Episodes from the Life of St Colman* (strong black line used) and in the Ulster Museum – *The Fate of the Children of Lir* (1930).

Evie Hone, who was trained in abstract painting, discovered the fascination of stained glass during a trip to France and joined An Túr Gloine in 1934. Her work, which was often inspired by Irish medieval sculpture, includes *The Ascension* (1948) for the Roman Catholic church in Kingscourt, Co Cavan, and *The Beatitudes* (1946) for a chapel in the Jesuit Retreat House at Tullabeg near Tullamore.

Harry Clarke (1889–1931), who trained under Childe at the Metropolitan School of Art, developed a distinctive personal style as early as 1915, drawing from iconography and legends in a symbolist manner. His first public commission, 12 windows for the Honan Chapel in University College Cork, is one of his greatest works. His "Geneva Window" (1928) is in the Municipal Gallery of Modern Art in Dublin. Just before his death he executed his most important ecclesiastical commission *The Last Judgement with the Blessed Virgin Mary and St Paul* for St Patrick's Church in Newport.

A current revival is headed by James Scanlon and Maud Cotter, both based in Cork.

Ecclesiastical Architecture

Little remains of most early Christian settlements as the buildings were made of perishable material – wood or wattle and daub. The records describe beautiful wooden churches made of smooth planks, constructed with great craft and skill, but none has survived. The Irish seem to have preferred to build in wood until the 9C when the monasteries were pillaged and set on fire by Vikings.

Early monasteries consisted of an area enclosed by a circular wall or bank and divided into concentric rings, as at Nendrum *(see p 375)*, or into sectors assigned to different uses. The most important sector was the graveyard, since it was seen as the gateway to heaven; a saint's grave brought a monastery fame and increased wealth as it was thought desirable to be buried near the grave of a saint. The drystone beehive huts at Nendrum were constructed on the corbel principle also seen at Dunquin (Dun Chaoin). The boundaries of monastic enclosures were often marked by stone pillars or high crosses. The times of worship were reckoned by means of a sundial.

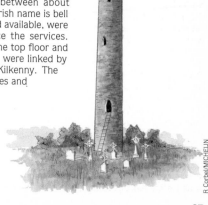

Round Towers – The slender tapering round towers, which are almost unique to Ireland, mark the site of early monasteries. They were built between about AD 950 and 12C as bell-towers – the Irish name is bell house – where hand bells, the only kind available, were rung from the top floor to announce the services. There were usually four windows on the top floor and one on each of the lower floors, which were linked by wooden ladders as at Devenish and Kilkenny. The towers were also used to store treasures and possibly as places of refuge; in almost every case the entrance was several feet (10ft/3m) above ground level, facing roughly towards the major church of the site.

Intact towers vary in height (from 50ft/17m to over 100ft/30m). All were surmounted by a conical cap, created on the corbel principle, which

R Corbel/MICHELIN

has sometimes been replaced by later battlements. About 65 survive in varying condition, with 12 intact. Most were constructed without foundations and all are tapered. Kilmacduagh is a very fine instance of a well-preserved 11C or 12C tower (about 100ft/30m tall).

Tomb Shrines – Some saints' graves are marked by a stone **mortuary house** which resembles a miniature church. These structures, such as St Ciaran's at Clonmacnoise, are among the earliest identifiable stone buildings in Ireland. There was usually a hand hole at one end through which the faithful could touch the relics.

Churches – Most early **stone churches** consisted of a single chamber with a west door and an east window; churches with a nave and chancel date from the 12C. In some buildings the north and south walls project beyond the west wall to form antae, probably a copy in stone of a feature required to support the barge-boards of a wooden structure. None of the surviving churches is very large but there are often several churches on one site. The very large stones employed accentuate the smallness of the churches. The roofs would have been made of thatch or shingles.

The rare **stone-roofed** churches, an Irish peculiarity, employ the corbelling technique. The simplest is Gallarus Oratory; St Doulagh's near Malahide is A 13C church still roofed with stone slabs; St Columba's House, St Mochta's House, St Flannan's Oratory and Cormac's Chapel have a small room between the vaulted ceiling and the roof. The earliest examples are devoid of ornament; an exception to this rule is found on White Island in Co Fermanagh, where seven figurative slabs are attached to the walls (which may be later insertions). Doorways were sometimes trabeated – ie the jambs incline somewhat and are covered by a massive flat lintel as at Reefert Church in Glendalough.

Romanesque – The first church in the Romanesque style, which was introduced from the Continent in the 12C, was Cormac's Chapel at Cashel finished in 1139. In Ireland Romanesque churches are always small; their typical features, to which carved decoration is limited, are round-headed doorways, windows and arches. Ornament includes fantastic animals, human masks and geometric designs such as bosses, zigzags and "teeth". There were no free-standing pillar capitals to carve. Cormac's Chapel has fine carvings, several series of blind arcades, painted rib vaults (the earliest in Ireland) and the earliest extant frescoes, now conserved.

Profusely ornamented west doorways are perhaps unique to Ireland, exemplified by Clonfert (after 1167), Ardfert and St Cronan's in Roscrea. At Clonfert the stylised foliage is of classical derivation – the inner arch is later than the main doorcase.

Gothic – Gothic architecture, introduced to Ireland in the late 12C, is on a much smaller scale than elsewhere. Most cathedrals show English and Welsh influences, whereas monasteries, founded by Continental monastic orders, are built according to their usual plan of a quadrangle enclosed by cloisters bordered by the church on the north side, the sacristy and chapter-house on the east, the refectory and kitchens on the south and the store on the west, with dormitories above the east and south ranges. At Jerpoint the church is in the form of a cross with a large vaulted chancel, nave and side aisles divided by arcades; the fine battlemented crossing tower is 15C. Holy Cross, in its present form predominantly 15C, retains its earlier layout with the convent buildings to the south of the church. The distinctive features are the narrow lancet windows. There was a distinctive tendency in the late 13C to light the choir with as many lancets as possible, as at Ennis, Sligo and Ardfert. Vaulting is unusual but Holy Cross Abbey has a very good vaulted east end.

Early in the 13C many cathedrals were remodelled; the two Anglican cathedrals in Dublin contain building from this period, although they have been much altered. St Patrick's Cathedral in Dublin, completed in 1254, to which a tower was added in 1372, is very English in its form and decoration. The flying buttresses to the Lady Chapel (reconstructed mid 19C) are relatively unusual.

A second period of building occurred in the 15C and coincided with the construction of many Franciscan houses in the west. Most existing churches were altered to conform to the new fashion. Broad traceried windows were inserted which let in more light and provided the stonemasons with opportunities for decoration. There is an Irish character to the capitals in the cloisters at Jerpoint (15C) and high-relief carving on the webs between the pillars.

Few medieval churches have survived but among those which have been in constant use for worship or have been restored in this century are the cathedrals in Dublin, Ballintubber Abbey in Co Mayo, Holy Cross Abbey north of Cashel, Black Abbey in Kilkenny and Duiske Abbey in Graiguenamanagh north of New Ross.

Planter's Gothic – This style was introduced in the early 17C by settlers from England and Scotland who built many parish churches throughout Ireland, a few of which survive unaltered; one of the best examples is St Columb's Cathedral in Londonderry. A parish church of the period is Waringstown in Co Down.

18C–19C Classical – Classical details began to be used in the 17C. St Michan's in Dublin (c 1685) and Lismore (1680) by William Robinson retain some details of 17C work. The early Georgian St Anne's in Shandon in Cork has an imposing west tower with an eastern flavour. The neo-Classical rectangular building with a pillared portico, inspired by the Greek temple, was popular with all the major denominations: St Werburgh's (1754–59), St George's (1812), St Stephen's (1825) and the Pro-Cathedral (finished after 1840) in Dublin, St John the Evangelist (1781–85) at Coolbanagher by Gandon and St George's (1816) in Belfast. Christ Church Cathedral (1790s) by John Roberts in Waterford has a good Classical interior although the galleries have been removed.

Gothic Revival – Many early 19C Gothic churches, such as the Church of the Most Holy Trinity (formerly the Chapel Royal) in Dublin Castle, are filled with ornament, with decorative galleries, plaster vaulting and rich oak carvings. Later the influence of Augustus Welby Pugin, who practised widely in Ireland, and JJ McCarthy promoted antiquarian correctness, as at St Fin Barre's in Cork (1862) by William Burges. The spate of building which followed the Emancipation Act was hampered by the Famine and limited funds. Nevertheless many Roman Catholic cathedrals and parish churches were constructed in eclectic Gothic variations, whereas those for dissenting congregations were quite austere in style.

20C Churches – Despite widespread eclecticism, as with the correct Classicism of Cavan Cathedral (finished 1942) by Ralph Byrne, some modern influences emerged. The earliest example, Christ the King (1927) at Turner's Cross in Cork by Barry Byrne of Chicago, is rigorously modern for its date. The changes in practice introduced by Vatican II, which favour the concept of churches in the round, have inspired many exciting modern designs, some of which reflect local physical features – St Conal's Church, Glenties, Co Donegal; St Michael's Church, Creeslough, Co Donegal; Dominican Church, Athy; Prince of Peace Church, Fossa, near Killarney; Holy Trinity, Bunclody.

Historical Table

6000-1750 BC	Stone Age; c 3000 BC men turned to farming from hunting and gathering. Construction of passage graves.
1750–500 BC	Bronze Age.
500 BC–AD 450	Iron Age; Celtic tribes arrived from Europe; inter-tribal strife for supremacy and the title of High King (Ard Rí).
55 BC	Roman invasion of Britain. Roman coins and jewellery, found at Drumanagh near Dublin.
4C–5C	Irish Celts (known as Scots) colonised the west of England and Scotland.
432–61	**St Patrick's mission** to convert Ireland to Christianity.
6C–11C	Monastic age; Irish missionaries travelled to the European mainland.
795	**Viking Invasions** – Vikings from Norway and Denmark made raids on the monasteries near the coasts and waterways; in 841 they began to settle.
1014	**Battle of Clontarf – Brian Ború**, king of Munster, gained a Pyrrhic victory against the combined forces of the Danish Vikings and the king of Leinster. His death was followed by a decline in the power of the church and the High King.
1156	Death of Turlough O'Connor, last powerful native ruler.
1159	Henry II (1154–89) received the title "Lord of Ireland" from Pope Adrian IV and the Pope's blessing to invade Ireland.
1168	Henry II invited by Dermot, King of Leinster, to mount an expedition against Dermot's enemies; the Anglo-Normans landed in Co Wexford the following year.
1177	**Anglo-Norman** invasion of Ulster under John de Courcy.
1185	**Prince John** visited Ireland, accompanied by Gerald of Wales (see p 254).
1210	**King John** again in Ireland.
1297	First **Irish Parliament** convened.
1315–18	**Bruce Invasion** – Edward Bruce, brother to King Robert of Scotland, landed at Carrickfergus with 6 000 Scottish mercenaries (gallowglasses) to prevent aid reaching Edward II of England, who had been defeated at the **Battle of Bannockburn** (1314) by Robert Bruce; he was crowned king in 1316 but died at the Battle of Faughart near Dundalk in 1318.
1348–50	**Black Death** – About one-third of the population died.

1366	**The Statutes of Kilkenny** prohibited fosterage, bareback riding, hurling, the Irish language and Irish dress and patronage of Irish story tellers and poets; in 1465 the laws against Irish culture were strengthened but failed to maintain the distinction between Anglo-Normans and native Irish.
1394 & 1399	**Richard II** landed in Ireland with an army to re-establish control.
1446	First mention of **The Pale** to describe the area of English influence in the Middle Ages; by the 15C it was only a narrow coastal strip from Dundalk to south of Dublin.
1471	The Earl of Kildare first appointed **Lord Deputy**.
1487	Lambert Simnel crowned Edward V of England in Dublin by the Earl of Kildare.
1491	Perkin Warbeck, pretender to the English throne, landed in Cork without the opposition of the Earl of Kildare.
1494	Sir Edward Poynings appointed Lord Deputy; under **Poynings' Law** the Irish parliament could not meet or propose legislation without royal consent.
1534–40	**Kildare (Geraldine) Revolt** which brought down the house of Kildare.
1539	**Reformation** and **Dissolution of the Monasteries**.
1541	Henry VIII declared **King of Ireland** by the Irish Parliament.
1556	Colonisation of Co Laois (Queen's County) and Offaly (King's County).
1579	**Desmond (Munster) Rebellion** severely crushed by Elizabeth I; confiscation and colonisation.
1585	Ireland mapped and divided into counties; 27 sent members to Parliament.
1588	**Spanish Armada** – After its defeat in the English Channel, the Spanish Armada, driven by the wind, sailed up the east coast of Great Britain and round the north coast of Scotland. Off the Irish coast stormy weather further depleted its ranks.
1598	**Battle of Yellow Ford** – Irish victory (see p 334).
1601	**Siege of Kinsale** – 4 000 Spanish troops landed in Kinsale to assist Hugh O'Neill but withdrew when besieged.
1603	Submission of Hugh O'Neill, Earl of Tyrone, and Rory O'Donnell, Earl of Tyrconnell, at Mellifont to **Lord Mountjoy**, Queen Elizabeth's Deputy.
1607	**Flight of the Earls** – The Earls of Tyrconnell and Tyrone sailed from Rathmullan (see p 203) into exile on the continent.
1607–41	**Plantation of Ulster** under James I in which Protestants from the Scottish lowlands settled in the northern counties of Ireland.
1641	**Confederate Rebellion** provoked by the policies of the King's Deputy and the desire of the dispossessed Irish to regain their land.
1642	**Confederation of Kilkenny** – The Irish and Old English Catholics formed an alliance to defend their religion, land and political rights.
1646	**Battle of Benburb** – Irish victory (see p 167).
1649	**Oliver Cromwell** landed in Dublin to avenge the Ulster Protestants; he stormed Drogheda and Wexford and transported thousands of Irish to the West Indies.
1657	First **Quaker settlement** established at Mountmellick in Co Offaly by William Edmundson, founder of the Irish Quaker movement; his Will was

Spanish Armada

Some 30 ships of the Spanish Armada were wrecked off the Irish coast between Antrim and Kerry. It has been estimated that they contained 8 000 sailors and gunners, 2 100 rowers, 19 000 soldiers and 2 431 pieces of ordnance. Those survivors who were not killed by the Irish were hunted by the English.

Port na Spaniagh on the Giant's Causeway marks the place where the *Gerona*, a galleass, was wrecked without survivors; some of its treasures, recovered by diving on the wreck in 1968, are on display in the Ulster Museum.

On the Inishowen Peninsula at Kinnagoe Bay many interesting military relics were found in the wrecks of *La Duquesa St Anna* and *La Trinidad Valencia*. A map on the clifftop (at the road junction) plots the sites of the many ships of the Spanish Armada which were wrecked on the Irish coast.

Three ships – *Juliana*, *La Levia* and *La Santa Maria de Vision* – were wrecked at Streedagh Point, north of Sligo; over 1 300 men are thought to have died. One of the survivors who came ashore at Streedagh, Captain Francisco de Cuellar, wrote an account of the shipwreck and of his journey from Sligo through Leitrim, Donegal and Derry to Antrim; from there he sailed to Scotland and returned via Antwerp to Spain.

witnessed by Thomas Winsloe of Birr, who played host to William Penn in 1698. Quakers were known for their industry and integrity and were the most active in providing relief during the Great Famine *(see below)*.

1653 Under the **Cromwellian Settlement** most Roman Catholic landowners judged unsympathetic to the Commonwealth were dispossessed and ordered to retreat west of the Shannon; the proportion of Irish land owned by Roman Catholics dropped to one-tenth whereas 30 years earlier it had been nearly two-thirds; by 1685 only 22% of Ireland belonged to Roman Catholics.

1658 Completion of the **Down Survey** in which the re-distribution of land under the Commonwealth was noted down *(see p 106)*.

1660 **Restoration** of Charles II who returned some land to Roman Catholic owners.

1678 **Oates Conspiracy,** which alleged the existence of a Jesuit plot to procure the death of Charles II and the succession of his brother; it was in fact invented by Titus Oates but led to the arrest and imprisonment and even the death of various Roman Catholics, among them Oliver Plunkett, Archbishop of Armagh *(see p 193)*.

1685 Revocation of the Edict of Nantes in France caused many **Huguenots** (Protestants) to flee to England and Ireland.

1688 **Glorious Revolution** – James II deposed; William of Orange accepted the English throne.

1690 **Battle of the Boyne** – King William III of England and his allies representing the Protestant interest defeated King James II of England, supported by Louis XIV of France. The Irish Army retreated west to Athlone.

1691 **Siege of Limerick** – Following the battles of Athlone and Aughrim *(see p 107)*, the Irish army again retreated to Limerick, where it was besieged and surrendered. Under the military terms of the **Treaty of Limerick** the Irish defenders were allowed to surrender with honour. Eleven thousand later joined the French army; at their head was Patrick Sarsfield and they were known as the **Wild Geese**. The civil terms, guaranteeing the religious and property rights pertaining to Roman Catholics under Charles II, were not upheld by the English parliament.

1695 **Penal Laws** *(see p 63)* curtailing the power of Roman Catholics.

1765 **Edmund Burke** (1729–97), the great orator, entered Parliament as a Whig; he defined the role of an MP as a representative not a delegate; he advocated Irish free trade and Catholic relief; in his last years he was particularly concerned by Irish political questions.

1778 **Volunteers** formed to defend Ireland against the French, as English troops were withdrawn to fight in the American War of Independence; they supported the demand for an independent Irish parliament.

1782 **Repeal of Poynings' Law** and the establishment of an independent Irish Parliament, known as Grattan's Parliament after Henry Grattan who had led the campaign for independence.

1791–93 **Catholic Relief Acts** *(see p 63)*.

1795 Foundation of the **Orange Order** (see p 313) in September 1795 in a farmhouse near the Diamond Hill in Co Armagh after a fight between two armed bands of tenant farmers in which the Peep O'Day Boys (Protestants) beat the Defenders (Roman Catholics). Owing to the increase in population and the competition for tenancies, the Protestants feared they would be underbid by the Roman Catholics and tried to frighten them into leaving the district.

1796	Abortive French invasion in Bantry Bay *(see p 109)*.
1798	**Rebellion of the United Irishmen** launched by Wolfe Tone; the main engagements were in Antrim, Wexford and Mayo; the rising was severely suppressed and 30 000 rebels died. The movement, which was founded in 1791 in Belfast, became a secret society dedicated to the establishment of a republic when suppressed by the government in 1794.
1800	**Act of Union** – Suppression of the Irish Parliament. Ireland was represented at Westminster by 100 seats in the House of Commons and 28 temporal and four spiritual lords in the Upper House: £1 250 000 was spent in compensation (£15 000 per seat) and Union peerages were conferred to secure compliance.
1803	**Emmet Rebellion** – An abortive rising led by Robert Emmet (1778–1803), who had been a political exile in France; he counted on the invasion of England by Napoleon and support from Thomas Russell in Ulster and Michael Dwyer in Wicklow. Emmet was hanged but his speech from the dock was an inspiration for future generations of nationalists.
1823	**Daniel O'Connell** (1775–1847), a Roman Catholic lawyer, known as the Counsellor and the Liberator, campaigned for the recognition of the rights of Catholics; he was elected MP for Clare in 1828; he denounced violence and organised mass meetings to rally support for repeal of the Act of Union.
1829	**Roman Catholic Emancipation Act** enabling Roman Catholics to enter Parliament.
1848	Abortive **Young Ireland Uprising** led by William Smith O'Brien (1803–64).
1858	Founding of the **Irish Republican Brotherhood (IRB)** to overthrow British rule in Ireland; it dissolved itself in 1924.
1867	**Manchester Martyrs** – The "martyrs" were three Fenians who were executed for the murder of a policeman during an attack on a police van in Manchester to release two Fenian prisoners. The doubtful nature of some of the evidence weakened Irish confidence in British justice.
1869	Disestablishment of the **Church of Ireland** (Anglican).
1870–1933	**Land Acts** – 17 acts which transferred the ownership of the large estates from the landlords to their tenants.
1874	**59 Home Rulers** elected to Parliament

Huguenots

The first Huguenots came to Ireland at the invitation of the Duke of Ormond to work in textiles in Chapelizod but the greater number came after 1685, in all about 5 000, who settled in Dublin, southeast of Ireland and Cork. The Huguenots were Calvinists, who recognised only two sacraments, baptism and communion. In Dublin they used the Lady Chapel in St Patrick's Cathedral from 1666 to 1816 and had burial grounds in Cathedral Lane (1668–1858) and in Merrion Row (fl 1693).

The army of William of Orange contained about 3 000 Huguenots, who played a leading role both at the Battle of the Boyne, where their leader Schomberg was killed, and at Aughrim under Ruvigny. When they were demobbed, many settled on the estate at Portarlington granted to Ruvigny.

In Dublin the Huguenots introduced the weaving of silk and also of poplin, a mixture of wool and silk. Louis Crommelin, who came from Picardy via Holland, was appointed to develop the Irish linen industry. In 1698 he settled in Lisburn, already home to many Huguenots, and introduced improved methods of flax cultivation and the use of water power to drive the looms.

Sir Francis Beaufort, who originated the Beaufort Scale of wind velocity, and William Dargan, who built most of the Irish railway system, were both of Huguenot descent. So too were James Gandon and Richard Castle, who designed some of Ireland's finest buildings.

Several Huguenots were talented artists. James Tabary, designer and woodcarver, worked with his brothers at Kilmainham Hospital; George du Noyer, a miniaturist, worked for the Ordnance Survey and sketched archaeological sites; Gabriel Béranger was employed by the Royal Antiquarian Society to make drawings of historical ruins. Many performed in the theatre and concert world as composers, organists, violinists and violin makers, or as singers and dancers.

From working as gold- and silver-smiths, at which they excelled, they moved into banking. The chain of the Chief Magistrate of Dublin was made by Jeremiah D'Olier in 1796; his sons and grandsons were governors of the Bank of Ireland. David La Touche III, whose grandfather arrived with William of Orange in 1690, was a merchant and banker and a founder member of the Bank of Ireland.

1875–91	**Charles Stewart Parnell** (1846–91), elected MP for Meath in 1875, became President of the Land League and leader of the Home Rule party.
1886	First **Home Rule** Bill, granting Ireland various degrees of independence in domestic matters, introduced by Gladstone but rejected by Parliament.
1879–82	**Land League** formed by Michael Davitt to campaign for the reform of the tenancy laws and land purchase by passive resistance. It proposed the extension of the Ulster Custom (fair rent, free sale, fixity of tenure) to the whole country. Parnell advocated that those who opposed the Land League be ostracised; the most well-known victim of this treatment, Captain Boycott, involuntarily gave a new word to the English language.
1891–1923	**Congested Districts' Board** – Funds from the disestablished Church of Ireland were used in the poorer districts of Ireland to construct harbours and promote fishing, fish curing and modern farming methods; after 1903 the Board was empowered to re-distribute large estates to smallholders.

National Gallery of Ireland, Dublin

Daniel O'Connell (1775–1847)
by George Mulvany (1809–69)

Great Famine (1845–49)

Potato blight *(phytophthora infestans)* destroyed the potato crop, on which the bulk of the population depended for food; 800 000 people died of hunger, typhus and cholera; hundreds of coffinless bodies were buried in mass graves. Thousands of starving people overwhelmed the workhouses and the depot towns from which the Indian corn imported by the government was distributed; the workhouse capacity was 100 000 but five times that number qualified for relief. The Quakers did most to bring relief to the hungry. Soup kitchens were set up by compassionate landlords and by Protestant groups seeking converts; 50 large cauldrons were imported in 1847 from the Darby works in Coalbrookdale in England. Public works were instituted to provide employment and relief. Some landlords evicted their penniless tenants (in 1847 16 landlords were murdered), others arranged for their emigration. So many died during the voyage or in quarantine that the vessels were known as coffin ships. One million Irish men and women emigrated to England, Scotland, Canada and the USA.

1893	Second **Home Rule** Bill introduced and rejected by Parliament.
1905–08	**Sinn Féin** (Ourselves) founded to promote the idea of a dual monarchy.
1912	Third **Home Rule** Bill introduced by Asquith, delayed by the veto of the House of Lords but finally signed by George V in September 1914; it was suspended for the duration of the First World War. Sinking of the *Titanic*.
1913	**Tramway Strike** in Dublin organised by James Larkin and James Connolly.
1914–18	**First World War** in which many Irishmen fought as volunteers as there was no conscription in Ireland.
1916	**Easter Rising** – On the outbreak of war in 1914 both nationalists and unionists agreed to the postponement of Home Rule but the Military Council of the Irish Republican Brotherhood, the more militant nationalists, secretly organised an uprising. Despite the capture of Sir Roger Casement and a cargo of arms from Germany and despite a last-minute confusion in orders, the rising was not cancelled. On Easter Monday columns of Volunteers marched into Dublin and took possession of various strongpoints including the General Post Office, where they set up their headquarters; from its steps Patrick Pearse announced the establishment of a republic. The insurgents were hopelessly outnumbered and outgunned and on Saturday they surrendered. Although intended to be a national rebellion, it was confined to Dublin and failed. The insurrection had not enjoyed public support but attitudes changed when the ringleaders were tried by court martial and executed.
1917	**Sinn Féin** reorganised under Eamon de Valera as a nation-wide movement for the independence of Ireland and withdrawal from Westminster.
1918	**General Election** at which Sinn Féin candidates won 73 seats.
1919	**Declaration of Independence** drafted on 8 January and read in Irish, English and French on 21 January at the meeting of the first Irish Assembly *(Dáil Éireann)* in Dublin.

Royal Visits

In the Middle Ages royal visits were rare. King John, whose name is attached to several ruined castles, visited Ireland in 1185 and again in 1210. In 1394 and 1399 Richard II arrived with an army to re-establish control.

Although the 10th Earl of Ormond, known as Black Tom, built Ormond Castle c 1568 to receive Queen Elizabeth, she never visited Ireland.

In 1821 George IV landed at Dún Laoghaire, renamed Kingstown in his honour. The state bedroom at Castle Coole was refurbished to receive him but he spent most of his visit at Slane Castle, as the guest of the 1st Marquess Conyngham, whose wife, Elizabeth Dennison, was his mistress. The 3rd Earl of Kingston rebuilt Mitchelstown Castle with a Royal Tower containing a bedroom for the king, but His Majesty never returned to Ireland.

The next royal visitor was his niece, Queen Victoria, who made her first tour in 1849 to Dublin, Cork and Belfast. In 1853 she returned to open the Dublin exhibition and in August 1861 she visited Killarney.

The state visit of King Edward VII and Queen Alexandra in 1907 was marred by the theft of the Crown Jewels from Dublin Castle four days before their arrival.

1919–20	**War of Independence – Irish Republican Army (IRA)** launched a campaign to make British administration in Ireland impossible; martial law was proclaimed; the Royal Irish Constabulary was reinforced by British ex-servicemen (Black and Tans).
1920	**Government of Ireland Act** provided for partition: the six counties of Northern Ireland remained within the UK, in accordance with the wishes of the Loyalists led by Edward Carson, with a separate parliament; dominion status was granted to the remaining 26 counties.
1921	**Anglo-Irish Treaty**
1922–23	**Civil War** between the Free State Army and the Republicans who were defeated; Michael Collins, who was pro-Treaty and a potential political leader, was assassinated.
1922	Constitution of the **Irish Free State**, which comprised the 26 counties; the two-tier legislature consisted of the Senate and *Dáil Éireann*.
1937	New Constitution which changed the official name of the country to **Éire**.
1938	Spike Island and Crosshaven fort in Cork Harbour, Bere Island and Lough Swilly handed over by the British Government.
1939–45	**Second World War** (known in Éire as the Emergency).
1949	Éire became the **Republic of Ireland** and left the Commonwealth.
1952	Republic of Ireland joined the United Nations; Irish troops involved in peace-keeping missions.
1965	Anglo-Irish Free Trade Area Agreement.
1967	Northern Ireland Civil Rights Association formed to demand reform in local government.
1969	**People's Democracy March** from Belfast to Derry. British troops deployed in Northern Ireland in peace-keeping role.
1971	**Provisional IRA** began a campaign of bombing to force the British to withdraw from Northern Ireland. Internment without trial introduced.
1972	Parliament of Northern Ireland at Stormont prorogued in March; direct rule from Westminster introduced.
1973	Republic of Ireland and Northern Ireland became members of the European Union (EU), then the EEC, leading to a period of agricultural prosperity and access to Community funds for development projects.
1974	Power-sharing Executive in Northern Ireland brought down by a Unionist strike.
1975	Northern Ireland Convention held; internment suspended.
1976	Collapse of the Convention; British Ambassador to Ireland killed in Dublin.
1979	Papal visit; murder of Earl Mountbatten in Co Sligo and of eight soldiers at Warrenpoint.
1981	Death of hunger-strikers in H blocks protest.
1983	Failure of the All-Ireland Forum; confirmation of ban on abortion in the Republic.
1985	**Anglo-Irish Agreement** accorded the government in Dublin a limited consultative role in the administration of Northern Ireland.
1986	Confirmation of the ban on divorce in the Republic.

1991	Series of tri-partite talks set in motion by Peter Brooke, Secretary of State for Northern Ireland, involving the political parties in Northern Ireland, the British Government and the Dublin Government.
1993	**Downing Street Declaration** made jointly by the Prime Minister of the United Kingdom and the Taoiseach of the Republic of Ireland in which it was stated that the British Government had no selfish, strategic or economic interest in Northern Ireland and that the Irish government accepted that the democratic right of self-determination by the people of Ireland as a whole must be achieved and exercised with and subject to the agreement and consent of a majority of the people of Northern Ireland.
1994	Declaration by the IRA of a complete **cessation of violence** on 31 August followed by an announcement by the Combined Loyalist Military Command that they would universally cease all operational hostilities as from midnight on Thursday 13 October.
1997	Declaration of **second ceasefire** by the IRA, following the cancellation of the first in February 1996; start of talks at Stormont attended by representatives of all political parties to negotiate an agreement.
1998	**Stormont Agreement** approved by referendum. Elections held for new Assembly in Northern Ireland.
	The Republic of Ireland adopted the euro as its official currency.
1999	**Northern Ireland Assembly** set up in December.
2000	**Northern Ireland Assembly** reconvened on 30th May, having been suspended on 11 February following disagreement about the decommissioning of arms.

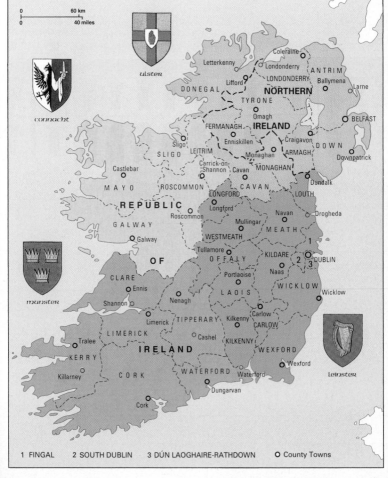

1 FINGAL   2 SOUTH DUBLIN   3 DÚN LAOGHAIRE-RATHDOWN   O County Towns

Custom House, Dublin

Republic
of Ireland

ABBEYLEIX

MAINISTIR LAOISE – Co Laois – Population 1 299
Michelin Atlas p 86 and Map 923 – J 9

Originally the site of a 12C abbey, Abbeyleix seems unchanged since the period when it was dominated by the de Vesci family, who laid it out in the mid 18C at the gates of their mansion. It is an excellent example of a planned estate settlement and has been designated a Heritage Town.

> **Adjacent Sights** – See Athy, Carlow, Cashel, Kildare, Kilkenny, Roscrea, Russborough, Tullamore.

Abbeyleix Heritage House ⊘ – The exhibition in the old school traces the history of Abbeyleix and its role in the evolution of the region, in which the actions of the de Vescis feature prominently. There is a fine model of the town in its setting as well as one of the Rock of Dunamase.

Abbey Sense Garden ⊘ – The old walled garden of a former Brigidine convent has been redesigned with elaborate planting and other features intended to appeal to touch, taste, smell and sound as well as sight.

EXCURSIONS

★★**Emo Court** ⊘ – *15mi/24km north-north-east of Abbeyleix by N 8, M 7 and R 422.* The **house** was designed in the Classical style by James Gandon in 1792 for Lord Portarlington, formerly John Dawson, a banker and an architect; the interior decor (1835–40) was completed by Louis Vulliamy. The tour of the house *(30min)* includes the reception rooms, all restored to their early glory and furnished with some fine pieces and varied examples of Wedgwood pottery.
An avenue of Wellingtonias, the first in Ireland, links the house to the Dublin Road. Extensive **gardens** spread from the house to the lake. The Clucker Garden is planted with azaleas, rhododendrons and Japanese maples; four statues of the Seasons and a ring garden adorn the lawns; the Grapery, which is planted with trees and shrubs, descends to the lakeside walk.

St John the Evangelist ⊘ – *Coolbanagher; from the gates of Emo Court take the road opposite through the village; turn left into R 419 (Portarlington–Portlaoise road).* James Gandon also designed this church, his only one, in 1785 for Lord Carlow. The interior is decorated with plaster swags and garlands.

★**Rock of Dunamase** – *15mi/24km north-east of Abbeyleix by R 245, R 247 and N 80 northwest.* The rock rising straight from the plain is crowned by the extensive and impressive ruins of the O'More clan fortress, destroyed by Cromwell's army in the mid 17C. Excellent **views**★ from the summit (200ft/60m high).

★**Stradbally** – *13mi/21km north-east of Abbeyleix by R 245, R 247 and N 80 south-east.* Population 1 046. The steeply sloping flower-lined Main Street climbs towards a range of low hills. An unusual pagoda-like structure with a red roof in the Market Place commemorates Dr William Perceval, a local doctor who died in 1899 after 54 years of local practice.

The **Steam Museum** ⊙ displays a collection of old steam-powered rollers and threshing machines. A narrow-gauge steam railway (1mi/1.6km) runs through the woods. A rally of steam machines is held in the village in August.

★**Timahoe Round Tower** – *9mi/15km north-east of Abbeyleix by R 430 east and a minor road north.* The round tower (96ft/29m high) was probably built in the 12C; the top leans from the vertical (2ft/0.6m); the Romanesque double doorway has steps to the interior.
The ruins of a 15C church *(east)* were converted into a castle in the 17C.
A **memorial** on the broad village green marks the visit of **Erskine Childers**, former President of Ireland, on 31 May 1974. **Richard Nixon**, President of the USA (1969–74), whose ancestors came from the village, visited Timahoe in 1970.

Heywood Gardens ⊙ – *Near Ballinakill; 3.5mi/6km south-east of Abbeyleix by R 432.* Although the mansion which they once graced has long since been replaced by a modern college building, these gardens (1906–10) are a fine example of the partnership between the architect **Edwin Lutyens** (1869–1944) and the garden designer **Gertrude Jekyll** (1843–1932). Architectural influences predominate, with terraces, massive retaining walls, gateways, flights of steps, pleached lime walk and hedges of clipped yew. The Italianate sunken garden has a pool and a pavilion; paths and lawns have a prospect of church towers and distant mountains, and a pergola is set high above a pond and wooded ravine.

ADARE★

ÁTHA DARA – Co Limerick – Population 1 042
Michelin Atlas p 84 and Map 923 – F 10

Adare is set on the west bank of the River Maigue, in the fertile wooded lands of west Limerick. The broad Main Street is lined with thatched cottages, mostly at least two centuries old. Adare has changed little since most of the other buildings were erected in the late 19C.
Nothing remains of the original settlement, built 1 000 years ago near the castle. During the 12C the Anglo-Normans settled in Adare; a century later the Fitzgeralds, Earls of Kildare, acquired the land. There is no trace of the town walls that were built when Adare was incorporated in the 14C.

Out and About

Adjacent Sights – See Kilmallock, Limerick, Tralee.

Where to Eat

The Wild Geese, Main St. ☎/Fax 061 396 451. Pretty little thatched cottage; well known for traditional Irish cooking.

Where to Stay

Sandfield House, Castleroberts. ☎ /Fax 061 396 119. *3.5mi/5.6km SE by N 21; on Croom rd.* Guesthouse (4 rm) offering comfortable B&B in quiet country location.
Berkeley Lodge, Station Rd. ☎/Fax 061 396 857. Small guesthouse (6 rm) with pleasantly decorated bedrooms providing good value accommodation.
Carrabawn Guesthouse, Killarney Rd. ☎ 061 396 067; 061 396 925. *0.5mi/0.8km SW by N 21.* Spacious house (8 rm) with generously sized bedrooms; on main road with garden and parking.

SIGHTS

Adare Heritage Centre ⊙ – There is more to Adare than picturesque thatched cottages. The historical exhibition tells of Norman invaders, medieval abbeys and the influential Dunraven family. Its highlight is a model which brings to life the town in 1500; there is also an audio-visual presentation *(15min)*.

★**Adare Friary** – *Access via Adare Golf Course; ask at the Club House.* Beside the River Maigue are the ruins of the Franciscan friary founded by the Earl of Kildare in 1464; extensions were built in the 15C and 16C. The nave, choir, south transept and cloisters are reasonably well preserved. The **Kilmallock Gate** was once the main entrance.

Desmond Castle – *Access via Adare Golf Course; ask at the Club House; restoration in progress.* The castle had already ceased to be of strategic importance when much of it was demolished by Cromwell's forces. A large square tower stands in the inner ward of the early 14C castle surrounded by a moat. The upper storey of the building in the southwest corner of the outer ward was the **great hall**. Nearby are the remains of **St Nicholas Church** (11C) and the **Desmond Chapel** (14C).

Adare Manor – The neo-Gothic limestone mansion, now a hotel open to non-residents, was begun in 1832; among the architects involved were James Pain and Augustus Welby Pugin. The carved inscriptions state that it was built by the Earl of Dunraven. The interior contains an elaborately panelled staircase and a long gallery (132ft/40m). The grounds, which include a maze and a lake, border the River Maigue.

Church of the Most Holy Trinity (Roman Catholic) – *Main Street facing the town park*. The square tower and the south wall of the present church were part of a monastery, the only house in Ireland of the Trinitarian Order, constructed about 1230 by Maurice Fitzgerald, 2nd Baron of Offaly. The 50 monks were put to death in 1539 at the Dissolution of the Monasteries. The ruins were restored by the 1st Earl of Dunraven and enlarged in 1852. At the rear stands a completely restored 14C **dovecot**.

★**Adare Parish Church (Anglican)** – The church consists of the nave and part of the choir of an Augustinian priory founded in 1315. The cloisters (north side) were converted into a mausoleum for the family of Quin, the Earls of Dunraven.

EXCURSIONS

Croom Mills ⊘ – *5mi/8km south of Adare by N 20*. The exhibition and audio-visual film trace the history of the mill built by Denis Lyons in 1788 on the River Maigue. The exhibits give hands-on experience of how the machinery worked. The windows of the restaurant overlook the mill race which drives the nearby waterwheel.

★**Castle Matrix** ⊘ – *Rathkeale; 7.5mi/13km W of Adare by N 21; concealed entrance on north side of busy main road*. The Norman tower was built in 1440 by the 7th Earl of Desmond; he and his father, the 4th Earl, are the earliest-recorded Norman poets in the Irish language. The Great Hall houses a fine **library** and objets d'art. The castle also houses an **international arts centre** and the **Heraldry Society of Ireland**. It was at Castle Matrix that Edmund Spenser, the poet, and Walter Raleigh, then a captain, met for the first time in 1580 and began a lifelong friendship.

> **"Crom Abu"**
>
> The battle cry of the Earls of Kildare derives from their estates and castle at Croom on the River Maigue in Co Limerick.

★**Irish Palatine Heritage Centre** ⊘ – *Rathkeale; 7.5mi/13km W of Adare by N 21*. The centre, housed in an old station-master's house re-erected on a new site, presents an exhibition of photographs, documents, arms, domestic articles and larger artefacts, recalling the settlement of South German Protestants in the area of Rathkeale in the early 18C, their innovative farming methods, their contribution to Methodism and their dispersion throughout the English-speaking world. There is also a genealogical service for tracing Palatine ancestors.

★**Newcastle West** – *16mi/26km W of Adare by N 21*. Population 3 287. This thriving market town, known for its spring water, takes its name from the **castle** (recently restored) in the town square. Originally the castle belonged to the Knights Templar but it later passed into the ownership of the Earls of Desmond. The banqueting hall, now known as **Desmond Hall** ⊘, with an oak minstrel's gallery (restored) and a hooded fireplace (reconstruction), stands over a 13C vaulted stone chamber, lit by ecclesiastical lancet windows. The remains of the castle include the adjoining Great Hall *(Halla Mór)*.

Askeaton – *13mi/20km NW of Adare by N 21 and R 518*. Population 893. On a small island in the River Deel stand the ruins of **Askeaton Castle**, probably founded by William de Burgo c 1199. The tower and walls (15C) are largely intact; the banqueting hall, erected between 1440 and 1459 by the 7th Earl of Desmond, was one of the largest of its kind in Ireland and has a blind arcade in the south wall and finely carved windows.

North of the town centre on the east bank of the river are the ruins of **Askeaton Franciscan Friary**, a 15C foundation. A representation of **St Francis** is to be found in the northeast corner of the cloisters.

Foynes Flying Boat Museum ⊘ – *21mi/34km W of Adare by N 21, R 518 and N 69*. Before and during the Second World War the small seaport of Foynes (population 650) in the Shannon Estuary, was the operational base for flying boats, the original Shannon Airport. The old terminal building now houses a **museum** displaying many models, photographs and log books. The film *Atlantic Conquest* contains original footage linked by a modern commentary. The radio and weather room houses the original equipment, which is still in operation and provided the first information used by the Irish Meteorological Service.

Irish Palatines

In 1709, following two invasions and a winter of extreme cold, the Irish Palatines emigrated from their native land, the Rhineland–Palatinate in South Germany (hence their name), and travelled to England in response to the provision of funds by the English Government to enable them to travel to Carolina in the USA. When the government funds ran out, many were stranded in London until the Dublin government offered to take 500 families; 821 families arrived in Ireland. Landlords were offered subsidies to accept the immigrants; some went to Counties Kerry, Tipperary and Wexford but the majority settled on the estate of Lord Southwell in Rathkeale, where their names – Bovenizer, Corneille, Delmege, Miller, Rynard, Piper, Sparling, Stark, Switzer, Teskey – sounded a foreign note. They were an industrious people, who introduced new farming techniques, and a pious, God-fearing people, mostly Lutherans or Calvinists. They responded with great enthusiasm to the preaching of John Wesley, who returned to visit them on several occasions after his first visit in 1756.

One of Wesley's preachers, Philip Embury, and his cousin Barbara Heck emigrated to America in 1760. The sermon preached by Philip in his house in New York in 1766 led to the founding of the Methodist Episcopal Church in America.

★Glin Castle ⊘ – *29mi/47km W of Adare by N 21, R 518 and N 69.* In the village of Glin (population 569) by the stream stands the ruined **keep** of the castle of the Knights of Glin, destroyed in 1600 by Queen Elizabeth's forces. The **modern castle** was built about 1780–85 west of the village; the battlements and tower were added about 1820 when the three Gothic turreted lodges were built at the entrances to the estate. The property has been owned by the unusually titled hereditary Knights of Glin since about 1300. The mild climate enables palm trees to grow in the **formal gardens** behind the house.

The **interior** is notable for its very fine neo-Classical plasterwork, particularly in the front hall which leads to the most unusual double flying **staircase** with a Venetian window overlooking the formal gardens. The main reception rooms have a notable collection of mahogany mid-18C Irish furniture. Inset into one of the library walls is a mahogany pedimented bookcase which conceals a hidden door leading to the staircase. Other rarities are paintings on chicken skin and a room warmer consisting of a wooden surround containing an open bronze pan holding charcoal. The rooms are hung with an interesting collection of family portraits and other Irish paintings.

Glin Heritage Centre ⊘ – The neo-Gothic church at the gates of Glin Castle houses an exhibition on the history of Glin and the Fitzgerald family.

Entrance Hall, Glin Castle

Irish Picture Library

ARAN ISLANDS★

OILEÁIN ÁRAINN – Co Galway – Population 2 000
Michelin Atlas p 88 and Map 923 – CD 8

The three Aran Islands extend in an oblique line across the mouth of Galway Bay. The smallest, Inisheer, is not far (5mi/8km) from the mainland; the middle island, Inishmaan, is slightly larger (6sq mi/7.77km²); the largest island, Inishmore, is about 7mi/11.3km from the coast of Connemara.

Literary Tradition

Gaelic is still spoken on the islands and the people are great story tellers and music makers. Local stories were the inspiration of JM Synge's play *Riders to the Sea*, which is set on Inishmaan, and of *The Playboy of the Western World*. His book *The Aran Islands* (1907) and the film *Man of Aran* (1934) by Robert Flaherty, an American, illustrate the traditional island way of life.

Although included for administrative purposes in Co Galway, the islands are geologically and historically linked to The Burren on the mainland. The land rises in natural terraces from a flat sandy shore facing Galway Bay to high cliffs (300ft/91m) confronting the Atlantic; constant sea erosion forms ledges used by fishermen. There are over 400 different wild flowers including fuchsias. Rainfall is lower than on the mainland and the islands are never touched by frost. Trees are rare and the tiny fields, created laboriously over the years out of layers of sand and seaweed, are divided by openwork drystone walls through which the wind can pass. Traditionally the white cottages were thatched with straw tied down against the wind. Fishing and farming are the main activities. Cows spent the summer grazing in Connemara but returned to Aran where it was dry for the winter; ponies however wintered in Connemara and worked on Aran during the summer months. Illicit whiskey and also peat for fuel were imported by boat from Connemara in exchange for potatoes and limestone.

Access ⊙

By air from Inverin *(20mi/32km west of Galway by R 336)*.
By sea from Galway, from Rossaveel *(23mi/37km west of Galway by R 336)* and from Doolin in the Burren (Inisheer only).

Despite or because of their remote situation the Aran Islands have been inhabited for centuries. The earliest surviving ruins are the great stone forts which date from the prehistoric era. The later more abundant ruins date from the early and medieval Christian period (5C–16C) when the Aran monasteries were important cultural centres.

Traditional crafts are still practised, particularly the production of the distinctive cream-coloured Aran knitwear using the symbolic stitches which represent elements in nature and the Aran way of life; originally the women spun the wool and the men did the knitting using goose quills for needles.

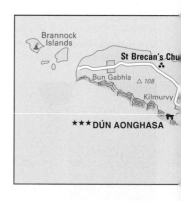

INISHMORE (ARAINN)

The island (population 1 000) (9mi/14.5km x 2.5mi/4km) is served by one road which runs from the airstrip along the shore of Killeany Bay *(Cuan Chill Éinne)*, through Kilronan *(Cill Rónáin)* to the remote hamlet of Bun Gabhla overlooking Brannock Island *(Oileán Dá Bhranóg)* and the lighthouse. The old tracks and walls (7 000mi/11 265km) run from northeast to southwest following the natural rifts and the traditional pattern of movement carting seaweed from the shore to fertilise the fields. At the roadside stand square pillars topped by crosses erected in memory of islanders who died abroad or at sea.

Aran Heritage Centre Ionad Arann ⊙ – *In Kilronin*. Ionad Arann, to give it its Irish name, provides an introduction to the landscape, traditions and culture of the islands.

★★★ **Dún Aonghasa** ⊙ – *4.5mi/7.2km west of Kilronan; 20min there and back on foot from Kilmurvy (Cill Mhuirbhigh)*. A path leads uphill to a great drystone fort set on the very edge of the cliffs (200ft/61m above sea-level). It is one of the finest prehistoric monuments in Europe and consists of three lines of defence. The ground between the outer and the middle wall is spiked with stone stakes set at an angle to impede attack. A square tunnel in the thickness of the wall leads into

Inishmore

the inner compound. The inner wall, which has steps up to wall walks, describes a semicircle beginning and ending on the cliff edge; it is not known whether the fort was originally this shape or whether some of it has collapsed into the sea.

St Brecan's Church (Teampall Bhreacáin) – *5.5mi/8.8km W of Kilronan*. In a hollow on the north coast overlooking a small bay is an ancient monastic site including an early church, greatly altered in the late Middle Ages, and dedicated to St Brecan whose grave is opposite the west door. In the southeast corner of the graveyard is a stone inscribed to seven Roman saints.

St Kieran's Church (Teampall Chiaráin) – *1mi/1.7km NW of Kilronan; bear right in Mainistir*. Half way down the slope to the shore stands a small ruined church dedicated to St Kieran of Clonmacnoise. Surrounding the church are four cross-inscribed stones and St Kieran's Well.

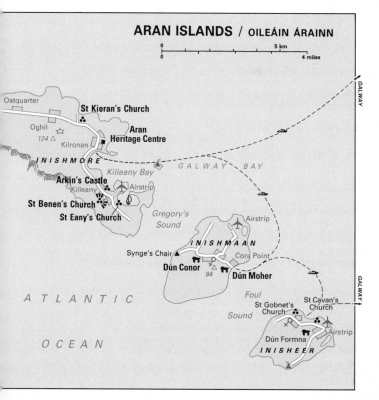

Arkin's Castle (Caisleán Aircín) – *1mi/1.6km S of Kilronan in Killeany.* On the south shore of Killeany Bay stand the ruins of a tower house which was probably built by John Rawson, to whom the islands were granted by Elizabeth I in 1588. It was fortified by Lord Clanrickard against the Cromwellians who captured it in 1652, lost it and recaptured it in 1653.

St Benen's Church (Teampall Bheanáin) – *1mi/1.6km S of Kilronan; in Killeany bear right; 10min there and back on foot.* A path climbs the hill past St Eany's oratory (6C or 7C) with a narrow north door and a slim east window. There is a good **view** of Killeany Bay and of the mainland.

St Eany's Church (Teaghlach Éinne) – *1.5mi/2.4km S of Kilronan.* On the coast south of the airstrip, almost submerged by the surrounding graves, are the ruins of an early church with antae and a round-headed window. St Enda is said to be buried here on the site of the monastery, which he founded in about 490. His reputation as a teacher attracted so many famous men to study under him – St Kieran of Clonmacnoise, St Finnian of Moville on Inishowen, St Jarlath of Tuam, St Colman of Kilmacduagh near Loughrea – that the island, where 227 saints are buried, became known as Aran of the Saints.

INISHMAAN (INIS MEAIN)

The island (3mi/5km x 1mi/2km) slopes from a bare rocky plateau northeast to a sandy shore. The houses are strung out in the lee of the high ground. JM Synge is said to have favoured a sheltered spot called Synge's Chair *(Cathaoir Synge)* on the western cliffs overlooking Gregory's Sound *(Sunda Ghrióra).*

Dún Conor (Dún Chonchúir) – The huge prehistoric fort (restored) stands on high ground in the centre of the island on the edge of a narrow valley; it consists of a thick stone wall (17.5ft/5.65m), stepped on the inside, round an oval enclosure (227ft/69m x 115ft/35m), which is flanked to the east by an outer court; the entrance is protected by a stone bastion.

Dún Moher or Dún Fearbhaigh – This smaller stone fort (103ft/31m x 90ft/27m) stands on the edge of the high ground overlooking the landing jetty at Cora Point.

INISHEER (INIS OIRR)

On the smallest island the houses cluster along the north coast.
Near the airstrip are the ruins of **St Cavan's Church** *(Teampall Chaomháin)*, threatened by the sand; the chancel with its round-headed east window dates from the early 10C; the chancel arch and south door are medieval, probably 14C. The grave of St Cavan, the brother of St Kevin of Glendalough, lies nearby *(NE.*
In the centre of the settlements stands **Dún Formna**, a stone fort (170ft/52m x 123ft/37m), which contains the ruins of a tower house, probably built by the O'Briens in the 14C and destroyed by the Cromwellians in 1652.
Northwest of the houses are the ruins of **St Gobnet's Church** *(Kilgobnet)*; the small medieval oratory has an altar, a round-headed east window and a flat-headed doorway narrowing towards the top.

ATHENRY★

BAILE ÁTHA AN RÍ – Co Galway – Population 1 612
Michelin Atlas p 89 and Map 923 – F 8

The importance of this Heritage Town lies in its Norman and medieval monuments. Now a quiet agricultural town on the Clarinbridge River, Athenry, meaning the King's Ford, was an important Norman stronghold and is still largely contained within its medieval **town walls** (1211), of which the best preserved section is the **North Gate**. In the town centre stands a 15C market cross depicting the Crucifixion.

Athenry Heritage Centre ⊘ – The display in the former Anglican church traces the history of the town and interprets the medieval monuments.

Entertainment – To recapture the taste of life in the Middle Ages sit down to a **medieval banquet** at Dunguaire Castle *(see below)* and listen to songs, poems and extracts from the writings of Synge, Yeats and Gogarty.

Events – The **Athenry Annual Medieval Festival** *(weekend nearest 15 August)* celebrates with an open air play and concert, exhibitions of archery, jousting competitions, a medieval crafts fair and fireworks.

Adjacent Sights – See Birr, Clonmacnoise, Galway, Portumna, Strokestown, Tuam.

Athenry Castle ⊘ – The castle, built by Meiler de Bermingham c 1239 but in ruins since 1597, consisted of a central keep, with a vaulted undercroft supported on pillars and a main entrance at first-floor level, enclosed within a stout wall reinforced by two towers.

Dominican Friary ⊘ – Beside the river on the east side of the town are the ruins of a friary founded in 1241 by Meiler de Bermingham. The choir of the church, which was dedicated to St Peter and St Paul, is 13C with lancet windows, but the pillars and aisle arches date from a 14C rebuilding in which the chancel was extended and a new east window was inserted. The tomb niches date from the 13C to the 15C. The north transept was probably added during repairs after a fire in 1423. In 1574 the friary was confiscated and burned by the Burkes. In 1627 it was returned to the friars, who restored the buildings, and in 1644 it became a university. Eight years later, however, the friars were expelled by the Cromwellians.

EXCURSIONS

East of Athenry

Loughrea – *11mi/18km S by R 348 and R 349*. The town lies on the north shore of Lough Rea facing the Slieve Aughty Mountains. Its origins lie in a Norman stronghold built in about 1300 by Richard de Burgo, who also founded the **Carmelite Priory**, now in ruins, where General St Ruth, who died at the Battle of Aughrim, is said to be buried under the tower. Part of one of the medieval **town gates** stands on the edge of the cathedral precinct.

★**St Brendan's Cathedral** ⊘ – The cathedral of the Roman Catholic diocese of Clonfert *(see p 261)* was designed by William Byrne in the neo-Gothic style in 1897. The **interior** is richly decorated in the spirit of the Celtic Revival. The work was commissioned by Edward Martyn *(see p 204)* and his relatives, the Smyth family of Masonbrook.

The stained glass is by Sarah Purser, Hubert McGoldrick and Evie Hone working for **An Túr Gloine** *(see p 87)*, and by Patrick Pye and Michael Healy.

The textiles were designed and woven by the Dun Emer Guild, which was founded by Evelyn Gleeson. The sculpture is from the hands of John Hughes and Michael Shorthall. The furnishings, metalwork and wood-carving are the work of William Scott.

The **Diocesan Museum** ⊘ displays a collection of vestments (15C–20C), chalices (16C–19C), statues, penal crosses, rosaries, crucifixes and missals.

★**Turoe Stone** – *10mi/1.6km S of Athenry by R 348 and a minor road S from Kiltullagh towards Bullaunpark in gateway*. In the middle of a field *(right)* stands a granite boulder (3ft/1m high). Its domed cap is carved in relief with curvilinear La Tène motifs and a "step" pattern arranged in four panels. Motifs include a stylised bird's head and the **triskele**. It is presumed to be a Celtic ritual stone and was found in a nearby hillfort, known as the Rath of Fearmore (Rath of the Big Man), which dates from the last pre-Christian centuries.

Kilconnell Franciscan Friary – *15mi/18km E of Athenry by R 348. Plan of layout in the nave*. The ruins are the remains of a monastery founded in 1353 for the Franciscans by William O'Kelly on the site of an earlier monastery begun in the 6C by St Conall. There are two fine tomb niches: one bears the figures of six saints, named in a manner which suggests a French influence; the other in the choir belongs to the O'Daly family. The tower was added later. The remains of the cloister include the refectory in the northwest corner. Although the friary was dissolved in 1541, there were still friars in residence shortly before the Battle of Aughrim in 1691.

Battle of Aughrim Centre ⊘ – *Aughrim; 5mi/8km S of Kilconnell by minor road*. The Interpretative Centre uses audio-visual, three-dimensional displays and many relics to recreate the bloody battle of Aughrim, based on the account of Captain Walter Dalton, one of the combatants.

B Lynch /Bord Fáilte, Dublin

St Joseph by Michael Healy
in Loughrea Cathedral

> ### Battle of Aughrim
>
> Aughrim was the last great battle in the War of the Two Kings *(Cogadh an Dá Rí)* between King James II of England, supported by Louis XIV of France, and King William III of England and his allies. After retreating west following the **Battle of Athlone**, the Jacobite forces, under the French general St Ruth, took up a defensive position at Aughrim against the army of William III of England, under the Dutchman General Ginkel. On 12 July 1691 45 000 men (20 000 Jacobites composed of Irish, French, Germans and Walloons and 25 000 Williamites composed of Irish, English, Dutch, Germans and Danish) met and fought; 9 000 died. The death of St Ruth at the height of the battle caused disarray among the Jacobites and gave victory to the Williamites. According to legend, the Williamite dead were buried at Clontuskert Priory while the Jacobite dead were stripped and left to rot and their bones were smashed on the walls of Kilconnell Friary.

Clontuskert Augustinian Priory – *10mi/16km SE of Aughrim by N 6 to Garbally and S by R 355; 5min on foot from roadside car park (left).*
The first monastery on the site was founded by St Baedán (d c 809). The Augustinians, who arrived in the 12C, had by the end of the 13C established one of the richest monasteries in the diocese. Most of the present ruined building dates from the 15C – east window, rood-screen, west door which bears carvings of St Michael, St John, St Katherine and an abbot or bishop. Although the building passed to the de Burghs at the 16C Dissolution, the monks returned in 1637 and made repairs to the fabric.

Kiltartan Country *S of Athenry*

★**Thoor Ballylee** ⊙ – *23mi/37km S of Athenry by R 348, R 349, N 6 and N 66 (sign).*
The 16C tower house, which was William Butler Yeats' summer house for 11 years, became a powerful symbol in his poetic work, as the inscription on the wall facing the road records. In 1917, the year of his marriage to Georgie Hyde-Lees, he was looking for a property near Lady Gregory's house at Coole Park *(see below)*, where he was a frequent visitor. He spent most of that summer converting the four-storey tower. Yeats abandoned the tower in 1928. In 1961 the local Kiltartan Society began its restoration, including the adjoining miller's cottage and millwheel.

Kiltartan National Museum ⊙ – *3.5mi/5km W of Thoor Ballylee by minor road and N 18 south.* The old schoolhouse, built by the Gregory family, displays memorabilia of Lady Gregory, co-founder with Yeats of the Abbey Theatre; outside are stones commemorating those connected with the Irish Literary Renaissance.

Coole Park ⊙ – *2mi/3km S from Kiltartan by N 18.* Coole was the home of Augusta, Lady Gregory (1852–1932).In the walled garden stands a great copper beech, the **autograph tree**★, on which many of the significant figures in the Irish Literary Renaissance – William Butler Yeats, George Bernard Shaw, G Russell (AE), John Millington Synge and Sean O'Casey – cut their initials while guests at the house (demolished). The **visitor centre** in the converted stables provides information on the national park – deer enclosure, nature trail; a forest walk *(0.5mi/0.8km)* leads to the lake, where petrified trees protrude from the water.

★**Kilmacduagh Churches and Round Tower** – *3.5mi/50km SW of Gort by R 460; car park.*
The ruins of the monastery, which was founded in the 7C by St Colman, son of Duagh, straddle the road. The monastery suffered many Viking attacks in the 9C–10C; after the Reformation it became the property of Richard, 2nd Earl of Clanrickard.
The **Glebe House**, a two-storey 13C building, was probably the Abbot's lodging. South of it stands the **Church of St John the Baptist**, a small 12C building with rounded and pointed windows and a later chancel.
Beside the well-preserved inclined **round tower** stands the **cathedral**; its west gable dates from the 11C–12C, the nave from 1200; the south doorway with a bishop's head above it, the two transepts, the west window and the chancel probably date from the 15C; the folk art Crucifixions were moved from the south to the north transept after 1765. **St Mary's Church**, across the road, was built c 1200.

O'Heyne's Church *(northwest)* contains early-13C carving on the chancel arch and east windows.

★**Dunguaire Castle** ⊙ – *20mi/32km NW of Kilmacduagh by minor road via Tirneevin and Killinny to Kinvarra; car park.* Facing **Kinvarra** (population 425), a charming little port at the head of Kinvarra Bay, stands a four-storey tower house with adjoining bawn, built in 1520 by the descendants of Guaire, King of Connaught in the 7C. The Martyns of Galway owned it from the 17C to 20C, when it was restored by Oliver St John Gogarty (1924) and by Christobel Lady Ampthill (1954). Traces of the wickerwork support used in its construction are visible on the ground-floor vault. The first and second floors are furnished for medieval banquets, the top floor *(76 steps)* as a 20C sitting room.

ATHLONE

BAILE ÁTHA LUAIN – Co Westmeath – Population 7 691
Michelin Atlas p 90 and Map 923 – I 7

Athlone, the "Ford of Luan", occupies a strategic position commanding a crossing point on the River Shannon south of Lough Ree. It is the county town of Westmeath. Early in the 20C, owing to its central position on the map, it was proposed as the capital of the new Republic. There is a **fine view**★ of Lough Ree from Ballykeeran Viewpoint *(4mi/6.4km NE by N 55)*.

John McCormack

The greatest lyric tenor of his day, John McCormack (1884–1945), was born in The Bawn, a narrow street in the centre of Athlone. He sang in the Palestrina Choir of the Pro-Cathedral in Dublin. At 23 he sang a major role at Covent Garden, where he appeared every year until 1914. After achieving fame on the operatic stage in Europe and the USA, he turned to the concert stage. He was made a Count of the Papal Court for his charity work.

Siege of Athlone – Following the Battle of the Boyne *(see p 116)* the Jacobite forces retreated to Athlone. In June 1691 the Williamite army under Ginkel made a determined assault on the bridge; Sergeant Custume, who died in its defence, is commemorated in the name of the local barracks.

After 10 days of bombardment the town and the castle fell. Ginkel was made Earl of Athlone. The Jacobites withdrew south-west to Aughrim *(see p 106)*.

SIGHTS

Athlone Castle ⊘ – *Market Square*. Early in the 13C John de Grey, Justiciar of Ireland, built a stone castle on the west bank. The curtain wall and its three fortified towers date

Boat Trips ⊘ – Excursions on Lough Ree from the marina at Coosan Point.

John McCormack Golden Voice of Athlone – A competition for young classical singers *(late June)* to honour John McCormack, to bring good music to the community and to provide assistance to young singers.

Adjacent Sights – See Athenry, Birr, Longford, Mullingar, Strokestown, Tullamore.

from the late 13C. The oldest part of the structure is the central polygonal **keep**; early in the 19C the upper part was greatly altered to accommodate heavy artillery supplemented by new defences, known as the Batteries, west of the town. From the battlements there is a good **view** of the river and the town.

The **Exhibition Centre** provides an audio-visual presentation of the Siege of Athlone and the life story of the world-famous tenor, **John McCormack**.

The **Castle Museum** ⊘, housed in the keep, covers local history and folk life and displays souvenirs (gramophone and silver cups) of John McCormack.

Church of St Peter and St Paul – *Market Square*. The church, with its twin towers and cathedral-like proportions, was designed by Ralph Byrne and consecrated in 1937. Most of the stained-glass windows were designed by the Harry Clarke studios but the one in the priest's sacristy is by Sarah Purser.

Town Centre – From the bridge the main street curves east towards the site of the Dublin Gate. In a side turning *(left)* stand the ruins of Court Devenish *(private)*, a Jacobean house (1620) ruined in 1622. The Bawn, a narrow street *(left)*, contains the **birthplace of John McCormack**. The **Franciscan Church** (1931), south of the main street, was built in the Hiberno-Romanesque style inspired by old Irish designs. The **Strand** along the river bank to Burgess Park provides a fine view of the weir, the eel fisheries and the old port on the west bank.

ATHY

BAILE ÀTHA – Co Kildare – Population 5 306
Michelin Atlas p 86 and Map 923 – L 9

Athy is a pleasant small town on the River Barrow, for many years the property of the Fitzgeralds, Dukes of Leinster. At the beginning of the Middle Ages it was the largest town in Co Kildare, clustered round a fortified crossing of the river. Athy marks the confluence of the River Barrow and the Barrow Line, a southern branch of the Grand Canal: pleasant riverside walks and fishing for coarse and trout anglers.

In 1944 **Macra na Feirme**, a cultural and social organisation for young farming people, was founded in the Town Hall.

Crafts – At the **Irish Pewter Mill** *(see below)*.

Adjacent Sights – See Abbeyleix, Carlow, Kildare, Kilkenny, Russborough, Tullamore.

Town Centre – The present bridge, known as Crom-a-Boo Bridge, from the war cry of the Geraldine family, dates from 1796. Beside it stands White's Castle (*private*) which was built in the 16C.

The main square beside the river is graced by the **Courthouse**, which was built in 1856 as the Corn Exchange. On the opposite side of the square stands the **Town Hall**, which dates from the mid 18C and has housed a market, council chambers and law courts. The brick-vaulted ground floor now houses the **Heritage Centre** ⊘; its displays evoke the history of the town and associated personalities and events, such as the Antarctic explorer Ernest Shackleton and the famous Gordon Bennett motor race.

Dominican Church – The fan-shaped modern church is furnished with stained-glass windows and Stations of the Cross by George Campbell, a noted North of Ireland artist of the earlier 20C.

EXCURSIONS

East of Barrow Valley

Ballitore – *7mi/11km E by minor road*. Population 293. The 18C **Quaker meeting house** ⊘ has been converted into a small library and museum describing Quaker settlements in the area; there is a Quaker graveyard on the far side of the village. **Crookstown Mill and Heritage Centre** ⊘, housed in a converted 1840 cornmill, contains material on the baking and milling industries, items of local historical interest, a graphic/photographic gallery and furniture workshops.

Irish Pewter Mill, Museum and Crafts Centre ⊘ – *Timolin; 11mi/16km E by minor road to Ballitore and S by N 9*. The museum displays moulds, tools and dies used as long ago as the Middle Ages. There are demonstrations of pewter vessels being cast and a video of the spinning, smithing and polishing. The building, which is about 1 000 years old, was originally a mill or part of a nunnery.

★**Moone High Cross** – *12mi/19km E by minor road to Ballitore and S by N 9*. The scanty ruins of a 6C monastery founded by St Columba enclose a high cross (17.5ft/5.3m high), elaborately restored in the 19C. The 51 carved panels show scenes from the Bible: the 12 Apostles are grouped in three tiers on the west face.

Baltinglass Abbey – *15mi/24km E by minor road to Ballitore, S by N 9 and a minor road east via Graney*. Beside the 19C Anglican church are the ruins of Baltinglass Abbey, which was founded by Dermot MacMurrough, King of Leinster, in 1148 and suppressed in 1536. Six Gothic arches flank the nave; the 19C tower and parts of the original cloisters (restored) still stand. Baltinglass, which was started by monks from Mellifont *(see p 119)*, sent out monks in its turn to found Jerpoint *(see p 220)*.

The town (population 1 066) lies at the foot of steep Baltinglass Hill; the main square is dominated by the 1798 memorial, commemorating Michael Dwyer, who was enabled to escape by his faithful comrade Sam MacAllister drawing the fire of the British soldiers on himself.

★**Castledermot High Crosses** – *9.5mi/16km SE by R 418*. The site of a monastery founded by St Dermot is marked by two granite **high crosses**, carved with biblical scenes, and a 10C **round tower**, topped by medieval battlements. Ruined chancel walls recall the Franciscan friary founded by Lord Ossory in 1302.

BANTRY★

BEANNTRAÍ – Co Cork – Population 2 936
Michelin Atlas p 77 and Map 923 – D 12

Bantry *(Beanntraí)*, a market and fishing town (population 2 777), has changed little since the 19C; it is situated on the south shore of Bantry Bay, a narrow deep-water bay in the lee of the Beara Peninsula which has long been known to mariners as a safe anchorage.

Out and About

Boat Trips – There is a **ferry** ⊘ from Bantry Pier to **Whiddy Island** and there are scenic cruises of Bantry Bay.

Facilities – The inner harbour, with two slipways and safe anchorage, is an ideal location for sailing, water-skiing, wind surfing, canoeing, scuba-diving and swimming. The indoor swimming pool, children's pool and toddlers' pool and leisure centre at the Westlodge Hotel in Bantry are open to the public throughout the year.

Events – The **Bantry Mussel Fair** is held in May *(second weekend)* each year and the **International Chamber Music Week** in July *(second week)*.

Adjacent Sights – See Kenmare, Killarney, Skibbereen.

1796 French Armada

In the winter of this year a French fleet commanded by General Hoche and inspired and accompanied by Wolfe Tone, an Irishman, set sail from Brest intending to invade Ireland and expel the British. The fleet, which carried 15 000 troops and consisted of 19 ships of the line, 13 frigates, six corvettes and luggers, and nine transport vessels, was dispersed by fog, and a contrary wind prevented some ships from entering Bantry Bay. Their appearance and the threat of invasion by 6–7 000 foreign troops caused great alarm. A storm blew up forcing the ships to retire. Some cut anchor and one of the anchors (17cwt/863kg), brought up by a local trawler in 1964, now stands beside the road south of Bantry (N 71). Ten French warships were destroyed, including the frigate *La Surveillante*, which was scuttled by its crew on 2 January 1797. By the time Hoche arrived in the second group of ships, the first had returned to France and he was obliged to retreat. One of the French longboats, which was captured, is now displayed in the National Maritime Museum in Dún Laoghaire.

★**Bantry House** ⊘ – Ten years after its construction in 1740, Bantry House was purchased by the White family, which had settled on Whiddy Island in the late 17C. In recognition of his loyal service against the French threat in 1796, Richard White (1767–1851) was raised to the peerage. His son, Viscount Berehaven (1800–68), enlarged the house and laid out the **terraced Italianate gardens** *(109 steps)* which rise behind the house on the south side. The north front overlooking Bantry Bay and Whiddy Island was added in 1820 and the house was further enlarged in 1840.

Bantry House

There are family portraits throughout the house. Many items among the furniture and furnishings were bought by Viscount Berehaven who travelled widely in Europe – four coloured panels from Pompeii, set into the hall floor. The impressive Russian travelling household shrine, containing many 15C and 16C icons, was brought from Russia in the 19C.

The **Rose and Gobelin Drawing Rooms** are furnished with late-18C Savonnerie carpets, a Gobelin tapestry and Aubusson tapestries. The **dining room**, a spectacular room with royal blue walls, is dominated by **portraits** of King George III and Queen Charlotte, presented by the king at the time of the ennoblement. The long **library**, heated by two fireplaces, contains many old and rare **books** and an 1897 Blüthner grand piano. 17C Spanish leather decorates the panelling on the walls of the main **stairs**. The **old kitchen**, with its range, now serves as a tea room next to the craft shop.

1796 Bantry French Armada ⊘ – *East stables*. The converted buildings now house a detailed exhibition on the French Armada *(see above)*. It describes the historical context of the expedition and the composition of the fleet and traces the sequence of events, using a cut-away model of *La Surveillante*, which was scuttled in Bantry Bay, exhibits rescued from the sea and extracts from the journal of Wolfe Tone, who is shown in his cabin on board one of the frigates.

Whiddy Island – The island has had a varied history as the many ruins testify: Kilmore church and graveyard; Reenavanig Castle, the first residence of the White family; fortifications, including three gun batteries, erected by O'Sullivan Bere in 1801. An American Sea Plane Base was in operation on the island for a few months at the end of the First World War. The oil refinery, built in 1968, ceased operations in 1979 following the explosion of the tanker *Betelgeuse*.

EXCURSIONS

★**Gougane Barra Forest Park** – *23mi/38km – half a day. From Ballylickey take R 584 E inland.*
The approach road climbs inland between the vertical rock walls of the **Pass of Keimaneigh** (2mi/3.2km).
West of the lake, which is the source of the River Lee, a **forest drive** (3mi/4.8km) makes a loop through the extensive forest park (walks and nature trails) which rises up the steep mountain slopes beside the tumbling mountain stream. St Finbar, the 6C founder of Cork, had a hermitage on the island in the lake. A small causeway leads to the modern island chapel, a popular place of pilgrimage, built in the Irish Romanesque style.

Kilnaruane Inscribed Stone – *2mi/3km S of Bantry by N 71; turn left at the Westlodge Hotel (sign). After 0.25mi/0.4km by the signpost; walk across the field (right).* On the hilltop marking the site of a now-vanished ecclesiastical establishment stands a 9C stone pillar, which may have been the shaft of a high cross. The stone bears panels of interlacing as well as *(north-east face)* a boat with four oarsmen, possibly a curragh, navigating through a sea of crosses, and *(south-west face)* a cross, a figure at prayer and St Paul and St Anthony in the Desert.

BIRR★

BIORRA – Co Offaly – Population 3 355
Michelin Atlas p 90 and Map 923 – I 8

Birr lies at the confluence of the Little Brosna and Camcor Rivers in the south midlands. It is an attractive Georgian town dominated by Birr Castle and its demesne. Owing to its central position, it was referred to as Umbilicus Hiberniae in the Down Survey *(see p 203)*.

Parsonstown – Until the establishment of the Irish Free State Birr was known as Parsonstown in King's County. In 1620 the small village was granted to Sir Lawrence Parsons, who started weekly markets, set up a glass factory and built most of the castle. In 1642 much of the new town was destroyed by fire during a siege by local clans; in 1690 Birr was garrisoned by the Williamites and besieged by the Duke of Berwick. During the more peaceful 18C and 19C the town and the castle and demesne were much extended.
The Parsons, later ennobled as the **Earls of Rosse**, constantly improved their property and inaugurated some notable "firsts". **Sir William Parsons**, a patron of Handel, enabled the composer to stage the first performance of *Messiah* in Dublin in 1742. His grandson, another Sir William, the 4th baronet, devoted much time to the late-18C Volunteers. **Sir Lawrence**, the 5th baronet, was more nationalist in political sentiment and a friend of **Wolfe Tone** but he retired from politics after the Act of Union in 1800. In the 19C the family genius made **scientific discoveries** and in the 20C was directed towards the collection and propagation of the **rare botanical species** to be found in the gardens.

Out and About

Events – **Birr Vintage Week** is an annual event *(second half of August)*, during which there is a Georgian Cricket Match played by men in period costume according to the 1744 rules, and the Irish Independent Carriage Driving Championships are held in the Castle demesne. An astronomy weekend takes place in September. Concerts are given in the Castle and the park; exhibitions are held in the **Castle gallery**.

Riverside Walks – On the south bank of the Camcor and in Birr Castle Demesne.

River Cruise ⊘ – Downstream on the mighty Shannon from Banagher to Victoria Lock at Meelick *(90min)*.

Adjacent Sights – See Abbeyleix, Athlone, Clonmacnoise, Portumna, Roscrea, Tullamore.

Where to Eat

The Thatch, Crinkle. *1.25mi/2km SE by N 62.* ☎ 0509 20682; Fax 0509 37284. Friendly, busy, dining pub, with good atmosphere.

Where to Stay

The Maltings, Castle St. ☎ 0509 21345; Fax 0509 22073. Converted stone-built mill (13 rm); friendly informal service; bistro restaurant; parking.

Dooly's, Emmet Sq. ☎ 0509 20032; Fax 0509 21331. Long established hotel (18 rm) in town centre; restaurant.

Kinnitty Castle, Kinnitty. ☎ 0509 37318; Fax 0509 37284. Medieval castle (37 rm) with 12C origins; quiet country location in spacious gardens and grounds.

★★BIRR CASTLE DEMESNE ⊙ 2–3hr

Gardens – The pleasure grounds (100 acres/40ha) have over 1 000 species of trees and shrubs. The 4th baronet started to landscape the park, creating the lake out of a bog and planting many trees. The 6th Earl, who collected seeds from the Americas and the Far East earlier this century, gave the demesne one of the world's finest collections of trees and shrubs, particularly strong on Chinese and Himalayan species. Some of the trees are so rare that seeds have been taken from them for the Royal Botanical Gardens at Kew in London.

The spring-flowering varieties include magnolias, crab apples and cherries while the chestnuts, maples and weeping beech provide strong autumnal colours. The **formal gardens** are subdivided by pleached hornbeam alleys and box hedges which appear in the *Guinness Book of Records* as the tallest in the world.

Extensive herbaceous displays adorn the terraces below the crenellated 17C **castle** *(private)*.

There are many attractive **walks**: the high and low walks near the castle, the lilac walk, the lagoon walk, the lake walk and the river walk with bridges over the Camcor and Little Brosna Rivers which bisect the gardens and form waterfalls.

★★ **Great Telescope** – In the 1840s the 3rd Earl of Rosse built a telescope, the **Leviathan of Parsonstown**, which enabled him to see further into space than anyone before; its mirror (72in/183cm) was cast in a furnace built at the bottom of the castle moat and fired with turf from nearby bogs. Astronomers came from as far as Australia, Russia and the USA to see the telescope, which was in use for 60 years until 1908. Lord Rosse used it to explore the nebulae and, as photography was not sufficiently advanced to record the results, he drew them. The restoration of the telescope to full working order was completed in 1997.

Great Telescope, Birr

Galleries of Discovery – The exhibition set in part of the stable yard celebrates the brilliant activities of the Parsons family – the building of the first-known example of a wrought-iron Suspension Bridge by the 2nd Earl of Rosse; the construction of the great telescope and the discovery of distant galaxies by the 3rd Earl of Rosse; the invention of the Steam Turbine Engine by Charles Parsons in the 1890s; the pioneering work in photography by Mary Countess of Rosse in the 1850s; the world-wide plant-collecting expeditions conducted by the 5th and 6th Earls of Rosse.

★BIRR TOWN

Oxmantown Mall leads from Birr Castle gates between a row of elegant Georgian houses and a line of mature trees to **St Brendan's** 19C Anglican church. **Oxmantown Hall** (1899), which has been restored and is used as a small theatre for the Birr Stage Guild, is decorated with carved wooden gables and heraldic beasts.

The town centre is formed by **Emmet Square**, formerly Cumberland Square after the Duke of Cumberland, whose statue (1747) once crowned the central column; among the Georgian houses is Dooley's Hotel (1740).

In **John's Mall** stands a statue of the 3rd Earl of Rosse, the astronomer. John's Hall was a schoolhouse built in 1833 in the style of a Greek temple to designs by Bernard Mullins. It is flanked by the **Birr Stone**, a large limestone rock, which was probably part of a

One of the signatories of the American Declaration of Independence in 1776, Charles Carroll of Carrollton, was the grandson of Charles Carroll, who emigrated in 1688 from Letterluna in the Slieve Bloom mountains to the USA, where he was granted land in Maryland.

megalithic monument near Seffin, the supposed meeting place of the mythical Fianna warriors; in 1828 it was removed to a mansion in Co Clare to be used as the Mass rock but returned to Birr in 1974. The Russian cannon dates from the Crimean War (1854–56).

EXCURSIONS

★**Slieve Bloom Mountains** – *Round tour of 46mi/73km – half or whole day. From Birr take R 440 E.* **Kinnitty** (population 265), a small unspoiled village with a wide main street, is the western gateway to the Slieve Bloom Mountains, which have been designated an environmental park. Maps and relevant information on exploring the uplands are available from the **Slieve Bloom Display Centre** ⊘. In the graveyard of the local Anglican church *(minor road S to Roscrea)* is the **Kinnitty Pyramid** (1830), inspired by the pyramid of Cheops in Egypt, as the burial place of the Bernard family from Kinnitty Castle.

The **Slieve Bloom Way** (44mi/70km), a long-distance footpath, provides a fine view of the heights (1 728ft/527m), which are covered in mountain blanket bog and several pine and spruce plantations; there are scenic routes, riverside and forest walks, picnic areas and hilltop **viewing points**.

A less adventurous tour may be accomplished by taking the road east from Kinnitty to Drimmo, which passes **Forelacka Glen** *(right)* in a fold of the hills and runs parallel with the Camcor river before veering south towards the Delour River. The minor road north to Clonaslee passes through **The Cut** before descending the Gorragh River valley.

Banagher (Beannchar) – *8mi/13km N by R 439.* Population 1 423. The town is situated on the south bank of the Shannon at an important crossing point. The plaque on the bridge, built in 1843, bears the name King's County, the former name of Co Offaly.

On the west bank of the Shannon stands Cromwell's Castle; its name derives from the fact that bastions were added to the original tower house in about 1650; in the Napoleonic period a cannon was mounted on the top.

Charlotte Brontë *(see p 358)* spent her honeymoon nearby and her husband, the Revd Arthur Nicholls, whose family owned Hill House and whose brother was Manager of the Dublin–Banagher stretch of the Grand Canal, resided in Banagher after her death.

Another literary resident was Anthony Trollope *(see p 129)*.

Shannon Harbour – *11mi/18km N by R 439 and minor roads from Banagher.* The junction of the Grand Canal and the Shannon is now a popular mooring for river cruisers. In its commercial heyday a dry dock, warehousing, a customs post and a hotel (now in ruins) were available beside the lock and canal basin; the local population numbered 1 000, up to 300 000 tons of produce were transhipped annually and over 250 000 people used the passenger barges, many of them emigrants on their way via Limerick and Cobh to Australia, Canada and America. The locality provides excellent coarse fishing and is a paradise for birdwatchers to see the rare birds, including the corncrake, which visit the wet grasslands known as the Shannon Callows.

Clonmacnoise and West Offaly Railway ⊘ – *16mi/25km N of Birr by N 52, N 62 and R 357.* The narrow-gauge railway takes passengers on a guided tour (45min – 5.5mi/8km) of the **Blackwater Bog**, which is part of the Bog of Allen (20 000 acres/8 090ha), one of the largest unbroken raised bogs in Ireland. The tour includes a view of the various stages in the process of harvesting the peat to fuel the electricity power station at Shannonbridge, and a half-way halt where visitors may step out onto the bog to see and try turf cutting with a *slane*, to study the bog plants and handle a piece of bog wood, 4 000 to 7 000 years old. The railway runs past two trial conifer plantations, established on worked-out bog, and an island farm, which occupies a patch of agricultural land completely surrounded by bog.

Cloghan Castle ⊘ – *12mi/20km N by R 439; in Banagher turn left; at Lusmagh Church keep straight on.* Cloghan Castle, a tower house built in 1336 by Eoghan O'Madden and extended by the Cromwellians, stands on the site of a 7C monastery founded by St Cronan on the north bank of the Little Brosna River. The tour starts in the Great Hall and passes up spiral stairs and through passages in the thickness of the walls to end on the roof with a fine view of the site. On display are pieces of armour and weapons, old furniture and china, silk pictures, four-poster and tester beds, and the family tree from the 3C AD to the 20C of the present owner, O'Donovan.

Gallen Grave Slabs – *14mi/22km N by N 52 and N 62. Turn right into the drive (0.5mi/0.8km) to Gallen Priory.* The ruins of a 13C church, on the site of a monastery founded in the 5C beside the River Brosna, contain a collection of early Christian grave slabs (8C to 11C); most are attached to the rebuilt west gable.

BOYLE

MAINISTIR NA BÚILLE – Co Roscommon – Population 1 695
Michelin Atlas p 96 and Map 923 – H 6

Boyle lies at the southern foot of the Curlew Mountains (867ft/264m) on the River Boyle. It is a good centre for trout and coarse fishing and the main town in the northern half of Co Roscommon, a region formerly known as Moylurg.

In 1617 the lands of the MacDermots, Lords of Moylurg, were granted to Sir John King; his fourth son, Edward, who drowned in 1636 while travelling from England to Ireland, was the subject of Milton's *Lycidas*.

SIGHTS

★**Boyle Abbey** ⊙ – *2mi/3.2km E of Boyle by N 4.* The ruins belong to a Cistercian house founded in 1161 by monks from Mellifont *(see p 119).* The church is an impressive example of Cistercian architecture, showing the transition from Romanesque to Gothic; the buildings were damaged by the Cromwellians and used as a military barrack from the 16C to 18C.

Events – Chamber music and piano recitals at King House *(see below).*

River Cruises – The **Slieabh an Iarann Riverbus**, based in Ballinamore, offers a variety of cruises on the Shannon-Erne Waterway.

Adjacent Sights – See Carrick-on-Shannon, Killala, Knock, Sligo, Strokestown.

The **gatehouse**, which houses a model of the abbey and information on the monastic life *(upstairs),* opens into the cloister garth. Little remains of the cloister buildings. The chancel and transepts (12C) are the oldest part of the **church**; the barrel vault and the pointed arches derive from Burgundy, the home of the Cistercian Order. The east window is 13C. Contrary to the usual Cistercian practice the tower seems to have been part of the original design although its windows are probably 14C. The five eastern arches on the south side of the nave date from about 1180, those on the north side from about 1190–1200; the capitals of the western pillars show West of England influence in the trumpet scallops and West of Ireland influence in the animal carving. The west window is Gothic and similar to Christ Church Cathedral in Dublin.

★**King House** ⊙ – At the east end of the main street stands the King mansion. It was probably designed for Sir Henry King c 1730 by William Halfpenny, an assistant of Sir Edward Lovett Pearce. It has a long narrow central hall terminating in Venetian windows, an 11-bay garden front facing the river and vaulted ceilings on all four floors; it was probably intended to have a fourth side enclosing the courtyard.

It now houses a detailed exhibition on the O'Connors, Kings of Connaught, on the MacDermots of Moylurg, on the house and its restoration after years of neglect, and on the King family (later Earls of Kingston) and their subsequent house at Rockingham *(see below),* and on the house as a military barracks occupied by the Connaught Rangers and the Irish Army. Visitors can try their hand at writing with a quill pen and listen to recordings – a Gaelic love poem, the words and even voices of members of the King family.

Frybrook House ⊙ – *Parking in front of the house.* This is a modest Georgian house (c 1750) built for Henry Fry, who was invited to Boyle by the Earl of Kingston *(see above)* and became Chief Magistrate of the area. The tour includes the reception rooms, the principal bedroom and the staircase. Among the furnishings, some of which are original, is a postbox designed by John Nash as a model of the gatehouse at Castle Leslie. The gardens are being restored.

EXCURSIONS

★**Lough Key Forest Park** ⊙
2mi/3.2km E of Boyle by N 4

Until 1959 the park (865 acres/350ha) was part of the Rockingham estate, which had been confiscated from the MacDermots under Cromwell (17C) and granted to the King family, later Stafford-King-Harman, Earls of Kingston.

The **Moylurg Tower**, a modern structure *(132 steps),* provides an excellent view of the ancient region of Moylurg: Lough Key and its islands *(north),* the Curlew Mountains *(north-west)* and the Plains of Boyle *(south).* It stands on the site once occupied by a 16C MacDermot castle and the two mansions built by the King family. The second mansion, which burned down in 1957, was designed by John Nash in 1810 to look the same from all sides; it was serviced by tunnels, one of which runs from the foot of the tower to the restaurant.

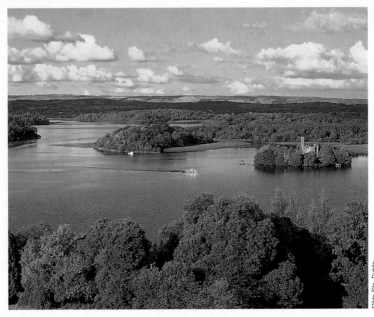

Slide File, Dublin

Castle Island, Lough Key

The grounds were designed by Humphry Repton. The **woodlands** include many of the ornamental trees planted in the 18C. A **nature trail** leads past the Wishing Chair and over the Fairy Bridge, built of local limestone in 1836, to the **Bog Garden** which contains a wide range of rhododendrons and azaleas and other peat-loving plants; the paths are paved with cross-sections of oak trunks. Another bridge leads to Drumman's Island.

There are **boat trips** on the lake among its many islands: Castle Island, where a 19C folly incorporates traces of a MacDermot castle; Church Island, which was occupied by a monastery from the 6C to 16C; Trinity Island *(private)*, where Sir Conyers Clifford *(see above)* was buried in a monastery of Premonstratensian canons.

★Mountain Drive

Round tour of 50mi/80km N of Boyle – half a day

From Boyle take N 4 N.

As it climbs over the Curlew Mountains (867ft/264m) the road provides splendid **views**★ of the lakes *(east)*.

In Ballinafad turn left.

Ballinafad Castle – The castle, now in ruins, was built in 1590 to a 13C design with four round corner towers which are square within. It was known as the Castle of the Curlews, as it protected the Curlew Mountain pass.

Battle of the Curlews

In 1599 the last Irish victory in the Elizabethan campaign to control the country was fought in the Curlew Mountains; the English under Sir Conyers Clifford *(see below)*, President of Connaught, who was killed, were defeated by the forces of Hugh Roe O'Donnell.

Continue N on N 4. In Castlebaldwin turn left (sign) to Carrowkeel Cemetery; at the fork bear left. Park at the gate if it is locked; 1hr on foot there and back.

Carrowkeel Megalithic Cemetery – The bleak hilltop in the Bricklieve Mountains (1 057ft/321m), which provides a fine

view★★ of the surrounding country, is the site of a megalithic cemetery. The stone mounds, mostly round, contain passage graves dating from the Late Stone Age (2500 to 2000 BC). On a lower ridge *(east)* are about 50 round huts, probably the dwellings of the people who built the tombs.

From Castlebaldwin take the road along the shore of Lough Arrow. At the end of the lake turn left. In Ballyfarnan turn left into a steep minor road (narrow entry between two houses) to Altgowlan.

★**Arigna Scenic Drive (Slí)** – From the **viewpoint** *(right)* there is a superb view of Lough Skean and Lough Meelagh. As the road crosses the watershed another fine view opens up of the steep Arigna Valley and the southern end of **Lough Allen**. The spoil heaps are the result of iron-ore mining. The charcoal required for smelting was obtained by felling rather than coppicing the local oakwoods.

At the T-junction turn right; after 2.5mi/4km turn left into Arigna.

Arigna – Arigna lies in a narrow river valley between steep mountains which contain some of the rare coal seams in Ireland. The coal, which was first mined to fuel the iron furnaces, later supplied the local power station until it closed in 1990.

In Arigna cross the river and turn left uphill; after 1.5mi/2.4km turn right (sign) onto a very steep and narrow road. At the next junction turn right.

★**View** – As the road descends from the bare and rugged heights there is an extensive view of Lough Allen, the most northerly of the great Shannon lakes. The river rises in a bog at Shannon Pot *(9mi/14.5km north)*. On the east shore stands Slieve Anierin (1 927ft/586m), the highest point in the Iron Mountains.

At the bottom of the hill turn right onto R 280 to Drumshanbo.

Drumshanbo (Droim Seanbho) – Population 588. The town at the southern end of Lough Allen is a major coarse fishing centre offering anglers not only the waters of the Shannon but also a string of lakes in the drumlin country extending east beyond Ballinamore, which are linked by the Ballinamore and Ballyconnell Canal. The **Sliabh an Iarainn Visitor Centre** ☉ presents an exhibition and an audio-visual presentation on the history of the area – iron and coal mines, the narrow-gauge Cavan and Leitrim Railway, sweathouses (an ancient form of sauna bath).

From Drumshanbo return N on R 280; turn left onto R 285 and drive through Keadew (Keadue).

Holy Well – The well on the lake shore is named after St Lasair, the daughter of St Ronan who founded the monastery.

Turlough O'Carolan (1670–1738)

The blind harpist (also known as Turlough Carolan) who wrote poetry and music, including the melody of *The Star-Spangled Banner*, was born in Nobber in Co Meath. In 1684 his family moved to Carrick-on-Shannon, where Mrs MacDermot Roe became his patron, providing for his education and musical studies. She gave him a horse so that he could perform his compositions at the big houses. After his marriage in 1720 he lived for several years in Mohill, where he is commemorated by a statue in the town centre. He died in 1738 in Keadew (Keadue) and his funeral lasted four days. Annual harp festivals *(see p 37)* are held in his honour in Keadew and Nobber.

O'Carolan's Grave – The tombstones *(right)* mark the site of Kilronan Abbey, founded in the 6C between Lough Meelagh and the Arigna Mountains. The doorway of the ruined church is 12C–13C. In the transept is the tombstone of **Turlough O'Carolan**.

Return to the last junction; turn right. In Knockvicar turn right to Corrigeenroe; in Corrigeenroe turn left to return to Boyle.

The road provides views of the lake and the mountains as it runs parallel with the Boyle River and skirts the north and west shores of Lough Key.

BOYNE VALLEY★★

Co Meath
Michelin Atlas p 93 and Map 923 – M 6

The fertile and well-wooded Boyne Valley holds a significant place in Irish and European history. The prehistoric inhabitants built huge grave mounds on the banks of the river and on hilltop sites such as Loughcrew *(see p 211)*.

In the pre-Christian era the High Kings of Ireland held court at Tara and the Celtic Feast of Samhain (November) was celebrated by the druids on the Hill of Ward near Athboy west of Navan.

Christianity was brought to the region by St Patrick himself. The early monastic sites at Kells and Monasterboice, which are typical of the early Irish church before its Romanisation in the 12C, contrast with the European style of monastery at Mellifont, Slane and Bective.

Battle of the Boyne

The battle fought on 12 July 1690 was the decisive engagement in the War of the Two Kings *(Cogadh an Dá Rí)* between King James II of England, supported by Louis XIV of France, and King William III of England (William of Orange) and his allies, who were engaged in a struggle for the domination of Europe. The soldiers involved – 36 000 in William's army and 25 000 in James's – were of many nationalities: British, Danes, Dutch, Finns, French, Germans, Irish, Poles, Prussians and Swiss.

Whereas the French troops supporting James were under orders to delay William, the latter wished to achieve a speedy victory. As he was making observations on the morning of the battle, he narrowly escaped death from a bullet which tore his coat and grazed his shoulder. He sent some of his force upstream to attack the French left flank and his main force crossed the Boyne at the ford at Oldbridge and attacked the Jacobite army drawn up on the south bank; five crossings were made between 10am and 2pm. On the north bank of the river overlooking the crossing point there is a viewing platform *(78 steps)* with a diagram.

During the battle the Duke of Schomberg, once a Marshal of France in Louis XIV's army, who had left France because he was a Protestant and become a soldier of fortune, was killed. William lost 500 men; James lost about 1 000. When he heard that William had crossed the river, he left for Dublin. The following day he rode to Duncannon near Waterford and took ship to Kinsale; from there he sailed to France. In the hope of reversing the Cromwellian land settlement, the Irish fought on until the following year when they suffered a series of defeats at Athlone, Aughrim and Limerick.

The Williamite victory meant the defeat of the Stuart cause in the United Kingdom and determined the balance of power in Europe. Its outcome is still a factor in Irish politics.

Adjacent Sights – See Drogheda, Fingal, Kells, Trim.

The Norman settlers from Wales and England built castles such as Navan motte and Trim to defend the territory under their control against the native Irish; the area, known as the Pale, fluctuated in size throughout the Middle Ages. Some castles were later converted into stately homes.

PREHISTORIC SITES

The prehistoric burial sites at Knowth, Dowth and Newgrange are the oldest in the British Isles; they are 500 years older than the pyramids in Egypt and 1 000 years earlier than Stonehenge.

The burial mounds contain passage graves, built by a farming and stock-raising community in the Neolithic Era (3000–2000 BC) on the south-facing slope overlooking the River Boyne, which was then the main artery of communication. There are some 40 graves, consisting of three major graves and many satellites.

Present knowledge suggests that Dowth was built first to align with the setting sun. It was followed by Newgrange where the rising sun penetrates the inner chamber at the winter solstice. Knowth was built later facing east–west to align with the rising sun in March and the setting sun in September.

Brú na Bóinne Visitor Centre ⊘ – *South bank; footbridge over the river and bus shuttle to graves from north bank; no other access.* The display shows the site by the river as a dwelling place, and describes the clothing, food and housing of the Neolithic people, their technical knowledge, how the stones were moved on rollers and the different phases of construction and decoration.

★★★ **Newgrange** ⊘ – Newgrange is one of the best examples of a passage grave in western Europe.

The **mound** (1.25 acres/0.5ha, 260ft/79m–280ft/85m in diameter and 37ft/11m high) consists of a cairn of medium-sized stones enclosed within a circle of 97 kerb stones, some of which are decorated, set on their long edges, ends touching, surmounted by a facing of round granite boulders.

Excavations in 1963 made it possible to reconstruct the original south front **revetment** of white quartz stones, except where the entrance has been enlarged to accommodate visitors.

Above the entrance, which was originally closed by an upright slab *(right)*, is the **roof box**, a unique structure with a finely decorated lintel, through which the rays of the rising sun penetrate to the inner chamber for 17 minutes at the winter solstice (21 December).

The passage, which is lined with large standing stones, some decorated and all dressed, leads into a corbelled **chamber** a third of the way into the mound. The three decorated recesses contain stone **basins**, which held the bones of the dead together with funeral offerings of stone and bone beads and pendants, bone pins and small stone balls resembling marbles. The corbelled vaulted roof, completed by a central capstone (4 tonnes), is quite waterproof as the outer face of the stones is grooved to drain off water.

The mound was surrounded at a distance (39ft/12m–49ft/15m) by a **great circle** of standing stones. The four opposite the entrance are among the largest; most have been broken off near ground level.

South of the mound are traces of a late-Neolithic – early-Bronze Age **pit circle** which was uncovered in 1982.

★ **Knowth** ⊘ – *Excavations in progress.* The mound (40ft/12m high, 220ft/67m in diameter) probably dates from 2500 to 2000 BC. It contains two decorated passage graves discovered in 1967 and 1968; one is simply an enlargement of the passageway but the other is circular and corbelled with side chambers. It is aligned east–west and is surrounded by smaller tombs facing the large central mound. In the early centuries AD the central mound was surrounded by deep defensive ditches. In about 8C AD the settlement expanded and several souterrains and rectangular houses were built. From the 12C to 14C the site was occupied by the Normans who constructed a rectangular stone structure on the top of the mound.

Excavations conducted since 1962 have made it possible to reconstruct the smaller tombs which had collapsed owing to the passage of time and conversion of the material to other uses.

Dowth – *Closed for excavation.* The mound, which was raised by man in 3000 BC (1 acre/0.4ha, 280ft/85m in diameter, 50ft/15.24m high), contains two tombs and a souterrain connecting with the north tomb. The base of the mound was enclosed by about 100 kerb stones, many ornamented, although most are covered by landslip.

Fourknocks – *11mi/18km S of Drogheda by R 108; after 10mi/16km turn right; park in the road. Key available from the last house on the right before the stile.*

Christopher Hill, Belfast

Newgrange

The passage grave, which dates from c 1500 BC, is unusually large compared with the size of the mound. The interior contains stones decorated with zigzags and other prehistoric designs and a human face. It contained over 60 burials.

★**Tara** ◷ – *5mi/8km S of Navan by N 3.* The name of Tara conjures up the spirit of Irish Celtic greatness; the Hill of Tara, also known as Tara of the Kings, played a significant part in Irish legends. Its origin as a religious site is lost in prehistory; it achieved its greatest prestige under the pagan High Kings of Ireland, and even after the introduction of Christianity it retained its significance as the nominal seat of the High King until it was abandoned in 1022.

During the 1798 rebellion a skirmish took place on the hill. In the 19C O'Connell chose it as the site of one of his monster meetings in the cause of Roman Catholic emancipation; 250 000 people came to hear him speak.

The **bare hill** ◷ pockmarked with earthworks does not readily suggest a royal palace. An effort of the imagination is required to envisage the many small buildings, of wood or wattle and daub, where the king held his court.

The history of Tara is recounted in an audio-visual presentation in the early-19C **St Patrick's Church**, which incorporates a medieval window.

In the churchyard stands a red sandstone pillar stone, known as **St Adamnán's Cross**, which bears a carved figure which may be the ancient Celtic god Cernunnos.

West of the graveyard is the **Rath of the Synods**, a ringfort with three banks. Further south is an Iron-Age ringfort, enclosed by a bank and a ditch, known as the **Royal Enclosure**. Within it is the **Mound of the Hostages**, a small passage grave which dates from about 1800 BC. In the centre of the enclosure are two ringforts, known as the **Royal Seat and Cormac's House**; at the centre of the latter, beside a statue of St Patrick, is a standing stone known as the **Lia Fáil**, which was moved from its original position near the Mound of the Hostages to be a memorial to those who died in 1798.

South of the Royal Enclosure is part of another earthwork known as **King Laoghaire's Rath**. To the north of the churchyard is a hollow flanked by two long parallel banks, which may have been the grand entrance but which is known as the Banqueting Hall. On the west side are three circular earthworks; the first is known as Gráinne's Fort, the other two as the Sloping Trenches.

South of the hill *(0.5mi/0.8km – visible from the road)* is part of another ringfort, known as **Rath Maeve**, surrounded by a bank and ditch.

MONASTIC SITES

★★**Monasterboice** – *8mi/13km N of Drogheda by N 1.* Three **high crosses** mark the site of the monastery founded by St Buithe (Boethius), who died in 521. It was a dual foundation for men and women and an important centre of learning closely connected with Armagh.

The **South Cross** was erected by Muiredach in the 9C. The west face shows the Crucifixion, Christ with Peter and Paul, the raised Christ flanked by Apostles and the Mocking of Jesus; on the east face are the Last Judgement, the Adoration of the Magi, Moses striking the Rock, David and Goliath, the Fall of Man, and Cain slaying Abel.

The **West Cross** *(between the two ruined churches)* is unusually tall (23ft/7m) and the subjects of some of the carvings are rare. The west face shows the Crucifixion; on the shaft are the Arrest of Christ, Christ surrounded by Apostles, the Resurrection of the Dead, the Soldiers at the Tomb. The east face shows Christ Militans with *(above)* Christ walking on the water, *(right)* Simon Magus and *(below)* the Fiery Furnace; on the shaft are Goliath, Samuel anointing David, the Golden Calf, the Sacrifice of Isaac, David killing a lion.

The **North Cross** *(northeast corner of the graveyard)* also shows the Crucifixion on the west face. The original shaft is contained in the same enclosure as well as a monastic sundial indicating the hours of the Divine Office.

Behind the north church lies an early **grave slab** bearing the name Ruarcan.

The **round tower** and its treasures were burned in 1097.

South Cross (east face), Monasterboice

★Mellifont Old Abbey ⊙ – *6mi/10km W of Drogheda by N 51, R 168 and a minor road west of Tullyallen.* Mellifont, the honey fountain, on the banks of the River Mattock, was founded by St Malachy in 1142 with four Irish and nine French monks. It was the first Cistercian house in Ireland. Modern Mellifont Abbey (1938) is at Collon *(3mi/4.8km N).*

Still standing are the ruined **gatehouse** *(right)* beside the approach road, the vaulted **Chapter House** (14C) and four faces of the two-storey **octagonal lavabo** (12C), where the monks washed their hands before eating in the refectory opposite. Excavation has revealed the outline of the monastic buildings.

The 12C church, which was consecrated in 1157, was designed by one of the Frenchmen; it had a crypt at the west end and three chapels in the transepts – two apsidal chapels flanking a central rectangular one. In 1225 the chancel and transepts were extended. In 1556 the abbey became a private house which was abandoned in 1727.

Hill of Slane – The hilltop site has been associated with Christianity since the 5C. In 433 St Patrick travelled from Saul by sea and on foot to Slane, where he lit a fire on the hilltop on Easter Eve to challenge the druids who were holding a festival at Tara. As anyone who kindled a fire within sight of Tara did so on pain of death, Patrick was brought before Laoghaire, the High King, to whom he preached the Gospel. Although the king remained a pagan, he allowed his subjects freedom of conscience. One of them, Erc, converted and founded a monastery at Slane; he is said to be buried in the ruined mortuary house in the graveyard.

The church, which was in use until 1723, was part of **Slane Friary**, a Franciscan house, founded in 1512 by Sir Christopher Flemyng; the Flemyng arms are on the west wall of the courtyard. The friary, which housed four priests, four lay-brothers and four choristers, was suppressed in 1540, occupied by Capuchins in 1631 and abandoned under Cromwell. On the west face of the hill is a motte raised by Richard le Flemyng of Flanders, who arrived in Ireland in 1175.

★Termonfeckin – *6mi/10km from Drogheda by R 167 E and R 166 N.* Population 589. Close to the shore stands a 15C or 16C three-storey **tower house** ⊙ which has an unusual corbelled roof *(45 steps)*: **view** of the coast from Drogheda *(south)* to Clogher Head *(N).*

In the graveyard of St Fechin's Church stands a 10C **high cross** depicting *(east face)* the Crucifixion and *(west face)* Christ in Glory; it marks the site of a monastery founded by St Fechin of Fore *(see p 258).*

SLANE

The centre of Slane, known as the "square", was laid out by Viscount Conyngham in the late 18C; it is lit by oil lamps and bordered by four detached houses, each flanked by two smaller houses.

The Gothic Gate *(S of the crossroads)* was designed by Francis Johnston c 1795 as an entrance to Slane Castle. From the bridge over the Boyne there is a **view** of Slane Castle, Slane Mill (1766), the weir and the canal; there is a towpath walk upstream to Navan and downstream to Drogheda.

Slane Castle ⊙ – *0.25mi/0.5km W of Slane by N 51.* The impressive raised **site** overlooking the River Boyne is surmounted by an elegant assembly of square turrets, crenellations and artificial machicolations. The present house was built between 1785 and 1821 on the site of a confiscated Fleming fortress purchased by the Conynghams in 1641. It is the work of James Gandon, James Wyatt, Francis Johnston and Thomas Hopper. Capability Brown designed the stables and grounds although he did not visit Slane.

Ledwidge Cottage Museum ⊙ – *0.5mi/0.8km E of Slane by N 51.* The cottage displays some of the manuscripts of the poet, Francis Ledwidge (1887–1917), whose work, first published through the patronage of Lord Dunsany, reflects his love of the Meath countryside. His childhood home, this four-roomed semi-detached cottage, built under the Labourers' Dwellings Act (1886), has been restored to its original appearance.

Use the key on page 9 to make the best use of this Michelin guide

BUNCRANA

This seaside resort has a long sandy beach facing west across Lough Swilly to the mountains of Donegal.

At the north end of the seafront an old six-arched bridge spanning the Crana River leads to **O'Docherty's Keep**, a Norman tower which was repaired in 1602 by Hugh Boy O'Docherty in anticipation of a Spanish invasion. It was burned in the English counter-attack but granted by Chichester to the Vaughans, who restored it as their family residence. The nearby mansion of seven bays and two wings, which stands at the top of the rise overlooking the sea, was built by Sir John Vaughan in 1718.

Out and About

Adjacent Sights – See Donegal, Donegal Coast, Donegal Glens, Londonderry, Sperrin Mountains.

Where to Stay

Lake of Shadows, Grianan Park. ☏ 077 61005; Fax 077 62131. Small hotel (23 rm) situated in popular residential district.

Inishowen Gateway, Railway Rd. ☏ 077 61144; Fax 077 62278. Comfortable hotel (63 rm) with extensive leisure facilities.

★★INIS EOGHAIN SCENIC DRIVE
100mi/160km – 1 day

The drive follows the coast of the Inishowen Peninsula (Inis Eoghain), which terminates in Malin Head, the most northerly point in Ireland. The landscape is composed of rugged mountains covered in blanket bog, fringed by steep cliffs or broad sweeps of sand. Flocks of sheep graze the stony ground. In the fishing villages the traditional cabins are roofed with thatch, tied down with ropes against the wind.

The peninsula is named after a son of Niall of the nine hostages, Eoghain, who was a contemporary of St Patrick in the 5C. The Vikings made several raids but were expelled. By the 15C the O'Dochertys held sway but when Sir Cahir O'Docherty, the young clan chief, was killed at Kilmacrenan *(north of Letterkenny)* in 1608, a year after the *Flight of the Earls (see p 162)*, the way was open to Sir Arthur Chichester, who took possession of the whole peninsula.

Take the coast road N to Dunree Head.

★**Dunree Fort** ⊘ – *Car park within the military compound*. A drawbridge spans the narrow defile which separates the fort from Dunree Head. The fort itself has been converted into a **military museum** containing the original guns; a film explains their role in a coastal defence battery; 180 years of records illustrate the evolution of the fort from a fortified earthen embankment, built in 1798 under the threat of French invasion, to an important element in a chain of forts on the shores of Lough Swilly defending a British Naval Base at Buncrana. In 1914 the entire British Grand Fleet sheltered behind a boom in the Lough. Knockalla Fort is visible across the narrow channel on the opposite shore.

Return to the junction and turn left; at the crossroads turn left.

★**Gap of Mamore** – The road climbs past rocky outcrops and grazing sheep to the **viewpoint** *(car park – right)* – an extensive view north to Dunaff Head.

Turn left past Lenan Strand to Lenan Head.

Lenan Head – The headland, where a gun battery (1895) used to command the entrance to Lough Swilly, is disfigured by a ruined army camp.

Take the road through Dunaff to Clonmany and continue N on R 238.

Ballyliffin (Baile Lifín) – Population 334. This attractive resort is set slightly inland from Pollan Bay and Pollan Strand, a long sandy beach backed by a golf course on Doagh Isle, a flat sandy peninsula.

Continue E on R 238.

★**Carndonagh High Cross** – At the top of the hill next to the Anglican church *(left)* stands an 8C **high cross**, decorated with an interlaced cross and a Crucifixion and flanked by two **pillars**, one of which shows David with his harp. In the graveyard stands a **cross pillar**, known as the Marigold Stone, which is decorated with a seven-pointed star, resembling a marigold, on one side and a Crucifixion on the other.

Continue N on R 238 and R 242.

Malin – The 17C Plantation village is centred on a triangular green.

★**Lag Sand Dunes** – Massive sand dunes rise up on the north shore of Trawbreaga Bay, the estuary of the Donagh River.

★★**Malin Head** – The tiny fishing village shelters from the prevailing wind in the lee of the great headland, the most northerly point in Ireland, which figures in the shipping forecasts. On the cliffs stands a tower, originally built in 1805 by the British Admiralty to monitor shipping and later used as a signal tower by Lloyds. North across the sound *(1.5mi/2.4km)* lies Inishtrahull Island, once the site of a hermitage but now deserted. The road circles the headland providing dramatic **views★★** *(southwest)* across the water to Pollan Strand and Dunaff Head.

Take the coast road S via Portaleen to Culdaff. Take R 238 S; turn right to Clonca.

Clonca Church and Cross – *Path across a field.* In the 6C St Buodán founded a monastery at Clonca. The ruined church dates from the 17C or 18C but the carved lintel is earlier. Inside is the 16C tombstone of Magnus MacOrristin, who probably came from the Hebrides, showing a sword and a hurley stick and bearing a rare Irish inscription. In the field opposite the church door is **St Buodán's high cross** depicting the miracle of the loaves and fishes *(east face)*.

Continue to the junction, turn left and then right.

Carrowmore High Crosses – The site of a monastery founded by Chionais, St Patrick's brother-in-law, is now marked by two **high crosses**, a decorated slab and a boulder inscribed with a cross.

Return to the last junction; turn right and then left and left again into R 238; turn right.

Bocan Stone Circle – In a field *(left)* are the remains of a stone circle which originally may have consisted of 30 standing stones.

Return to R 238; continue S through Gleneely; turn left to Leckemy and take the minor road NE to Kinnagoe Bay.

Kinnagoe Bay – The sandy beach is sheltered by steep headlands. A map *(at the road junction)* plots the sites of the many ships of the Spanish Armada which were wrecked on the Irish coast; many interesting military relics were found in *La Duquesa St Anna* and *La Trinidad Valencia*, which were wrecked in the bay. *Clifftop footpath to Inishowen Head.*

Take the minor road S to Greencastle.

Viewpoint – *Car park.* The view embraces open moorland used for turf cutting and sheep pasture extending east to Lough Foyle.

On the edge of Greencastle turn leftt to Inishowen Head.

★**Inishowen Head** – The headland (295ft/90m) above the tiny harbour next to the lighthouse on Dunagree Point commands a fine view east along the Antrim coast as far as the Giant's Causeway. *Clifftop footpath to Kinnagoe Bay.*

Take the coast road S past the golf course.

Greencastle – Population 588. A fine beach makes this a pleasant and popular resort. North of the town on the cliffs opposite Magilligan Point commanding the narrow entrance to Lough Foyle stand the overgrown ruins of a castle built in 1305 by Richard de Burgo, the Red Earl of Ulster, so-called because of his florid complexion. It was captured by Edward Bruce in 1316, fell into the possession of the O'Donnells in the 14C and was granted to Sir Arthur Chichester in 1608. The adjoining fort (1812) was used in the defence of Lough Foyle until the end of the 19C.

From Greencastle take R 241 S.

Moville (Bun an Phobail) – Population 1 392. Moville (pronounced with the accent on the second syllable), once a bustling port where emigrant ships set sail for the United States, is now a seaside resort. **St Pius' Roman Catholic Church** (1953) is an impressive granite building with a handsome mahogany interior. The cliffs and beaches overlooking Lough Foyle have been incorporated into a landscaped coastal walk, **Moville Green**, interspersed with lawns and shrubberies and sporting facilities.

From Moville take R 241 S; after 2mi/3.2km turn right.

In **Cooley** at the graveyard gate stands a **high cross** (10ft/3m) with a hole in its head through which people clasped hands to seal an undertaking. The graveyard contains a **mortuary house**, a tomb shrine known as the Skull House and thought to be associated with St Finian, the abbot of the monastery, which was founded by St Patrick and survived until the 12C.

Continue S on R 241. In Muff turn right to Burnfoot; take the minor road to Speenoge.

Grianán of Aileach

B Lynch /Bord Fáilte, Dublin

★★Grianán of Aileach – *Car park.* The circular stone fort, which crowns the exposed hilltop and provides an excellent protection against the wind, is a reconstruction dating from 1870. A tunnel pierces the stone wall (13ft/4m thick) which contains small chambers and steps to the ramparts and encloses a circle (77ft/23m in diameter).

It is not known to what extent this structure resembles the original stone fort, which was built early in the Christian era and served as the royal seat of the O'Neill clan from about the 5C to 12C.

It was destroyed in 1101 by the King of Munster, Murtogh O'Brien, in retaliation for the destruction of his own royal seat at Kincora near Killaloe.

From the ramparts there is an extensive **view★★** *(east)* of Londonderry and the Sperrin Mountains, *(northeast)* of Lough Foyle, *(north)* of the Inishowen Peninsula, and *(west)* of Inch Island, Lough Swilly and Knockalla Mountain.

The circular shape of the stone fort is echoed at the foot of the hill in **St Aengus Church**, which was designed by Liam McCormack.

Return downhill to N 13; turn left towards Letterkenny.

Grianán Ailigh Centre ⊘ – *Burt; beside N 13.* An exhibition of storyboards and models relating the legends associated with the site is housed on the upper floor of a redundant Anglican church, which has been converted into a restaurant. Other displays describe similar Irish stone forts and the restoration of the church.

Return N on N 13 and the minor road to Burnfoot. Take R 238 N to Fahan.

> **Coirrgend, the warrior**
>
> His punishment for murdering the king's son was to carry the body and a burial stone to Grianán Mountain. The burden killed him and he died crying «Á, leac!» ("Alas, stone!") – the origin of the name of the site.

Fahan Cross-Slab – On the south side of the village (population 309) in the old graveyard beside the Anglican church stands a 7C **cross-slab**, which is decorated on each face with a cross formed of interlaced bands; one of them is flanked by two figures. It marks the site of a monastery which was founded by St Mura in the 7C and survived until at least 1098.

Take R 238 N to Buncrana.

The BURREN★★

BOIREANN – Co Clare

Michelin Atlas pp 88–89 and Map 923 – E 8

The vast limestone plateau which covers much of Co Clare is gradually being established as a national park. The limestone is deeply fissured and most of the rivers have gone underground creating an extensive cave system and many swallow holes. When the water table rises sufficiently high, a hollow with a porous bed may fill with water and become a *turlach*.

The Burren is noted for the "opposite" contrasts of its flower population with Mediterranean and Alpine species flourishing side by side, on the dry horizontal surfaces (clints) or in the fissures (grykes).

Four thousand years of farming has largely denuded the country of trees and vegetation and the old Celtic practice of booleying *(see p 49)* is practised in reverse: in winter the cattle are kept on the higher ground, which remains relatively dry and warm owing to the Gulf Stream, and in summer, when the uplands may suffer from drought, they are kept near the homesteads, where they can be tended and watered.

Out and About

Irish Traditional Music – **Doolin** has an international reputation both for the audience and for the quality of the musicianship. Other places for sessions in summer are Ballyvaughan, Kilfenora, Lisdoonvarna and Ennistymon.
The **Willie Clancy Summer School** *(July)* in Milltown Malbay is a major music festival, particularly of the uilleann pipes.

Lisdoonvarna Fair – In September bachelors from Ireland and beyond come to town to seek a wife at the match-making events – dancing, singsongs, evening pub sessions and walks.

Seaside Resorts – To the south at **Liscannor**, **Lahinch** (long sand beach with lifeguard on duty) and **Milltown Malbay**.

Burren Way – Walking trail *(26mi/42km)* from Ballyvaughan to Liscannor *(leaflet from TIC)*.

Aran Islands – From Doolin there is a ferry to the Aran Islands *(see p 102)*.

Adjacent Sights – See Aran Islands, Athenry, Connemara, Ennis, Galway.

Where to Stay

Sheedy's, Suphir Hill, Lisdoonvarna. ☎ 065 707 4026; Fax 065 707 4555. Personally run hotel (11 rm) offering comfortable accommodation and contemporary Irish cooking; at the top of the town.
Rusheen Lodge, Ballyvaughan. *0.75mi/1.2km SW of Ballyvaughan by N 67.* ☎ 065 707 7092; Fax 065 707 7152. Family run guesthouse (8 rm) with spacious well decorated bedrooms.

SIGHTS *In rough clockwise order starting in the north*

★**Corcomroe Abbey** – The ruins of this Cistercian abbey are almost indistinguishable from the stone of the surrounding Burren. The abbey of St Mary of the Fertile Rock was founded in about 1180 by Donal Mor O'Brien or more likely his son Donat. There are carved capitals and fine vaulting in the choir and transept chapels. It was here that William Butler Yeats set his verse play *The Dreaming of the Bones*. On the north slope of Turlough Hill (925ft/282m) are the ruins of three 12C churches.

Cliffs of Moher

Slide File, Dublin

Burren eXposure ⊘ – *Ballyvaughan; just E of the village centre by N 67.* This interpretation centre occupies a splendid setting overlooking the harbour; it uses a series of audio-visual presentations to describe the geology, flora and human history which have combined in the unique landscape of the Burren.

Newtown Castle and Trail ⊘ – *2mi/3km SW of Ballyvaughan by N 67.* The stone spiral staircase of this fine 16C defensive tower house leads to a series of exhibits illustrating the recent restoration of the building and the importance of the region in medieval times as a centre for the study of law. The gallery of the Great Hall beneath the new domed roof leads to a balcony with extensive views over the Burren. A trail on the hillside behind the tower leads to a variety of natural and historic man-made features including an early lime kiln and a Victorian gazebo.

Corkscrew Hill – There is a good **view** of the limestone terraces from Corkscrew Hill on the road between Ballyvaughan and Lisdoonvarna *(N 67).*

Aillwee Cave ⊘ – *Park in the upper car park.* The single tunnel stretching deep into the Burren (0.75mi/1km) presents stalactites and stalagmites and a **waterfall**★ which is impressively floodlit from below. The bones of a brown bear were found in one of the hibernation pits near the entrance. At the back of the Highway, the largest chamber, there is a vertical drop; even in dry weather the sound of flowing water can be heard.

The **visitor centre**, built in the style of a stone fort in harmony with its surroundings, explains the formation of the cave and its discovery in 1940 by a local herdsman, Jack McCann. Adjacent is the tiny entrance to the extensive cave systems discovered in 1987.

★**Poulnabrone** – The most famous of the many **megalithic tombs** in the Burren lies on the east side of the road between Aillwee and Leamaneh Castle *(R 480).*

Burren Perfumery ⊘ – *Carran (signed).* In this seemingly inhospitable limestone landscape an astonishing diversity of Mediterranean and Alpine flowers live side by side; they are the floral inspiration for a range of perfumes made here by traditional methods of distilling and blending. An audio-visual *(9min)* and photographic display give a close-up view of some of the many species of flowers growing nearby.

Leamaneh Castle ⊘ – Only the shell remains of a four-storey Elizabethan-style fortified house with mullioned windows which was built in the 17C by Conor O'Brien, who was killed in 1651 during the Cromwellian wars. From the top *(88 steps)* of the adjoining 15C **tower house** there is a fine **view**.

★**Kilfenora High Crosses** – In the past Kilfenora (population 200) was an important episcopal see. The site of a monastery founded by St Fachtna in the 6C is marked by the remains of three 12C high crosses; a fourth cross *(100yd/90m W in a field)* shows the Crucifixion.

The partially ruined cathedral was built about 1190 and altered in the 15C. The chancel is noted for its finely carved triple-light east window and two effigies of bishops, thought to be 14C.

Burren Centre ⊘ – *Kilfenora.* The centre provides information on the district through an audio-visual presentation *(20min)* and static displays.

Ennistimon (Inis Díomáin) – Population 917. The **waterfalls** on the River Cullenagh are visible from the seven-arch bridge that spans the river, from the river bank *(through arched entry in the Main Street)* and from the grounds of the Falls Hotel. The town is noted for its fine shop façades, many in Irish and preserving their traditional character.

Birchfield House – The ruins of the vast house, built by Cornelius O'Brien, local MP for over 20 years, are dominated by a tall column erected in his honour in 1853.

★★★**Cliffs of Moher** ⊙ – *As the cliff edge is extremely dangerous the clifftop path is fenced. The site attracts large numbers of tourist coaches.* Great dark sandstone cliffs (600ft/182m high – nearly 5mi/8km long) rise sheer from the Atlantic; screaming sea birds throng the ledges or wheel and swoop above the waves. The best view is from **O'Brien's Tower**, built in 1853 by Cornelius O'Brien. The **Visitor Centre** provides much information on the flora and fauna of the area, including examples of local bird life.

Lisdoonvarna (Lios Dúin Bhearna) – Population 842. Ireland's only spa developed in the 19C round three mineral springs; water from the sulphur spring is served by the glass or the bottle at the Spa Wells; the health centre provides sulphur baths, massage and other treatments. A 17C crucifix adorns the Roman Catholic Church of Our Lady of Lourdes (1878).

★★**Scenic Route** – The coast road *(R 477)* south of Black Head provides a fine view of the huge boulders, deposited at the end of the Ice Age, which rest on the bare limestone pavement; in fine weather the Aran Islands, of similar geological formation, are visible offshore.

Use the Map of Principal Sights to plan an itinerary.

CAHER

AN CATHAIR – Co Tipperary – Population 2 236
Michelin Atlas p 85 and Map 923 – I 11

Caher (or **Cahir**, pronounced Care) is an attractive historic town in south Tipperary beside the River Suir which provides attractive walks.

The town, which is dominated by its 13C castle, was largely developed by the Butler family in the 18C; from this period date the mills, the Market House, now the library, and Caher House, now a hotel, which was used by Lord Caher as the family seat after the castle had fallen into disrepair.

In spite of two 19C bankruptcies, which brought the town near to ruin, Caher developed a milling industry, owing to the diligence of six local Quaker families. The Great War Memorial, which commemorates the many local men who died in the First World War, mostly in Irish regiments, is a rarity in an Irish town.

> **Adjacent Sights** – See Cashel, Clonmel, Lismore, Tipperary.

SIGHTS

★★ Caher Castle ⊙ – The castle (restored) stands on a strategic riverside site where Brian Ború, High King of Ireland (926–1014), had a residence. It was begun in the 13C by either the Worcester or the de Bermingham families and was extended early in the 15C by the Anglo-Norman Butlers, who retained possession until the castle passed into State care in 1961. An **audio-visual presentation** surveys the neighbouring historic sites.

The high enclosing walls of the castle embrace an outer, middle and inner ward; there are three towers and a keep. The middle gate incorporates a **portcullis**, restored to working order. The battlements in the inner ward were built in the 19C. The **keep** was originally a 13C gate tower with a spiral stairway to the upper levels. The next largest building is the **northwest tower**, which dates from the 13C. The large room on the first floor has a 15C double-light window, while a similar window is to be found in the main room of the second floor. The roof and two walls of the **great hall** date from the 1840s. Both buildings display period furniture.

Town Centre – The split-level square is surrounded by shops and houses little changed since the 1950s.

The ruined church *(Old Church Street, N 24 to Clonmel)*, last used in the 1820s, had a curtain wall, which allowed Roman Catholics and Protestants to worship simultaneously; in the 19C, when Caher was an important garrison town, part of the adjoining cemetery was reserved for military burials.

St Paul's Church *(Church Street, N 8 north towards Cashel)*, the Anglican church, was designed in 1820 by John Nash, the famous Regency architect who also worked in Antrim and Cookstown.

Dúchas, Dublin

Swiss Cottage, Caher

EXCURSIONS

★**Swiss Cottage** ⊘ – *1mi/2km S of Caher by R 670*. The ornate two-storeyed thatched cottage (restored) was designed by John Nash and built between 1812 and 1814 as a fishing and hunting lodge for Lord Caher. In one of the two ground-floor rooms, the hand-painted French wallpaper shows views of the Bosporus. Nearby an elegant cast-iron bridge spans the River Suir.

Burncourt House – *8mi/13km W by N 8; in Boolakennedy turn left. Access through farmyard and across a field*. The ruined house, with its 26 gables and many chimneys, was built in 1640. Ten years later it was set on fire by the wife of its owner, Sir Richard Everard, to deny it to the Cromwellian army.

Mitchelstown Cave ⊘ – *9mi/14.5km W by N 8; in Boolakennedy turn left*. A flight of 88 steep steps leads into three massive caverns (1mi/2km) containing dripstone formations – stalactites and stalagmites. The most impressive is the Tower of Babel, a huge calcite column, in the very straight Kingston Gallery (250ft/76m long). The cave system was discovered by a quarryman in 1833. The nearby Old Caves are open only to experienced potholers.

Ronald Reagan Centre ⊘ – *Ballyporeen; 11mi/18km SW by R 668 and R 665*. The centre shows videos, photographs and other souvenirs of the visit made in 1984 by Ronald Reagan, former US President, whose great-grandfather was born in 1829 in the vicinity of Ballyporeen (population 319).

CARLOW

CEATHARLACH – Co Carlow – Population 11 721
Michelin Atlas p 86 and Map 923 – L 9

The administrative centre of Ireland's second-smallest county, Carlow is situated on the east bank of the River Barrow where it is joined by its tributary the Burren. Below the bridge (1815) old warehouses line the quays; upstream there is a riverside walk. Carlow's most important traditional industry is sugar beet refining; in recent years the town has attracted a number of international manufacturing firms.

Frontier Town – Set on the southern frontier of the Pale, Carlow saw many battles for its possession between its Anglo-Norman rulers and the displaced native Irish. Except for the west wall and two towers (in the grounds of Corcoran's mineral water factory), the Norman **castle** (1207–13) was demolished in 1814 when a local Dr Middleton, who wanted to turn the building into an asylum, placed explosives round the walls to reduce their thickness.
The town walls, built in 1361, came under bombardment in 1650 from Ireton, Cromwell's general and son-in-law.
The last battle between the English and the Irish took place on 25 May 1798 when an army of insurgents was confronted by Crown forces in Tullow Street. Six hundred and forty United Irishmen were killed; some 400 were buried in gravel pits in Craiguecullen, a suburb of Carlow on the west bank of the river. The dead are commemorated by a memorial of Celtic design at Governey Park.

Adjacent Sights – See Abbeyleix, Athy, Enniscorthy, Glendalough, Kilkenny, New Ross, Wicklow Mountains.

SIGHTS

Carlow Museum ⊘ – A reconstructed dairy, forge and kitchen show what farm life was like in the 19C; the printing press (1856) was used by the *Nationalist and Leinster Times*, Carlow's weekly newspaper.
Other curiosities include an Irish deer's head, lacking only its teeth, which dates from about 10 000 BC.

Cathedral – The Roman Catholic cathedral, started in 1829, the year of the Emancipation Act, and completed four years later, is a cruciform structure in the late English Gothic style surmounted by a striking slender tower, terminating in a lantern.
A **marble monument** by John Hogan commemorates Bishop Doyle (1786–1834), otherwise known as JKL (James of Kildare and Leighlin), a prolific writer on current affairs and politics; the allegorical female figure represents Ireland raised to one knee as a result of the bishop's efforts.

Courthouse – According to tradition, the neo-Classical courthouse (1830), designed by William Vitruvius Morrison, should have been erected in Cork but the plans were sent to Carlow by mistake.

Surrounded by impressive railings, the polygonal building has an extended porch and an Ionic portico overlooking a broad flight of steps, interrupted halfway by a plaza.

Cigar Divan – *50 Dublin Street*. The name of this shop, which has an authentic Victorian shopfront with advertisements engraved on the glass, derives from the late 19C, when Turkish cigarettes were fashionable.

EXCURSIONS

Browneshill Portal Tomb – *2mi/3km east of Carlow; from lay-by on the eastern by-pass (sign) 500yd/0.5km on foot.* Just below the brow of the low range of hills east of Carlow is this massive Megalithic dolmen, erected at some point between 3000 and 4000 BC. Its tilted capstone may weigh as much as 150 tons, making it the heaviest in Europe.

Altamont Gardens ⊙ – *12mi/19km east by R 725 to Tullow; turn right onto N 81 and left (sign).* Designed in both formal and informal styles, the gardens have many specimen trees, an arboretum and a small garden with species of flowers normally found growing in Ireland's marshy bogs. The lake was dug out by hand to provide employment during the Famine.
On the horizon rise Mount Leinster *(south)* in the Blackstairs Mountains, and the Wicklow Mountains *(northeast)* across the River Slaney.

Leighlinbridge – *7.5mi/13km south either by N 9 down the east bank of the Barrow or by the minor road down the west bank.* Population 510. This attractive small village is set on the banks of the River Barrow, spanned by a bridge built in 1320.
The mound of Dinn Righ *(south of the village)* is the site of the ancient palace of the kings of Leinster.
At Old Leighlin *(2mi/3km west)* is the 12C Anglican cathedral, largely rebuilt in the 16C.

Killeshin Church – *2.5mi/4km west by R 430.* This idyllically located little ruin, its nave long since used as a graveyard, has a Romanesque west door with superb carving featuring animal heads and an inscription reading "A Prayer for Diarmit King of Leinster".

CARRICK-ON-SHANNON★
CORA DROMA RÚISC – Co Leitrim – Population 1 868
Michelin Atlas p 96 and Map 923 – H 6

Carrick-on-Shannon, now the county town of Co Leitrim, is an important crossing point on the River Shannon. Until the 16C the district, known as West Breifne, was held by the O'Rourkes, who ruled from their main stronghold at Leitrim. The town was fortified at the time of the Plantation when it was granted a charter by James I. It benefited from the improvements to the Shannon Navigation in 1846 and from the arrival of the Midland Great Western Railway in 1862. The town marks the upper limit of navigation on the Shannon and is a centre for cruising and angling.

SIGHTS

Costello Chapel ⊙ – *Bridge Street*. At the top of the street *(right)* stands a tiny mortuary chapel (16ft/5m x 12ft/4m), which was built by Edward Costello as a memorial to his wife, who died in 1877. She was buried in April 1879 under a thick glass slab (left) and her husband was interred in 1891; during the intervening 12 years mass was celebrated in the chapel on the first Friday of the month.

Shannon–Erne Waterway

This canal was built (1847–58) as the Ballinamore–Ballyconnell Navigation by the engineer John McMahon to join the River Shannon with Lough Erne, the final link in a waterway system which enabled barges to travel between Dublin, Belfast, Limerick and Waterford. Because of railway competition and the lack of industry the hoped-for traffic failed to develop and the canal was abandoned in 1869; by 1880 it was derelict. In 1994 it was reopened for leisure use. The waterway (40mi/65km – 13hr) passes through 16 locks and under 34 stone bridges, traverses a chain of lakes – Lough Scur, St John's Lough, Garadice Lough – and follows the course of the Woodford River. The western end joins the River Shannon in Leitrim *(4mi/8km north of Carrick by R 280)*.

St George's Terrace – At the east end of the street stands the **Town Clock**, erected in 1905. The **Market house** and yard *(south side)* were built in 1839 by the local landlord, CM St George, whose elegant house, **Hatley Manor** *(north side)*, was built in the 1830s and named after his ancestral home in Cambridgeshire.

> **River Cruises** – The **Slieabh an Iarann Riverbus**, based in Ballinamore, offers a variety of cruises on the Shannon-Erne Waterway.
>
> **Adjacent Sights** – See Boyle, Cavan, Knock, Longford, Strokestown.

Next to it stands the Courthouse, designed in 1821 by William Farrell but now without its entrance portico, which was supported on four Doric columns. An underground passage linked it to the neighbouring County Gaol (1822–1968). The gaol site, ideally placed in a bend of the River Shannon, is now occupied by a modern **marina**.

SHANNON VALLEY *Drive of 25mi/40km*

From Carrick-on-Shannon take N 4 southeast.

Jamestown – The stone arch through which the road enters from the north was part of the defensive wall enclosing the village which was established in 1622 to guard the river crossing.

Drumsna – Population 160. It was here that Anthony Trollope was inspired by the ruins of the Jones family mansion and the history of their downfall to write his first novel.

Anthony Trollope (1815–82) in Ireland

In 1841, having been in the employ of the Post Office since 1834, Trollope was appointed a Surveyor's Clerk in Ireland, where he was based until 1859 when he returned permanently to England.

His first appointment, to which he travelled from Dublin by canal boat, was in **Banagher**, where he took up hunting, a sport he pursued with great enthusiasm for the next 35 years. He was acquainted with Sir William Gregory of Coole Park *(see LOUGHREA)*, a contemporary of his at Harrow School. In 1843 during a visit to Drumsna *(see above)* he was inspired to begin his first novel, *The Macdermots of Ballycloran*, published in 1847. On 11 June 1844 he married Rose Heseltine, whom he had met in 1842 while on business in Dún Laoghaire (then known as Kingstown).

Later that year they moved to **Clonmel**, where they lived in rented rooms on the first floor of a house in O'Connell Street (then High Street) and there two sons were born - Henry Merivale in March 1846 and Frederic James in September 1847. In 1845 Anthony began his second novel, also on an Irish theme, *The Kellys and the O'Kellys*, which was published in 1848.

Their next move took the family to **Mallow**, where they leased a house in the High Street from 1848 to 1851 and Anthony was able to indulge his passion for hunting with the Duhallow, the oldest hunt in Ireland, the Limerick, the Muskerry and the United.

While on secondment in the Channel Islands in 1853, Trollope took up an existing idea and introduced the first **post boxes**, which were painted sage green.

In 1854, after a year in Belfast as Acting Surveyor, he was appointed Surveyor of the Northern District of Ireland but obtained permission to reside in Dublin, where he lived at 5 Seaview Terrace, Donnybrook. As his work involved a good deal of travelling, he created a portable desk *(see p 318)* so that he could write on the train.

His third Irish novel, *Castle Richmond*, in which the action takes place during the Great Famine, was begun in 1859, the year in which he was transferred permanently to England. At the end of his life he began a fourth Irish novel, *The Landleaguers*, about agrarian reform but died in December 1882 before it was finished.

South of Drumnsa turn left onto R 201 to Mohill.

Mohill – Population 796. At the centre of the town there is a statue of Turlough O'Carolan (Carolan) *(see BOYLE)* seated at his harp; he lived in Mohill for several years.

Leave Mohill by R 201 which bears right at the end of the main street; at the fork bear right onto L 112; at the next fork bear right; after 0.75mi/1.2km turn left onto a narrow road (sign).

★**Lough Rynn Demesne** ⊘ – Three **walled gardens** (3 acres/1.2ha), created in 1859 and now planted in the manner of a Victorian pleasure garden, ascend in three terraces from a turreted gazebo (1867) on the lake shore.

The **Blue Gate** leads to the **arboretum** which contains some rare trees (labelled): Californian redwoods, palm trees, a tulip tree, a Japanese cedar which is 140 years old and a Chilean pine (monkey puzzle) which is said to be the oldest in Ireland. The **dairy yard** (1830) has retained the original tiles and marble slabs; the **coach yard** (1850) is fitted with sliding doors; the farmyard (1840) was greatly extended in 1858; the former estate office, now a restaurant, has a small **rent window** and unusual shutters raised by leather straps.

The estate was acquired by the Clements family in 1750 and the estate buildings were erected by the 3rd Earl of Leitrim after 1854; his hasty temper, aggravated by a painful war wound, led to his assassination in 1878 for harsh treatment of his tenants.

On leaving the demesne turn right. At the T-junction turn right; after two side turnings and two crossroads bear right to Dromod.

Dromod and Roosky (population 249) are two attractive Shannonside villages where river cruisers can moor and replenish their supplies.

From Roosky continue south on N 4; after 3mi/4.8km turn left (sign) to Cloonmorris Abbey (1mi/1.6km).

Cloonmorris Ogham Stone – Beside the entrance to the graveyard of the ruined 12C church stands an Ogham stone bearing the name Qenuven.

Return to N 4 and continue south; in Newtown Forbes bear right onto a minor road (direction Killashee); turn right onto N 4 and then bear left to Cloondara.

At **Cloondara** the junction of the Royal Canal, the Camlin River and the Shannon is marked by two locks, a picturesque cluster of houses beside the canal basin, a hump-backed bridge, an old watermill and a ruined church.

Rejoin N 5 west of the village and continue to Termonbarry.

The bridge at **Termonbarry** has a lifting section to allow boats to pass and provides a fine view of the lock and weir on the Shannon.

CASHEL★★★

CAISEAL – Co Tipperary – Population 2 346
Michelin Atlas p 85 and Map 923 – I 10

The Rock of Cashel, an outcrop of limestone (200ft/61m) rising from the Tipperary plain, is the focal point of the town and the surrounding district. Topped by one of the most striking ecclesiastical ruins in Ireland, St Patrick's Rock has outstanding architectural remnants of the early Christian era.

Royal Seat – From about 370 until 1101 the rock was the seat of the kings of Munster, and therefore the provincial capital, and comparable in regal stature to Tara *(see p 54)*, home of the High Kings of Ireland. St Patrick visited Cashel in 450 when he baptised King Aengus; there is a legend that during the ceremony, St Patrick accidentally pierced the king's foot with the point of his staff but the king, believing it to be part of the ritual, remained composed. Cashel was a place of much importance during the 10C when the holy Cormac MacCullinan was king of Munster; he was also a bishop but not of Cashel.

Ecclesiastical Site – In 1101 the site was given to the ecclesiastical authorities whose first building, Cormac's chapel, was consecrated in 1134. The first cathedral was founded in 1169.

The arrival of Henry II in Ireland three years later marked the start of a prolonged period of unrest for Cashel. In 1494 the cathedral was burned down by Gerald Mor, the Great Earl of Kildare. The greatest act of desecration came in 1647, when Lord Inchiquin, seeking the presidency of Munster under the Cromwellian regime, attacked the town of Cashel. Hundreds of people fled to the rock. Lord Inchiquin ordered turf to be piled against the walls of the cathedral and in the subsequent fire many were roasted to death.

By the end of that terrible day, most of the population of 3 000 had been killed. In 1749 the Anglican Archbishop of Cashel decided to move the cathedral into town. The great storm of 1847 did much damage to the abandoned building. In 1874 the Rock became a National Monument and was subsequently restored.

> **Access** – There is a footpath up to the Rock from the gardens of the Cashel Palace Hotel.
>
> **Entertainment** – For a **traditional Irish evening** visit the Brú Ború theatre and sit down to a banquet *(see below)*.
>
> **Adjacent Sights** – See Abbeyleix, Caher, Clonmel, Kilkenny, Roscrea, Tipperary.

C. Boisvieux

Rock of Cashel

★★★ROCK OF CASHEL ⊘

Public car park beside the Rock. Access to the Rock via the Hall of the Vicars Choral (see below).

★★**Cormac's Chapel** – The highly ornate Romanesque building, which is flanked by twin towers, is divided into a nave and a chancel. It is decorated with some of the earliest frescoes in Ireland. Almost every stone of the interior is adorned with carvings. The south tower gives access to the chamber contained between the barrel vault and the stone roof. The chapel was started by Cormac MacCarthy, king and bishop of Cashel, in 1127 and consecrated in 1134. Legend says that it was built of local sandstone and every block was passed from hand to hand from the quarry to Cashel *(12mi/19km).*

★**Round Tower** – In perfect condition, the round tower is built from irregularly coursed sandstone (92ft/28m high). The round-headed doorway (12ft/3.5m above ground-level) has an architrave and the four top-storey windows are pointed.

Cathedral – Most of the ruin, including the high-set lancet windows, dates from the 13C. The cathedral was built to a cruciform plan without aisles; the central tower probably dates from the 14C. The transepts have two east chapels each. In the south wall of the choir is the tomb (1) of Archbishop Miler MacGrath, the Scoundrel of Cashel, who changed his religious beliefs several times and served as both Anglican and Roman Catholic bishop of Cashel during the reign of Elizabeth I; he died in 1621 at the age of 100.
The west tower (91ft/28m), also called the **castle**, was built as a fortified residence by Archbishop O'Hedigan in 1450. The first three storeys are covered by a pointed vault supporting the principal room.

★**Museum** – The museum, which is housed in the undercroft of the Hall of the Vicars Choral, displays articles associated with the Rock – the stone cross of St Patrick (12C) which has lost one arm, an evil eye stone and replicas of the 9C Cashel bell and brooch (originals in the Hunt Museum in Limerick), and of a 17C wine cup and jug (originals in the GPA Bolton Library – *see below*).

Hall of the Vicars Choral – The building (extensively renovated in the 1970s) was the clergy residence. The main hall *(upstairs)* contains a huge 17C stone fireplace and fine items of medieval-style furniture made by modern craftsmen. The kitchen has been restored to its original state: butter churns and three-legged stools. A video presentation in the Dormitory sets Cashel in the context of Irish history.

Brú Ború ⊘ – *At the foot of the Rock.* A modern village green is a fitting focal point for this cultural centre, which presents performances of native Irish music, song and dance, story-telling and folk theatre; it also houses Celtic Studies and a genealogy centre.

TOWN CENTRE

Cashel Heritage Centre ⊘ – The display traces the history of Cashel with a model of Cashel and commentary – display of royal heirlooms and relics of the house of McCarthy Mor.

ROCK OF CASHEL

★ **Cashel Palace Gardens** ⊘ – The gardens, which lead to the Rock of Cashel, contain a 1702 mulberry tree and hop plants, descendants of those used in 1759 to brew the first Guinness dark beer, which was invented by Richard Guinis, agent to the Archbishop of Cashel; his son Arthur founded the world-famous brewery in Dublin. The Palladian mansion, now a luxury hotel, was built in 1730 as the archbishop's palace, designed by Edward Lovett Pearce for Archbishop Theophilus Bolton. The original panelling and plasterwork in the hall is complemented by the red pine staircase, as impressive as that in the Damer House (see ROSCREA).

★ **GPA Bolton Library** ⊘ – This small building, standing in the grounds of the Anglican cathedral, dates from 1836 (renovated in 1986).
The oldest of its 12 000 books is a monk's encyclopedia dating from 1168; it also contains two leaves from Chaucer's *The Book of Fame*, printed by William Caxton at Westminster in London in 1483, a note signed by Jonathan Swift (see p 180) and a collection of ecclesiastical silver.

Cathedral ⊘ – The austere Anglican cathedral was built, with little ornamentation, between 1749 and 1784; it occupies the site of the old parish church of St John the Baptist and is dedicated jointly to St John and to St Patrick of the Rock. The five gates and two towers of the town defences (14C) were demolished in the 18C but substantial remains of the walls still enclose the graveyard; a number of 13C carved stone coffin lids have been placed against the walls.

Hore Abbey – 0.5mi/0.8km west of the Rock of Cashel. The last Cistercian house to be founded in medieval Ireland, Hore Abbey was established by monks from Mellifont (see BOYNE VALLEY) in 1272. Most of the present extensive ruins date from the late 13C. The church was built in cruciform shape, with a chancel, two eastern chapels to each transept and an aisled nave.

Dominican Friary – The friary was founded by Archbishop David MacKelly (Dáibhí Mac Ceallaigh), a Cork Dominican, in 1243 and suppressed in 1540. The church, which was rebuilt after a fire in 1480, has a long narrow nave and choir; the chancel walls and tower are in a good state of preservation.

Parish Church – The Roman Catholic church of St John the Baptist, the oldest RC church in use in Ireland, was opened in 1795, screened by a row of cottages. The mosaics on the façade were added to commemorate the Eucharistic Congress held in Ireland in 1932; another mosaic of Christ the King decorates the baptistery. The interior is unusual in that two galleries run the full length of the building and the ceiling resembles the upturned hull of a ship.

Folk Village ⊘ – The folk village is a small reconstruction of 18C Irish rural life.

EXCURSIONS

★★**Holy Cross Abbey** ⊘ – *9mi/16km north of Cashel by R 660.* The abbey was founded for the Benedictines by Donal O'Brien, King of Munster, in 1168. Fourteen years later it was transferred to the Cistercians and became a major place of pilgrimage, as it was reputed to contain a relic of the True Cross. It was suppressed in 1536 and given to the Earl of Ormond in 1563. Through the intercession of the Butler family the monks stayed at Holy Cross until the 17C. After falling into considerable disrepair the roofless abbey was abandoned for 200 years but is now used as a parish church.

Holy Cross Abbey

The church contains three windows – east, west and south transept – with **stained glass**. There is fine 15C stonework and an early-15C **wall painting**, one of the few from this era surviving in Ireland; it is a secular work, showing two hunters and a stag resting beneath an oak tree.

The west range of the restored **cloisters** contains an exhibition and audio-visual presentation and a tourist information office. There is a mill wheel in the adjacent outbuildings.

The **grounds** contain a replica of the Vatican gardens, including the Stations of the Cross and an altar, commemorating the Italian stigmatist Padre Pio.

The eight-arch **bridge** spanning the River Suir, a copy of the original, was constructed in 1626 by James Butler, Baron of Dunboyne, and his wife, Margaret O'Brien; it is ornamented with their arms and carries a short prayer: "May the two who built it escape the pit of hell".

★**Athassel Priory** – *5mi/8km west by N 74 and minor road south from Golden; across two fields.* The extensive ruins of a 12C Augustinian priory stretch over a wide area. It was destroyed in 1447 but the central tower of the main church, the nave and chancel walls are reasonably preserved. In the church is a tomb, believed to be that of the Norman, William de Burgh, the founder of the priory. The town which once surrounded the priory was destroyed twice, first in 1319 and finally in 1329.

Lár na Páirce ⊘ – *14mi/23km north by N 8 and N 62 to Thurles; Slievenamon Road.* An elegant 19C building now houses a detailed display tracing the history of the Gaelic Games. The GAA *(see p 59)* was formed, at a meeting held on 1 November 1884 in Miss Hayes' Commercial Hotel in Liberty Square in Thurles, not only to revive Gaelic games but also to give active support to the Irish language, traditional dancing, music and song. Here one can learn that hurling (the men's game) and camogie (the women's game) are played with a hurley, study the rules of Gaelic football and handball, gaze at souvenirs of former champions or use the computer to look up information on current players and teams.

Consult the Touring Programmes suggested at the beginning of the guide
Plan a tour with the help of the Map of Principal Sights

CAVAN

AN CABHÁN – Co Cavan – Population 3 509

Michelin Atlas p 97 and Map 923 — J 6

Cavan, the county town, lies in drumlin country – a tranquil, undulating, well-wooded landscape, scattered with countless small lakes which provide extensive coarse fishing and boating facilities. Nearby is Lough Oughter, the largest lake in Co Cavan, which is fed by the River Erne.

Literary Associations – Several famous penmen are connected with County Cavan. The playwright, **Richard Brinsley Sheridan**, was the grandson of Dr Thomas Sheridan, headmaster of Cavan Royal School and a good friend of Jonathan Swift, who often stayed at his home, Quilcagh House near Mullagh. An ancestor of **Edgar Allan Poe** (1809–49) emigrated to America from Killeshandra in the mid 18C. William James, a native of Baillieborough, who emigrated to America because he was a Presbyterian, was the grandfather of **Henry James** (1843–1916). Though born at Cloonyquin (west of Strokestown) **Percy French** (1854–1920), a famous songwriter and gifted painter, is celebrated in Cavan, where he worked for seven years as inspector of loans to tenants. It was while studying engineering at Trinity College in Dublin that he began to write the songs which capture the humour and spirit of his native land. He died in Formby in Lancashire, having moved to England in 1908.

Craft – **Cavan Crystal** ⊙ (SE of Cavan on N 3), the second-oldest glass factory in Ireland, produces lead-crystal glass and enables visitors to watch the various processes – blowing, marking, hand-cutting, polishing.

Adjacent Sights – See Carrick-on-Shannon, Enniskillen, Longford, Monaghan.

SIGHTS

Life Force Mill ⊙ – In the town centre on the River Cavan stands an old flour mill which ceased production in the early 1950s and has been restored to working order. A video (25min) presents the history of the mill and its restoration. The tour (1hr) starts with the participants mixing the dough for a loaf of soda bread, shows the milling machinery in operation and returns to the kitchen when the bread is cooked.

Town Centre – At the north end of the town stands the Roman Catholic **cathedral** (1942), a composite of styles by Ralph Byrne, with sculptures by Albert Power. South stands the **Anglican Church**, an aisleless, galleried church with crenellations, a west tower and steeple, by John Bowden, who also designed the Classical **Courthouse** (opposite). There is a Genealogical Centre at the Tourist Information Office.

EXCURSIONS

Ballyjamesduff – 10mi/16km S of Cavan by N 3, N 55 and a minor road via Cross Keys. Population 53 000. The town is named after an English officer who was involved in the 1798 uprising. It clusters round the Market House (1813) at the junction of five broad streets; during the 18C, it was a lively place on the main coach road between Cavan and Kells, with a weekly market, nine fairs a year and a reputation for selling black cattle.

Cavan County Museum ⊙ – The museum traces the history of County Cavan with archaeological finds from the Stone Age to the Middle Ages (three-faced pre-Christian Corleck Head; 1 000-year-old dug-out boat), a display of 18C, 19C and 20C costume from the **Pighouse Collection**, a gallery on folk life, one on the Gaelic Athletic Association (see p 59) and another hung with banners and sashes belonging to various orders – Loyal Orange , Royal Black Preceptory, the Apprentice Boys of Derry. the Ancient Order of Hibernians and the Irish National Foresters – showing religious scenes; King William III; Death of Schomberg; Mountjoy breaking the boom at the siege of Londonderry. The building is a converted 19C convent set in a typical conventual garden.

Basketry

In past centuries in Ireland there was a willow tree – there are 260 sorts of willow – outside each house, mostly in Donegal, Mayo and Galway, to provide material for making baskets. The trees were coppiced to produce long straight shoots, known as withies. Natural withies are dark, stripped withies are white; boiled and stripped withies have a red tinge. Different patterns of weaving and design developed in different parts of the country.

Carraig Craft Centre and Basketry Museum ○ – *Mount Nugent; 15mi/24km S of Cavan by N 3, N 55 and R 154.* This unusual little museum displays baskets of every sort – donkey creels (panniers), baskets for pigeons, eggs, turf, potatoes, fish, salmon and eel traps, egg laying, hens and ducks, bee skeps, flower baskets, potato sieves and serving

dishes – made not only from willow but also from straw and reed, which are less rigid and need a frame; the owner specialises in rush work using rush gathered each summer from Lough Sheelin. The tour begins with a short video on baskets and basket weaving.

Kilmore Cathedral ○ – *2mi/3.2km W of Cavan by R 198.* The Anglican cathedral, which stands isolated in rolling parkland, is dedicated to St Felim *(Fethlimidh)*, who brought Christianity to the region in the 6C; it is also known as the Bedell Memorial Church. It was completed in 1860 in the neo-Gothic style and incorporates *(north side)* a 12C Romanesque doorway which may have belonged to an earlier church or to the abbey on Trinity Island in Lough Oughter. On display in the chancel is a copy of the Old Testament (printed in 1685) translated into Irish by Bishop William Bedell (1571–1642), whose memorial is over the west door; he is buried in the neighbouring graveyard.

★**Killykeen Forest Park** – *5mi/8km W of Cavan by R 198.* The Forest Park (600 acres/243ha), a patchwork of land and water, is in two sections linked by a footbridge. The woodland, which is mostly spruce grown for commercial exploitation, includes about 10% deciduous trees. There are three marked nature trails *(maximum 2mi/3.2km)* which follow the shore, identifying the trees and the habitats of birds and animals, and a wildfowl sanctuary in Sally Lake.

On Trinity Island at the southern end of Lough Oughter there is the ruin of a Premonstratensian Priory, established in 1250 by monks from Lough Key *(see p 114).* On an island in the northeast arm of the lake stands Clogh Oughter Castle, a 13C or 14C tower house.

CLONMACNOISE★★★

CLUAIN MHIC NÓIS – Co Offaly
Michelin Atlas p 90 and Map 923 – I 8
13mi/21km S of Athlone by N 6 and N 62

The monastery of Clonmacnoise, which was founded in 545 by St Kieran (Ciarán), was the burial place of the Kings of Connaught and Tara, and one of the most famous monastic sites in Ireland, second only to Armagh.

Its position beside the Shannon now seems remote and inaccessible but in earlier centuries transport was easier by water than over land. The old Pilgrims' Road approached from the north along the esker. On St Kieran's Day (9 September) people still make a pilgrimage to Clonmacnoise.

Monastic Settlement – As its reputation grew the settlement expanded from an original wooden oratory to a cluster of stone churches, numerous monks' dwellings and a round tower within an earth or stone enclosure. None of the surviving ruins is earlier than the 9C. The monastery was plundered many times from the 9C onwards by the Irish, the Vikings and the Anglo-Normans, until it was finally reduced to ruin in 1552 by the English garrison from Athlone. A castle built by the Normans c 1212 on the river bank was slighted in the Cromwellian period.

Adjacent Sights – See Athenry, Athlone, Birr, Portumna, Tullamore.

TOUR *1hr*

Visitor Centre ⊙ – The **Visitor Centre** displays the original **high crosses**, which have been replaced on site by replicas, and a collection of **grave slabs**★ uncovered at Clonmacnoise which must have been an important stone-carving centre from the 8C to 12C.

South Cross – The cross (12ft/3.6m), which dates from the early 9C, bears a carving of the Crucifixion on its west face. The decorative spirals and interlacing are similar to those on the crosses at Kells *(see p 210)* and to those at Iona and Kildalton in Scotland.

Temple Doolin – The church, which is named after Edward Dowling, who restored it in 1689 to serve as a mausoleum, is probably pre-12C with antae and a round-headed east window. In the 17C **Temple Hurpan** was added to the east end.

Temple Meaghlin or Temple Rí – The east windows of this church, which dates from about 1200, are similar to those at Clonfert *(see p 261)* and O'Heyne's Church at Kilmacduagh *(see p 106)*; there was once a wooden gallery at the west end.

Temple Kieran – Parts of this tiny church, which is said to contain the grave of St Kieran, are pre-12C.
From the south side a stone path leads out of the enclosure to the Nun's Church *(see below)*. On the north side is the outline of **Temple Kelly** (12C).

North Cross Shaft – The shaft (c 800) is decorated with lions biting their tails, and a cross-legged figure thought by some to be the Celtic god Cernunnos.

Cathedral – The simple rectangular building has been modified many times. The oldest parts probably date from the 10C, when the original wooden church was replaced with a stone structure. The Romanesque west doorway dates from the 12C, the two-storey sacristy may be 13C; in the 15C the elaborate north doorway, surmounted by three plaques depicting St Dominic, St Patrick and St Francis, was constructed by Dean Odo and the chancel was divided into three vaulted chapels.

★**Cross of the Scriptures** – The cross, which is made of sandstone and is related to the crosses at Monasterboice *(see p 118)*, was erected in the 10C possibly by King Flann (d 916). The decoration includes the Last Judgement on the east face and the Crucifixion on the west; the lowest panel on the east face may represent St Kieran and King Diarmaid founding the first church, or Abbot Colman and King Flann setting up the cross or beginning the cathedral.

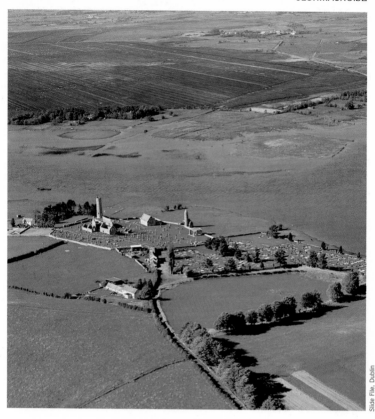

Clonmacnoise

Round Tower – This is a good example of a round tower although it has lost its conical cap. It may have been built in the 10C by Fergal O'Rourke and been repaired in 1120 by Abbot O'Malone, but the arched doorway is most likely 12C.

Temple Connor ⊘ – The church may date from 1010, when it was endowed by Cathal O'Connor; the small window in the south wall is original. The building was restored in 1911 and is used by the Church of Ireland (Anglican) for services.

Temple Finghin – The 12C church consists of a nave and chancel. The Romanesque chancel arch was modified and strengthened in the 17C. It is unusual in having a south door and a mini round tower incorporated into the chancel.

From the centre of the enclosure follow the old path E across the extended grave-yard and along the road; 10min there and back on foot.

Nun's Church – The ruined church consists of a nave and chancel and according to the Annals of the Four Masters *(see p 158)* it was completed in 1167 by Dervorgilla. The west doorway and the chancel arch are beautifully decorated in the Irish Romanesque style.

EXCURSION

Clonfinlough Stone – *2mi/3km E by the minor road and 0.5mi/0.8km S by the minor road; park by the church; 10min there and back on foot up the path and over the stile.* Near the edge of the field stands a large boulder which bears symbols similar to some Bronze Age rock art in Galicia in Spain. The natural indentations in the rock have been modified to suggest human figures.

To the south there is a **view** of the Brosna and Shannon river valleys where peat extraction is conducted on a large scale.

The key on page 9 explains the abbreviations and symbols used in the text or on the maps.

CLONMEL★

CLUAIN MEALA – Co Tipperary – Population 15 215
Michelin Atlas p 80 and Map 923 – I 10

Clonmel, the principal town of Co Tipperary, is set on the northern bank of the River Suir which at this point forms the boundary between Co Tipperary and Co Waterford. Directly to the south beyond the river rise the Comeragh Mountains, providing an impressive backdrop to the many historic buildings of the town.

HISTORICAL NOTES

The town is believed to pre-date the Vikings; its name comes from the Irish words for "a meadow of honey", an early Christian reference to the great fertility of the Suir valley. Viking longships sailed up the River Suir from Waterford in the early 10C and, according to tradition, a battle was fought at Clonmel in 916 or 917 between the local O'Neill clan and the Vikings. Edward I granted the town a charter and the walls were built in the early 14C. The town became an important stronghold of the Butler family, the Earls of Ormond *(see KILKENNY)*. The garrison at Clonmel put up more resistance to Cromwell in the mid 17C than any other Irish town.

Out and About

Events – **Greyhound** racing Monday and Thursday evenings. Major annual **coursing** festival in February.
Annual **Writers' Weekend** in September particularly for short story writers and poets.

Crafts – At **Tipperary Crystal** ⊘ *(10mi/16km E by N 24)* visitors may watch the production and buy pieces of hand-decorated crystal glassware.

Adjacent Sights – See Caher, Cashel, Kilkenny, Youghal.

Literary Associations – Four major figures in English literature had close associations with Clonmel. **Anthony Trollope** *(see p 129)* wrote his first two novels while living in the town from 1844 to 1848. **George Borrow**, who was at school in Clonmel, mentioned the town in two chapters of *Lavengro*. **Marguerite Power**, the Countess of Blessington, a noted early-19C literary figure, was born at Suir Island in 1789; she died in Paris in 1849. **Laurence Sterne** (1713–68), author of *Tristram Shandy*, was born in Mary Street; his family lived at Suir Island.

Bianconi Cars

Charles Bianconi (1786–1875), son of an Italian immigrant from Lombardy and twice Mayor of Clonmel, began a horse-drawn car service in 1815 linking Clonmel to Limerick and Thurles. Following the battle of Waterloo, horses were in plentiful supply at about £10 each; by 1844 he had over 100 in his stables. By 1851 his open long cars, known as Bians, operated in 22 counties with central depots in Clonmel, Galway and Sligo. At its peak the service employed 1 400 horses and 100 vehicles, painted crimson and yellow. It created a nation-wide revolution in the carrying of mail, freight and passengers, which was superseded only by the building of the railway network in the later 19C.

Bianconi retired in 1865 but one of the Bianconi horse-drawn mail cars was used between Clonmel and Dungarvan as late as the 1920s. A coach-horn from a Bianconi mail coach, together with the clock, now handless, by which the departures were timed, are displayed in the foyer of Hearn's Hotel (**A**).

SIGHTS

★**County Museum** ⊘ (**M¹**) – The display depicts the history of the South Riding of Co Tipperary from the Stone Age to the 20C – Roman coins found in Clonmel, the scrapbook associated with the Young Irelanders' trial held in Clonmel in 1848 and the uniform jacket of the Royal Irish Regiment, which had a depot in the town until it was disbanded in 1922 after the signing of the Anglo-Irish Treaty. There is also a small collection of paintings by Irish artists.

CLONMEL

★ **St Mary's Church** ⊘ – The present Anglican church, with its unusual octagonal tower, was built in the 19C, incorporating parts of earlier 14C buildings. Written references suggest the existence of a building as early as the 13C. In the grounds there are extensive sections of the town walls.

Riverside – The 17C **Old Bridge** (**18**) crosses the River Suir three times from Little Island and Suir Island *(downstream)* to Stretches Island *(upstream)*, derived from the name of 16C Italian immigrants called Stroccio.
The north bank between the Old Bridge and the 18C **Gashouse Bridge** (**12**) (named after the nearby gas-works) forms the town **quay**, where ships used to unload their cargoes; it is marked by a memorial to the Manchester Martyrs *(see p 93)* of 1867 and is lined by terraces of **Georgian** houses and tall warehouses.

Main Guard – The three-storey, five-bay building is crowned by a cupola and bears the **Arms of Clonmel**. It was commissioned by the Duke of Ormond to replace the original 17C courthouse, which was destroyed during the Cromwellian siege in 1650.

West Gate – The original 14C gate was rebuilt in 1831 in the mock-Tudor style with a castellated top.

Museum of Transport ⊘ (**M²**) – Two floors of a handsome six-storey mill building now house some two dozen vintage, veteran and classic cars as well as much motoring memorabilia.

EXCURSIONS

★★ **Nier Valley Scenic Route** – *Round tour of 40mi/64km. From Clonmel take R 678 S. After 5mi/8km turn right; after 4mi/6km make a detour left to a viewpoint. In Ballymacarbry turn right onto R 671 to return to Clonmel.*
The road climbs into the Comeragh Mountains – there are **views** of mountains and forests at most points on the route – before descending the Nier and Suir river valleys.

Carrick-on-Suir – *13mi/21km E by N 24.* This bustling town (pop 5 143) has an enviable location on the tidal Suir between Slievenamon *(NW)* and the Comeragh foothills *(S)*. Its 15C Old Bridge is evidence of its former importance as the lowest crossing point of the river before the estuary. The **Heritage Centre** ⊘ traces local history.

★ **Ormond Castle** ⊘ – The great treasure of Carrick is the partially ruined 15C castle and adjoining Elizabethan mansion which stand in a wooded park. The restored mansion, a very fine example of its type, was built about 1568 by the 10th Earl of Ormond, known as Black Tom, to receive his cousin, Queen Elizabeth, who never visited Ireland. The exterior has fine mullioned windows and gabled roofs; the interior is noted for its **ornamental plasterwork** and long gallery.

Kilkeeran High Crosses – *17mi/27km E by N 24 and R 697.* The three crosses, which probably date from the 9C, mark the site of an early monastery. There are eight horsemen on the base of the **West Cross** which otherwise is decorated with interlacing and bosses. It bears an unusual cap, as does the East Cross which was probably not finished as it is undecorated.

Ormond Castle, Carrick-on-Suir

★**Ahenny High Crosses** – *19mi/31km E by N 24 and R 697*. The two crosses, which bear unusual caps, may date from the 8C since the decorative interlacing and spirals are similar to those in the Book of Kells. The figures on the base represent seven clergy carrying croziers, led by a clerical cross-bearer.

★**Fethard** – *8mi/13km N by R 689*. Population 946. The small town retains several relics of the Anglo-Norman settlement; most sections of the late-14C town walls remain intact. **Fethard Castle** in the town centre is one of three keeps probably dating from the 15C. The **church**, which has a late-15C crenellated tower, includes earlier buildings much restored between 1400 and 1600. The huge roof-span of the nave is a notable architectural feature and the east window is copied from Kilcooley Abbey. There are many 16C and 17C tombs among the ruins of the 12C Augustinian priory.

The **museum** ⊘ in the old railway station has numerous items of rural and domestic life in Ireland in earlier centuries.

COBH★

AN CÓBH – Co Cork – Population 6 468
Michelin Atlas p 78 and Map 923 – H 12

Cobh (pronounced Cove) began to expand during the late 18C, when Cork harbour became an assembly point for Royal Navy fleets engaged in the American War of Independence and later in the war against France. Its main architectural development, neo-Gothic villas and Italianate buildings, came in the early 19C when Cobh was a health resort. The elegant waterfront pavilion (1854) which used to be the

Out and About

Cork Harbour Car Ferry ⊘ – There is a car ferry across the River Lee between Carrigaloe *(east bank)* and Glenbrook *(west bank)*.

Cork Harbour Cruises ⊘ – There are cruises from Kennedy Pier via the harbour forts, Spike Island, the naval base and major harbour industries.

Rail Service – From Cork and Cobh to Fota Island.

Adjacent Sights – See Cork, Kinsale, Midleton, Youghal.

Where to Stay

Robin Hill House, Rushbrook. ☎ 021 4811 395. Former 19C rectory (6 rm); individually furnished bedrooms and a comfortable restaurant serving contemporary cuisine; overlooking Cork Harbour.

Bella Vista Manor House, Bishop's Rd. ☎ 021 812 450; Fax 021 812 215. Hotel (16 rm) with comfortable spacious bedrooms and a small informal restaurant; good view over the port.

home of the Royal Cork Yacht Club was designed by the architect Anthony Salvin; the RCYC, now based in Crosshaven *(see CORK)*, was the successor to the world's first yachting fraternity, the Water Club of 1720. In 1849 Cobh was renamed Queenstown in honour of Queen Victoria, who visited the town in August of that year. Until the 1960s Cobh was a port of call for the *Queen Mary*, the *Queen Elizabeth* and other great ships from lines such as Hamburg Atlantic and North German Lloyd; photographs and paintings of that period hang in the bar of the Commodore Hotel. The traffic was not all tourist class; Cobh was also the port of departure for hundreds of thousands of Irish emigrants who sailed to North America in the late 19C and early 20C.

★**St Colman's Cathedral** ⊘ – The neo-Gothic Roman Catholic cathedral, which stands on the heights above the town, was designed by Pugin and Ashlin and built between 1868 and 1915. Its tall **spire**, which houses a carillon of 47 bells, is a landmark for miles. The interior is decorated with columns of polished marble, mosaic flooring and a detailed marble reredos.

★**Lusitania Memorial** – *Casement Square*. The 1 500 victims of the *Lusitania*, which was torpedoed in 1915 *(see KINSALE)*, are commemorated by an elaborate carving of an angel flanked by two sailors; it was designed by Jerome Connor (1876–1943), a Cork sculptor, and completed after his death by Seamus Murphy. In nearby Pierce Square a more modest memorial recalls the victims of the *Titanic*; the supposedly unsinkable liner made her last call at Cobh on 11 April 1912 before setting off on her fateful maiden voyage.

Cobh Heritage Centre: The Queenstown Story ⊘ – Part of Cobh railway station now houses an exhibition recalling the days when Cobh was a great port – evocation of shipboard life in the days of sail for emigrants and convicts; emigrant lodging houses in Cobh; audio-visual presentation on the development of Cork Harbour as a naval base; embarkation of troops for the Boer War and the First World War; introduction of steam ships in 1838 and the heyday of the great liners between the wars; the sinking of the *Titanic* and the *Lusitania*.

Cobh Museum ⊘ – A former Presbyterian Church houses a collection of local artefacts with a strongly maritime theme.

EXCURSION

★**Fota Island** – *4mi/6km N by R 624*. The island was the estate of the Smith-Barry family until 1975, when it was purchased by University College, Cork. **Fota House** ⊘, originally an 18C hunting lodge, was designed in the 1820s by Sir Richard Morrison and contains some of Ireland's finest Regency interiors *(renovation in progress)*.

The **Wildlife Park**★ ⊘ (70 acres/ 28ha) was established by the Zoological Society of Ireland in 1983 with the main aim of conserving endangered species, like the cheetah which is one of its main attractions. Fota is one of the most popular establishments of its kind in Ireland, with a fine array of creatures, with many of its species wandering freely around the park. A grassy plateau in the centre of the island is sufficiently like the savannah to provide a convincing habitat for giraffes,

Fota Wildlife Park

B Lynch /Bord Fáilte, Dublin

zebras and antelopes. Various species of monkey disport themselves on a series of islands on the lower part of the site, while flamingoes, pelicans, penguins and other waterfowl are accommodated on and around the surrounding pools. A "train" helps footsore visitors experience the whole of the extensive grounds and there is a playground for children.

The **Arboretum** ⊘ is planted with many sub-tropical trees and shrubs which flourish in the mild climate; the collections have come from all over the world, including Australia, Chile, China, Japan and New Zealand. Unusual species of coniferous trees grow in the garden.

For historical background on the country see the Historical Table and Notes in the Introduction

CONNEMARA★★★
Co Galway
Michelin Atlas p 88 and Map 923 – C 7

Connemara is a wild and beautiful region of mountains, lakes, tumbling streams, undulating bog, sea-girt promontories, unspoilt beaches and panoramic views. It is a Gaelic-speaking region and has attracted many artisans, who can be visited at work in their studios – handweaving, knitting, screen printing, pottery, jewellery, marble inlay and carving.

The centre of Connemara is composed of mountain peaks, the **Twelve Bens** or **Pins**, which culminate in Benbaun (2 388ft/728m). The sharp grey peaks of quartzite rock, which is resistant to weathering, are too steep and hard to be clothed in blanket bog. The Bens are drained by mountain streams and ringed by a chain of lakes where trout are plentiful. The region is now largely uninhabited, although in the past the more fertile lowlands were cultivated and the uplands were used as pasture for cattle and sheep. Between the foot of the Twelve Pins and the deeply indented southern coastline extends the level **Connemara Bog**, dotted with innumerable tiny lakes. On a bright day the stretches of water act like mirrors reflecting the sun; in the rain the whole environment seems to be made of water.

John D'Arcy (1785–1839)

In 1804 the D'Arcy estates in Connemara, then an inaccessible and sparsely populated region, were inherited by John D'Arcy, who had earlier converted to the established church to avoid exclusion as a Roman Catholic under the Penal laws. He was the seventh generation of a family of Anglo-Norman origin, which had settled in Galway in the reign of Elizabeth I. After the death of his first wife in 1815 he moved to Connemara and devoted the rest of his life to the development of a town, which he named Newtown Clifden. He importuned the authorities constantly for funds to build roads to link his new settlement to Galway and Westport.

CLIFDEN

Clifden (population 808) lies in a hollow at the head of Ardbear Harbour, a safe anchorage in a long sea-inlet on the west coast; the site was chosen deliberately as in the early 19C all heavy goods were carried by sea. The harbour **quay**, begun in 1822, was not completed until 1831 owing to lack of funds. The road to Galway, which runs east–west between the Twelve Bens and the Connemara bog, was built in the 1820s. As it passed through uninhabited country, tents and cooking utensils had to be supplied for the workmen. The railway from Galway, which was laid in 1895, closed in 1935.

NORTH CONNEMARA *Round tour of 60mi/96km – 1 day*
From Clifden take the cliff road W.

Clifden Bay – There is a long sandy beach on the north shore of Clifden Bay west of the harbour *(1.5mi/2.4km – car park)*.

★★**Sky Road** – A steep and narrow road climbs along the cliffs on the north side of Clifden Bay past the site of Clifden Castle, John D'Arcy's house. To the south across Clifden Bay rises the round hump of Errisbeg (987ft/300m).
As the road bears north-west over the ridge, a magnificent **view**★★ unfolds *(NW)* of the indented coastline and the islands offshore *(viewing point car park)*. The road descends in a curve to the head of Kingstown Bay and then continues inland along the south shore of Streamstown Bay, a narrow inlet (4mi/6.4km long).
At the T-junction turn left onto N 59. To visit Inishbofin make a detour (4mi/6.5km) W to Cleggan. Otherwise continue N.

Inishbofin – *Ferry from Cleggan.* The island of the White Cow, where St Colman of Lindisfarne founded a monastery in the 7C, is inhabited by farmers and fishermen. The fort was used by Grace O'Malley *(see p 285)*, whose ancestors seized the island from the O'Flahertys in the 14C.

★**Connemara National Park (Páirc Náisiúnta Chonamara)** ⊘ – *1.5mi/2.4km to car park.* The park (4 942 acres/2 000ha) covers part of the Twelve Bens range of mountains and consists of heath, blanket bog and grassland with some natural woodland of oak and birch. The flora ranges from Mediterranean species to alpine and arctic plants on the upper slopes. The **red deer**, once native to Connemara, and the **Connemara pony**, are established in the park.

Out and about

Rambling – Visitors intending to walk in the hills should be properly equipped (map and compass, stout waterproof footwear, warm clothes and food) and should advise someone, preferably the **National Park Visitor Centre** *(see below)*, of their route and expected time of return; no one should walk alone. There is a guided walk up to *(2hr)* and through *(2–4hr)* the **Pass of the Birds** *(first Sunday in August)* from Recess northeast up Owentooe River Valley, southeast of Maumeen Peak, through the Pass of the Birds, past St Patrick's Bed and Holy Well, down into Failmore and Joyce River valleys. For a description of the road see North Connemara below.

Coastal Cruise – Ferries ⓥ from Cleggan to Inishbofin *(see below)*. Maritime Wildlife cruises and sea angling cruises from Letterfrack.

Sports – For scuba diving **Scubadive West** in Renvyle; for fishing the **Roundstone Sea Angling Centre**.

Crafts – IDA craft village at Roundstone *(see below)*, the Craft Shop at Kylemore Abbey *(see below)* and, for Woollen goods, the Leenane Cultural Centre *(see below)*.

Adjacent Sights – See Aran Islands, Galway, Westport.

Where to Eat

John J Burke, Clonbur. ☎ 092 46 175. Traditional Irish pub, offering carefully prepared food; live music at weekends.

High Moors, Dooneen, Clifden. *0.75m SE off Ballyconneely rd.* ☎ 095 21342. Busy, family run restaurant using home-grown produce; views across countryside.

Where to Stay

Buttermilk Lodge, Westport Rd, Clifden. ☎ 095 21951; Fax 095 21953. Purpose built, friendly home (11 rm) with spacious modern rooms; home baking; 400m from town centre.

River Run Lodge, Glann Rd, Oughterard. *0.5mi/0.8km NW.* ☎ 091 552 697; Fax 091 552 669. Spacious guesthouse (6 rm) on Owenriff River, offering modern Irish dishes.

Eldon's, Roundstone. ☎ 095 35933; Fax 095 35722. Family run village centre hotel (18 rm incl 6 very spacious annexe rooms); Beola restaurant specialising in lobster; views across harbour.

Erriseask House, Ballyconneely. ☎ 095 23553; Fax 095 23639. Period farmhouse (12 rm), overlooking Mannin Bay and the Twelve Bens; award winning food; good walking nearby.

Currarevagh House, Oughterard. ☎ 091 552 312; Fax 091 552 731. Early Victorian country house (15 rm) in parkland beside Lough Corrib; very quiet location. 55-110

Ballywarren House, Cong. ☎ 092 46989; Fax 092 46989. Stylish, spacious, personally run, country house guesthouse (3 rm) on main road.

Quay House, Beach Rd, Clifden. ☎ 095 21369; Fax 095 21608. Extended period property (14 rm) informally run; good views across harbour; 5min walk from town centre.

Lough Inagh Lodge, Recess. *4.75m NW by N 59 on R 344.* ☎ 095 34706; Fax 095 34708. Converted Victorian fishing lodge (12 rm) specialising in outdoor activities; isolated location, superb views.

Cashel House, Cashel. ☎ 095 31001; Fax 095 31077. Traditional country house (32 rm) with antiques and paintings, set in idyllic gardens.

Renvyle House, Renvyle. ☎ 095 43511; Fax 095 43515. Family oriented coastal hotel (63 rm) offering themed weekends and sports facilities.

The **Visitor Centre**, housed in old farm buildings, provides information on guided walks and nature trails, an audio-visual film and an interpretative exhibition about the Connemara landscape.

Rising behind the Visitor Centre is Diamond Hill (1 460ft/445m), the highest point, which provides a good view. At the foot of its east face the Polladirk River flows north from a large valley, Glanmore, and through a spectacular gorge.

Continue N on N 59. In Letterfrack make a detour left to Rinvyle.

Rinvyle Peninsula – At the end of the peninsula, which is dominated by Tully Mountain, stands **Rinvyle (Currath) Castle**, a ruined tower house, belonging to the O'Flaherty clan. The northeast corner has collapsed revealing a spiral stair, a vaulted third storey and a huge fireplace. There is a fine view of the Mweelrea (Muilrea) Mountains *(northeast)* and of the islands offshore – Inishbofin *(west)*, Inishturk and Clare Island *(north)*. The Rinvyle House Hotel was once the home of the author, Oliver St John Gogarty.

Return to N 59 and continue E.

★**Kylemore Abbey** ⊘ – The name, *Coill Mhór* in Irish, which means the big wood, refers to the oak, birch, holly and conifers which grew on the north shore of Lough Pollacappul at the foot of Doughrough Mountain. The turreted and crenellated neo-Gothic castle, built (1860–67) of Dalkey granite, now houses a community of Irish Benedictine nuns and a convent school. **Kylemore pottery** is made and decorated by hand in the **Craft Centre**, which sells a wide variety of goods.

The lavish mansion was commissioned by Mitchell Henry (1826–1901) and his wife Margaret Vaughan of Co Down, who entertained on a grand scale until her death in 1874. The history of the castle and convent is traced in photographs and text and an audio-visual presentation in three rooms of the castle, including the entrance hall with its magnificent staircase and ceiling.

The huge walled garden is being restored to its former glory.

A walk *(10min there and back on foot)* along the wooded shore past rushing streams leads to the **Gothic church** (1868), a replica of Norwich Cathedral, which is used for ecumenical services and concerts.

Continue E on N 59.

Leenane – *Car park.* There is a fine view of **Killary Harbour**★, a deep fjord which is the drowned estuary of the Erriff River. *(See also p 286).*

Leenane Cultural Centre ⊘ – The Centre houses a demonstration of the processing of wool – from the fleece to the finished product – carding, spinning, dyeing with natural plant dyes and weaving. There is a selection of hand-made goods on sale in the shop. Outside, several different breeds of sheep, some very ancient, graze on the turf.

Take R 336 south; after 4.5mi/8km turn left onto a steep and narrow mountain road.

★**Joyce Country** – This area takes its name from a Welsh family which settled in the mountains between Lough Mask and Lough Corrib after the Anglo-Norman invasion in the 12C. The route provides many beautiful perspectives of lake and mountain.

★**Lough Nafooey** – East of the watershed there is a superb **view** of Lough Nafooey at the foot of Maumtrasna (2 207ft/671m). From the north shore there is a view of the waterfall at the west end of the lake.

Lough Mask – From the Ferry Bridge the full extent of Lough Mask is revealed stretching north at the foot of the Partry Mountains *(west)* towards the Plains of Mayo.

At the T-junction turn left; in Clonbur turn right onto R 345.

★★**Lough Corrib** – The wooded shore road provides a **view** of the lake and islands. In the northwest arm of Lough Corrib on an island stands the ruin of an O'Flaherty stronghold, **Hen's Castle**, which was twice defended by Grace O'Malley *(see p 285)*. In 1570 the Joyces, who had murdered her husband, Donal O'Flaherty, tried in vain to gain possession of the castle. Several years later, when it was besieged by English troops from Galway, Grace drove them back by pouring melted roof-lead on their heads and summoned help by sending a man through the underground passage which linked the castle with the shore, to light a beacon on Doon Hill, a promontory on the north shore.

At the T-junction turn left onto R 336. In Maam Cross turn right onto N 59 to return to Clifden.

Lough Inagh

Alexander Nimmo (1783–1832)

Alexander Nimmo was a Scot who came to Ireland in 1809 to assist in bog surveys. In 1822 he was appointed engineer of the Western District and engineered the Galway to Clifden road; while work was in progress in the 1820s he lived at Corrib Lodge at Maam Cross. He also designed piers and harbours.

Maam Cross (An Teach Dóite) and **Recess (Sraith Salach)** – These are two popular angling villages on the Galway to Clifden road. Beyond Recess the many islands of **Derryclare Lough** come into view. North of this lake in the glaciated valley between the Maumturk Mountains *(east)* and two of the Twelve Pins, Bencorr and Derryclare *(west)*, lies **Lough Inagh** *(picnic places)*; the bog is dotted with turf stacks and sheep. On the south shore of Ballynahinch Lake stands **Ballynahinch Castle** (now a hotel), formerly the property of the Martin family who acquired the estate from the O'Flaherty clan in the 16C; it was the home of Richard Martin, also known as "Humanity Dick", who founded the Society for the Prevention of Cruelty to Animals.

SOUTH CONNEMARA *Round tour of 75mi/121km – 1 day*
From Clifden take R 143 S.

Owenglin Cascade – On the southern edge of the town the Owenglin River plunges over a waterfall before entering Ardbear Harbour.
Continue S on R 341 for 2mi/3.2km.

Alcock and Brown Monument – The monument on the hill *(northwest)* commemorates the first non-stop transatlantic flight made in 1919 by Alcock and Brown who landed in Derryginlagh Bog *(south)*.
Continue S on R 341.

Errisbeg – The outcrop of dense gabbro rock (987ft/300m) shelters two sandy coves.

★ **Roundstone (Cloch na Rón)** – Population 281. The resort was laid out by Alexander Nimmo *(see above)*, a Scot, who invited fellow Scots to live there. On the south side of the town is a **craft village**, one of those established by the Industrial

Irish Picture Library

Development Authority. It is best known for the workshop of Malachy Kearns who makes the traditional goatskin drum (*bodhrán* pronounced "borawn") which accompanies folk music.

In Toombeola turn right onto R 342.

★**Cashel** – This attractive little resort, a good angling and shooting centre, nestles at the foot of a hill overlooking Bertraghboy Bay.

Turn right onto R 340.

Carna Peninsula – A string of villages punctuates the shoreline.
Offshore *(south)* lies **St MacDara's Island** ⊘ where the 6C saint founded a monastery; the church (restored), which was built of very large stones, has unusual antae meeting at the roof ridge; sailors used to dip their sails in veneration of St MacDara. The island can be reached from **Carna**, a lobster fishing village, where, on St MacDara's feast day (16 July) a pattern takes place; local people and visitors journey to St MacDara's island for Mass and other prayers; later in the day there are boat races and celebrations.

Kilkieran *(Cill Chiaráin)* on the east coast offers a fine view of the patchwork of islands and peninsulas which lie offshore.

7mi/11.3km N of Kilkieran, turn right (sign) to Patrick Pearse's Cottage.

Patrick Pearse's Cottage ⊘ – *Car park*. Nestling against a rocky outcrop on the west shore of Lough Aroolagh is the three-roomed thatched cottage built by Patrick Pearse *(see p 193)* where he spent his holidays and studied the Irish language.

Return to R 340; continue east. At the T-junction turn left onto R 386. In Maam Cross turn left onto N 59 to return to Clifden.

CORK★★

CORCAIGH – Co Cork – Population 127 187
Michelin Atlas p 78 and Map 923 – G 12

Ireland's third-largest city, after Dublin and Belfast, Cork is a major commercial city, the administrative centre of Co Cork and a university town.
The city centre, built on reclaimed marshland, is flat but the northern suburbs, including **Montenotte**, Cork's most exclusive residential district, are set on the steep northern heights. The River Lee flows through the centre forming attractive channels on the western side; its estuary forms the largest natural harbour in Europe. Until the 19C many of the city streets were open waterways where ships moored; in 1780 Arthur Young compared Cork to Dutch towns.
The city has a strong historical and cultural identity. The people of Cork speak with a distinctive accent and relish two local specialities, black pudding *(drisheen)* and pig's trotters *(crúibíní – crubeens in English)*; both can be appreciated on a visit to the **English Market**, where the stall holders have a lively line in Cork banter.

"A Marshy Place" – Cork derives its name from the Irish for a "marshy place", where St Finbar founded a church in 650 on the banks of the River Lee near the present site of University College. Its early development was disrupted in 860 by Viking raids, and in 1172 by the invasion of the Anglo-Normans who eventually broke the Danish hold on the city.

"Rebel Cork" – Owing to its commercial strength Cork early developed a political independence which has survived to the present day. In 1492 **Perkin Warbeck**, the pretender to the English throne, arrived in Cork; he won the support of the mayor and some leading citizens who accompanied him to England, where he proclaimed himself Richard IV, King of England and Lord of Ireland. Warbeck and his Cork supporters were hanged at Tyburn.
In the 1640s Cork supported the royal cause. Cromwell entered the city in 1649 causing much damage. Cork's humiliation was complete in 1690 when, after a five-day siege, the army of William III entered the city and the walls and other fortifications were destroyed.

Out and About

Cork City Tourist Office, Áras Fáilte Tourist House, Grand Parade ☎ (00353) 021 273 251; Fax (00353) 021 273 504. Alternatively consult the website at www.iii.ie/iii

Public Transport – For **bus travel** contact the Bus Éireann Travel Centre, Parnell Place ☎ 021 508 188, or consult the website at www.infopoint.ie/buse/
For frequent use of the bus network, purchase a Bus Éireann Rambler ticket, available for 3-day, 8-day or 15-day periods.

For information on **rail travel** contact Iarnród Éireann, Travel Centre, 65 Patrick Street ☎ 021 504 888 or consult the website at www.club.ie/RailNet/

Cork Harbour – There is a **car ferry** from Glenbrook (southeast of the city centre) to Carrigaloe near Cobh on Great Island. There are also **harbour cruises** from Penrose Quay.

Shopping – Most of the well-known brands are to be found in **Patrick Street**, the main shopping street running through Cork City centre, and in **Merchants Quay Shopping Centre**, which is also in Patrick Street. **North Main Street** is one of the oldest shopping streets in Cork. For something a little different try the **Huguenot Quarter**, a bohemian district which houses a variety of cafés and boutiques, as well as several antique shops, or the **Shandon Crafts Centre**. The **English Market** *(just off Patrick Street)* offers market-lovers a wide range of fresh produce to choose from.
For woollen goods visit the **Blarney Woollen Mills** *(see below)*.

Festivals – **Cork Guinness Jazz Festival** is an annual jazz festival, established over 20 years ago, which takes place in the last week of October and attracts over 35 000 visitors. For further details ☎ 021 270 463.

Murphys Cork Film Festival, which has been running for over 40 years, takes place in October and celebrates the best in world cinema. ☎ 021 271 711.

Entertainment – **Everyman Palace Theatre**, *MacCurtain Street* ☎ 021 501 673.
UCC Granary Theatre ☎ 021 904 275 – Range of amateur and professional productions.
The **Opera House**, *Emmet Place* ☎ 021 270 022 – Touring theatre companies and local productions.
Kino Cinema, *Washington Street* ☎ 021 271 571 – Wide selection of films.
The Half Moon Club, *just to the rear of the Opera House* ☎ 021 274 308 – Variety of jazz, blues and rock music acts.
Triskel Arts Centre ⊙ (Z F), *Tobin Street* – Film shows, art exhibitions and other activities.

Adjacent Sights – See Cobh, Kinsale, Mallow, Midleton, Youghal.

Where to Eat

Café Paradiso, 16 Lancaster Quay, Western Rd. ☎ 021 277 939; Fax 021 307 468. Very busy informal vegetarian café; good value eclectic cooking.

Isaacs, 48 MacCurtain St. ☎ 021 503 805; Fax 021 551 348. Busy and buzzing large restaurant serving eclectic brasserie dishes; good value.

Jacques, Phoenix St. ☎ 021 277 387; Fax 021 270 634. Mediterranean bistro, using good quality local ingredients; short menu but good value.

The Ivory Tower, The Exchange Buildings, 35 Princess St. ☎ 021 274 665. One of the city's best well known restaurants using local ingredients in highly individual and creative style.

Jacobs on the Mall, 30A South Mall. ☎ 021 251 530; Fax 021 251 531. Modern restaurant in converted Turkish bath; contemporary European cooking with creative touches.

Where to Stay

Killarney House, Western Rd. ☎ 021 270 290; Fax 021 271 010. Traditionally furnished house (19 rm); comfortable sensibly priced rooms with typical facilities.

Garnish House, Western Rd. ☎ 021 275 111; Fax 021 273 872. Large Victorian house (14 rm) within walking distance of the town; traditional guesthouse comforts.

Seven North Mall, 7 North Mall. ☎ 021 397 191; Fax 021 300 811. Attractive Georgian house (7 rm) providing pleasantly furnished stylish accommodation; overlooking the river.

Victoria Lodge, Victoria Cross. ☎ 021 542 233; Fax 021 542 572. Former monastery (30 rm) now offering good value no-frills accommodation, 5min from the city.

Jury's Cork Inn, Anderson's Quay. ☎ 021 276 444; Fax 021 276 144. Good value businessmen's hotel (133 rm); cheaper for tourists at weekends.

Lancaster Lodge, Lancaster Quay. ☎ 021 251 125; Fax 021 251 126. Modern hotel (39 rm) close to the city; well-equipped bedrooms with all facilities.

CORK

In the early 18C Cork received many of the Huguenots who fled from religious per-
secution in France; their presence is recalled in the name of French Church Street.
In the 19C the city lived up to its reputation of rebelliousness by being a stronghold of
Fenian agitation. The *Cork Examiner*, the city's daily newspaper, was founded in 1841.
The War of Independence and the subsequent Civil War were bitterly fought in and
around Cork. In 1920 the Black and Tans set fire to a substantial portion of the city
centre, which was later rebuilt in anonymous modern style. The political unrest was
aggravated by the deaths of two Lord Mayors of Cork. Terence McSwiney died on
hunger strike in Brixton Prison; Tomás McCurtain was shot in his bed by Crown Forces
in the presence of his wife and children.

Commercial and Industrial Centre – Cork began its involvement in trade in the 12C
exporting hides and cloth and importing wine from Bordeaux.
By the 18C the city had extended its commercial activities through the production and
sale of butter to Great Britain, Europe and America.
In 1852 Cork staged Ireland's first national Industrial Exhibition, modelled on the
Great Exhibition held in London the year before. In 1917 the Ford car company
set up its first overseas factory at the Marina in Cork; **Henry Ford**, the founder of
the American firm, was born at Ballinascarty, north of Clonakilty. The Ford factory
closed down in 1980 at the same time as the Dunlop tyre plant, set up in the
1930s. Shipbuilding also came to an end in the 1980s. Commercial activity is now
concentrated in computer manufacturing companies.

CITY CENTRE

★**Grand Parade** (Z) – The main business street of Cork contains some handsome
late-18C bow-fronted buildings hung with grey slates. Until 1800 the street was
an open channel of the River Lee lined by merchants' houses; the steps that led
down to the boats can still be seen.

★**South Mall** (Z) – The Commercial Rooms, now incorporated in the Imperial Hotel
at the eastern end of South Mall were built in 1813 for the merchants who ran
the Butter Exchange; directly opposite, at the corner of Pembroke Street, is a
doorway with the inscription *Cork Library* (**E**), the city's first major library, funded
by private subscription.

★**St Patrick's Street** (Z) – Cork's main shopping thoroughfare offers a wide variety
of departmental and speciality shops, supplemented by a large new shopping centre
in Merchant's Quay.

Grand Parade, Cork City

★Crawford Art Gallery ⊘ (Y) – The gallery, which is named after its founding benefactor, WH Crawford, presents a representative collection of 19C and 20C works by Irish artists such as William Conor, John Keating, Sir William Orpen and Seán O'Sullivan, together with works by John Hogan and Daniel Maclise, two noted 19C Cork artists, and works by modern Irish artists.

Other exhibits include late-19C Japanese Samurai armour and a collection of Classical casts from the Vatican. There are frequent touring exhibitions of contemporary Irish and European art.

The gallery building, erected in 1724 as the Custom House, was given in 1832 to the Royal Cork Institution, a scientific society, from which the gallery inherited its collection of casts.

Busker in Cork City

Slide File, Dublin

Cork Archives Institute ⊘ (Z B) – *South Main Street*. The copious material held by the Institute consists chiefly of historical records relating to business, local government and trade union activities, as well as family and private papers, some of potential genealogical interest.

The archive is administered jointly by Cork Corporation, Cork County Council and University College, Cork.

It is housed in Christ Church, built in 1726 on the site of a medieval church destroyed in the 1690 siege; ancient gravestones survive in the old churchyard.

Cork Vision Centre ⊘ (Y) – This urban information centre, located in the deconsecrated 18C St Peter's Church, has displays on the past, present and future of Cork, arranged around a large model (1:500) of the city.

Beamish and Crawford Brewery (Z) – The attractive old-English half-timbered façade belongs to one of the two local breweries.

University College ⊘ (X U) – University College Cork (UCC) was founded by charter in 1845, together with two other colleges in Galway and Belfast, and is now part of the National University. The original buildings were designed by Benjamin Woodward (1816–61). A walking tour starting from the main gates includes the Main Quadrangle building with its outstanding Stone Corridor, the Boole Library, the Honan Chapel which is noted for its **stained-glass windows★** by Harry Clarke, the Crawford Observatory, the Republican Grave Plot and Gaol.

SOUTH CITY

★Cork Public Museum ⊘ (X M) – The exhibits, which are attractively presented in a house in Fitzgerald Park, trace life in the Cork area since prehistoric times. The entrance hall displays the City Coat of Arms, rescued from the old City Hall which was burned in a fire in 1920. The collection of maces and other Corporation regalia includes the 1500 **silver dart**, thrown into the sea by Lord Mayors to assert the limits of the city's jurisdiction. A model of the walled city shows the extent of Cork in 1185. Prehistoric life is illustrated by a model of Iron Age metal-making methods. Local crafts include needlepoint lace made in Youghal and 18C Cork silver. The rare **Cork Republican Silver** dates from early 1922, when the fighting in the city made it impossible to send silver to Dublin to be assayed.

The adjoining park exhibits **sculptures** by five contemporary Irish sculptors.

★★St Fin Barre's Cathedral (Anglican) ⊘ (Z) – Cork's most exuberant church building (1865) was designed by William Burges in an early pointed French Gothic style and built in white limestone. It replaced an earlier church (1735) which was preceded by a medieval structure. The church has three spires, the central one rising to 240ft/73m. The apse is lit by 18 windows of stained glass. A brass plate

149

in the floor marks the burial place of Elizabeth Aldworth; she is said to have hidden in a clock-case during a Masonic lodge meeting in her husband's house in 1712 and was made a Mason to secure her silence.

The **cannonball** hanging south of the altar is said to have been fired at the tower of the previous church during the 1690 siege.

★**Christ the King Church** (X D) – *Turner's Cross.* This striking modern church was built in 1937 to a design by Barry Byrne, a Chicago-based Irish-American architect, and his partner, JR Boyd Barrett. The interior is devoid of ornamentation but the façade has a Cubist-style sculpture of Christ by American artist John Storrs. From the front of the church there is a magnificent **panorama** of the city.

★**Elizabethan Fort** (Z) – Originally built in the 1590s for "overawing the citizens of Cork", the fort was rebuilt on its present lines in about 1624 and was converted to a prison in 1835. It was burned down in 1922 by the Anti-Treaty forces before they withdrew from the city. The extensive parapets provide one of the best vantage points in Cork.

Cork Lough (X) – Despite the proximity of the houses, the large grass-fringed lake is a thriving bird sanctuary inhabited by many species, including Mandarin duck, mallard, moorhen and a large population of swans.

Nano Nagle

This relative of Edmund Burke was born near Mallow but she spent her life in teaching and in feeding and clothing the poor children of Cork. She was an early educational pioneer and in 1776 she founded South Presentation Convent, which contains her tomb and some of her personal possessions.

South Chapel (Z) – The chapel (1766) contains a sculpture of the Dead Christ, beneath the high altar; it is the work of John Hogan (1800–58), who spent his boyhood in nearby Cove Street.

Red Abbey (Z) – The square tower is all that remains of Cork's oldest building, an Augustinian friary founded in 1300. During the siege of 1690, a cannon was mounted on top of the tower, then outside the city, to batter Cork's eastern walls.

Cork Heritage Park ⊘ (X) – *Blackrock; 2mi/3km east.* The centre is housed in the outbuildings of the Bessboro estate, the home of the Pikes, a local Quaker family. The flora and fauna to be found on the estate and the adjacent Douglas estuary are presented in the Environmental Centre.

The Maritime Museum traces the history of the Pike family, who came from Newbury in Berkshire in England, their trading in wool, their shipbuilding yards and their charitable works during the Famine; it shows a scale model of Cork Harbour with its islands and tributaries, and accounts of shipwrecks.

Horse-drawn forms of transport are displayed in the stables.

The history of Cork City fire service is demonstrated with obsolete equipment.

NORTH CITY

★★**Shandon Bells** ⊘ (Y) – *St Anne's Anglican Church.* Cork's most famous attraction is the carillon of eight bells hung in 1752 in the church tower; among the tunes which visitors may play is Cork's own "anthem", *On the Banks of My Own Lovely Lee.*

The tower, which is faced in limestone on two sides and sandstone on the other two, is built of four blocks of diminishing size and has the largest clock faces in Cork. The church (1722), which has a wooden ceiling, replaces an earlier building destroyed in the 1690 siege; there has been a religious foundation on this site since 1100. Fine view from the top of the tower (133 steps).

The interior houses a collection of 17C books – a 1648 medical textbook, the *Letters of John Donne* printed in 1651 and a Bible printed in Geneva in 1648 – which belonged to the Green Coat charity school built nearby in 1716.

Cork Butter Museum ⊘ (M¹) – The museum traces the history of the most lucrative export business in Cork in the 19C, which ended only after the First World War. The neighbouring **Butter Exchange** (1750) provided a centralised system for exports and in 1769 a Committee of Merchants was set up to control the trade; it established first three then six standards of quality and its influence prevailed until the late 19C. The display includes samples of bog butter and traditional and modern butter-making equipment.

Shandon Crafts Centre (Y A) – The old Cork Butter Market is now a crafts centre where visitors may watch such articles as crystal, jewellery and textiles being made.

Cork City Gaol ⊘ (X G) – *Convent Avenue.* The prison, designed by Sir Thomas Deane, opened in 1825 and closed in 1923. After 1878 it was used for women only, except during the period when Ireland gained its independence, when it housed men and women.

CORK

The display recalls the prison diet (porridge) and regime (oakum picking, treadmill, solitary confinement), the sort of crimes the prisoners might have committed, the role of the school (1856–79) and the hospital, the graffiti left by 20C prisoners. The audio-visual presentation, which takes place in the eastern rotunda, provides a dramatic insight into the social conditions of 19C Cork.

The **Radio Museum** shows a film about Marconi, who made some of his early transmissions in Ireland *(see p 307)*, and displays pices of transatlantic cable and relics of the early days of Cork Radio, which made its first broadcast in 1927 from the prison.

Railway Locomotive (X) – In the railway station entrance hall stands a steam **locomotive**, a 2-2-2 built in 1848; it was withdrawn in 1874 after 30 years of service.

EXCURSIONS

North of Cork

★★**Blarney Castle** ⊘ – *5mi/8km NW by N 20 and W by a minor road.* The gift of eloquent speech is said to be bestowed on all those who kiss the **Blarney Stone.** This is harder than it sounds since the famous piece of rock is set inside the parapet at the top of the castle and can be reached only by lying upside-down with a guide holding one's legs. The stone is believed to have been brought to Ireland during the Crusades. In the 16C Queen Elizabeth I commanded the Earl of Leicester to take the castle from the head of the McCarthy clan. The Earl was frustrated in his mission but he sent back numerous progress reports which so irritated the Queen that she referred to them as "all Blarney".

Much of the present castle, which is a tower house, dates from 1446; it includes the Great Hall, the Banqueting Hall, the Earl's Room and the Young Ladies' Room. It surmounts a series of passages leading to the dungeons.

Blarney Castle House★ *(private)* was built in the 1870s in the Scottish baronial style with fine corner turrets and conical-roofed bartizans; it is surrounded by formal gardens and walks giving extensive views of Blarney lake.

B Lynch /Bord Fáilte, Dublin

Blarney Castle

Rock Close, the 19C gardens, which are built on a druidic site beside the Blarney River, contain wishing steps, which should be negotiated up and down with one's eyes closed. Two dolmens are sited in the close, which has a Fairy Glade with a sacrificial rock, also said to have druidic connotations.

The **Agricultural Museum** displays a variety of 19C agricultural implements which have become obsolete owing to the application of modern technology to farm machinery.

Blarney Woollen Mills,⊘ a 19C woollen factory (restored) is operated as a commercial enterprise; visitors may make purchases in the enormous ground-floor shop.

★**Dunkathel House** ⊘ – *3mi/5km E of Cork by N 8; after the Dunkettle/Glanmire roundabout turn left (sign).*
This Georgian house was built about 1790 and stands on rising ground with a superb prospect of the estuary of the River Lee. The live-in interior is particularly appealing, with fascinating items of furniture including a rare barrel organ of 1880 which may be played. To the rear of the hall, where the ceiling and walls are hand-painted, is a bifurcating staircase with a cast of the *Three Graces* on the half-landing. An upper room is profusely hung with attractive water-colours by a daughter of the house, Beatrice Gubbins (1878–1944); some are of local inspiration; others were painted in the course of the travels which took her around the Mediterranean and to the West Indies.

Riverstown House ⊘ – *5mi/8km E of Cork by N 8; at the Dunkettle roundabout turn left onto R 639 to Glanmire; continue for 2.5mi/4km; at the crossroads in Riverstown turn right (sign).*
In 1745 the original house (1602) was rebuilt with fine **plasterwork★** by the Lafranchini brothers for Dr Jemmett Browne, Bishop of Cork.

South of Cork

Crosshaven – *15mi/24km SE of Cork by N 28, R 611 and R 612.* This popular little resort, located at the point where the Owenabue River widens to form a sheltered inlet of Cork Harbour, is a yachtsman's paradise and, since 1969, the home of the Royal Cork Yacht Club.

Boatbuilders thrive here; among their past achievements are the *Brendan (see p 200)* and the *Gypsy Moth V* in which Sir Francis Chichester sailed round the world in 1971. **Fort Meagher**, a fine example of a coastal artillery fort, commands the approach from the sea while **Crosshaven House** (mid-18C) looks down on the activity of the waterfront.

Ballincollig Gunpowder Mills ⊙ – *Ballincollig; 4mi/6.4km W by N 22.* The display in the Visitor Centre and the audio-visual presentation describe the production of gunpowder, which was discovered by the Chinese, and illustrate the history of the gunpowder mills on the south bank of the Lee.

The guided tour includes a Change House, where the powder was stored temporarily, and one of the 24 mills, a wooden building, where the powder was incorporated by two vertical millstones turning in a circular trough; one waterwheel drove two mills and each pair of mills was isolated from the others by blast walls. Many of the original buildings still stand on the site and are being restored.

Gunpowder at Ballincollig

The mills were started in 1794 by Charles Henry Leslie, a Cork banker. In 1805, under the threat of invasion by Napoleon, the British Board of Ordnance bought the mills for £17 000, increased the production and capacity and dug a canal to provide water power and transport. On Napoleon's defeat in 1815 the demand for gunpowder decreased and the mills closed. In 1833 they re-opened and by the mid 1850s Ballincollig was one of the largest industrial establishments in the Cork area, employing about 500 men and boys with a wide range of skills – coopers, millwrights, carpenters – who lived in the workers' cottages nearby. The discovery of dynamite and nitroglycerine made gunpowder obsolete and in 1903 the mills closed.

Lee Valley – *25mi/40km W of Cork by N 22. After 9mi/14.5km turn right (sign).*

Farran Forest Park – The valley of the Lee upstream from Cork has been partly drowned to provide hydro-electric power but here in the forest park the surrounding landscape remains attractive.

Continue W by N 22; 1mi/1.5km before Macroom turn left onto R 584 towards Bantry; after 2mi/3km park in the lay-by (left). It is dangerous to venture off the causeway running from the lay-by without taking local advice; water-levels can change rapidly and many parts of the area are very swampy.

The Gearagh – A great rarity, the post-glacial alluvial oak forest, known as the Gearagh, was also inundated but has recovered and is now protected as a National Nature Reserve. In the distant past, its many-branched stream, treacherous reed-beds, mud-banks and countless islands provided a refuge for fugitives from the law, notably distillers of illicit whiskey *(potheen)*. Today despite its forlorn appearance, with blackened tree-stumps protruding from the surface of the water, it is home to an extraordinary variety of flora and fauna, best visited from October onwards when vast numbers of migrant birds arrive, among them whooper swans and greylag geese, many species of duck, curlew, lapwing and golden plover.

On the cover of Michelin Green Guides,
the coloured band on top indicates the language:
*   pink for English*
*   blue for French*
*   yellow for German*
*   orange for Spanish*
*   green for Italian etc.*

DINGLE PENINSULA★★

Co Kerry
Michelin Atlas p 82 and Map 923 – AB 11

The Dingle Peninsula is a Gaelic-speaking area and contains a large number of ancient stone monuments, many from the early-Christian period. It is appreciated for its scenery and dramatic views. Brandon Mountain (3 121ft/951m) on the north coast, the second-highest in Ireland, is clothed in mountain blanket bog and takes its name from St Brendan of Clonfert *(see p 200)*, a 6C monk, who is reputed to have set out on a transatlantic voyage from **Brandon Creek**, the narrow sea-inlet at the west foot of the mountain.

HISTORICAL NOTES

From the 12C onwards Smerwick Bay and Ventry Bay were superseded by the great natural harbour of Dingle, which is almost totally enclosed. Its possibilities were quickly realised by the Anglo-Normans; in 1257 Henry III of England imposed customs duties on exports. The peak of its commercial importance was reached in the 16C when Dingle had particularly strong trading links with Spain; in 1583 the town received permission to build a wall of enclosure.

In the same year a long period of local rule by the house of Desmond came to an end when Gearóid, the rebel Earl, was killed. Three years earlier 600 Spanish and Italian troops sent to aid the Desmond Rebellion had been massacred by government forces at Dún an Óir on the west side of Smerwick Harbour. Following the rebellion of 1641 and the Cromwellian wars Dingle declined significantly as a port for nearly a century, although during the late 18C it had a substantial linen industry.

SIGHTS *In clockwise order starting in Dingle town*

★**Dingle (An Daingean)** – Population 1 536. Dingle, the principal centre of population, is the home port of one of Ireland's largest fishing fleets; when the catch is unloaded, the pier (0.25mi/0.4km long) is a scene of frantic activity; at other times it is ideal for a quiet stroll. The town has developed as a popular tourist resort with numerous restaurants.

Out and About

Crafts – In addition to the many craft shops; there is a **Craft Centre** ☉ *(Ceardlann na Coille in Ventry Road, Dingle)* with a cluster of workshops – jewellery, making of uilleann pipes and violins, knitting, feltwork, leatherwork, hand-weaving, upholstery, wood-turning and cabinet-making.

Beaches – At Smerwick Bay, Ventry Bay, Stradbally Strand.

Adjacent Sights – See Killarney, Tralee.

Where to Eat

Lord Baker's, Main St. ☎ 066 915 1277. Busy pub well known for its food–simple Irish or local seafood.

Doyle's Seafood Bar, 4 John St. ☎ 066 915 1174; Fax 066 915 1816. One of Ireland's best well-known seafood eateries; choose the bar or the restaurant.

The Chart House, The Mall. ☎/Fax 066 915 2255. Pleasant little wood-panelled restaurant serving sensibly priced modern Irish cooking.

Where to Stay

Cleevaun, Lady's Cross, Milltown. *1.5mi/2km on R 559 following signs for Slea Head Drive.* ☎ 066 915 1108; Fax 066 915 2228. Comfortable out of town guesthouse (9 rm) with pleasant views; particularly good Irish breakfast.

Pax House, Upper John St. *1mi/1.3km NE.* ☎ 066 915 1518; Fax 066 915 2461. Guesthouse (13 rm) with individually decorated rooms; quiet situation above the town; good view of town and sea.

Captain's House, The Mall. ☎ 066 915 1531; Fax 066 915 1079. Hospitable personally run guesthouse (8 rm) with pleasantly furnished rooms and many extra little touches.

Heatons, the Wood. ☎ 066 915 2288; Fax 066 915 2324. Modern spacious and very comfortable small hotel (12 rm); out of town with pleasant views of the sea.

Milltown House. *0.5mi/0.8km W by R 559 (Slea Head Drive).* ☎ 066 915 1372; Fax 066 915 1095. Small hotel (10 rm) providing comfort with a personal touch; quiet location by the sea.

The **Oceanworld Aquarium** ⓥ displays a spectacular variety of fish, some in a touch tank. The fine collection of stained glass (1924) in **Presentation Convent Chapel★** ⓥ consists of 12 lights, featuring biblical scenes by Harry Clarke.

St Mary's Church★ dates from 1862 when the earlier church (1812) was replaced; the red sandstone was quarried near Minard Castle *(see below)* and substantial financial backing was provided by Clara Hussey, a prominent Dingle businesswoman. Extensive renovation work was carried out between 1965 and the late 1970s.

In **Dingle Library** ⓥ *(next to St Mary's Church)* there is a large display of printed material relating to local history, as well as a permanent exhibition on **Thomas Ashe** (1885–1917), who took a leading role in the 1916 Easter Rising and was born at Lispole *(5mi/8km east)*.

The **Holy Stone** beside the pavement *(junction of Upper Main Street and Chapel Lane)* is a large stone (10ft/3m long) with several deep cup marks on it, which may have been cut in prehistoric times.

Slea Head (Ceann Sléibhe) – *10mi/16km W of Dingle by R 559 (sign: Ceann Sléibhe). The scenic route skirts the fine sandy beaches of Ventry Harbour.* On the south face of Mount Eagle (1 696ft/516m), both east and west of the ford at Glenfahan *(parking)*, there are many prehistoric remains – over 400 **beehive huts★** *(privately owned)* made with dry stone and mostly in perfect condition, nearly 20 souterrains and as many inscribed stones.

In good weather there is a fine **view** from Slea Head across the Blasket Sound to the Blasket Islands *(see below)*.

Great Blasket Centre ⓥ – *10mi/16km W of Dingle by R 559 via Ventry and Dunquin or via Slea Head.* The stark modern building houses a display celebrating the fine Gaelic literary tradition of the Blasket Islands, based on local folktales, which attracted the interest of foreign scholars. The centre also illustrates the traditional way of life, based on farming, with spade cultivation and donkey transport, and on fishing in the island boats made of skin stretched over a timber frame. Some islanders emigrated to America; the last inhabitants moved to the mainland in 1953.

> ### Blasket Island authors
>
> Among the better-known works are *Western Island* by Robin Flower and three novels translated from Irish: *Twenty Years A-Growing* by Maurice O'Sullivan, *The Islandman* by Tomás Ó'Criomhthain, *Peig* by Peig Sayers.

★**Blasket Islands** ⓥ – *Accessible by boat from Dunquin.* The group consists of four large and three smaller islands, as well as many rocks and reefs. The largest of the islands is the mountainous **Great Blasket** (4mix0.75m/6kmx1.2km), now a national historic park where some of the ruined buildings are being restored. Inishvickillane has monastic ruins, a house and cottage and helicopter landing-pad but for most of the year is accessible only by air; from 1974 to 1997 it was owned by Charles Haughey. In 1586 two ships from the Spanish Armada – *San Juan* and *Santa Maria de la Rosa* – foundered near the Blaskets.

Gallarus Oratory

155

★**Corca Dhuibhne Regional Museum** ⊘ – *Ballyferriter; 8mi/13km W of Dingle by R 559.* The centre illustrates many details of life and history on the Dingle peninsula: ancient monuments, Blasket Island literature, 190 folk scenes.

★★**Gallarus Oratory** – *5mi/8km NW of Dingle by R 559 (sign).* Built probably in the 9C in the shape of an inverted boat, using dry stone, this is a fine example of a corbel-built oratory in perfect condition. There are two openings, the west doorway and the east window; the doorway has a double lintel above which project two stones, each pierced with a round hole, indicating that the entrance may have been closed with a wooden door.

★**Kilmalkedar** – *5mi/8km W of Dingle by R 559 and minor road (right).* The ruined Romanesque church, probably built in the 12C, is part of a medieval religious complex and has an alphabet stone and an Ogham stone. Similar in style to Cormac's Chapel at Cashel, it has a tympanum on the east doorway and blind arcading in the nave, the walls of which survive to their full height.
The chancellor's house *(404yd/369m south)* was once occupied by the chancellor of the diocese of Ardfert *(see p 275).* St Brendan's House, a two-storey ruin, may have been a priest's residence in medieval times.
From here an old track, the **Saint's Road** *(7mi/12km),* runs up the southwest face of Brandon Mountain to the summit which is crowned by an oratory and shrine dedicated to St Brendan *(see p 200).*

★★**Connor Pass** – *5mi/8km from Dingle by the minor road (sign) NE.* From the highest mountain pass in Ireland open to vehicles (1 496ft/456m – *car park*) there are clear views *(S)* of Dingle Harbour and *(N)* of Brandon Mountain overlooking Brandon Bay and Tralee Bay separated by the Castlegregory Peninsula.

Brandon Bay – *N of Dingle via the Connor Pass.* The beautiful horseshoe bay is dominated *(E)* by Brandon Mountain and lined *(S and W)* by **Stradbally Strand★★**, the longest sandy beach (12mi/19km) in Ireland; several trackways link the main road to the beach.
Offshore at the north end are the **Magharee Islands**, also known as The Seven Hogs. At low tide it is possible to walk from Illauntannig, the largest island, on which there is an early-Christian monastery, to Reennafardarrig Island.

Minard Castle – *9mi/14.5km E of Dingle by N 86; turn right onto a minor road (sign).* The ruin *(in a dangerous condition)* occupies an excellent vantage point overlooking Dingle Bay. The great square fortress was built by the Knight of Kerry in the 15C and largely destroyed by Cromwellian forces in the 17C.

DONEGAL

DÚN NA NGALL – Co Donegal – Population 2 296
Michelin Atlas p 100 and Map 923 – H 4

Donegal is an attractive small town at the mouth of the River Eske which rises in the Blue Stack Mountains. It is a good centre from which to explore northwards into the glens and mountains, westwards through dramatic coastal scenery or southwards to the seaside resorts on Donegal Bay.

HISTORICAL NOTES

Donegal, the fort of the foreigners, was established by the Vikings. It then became the stronghold of the O'Donnell clan for 400 years until the flight of the Earl of Tyrconnell in 1607. In 1610 it was granted by the English crown to Sir Basil Brooke who laid out the town round the central triangular Diamond.
The Irish mounted an unsuccessful attack during the 1641 rebellion; during the Williamite war the town was burned by the Jacobite Duke of Berwick but the castle held out. In 1798 two French ships, carrying reinforcements for General Humbert's army *(see KILLALA),* anchored in Donegal Bay but cut their cables on learning of his defeat. The anchor abandoned by the *Romaine* is now displayed on the quay.

SIGHTS

★**Donegal Castle** ⊘ – *The Diamond.* The castle stands on a bluff on the south bank of the River Eske. The O'Donnell stronghold consisted of a tower house which was largely destroyed by Hugh Roe O'Donnell to prevent it falling into the hands of the English. The remains were incorporated into the Jacobean mansion built in the courtyard by Sir Basil Brooke, who also built the gatehouse. The five-gable façade contained living accommodation on the first floor with the kitchens below. Above the original entrance to the O'Donnell tower a large mullioned bay window was inserted to light the great hall on the first floor; its stone chimney-piece is carved with the Brooke family coat of arms.

Out and About

Craft – The famous woollen **Donegal tweed**, which is made locally, is on sale in the shops; there are demonstrations of **hand-loom weaving** ⊘ in the summer season.

For ceramics visit **Donegal Parian China** *(Ballyshannon)*.

There is a craft village on the southern outskirts of the town.

Sport and Leisure – **Rossnowlagh Strand** is ideal for bathing, surfing and horse riding.

Bundoran has sandy beaches for bathing (up and down the coast) but the town beach can be dangerous; indoor facilities at **Waterworld** ⊘ – tidal wave, aqua volcano, tornado slide, water rapids.

Adjacent Sights – See Buncrana, Donegal Glens, Enniskillen, Londonderry.

Where to Eat

The Restaurant (in Harvey's Point Country House – *see below*). Lough Eske, Donegal. *4.5m NE by T 27 Killibegs rd*. ☎ 073 22208; Fax 073 22352. Formal restaurant serving local produce in season.

Where to Stay

Island View House, Ballyshannon Rd, Donegal. *0.75mi/2km SW on N 15*. ☎ 073 22411. Friendly personally run house (4 rm); good value.

Harvey's Point Country House, Lough Eske, Donegal. *4.5m NE by T 27 Killibegs rd*. ☎ 073 22208; Fax 073 22352. Spacious period hotel (20 rm) in a picturesque laleside setting.

Sand House, Rossnowlagh. *10mi/16km S of Donegal by N 25 and R 231*. ☎ 072 51777; Fax 072 52100. Large Victorian sandstone hotel (45 rm) on the coast.

The tower has been re-roofed (1988–96), and the rooms are furnished in the style of the 1650s and present visual histories of the O'Donnell and Brooke families.

Donegal Railway Heritage Centre ⊘ – An exhibition in the old station house traces the history of the County Donegal Railway. From 1900 until its closure in 1959 its steam and later diesel trains took market produce, farmers, fishermen, shoppers and schoolchildren along the route from Derry and Strabane to the Atlantic Coast. Displays include photographs, contemporary film footage, timetables and a 1940s model of part of the railway. Carriages are being restored with a view to operating vintage train rides on a re-opened stretch of scenic line.

Donegal Friary (Abbey) – On the south bank of the estuary overlooking Donegal Bay are the ruins of a Franciscan house consisting of a church with cloisters and conventual buildings on the north side. The buildings were greatly damaged by an explosion in 1601 when the friary was occupied by the English and their ally, Niall Garbh. The friary church was used for Anglican worship until the present church in cut stone was built in 1828 beside the castle.

The friary, which was founded in 1474 by Red Hugh O'Donnell and his wife Nuala and richly endowed by the O'Donnell family, acquired a reputation as a centre of learning.

Slide File, Dublin

Donegal Castle

157

Four Masters

The four masters were Michael O'Cleary (b 1580), a Franciscan from Donegal Abbey, and three lay Gaelic scholars, who compiled the *Annals of the Kingdom of Ireland*, an account of Irish history known as the Annals of the Four Masters; the work was done in the 17C while the authors were in refuge at a Franciscan house by the River Drowes south of Bundoran *(see below)*. They are commemorated by the obelisk erected in 1967 in the Diamond in the town centre, and are also recalled in the dedication of the Roman Catholic church which was built in 1935 in local red granite in the Irish Romanesque style.

Drumcliffe Walk – From the river bridge there is a pleasant wooded walk downstream along the north bank of the River Eske overlooking the estuary.

EXCURSIONS

South of Donegal

Drive of 22mi/36km – half a day

From Donegal take N 15 S. After 4mi/6.4km in Ballintra turn right onto R 231 to Rossnowlagh.

★★**Rossnowlagh Strand** – A small village and a large hotel overlook the great sweep of sand (2.5mi/4km) which is excellent for bathing, surfing and horse riding; northwest across Donegal Bay rises Slieve League *(see p 159).*

Continue S on R 231.

Abbey Assaroe – In the late 12C Cistercian monks from Boyle Abbey settled by the Erne estuary. The history of their monastery and mill is retold in an audio-visual presentation at **Water Wheels** ⊘ in the restored mill buildings.

Ballyshannon – Population 2 420. The town, which was created a Borough by Royal Charter in 1613, is set on a steep slope guarding an important crossing point on the River Erne. In 1597 the English under Sir Conyers Clifford *(see p 114)* were defeated here by Red Hugh O'Donnell.

William Allingham (1824–89), the poet, was born in the Mall and is buried in St Anne's churchyard at the top of the hill. Another famous native was "Speaker" Conolly *(see p 251)*, son of a local publican.

Upstream is **Assaroe Lake**, which has been formed by a dam to provide power for two generating stations.

From Ballyshannon take N 15 S.

Bundoran (Bun Dobhráin) – Population 1 463. Bundoran is one of Ireland's major seaside resorts with a fine view across Donegal Bay to Slieve League; to the south rises the distinctive square mass of Benbulben north of Sligo. The rocks at the north end of the resort have been fashioned into strange shapes by the waves. On the cliffs above there is a golf course where for many years Christy O'Connor was the professional.

DONEGAL COAST★★

Co Donegal
Michelin Atlas p 100 and Map 923 – FGHI 2, 3

The coast of Donegal is a remote and sparsely inhabited region facing the full force of the Atlantic gales in winter. It has a rugged, broken coastline of deep sea-inlets and sandy beaches, backed by spectacular mountains and blanket bog. On the north coast the land is divided into fields by walls of huge round stones and dotted with tiny white houses, each with its own turf stack; the thatched roofs are roped down against the winter gales.

Out and About

Crafts – The famous Donegal tweed is on sale in several centres - Kilcar, Ardara and Downies; carpets are made in Killybegs *(see below)*. The traditional Weavers' Fair is held annually *(late-June to early-July)*.

Adjacent Sights – See Buncrana, Donegal, Donegal Glens, Londonderry.

Where to Stay

Castle Murray House, St John's Point, Dunkineely. *1.5mi/2.4km SW by N 56 and St Johns Point rd turning left at T-junction.* ☎ 073 37022 ; Fax 073 37330. Picturesque position overlooking bay (10 rm); rustic French dishes.

Bay View, Main St, Killybegs. ☎ 073 31950; Fax 073 31856. Comfortable hotel (40 rm) in town centre.

DONEGAL TO LETTERKENNY

Donegal to Naran *Drive of 70mi/113km – 1 day*

From Donegal take N 56 W. West of Dunkineely, after the turning to St John's Point, turn left; park beyond the old railway embankment.

Killaghtee Cross – In the graveyard of the ivy-covered ruins of Killaghtee Church (12C) stands a 7C **cross-slab**.

Return to N 56 and continue W. After 3mi/4.8km turn left.

Killybegs – Population 1 522. The town, a major port in the Irish fishing industry, is set on a steep hill, where the River Strager enters a deep sea-inlet. It is also famous for the hand-tufted carpets which were first produced in the middle of the 19C.

Within the gates of St Catherine's Church *(turn right uphill; car park)*, which was designed by JB Papworth in about 1840, stands the **tomb slab** *(left)* of Niall Mor MacSweeney, showing several gallowglasses.

Continue W on R 263; after 3mi/4.8km turn left onto the Coast Road.

Kilcar (Cill Cárthaigh) – Population 1 307. Kilcar is a centre for Donegal tweed; visitors can watch the weaving and buy the cloth. It stands where two rivers meet in a narrow sea-inlet with several sandy beaches in the vicinity.

Continue W. In Carrick turn left to Teelin (Teileann); take the second right to Bunglass, a steep, narrow, gated road (passing places).

★★Cliffs of Bunglass – After climbing steeply (over 1 000ft/305m) and skirting Lough O'Mulligan the road reaches the cliff top (car park) facing one of the most spectacular views in Ireland: the south face of **Slieve League** (1 972ft/601m) dropping sheer into the sea. In winter the cliffs seem dark and menacing but on a fine day the sunlight picks out the different hues of the minerals in the rock face.

Return to Carrick and turn left onto R 263. After 2mi/3.2km bear left to Malin Beg (Málainn Bhig).

Glenmalin Court Cairn – *Park in the road; 5min return on foot over the stile and along the concrete path.* In marshy ground beside a small stream are the substantial remains of a court tomb, known locally as Cloghanmore, meaning the Big Stone.

Continue to the crossroads; turn left along the coast.

★Trabane Strand – *Car park; steep steps.* The sheltered sandy bay faces south across Donegal Bay to Benbulben *(see SLIGO).*

Return to the crossroads and go straight ahead to Glencolumbkille.

★★Glencolmcille Folk Village ⊘ – The folk village was the idea of Father James McDyer (d 1987) who set up a cooperative to improve economic conditions in his poor and remote parish. Three cabins, each appropriate to a certain period – the 1720s, the 1820s and the 1920s – are furnished to reflect the local way of life: household utensils, tools for spinning and weaving, items from the dairy, turf spades and fishing tackle. Local history can be traced in the School House. Local preserves and wines are on sale and available for tasting in the **Shebeen**.

The ordinary village of Glencolumbkille *(Gleann Cholm Cille)* (population 259) lies inland from its sandy beaches guarded by a Martello tower on Glen Head (745ft/227m). In this remote and rugged valley St Columba *(Colmcille* in Irish – *see p 164)* built himself a retreat house for quiet prayer. On his feast day (9 June) pilgrims make a penitential tour (3mi/5km) of the glen between midnight and three in the morning stopping at the Stations of the Cross, which are marked by cairns, boulders, pagan standing stones and early-Christian cross-slabs.

On the edge of the village stands the **Ulster Cultural Institute** ⊘ *(Foras Cutúir Uladh),* a centre for Gaelic studies and activities, with a display on local archaeology, an archive of traditional music and a shop selling Gaelic books and tapes.

Take the road to Ardara. After 10mi/16km viewing point (left).

★★Glengesh Pass – *Car park at viewpoint.* From the head of the pass there is a fine view of the glaciated, green valley, enclosed between steep and rugged mountains. Hairpin bends carry the road down to join the river.

Ardara (Ard an Rátha) – Population 653. Ardara (pronounced with the accent on the last syllable) is an attractive market town on the Owentocker River at the head of a deep sea-inlet. It is an important centre for the production and sale of homespun Donegal tweed. The **Ardara Heritage Centre** ⊘ traces the history of the tweed industry, its devastation by government export restrictions in 1699 and its 19C revival, largely due to the efforts of philanthropists Ernest and Alice Hart. Weaving demonstrations are given and the products – rugs, jumpers etc – are on sale.

Take N 56 E.

Glengesh

Glenties (na Gleannta) – Population 802. Glenties is an angling centre at the confluence of the Owenea and Stracashel Rivers, and the home town of Patrick MacGill (1896–1937), known as the "Navvy Poet", who is honoured in a festival each August.

St Conall's Museum and Heritage Centre ⊘ is housed partly in purpose-built premises and partly in the adjoining Courthouse (1843) which contains the original courtroom, still used once a month, and three basement cells. It traces the local history through slides, films and early photos, archaeological artefacts, records of the Great Famine, relics of the Donegal Railway, 19C souvenirs of the relationship between landlord and tenants, obsolete implements and school equipment, and a display of local wildlife. St Conall, a cousin of St Columba, founded a monastery on Inishkeel *(see below)* where he died in 596.

Opposite the museum stands **St Conall's Church** (Roman Catholic) designed by Liam McCormack; beneath the steep pitched roof the windows descend to floor level revealing the surrounding water garden; the detached triangular shingled belfry echoes the sheltering conifers.

Take N 56 west. In Maas take R 261 west; after 3mi/5km turn right.

Naran and Portnoo – The twin resorts, which face Inishkeel in Gweebarra Bay, provide broad sandy beaches, cliff walks, surfing, sailing, fishing and golf.

Naran to Dunfanaghy *70mi/113km – 1 day*
E of Naran take R 261 E. In Maas take N 56 N.

★**Gweebarra Estuary** – A long bridge spans the beautiful estuary.
Continue N on N 56.

★**The Rosses** – Dunglow *(An Clochán Liath)* is an attractive small town (population 988), known as the capital of The Rosses, a bleak flat rocky Gaelic-speaking region (100sq mi/259km²) which is dotted with over 100 tiny lakes.
Take R 259 NW.

Burtonport (Ailt an Chorráin) – Population 278. This remote and tiny harbour provides a regular ferry service *(2mi/3.2km)* to Arranmore Island.

Arranmore Island ⊘ – Population 1 000. The island has an annual festival in August. The scenic attractions are rugged cliffs on the northern and western shores, and several lakes. There are six pubs which hold regular traditional music sessions; local crafts – incuding Aran knitwear – are on sale.
Continue N on R 259. In Crolly turn left onto N 56. After 1mi/1.6km turn left onto R 258; turn left to Bunbeg.

Bunbeg (An Bun Beag) – Population 1 427. Beyond the signal tower on the narrow winding Clady estuary is the tiny harbour; old warehouses line the quay. Boats sail from here to Tory Island *(see below)*.
Take R 257 N.

Bloody Foreland Head – The headland owes its name to the reddish colour of the rocks, which is enhanced by the evening sun.
Beyond the headland is a wild and remote area with many abandoned houses. Offshore Inishbofin and its sister islands point north towards Tory Island.

Tory Island (Toraigh) ⊘ – *Access by boat from Meenlaragh (Magheroarty) and Gortahork; from Gortahork follow the signs (Bloody Foreshore) and turn right down a steep hill to the pier.* The island *(7mi/11km from the mainland)* is still inhabited by Gaelic-speaking fishermen. Little is left of the monastery founded in the 6C by St Columba (Colmcille): a round tower, a Tau cross and two ruined churches. At the Tory School of Primitive Art islanders produce striking paintings in a "folk" style, including depictions of ships at sea, in strong, simple shapes and colours. Examples can be seen at the Glebe House *(see DONEGAL GLENS).*

Turn left onto N 56.

Ballyness Bay – This sheltered sea-inlet is overlooked by two Gaelic-speaking villages (population 951), **Gortahork** *(Gort an Choirce)* and **Falcarragh** *(An Fál Carrach).*

Dunfanaghy – Population 280. The small town, sited on a flat isthmus in the shelter of Horn Head, was a busy fishing port until the harbour silted up; it is now a seaside resort, with extensive sandy beaches and facilities for sailing, surfing, water-skiing and fishing. The exhibition in the **Workhouse** ⊘ illustrates life both inside and out.

★**Horn Head Scenic Route** – *30min – viewpoint.* The headland, a breeding colony for a great variety of seabirds, rises to high cliffs (over 600ft/183m) on the north coast; there is a blow-hole known as McSwyne's Gun *(SW).*
The road circles the headland providing magnificent **views**: *(W)* Inishbofin, Inishdooey and Inishbeg, three islands, backed by Bloody Foreland Head; *(NW)* Tory Island further offshore; *(E)* Sheep Haven Bay backed by the Rosguill Peninsula *(see below);* *(NE)* Melmore Head and Malin Head and on a clear day Scotland; *(inland)* Muckish Mountain and Errigal Mountain.

Dunfanaghy to Letterkenny *80mi/130km – 1 day*
From Dunfanaghy take N 56 E.

Portnablagh – From a scattered fishermen's hamlet Portnablagh began to develop into a seaside resort with the opening of the Portnablagh Hotel in 1923. The golf course is a links course designed in 1905 by Harry Vardon.

Ards Forest Park – The park (1 188 acres/481ha) extends along the north shore of the Ards Peninsula, rising to a headland, Binnagorm, overlooking Sheep Haven Bay *(bathing beaches).* Several waymarked **walks** and **nature trails** (1.5mi to 8mi/2.5km to 13km) explore the many different features: mixed woodland, Lough Lilly where white and yellow water-lilies flower in August, the Derryart River, fenland, sand dunes, salt-marsh, red deer enclosure, dolmen, ringforts, viewpoints. The whole peninsula was once a huge estate (2 000 acres/4 942ha), bought in 1782 by Alexander Stewart, brother of the Marquis of Londonderry *(see p 352),* from the eccentric William Wray who always made provision for 20 guests at dinner; in 1930 the southern part was bought by the Franciscans who replaced Ards House (c 1830) with the present Friary buildings (1966); the grounds are open to the public.

Continue S on N 56.

Creeslough – Population 299. The village sits in the shadow of Muckish Mountain (2 197ft/670m), which is reflected in the shape of **St Michael's Church** (Roman Catholic), designed in 1971 by Liam McCormack and Partners. Artists and writers such as William Butler Yeats, AE Russell, Percy French and GK Chesterton were frequent visitors.

In Creeslough turn left (E) onto a minor road.

★**Doe Castle** ⊘ – The ruined castle stands in a strategic and beautiful position on a promontory in Sheep Haven Bay protected by the sea and a rock-cut moat which was spanned by a drawbridge. A bawn encloses a four-storey keep to which an L-shaped building, two round towers and a Great Hall were added later. It is difficult to date as it was frequently attacked, damaged and repaired until its military importance declined after the Battle of the Boyne (1690).
The initials over the east entrance belong to a relative of the Vaughans of Buncrana, General George Vaughan Harte, who had served with distinction in India. At the end of the 18C he made the castle habitable and mounted several cannon from the Siege of Serringapatam on the turrets and sea front.
The **tomb slab** standing against the tower near the entrance gate is carved with an elaborate cross; until 1968 it stood in the ruins of the neighbouring Franciscan monastery. It is thought to have belonged to one of the McSweeneys, medieval mercenaries from Scotland, who by 1544 held Doe Castle and allied themselves with the English or Irish in their family disputes for possession.

On leaving the castle turn left over a hump-backed bridge; turn left onto R 245.

Carrigart (Carraig Airt) – The village is a popular seaside resort on a deep inlet.
Take R 248 NW.

Hand-loom weaving, Co Donegal

Slide File, Dublin

★Rosguill Peninsula Atlantic Drive – *9mi/ 14.5km*. The **Atlantic Drive** is a modern road which circles the Rosguill Peninsula. From the great curve of sand dunes flanked by the Rosapenna golf links, the road climbs to **Downies** *(Na Dúnaibh)*, a resort and centre for Donegal Tweed, and then skirts the high ground overlooking *(W)* the deep inlet of Sheep Haven Bay backed by Horn Head, *(NW)* the sheltered beach of Tranarossan Bay, *(N)* the promontory extending to Melmore Head and *(E)* the sandy coves and islands in Mulroy Bay.

In Carrigart take R 245 E.

The road follows the wooded west shore of Mulroy Bay to **Millford**, a good centre for fishing in Lough Fern and the Leannan River *(2mi/3.2km southwest)*.

In Millford turn left onto R 246. 2mi/3.2km N of Carrowkeel fork left onto the coast road.

Fanad Peninsula – A string of hamlets lines the east shore of Mulroy Bay and Broad Water. North of Kindrum, grass-covered dunes, dotted with white cottages and small lakes, extend to the sandy shore. The lighthouse on Fanad Head *(no access)* marks the entrance to Lough Swilly. Dunaff Head, the Urris Hills and Dunree Head come into view on the opposite shore. **Portsalon** is a small resort at the north end of Warden Beach.

From Portsalon take R 246; after 1mi/1.6km turn left onto the coast road.

★Knockalla Viewpoint – *Car park*. The north end of Knockalla Mountain (1 194ft/364m) provides a superb **view**.

At the junction bear left onto R 247.

Rathmullan (Ráth Maoláin) – Population 536. The **Flight of the Earls' Exhibition** ⊘, housed in the old Napoleonic battery beside the pier, recalls the incident in 1607 when Hugh O'Neill and Rory O'Donnell, the Earls of Tyrone and Tyrconnell took ship with their families in Rathmullan harbour, never to return to Ireland; they were bound for Spain but were forced by bad weather to land in France. In 1608 they arrived in Rome; they are buried before the high altar in the church of San Pietro in Montorio. Their confiscated estates were granted to new settlers from England and Scotland. The harbour was also the site of the kidnap of Red Hugh O'Donnell by Sir John Perrot in 1587.

By the shore stand the ruins of a Carmelite Priory, founded in the 15C by McSweeney, Lord of Fanad, who built the tower and chancel. In 1617 the Bishop of Raphoe *(see p 166)*, Knox, converted the nave and south transept into a residence, adding several windows, two corbelled corner turrets in the Scottish style and a new doorway bearing the date and his initials.

Continue SW on R 247.

★Rathmelton (Ráth Mealtain) – Population 920. This very attractive town, on a salmon river flowing into Lough Swilly, was founded early in the 17C by William Stewart. The Mall, a tree-lined street, along the south bank of the river, opens into the Square; warehouses line the quay. The ruined 17C church at the top of the hill contains an interesting perpendicular east window and Romanesque carving from Aughnish Island further down the creek.

The **Mackemie Hall** *(Back Lane)*, which now houses **Donegal Ancestry** ⊘, a family history research centre, was formerly a **meeting house** and is named in honour of the Revd Francis Mackemie, who was Rector in Rathmelton until he emigrated in 1683 to Virginia in America, where he founded the first Presbyterian church.

Take R 245 S to Letterkenny.

DONEGAL GLENS

Co Donegal
Michelin Atlas p 100 and Map 923 – I 3
Local map below

The centre of County Donegal is mountainous country traversed by long and sometimes serpentine glens: the Barnesmore Gap running south of the Blue Stack
Mountains (2 205ft/672m) to Donegal, the Barnes Gap north of Kilmacrenan to the
east of Muckish Mountain (2 197ft/670m), and Muckish Gap at the foot of the south
face. The most spectacular of the high peaks is Errigal (2 466ft/752m), a cone of
white quartzite, which towers over Dunlewy.

The county town is Lifford but
Letterkenny is the largest town
and, owing to its position, is a
good centre from which to tour
the county.

> **Adjacent Sights** – See Buncrana, Donegal,
> Donegal Coast, Londonderry.

SIGHTS *In rough clockwise order from Letterkenny*

Letterkenny – Population 7 166. The town on the River Swilly has the longest
main street in Ireland and is the seat of the bishop of the Roman Catholic diocese
of Raphoe. **St Eunan's Cathedral** was built from 1895 to 1900 in the neo-Gothic style;
the interior is decorated with Celtic carving, and the ceilings in the choir and sanctuary chapels are the work of Amici, an Italian from Rome; the Four Masters *(see
DONEGAL)* are among the figures on the pulpit, which is made of Carrara marble
with Irish marble columns.

The **County Museum** ⊘ *(High Road)*, which is housed in the old 19C workhouse,
traces the folk life and traditions of Donegal, its history, archaeology and geology.

Newmills ⊘ – The corn mill and flax mill were operated by the water power of
the River Swilly. The tour explains how the corn was dried and milled and how the
flax was treated by retting, rolling, scutching and buffering to produce linen thread.

Lake Finn – *19mi/31km west of Letterkenny by R 250 to Fintown.* From the roadside village, which faces the lovely Aghla Mountains across the lake, a track leads
down to the pier, where paddle boats are available for hire. The lakeside scenery
can also be explored by taking a ride on the **Fintown Railway** ⊘ along a narrow-
gauge track beside the lake *(30min there and back)*. The bumpy and noisy vintage
snub-nosed carriages, which give the railway its name, **Black Pig Train** (An Mhuc
Dhubh), are somewhat at odds with the serenity of their surroundings.

Colmcille Heritage Centre ⊘ – *Church Hill; car park.* The modern building beside
Gartan Lough presents a detailed exhibition on the life of **St Columba** (**Colmcille** in
Irish). There is a detailed display on the preparation of materials required for pro-
ducing illuminated manuscripts: parchment, ink, pigments.

★**Glebe House and Gallery** ⊘ – *Church Hill; car park.* The gallery stands in the
attractive lakeside grounds of an old rectory (1828), which was bought by the
artist, Derek Hill, in 1953; he was born in Southampton in 1916 and worked as
a stage designer in Munich.

Newmills, Co Donegal

Dúchas, Dublin

163

The **gallery** was built in 1982 to house the **Derek Hill Collection** of paintings by 20C artists, consisting of works by important Irish artists and inhabitants of Tory Island who paint in a primitive style producing striking "folk" works; textiles by William Morris and Middle Eastern ceramics.

The **house**, which is furnished with Japanese and Chinese prints from his travels, William Morris fabrics, William de Morgan tiles, a Tiffany lamp and Wemyss ware pottery, displays a bronze bust of Derek Hill by John Sherlock and works by Derek Hill, Victor Pasmore, Basil Blackshaw, Augustus John, Evie and Nathaniel Hone, Sir William Orpen, Oskar Kokoshka, Cecil Beaton and John Bratby.

St Colmcille's Oratory – On the hillside facing southeast over Lough Akibbon are the scanty remains of a monastery associated with St Colmcille: a holy well, two crosses and the ruins of a church in a graveyard.

★★**Glenveagh National Park** ⊘ – The park (23 887 acres/9 667ha) consists of Lough Beagh and the surrounding bog and open moorland and natural woodlands of oak and birch; in sharp contrast, on a promontory beside the lake are luxuriant gardens surrounding a romantic granite castle. The estate was created by John George Adair by the amalgamation of several smaller holdings from which he evicted all the tenants in 1861. In 1937 it was bought by Henry McIlhenny, of Philadelphia, USA, who sold the land to the Irish National Parks Service in 1975 and in 1983 donated the castle and gardens.

The **Visitor Centre**, a cluster of grass-topped pavilions, hidden in a depression, traces the history of the park and offers a short audio-visual show about the conservation of the flora and fauna, including the largest herd of red deer in Ireland contained by a fence (28mi/45km long).

The beautiful **gardens**★★ were begun by Mrs Adair and cherished and extended over 40 years by Henry McIlhenny. The planting is designed to provide colour and interest at all seasons; the stone statues and ornaments add a formal note particularly on the **Terrace** (1966) and in the **Italian Garden** (1958). From the long lawn at the centre of the

---

St Columba

St Columba (known in Irish as St Colmcille) (521–597), who was a native of Donegal, was active during the transition from pagan to Christian Ireland. He was born in Gartan of a noble family, the O'Neill, and in accordance with the custom of the times was fostered at Kilmacrenan as a boy. There are several sites in Donegal associated with his life.

Over a period of 15 years he founded monasteries at Tory, Drumcliffe, Kilmore, Swords, Moon and Durrow (553). In c 560 he embraced the white martyrdom by giving up all he loved and left Ireland for Iona off the coast of Scotland, where he established a famous monastic community. He died in 597, the year in which Augustine landed in Kent.

Pleasure Grounds, paths lead up to the **Belgian Walk**, which was constructed during the First World War by convalescent Belgian soldiers staying in the house. The **walled garden** contains an Orangery (1958) designed by Philippe Jullian. From the south end of the gardens there is a long **view** up Lough Beagh to the head of the glen below the peak of Slieve Snaght (2 441ft/683m).

The castellated façade of the **castle** conceals a large Victorian house, designed in 1870 by John Adair's cousin, John Townsend Trench. It was lit by oil lamps until 1957 and heated by a boiler which was fed with turf every three days. The furnishings, left by the last American owners, include a carpet woven in Killybegs (*see DONEGAL COAST*) to match the **drawing room** furnishings; there are paintings by George Russell in the Library.

Dunlewy Centre (Ionad Cois Locha) ⊘ – On the shore of the lake stands an old weaver's homestead, which offers weaving displays, a guided tour of the original weaver's cottage, pony treks and special activities such as story-telling boat trips. The restaurant has good views of Errigal Mountain.

The road from Dunlewy east to Letterkenny (R 251) offers wonderful **views** of the lake and its valley, known as the **Poisoned Glen**; a derelict white-stone church forms a striking landmark on the slopes.

Doon Well and Rock – *Car park.* The rags on the bush show that people still believe in the curative properties attributed to the well in the Penal Period. Until the 16C the **Doon Rock** was the place of inauguration of the O'Donnells, the chiefs of Tirconaill. Its flattened top *(5min there and back on foot)* provides a fine **view** of the surrounding country. It was near here that Sir Cahir O'Docherty *(see p 120)* was shot dead in 1608.

Errigal Mountain, Co Donegal

165

Kilmacrenan – St Columba built the first church here. The site, between the road to Millford and the Leannan River, is now marked by the ruins of a 17C church and traces of Kilmacrenan Friary, which was founded in 1537 by the local chieftain, Manus O'Donnell.

Raphoe – Population 1 900. The village of Raphoe (pronounced with the stress on the last syllable) is grouped around an attractive triangular green. In the south corner stands **Raphoe Cathedral** ☉, a Gothic church, with 18C tower and transepts, incorporating several carved fragments dating from the 10C to 17C. The see of Raphoe was established in the 12C at the monastery founded by St Adomnan (625–704), ninth Abbot of Iona, which lasted until 1835.
The gaunt ruin south of the church was the Bishop's Palace, built in 1636 by Dr John Leslie with flanking towers similar to Kanturk and Rathfarnham; it was damaged during the 1641 Rebellion and the Williamite Wars but was repaired, only to be destroyed by fire in 1839.

Beltany Stone Circle – *Due south of Raphoe; west up a stone track (sign "Stone Circle"); park at the entrance to The Potato Centre; 10min there and back on foot.* The stone circle (150yd/137m circumference; about 4ft/1m high) dates from the Bronze Age; it consists of 64 stones although there were originally many more.

Lifford – Population 1 359. The old **courthouse** *(Main Square)*, built in 1746, has been converted into the **Seat of Power Visitor Centre** ☉, containing a genealogical centre and a display on local history and the evolution of the legal system from the period when the O'Donnell clan held sway, through the Plantation of Ulster to more recent centuries, using models, talking heads, artefacts, audio-visual re-enactments of famous trials and a tour of the prison cells.

Cavanacor House ☉ – *At Ballindrait, 2mi/3km west of Lifford by N 14; turn left at sign.* The house, the oldest in Donegal, was built c 1611 by Roger Tasker, whose younger daughter Magdalen was the great-great-great-grand-mother of James Knox Polk, 11th President of the USA. It was saved from destruction during the retreat of James II from the Siege of Derry in 1689 because he had earlier dined under a sycamore in the garden. The tour of the principal rooms shows a simple Plantation house; the outbuildings contain a museum about the history of the house and a display of hand-made pottery.

DROGHEDA★

DROICHEAD ÁTHA – Co Louth – Population 24 460
Michelin Atlas p 93 and Map 923 – M 6

Drogheda is a major port on the Boyne estuary; there are extensive beaches at Bettystown to the south and an attractive coastline to the north. Inland lies the **Boyne Valley** *(see p 115)*, rich in Irish history.

HISTORICAL NOTES

The town was founded in 911 by the Norsemen, under the Dane Thorgestr. In the late 12C Hugh de Lacy, Lord of Meath, developed it into an important Norman stronghold with two separate parishes, one in the diocese of Armagh and one in Meath. Little remains of the many monasteries which flourished in Drogheda in the Middle Ages; the roofless nave and crossing tower are the only relics of **St Mary's Abbey** (Y), which was founded in 452; the **Magdalene Tower** (14C) recalls the Dominican friary, founded in 1224, where in 1395 four Irish princes submitted to Richard II. Only the **Butter Gate** on Millmount and St Laurence Gate *(see below)* remain of the town walls which were begun in 1234.
Parliament often met in Drogheda and it was during one of these sittings that Poynings' Law was enacted in 1494.

Cromwell's Massacre – During the Confederate Rebellion Drogheda was twice besieged. In 1641 Sir Henry Tichborne and Lord Moore withstood the forces of Sir Phelim O'Neill until the Earl of Ormond brought relief. When the town was again besieged in 1649 by Cromwell it was stoutly defended by Sir Arthur Aston and 3 000 men. During the siege many people who had taken refuge in St Peter's Church were burned to death when the wooden steeple was set alight. Eventually the city wall was breached on the southeast side of Millmount near St Mary's Church and, according to Cromwell's own estimate, 2 000 died by the sword in the ensuing massacre. Most of the survivors were transported to Barbados.

MILLMOUNT

The eminence on the south bank of the Boyne, possibly an ancient passage grave, was crowned by an Anglo-Norman motte and then by 18C fortifications. From the highest point there is a good **view** of the town centre on the north bank of the Boyne and of the **railway viaduct** which was built in 1855 across the Boyne estuary. Until then passengers travelling between Dublin and Belfast by rail had to leave the train on the south bank and take a coach over the river bridge to join another train on the north side.

The point where Cromwell breached the city walls is visible in the churchyard *(south-east)* of St Mary's Church (Anglican), which stands on the site of a Carmelite convent.

★**Drogheda Museum** ⊙ (Z) – The museum is housed in the old Officers' quarters (1820). The excellent display covers various aspects of local history: the medieval period; Drogheda's maritime activities; three **guild banners**; souvenirs of Friendly Societies and Temperance Groups; Victoriana; domestic utensils set out in a 19C kitchen; obsolete industrial equipment; local battles; geological collection. The neighbouring Martello Tower (restored) was seriously damaged during the Civil War.

TOWN CENTRE

The town centre is set on the steep north bank of the river; narrow lanes and flights of steps link the different levels.

★**St Laurence Gate** (Y) – Despite its name the structure is a barbican which protected the 13C gate; a section of the town wall still stands on the south side.

St Peter's Church ⊙ (Y) – The neo-Gothic building (1881) contains the shrine of Oliver Plunkett (1625–81), Roman Catholic Archbishop of Armagh, who was implicated in the Oates conspiracy, executed for high treason at Tyburn in 1681 and canonised in 1975: his head, his letters from Newgate gaol and his cell door.

St Peter's Church ⊙ (Y) – The Anglican church was built in 1753; the porch and spire were added by Francis Johnston in 1793. In the graveyard, beside the east gate, is a cadaver tombstone; beyond the gate are three rows of houses (c 1730) built for clergy widows.

Courthouse (Y) – The building with its distinctive weather vane was designed by Francis Johnston and completed in 1790.

Tholsel (Z) – The Tholsel stands at the crossroads in the town centre; a clock tower and a lantern surmount the limestone building (1770) where Corporation meetings and law courts were held until 1889.

Oliver Plunkett (1629-81)

Oliver Plunkett was a member of a notable Anglo-Irish family from Loughcrew in Co Meath. He was educated in Rome and trained by his kinsman Patrick, who became Bishop of Meath. In 1670 he was appointed Archbishop of Armagh and Primate of Ireland. Using his family connections with the establishment, particularly Viceroy Berkeley, he began to impose his authority and reverse the effect of years of neglect following the Cromwellian era and the Penal Laws. He travelled extensively in the north of Ireland administering the Sacrament of confirmation; a school was set up for pupils of all ages, priests were ordained, bishops appointed.

In response to a new wave of repression, occasioned by the marriage of the Charles II's bother, James Duke of York, to Mary of Modena, a Roman Catholic, Plunkett chose to go into hiding. Anti-monarchists in London accused him of complicity in the "Popish Plot" fabricated by Titus Oates; he was said to have organised an invasion of 40 000 men who would land in Carlingford. Plunkett was arrested in 1679 and brought to trial in Dundalk but no one would give evidence against him. He was later tried in London for treason and condemned to be hung, drawn and quartered at Tyburn. Through the intervention of his friends his body was preserved and eventually various relics were returned to Ireland.

EXCURSION

Whiteriver Mills – *Dunleer; 9mi/14.5km north of Drogheda by N 1 and R 132.* On the southern edge of Dunleer stands a three-storey 18C mill, which has been lovingly restored to working order; all the processes involved in milling are expertly demonstrated.

Cadaver tombstone, Drogheda

DUBLIN★★★

The capital of Ireland is situated on the banks of the River Liffey; downstream the port of Dublin straddles the estuary on the shores of Dublin Bay. In the 18C Dublin enjoyed a period of prosperity from which it has preserved many of its neo-Classical buildings and elegant Georgian terraces. Several garden squares and the broad green acres of Phoenix Park, as well as the banks of the canals, provide oases of tranquillity. The residential suburbs extend north to the Ben of Howth and south to Dalkey Headland. For recreation Dubliners can retreat to the sandy beaches of the east coast, or inland to the rich farming country west and north, and the wooded heights of the Wicklow Mountains to the south. At the turn of the millennium Dublin, with its lively public bars and its reputation for enjoyment, is an exciting destination for a long weekend.

HISTORICAL NOTES

Viking Settlement – The name Dublin is derived from *Dubh Linn,* the Dark Pool at the confluence of the Poddle and the Liffey; the Irish name, *Baile Átha Cliath,* means the city by the hurdle ford. The first permanent settlement beside the Liffey was established by the Vikings in the 9C at Wood Quay; at the Battle of Clontarf on the north shore of Dublin Bay in 1014 their power was curbed by Brian Bórú.

Anglo-Norman Stronghold – After the Anglo-Norman invasion late in the 12C Dublin was granted to the port of Bristol as a trading post by Henry II in 1172. Under constant harassment by the Irish tribes and an unsuccessful attack in 1316 by Edward Bruce of Scotland, the extent of the Anglo-Normans' influence waxed and waned but they never lost control of Dublin, which gradually became the seat of Parliament and also the centre of government.

Georgian Dublin – In the relative peace of the 18C, restrictions eased and trade flourished. Buildings were constructed to house public bodies; elegant terraces of houses were erected first north and then south of the river; men of property, drawn to the capital on parliamentary and other business, commissioned fine mansions.
Under the activities of the Wide Streets Commissioners, established in 1758, Dublin developed into an elegant city, embraced by the Royal and Grand Canals and bisected by the Liffey, now embanked between quays and spanned by several bridges.

Capital of the Republic – With the Act of Union (1800) political affairs removed to London and, despite being known as the "second city of the Empire", Dublin stagnated. After the brief rage of the Civil War, the city restored the Four Courts, the GPO and the Custom House to something like their former glory. The refurbishment projects carried out in the last decades of the 20C mean that Dublin well deserved the title European City of Culture awarded in 1991 by the European Union. The major public buildings have been restored and are floodlit at night. Temple Bar was transformed from a dilapidated district into a network of pedestrian streets, vibrant with pubs, restaurants, hotels, craftshops and cafés. The district west of O'Connell Street is being regenerated under the Harp Project, which began in 1999.

Literary Dublin

Several Nobel Prize winners figure in the long roll of Dublin-born writers who have achieved international fame – Swift, Mangan, Wilde, Shaw, Yeats, Synge, O'Casey, Joyce, Behan, Beckett. Their places of residence are marked with plaques or converted into museums. The major figures are named together with their work in a literary parade in St Patrick's Park. Their literary achievement, past and present, is analysed in the Dublin Writers Museum.

★★DUBLIN CASTLE ⊘ (HY) *South bank*

Symbol of British Rule – For 700 years until 1922 Dublin Castle represented British rule in Ireland. People under suspicion languished in its prisons; traitors' heads were exhibited on spikes over the gate. Early Lord Deputies operated from their own power bases in the Pale – Trim, Maynooth and Kilkenny – but in the 16C Sir Henry Sidney, who was four times Lord Deputy, took up residence in the castle and put it in good repair. Gradually the medieval fortress evolved into an administrative centre and viceregal court. In the 19C the Lord Deputy usually resided in Vice-Regal Lodge in Phoenix Park *(see below)*, staying at the Castle only for the few winter weeks of the Castle Season, which was a glittering round of levées, balls and receptions.

Construction – In 1204, 30 years after the Anglo-Norman landing in Ireland, King John ordered a castle to be built. The site chosen was high ground southeast of the existing town and protected to the south and east by the River Poddle. The original structure expanded into a rough quadrangle with a round tower at each corner on the site of the present Upper Yard. In 1684 much of the medieval castle was destroyed by fire. New apartments designed by Sir William Robinson were completed in 1688 but most of them were replaced in the middle of the 18C.

Out and About

Tourist Information – The various tourist information centres provide information to people calling in person:

– Dublin Tourism Centre, Suffolk Street;
– Irish Tourist Board (Bord Fáilte), Baggot Street Bridge;
– Dublin Airport, Arrivals Hall;
– Dún Laoghaire, New Ferry Terminal;
– Tallaght, The Square, Town Centre.

For information by phone:
– 1859 230 330 (Irish Tourist Board);
– 0171 493 3201 (Irish Tourist Board from London).

For information by fax:
– 066 979 2035.

For information by e-mail: information@dublintourism.ie

For information via the internet consult www.visitdublin.com

For credit card accommodation reservations in Dublin:
– by e-mail to: reservations@dublintourism.ie

For credit card accommodation reservations International free phone:
– 00 800 668 668 66 (from Ireland,UK, France, Germany, Italy, Sweden and Norway);
– 011 800 668 668 66 (from the USA);
– 001 353 66 92082 (from other countries).

Public Transport – Dublin city is served by a bus network and a railway line along the coast.

The **DART** (Dublin Area Rapid Transport) is a **rail service** along the coast (25mi/40km) from Howth in the north to Bray in the south. It serves three stations in central Dublin – Connolly, Tara Street and Pearse. The service operates daily between 6am (9am Sunday) and 11.45pm with trains running every 5–10min during peak times and every 15min off-peak. All-day tickets available at any station – rail only up to £3.20 according to distance; rail and bus £4. Further details from 35 Lower Abbey Street; ☎ 01 836 6222, 01 703 3592 (Customer Services); Fax 01 703 4690.

Air Link is a bus service operated by Dublin Bus *(see below)* between Dublin Airport and central Dublin; pick-up points – O'Connell Street, Central Bus Station (Store Street); Connolly Railway Station; Parnell Square West.

Dublin Bus (CIE) operates the **bus network** which covers the whole city from the Central Bus Station (Busáras) in Store Street (behind the Custom House); any bus bearing the direction *An Lár* is going to the city centre. All-day tickets available either exclusively for bus travel or for bus and rail travel combined – bus only £3.50; all-day bus and rail £5.20. All-day tours are available (north along the coast to Howth and Malahide; south along the coast to Bray and Greystones returning inland via Enniskerry. Further details from Dublin Bus, 59 Upper O'Connell Street, Dublin 1; ☎ 01 873 4222; 01 703 3028 (ticket sales); Fax 01 703 3077; www.dublinbus.ie

Nitelink buses run from the City Centre to the suburbs, every Thursday, Friday and Saturday, at midnight, 1am, 2am and 3am.

Parking – In the city centre there are **paying car parks**, **parking meters**, **pay and display machines** and **disc parking areas**; an electronic panel, advertising parking spaces, is visible from the west side of St Stephen's Green.
There is **no parking** on **double yellow lines** at any time; no parking on **single yellow lines** during the hours indicated on the time plate; no parking in **clearways and bus lanes** during the hours indicated on the time plate.

Parking bays for the **disabled** may be used only if a disabled parking permit is displayed. Cars parked illegally may be **clamped**; declamping costs £65 payable by phone by credit card only or at the Parking shop (16 Bachelor's Walk, Dublin 1; ☎ 01 602 2500) by credit card, cash or cheque (with cheque card).

Sightseeing – A **Supersaver Card**, available from the Dublin Tourism Centre, provides entry to the following tourist attractions and saves up to 30% on admission prices: Dublin's Viking Adventure, Dublin Writers Museum, James Joyce Museum, Shaw Birthplace, Malahide Castle, Fry Model Railway and Newbridge House.
Several companies organise **circular bus tours** ⊙ of the city centre on an open-top bus comprehensive tour (2hr 45min) including all the famous sights and a running commentary given by an approved guide; **hop-on-hop-off bus tours** giving unlimited travel throughout the day, with the flexibility of stopping off and visiting various sights and then catching a later bus for no extra charge.

More active sightseers may consider a **bicycle tour** ⊘ (bicycles provided) of Dublin, accompanied by a guide, who will point out the cultural and historical sights and avoid the busier roads.

A ride in a **horse-drawn open carriage** ⊘ is a more romantic and leisurely way of seeing the city; departure point St Stephen's Green *(northeast corner)*.

For sightseers prepared to go further afield there are **steam train excursions** ⊘, starting from Dublin and travelling to various provincial towns and cities.

Adjacent Sights – See Fingal, Kildare, Maynooth, Powerscourt, Russborough, Tara, Trim, Wicklow Mountains.

Dublin Region – Full-day and half-day tours to attractions in the Dublin area are organised by various bus companies: Dublin Bus *(see above)*; Irish City Tours *(see Dublin Tourism)*.

Walking Tours – Three different **heritage trails**, walking tours with historical themes, are organised by Dublin Tourism; further details from the Dublin Tourism Centre or from the website *(see above)*.

To see the famous Dublin landmarks while learning about key events in Irish history, join a specialised walking tour – **historical walking tours** ⊘, the **1916 Rebellion Walking Tour** ⊘, a **Literary Tour** ⊘, **The Real Irish Pub Crawl** ⊘, a **Musical Pub Crawl** – details from Dublin Tourism.

Shopping – The **central shopping** area extends from Grafton Street *(south bank)* to O'Connell Street *(north bank)*. Nassau Street *(parallel with the south side of Trinity College)* contains several good shops selling a range of **Irish goods** from high fashion to modest souvenirs – clothing, craftwork, pottery, Irish music and instruments, family crests.

The **Temple Bar** area offers an eclectic mix of individual little shops and outdoor stalls. Market-lovers should try the **Moore Street market** *(Mon-Sat)*, where barrow boys sell fresh fruit and vegetables; **Dublin Corporation Fruit and Vegetable Market** under a cast-iron roof *(Mary's Lane; Sat am)*, **Mother Redcaps Market** *(Back Lane near Christchurch; Fri-Sun, 10am-5.30pm)*, the oldest market in Ireland, which offers a wide assortment of goods, including antiques, bric-a-brac, knitwear and crafts; Temple Bar Market *(Meeting House Square; Sat am)* selling local produce (cheeses, sauces, bread, chocolates, vegetable drinks, pizzas, pies and sausages). For **antiques** go to Francis Street.

Craft Shops – The following offer an interesting selection of goods -

Crafts Council Retail Gallery, Powerscourt Centre, South William Street, Dublin 2 ☎ 01 679 7368.

DESIGNyard, Temple Bar, Dublin 2

Kilkenny Shop, Nassau Street, Dublin 2 ☎ 01 777 066 - for wooollen goods and domestic items

North Earl Street, Dublin

Blarney Woollen Mills, 21-23 Nassau Street, Dublin 2 ☎ 01 710 086 - for wooollen goods

Club Tricot (Blarney Woollen Mills), 49 Grafton Street, Dublin 2 ☎ 01 772 700

National Museum Shop, Kildare Street, Dublin 2

National Museum Shop, Benburb Street, Dublin 7

Angles, 10 Westbury Centre, Harry Street, Dublin 2 - for jewellery.

Claddagh Records, 2 Cecilia Street, Dublin 2 ☎ 01 677 0262 - for specialist folk, traditional and ethnic music.

Celtic Note, 14-15 Nassau Street, Dublin 2 ☎ 01 670 4157; Fax 01 670 4158; sales@celticnote.com; www.celticnote.com for Irish music.

Entertainment

Music – The **National Concert Hall** ☉ *(Earlsfort Terrace)* – regular programme of classical and modern orchestral music. Recitals at the **Bank of Ireland Arts Centre** ☉ *(Foster Place, Dublin 2)*.
Smaller venues offering more specialised music, such as jazz, blues etc are to be found in Temple Bar *(see p 181)*. Many pubs offer live music in the evenings *(see below)*.

Theatre – Modern and classic plays are performed at the historic **Abbey Theatre** (Abbey Street, ☎ 01 878 7222; www.abbeytheatre.ie) or at the **Gate Theatre** (Parnell Square East, ☎ 01 874 4045). Opera and musicals are performed at the **Olympia Theatre** (72 Dame Street, ☎ 01 677 7744) and the **Gaiety Theatre** (☎ 01 677 1717; Fax 01 677 1921; boxofffice@gaietytheatre.com; www.gaietytheatre.com). In October the Dublin Theatre Festival takes place.

Cinema – There is plenty to choose from at several **cinemas**, including two art-house cinemas and the **Imax Experience**, a nine-screen complex in Parnell Street.

Sports – Sporting venues include **Croke Park**, the home of Gaelic games (football, hurling), **Shelbourne Park** for greyhound racing, and **Leopardstown** (south) and **Fairy House** (north) for horse racing.

Musical Pubs

The greatest concentration of pubs is in Temple Bar. The following is a selection of pubs offering traditional Irish music:

North Bank

Keatings Pub, *Jervis Street, Dublin 1* ☎ 01 873 1567 – Traditional music every Tuesday, Wednesday, Thursday and Saturday night.

Clifton Court Hotel, *O'Connell Street Bridge, Dublin 1* ☎ 01 874 3535 – Traditional music every night.

South Bank

Brazen Head Pub, *20 Lower Bridge Street, Dublin 8* ☎ 01 679 5186 – Traditional music every night in Ireland's oldest pub (1688).

Castle Inn, *5–7 Lord Edward Street, Dublin 2* ☎ 01 475 1122 – Traditional music every Friday night.

Harcourt Hotel, *Harcourt Street, Dublin 2* ☎ 01 478 3677 – Traditional music every Monday, Tuesday and Wednesday.

The Norseman, *29 East Essex Street, Dublin 2* ☎ 01 679 8372 – Traditional music every night except Monday.

Oliver St John Gogarty, *Temple Bar, Dublin 2* ☎ 01 671 1822 – Traditional music every night (Saturday at 4.30pm; Sunday at noon).

O'Shea's Merchant Pub, *12 Lower Bridge Street, Dublin 1* ☎ 01 679 3797 – Traditional music every night.

Kitty O'Shea's, *23–25 Upper Canal Street, Dublin 4* ☎ 01 660 8050 – Traditional music every night except Thursday.

Northern Suburbs

Clontarf Castle Hotel, *Castle Avenue, Dublin 3* ☎ 01 833 2321 – Traditional music every Saturday night.

Abbey Tavern, *Howth, Dublin* ☎ 01 832 2006 – Traditional music every weekend, booking essential.

Southern Suburbs

Sean Doherty's, *Edmonstown Road, Rockbrook, Rathfarnham, Dublin* ☎ 01 493 1495 – Pub and restaurant (20min south of the city centre).

Culturlann na hEireann, *Belgrave Square, Monkstown, Dublin* ☎ 01 280 0295 – Traditional music every Friday and Saturday night; *céili* every Friday night.

Johnny Fox's Pub, *Glencullen, Dublin* ☎ 01 295 5647 – Traditional music every night *(south by N 11 and R 116)*.

Other pubs and restaurants worth a mention include:

North Bank

Slattery's, *129 Capel Street, Dublin 1* ☎ 01 872 7971 – For carvery lunches and evening snacks. Live music every night.

South Bank

Lord Edward, *23 Christchurch Place, Dublin 8* ☎ 01 454 2420 – This well-established pub and seafood restaurant is situated opposite Christchurch Cathedral.

Il Pasticcio, *12 Fownes Street, Temple Bar, Dublin 2* ☎ 01 677 6111 – Enjoy authentic Italian food in the heart of Temple Bar.

Cookes Café, *14 South William Street, Dublin 2* ☎ 01 679 0536 – One of Dublin's most fashionable restaurants draws culinary inspiration from the Mediterranean, and also serves seafood and Californian cuisine.

Davy Byrnes, *21 Duke Street, Dublin 2* ☎ 01 677 5217 – Renowned for its seafood and **mentioned in James Joyce's works.**

La Cave, *28 South Anne Street, Dublin 2* ☎ 01 679 4409 – Just off Grafton Street is Dublin's oldest French wine bar serving French food and wine.

Whelan's, *25 Wexford Street, Dublin 2* ☎ 01 478 0766 – Live music every night, including jazz, country and traditional Irish music.

Marrakesh, *11 Ballsbridge Terrace, Dublin 4* ☎ 01 660 5539 – For authentic Moroccan cuisine.

Where to Eat

Jacob's Ladder, 4-5 Nassau St, Dublin 2. ☎ 01 670 3865; Fax 01 670 3868. Informal 1st floor restaurant offering good value modern Irish fare; view of Trinity College grounds.

Cavistons, 59 Glasthule Rd, Dun Laoghaire. ☎ 01 280 9120; Fax 01 284 4054. Family run delicatessen with a lunch time fish restaurant adjacent; booking advised.

Mermaid Café, 69-70 Dame St, Dublin 2. ☎ 01 670 8236; Fax 01 670 8205. Simple, well run, busy restaurant, offering tasty modern classic dishes; Sunday brunch.

Roly's Bistro, 7 Ballsbridge Terr, Dublin 4. ☎ 01 668 2611; Fax 01 660 8535, Well run, very busy, fun bistro offering classic Irish dishes.

King Sitric, Harbour Rd, East Pier, Howth. ☎ 01 832 5235; Fax 01 839 2442. Modern establishment (8 rm) minimalistic bedrooms with lighthouse theme; strong seafood bias in restaurant.

Where to Stay

Red Bank, 7 Church St, Skerries. ☎ 01 849 1005; Fax 01 849 1598. Personally run comfortable modern bedrooms, seafood oriented menu.

Eglinton Manor, 83 Eglinton Rd, Dublin 4. ☎ 01 269 3273; Fax 01 269 7527. Red-brick Victorian House (8 rm) in elegant suburb.

Tudor House, off Castle St, Dalkey. ☎ 01 285 1528; Fax 01 284 8133. Elegant manor house (6 rm) with individually decorated bedrooms; secluded grounds; views of Dublin Bay.

Hedigan's, Tullyallan House, 14 Hollybrook Park, Clontarf, Dublin 3. ☎ 01 853 1663; Fax 01 833 3337. Late Victorian listed residence (9 rm); 15min from Dublin Airport.

Trinity Lodge, 12 South Frederick St, Dublin 2. ☎ 01 679 5044; Fax 01 679 5223. Personally run accommodation (10 rm) in a Georgian house near Trinity College.

Bewley's, Merrion Rd, Ballsbridge, Dublin 4. ☎ 01 668 1111; Fax 01 668 1999. Modern accommodation behind Victorian façade; good value; informal modern basement restaurant.

Harrington Hall, 70 Harcourt St, Dublin 2. ☎ 01 475 3497; Fax 01 475 4544. Pair of Georgian townhouses (30 rm), personally run with bright, spacious bedrooms.

Adams Trinity, 28 Dame St, Dublin 2. ☎ 01 670 7100; Fax 01 670 7101. City centre hotel (28 rm) offering spacious traditional bedrooms; award winning Mercantile bar and restaurant.

Chief O'Neills, Smithfield, Dublin 7. ☎ 01 817 3838; Fax 01 817 3839. Modern hotel (73 rm), Kelly & Ping Asian influenced restaurant.

Brownes Townhouse, 22 St Stephen's Green, Dublin 2. ☎ 01 638 3939; Fax 01 638 9000. Elegant restored Georgian townhouse (12 rm), well appointed stylish bedrooms; pleasant busy brasserie.

The Mercer, Mercer St Lower, Dublin 2. ☎ 01 478 2179; Fax 01 478 0328. Adjacent to St Stephen's Green, boutique style hotel (21 rm) with informal modern restaurant.

Brooks, Drury St, Dublin 2. ☎ 01 670 4000; Fax 01 670 4455. Designer/boutique style hotel (75 rm) in contemporary style in heart of city centre.

The Shelbourne Meridien, 27 St Stephen's Green, Dublin 2. ☎ 01 676 6471; Fax 01 661 6006. Long established hotel (168 rm); retaining traditional, grand style, famous for afternoon tea.

Clarence, 6-8 Wellington Quay, Dublin 2. ☎ 01 670 9000; Fax 01 670 7800. Contemporary boutique style hotel (45 rm) in Temple Bar district overlooking River Liffey; busy Octagon bar and imposing **Tea Rooms** restaurant serving modern Irish food.

The Merrion, Upper Merrion St, Dublin 2. ☎ 01 603 0600; Fax 01 603 0700. Imposing series of Georgian townhouses (135 rm); discreet service; most rooms overlooking gardens; selection of restaurants; informal cellar bar and brasserie.

Under Attack – The most serious siege occurred in 1534 when Thomas Fitzgerald, known as "Silken Thomas" because of the silk embroidery on his men's apparel, was acting as Vice Deputy during his father's absence in London. On hearing a false report that his father had been beheaded, he relinquished the sword of state and threatened the citizens to allow him to lay siege to the castle in what was known as the Kildare or Geraldine Revolt. The citizens warned the Constable of the castle and supplied him with stores; when they heard that the king's men were coming they turned against Fitzgerald. The besieged proclaimed the arrival of the king's army and made a sortie; the besiegers took fright and scattered. Fitzgerald himself escaped but he was forced to surrender some months later and was executed in London together with his five uncles.

The last attack on the castle was during the Easter Rising in 1916 when the rebels commanded the approaches and main gate from the roof of the City Hall; after about three hours the regular soldiers regained command of the Upper Yard.

Tour *1hr; entrance via Lower Yard*

State Apartments – *Upper Yard.* The upper floor on the south side of the Upper Yard was built between 1750 and 1780 and altered on several occasions. All the carpets were made in Killybegs *(see DONEGAL COAST)*.

Beyond the hexagonal sentry boxes flanking the entrance the **Grand Staircase** ascends to the **Battleaxe Landing**, named after the weapons carried by the Viceroy's bodyguard.

A suite of rooms includes the one where James Connolly, one of the leaders of the Easter Rising, was held prisoner: Sheraton, Regency and Louis XIX furniture and two fine Irish **plasterwork ceilings**, from Mespil House (demolished). The windows overlook Castle Green and Queen Victoria's Wall, which was built to hide the stables.

The **Apollo Room** is furnished with an original 18C mantelpiece and a ceiling (1746) depicting Apollo, the sun god and patron of the arts and music.

The modern colour scheme in the 18C **Drawing Room** is based on a late-Ming vase. The ovals and four roundels depicting Jupiter, Juno, Mars and Venus, which decorate the **Throne Room**, are attributed to Giambattista Bellucci, an early-18C Venetian.

Portraits of the Viceroys and Venetian chandeliers hang in the **Picture Gallery**, originally the Dining Room.

Four black **Wedgwood plaques** ascribed to John Flaxman (1755–1826) adorn the Wedgwood Room; the three paintings are ascribed to Angelica Kauffmann (1741–1807).

The carpet in the **Bermingham Tower Room** echoes the rose, thistle and shamrock on the chandelier and ceiling (1777).

St Patrick's Hall was built after 1746 as a ballroom. Typical crests, helmets and banners hang above the stallplates recording the names of the members of the Order of the Knights of St Patrick. The ceiling, a symbolic representation of the relationship between Britain and Ireland, was painted by Vincenzo Valdré (1742–1814), an Italian who came to Ireland in 1774 with the Viceroy, the Marquess of Buckingham, for whom he had worked at Stowe.

Powder Tower Undercroft – *Lower Yard*. Excavations beneath the Powder Tower have revealed parts of the Viking and Norman defences – a 13C arch and relieving arch in the **Old City Wall** which enabled boatmen to enter the moat to deliver goods to the postern gate.

Church of the Most Holy Trinity – *Lower Yard*. The building, which stands on the site of an earlier and smaller Chapel Royal, was designed by Francis Johnston and consecrated in 1814. The exterior is decorated with over 100 heads carved in Tullamore limestone by Edward Smyth and his son John; the interior plasterwork is by George Stapleton and the woodwork by Richard Stewart. The scenes from the Passion of Christ in the east window are composed of old stained glass from the Continent. The arms of all the Viceroys from 1172 to 1922 are represented in wood on the galleries and chancel walls and in stained glass in the gallery windows.

Castle Hall – *Upper Yard*. The attractive two-storey building *(not open)* on the north side of the upper yard was designed c 1750 by Thomas Ivory for the Master of Ceremonies. It incorporates the **Bedford Tower**, which was named after John Russell, Duke of Bedford and Lord Lieutenant, and built on the base of the west tower of the original castle gate. Four days before the state visit of Edward VII and Queen Alexandra in 1907 the Crown Jewels were stolen from the Office of Arms in the Bedford Tower; they have never been recovered.

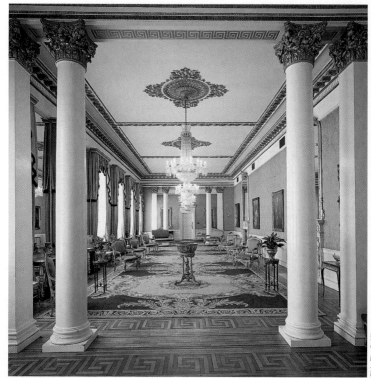

Slide File, Dublin

Drawing Room, Dublin Castle

Flanking Castle Hall are two gates surmounted by statues by Van Nost: *Fortitude* on the west gate and *Justice* on the east gate, which was the sole entrance until the west gate was opened in 1988 and a new bridge built; the fountain and pool recall the old moat. In wet weather the scales of Justice used to dip unevenly until holes were bored to drain the rainwater from the outer pan.

★★★**Chester Beatty Library** ⊘ – The collection of Islamic and Far Eastern Art, made by Sir Alfred Chester Beatty (1875–1968), is sympathetically displayed in an extended 18C building known as the Clock Tower; good **view** from the roof.

The Library has a large and renowned collection of **Arabic, Persian and Turkish manuscripts.** There are over 270 copies of the **Koran** among the Islamic manuscripts, including illuminations by some of the greatest master calligraphers.

Biblical material consists of Syriac, Armenian, Ethiopian and Coptic texts, also early Western Bibles and Books of Hours. Of international importance are the biblical papyri dating from the early 2C to 4C.

The **Japanese and Chinese collection** includes paintings and prints of the highest quality, including Japanese woodblock prints which influenced 19C European art, and a large collection of snuff bottles, *netsuke*, jade books and rhinoceros-horn cups.

The **Western European collection** contains many important printed books. The print collection includes works by Dürer, Holbein, Piranesi, Bartolozzi and many others.

OLD TOWN *South bank – 1 day*

The heart of old Dublin occupies the ridge between the Liffey and its southern tributary, the Poddle River, which now flows underground. The Vikings settled on the south bank of the Liffey at **Wood Quay** (HY **196**) (4 acres/1.62ha), where the modern Civic Offices of Dublin Corporation now stand; excavations (1974–81) revealed the remains of 150 Viking buildings at 13 different levels (AD 920–1100). Dublin Castle was raised on the south side of the ridge overlooking the Poddle. The town expanded westwards along the **High Street** (HY **78**) into the **Cornmarket** (HY **49**), where vast quantities of grain were sold for export in the Middle Ages. Little remains of the old buildings in **Fishamble Street** (HY **67**), where Molly Malone was born and Handel conducted the first performance of *Messiah* to raise funds for the Rotunda Hospital *(see below).* The **Liberties** was the name given to the area further south and west, which lay outside the jurisdiction of the medieval city; here the buildings vary from 17C high-gable houses built by French Huguenot refugees to 19C mansion flats and 20C modern housing estates.

★★**Christ Church Cathedral** ⊘ (HY) – The cathedral, which is a combination of the Romanesque and Early English Gothic styles, is the seat of the Anglican Bishop of Dublin and Glendalough and the Metropolitan Cathedral of the Southern Province of the Church of Ireland, second only to Armagh. Until 1871 it was also the state church where the officers of the Crown were instituted. The foundation dates from 1038 when a wooden church was built by Dunan, the first Bishop of Dublin, on land provided by Sitric, the Viking King of Dublin. Soon after 1170 this building was replaced by a stone church built by the Anglo-Normans and served by a community of Augustinian canons, who were replaced at the Dissolution (1541) by the Dean and Chapter.

In the 19C restoration, carried out under George Street, the Long Choir of John de St Paul (1358) was demolished. The floor is paved with encaustic tiles copied from the 13C originals in the Chapel of St Laud.

The elegant **Romanesque south door** overlooks the ruins of the Chapter House.

The **nave** was built early in the 13C in the Early English Gothic style; the north wall, supported by buttresses, is original but the south wall collapsed in 1562 and was rebuilt in the 19C. Some of the cathedral musicians are commemorated in the northwest corner. George Street converted the north porch into the **baptistery**; the **font** is composed of different-coloured Irish marble. The coat of arms in the north transept belongs to Sir Henry Sidney, Lord Deputy of Ireland under Elizabeth I. The **brass eagle lectern** is medieval but the pulpit and the choir screen, which is surmounted by a replica of the Cross of Cong, date from 1872. The sanctuary contains the bishop's throne and the carved oak stalls for the canons. The ambulatory leads to the Chapel of St Laud, which is paved with some of the original 13C tiles; hanging on the wall *(right)* is a casket containing the heart of St Laurence O'Toole, the second Archbishop of Dublin. The south transept shows the transition from Romanesque to Gothic.

The **"Strongbow" monument** in the south aisle commemorates Richard de Clare, Earl of Pembroke, known as "Strongbow", who initiated the building of the cathedral and died in 1176. The short stone figure is probably the original, which was broken when the south nave wall collapsed; the full-length figure, which bears the arms of the FitzOsbert family from Drogheda, was supplied by Sir Henry Sidney; "Strongbow's tomb" was frequently specified in legal contracts as the place of payment.

The 12C Norman **crypt** *(access in the south aisle)* was originally used for services, then let to shopkeepers and afterwards used for burials until the mid 19C; it now houses the **stocks** (1670) which formerly stood in the churchyard.

DUBLIN
CENTRE

Dublinia ⏱ **(HY)** – The Synod Hall, linked to the cathedral by an arch, presents an informative review of the early years of local history (1170–1540) using artefacts on loan from the National Museum and an interactive exhibition of a medieval fayre, a scale model of the city *(upstairs)* and reconstructions based on the dockside at Wood Quay and a medieval merchant's house.

From the top of St Michael's Tower *(96 steps)* there is a fine **view**.

★★St Patrick's Cathedral ⏱ **(HZ)** – As John Comyn, who was appointed Archbishop of Dublin by Henry II in 1181, disliked living next to Christ Church *(see above)* under the jurisdiction of the City Provosts, he moved south to the site of a holy well where, according to tradition, converts were baptised by St Patrick in the 5C. Comyn's immediate successor, Henry de Loundres, promoted the church to a cathedral and began a new building in the Early English style which was dedicated in 1254; the Lady Chapel was added c 1270. The present tower dates from 1370. Little of the original fabric remains owing to a fire in 1362 and extensive restoration work commissioned by the Guinness family in the 19C.

The tomb of **Jonathan Swift**, Dean of St Patrick's from 1713 to 1745, is marked by a bronze plaque in the floor near the main door beside that of his friend "Stella"; his epitaph, which he himself wrote, is inscribed over the door in the south wall next to his bust. In the north transept are displayed his death-mask, publications by and about him, his chair, altar-table and movable pulpit. He composed the inscription on the black marble tomb of the **Duke of Schomberg** *(see p 116) (north choir aisle)*, and put up a plaque *(south transept)* to his servant, Alexander McGee.

The vaulted **baptistery** in the southwest corner of the nave was probably the entrance to the church built by Comyn. The 13C floor tiles, transferred from the south transept in the 19C restoration, have been copied throughout the cathedral. At the west end of the nave stands the old door of the Chapter House; the hole was cut in 1492 so that the Earl of Kildare could "chance his arm" in a conciliatory gesture to Black James Ormond who had taken refuge in the Chapter House; they had quarrelled because Lord Ormond had been appointed Lord Deputy in place of Kildare who had failed to oppose Perkin Warbeck, a pretender to the English throne. The huge **Boyle Monument**, erected by the Great Earl of Cork in memory of his second wife Catherine, is the work of the sculptor, Edward Tingham. On the west wall are the arms of five of the Archbishops of Dublin between 1555 and 1678, painted in oil on wooden panels. One of the Celtic **cross-slabs** once marked the site of St Patrick's Well. An attractive sculpture commemorates **O'Carolan** *(see BOYLE)*, a friend of Swift. In the north aisle stands a statue by Edward Smyth of the Marquess of Buckingham, Viceroy and first Grand Master of the **Order of St Patrick** instituted in 1783 by George III. Until 1871 the cathedral was the chapel of the Order; the knight's banners hang in the choir above the stalls, which are labelled with their escutcheons.

Jonathan Swift (1667–1745)

The famous Dean of St Patrick's Cathedral was born in Dublin in 1667 and educated at Kilkenny and Trinity College, Dublin. In 1689 he became Secretary to Sir William Temple of Moor Park in England but failed to secure advancement. Back in Ireland he was ordained in 1694 and appointed as prebendary of Kilroot, near Carrickfergus, where he wrote his first book, *A Tale of a Tub*, a satire on "corruptions in religion and learning", published in 1704 together with *The Battle of the Books*. He tried a second time to advance his career in England but, on Temple's death in 1699, he again returned to Ireland; in 1701 he became Vicar of Laracor, south of Trim, and a prebendary of St Patrick's Cathedral; he was appointed Dean of St Patrick's in 1713.

Swift is best remembered as the author of *Gulliver's Travels* but he wrote many pamphlets on church matters, on politics and about Ireland, including the delightfully satirical *A Modest Proposal* (1729) for disposing of unwanted babies. His *Journal to Stella*, a collection of intimate letters, was addressed to Esther Johnson, whom he met in 1696 at Moor Park; in 1700 she settled in Ireland with a companion, Rebecca Dingley; according to some reports she and Swift were married in the Deanery garden but they never lived together as man and wife.

Swift was also associated with Vanessa van Homrigh of Celbridge, whom he met in London in 1708; she died in 1723 apparently of a broken heart three years before Stella.

Swift spent one-third of his income on the poor and saved another third which he bequeathed for the founding of a hospital for the insane. At the end of his life he suffered from Ménière's disease and lost the use of many of his faculties.

The arches along the east side of **St Patrick's Park** form a literary parade of Dublin-born writers, with their dates and major works; three won a Nobel Prize for Literature.

★★**Marsh's Library** ⊘ (HZ) – The building was designed in 1701 by Sir William Robinson to house the first public library in Ireland. A portrait of the founder, Archbishop Narcissus Marsh, hangs above the stairs. The dark oak bookcases, surmounted by a mitre, divide the long room into seven bays. Beyond the office are three "cages" where precious books can be consulted behind locked wire screens. The total of 25 000 books is composed of four individual collections and contains many rare early works..

★**Tailors' Hall** ⊘ (HY) – The Tailors' Hall, built between 1703 and 1707, is the only surviving guild-hall in Dublin; it is now the head office of *An Taisce*, an organisation devoted to the conservation of the Irish environment. The elaborate entrance gate dates from 1706. The Great Hall has a stage, a handsome marble fireplace and a minute gallery with a wrought-iron railing, approached by an elegant pine staircase.

★**City Hall** ⊘ (HY) – The City Hall (1769–79) was designed by Thomas Cooley as the Royal Exchange. It was bought by the City Corporation in 1852 when economic activity declined after the Act of Union (1800). The domed **rotunda** *(entrance hall)* is decorated with **frescoes** (1914–19) by James Ward, illustrating the city's history, and **a coffered ceiling** (18C) by Charles Thorp; Thorp also created the rich stuccowork above the doors and on the ceiling of the **east staircase**, which has an elegant wrought-iron balustrade and mahogany handrail. In 1916 the building was garrisoned by the insurgents *(explanatory panel on exterior west side)*.

St Audoen's Gate (HY B) – The river gate (1275) is one of the 32 gates which pierced the Norman city walls.

St Werburgh's Church ⊘ (HY) – The foundation dates from the 12C. The present building (1715) was remodelled in 1759; in 1810 the spire was dismantled as it overlooked the castle courtyard. Lord Edward Fitzgerald, who was mortally wounded while being arrested for his involvement in the 1798 rebellion, is buried in the vaults; his captor, Maj Henry Sirr, is buried in the graveyard. A plaque commemorates **John Field** (1782–1837), composer and creator of the Nocturne, who was born nearby in Golden Lane and baptised in St Werburgh's.

St Audoen's Church ⊘ (HY A) – The old church (Anglican) was founded by the Anglo-Normans and dedicated to St Audoen of Rouen in France. The west doorway dates from the 12C; the original 13C nave is lit by 15C windows.

Brazen Head (HY S) – The old public house (1688) was the headquarters of the United Irishmen in the 18C.

TEMPLE BAR (HJY) *South bank*

The area now known as Temple Bar (28 acres/11ha) takes its name from Sir William Temple, Provost of Trinity (1628–99), who owned land which included a sand bar on the south bank of the river. A stroll through its medieval network of narrow streets and alleys and courts reveals a variety of old buildings – Georgian houses, warehouses and chapels – restored and converted to new uses, interspersed with new purpose-built property.

The area, a successful case of urban renewal, has been re-developed as a **cultural district** with theatres, cinemas, nightclubs and bars, seven centres – including DESIGNyard, an applied arts centre, and the Irish Film Centre, a national centre for film in Ireland – galleries, "alternative" shops, ethnic restaurants, hotels and public and private residential accommodation. Open spaces have been created on derelict sites – Meeting House Square for open-air performances and a market, Central Bank Plaza among the banks and insurance offices in Dame Street, and Temple Bar Square, a shopping centre.

The **Temple Bar Information Centre** ⊘ *(18 Eustace Street)* provides a list of interesting things to do and see. **Sunlight Chambers** *(corner of Essex Quay and Parliament Street)* was built as the headquarters of Lever Brothers with coloured terracotta friezes telling the story of soap. **Merchants' Hall** was designed by Frederick Darley for the Merchants' Guild, also known as the Fraternity of the Holy Trinity, the first of Dublin's 25 guilds; the arched passage through the building links Temple Bar with the river bank.

Viking Adventure ⊘ (HY) – The tour embarks on a simulated rough sea voyage which lands its passengers in Viking Dublin; the inhabitants escort them on a guided tour explaining how they first raided, then traded and settled, building wooden houses, practising their crafts, and building a church near a well as Christianity was introduced beside the old Norse religion.

A long ramp leads up round an archaeological model dig to a scaled-down cross-section of a Viking ship and a film about the voyages made by the Vikings, who navigated by the sun and stars and travelled to Russia and Istanbul.

★**Liffey Bridge** (JY) – The delicate cast-iron footbridge linking the quays was built in 1816 as the Wellington Bridge but its popular name, the **Ha'penny Bridge**, derives from the toll (a half penny) which was levied until 1919.

Millennium Bridge – This footbridge was opened in 2000.

★★TRINITY COLLEGE (JY) *South bank*
Entrances in Nassau Street and College Green

Trinity College, Dublin, sometimes known as TCD, was founded in 1592 by Elizabeth I on the site of All Hallows, an Augustinian monastery suppressed at the Dissolution. It developed according to the tradition of the Oxford and Cambridge colleges and was an Anglican preserve until the late 18C. It stands in its own grounds, **College Park**, an open space devoted to sports – cricket, rugby, running and hurling – which has diminished as buildings to accommodate the science and medical faculties have been built at the east end. The film *Educating Rita*, starring Michael Caine and Julie Walters, was filmed here.

★★★**Old Library** ⊘ – The austere building (1712–32) was designed by Thomas Burgh, Chief Engineer and Surveyor-General of Her Majesty's Fortifications in Ireland, and paid for with a government grant of £5 000. The library acquired its books by purchase or donation until 1801, when it became a copyright library. Since then the increased pace of acquisition has required new buildings: the Reading Room built in 1937 and the Berkeley Library designed by Paul Koralek in 1967. Until 1892 the ground floor was an open colonnade designed to protect the books from damp; in 1992 part was converted to provide two galleries: The Colonnades for annual themed exhibitions, and the Treasury.

★★★ **Treasury** – This gallery displays the great treasures of Trinity College Library. The **Book of Kells**, the most famous of the library's treasures, is an illuminated manuscript of the four Gospels in Latin on vellum, produced c 800; although it was kept at Kells *(see p 210)* until the 17C, it is not known if it was produced in that monastery or elsewhere. The **Book of Durrow** (c 700) is another illustrated manuscript of the Gospels in a simpler style. The **Book of Armagh** (c 807) contains the complete text of the New Testament in Latin, as used by the Celtic Church, as well as the lives of St Patrick and St Martin and the Confession of St Patrick. The **Book of Dimma** contains both the Gospels and some liturgical text; its silver shrine dates from c 1150.

★★ **Long Room** – Above the entrance door at the top of the stairs are the **arms of Elizabeth I**, a relic of the original college. The **Long Room** (209ft/64m x 40ft/12m) consists of 20 bays lined with bookcases surmounted by a gallery. The original flat ceiling was replaced in the mid 19C by the present higher wooden barrel vault to provide more shelving.
The **Irish harp** (restored), the oldest in Ireland, is at least 500 years old; it was found in Limerick in the 18C; it is made of willow and has 29 strings.

Dublin Experience ⊙ – Through photography, music and voices the audio-visual presentation *(40min)* gives an entertaining and informative account of a thousand years of Dublin history from the Viking settlement to the modern city.

Library Court – The **Campanile** (1853) was designed by Charles Lanyon. Among the trees in the centre is a sculpture by Henry Moore, *Reclining Connected Forms* (1969). The area behind the north range is called Botany Bay, after the Australian penal colony, possibly because of the students' unruly behaviour. The red-brick range on the east side, known as Rubrics, is the oldest building in the college. The south side is closed by the Library.

Front Court – Statues by Foley of Oliver Goldsmith and Edmund Burke flank the main gate. The gateway itself is paved with hexagonal wooden blocks.
The buildings date from the mid 18C; the wings terminate in the **Theatre** *(south)* and the **Chapel** *(north)*, both designed by Sir William Chambers with stuccowork by Michael Stapleton. The chapel is mainly lit by high semi-circular windows; the organ case dates from the 18C. The theatre (1777–91) is used for degree ceremonies, Senate meetings and musical and theatrical performances; it is hung with portraits: Elizabeth I, Edmund Burke, George Berkeley, Jonathan Swift.

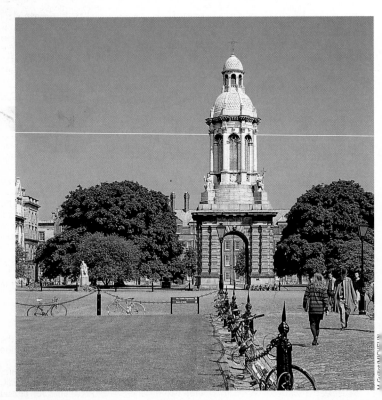

Trinity College, Dublin

Provost's House – South of the entrance gates facing College Green stands an elegant Georgian house built for the Provost in 1758.

Museum – *South side of New Square*. The Museum (1850) was designed by Sir Thomas Deane and Benjamin Woodward in the Venetian style promoted by Ruskin; the delightful stone carving of flowers, leaves and animals is by the O'Shea brothers from Cork.

COLLEGE GREEN DISTRICT *South bank*

Until the Old Parliament was built in 1728 there was nothing east of the old town but the buildings of Trinity College facing College Green (JY **45**), known as Hoggen Green, a triangular open space, formerly an old Viking burial ground *(haugen)* and meeting place *(thengmote)*.

College Green (JY **45**) – At the centre stands a statue of **Henry Grattan** by John Foley (1879) and a modern iron sculpture designed by Edward Delaney in memory of **Thomas Davis** (1814–45), poet, leader of the Young Ireland movement and founder of *The Nation*.

★★**Bank of Ireland** ⊙ (JY) – *Entrance in Foster Place*. Several architects contributed to this elegant building. The central block was designed by Pearce in 1728 to house the Irish Parliament; the south façade consists of an Ionic portico facing a square court which is flanked by two curved wings; above the pediment are replicas of three statues by Edward Smyth (1809) representing *Hibernia* between *Fidelity* and *Commerce*. James Gandon designed the east portico in 1785 and the west portico in 1797. In 1803 the building was converted by Francis Johnston for the use of the Bank of Ireland and in 1811 he designed the Armoury in Foster Place as a guardhouse for the bank.

In the **Story of Banking** an audio-visual presentation *(8min)* and exhibits of currency, bank notes and an old money cart form part of an excellent interpretation of the role of the Bank of Ireland in the commercial development of the country, since its establishment in 1783.

The old **House of Lords**, with its coffered ceiling, Irish glass chandelier (1788) and original oak mantelpiece to a design by Inigo Jones, is still intact; the tapestries (1733), woven by John Van Beaver and probably designed by Johann van der Hagen, depict William of Orange at the Battle of the Boyne and James II surveying the siege of Londonderry; the mace (1765) was retained by the last Speaker, sold by his descendants and bought from Christie's in 1937; a Bible (1772); coins, banknotes and scales for weighing sovereigns.

★**Grafton Street** (JYZ) – The most elegant shopping street in Dublin is now a pedestrian precinct; in the 19C it was paved with pine blocks to deaden the sound of carriage wheels. **Bewley's Oriental Café** ⊙ (JY **R**) with its distinctive mosaic façade and stained-glass windows by Harry Clarke was opened in 1927; the obsolete equipment in the **museum** *(top floor)* illustrates the evolution of the business which began c 1840. It stands on the site of Whytes School, which was attended by Robert Emmet, Thomas Moore, Richard Sheridan and the Duke of Wellington.

★**Powerscourt Centre** ⊙ (JY) – A most attractive modern shopping centre has been created in an 18C town house which contains some fine stucco ceilings. The house was designed in 1771 by Robert Mack for Viscount Powerscourt.

Civic Museum ⊙ (JY **M¹**) – The history of Dublin can be traced in the old City Assembly House. The Octagon Room displays maps, prints, postcards, photographs, relics of old buildings and a set of Malton's views of Dublin (1792–99). Early forms of transport are illustrated together with relics of earlier commercial practices.

St Ann's Church ⊙ (JZ) – The parish was founded in 1707 on a site provided by Sir Joshua Dawson. The building, one of the earliest Georgian churches in Dublin, was designed by Isaac Wills; the neo-Romanesque west front dates from 1868. The stained glass is Victorian; three windows in the south aisle are by Wilhelmina Geddes, a member of *An Tur Gloine (see p 87)*. The bread shelf in the chancel was established in 1723 by a charitable bequest to provide 120 loaves of bread each week for the poor.

Mansion House (JZ) – The house was built in 1705 by Joshua Dawson, a builder, and bought by the City of Dublin in 1715 as the residence of the Lord Mayor. The Round Room was added for the visit of George IV in 1821; it was here that the first Irish parliament met in 1919 to adopt the Declaration of Independence.

MERRION SQUARE DISTRICT *South bank*

The district began to develop into a fashionable suburb in the 1750s when the Duke of Leinster built the first nobleman's house south of the river; his prediction that fashionable society would follow soon proved true.

In 1815 his mansion was bought by the Royal Dublin Society; the National Museum, the National Library and the National Gallery were built in the grounds. In the 20C the mansion was converted to house the new Republican parliament *(see below)* set up in 1922.

★★**National Museum** ⊘ (KZ) – *Kildare Street. The collections of the National Museum are displayed here and at Collins Barracks (see p 190).* This museum, purpose-built in 1890 with a circular colonnaded portico, domed vestibule and elaborate decoration, concentrates on displaying the riches of the national archaeological collections.

Ground floor – An audio-visual presentation *(15min)* helps put into context the masterpieces of Irish art brought together in **The Treasury★★**. Precious objects range in date from the Bronze Age to the 15C and include: a model boat in gold from the Broighter Hoard (1C); the Loughnashade Trumpet (1C BC) *(see p 314)*; the Ardagh Chalice (8C); the Tara Brooch (8C); the Shrine of St Patrick's Bell in bronze, gold and silver (c 1100); the "Cathach", a book shrine made to contain the Psalter of St Columba (Colmcille) (12C–15C); the Kavanagh Charter Horn of ivory and brass, the only surviving object associated with Irish kingship (12C–15C).

The section on Prehistoric Ireland has a reconstruction of a passage tomb as well as the huge Lurgan Longboat, hollowed from a tree-trunk around 2500 BC. **Ireland's Gold** displays a gleaming array of artefacts, some from hoards preserved for thousands of years in the Irish boglands.

The **Road to Independence** commemorates those involved in the Easter Rising in 1916 through photos, MSS, documents, uniforms and death-masks.

Upper floor – Among the objects shown in **Viking Ireland** are artefacts from the Viking settlement at Wood Quay in Old Dublin: iron, bone, wood utensils, clothing and ornaments. St Manchan's Shrine, a spectacular reliquary, is one of several ecclesiastical treasures on display in the section entitled **The Church**.

Small in number but superb in quality, the objects on show from **Ancient Egypt** benefit from their dramatically lit display. **Irish Glass** has fine examples of this craft in which the country has long excelled.

★★**National Gallery** ⊘ (KZ) – *Kildare Street. A list of the highlights of the collection is available at the entrance; multimedia service in Gallery 7.* The statue at the entrance is of William Dargan (1799–1867), the railway magnate who sponsored the Irish Industrial Exhibition (1853), which included a Fine Art Hall. The Gallery, which displays over 2 000 works, was refurbished and rehung in 1989. Although it contained no masterpieces when the Gallery opened in 1864 in the Dargan Wing designed by Francis Fowke, a representative collection of Dutch 17C masters was soon acquired. The Milltown Rooms were added to house the Milltown Collection *(see RUSSBOROUGH)* donated in 1897. Thirty-one Turner watercolours were presented in 1900 by Sir Henry Vaughan. Sir Hugh Lane enhanced the collection with gifts and bequests. George Bernard Shaw made a generous donation in his Will including royalties from *My Fair Lady*.

Ground Floor – The Shaw Room *(Room 1 a)* presents portraits and sculpture of Irishmen and women or by Irish artists – *a Statue of Shaw* by Paul Troubetzky (1866–1938), *Earl of Bellamont* by Joshua Reynolds (1723–92). The **Yeats Gallery** presents work by Jack B Yeats – paintings of horses and portraits of family and friends. The octagonal Milltown Rooms *(Rooms 2–8)* exhibit work including furniture by Irish artists – portraits and landscapes by Hugh Douglas Hamilton, Nathaniel Hone, Francis Darby, Jeremiah Mulcahy, Daniel Maclise, William Orpen (1878–1931), Jack B Yeats (1871–1957), Seán Keating (1889–1971), John Lavery (1856–1941), 20C painters and artists who worked in France. There is a fine collection of portraits *(Room 32)*. The rest of the **North Wing** *(Rooms 33–36)* is devoted to British Painting – Hogarth, Richard Wilson, Kneller, Angelica Kauffmann, Thomas Gainsborough, Joshua Reynolds, George Romney, Richard Bonington, John Crome.

First Floor – The Dargan Wing is devoted to Baroque painting *(Room 9)* and to **French painting** (17C–20C) *(Rooms 10–13 and 15–16)*, which includes works by Claude (1600–82), Chardin (1699–1779), Géricault (1791–1824) and Sisley (1839–99). The Italian collection *(Rooms 17–21)* includes works from the Early Renaissance to the 18C, as well as 16C Venetian paintings. The North Wing *(Rooms 23-31)* contains Greek and Russian icons, early Italian religious subjects and 17C Italian works, German and Early Netherlandish works, later Flemish, Dutch paintings – genre and marine, Rembrandt and his circle, Dutch landscapes – and 15C to 18C Spanish.

★**Merrion Square** (KZ) – *Floodlit at night.* The square was laid out in 1762 by John Ensor for the 6th Viscount Fitzwilliam under the policy of the Wide Streets Commissioners. Delicate fanlights surmount the elegant doorways; commemorative plaques mark the homes of famous people – William Butler Yeats at no 82. The mature **gardens** provide a welcome contrast to the busy streets.

The southeast vista is closed by **St Stephen's Church** ⊘ (BT X), designed in 1821 by John Bowden and completed by Joseph Welland; its Greek façade, surmounted by a domed tower known as the "Pepper Canister", was inspired by three famous Athenian buildings – the Erecheum, the Tower of the Winds and the Monuent of Lysicarates. The Victorian apse (1852) is lit by a stained-glass window depicting the martyrdom of St Stephen.

★**Number Twenty-Nine** ⊘ (**KZ D**) – From 1794 to 1806 the 18C terrace house was occupied by a widow with three children, who bought it for £320 and sold it for £700. Throughout, the house is furnished with original or reproduction wallpaper, carpets and curtains, and contemporary furniture and paintings.

Features of particular interest are a water filter, a sugar cone, a hastener (for accelerating the cooking of food) and wood, tin, pewter and Delftware vessels in the stone-floored kitchen; the typical cloak rail and massive door lock in the entrance hall; knife boxes, a wine cistern designed by Francis Johnston and a plate bucket in the dining room; chandeliers and a spinet in the drawing rooms; a curved belly warmer and hair and feather mattresses in the bedrooms; a stencilled floor in the governess' room; oilcloth and dolls' houses in the nursery.

Natural History Museum ⊘ (**KZ M²**) – On entering the pillared hall and galleries the visitor is confronted by three skeletons of the Great Irish Deer, now extinct. The specimens in the display cabinets cover the full range of mammals, birds, fish and insects ever to have lived in Ireland.

Heraldic Museum ⊘ (**KZ M³**) – The display presents the banners of the recognised heads of Irish families; the arms of the provinces, counties, cities and towns; the colours of Irish Regiments which served in France in the 17C and 18C; various heraldic artefacts. The building, designed in 1860 by Thomas Deane and Benjamin Woodward as the **Kildare Street Club**, bears unusual carvings by Charles W Harrison.

Parliament ⊘ (**KZ G**) – The two houses (**Dáil Éireann and Seanad Éireann**) meet in **Leinster House**, which was designed in 1745 by Richard Castle for the Duke of Leinster and converted to house the republican parliament in 1922. The public are admitted to the public gallery which overlooks the chamber of the lower house (*Dáil*).

Government Buildings ⊘ (**KZ**) – This imposing structure in Edwardian Baroque, opened in 1911 by George V, was the last major public building project carried out in Dublin under British rule. Until 1989 parts of the building were occupied by Trinity College. A major restoration programme, the provision of well-chosen modern furniture and the display of a fascinating range of contemporary art works make a fine setting for some of the business of government, carried out in committee and conference rooms and in the office of the Prime Minister *(Taoiseach)*.

ST STEPHEN'S GREEN (JZ) *South bank*

Formerly common land first enclosed in 1663, the **gardens** ⊘ (22 acres/9ha), a delightful combination of water, flower beds and lawns, were laid out in 1880 by Lord Ardilaun, whose statue stands on the west side. A bronze sculpture by Henry Moore was erected in memory of **William Butler Yeats** in 1967. The gateway in the northwest corner commemorates those who died in the Boer War.

The green is bordered by some buildings of note. The **Shelbourne Hotel** *(north side)* was built in 1867; exotic figures flank the elegant porch and entrance. The **Royal College of Surgeons** *(west side)*, designed by Edward Parke in 1806, was captured during the Easter Rising in 1916 by a party of insurgents led by Constance Markievicz *(see p 269)*. **Iveagh House** *(south side)*, designed by Richard Castle, is now the Department of Foreign Affairs.

Harcourt Street curving from the southwest corner is lined by elegant terraces of red-brick Georgian houses with handsome door frames and fanlights.

Much of the district south of St Stephen's Green is covered by elegant Georgian terraces.

★★**Newman House** ⊘ – The two 18C town houses are named after Cardinal Newman, the first Rector of University College, which started there in 1854. The smaller house was designed by Richard Castle in 1738 and was then flanked by gardens. It has regained its original 18C appearance: glazing bars designed by Castle, marble tiled floor, early Cuban mahogany staircase. The original colour scheme of the Apollo Room has been revealed through paint scrapes; the stucco figures of Apollo and the nine Muses are the work of the Lafranchini brothers. They also decorated the Saloon on the first floor; two of the nude figures were covered in 1883 when the room became a Jesuit chapel. The larger house, which dates from 1765, contains the Bishops' Room, which is furnished with a reproduction of the original wallpaper (c 1780), a portrait of Cardinal Newman and the chair given him as Rector of the University; the staircase is decorated with Rococo plasterwork – birds and musical instruments – by Robert West.

University Church ⊘ (JZ) – The church (1854) was designed at the behest of Cardinal Newman by John Pollen in the Byzantine and Italian early-Christian style advertised by John Ruskin.

Iveagh Gardens ⊘ (JZ) – *Access from Harcourt Street or Earlsfort Terrace.* The gardens form an unexpected haven of lawns and tree-lined walks, enhanced by statuesque fountains, a rosarium and a maze.

National Concert Hall (BT **T**) – *Earlsfort Terrace*. The building, which was opened for its present purpose in 1981, was completed in 1865 as the Exhibition Palace to house the successful International Exhibition, which was opened by Queen Victoria. The Winter Gardens of glass and steel were later dismantled. The main auditorium (capacity 1 200) was inaugurated in 1865 with a concert of music by Handel, Mendelssohn and Haydn, followed four days later by a great ball. From 1908 to 1981 it was used mainly as an examination hall by University College (UCD). The new organ has four keyboards and a tracker action. The **John Field Room** (capacity 250), formerly the Sculpture Hall, is lit by a chandelier of 14 564 hand-cut pieces of Waterford crystal (20ft/6m high, 10ft/3m wide, 1 000lb in weight).

O'CONNELL STREET – PARNELL SQUARE (JKX) *North bank*

By the 18C this area had become the fashionable residential district of Dublin, centred on O'Connell Street, then known as Gardiner's Mall. The site of Parnell Square, formerly Rutland Square, was developed by Bartholomew Mosse to raise money for his maternity hospital, which occupied the south side. The houses on the other three sides were completed in the 1770s and inhabited by peers and bishops and members of Parliament. Public entertainments were held in the walled **pleasure gardens** extending behind the hospital; they were laid out with a wilderness, temples of refreshment and a terrace, called the Orchestra, where music was played. Funds were also raised from entertainments given in the **Rotunda**, designed in 1764 by John Ensor and now a cinema, and from functions held in the **Assembly Rooms**, designed by Richard Johnston in 1786 and now occupied by the **Gate Theatre** (JX **T**[1]), founded in 1928 by Hilton Edwards and Micheál MacLiammóir.

Many of the once-elegant Georgian terraces in the neighbourhood, particularly **Mountjoy Square** (BS), have passed through neglect and decay to demolition or restoration. **St George's Church** (BS), where the Duke of Wellington married Kitty Pakenham in 1806, was designed by Francis Johnston in the Greek Ionic style (1802–14) with a marked similarity to St Martin's-in-the-Fields in London.

The tradition of **public entertainment**, begun in the 18C, continues in the cinemas and theatres.

★**O'Connell Street** – The famous street, which is now lined with shops and cinemas, was laid out by Luke Gardiner in the 18C as a mall and then converted into a narrow residential square. Renamed Sackville Street, it developed into the most important street in 18C Dublin; later it was extended south to Carlisle Bridge (1794); the street and the present bridge (1880) were renamed after O'Connell in 1922.

Down the centre of the street stands a row of **monuments**: *(south to north)* statue by John Foley of Daniel O'Connell; William Smith O'Brien (1803–64), the leader of the Young Ireland Movement who was sentenced to death for treason in 1848; Sir John Gray, who organised Dublin's water supply; James Larkin (1876–1947), founder of the Irish Transport and General Workers' Union (1909); Father Theobald Mathew of the 19C temperance movement.

The **Anna Livia Fountain**, a female personification of the Liffey, soon nicknamed the Floozie in the Jacuzzi, was erected to commemorate Dublin's Millennium in 1988; it occupies the site of Nelson's Pillar (1808), which was damaged by a bomb in 1966 and demolished.

The **GPO building**★ with its Ionic portico was designed by Francis Johnston in 1814. It was the headquarters of the rebels in the Easter Rising in 1916 and still bears scars of the fighting.

The north end of the street is marked by a statue of Charles Stewart Parnell.

Irish Music Hall of Fame (IMHF) ⊘ – *Middle Abbey Street*. Through the visual panels and the sound track on the headphones the story of Irish music unfolds from the presence of Irish harpers at the court of Elizabeth I via traditional Irish music, the showbands of the 1950s, the three years of success in the Eurovision contest to Celtic rock and the 1 000 bands in 1990s Dublin.

Parnell Square (JX) – The north end has been converted into a **Garden of Remembrance** ⊘ designed by Daithí P Hanly. Celtic motifs are incorporated into the design of the gates. The central sculpture by Oisín Kelly echoes Yeats' poem *Easter 1916* with the mythological theme of the transformation of the Children of Lir into swans *(see p 257)*. The broken spears in the mosaic reflect the Celtic custom of throwing weapons into water after a battle.

The site is significant; the plans for the Easter Rising (1916) were made in a house *(plaque)* on the north side of the square and the rebels were held prisoner in the square overnight.

★**Hugh Lane Municipal Gallery of Modern Art** ⊘ (JX **M**[4]) – The gallery houses an extensive collection of late-19C and 20C works by Irish and Continental artists including the works collected by Sir Hugh Lane (1875–1915), who drowned on the *Lusitania*. The building, a three-storey mansion of Portland stone and granite, flanked by curved screen walls, was designed in 1762 by Sir William Chambers for an earlier connoisseur of art, James Caulfield, 1st Earl of Charlemont *(see p 122)*, who also built the Marino Casino *(see p 140)*.

The permanent collection includes many fine British and French paintings, among the latter several Impressionists as well as pictures by Corot and Courbet. Contemporary artworks include a characteristic project by Christo for swathing the pathways of St Stephen's Green but the most interesting rooms are perhaps those devoted to works by Irish artists. *Lakeside Cottage* (c 1929) is a typically atmospheric landscape by Paul Henry, while the dramatic canvas *The Rescue of the Prison Van at Manchester* by Maurice MacGonical reconstructs a famous Fenian attack in 1867 *(see p 93)*. A whole room is devoted to the paintings of Roderic O'Conor (1860–1940), a friend of Gauguin and an important link between artistic life in France and the British Isles; his pictures reflect the influence of his French colleagues, from Seurat to Van Gogh.

Dublin Writers' Museum ⊘ (JX **M⁸**) – The museum illustrates the personalities of those Irish writers who were associated with the city of Dublin. On display are personal items, photos, portraits, busts, manuscripts and copies of their major works. The museum also traces the written tradition in Ireland from the illuminated manuscripts of the Celtic Christian church such as the Book of Kells *(see Trinity College above)* to the present day through Jonathan Swift and his contemporaries, writers who made their names in England such as Oscar Wilde and Bernard Shaw, writers who lived abroad such as James Joyce and Samuel Beckett, the great names who promoted the 19C revival of interest in Irish folklore such as WB Yeats, Synge and O'Casey and those who lived and worked in Dublin such as Flann O'Brien, Brendan Behan and Patrick Kavanagh. Temporary exhibitions are held in the elegant reception rooms, readings and workshops in the children's section.

The museum occupies two Georgian terrace houses with **elegant stucco ceilings★**: the one in the library is by Michael Stapleton. Alterations made in 1891–95 by Alfred Darbyshire for George Jameson include stained-glass windows bearing the Jameson monogram, four female figures representing Music, Literature, Art and Science, and, in the first-floor saloon, a series of painted door panels by Gibson and an ornamental colonnade and gilded frieze.

★ **Rotunda Hospital Chapel** ⊘ (JX) – The exuberant Rococo chapel is decorated with superb stuccowork by Bartholomew Cramillion and carved mahogany woodwork by John Kelly. It is lit by an 18C lantern and a Venetian window which is filled with modern stained glass and surmounted by the Lamb of God on a book with seven seals and the figure of Charity with three children. The chapel is part of the lying-in hospital designed by Richard Castle in 1752 for Dr Bartholomew Mosse (1712–59).

James Joyce Centre ⊘ (JX) – *35 North Great George's Street*. The centre, which aims to promote an interest in the life and work of James Joyce, offers talks, conducted tours of the house and walks through the north inner city. As a boy Joyce lived nearby in Fitzgibbon Street and attended Belvedere College *(Denmark Street)*. The centre is housed in a restored terrace house, which was built in 1784 by Francis Ryan as the town house of Valentine Brown, Earl of Kenmare; the very fine plasterwork is mostly by Michael Stapleton. Portraits of members of the Joyce family line the staircase; there are family photographs in the exhibition room.

National Wax Museum ⊘ (HX **M⁵**) – The display of waxwork figures combines fantasy and reality. The tableaux on the upper floor illustrate traditional fairy tales. Those on the ground floor are peopled by national figures such as O'Connell, the heroes of the Easter Rising, the Presidents of Ireland, theatrical stars, church leaders, poets and writers, politicians, sportsmen and pop stars.

★ **Pro-Cathedral** ⊘ (JX) – The Church of the Conception of the Virgin Mary, which is in the style of a Greek temple with a Doric portico and a dome, was completed in 1821. The design has been attributed to John Sweetman, who went into exile after the 1798 rebellion, but the architect may be Louis Hippolyte le Bas, who worked for Napoleon. St Mary's has been known as the Pro-Cathedral since the 1880s, as the title of cathedral was granted by the Pope to Christ Church in the 12C.

In 1851 John Newman made his profession of faith to Cardinal Cullen in this church. The Palestrina Choir was endowed in 1902 by Edward Martyn *(see LOUGHREA)*; one of its early members was John McCormack *(see ATHLONE)*.

Tyrone House (JX) – The elegant mansion, now occupied by the Department of Education, was designed by Richard Castle in 1741.

Abbey Theatre (JX **T²**) – The foyer is hung with portraits of the actors and writers who have contributed to the Irish Theatre. The Abbey, which first opened in 1904 under the direction of William Butler Yeats and Lady Gregory, now occupies a modern building (1950s), which includes the smaller Peacock Playhouse (157 seats).

★★**Custom House** ⊙ (KX) – *Entrance in south front; floodlit at night.* The Custom House, with its long façade and central dome, is one of the most impressive pieces of architecture in Dublin. It was designed by James Gandon and completed in 1791. The building has been extensively restored, after being seriously damaged by fire in 1921, and houses government offices. The **Visitor Centre** occupies the ceremonial vestibules behind the south portico, little altered since Gandon's day. The detailed and fascinating display examines the construction of the building, the fire and restoration, Gandon's career and the work of the government offices which were housed there – excisemen, roads, canals and railways.

Famine Memorial – Six bronze figures by Rowan Gillespie, standing on the quay beside the River Liffey, recall the mixed emotions – ranging from despair through suffering to hope – of the many victims of the Great Famine *(see p 93).*

FOUR COURTS DISTRICT *North bank*

This part of the north bank of the Liffey, which was known as Oxmantown, had been settled by Norsemen. In the Middle Ages it was dominated by St Mary's Abbey. In the 17C it was built up on a grid plan around Oxmantown Green, now Smithfield, and provision was made for a hospital and free school, now the Bluecoat School.

Four Courts (HY) – The building (1785), which was designed to house four major courts – Chancery, King's Bench, Exchequer and Common Pleas – was the work of Thomas Cooley and James Gandon. In 1922 during the first hostilities of the Civil War, exploding mines and ammunition gutted the building and destroyed the Public Records Office which contained national archives dating from 1174.

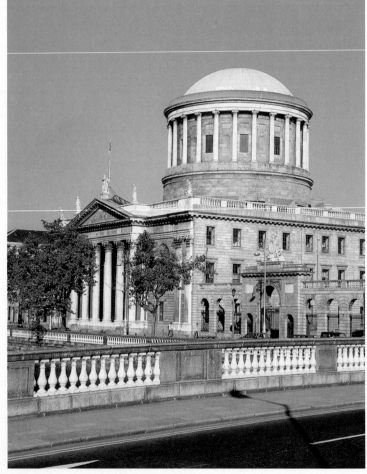

Slide File, Dublin

Four Courts

St Michan's Church ⊘ (**HY E**) – The first church on the site was probably built by the Danes as St Michan is thought to be a Danish saint. The present church dates from 1095 but its present appearance from 1686.

The **vaults** beneath the church contain some **mummified corpses** which have been preserved for over 300 years by the very dry air and the constant temperature. The **interior** displays several features of interest: the **organ** (1724), which was played by Handel; a wooden panel carved with **musical instruments** on the organ loft; the 18C **font** where Edmund Burke was baptised; the 18C **pulpit** with its curving stair; the **Penitents' Pew** where malefactors knelt to make public acknowledgement of their guilt; the **Ten Commandments** flanking the Venetian east window; the stone effigy of a **12C bishop** *(south chancel wall)* which may mark the tomb of Samuel O'Haingli (d 1121), appointed Bishop of Dublin in 1095.

Smithfield Village – The regeneration of this part of Dublin centres on an old whiskey distillery and combines both residential and commercial elements. The latter foster traditional Irish music and examples of Irish craftsmanship, available in **Cobblestones**.

Jameson Chimney ⊘ – The chimney (175ft/60m), constructed in 1895, is now flanked by a glass-walled lift and crowned by a glass observation platform – fine views of the city, the bay and the mountains to the south.

Old Jameson Distillery ⊘ (**BS V**) – Part of the old distillery, last used as such in 1971, has been converted to show current and earlier methods of production of whiskey. A video *(8min)* is followed by a tour *(20min)* which passes from the centre of a kiln, through the yard where the barley was delivered from the farms to the grain store; the mystery of worts and wash-backs in the process of making and maturing whiskey is explained. The tour ends in the bar where visitors are invited to take part in a whiskey tasting.

★**Ceol** ⊘ – The Irish word for music is the name of this centre which celebrates Irish traditional music, song and dance; the musical heritage of Ireland is presented through inter-active multi-media consoles and in the widescreen auditorium – see the soles of tap dancing shoes in action, watch the intricate steps of set-dancing, listen to folk songs and old people describing traditional musical entertainment.

Chief O'Neill's Café Bar – The bar hosts live performances by leading traditional musicians and the adjoining **White Room** is a venue for music workshops, exhibitions and live recording sessions. Chief O'Neill was one **Francis O'Neill**, who left Ireland aged 17 in 1865 to go to sea and in 1901 became Chief of Police in Chicago; despite living abroad, he collected and published many hundreds of traditional Irish tunes and melodies, thus preserving them for posterity.

St Mary's Abbey ⊘ (**HY**) – All that remains of the abbey are the **Slype** and the rib-vaulted **Chapter House**, which now contains a reconstruction of the 15C cloister arcade (the pieces were recovered in 1975 from a 17C building in Cork Street) and information about the foundation, architecture and history of the abbey and the Cistercian way of life.

St Mary's was founded in 1139 by Benedictines from Savigny but in 1147 the community adopted the Cistercian Rule and eventually came under the control of Buildwas Abbey in Shropshire, England.

It became the richest monastery in the Pale, with extensive estates both north and south of Dublin, and was closely associated with the city, acting as a repository, treasury and meeting place for the Council of Ireland. It was here that Silken Thomas renounced his allegiance to Henry VIII in 1534 and precipitated the Kildare Revolt, also known as the Geraldine Revolt.

★**Bluecoat School** (**BS F**) – The building, which is now owned by the Incorporated Law Society, was designed by Thomas Ivory in 1773; his tall central tower was replaced by the squat dome for reasons of economy. Until 1970 the building housed the Hospital and Free School of King Charles II, which was founded in 1670 for the education of poor boys; it was usually known as the Bluecoat School because the pupils wore a military-style blue uniform.

King's Inns (**HX**) – The building where barristers used to live as well as study was begun in 1795 and completed in 1827. It is the last great public building designed by James Gandon and the dining room is the only Gandon interior to survive. The west front overlooks an extensive park.

Dublin Waterways

The urban landscape of Dublin is greatly enhanced by the five waterways which traverse the city – **River Liffey**, personified as Anna Livia Pluribella, which bisects the centre as it flows out to sea in Dublin Bay; two tributaries, the **River Dodder** on the south bank and the **River Tolka** on the north bank; and two canals, the **Grand Canal** (1757–1803), which passes through the southern suburbs to join the Shannon at Shannon Harbour, north of Birr, and the **Royal Canal** (1790–1817), which passes through the Northside to join the Shannon west of Longford.

WESTERN SUBURBS *North to south*

★★**National Museum** ⊘ **(BS)** – *The collections of the National Museum are displayed here and at Kildare Street (see p 184).* This great complex, which once housed 3 000 men and 1 000 horses, was built in 1700 on the orders of King William III and designed by Thomas Burgh. It was intended to be "plain and useful, without any unnecessary ornament" and in its day was the largest institution of its kind in the British Isles, a progressive alternative to the contentious practice of billeting soldiers on the population. It has been converted to provide accommodation for several sections of the National Museum including the decorative arts, folklife, history and geology.

As well as space for temporary exhibitions, the **West Block** has galleries devoted to the work of the museum, and an enthralling array of special treasures – 25 highly varied pieces grouped together under the heading of **Curators' Choice**; they include a rare astrolabe from Prague, an elongated late-13C or early-14C wood statue of St Molaise *(see p 270)* and Bow figurines made by Thomas Frye, some of them modelled on his fellow London Irishmen.

The **South Block** has three floors of galleries: *(third floor)* Irish country furniture and woodcraft, with period furniture showing the development of furniture from Baroque to Modern, including the fascinating late-19C style unique to Ireland, Neo-Celtic, inspired by objects like the Tara Brooch discovered in 1850; *(second floor)* scientific instruments; *(first floor)* Irish silver from the early 17C to the striking work of modern silversmiths.

★★**Phoenix Park (AS)** – *Restricted access by car.* The park (1 752 acres/709ha), the largest enclosed urban park in Europe, derives its name from the Gaelic for clear water *(Fionn Uisce)*. The land, confiscated from Kilmainham Priory *(see below)* in 1543 by the Crown, was enclosed in 1662 by the Duke of Ormond who introduced a herd of fallow deer which still roam the Fifteen Acres (actually approximately 300 acres/121ha).

The history of the park is presented in the **Phoenix Park Visitor Centre**,⊘ housed in an old stable block, beside a 17C tower house which was for many years the residence of the park keeper before being incorporated into a private house (now demolished).

The southeast gate is flanked by the **Wellington Monument (N)**, designed by Sir William Smirke in 1817, and the **Peoples' Garden** *(right)*, a flower garden sloping to a small lake. Opposite are the **Zoological Gardens** *(see below)*, designed initially by Decimus Burton.

The main road, lit by gas lamps, leads to the **Phoenix Monument (L)**, which was erected by Lord Chesterfield in 1745. To the south stands the residence of the Ambassador of the USA and the **Papal Cross** erected to mark the visit of Pope John Paul II in 1979.

To the north stands the **official residence** ⊘ of the President of Ireland **(Aras an Uachtaráin)**, formerly Vice-Regal Lodge, which was built (1751–54) as a private house by Nathaniel Clements and in 1815 acquired its Ionic portico by Francis Johnston.

It was near here in 1882 at the height of agitation over the Land Act that the newly appointed Chief Secretary, Lord Frederick Cavendish, and the Under-Secretary, Thomas H Burke, the intended victim, were stabbed to death by the "Invincibles", members of a secret society.

★**Zoological Gardens** ⊘ **(AS)** – *Phoenix Park.* The Zoo, which was founded in 1830, is set in attractive parkland (30 acres/12ha). As well as keeping animals of many types from all parts of the world, it is involved in breeding programmes with other zoos and is under constant development. The **World of Cats** presents snow leopards as well as lions and other felines, while the **World of Primates** with its vivacious monkeys and sad-faced orang-utans exercises a constant appeal. Arctic foxes and snowy owls inhabit **Fringes of the Arctic**, while the lakes and their banks provides a habitat for water fowl, flamingoes, penguins and sea-lions. **City Farm** and **Pets Corner** are especially popular with children.

★**Guinness Hopstore** ⊘ **(BT M⁷)** – *Crane Street.* A free glass of the famous dark stout with the creamy head is served in the visitors' bar in the **old hop store**, at the end of a fascinating survey of the Guinness production process. The history of the Guinness family firm is traced through 140 years by means of a film *(20min)* supplemented by text, pictures and obsolete machinery.

Further west in Thomas Street is the house built by Arthur Guinness in the 18C next to the main gate of the brewery where the new date is painted up every year. St James' Gate, which pierced the old city wall, has given its name to the brewery.

Irish Museum of Modern Art ⊘ **(AT)** – *Military Road. Car park.* The role of the museum (opened in 1991) is to present 20C Irish and international art and allied theatrical and musical performances, and to establish a permanent collection through purchases and commissions. Its exciting and wide-ranging programme includes exhibitions by some of the 20th century's most influential artists and work by leading young artists from Ireland and abroad. The range of buildings facing the south front of the museum has been converted into artists' studios.

The museum is housed in **Royal Kilmainham Hospital★★**, the earliest-surviving Classical building in Ireland. It was commissioned by the Duke of Ormond, James Butler of Kilkenny, who was appointed Viceroy in 1669 after living in exile in France, and inspired by Les Invalides in Paris. The architect was William Robinson, Surveyor-General since 1670, who designed (1680–84) four ranges of buildings round a courtyard providing accommodation for 300 old soldiers, the last of whom left in 1929.

The **North Range** is occupied by the Master's Quarters, Great Hall, now used for concerts and government receptions, and Chapel.

The **Great Hall**, the soldiers' dining and recreation room, is hung with portraits specially commissioned between 1690 and 1734. The stained glass (1908) is the work of AE Child. Over the door is an oak carving

Kilmainham Gaol, Dublin

Dúchas, Dublin

(1683) by Jacques Tabary. The **chapel ceiling** is a papier mâché replica, made in 1903, of the unique Baroque stucco ceiling created in 1687 by English plasterers; after three centuries some of the fruit and vegetable motifs (max 12in/30cm long) had begun to break off. The altar, reredos and rails (1686) were carved by Tabary in Irish oak. The north front overlooks the formal gardens, designed (1710–20) by Edward Pearce to represent the crosses of St George and St Andrew.

The site, once part of Phoenix Park, was previously occupied by a monastery, founded in the 7C by Irish monks, which in 1100 passed to the Knights of St John and was later used as the Vice-Regal Lodge until demolished in 1670.

★★Kilmainham Gaol Museum ⊙ (AT M⁶) – *Inchicore Road*. The Irish struggle for political independence is excellently presented in the prison where so many Irishmen were incarcerated for offences against the Crown.

The exhibition of souvenirs, photographs, letters and press cuttings explains and illustrates the many incidents and rebellions which took place between 1796 and 1924 and their social and political context.

The **tour** includes the Central Hall (1862) containing 100 cells, the chapel with an audio-visual presentation on the history of the prison, individual cells in the 1798 corridor, and the yards where the prisoners took exercise and executions were carried out.

The New Gaol, as it was known for many years, was built in 1792 and consisted of a central range flanked by an east and a west courtyard divided into exercise yards; one contains the *Asgard (see p 192)*. In 1862, when the east wing was rebuilt, a high outer wall was constructed.

Drimnagh Castle ⊙ (AT) – *Long Mile Road*. Drimnagh is a 13C moated castle consisting of a medieval Great Hall over a vaulted undercroft, flanked by a battlemented tower. It has been restored to its medieval appearance with a formal 17C garden – box hedges, lavender bushes and herbs – at the rear.

NORTHERN SUBURBS *West to east*

★★National Botanic Gardens ⊙ (BS) – The gardens were established in 1795 on an attractive site beside the Tolka River. The glasshouses include the **Curvilinear Range** (1843–69), designed by Richard Turner, and the **Great Palm House** (1884). There is a delightful **walk** along the river bank from the **rose garden**, past the mill race, through the **peat garden** (walled) and the **bog garden** beside the ornamental pond to the **arboretum**. The specimens in the rock garden, cactus house and fern house are among the 20 000 species grown here.

GAA Museum – *Clonliffe Road*. **Croke Park** is the home of the national games of Ireland – hurling and Irish football. The museum traces the development of the **Gaelic Athletic Association** *(see p 59)* and its influence on the sporting, cultural and social traditions of Ireland. Touch-screen technology provides a view of the highlights of past games and the champions in action; visitors can test their speed of reaction and high-jumping ability or try hitting the *sliothar* with a *camán* in the practice nets.

★★**Marino Casino** ⓥ (CS) – The charming Palladian casino, designed by Sir William Chambers in 1765, was built in the grounds of Marino House (demolished 1921), the country seat of James Caulfield, Earl of Charlemont *(see pp 187 and 122)*, who had met Chambers while making the Grand Tour (1746–54). The casino is built of Portland stone in the French neo-Classical style in the shape of a Greek cross on a rusticated basement; 12 Doric columns support a frieze and cornice topped by pediments, statues and urn-shaped chimneys. The sculpture is by Simon Vierpyl and Joseph Wilton.
The interior contains four state rooms, decorated with elaborate plaster ceilings and inlaid floors using eight different kinds of wood, and four small bedrooms on the upper floor; plans of the building are displayed in the basement service rooms.

North Bull Island ⓥ – *North of Dublin by the coast road to Howth*. The island, which accommodates two golf links and attracts many summer visitors to its sandy beaches, consists of sand dunes, salt-marshes and mud-flats. It is an important **nature reserve** where many wildfowl and wading birds spend the winter; at high tide the 30 000 shore birds which feed in Dublin Bay all roost on North Bull Island. An exhibition on the wildlife and natural habitats of the island is housed in the **Interpretive Centre** *(at the end of the central causeway)*. For many years the only link with the mainland was a plank bridge to the southern end of the island. Since the Bull Wall was built in the late 18C to protect Dublin harbour from silting up, the island, which at first was only a sandbank covered at high tide, has grown to its present size (3mi/4.5km long) and continues to increase in width seawards.

★**The Ben of Howth** – The Ben of Howth is a steep rounded peninsula of rock rising from the sea on the north side of Dublin Bay.
From the high point on the east side of the headland *(car park)* there are two **cliff walks**: south past the Baily Lighthouse on the point and along the cliffs for a fine **view★** over Dublin Bay; or north past the Nose of Howth and Balscadden Bay to the picturesque village of **Howth**, which clings to the steep north face of the headland. At its heart are the ruins of **St Mary's Abbey** ⓥ; in the chancel is the splendid tomb of a late-15C knight and his lady. Below is the harbour (1807–09), which now shelters sailing craft and fishing boats; for 20 years from 1813 it was the packet boat station until Dún Laoghaire (then Kingstown) took over in 1833. Offshore lies **Ireland's Eye** ⓥ, now a bird sanctuary, where the early Christians built a church (in ruins) in the 6C.

Grand Canal, Dublin

West of the village is Howth Castle Demesne. In the grounds is the **National Transport Museum** ⊘, a varied and comprehensively labelled collection of commercial and military vehicles, horse-drawn or motorised, neatly parked in a large shed.

The castle *(private)*, a medieval keep with a 15C gatehouse, contains work by Morrison and Lutyens. Legend has it that when Grace O'Malley *(see p 285)* was refused hospitality on her return journey from London, she abducted the Earl of Howth's son and returned him only when the Earl promised always to keep his door open to her family at mealtimes.

SOUTHERN SUBURBS *East to west*

Waterways Visitor Centre ⊘ (**CT K**) – The modern building, which stands on an island in the Grand Canal basin, houses a display which, explains canal engineering and the history of the countrywide network of canals which was established in the 18C. The flat roof provides a view of the warehouses lining the canal basin.

Shaw Birthplace ⊘ (**BT W**) – *33 Synge Street*. The modest house, where George Bernard Shaw (1856–1950) was born and spent his early years, is furnished in the style of the mid 19C.

Jewish Museum ⊘ (**BT**) – *Walworth Road*. The museum was opened in 1985 by Chaim Herzog, President of Israel and son of the first Chief Rabbi of Ireland, in the old Walworth Road Synagogue (1917–c 75). The showcases on the ground floor display material on the history of the Jews in Ireland from the 11C to the 20C. In the kitchen, which is fitted with separate sinks for meat and milk, the table is laid for the Sabbath evening service.

The **synagogue** upstairs retains all its ritual fittings. The women's gallery has been converted to display religious artefacts: Torah Scrolls with their handles and covers, an Ark Cover (c 1750), the wedding canopy, skullcaps and prayer shawls, circumcision instruments, candlesticks, ram's horns, tabernacles and a Hebrew clock.

★ Rathfarnham Castle ⊘ – *3mi/5km south of Dublin by N 81 and R 115*. The magnificent but forbidding exterior gives no hint of the elegant 18C interior designed by Sir William Chambers and James "Athenian" Stuart. The rectangular central keep with four flanker towers was built c 1593 by Adam Loftus, a Yorkshireman

Slide File, Dublin

who became Dean of St Patrick's Cathedral, Archbishop of Armagh and then of Dublin (then a more important see than Armagh). The remodelling of the interior in the 1770s was commissioned by Henry Loftus. After being abandoned in the early 20C and then occupied by a Jesuit seminary, the castle was in need of restoration. The tour enables visitors to see this painstaking work in progress, to admire the 18C plaques in the Front Hall, the grand dimensions, original fireplaces and curved doors of the Drawing Room, the bow window in the Dining Room where the work of Chambers and Stuart seems to overlap, the elaborate Stuart ceilings in the Boudoir and in the Gilt Room.

Pearse Museum ⊘ – *4.5mi/7.2km south of Dublin by N 81. In Terenure fork left. In Rathfarnham bear left (direction: Bray); turn first right onto Grange Road; after 0.5 mile/0.8km turn right onto Sarah Curran Avenue. 10min there and back on foot from the car park by the footpath parallel with the road.*

Through pictures and manuscripts the museum traces the life of Patrick and William Pearse, founder members of the Irish Volunteers (1913), who were executed in 1916 for their leading role in the Easter Rising.

The house (1797) was acquired by the Pearse brothers in 1910 for their boys' school, named after St Enda of Aran *(see p 146)*. Their desire to encourage Irish culture and to allow children to develop their talents free from the pressure of exams was reflected in the curriculum, which included Gaelic language, literature and history, theatrical performances, nature study and games.

The **grounds** contain an avenue of trees, called Emmet's Walk in memory of Robert Emmet who courted Sarah Curran in the grounds, a walled garden, where the pupils grew vegetables, and a nature walk, called *The Wayfarer*, which follows the river from the lake where the pupils used to swim, to the car park.

Patrick Pearse (1879–1914)

He was the second of four children born to Margaret Brady, whose family had moved to Dublin from County Meath during the Great Famine, and James Pearse, a stone carver from England, who came to Ireland in the 1850s, during a boom in church building. From his father's library he acquired a love of English literature and from his maternal great-aunt, Margaret, a love of the Irish language. In 1895, aged sixteen, he joined the **Gaelic League** and in 1903 became editor of the League's newspaper. Two years later he went to Belgium to study bilingualism in the schools. He wrote many articles proposing the same policy for Ireland and set up his own school for boys. Great names - William Butler Yeats, Patrick MacDonagh and Padraic Colum - took an interest in the pupils' theatrical productions. Pearse spent his holidays in Rosmuc *(see p 104)* in order to study Gaelic. Over the years his original intention simply to promote a pride in things Irish evolved into more active political engagement. In November 1913 he joined the Irish Volunteers to campaign for Home Rule and in February 1914 he joined the IRB. He took a prominent part in the Easter Rising and was executed at Kilmainham Gaol on 2nd May 1916, not knowing that his brother was to be executed the following day.

DÚN LAOGHAIRE

The town, which is the main port of entry to Ireland from Great Britain, is named after Laoghaire (pronounced Leary), the High King of Ireland in the 5C, who built a fort here. The growth of trade with Britain in the 18C turned the small fishing village into a busy port.

The **harbour** (251 acres/101ha) was designed by John Rennie and begun in 1817; the main work, built of Dalkey stone, was complete by 1842.

For 100 years the port was known as **Kingstown** in honour of **George IV**, who landed here in September 1821; an **Obelisk**, erected in memory of the king's visit to Ireland, stands on the waterfront south of the harbour.

National Maritime Museum of Ireland ⊘ – *Haigh Terrace*. The museum is housed in the Mariners' Church (1835–60) on the south side of Moran Park. The exhibits include a cannon from the Spanish Armada; a French longboat, painted red, white and blue, captured during an attempted landing in Bantry Bay in 1796; the lamp from the Baily lighthouse *(see p 192)* in working order; the chart used by the Commander of the German U-boat which landed Roger Casement on Banna Strand; models of a Guinness barge, Irish coastal curraghs, a Rosslare cot (a sea-going flat-bottomed boat), Galway and Donegal hookers (sailing ships – *see p 36*), an

Arklow schooner, racing skiffs, ferries, cargo ships, the first transatlantic steam ship *Sirius* (1838); the Halpin Collection, including a model of the *Great Eastern*, and the Cornelissen Collection of model ships showing the evolution from a Greek trireme to the fighting ships of the Second World War.

James Joyce Museum ⊘ – *0.5mi/0.8km east of Dún Laoghaire by the coast road to Sandycove.* The Martello Tower (1804) on the point at Sandycove now houses a **Joyce Museum**: first editions, letters, photos, his death-mask, piano, guitar, cabin trunk, walking stick, wallet and cigar case. Joyce stayed there for six days in 1904 as the guest of the poet Oliver Gogarty, who had rented the tower from the government. The upper room, which was the location of the breakfast scene in *Ulysses*, is furnished appropriately, while the **view** from the roof embraces Dún Laoghaire Harbour *(northwest)*, the coast to Dalkey Island *(southeast)* and the Wicklow Mountains *(southwest)*.

DALKEY VILLAGE *1mi/1.6km south of Dún Laoghaire by the coast road*

Dalkey (pronounced Dawkey), now incorporated in Dún Laoghaire, was once a walled town with seven fortified buildings. **Bulloch Castle** by the shore was built in the 12C by the monks of St Mary's Abbey in Dublin to protect the harbour. Two late-medieval tower houses survive in the heart of the village. **Archbold's Castle** stands opposite the **Goat Castle**, which now houses the **Dalkey Heritage Centre** ⊘ with excellent displays on local history and a splendid all-round view from the battlements. A modern extension has been sensitively integrated with the adjoining graveyard of the ruined **St Genet's Church**, which may date from the 8C. Many writers, among them LAG Strong, Lennox Robinson, James Joyce and Hugh Leonard, have associations with Dalkey; as a child (1866-74) George Bernard Shaw (1856–1950) lived in Torca Cottage on Dalkey Hill and learnt to swim at Killiney beach. Offshore lies **Dalkey Island**, which is now a bird sanctuary.

From the coast road south of Sorrento Point there is a magnificent **view★★** of Killiney Bay extending south to Bray Head.

Killiney Hill Park – *Entrance and car park on the northwest side of Dalkey Hill.* The park, which covers the south end of Dalkey Hill, was once the property of Col John Mapas who lived in Killiney Castle, now a hotel; it was opened to the public in 1887 to celebrate Queen Victoria's Jubilee. A **nature trail** winds through the trees and over the heath to the **obelisk**, which was built by John Mapas in 1742 to provide work for his tenants: panoramic **view**.

B. Lynch/BORD FÁILTE, Dublin

Dalkey Island and Vico Road

DUNDALK

DÚN DEALGAN – Co Louth – Population 25 762
Michelin Atlas p 98 and Map 923 – M 5, 6

Dundalk, the county town of Louth and one of the largest provincial towns in Ireland, is also a port on the south bank of the Kilcurry estuary. The salt-marshes and mud-flats *(east)* are a vast bird sanctuary.

The Normans seem to have settled at Dún Dealgan *(1mi/1.5km west of Dundalk by N 53)* where their motte is now covered in trees. Dundalk is a medieval town which was granted a charter in 1189 and flourished until destroyed by the forces of Sir Henry Tichbourne in 1642. Charles II granted all the corporation property to Viscount Dungannon, who was succeeded as landlord by the Hamiltons, Earls of Clanbrassil, and the Jocelyns, Earls of Roden.

Out and About

Walking Tour – There is a **historical walking tour** ⊘ once a week.

Craftwork – The **Carlingford Craft Gallery** for a variety of craftwork.

Beaches – South at **Blackrock**, north at Clogherhead (Long Strand) and north-east on the Cooley Peninsula at **Giles Quay**, facing south, and at **Omeath**, on the shore of Carlingford Lough.

Rambling – The **Táin Trail** is a footpath *(19mi/30km)* encircling the Cooley Peninsula starting and finishing in Carlingford.

Adjacent Sights – See Boyne Valley, Drogheda, Kells, Mourne Mountains, Newry.

Louth County Museum ⊘ – *Jocelyn Street*. A restored 18C warehouse presents a clear and comprehensive review of local history (archaeological finds, farming and industry, the port and railway) through audio-visual presentations, touch-screens, films and graphics.

Town Centre – Dundalk was laid out c 1740 by James, 1st Earl of Clanbrassil. South of the river bridge *(Church Street)* stands **St Nicholas' Church** (Anglican); the tower is 14C but the body of the church was rebuilt in 1707 and the transepts were added in the 19C; the spire is by Francis Johnston. In the graveyard is the tomb of Agnes Burns, near to a pillar erected in memory of her brother Robert Burns (1759–96), the celebrated poet who wrote in the Scots dialect.

The **Courthouse** *(south)* was designed in the Doric style (1813–18) by Park and Bowden. An elaborate porch-screen *(Roden Place – east)* leads to **St Patrick's Church** (Roman Catholic), which is modelled on King's College Chapel in Cambridge; mosaics decorate the sanctuary and the side chapels.

Northeast *(Castle Road)* stands the **bell-tower** (known locally as the Castle) of a Franciscan friary, which was founded c 1240, burned by the soldiers of Edward Bruce in 1315 and razed to the ground in 1539. Further east is the seven-storey conical stump of a **windmill** *(inaccessible)* devoid of its sails.

EXCURSIONS

Cooley Peninsula

The Cooley Peninsula is a mountainous granite promontory, which provides mag-nificent land- and seascapes – *(south)* over Dundalk Bay and – *(north)* over Carlingford Lough which forms the boundary between the Republic of Ireland and Northern Ireland.

From 1873 to 1926 Greenore, at the entrance to Carlingford Lough, was the ter-minal of a ferry service to Holyhead; since 1960 the port has handled freight.

★**Proleek Dolmen** – *5mi/8km N of Dundalk by N 1 and E by R 173. Park in the grounds of the Ballymascanlon Hotel; 20min there and back on foot through the yard and along the tarmac path between the fields.* The massive capstone (40 tons/47 tonnes) on its two supports dates from 3000 BC; according to legend the wish will be granted of anyone who can make three pebbles land on the top. Nearby is a wedge-shaped gallery grave.

Continue E and turn left into the mountain road north to Omeath.

★**Windy Gap** – The road climbs towards Carlingford Mountain (1 932ft/587m). Beyond the site of the Long Woman's Grave *(plaque)* the road enters the aptly named **Windy Gap**, a narrow pass between rocky crags; fine view south over Dundalk Bay. Further north there is a **viewpoint** *(car park)* overlooking the mouth of Newry River at Warrenpoint and the Mourne Mountains rising from the eastern shore of Carlingford Lough.

Omeath – Population 315. Once a Gaelic-speaking fishing village, Omeath is now a little resort with a rocky shoreline, where one can savour freshly caught seafood. In summer jaunting cars carry fares to the outdoor Stations of the Cross at the monastery of the Rosminian Fathers, and the Carlingford Lough Ferry plies across the border to Warrenpoint.

From Omeath take the coast road S.

★**Carlingford** – Population 650. The Viking and Norman monuments add to the charm of this attractive resort, set at the foot of the Cooley Mountains and facing the Mourne Mountains across Carlingford Lough (marina and boat trips).

Local history from the Vikings to the present day is traced on great triptychs in the **Carlingford Heritage Centre** ⊘, housed in the deconsecrated Anglican church, which is the starting point for a guided tour of the town centre.

Spanning the main street is a gateway, once three storeys high, known as the **Tholsel**, where Parliament is said to have promulgated laws for the Pale *(see TRIM)*. South of the town square stands a 15C fortified house *(right)* with Celtic-style designs on the door and window mouldings; although it is known as the **Mint**, there is no proof that the local mint, founded in 1467, ever operated there.

Overlooking the harbour is **Taaffe's Castle**, a late-15C square tower fortified with machicolations, crenellations, arrow slits and murder holes; the vaulted basement may have been a boat-house since the tide used to reach the foundations. It was built by the Taaffe family, created Earls of Carlingford in 1661.

The ruins of **King John's Castle** stand on a bluff on the north side of the harbour commanding the entrance to Carlingford Lough; the western bailey was probably built by Hugh de Lacy, before King John's visit in 1210; the eastern apartments were added in 1261.

South and West of Dundalk

★**St Mochta's House** – *9.5mi/15km SW of Dundalk by N 52; bear right onto R 171 to Louth.* In a field behind the ruins of a Franciscan friary (14C–15C) stands a stone oratory with a **corbelled** roof. Between the steep roof and the vaulted ceiling is a tiny chamber reached by a steep stone stair. The oratory, which has been much restored, probably dates from the second half of the 12C; it is said to have been built in a night as a resting place for St Mochta who died in 534. The little village, which has given its name to the county, was the centre of the kingdom of Oriel in the 11C and 12C.

★**Dún A' Rí Forest Park** – *21mi/34km W of Dundalk by R 178 and R 179.* The forest park, until 1959 part of the Cabra estate, is set in a valley beside the Cabra River. A **nature trail** and four sign-posted **walks** reveal its secluded features: red deer enclosure; a waterfall downstream from Cromwell's Bridge; a wishing well; Cabra Cottage, the Pratt family mansion until Cabra Castle *(east)* was built in 1814; a ruined flax mill; an ice house; the ruins of Fleming's Castle (1607), named after an Anglo-Norman family who lost their land for supporting James II *(see p 119)*.

Traditional cottage, Carlingford

Slide File, Dublin

197

Carrickmacross – *14mi/22km W of Dundalk by R 178.* Population 1 678. The town grew up round a castle built by the Earl of Essex, to whom the land was granted by Elizabeth I. It has a reputation for angling and hand-made lace. **Carrickmacross Lace Gallery** ○ *(Market Square at the north end of the main street)* displays examples of the local work, which is a "mixed lace", composed of cambric patterns applied to machine net and embellished with point stitches and loops; both traditional and modern designs are executed. The Roman Catholic church (1866) was designed by JJ McCarthy, with stained glass (1925) by Harry Clarke.

Inniskeen – *10mi/16km west of Dundalk by R 178 turning north in Chanonrock.* The village is the birthplace of Patrick Kavanagh (1904–67), poet, author and journalist, who is buried in the old churchyard; his life and work are sympathetically presented in the **Patrick Kavanagh Centre** ○, housed in the old church, as well as local history. The remains of a round tower mark the site of a 6C monastery founded by St Daig beside the Fane River.

Ardee (Baile Átha Fhirdhia) – *13mi/21km south of Dundalk by N 52.* Population 3 269. The name means the Ford of Ferdia *(see p 57)*. On the east side of the main street stand two fortified buildings: **Hatch's Castle,** a late-medieval fortified house; and **Ardee Castle,** built in 1207 by Roger de Peppard, although much of the present building dates from the 15C. In the 17C the castle was granted to Theobald Taaffe, Earl of Carlingford.

ENNIS

INIS – Co Clare – Population 15 333
Michelin Atlas p 83 and Map 923 – F 9

Ennis, the county town and administrative centre of Co Clare, has much of historic interest in its narrow winding streets.
Harriet Smithson, the wife of Hector Berlioz, was born in Ennis; her father was the manager of the first theatre built in the town in the late 18C.

Royal Origins – The town traces its origins back to the 13C when the kings of Thomond built their royal residence nearby and one of the O'Brien royal family founded the Franciscan friary. Because of its central position Ennis became the county town of Clare during the shiring of Ireland in the reign of Elizabeth I. In 1610 the town was granted permission to hold fairs and markets; two years later it received a corporation charter from James I.

Medieval Banquet – For a taste of Ireland in the Middle Ages, sit down at a medieval banquet in **Knappogue Castle** *(see below)* accompanied by a pageant on the role of women in Irish history.

Traditional Folk Music and Dancing – Demonstrations in **Cois na h'Abhna,** a modern circular building on the Galway road *(N 18).*

Adjacent Sights – See Adare, The Burren, Killaloe, Kilrush, Limerick, Tralee.

Famous Statesmen – Two famous Irishmen are commemorated in the town. A great Doric column was erected in 1867 in O'Connell Square where **Daniel O'Connell** was declared MP for Clare in 1828.
A modern statue of **Eamon de Valera**, who was first elected to Parliament as MP for Ennis in 1917, stands in front of the old Courthouse (1850), a neo-Classical building with a pedimented Ionic portico *(Galway Road N 18).*

SIGHTS

★**Ennis Friary** ○ – This 13C church was augmented with a south transept and central tower in the 15C. An **Ecce Homo** shows Christ with the Instruments of the Passion. St Francis is shown with a cross-staff in his left hand and the stigmata on his right hand, side and feet. The most notable feature is the Creagh tomb (1843) in the chancel; it consists of five carved panels showing the Passion, taken from the MacMahon tomb (1475), and figures of Christ and the Apostles from another tomb. In the 14C the Franciscan friary was occupied by 350 friars and its school had over 600 students. It was finally suppressed in 1692.

Clare Museum ○ – The *Riches of Clare Exhibition* traces local history via four themes – Earth, Power, Faith and Water – using interactive screen and audio-visual presentations and artefacts on loan from the National Museum – the decorated barrow and inscribed spade with which Charles Stewart Parnell turned the first sod for the construction of the West Clare railway and the pen used by de Valera and Chamberlain to sign the Anglo-Irish financial agreement of 1938. The building was formerly a school, part of the convent of the Sisters of Mercy congregation.

Cathedral – The Roman Catholic Cathedral, dedicated to St Peter and St Paul, was built between 1831 and 1843 in Tau-cross shape; the tower with its spire was added between 1871 and 1874. Rows of pointed arches divide the nave and aisles and support the decorated panelled ceiling.

Railway Locomotive – *Railway Station*. On a plinth stands one of the steam engines from the West Clare railway, immortalised by Percy French's song *Are You Right There, Michael, Are You Right?* The railway, which ran to Kilkee *(see KILRUSH)* closed down in 1961 and the station is now used only for freight and buses.

EXCURSIONS

Dromore Wood National Nature Reserve ⊘ – *Barefield; 8mi/13km north by N 18 (signed)*. This nature reserve (1 000 acres/400ha) encompasses a variety of habitats, including lakes, limestone pavement and turloughs, river, fen and semi-natural woodland, together with several examples of human habitation, notably the ruins of the 17C O'Brien castle. A guidebook available from the visitor centre describes species such as the grey heron, badger and pine marten living near to the two self-guided trails.

★**Dysert O'Dea** – *6mi/10km north by N 85, R 476; after 4mi/6.4km turn left (sign); after 1mi/1.6km turn right.*
The **Archaeology Centre** ⊘ and a small **museum** devoted to the prehistoric and later culture of the neighbourhood *(audio-visual film (20min); leaflet of walks)* are housed in a 15C tower house, which has a murder hole above the entrance. From the roof there is a fine **view** of the surrounding country and nearby ruins.
In a neighbouring field *(access on foot or by car)* stand the late-12C **White Cross of Tola** showing the Crucifixion and a bishop on its east face, the stump of an 11C **round tower** and much of the chancel arch and outer walls of an 11C **church**; the Romanesque doorway is a reconstruction of the original. They were built on the site of a monastery founded by St Tola in the 8C.

★**Clare Heritage Centre** ⊘ – *Corrofin; 8.5mi/14km north by N 85 and R 476*. The centre, housed in the former Anglican church, illustrates life and work in Co Clare in the 19C through text and exhibits – a flax teaser, a butter spade, a melodeon and the workhouse keys. A section of oak trunk is marked with the dates of historic events which took place during the growth of the tree.
Extensive genealogical records make it possible to trace people who emigrated from Clare in the last century; in the aftermath of the Great Famine between 1851 and 1871 at least 100 000 people left the region.

Clare Abbey – *1mi/1.6km southeast by R 469; turn right before the railway station, then left; park at the corner; 0.5mi/0.8km on foot over the level crossing and right.* On the west bank of the River Fergus stand the substantial ruins of an Augustinian friary founded in 1189 by Dónall Mór O'Brien, last king of Munster; they include the central tower, much of the nave and a tall chimney stack, part of the domestic buildings, leaning at a steep angle.

Brendan

Craggaunowen, Shannon Heritage

★**Quin Franciscan Friary** ⊙ – *6.5mi/10.5km southeast by R 469; in Quin turn left.* The extensive ruins of the friary, built about 1430 by Sioda McNamara, include the **cloisters**, the tower and the south transept. The friary was built on top of a ruined Norman castle (1280–86) which had three round towers and was built on the site of an earlier monastery.

★**Knappogue Castle** ⊙ – *8mi/13km southeast by R 469.* The castle (restored), which from 1467 to 1815 was the seat of the McNamara family, is now used for medieval banquets. The gardens and orchards have been replanted.

★**Craggaunowen Centre** ⊙ – *11mi/18km southeast by R 469 (sign).* Various prehistoric Irish constructions have been re-created in a lakeside setting: a Crannóg, a wooden marsh track *(togher)*, a ringfort, a cooking site. The project was started by John Hunt, a medievalist, some of whose Collection is housed in the **tower house**; most of it is on display in the Hunt Museum in Limerick *(see p 240).*

The last exhibit is the *Brendan*, an ocean-going curragh built of wood and leather, in which Tim Severin and his crew sailed the Atlantic in 1976–77; the patch where the leather hull was holed by an ice floe is clearly visible.

An enclosure in the woodlands nearby is home to a group of Wild Boar *(Porcus sylveticus)*; other early breeds, such as the goatlike Soay sheep, can be seen grazing in fields near the entrance to *Craggaunowen – the Living Past.*

The Brendan Voyage

St Brendan of Clonfert, also known as Brendan the Navigator, was a seafaring monk, who in the 6C set sail from Brandon Creek, the narrow sea-inlet at the west foot of Brandon Mountain *(see p 156)* on the Dingle Peninsula. His account of the voyage, *Navigatio*, written in medieval Latin, was usually thought to be fanciful until Tim Severin built the *Brendan* and set sail with a small crew, to prove that the earlier voyagers could have reached America several hundred years before Christopher Columbus. The exploits of the 20C adventure, which in many respects substantiate the 6C narrative, are recorded in *The Brendan Voyage.*

ENNISCORTHY

INIS CÓRTHAIDH – Co Wexford – Population 3 788
Michelin Atlas p 81 and Map 923 – M 10

Enniscorthy, which is built on the steep slopes of the River Slaney, has a special place in the history of Ireland, because of its involvement in the 1798 rebellion.

It has two public buildings of exceptional interest in its castle and cathedral; its many 19C architectural characteristics have been little changed in the intervening years. Local events are commemorated in the 1798 memorial *(Market Square)*, designed by Oliver Sheppard, showing Fr Murphy, a leader of the uprising, and a pikeman, and in the 1916 Easter Rising memorial *(Abbey Square)* which portrays Seamus Rafter, a local commander.

The surrounding country is well suited to the growing of soft fruits, and the Strawberry Fair in early July attracts people from miles around.

Monastic Foundation – In the 6C St Senan arrived from Scattery Island *(see KILRUSH)* in Co Clare to found a monastic settlement at Templeshannon. In 795 the Vikings pillaged the monastery. From the 12C its fortunes were controlled by the Normans, who ruled from their castle in Enniscorthy until some time in the 15C when a local clan, the MacMurrough Kavanaghs, gained control. In the latter part of the 16C Queen Elizabeth I appointed two of her own men to put an end to local rule.

Commercial Development – Commercial exploitation was started in the 16C by Queen Elizabeth's men. Sir Henry Wallop felled timber in the rich woodlands and exported it to

---

Vinegar Hill

21 June 1798 is the most well-known date in the history of Enniscorthy. Following the rebellion that year, centred mostly in Co Wexford and Co Wicklow, the insurgents, known as the pikemen after their weapons, made their last stand on Vinegar Hill, which they held for nearly a month. The 20 000 insurgents, accompanied by many women and children, were faced by an equivalent number of English troops led by General Lake; the armed men killed in the battle were far outnumbered by the defenceless people killed by the English army. The defeat at Vinegar Hill marked the end of the 1798 rebellion.

France and Spain through the port of Wexford; Philip Stamp set up an ironworks, which survived until the 1940s, and brought many English families to settle in Enniscorthy, which expanded across the River Slaney. Towards the end of the 18C distilleries and breweries were set up; by 1796 Enniscorthy had 23 malthouses. Today Enniscorthy is noted for its bacon curing, fruit growing, cutlery and potteries.

Enniscorthy Tour ⊘ – Guided tour of the town in summer.

Craftwork – **Arts and Crafts Gallery** *(Tinnock, Gorey)* displaying wood turning, stained-glass, pottery etc. **Kiltrea Pottery** *(off R 890 to Kiltealy)* for handthrown pottery and terracotta.

Adjacent Sights – See New Ross, Wexford, Wicklow Mountains.

SIGHTS

1798 Visitor Centre ⊘ – *Parnell Road; south of town centre*. The rebellion of 1798, particularly the three weeks of disruption in Co Wexford, is presented in detail via touch screens, sensory-activated displays, film and story boards. This significant event in the development of popular democracy in Ireland is reviewed in the context of events in France and America at that time and of the development of modern political parties in Ireland as a whole.

★**Enniscorthy Castle** – The present building, which dates from 1586, houses the **Wexford County Museum**★ ⊘. The local history section includes the **1798 room**, containing a collection of pikes, and the **1916 room**, displaying many photographs and other material illustrating Enniscorthy's active participation in the Easter Rising. Among the model ships is one of a 19C emigrant ship wrecked on the Blackwater sandbar near Youghal. The old-style kitchen and dairy are equipped with old artefacts such as butter churns.

The original castle was built either by Raymond le Gros, who led the first Anglo-Norman soldiers into the town in 1169, or by the Prendergasts early in the 13C. It was held by the Prendergast family until the mid 15C when it was won in battle by the MacMurroughs. In 1581 the castle reverted to the crown and was leased to Edmund Spenser, the poet, for three days. Early this century the present castle was restored as a residence by the Roches, a local family of maltsters.

St Aidan's Cathedral – The Gothic-style building, which stands on the site of the former parish church, was designed by Pugin. The foundation stone was laid in 1843 and the building was roofed in 1846. Many of the stones used in its construction came from the ruined Franciscan friary in Abbey Square, dissolved in 1544.

Enniscorthy

EXCURSIONS

Carley's Bridge Potteries ⊙ – *1mi/1.5km W of Enniscorthy past the greyhound track.* Carley's Bridge Potteries, the oldest in Ireland, were founded in 1659 by two brothers from Cornwall. The local clay is used to make a variety of earthenware pots. It takes three months to make enough pots to fill the kiln and four days for them to be fired and cooled.

Also at Carley's Bridge are the Hillview Potteries.

*★**Ferns** – *8mi/13km NE of Enniscorthy by N 11.* The small village of Ferns (population 859), once the capital of the province of Leinster, is renowned for its **ruins**. The tower, square at the bottom and round at the top, and part of the north wall of the church are all that remain of an abbey founded in the 12C by the King of Leinster, Dermot MacMurrough Kavanagh, which was burned down in 1154; he rebuilt it in 1160 and gave it to the Augustinians. Little remains of the cathedral, where MacMurrough is said to be buried in the graveyard.

The 13C **castle**, one of the best of its kind in Ireland, has a rectangular keep and circular towers; the first-floor **chapel** has a fine vaulted ceiling.

Bunclody – *12mi/19km north of Enniscorthy by N 11 and N 80.* Population 1 316. The town is attractively sited on the River Clody, a tributary of the Slaney, at the north end of the Blackstairs Mountains. The broad central mall is bisected by a stream that falls in steps. The Church of the Most Holy Trinity, consecrated in 1970, is an interesting modern design by EN Smith.

Bunclody was the last bastion in Co Wexford of the Irish language, which was in widespread use in the town until a century ago; even today Gaelic is quite often used in shops, notices and signs.

*★**Mount Leinster** – *17mi/28km N of Enniscorthy by N 11 and N 80. In Bunclody take the minor road W; after 4mi/6.4km turn left onto the summit road which ends 0.25 mi/0.4km from the peak.*

From the summit (2 602ft/793m) on a clear day there are the best views in southeast Ireland: much of Wexford and Wicklow and even the mountains of central Wales across the sea.

FINGAL★

Co Fingal

Michelin Atlas p 93 and Map 923 – N 7

The area north of Dublin, which re-adopted the ancient name of Fingal in 1994, consists of rich farmland fringed by a long coastline. The seaside resort of **Skerries** (population 7 339) has a colony of grey seals and a fishing harbour where famous Dublin Bay prawns are landed. **Portmarnock** (population 9 175), another popular resort, is known for its championship golf course. In the Middle Ages Fingal formed part of **The Pale** *(see TRIM)* and contains several historic sites, elegant parks surrounding old stately homes and the charming town of Malahide.

Beaches – At Portmarnock (Velvet Strand) and Skerries.

Adjacent Sights – See Boyne Valley, Drogheda, Dublin, Kells, Trim.

SIGHTS

*★★**Malahide Castle** ⊙ – The castle was the home of the Talbot family for 791 years, except for seven years (1653–60) under Cromwell; in 1177 the land at Malahide was granted to Richard Talbot who came to Ireland with Henry II.

The house, which consists of the original 14C tower, the 15C Great Hall and 18C reception rooms, still contains some of the original furniture and is hung with portraits from the National Portrait Collection, family portraits, pastels and 12 oils by Hugh Douglas Hamilton, an Irish artist, a portrait of *James Gandon*, the architect, and *The Battle of Ballynahinch* by Thomas Robinson, which was painted in 1798, the year of the battle. The **Rococo plasterwork** in the drawing rooms is probably by Robert West of Dublin.

The 15C **Great Hall** is dominated by the *Battle of the Boyne* by Jan Wyck; it is said that 14 of the Talbot cousins, all Jacobites, who breakfasted at Malahide on the morning of the battle, were killed in the fighting. Facing the minstrels' gallery is a collection of family portraits.

The **Botanic Gardens** (19 acres/7.5ha with 4 acres/1.5ha of walled garden) were largely created by Milo Talbot between 1948 and 1973.

Fry Model Railway Museum ⊙ – *Malahide Castle Yard.* The model engines and rolling stock made by Cyril Fry of Dublin are displayed together with information on the development of railways in Ireland and a working-gauge model railway incorporating replicas of various railway stations.

Tara's Palace ⊘ – The grandeur and elegance of three great 18C Irish mansions are recreated in miniature in this magnificent dolls' house.

★Newbridge House ⊘ – This early-18C Georgian house, designed by George Semple, stands on the western edge of Donabate in extensive grounds, one of the finest remaining examples in Ireland of a landscape park.

It has been the home of the Cobbe family since it was built c 1740 for Charles Cobbe (1686–1765), who came to Ireland in 1717 as Chaplain to the Lord Lieutenant, his cousin the Duke of Bolton, and became Archbishop of Dublin in 1746 (portrait in the hall).

The **guided tour** of the ground floor and basement includes the dining room, with its **Rococo ceiling**, and the Library, with its Baroque ceiling depicting the Four Seasons. The family **museum**, begun in 1790, displays souvenirs and trophies from foreign parts. Many members of the family travelled abroad, including Frances Power Cobbe (d 1909) who toured in Egypt and Greece and earned her living as a journalist. The Chinese decor (restored) and the cabinets are original.

The **Red Drawing Room**, a fine example of a Georgian interior, has hardly changed since the wallpaper, curtains and carpet were installed in 1820. The Rococo plasterwork is attributed to Richard Williams, a pupil of Robert West. Much of the furniture was supplied by Dublin craft firms. The room was added to the house in about 1760 by the Archbishop's son, Thomas, and his wife, who entertained on a large scale and needed a gallery for their **art collection**.

The basement **laundry** and the magnificent 18C **kitchen** are fitted with much of their original equipment.

Traditional Farm – A museum of traditional rural life is presented in the buildings round the large cobbled **courtyard** (1790) – dairy (19C), estate worker's dwelling, carpenter's shop, forge, stables and coach house containing a park drag, which could carry 13 passengers, and the Lord Chancellor's State Coach (1790). Domestic animals live in the paddocks; the large walled garden was converted to an orchard during the Second World War.

Ardgillan Castle ⊘ – *Parking at the entrance to the park and beside the house.* On the coast north of Skerries lies the demesne (198 acres/80ha) of a country house, acquired in 1737 by the Revd Robert Taylor, Dean of Clonfert; it remained the home of the Taylor (also Taylour) family until 1962. His ancestor Thomas Taylor, a professional surveyor, had come to Ireland from Sussex in 1650 to work on the Down Survey.

The original Georgian house, which was enlarged in the late 18C, includes a billiard room, drawing room, dining room, morning room and library, which contain some mementoes and furniture of the Taylor family. Kitchens, larder and scullery occupy the extensive basement. There is an exhibition on the **Down Survey** on the upper floor.

Beyond the rose gardens are the walled gardens, laid out with lawns and flowers and vegetables in geometric plots. The west front is

> ### Down Survey
>
> The survey, which took 13 months (1655-6) and was conducted by Sir William Petty *(see p 212)*, was known as the Down Survey because it noted down on paper an account of ownership of the Baronies and Parishes of Ireland at the time of the redistribution of land following the Cromwellian Settlement. The maps were individually drawn and coloured and several sets were made. While at sea between Dublin and London in 1707 the Petty set was captured by the French. The barony maps were presented to the French King's library and are now in the French National Library; the rest were sold.

screened by a row of 21 Irish yew trees. The great sweep of the grass and woodland down to the shore is a sanctuary for many species of birds and mammals.

Skerries Mills ⊘ – From one mill in the 16C the complex grew to consist of a watermill, two windmills – one with five sails and one with four, mill races, a mill pond and wetlands. This rare survival of 17C-19C industrial technology, has been restored to working order.

Swords (Sord) – Population 22,314. The bustling county town of Fingal has a history going back to the 6C when St Columba founded a monastery on a low hilltop just to the west of the modern town centre. Its site is marked by the Anglican church, a 9C **round tower** and a 12C **Norman tower**. At the northern end of the town stands **Swords Castle** ⊘, the summer palace of the Archbishops of Dublin; the substantial remains include the craggy twin-towered Constable's Tower (fully restored).

Lusk Heritage Centre ⊘ – *Lusk.* The centre is housed in the tower of Lusk Church, which incorporates an earlier round tower; it presents the history of Lusk monastery and the medieval churches of the area, and the magnificent 16C effigy tomb of Sir Christopher Barnewall and his wife Marion Sharl.

GALWAY★★

GAILLIMH – Co Galway – Population 57 241
Michelin Atlas p 89 and Map 923 – E 8

Galway is not only a county town but also the largest conurbation in the west of Ireland. Its position at the mouth of the Corrib River in the northeast corner of Galway Bay makes it an excellent port; from the original quays on the east bank of the river the docks have extended southeast into Lough Atalia where they are still expanding. Galway has grown from a medieval core of narrow streets into a lively cathedral and university city with many modern industries. Galway is well placed as a centre for excursions westwards into the wild mountainous country of Connemara; east and south lies the fertile Galway plain.

City of the Tribes – The city was founded on the east bank of the river late in the 12C by the Anglo-Norman family de Burgo (later Burke) *(see p 262)*; it attracted many Welsh and Norman merchants who enclosed the city within a defensive wall. Under the control of the 14 leading families, known as the "tribes", an extensive trade developed not only with the Continent, importing French and Spanish wine, but also with the West Indies. This prosperity however did not survive the religious disputes of the Reformation and their political consequences. After two lengthy sieges – by the Cromwellians in 1652 and by William of Orange's forces in 1691 – Galway went into decline.

The Claddagh – Long before the arrival of the Normans there was a fishing village on the west bank of the Corrib River, an Irish-speaking community which preserved its own traditions and elected its own leader, known as the King. The name derives from the Gaelic word *cladach* meaning a rocky or pebbly shore. The men fished by night while by day the women sold the catch on the Spanish Parade. The picturesque whitewashed thatched cottages sited at random were replaced in the 1930s by a modern uniform housing scheme. The Claddagh finger ring, which bears the device of a heart enclosing two clasped hands, is popular throughout Ireland.

Gaelic Galway – The city adjoins the most extensive Gaelic-speaking region in Ireland: the Aran Islands, Connemara and the Joyce Country. The 19C revival of interest in the language brought many visitors to the region; two of the oldest summer schools were founded at the turn of the century at Spiddal *(west)* and Tormakeady on the west shore of Lough Mask.

Since the founding of the Republic, the Gaelic character of the region has been re-inforced: University College, Galway, founded in 1849 as Queen's College, was created a bilingual institution in 1929 and is an important centre for the study of Gaelic language and literature; a state-sponsored Irish Theatre *(Taibhdhearc na Gaillimhe)* was launched by Micheál Mac Liammóir and Hilton Edwards; the offices of the Gaelic Development Authority were moved to Na Forbacha in 1969 and Gaelic Radio has been operating from Casla since 1972.

Literary Galway – Galway city and its environs have produced or fostered several literary personalities. Patrick O'Connor (1882–1928), who wrote short stories in Gaelic, Nora Barnacle (1884–1951), who lived in Bowling Green and married James Joyce, and Frank Harris (1856–1931) are natives of the city. Violet Martin, the second half of the Somerville and Ross partnership, lived at Ross House on the west shore of Lough Corrib. In 1896 Edward Martyn, who lived at Tullira Castle in south Galway, introduced William Butler Yeats to Lady Gregory; together they co-founded the Irish Literary Theatre, which became the Abbey Theatre in Dublin.

SIGHTS

★**St Nicholas' Church** ⊘ **(BY)** – The medieval church, where Christopher Columbus is said to have worshipped, is dedicated to St Nicholas of Myra, the patron saint of sailors. The **exterior** is decorated with gargoyles and carved mouldings; the **interior** includes a medieval water stoup, a font and numerous tombstones. The south transept was extended to include the Lynch tomb which bears the family crest. The **Lynch Memorial (A)** recalls the legend that in the 15C Judge James Lynch condemned his son Walter to death for murder and acted as hangman since no one else would carry out the sentence.

★**Lynch's Castle (BY)** – The 16C building belonged to the most powerful of the 14 tribes. The grey stone façade bears some fine carving: gargoyles, hood mould-ings over the windows, medallions bearing the lynx, the family crest and a roundel bearing the arms of Henry VII.

★**Roman Catholic Cathedral (AY)** – The cathedral, which is dedicated to Our Lady Assumed into Heaven and St Nicholas, was designed by John J Robinson in 1957 and built of black Galway "marble", the local limestone which takes a good polish.

Out and About

Events – The **Galway Arts Festival** held annually *(10 days in July)* commands as much interest as the traditional **Oyster Festival** *(late September weekend)* with the World Oyster-opening Championship, the selecton of the Oyster Pearl and the singing of *The Fields of Athenry*. The **Gathering of the Boats** *(August in Kinvarra Bay)* features Galway hookers, workboats lovingly restored.

Theatre – Galway is known for the **Druid Theatre** ⊘ (**BZ K**), *Courthouse Lane*, which specialises in experimental/avant-garde works, and the **Irish Theatre** (An Taibhdhearc na Gaillimhe)⊘ (**BY F**), *Middle Street*, which stages Irish productions – music, singing, dancing and folk drama.

Excursions – There are **boat trips** from Wood Quay to Lough Corrib *(see below)*.
There is an air service to the **Aran Islands** from the airfield at Inverin *(20mi/32km west of Galway by R 336)* and a ferry service from the docks.

Adjacent Sights – See Aran Islands, Athenry, The Burren, Connemara, Tuam.

Where to Eat

Archway, Victoria Pl, Galway. ☏ 091 563 693; Fax 091 563 074. Small well run restaurant serving carefully prepared French/Irish dishes; set lunch menu is good value.

Moran's Oyster Cottage, The Weir, Kilcolgan. ☏ 091 796 113; Fax 091 796 503. *1.25mi/2km NW by N 18*. Part 18C thatched cottage overlooking the weir; fresh seafood dishes.

Moycullen House, Moycullen. *1mi/1.6km S by Spiddle rd*. Country house (3 rm) with antique furniture and pleasant gardens; formal restaurant with home cooked fare; remote location.

The Old Schoolhouse, Clarinbridge. *1.25mi/2km NW by N 18*. ☏ 091 796 898; Fax 091 796 117. Converted Victorian schoolhouse, offering local seasonal produce; oysters a speciality.

Where to Stay

Norman Villa, 86 Lower Salthill, Salthill. *2mi/3.2km SW*. ☏/Fax 091 521 131. Ivy-clad, stylish period guesthouse (5 rm) on main road with modern Irish artwork.

Killeen House, Killeen Bushypark, Galway. *4mi/6.4km NW on N 59*. ☏ 091 524 179; Fax 091 528 065. Victorian country house (5 rm); spacious bedrooms with Regency, Victorian, Edwardian and Art Nouveau decorations.

Spanish Arch, Quay St, Galway. ☏ 091 569 600; Fax 091 569 191. City centre boutique style hotel (20 rm) with unique Victorian bar.

Park House, Forster St, Eyre Sq, Galway. ☏ 091 564 924; Fax 091 569 219, Refurbished, spacious hotel (57 rm); private parking.

Above the altar in St Nicholas' Chapel in the east transept are the early-17C carved stone plaques, depicting the three persons of the Trinity surrounding the Virgin, which were rescued during the Cromwellian period from St Nicholas' Church.

Spanish Arch (BZ) – The name is a reminder of the city's trading links with Spain. The arch itself seems to have been part of a bastion, incorporating four blind arches, one of which was opened in the 18C to give access to a new dock beside Eyre's Long Walk. Part of the medieval **town wall** (20yd/20m long) is visible on the south side of the arch, together with the tidal quays dating from 1270.

Galway City Museum ⊘ – The buildings adjoining the Spanish Arch house a miscellany of articles illustrating daily life in the area in past centuries. From the rooftop terrace *(open in fine weather only)* there is a fine view of the River Corrib as it enters inner Galway Bay.

Nora Barnacle's House ⊘ (BY) – Nora Barnacle, the wife of James Joyce, lived in this two-up-two-down cottage until she left Galway to work in Dublin, where she met Joyce – souvenirs, photos and letters.

GALWAY

Salmon Weir Bridge (AY) – The bridge was built in 1818 to link the old prison (1802–1939), which stood on the cathedral site, with the **County Courthouse** (**B**), built (1812–15) on the site of the Franciscan Abbey. Upstream is the **salmon weir**; beyond are the pontoons of the Galway–Clifden railway viaduct (1890–1935).

Eyre Square (BY) – The focal point of the modern city between the old town and the docks centres on a small park, named after John F Kennedy, President of the USA, who visited Galway in 1963 *(plaque)*. There are several monuments: the **Browne doorway** removed from their house in 1906; cannons from the Crimean War presented to the Connaught Rangers; a statue by Albert Power RHA of **Patrick O'Connor** (1882–1928); a statue of **Liam Mellows** who took part in the 1916 Easter Rising and was executed by the Free State army during the Civil War.

The **sword and mace**★ of the city corporation, which was instituted by Richard III in 1484 and abolished in 1841, are displayed in the **Bank of Ireland Building** ⊙: the sword (1610) bears two Galway silversmiths' marks; the mace, a massive highly decorated piece made in Dublin (1710), was presented by Edward Eyre in 1712.

Galway Hooker

EXCURSION

★★Lough Corrib

By road 17mi/27.5km NW of Galway by N 59; by boat ⊘ from Wood Quay in Galway.

Lough Corrib, the second-largest lake in Ireland (36mi/58km long), is dotted with numerous islands, known as **drumlins**, varying in size from a tuft of grass to Inchagoill which was once the site of a monastery

★**Aughnanure Castle** ⊘ – *16mi/26km NW of Galway by N 59; turn right (sign). Car park; 5min there and back on foot.* The ruins of Aughnanure, an Irish tower house and bawn probably built by Walter de Burgo, stand on an outcrop of rock, partially defended but also undermined by the Drimneen River. The circular **watch tower** is all that remains of the original bawn wall. Most of the **Banqueting Hall** has collapsed into the river leaving the east wall with its decorated windows. The **keep** rises through six storeys from a battered base to Irish-style crenellations with a machicolation on each side. A spiral stair *(73 steps)* climbs to the top-floor living room. The garderobe on this floor leads into the space above the third-floor vault. From the roof there is a fine view of Lough Corrib.

★**Oughterard (Uachtar Ard)** – The attractive town on the west shore of the lake is a famous angling resort and a popular tourist centre.
The shore road north of the village, which ends near the head of the lake at Curraun *(8mi/13km there and back)*, provides an ever more spectacular **view**★★ of the lake and its backdrop of mountains.

Glengowla Mine ⊘ – *2mi/3.2km W by N 59.* The silver and lead mine, which contains its original timbers although it closed in 1865, is now open for guided tours down to 70ft/20m.

The star ratings are allocated for various categories:
– regions of scenic beauty with dramatic natural features
– cities with a cultural heritage
– elegant resorts and charming villages
– ancient monuments and fine architecture, museums and picture galleries.

GLENDALOUGH★★★
GLEANN DÁ LOCHA – Co Wicklow
Michelin Atlas p 87 and Map 923 – M 8

This once-remote valley among the Wicklow Mountains where St Kevin sought solitude and later founded a great monastery has long been a place of pilgrimage and continues to attract innumerable visitors. The "Glen of the Two Lakes" is one of the most evocative of all Irish monastic sites, both for the beauty of its setting and for the array of buildings, intact or in ruin, which conjure up a vivid picture of the early days of Christianity in Ireland.

Glendalough

The monastery founded by St Kevin flourished for many years after his death around 617, drawing pilgrims who were deterred from making the journey to Rome by the unstable conditions of the time. Seven pilgrimages to Glendalough were said to be the equivalent of one to far-off Rome. Despite repeated raids and destruction by both Vikings and Irish the monastery enjoyed a golden age in the 10C and 11C, a period of Celtic revival. Glendalough also prospered under the reforming leadership of St Laurence O'Toole (1128–80), who became abbot at the age of 25 and was made Archbishop of Dublin in 1163. Decline began in the 13C and an English attack in 1398 caused much destruction. Dissolution followed during the reign of Henry VIII but the pilgrimages continued until the disorderly behaviour of many participants caused their suppression in the 1860s.

The two lakes at Glendalough were once one. They are set in a valley whose dramatic contours were shaped by an Ice Age glacier descending from the Wicklow Mountains. The splendidly-wooded southern shore of the Upper Lake, the site of several features associated with St Kevin, is particularly striking, with cliffs (100ft/30m) dropping precipitously into the dark waters of the lake. For many years the area was the scene of mining activity, with the woods being cut to smelt lead, zinc, iron, copper and silver

---

St Kevin

Probably born around the middle of the 6C, the young Kevin soon attracted attention for his miracle-working abilities. He was put into the care of three clerics but he escaped his tutors into the bosom of Nature, supposedly dwelling in the hollow of a tree above the Upper Lake at Glendalough. Though persuaded to take up his studies again, Kevin had fallen under the spell of Glendalough, and it was to the lower part of the valley that he returned with a group of monks to found a monastery. The foundation flourished under the leadership of Kevin as abbot but, tiring of his fame, he once more retired to the wilderness, living in complete solitude "in a narrow place between the mountain and the lake", probably the area above the Upper Lake now known as Temple-na-Skellig. The story is told of the blackbird who lays her egg in the saint's hand as he stands in ascetic contemplation, his arms outstretched in the shape of the Cross, a posture he holds

> "*in the sun and rain for weeks*
> *until the young are hatched and fledged and flown*" (Seamus Heaney).

ores. The Miners' Road, which runs along the northern shore of the lake to a deserted mining village at the top of the valley, provides the best view of St Kevin's Bed and the ruins of Temple-na-Skellig.

Access – **Bus service** ⊙ from Dublin via Bray and Roundwood.

Adjacent Sights – See Athy, Kildare, Powerscourt, Russborough, Wicklow, Wicklow Mountains.

TOUR *2–5hr*

Visitor Centre ⊙ – This spacious modern building has a number of displays including a fine model, based on Glendalough, of a typical monastery complex as it would have appeared in medieval times. Old photographs show the site as it was before restoration and reconstruction in the late 19C; an audio-visual show traces the monastic history of Ireland.

*****Monastic Site** – The ruins of the later monastic settlement, east of the Lower Lake, form the most important part of the Glendalough site. It is approached through the gateway, the only surviving example in Ireland of such an entrance to a monastic enclosure. Set in the wall just beyond the first of two arches is a great slab of mica schist with an incised cross, probably marking the point at which sanctuary would be granted to those seeking it.

****Round Tower** – This fine example of a round tower (100ft/30m high) is the dominant feature of the site. Probably constructed in the early 10C, it would have served as landmark, storehouse, bell-tower, look-out and refuge; its entrance is some way above the ground (12ft/4m). The thick walls (3ft/1m at the base) taper slightly towards the tip. Internally the tower was divided into six storeys, connected by ladders.

****Cathedral** – This roofless structure, once the focal point of the communal life of the monastery, is still a substantial presence on the site, its nave one of the widest of early Irish churches. Built in stages, perhaps from the late 10C onwards, it consists of a nave and chancel with a small sacristy attached to the latter on the south side. The principal features of the nave are the corner pilasters, the west doorway and the south windows. A gravestone set against the north wall of the chancel bears carved crosses and inscriptions in Irish; an adjacent slab has outstanding scroll designs.

St Kevin's Cross – This early, undecorated Celtic high cross (12ft/3.5m high) is the best preserved of the many crosses on the site.

****St Kevin's Church** – This early Irish oratory with its high-pitched roof of overlapping stones dates from the 11C. Its alternative popular name – St Kevin's Kitchen – is because of its unusual circular tower resembling a chimney or perhaps because of the scullery-like sacristy at its eastern end. The sacristy was once entered from a chancel, now demolished, whose outline can be traced in what remains of its foundations and in the line where its roof met the wall of the nave. Inside there is a sturdy barrel vault with a croft between it and the roof.

St Kieran's Church – The remains of a very small nave and chancel were discovered in 1875 close to St Kevin's Church but outside the stone wall surrounding the monastic enclosure.

***St Saviour's Priory** – *East of the Lower Lake by the Green Road*. The Priory may have been founded by St Laurence O'Toole, Abbot of Glendalough, but is probably earlier in origin. The buildings (reconstructed in 1875), now enclosed within a forestry area, include a nave and chancel with a small group of domestic buildings on the north side. The chancel arch and the east window are impressive features in the Irish Romanesque style with much fine carving.

****Upper Lake** – *1.5mi/2.5km on foot west of the Visitor Centre by the Green Road – or 0.5mi/0.8km on foot from the Upper Lake car park. The approach to St Kevin's Cell is by a pathway which is steep and even muddy in places. There is no access to St Kevin's Bed or Temple-na-Skellig, which are best viewed from the far side of the lake.*

Crosses – *East shore of Upper Lake*. The crosses, which originally marked the boundary of the monastic site, were later used as Stations of the Cross when Glendalough became an important pilgrimage centre.

***Reefert Church** – Traditionally the burial place of kings, and even perhaps of St Kevin himself, this roofless church is set among the oak and hazel woodland of the lower slopes above the lake. With a plain but beautiful chancel arch, round-headed windows in the south wall of the nave and an imposing granite doorway with sloping jambs, the building may date from the late 10C. In the graveyard are grave slabs and two crosses, one with fine interlaced carving.

St Kevin's Cell – Nothing remains of the cell where St Kevin dwelt alone save for a ring of foundation stones, colonised by three oak trees. His lonely abode was probably built with corbelled stones *(see p 83)* on the pattern of the beehive dwellings on Skellig Michael. The doorway faced eastward down the valley and there may have been a window overlooking the lake.

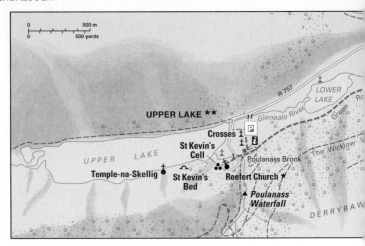

St Kevin's Bed – This tiny cave in the rockface (30ft/9m above the lake) was probably a Bronze Age tomb. Believed to be the place where St Kevin would go to pray and fast, it used to be the focal point of a pilgrimage to Glendalough; having arrived at Temple-na-Skellig by boat, the pilgrims would make their way along the lake shore, climb steps hewn in the cliff and then be helped, one by one, into the "bone-rock bed of the austere saint" (Richard Hills).

Temple-na-Skellig – The first church on this site (about 20ft/6m above the lake) may date from the time of St Kevin himself, though the present ruined structure was probably a 12C rebuilding and was restored in the 1870s. It has an east window with narrow round-headed twin lights and a huge granite lintel above the incomplete west doorway. The huts of the earliest monastic community were probably built in the raised enclosure to the west of the church.

Poulanass Waterfall – From close to the cottage housing the National Park Information Centre, a path follows the miniature chasm of the Lugduff Brook steeply upstream to a lovely waterfall set among the oaks and holly trees of the surrounding forest.

KELLS★

CEANANNAS MÓR – Co Meath – Population 2 183
Michelin Atlas p 92 and Map 923 – L 6

Kells is an attractive market town in the valley of the River Blackwater, which owes its fame to its monastic past. The Courthouse and the Roman Catholic Church were designed by Francis Johnston.

The Book of Kells – The famous illuminated manuscript of the Gospels, now in Trinity College library *(see DUBLIN)*, was produced in the local monastery in the 8C; it was stolen from the sacristy in 1007 but found two months later minus its gold ornament. The monastery was founded by St Columba *(see p 164)* in the 6C; in 807 monks from Iona sought refuge at Kells from the Vikings and in 877 St Columba's relics were moved to Kells. In the 10C, however, Kells itself was raided by the Vikings. Further raids, by the Irish, occurred in the 11C and the monastery was burned in 1111 and 1156. The Synod of Kells in 1152 raised the monastery to the status of a diocese but it was later reduced to a parish.

> **Adjacent Sights** – See Boyne Valley, Cavan, Drogheda, Dundalk, Mullingar, Trim.

SIGHTS

★★ **Round Tower and High Crosses** – *Market Street.* In the churchyard of **St Columba's Anglican Church** ⊘ stand various relics of the early monastery.
The **round tower**, built before 1076, has lost its conical cap, and the heads carved on the doorway are severely weathered.
Next to it stands the **South Cross**, probably 9C, which depicts Daniel in the Lions' Den, the Three Children in the Fiery Furnace, Cain and Abel and Adam and Eve *(south face)*, the Sacrifice of Isaac *(left arm)*, St Paul and St Antony in the desert *(right arm)*, David with his harp and the miracle of the loaves and fishes *(top)*, the Crucifixion and Christ in Judgement *(west side)*; interlacing, foliage and birds and animals fill the interstices. Nearby stands the stump of a cross showing various

biblical scenes and geometric decoration. South of the church stands an unfinished cross with raised panels ready to be carved and the Crucifixion on one face. North of the church is a medieval church tower with grave slabs inserted at the base. Detailed information about the monastery, the crosses, the Kells crozier *(in the British Museum)* and the Book of Kells is displayed in the gallery of the church.

★**St Columba's House** – *Keys available at the house with the vehicle entrance in the lane beside the east churchyard gate.* Higher up the lane stands an ancient stone oratory with a corbelled stone roof which probably dates from the 11C or 12C. The original entrance is visible in the west wall; the intervening floor is missing. Between the ceiling vault and the steep roof there is a tiny chamber *(access by ladder)*.

EXCURSIONS

St Kilian's Heritage Centre ⊘ – *8mi/13km north of Kells by R 164.* The centre celebrates the life of St Kilian (640–689), the "Apostle of the Franks" who became the patron saint of Würzburg and died a martyr's death. North of Mullagh stands a ruined church known as Kilian's church *(Teampall Ceallaigh)*. People still pray at his holy well, although formal observances ended early in the 19C.

Castlekeeran High Crosses – *5mi/8km west of Kells by R 163; after 3mi/5km turn right at the crossroads. Park beside the road. Through the farmyard and across the field and stile.* Round the edges of the graveyard are three undecorated early crosses which pre-date the scriptural crosses at Kells. Beside the yew tree stands an Ogham Stone. They mark the site of an early monastery which grew up round the hermitage of Kieran, a monk from Kells.

★**Loughcrew Passage Graves** ⊘ – *15mi/24km west of Kells by R 163. Beyond Ballinlough bear right onto R 154; after 3mi/5km turn left onto L 3. After 3mi/4.6km turn left; after 0.5mi/0.8km turn left again onto narrow rough road. Car park.* The cemetery covers two adjoining peaks, Cairnbane East and Cairnbane West, on either side of the road, on Slieve na Calliagh (908ft/277m). It consists of at least 30 graves, some of which have been excavated. Most of them date from between 2500 and 2000 BC, although excavations in 1943 in Cairn H on Cairnbane West uncovered objects bearing Iron Age La Tène style decoration. **Cairn T** (120ft/37m in diameter), the largest grave on Cairnbane East, is decorated with concentric circles, zigzag lines and flower motifs.

St Kilian

Kilian was born in the 7C in Mullagh in Co Cavan and was educated at the monastic school in Rosscarbery *(see p 237)*. As a pilgrim for Christ, he went to Würzburg in Franconia to convert the people to Christianity. According to tradition he disapproved when the local ruler, Gozbert, whom he had converted, married his brother's wife and so she had St Kilian beheaded. In 782 his remains were moved to a round church on the Marienberg but in 1991 they were returned to Mullagh.

KENMARE★

NEIDÍN – Co Kerry – Population 1 420
Michelin Atlas p 76 and Map 923 – D 12

The small market town is set in a horseshoe of mountains where the Roughty River widens into the Kenmare River. Kenmare is a popular tourist centre, with a wide range of hotels and restaurants and elegant shops (jewellery, linen, delicatessen, books and foreign newspapers) catering for visitors from many countries.

The attractive site was chosen by Sir William Petty (1623–87), a man of many talents, who arrived in Ireland as physician-general in Cromwell's Army and organised the Down Survey *(see p 203)*. In 1775 the first Marquess of Lansdowne laid out the two principal streets, which intersect one another to form an X-shape, with space for a market at the crossing point.

Out and About

Adjacent Sights – See Bantry, Killarney.

Where to Eat

The Square Pint, The Square. ☎ 064 42357; Fax 064 42358. Popular and lively pub with frequent live Irish music sessions; serving food and beer.

An Leath Phincrin, 35 Main St. ☎ 064 41559. Unpretentious little restaurant serving rustic Italian dishes; good value.

Packies, Henry St. ☎ 064 41508. Best known local restaurant, cosy and rustic, serving good fresh Irish cooking.

The Lime Tree, Shelburne St. ☎ 064 41225; Fax 064 41839. Former schoolhouse serving contemporary Irish cuisine; busy but good value.

Where to Stay

Ceann Mara. *1mi/1.6km E on R 569 Cork rd.* ☎ 064 41220. Pleasant small guest house (4 rm) in quiet setting; attractive garden and beautiful views.

Mylestone House, Killowen Rd. *0.25mi/0.4km E on R 569 Cork rd.* ☎ 064 41753. Modern house (5 rm) providing simple friendly comfort.

Sallyport House. *0.25mi/0.4km S on M 71.* ☎ 064 42066; Fax 064 42067. Modern house (5 rm) well furnished with antiques; spacious comfortable bedrooms and lounges; pleasant views.

The Lodge, Killowen Rd. ☎ 064 41512. Spacious modern house (11 rm) with large well appointed and furnished bedrooms.

Shelburne Lodge. *0.5mi/0.8km E on R 569 Cork rd.* ☎ 064 41013; Fax 064 421 35. Attractive 18C country house (7 rm) with its own charm; individually decorated and comfortably furnished rooms.

Kenmare Heritage Centre ☉ – *Main Street*. The centre traces the history of Kenmare, originally called Nedeen (*Neidín* in Irish), and its buildings, its sufferings during the Famine and the story of the Nun of Kenmare.

There is a display of antique Kenmare Lace. The **Lace and Design Centre** gives demonstrations of lace-making and sells lace made by a local cooperative working from the designs created by the nuns.

Stone Circle – *Market Street*. On the edge of the town there is a prehistoric stone circle consisting of one central stone surrounded by 15 upright stones.

Sheen Falls – *Take N 71 south across the Kenmare River and turn left (sign)*. Here the Sheen River swirls and tumbles over rocks and boulders before joining the Kenmare River.

Kenmare Lace

Kenmare lace is needlepoint lace, a technique introduced from Italy in the 17C. It is the most difficult kind as it is worked in needle and thread without any supporting fabric. The design is drawn on parchment or glazed calico and outlined with skeleton threads which are later removed together with the backing. Its distinctive characteristics are braided outlines and the use of linen rather than cotton thread. Raised point is created by using button-hole stitches over cords or horsehair.

★RING OF BEARA★ *Round tour of 85mi/137km – 1 day*

The Ring of Beara reveals the natural beauty of the long coastline backed by the Caha and Slieve Miskish Mountains. The copper mines, which started in 1812 and attracted many Cornish miners, produced great wealth until 1842; they continued to be worked intermittently until 1962 but only disused workings remain.

From Kenmare take N 71 south over the Caha Pass.

Caha Pass – In about 1839 work started on blasting the tunnels that carry the road over the Caha Mountains between Kenmare and Glengarriff; south of the pass there is a fine **view** of Glengarriff and Bantry Bay.

★**Glengarriff (An Gleann Garbh)** – The town consists of little more than a main street with shops and pubs, hotels and guesthouses. It has been a tourist resort since the mid 19C; as early as the 1830s visitors to the area were publishing their impressions of the exotic flora which flourish in the mild climate of southwest Cork. Queen Victoria stayed at the **Eccles Hotel**, which was built in 1833 as a coaching stage and has retained its original façade and some interior features. George Bernard Shaw wrote part of his play *St Joan* in the dining room and the remainder on Garinish island.

There are pleasant walks along the wooded shore of the Blue Pool (*poll gorm* in Irish) in the northwest corner of Glengarriff Harbour. The best view of Glengarriff is from the top of **Shrone Hill** (919ft/280m – *southwest*).

★★**Ilnacullin** ⊘ – Garinish Island (37 acres/15ha), also known as **Ilnacullin**, lies in Glengarriff Harbour. Early this century it was turned into a meticulously planned Italianate garden, featuring Classical pavilions and an extensive variety of exotic floral species; flowers are in bloom all year because of the mild weather and the garden's protected position. A path leads to the **Martello Tower** (135ft/41m above sea-level), the highest point on the island.

Bamboo Garden ⊘ – The climate is ideally suited to the oriental bamboo; an exotic forest is being created of 30 different species of this plant and 12 different species of Palm Trees. The slim green leaves of the bamboo contrast with the darker green of the myrtle and hydrangeas; take a stroll in the old garden, enjoy the exotic flora of the new or swim from the South Beach. There are fine fine views of Glengarriff Harbour and Bantry Bay from the Tower and from the waterfront, which is embellished with 13 stone pillars.

From Glengarriff take R 572 west; in Adrigole turn right (sign) to the Healy Pass.

★★**Healy Pass** – *The road is particularly steep near Glanmore Lake.* The road, which was opened in 1931, climbs through a series of tortuous hairpin bends *(7mi/11km)* to the summit; on a clear day the **views★★** are very impressive.

The **Healy Pass** was named after Tim Healy, who was born in Bantry in 1855. He was a Nationalist MP at Westminster from 1880 until 1916 and in 1922 he was appointed the first Governor-General of the Irish Free State. At a presentation in the Anchor Bar, Bantry, on his retirement as Lord Chief Justice of Ireland, he was invited to choose a leaving present; he asked for improvements to be made to the bridle pass from Adrigole to Lauragh on the Beara Peninsula.

At the crossroads turn left to Derreen Gardens (sign).

★**Derreen Gardens** ⊘ – The gardens were planted 100 years ago by the 5th Lord Lansdowne beside Kilmakilloge Harbour, an inlet on the south shore of the Kenmare River. The woodland gardens contain many azaleas and rhododendrons; the most notable attraction is the grove of New Zealand tree ferns.

Take R 571 west for 8mi/12.9km to the Ballycrovane junction.

Ballycrovane Ogham Pillar Stone – *Donation to enter the field.* In a field stands the tallest pillar stone in Ireland (15ft/5m high); the Ogham inscription - MAQI-DECCEDDAS AVI TURANIAS - of the son of Deich descendant of Torainn - was probably added later.

Continue west to Eyeries.

Eyeries – This typical Irish mountain settlement, with four pubs, a couple of shops and scattered cottages, is the home of Milleens cheese. There is a beach *(1mi/1.6km west)*.

Take R 575 west along the coast to Allihies.

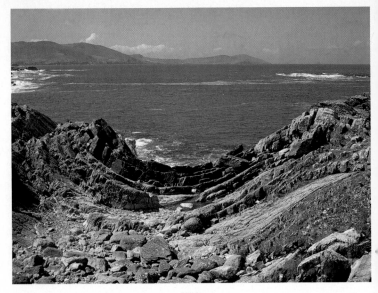

Allihies

Allihies – In the 19C Allihies was a prosperous mining community; above the straggling village *(sign)* are the extensive remains of the **copper mines★**. Old engine houses and spoil heaps are visible among the many invisible but dangerous abandoned mineshafts. **Ballydonegan Strand** *(1mi/1.6km south)* is a magnificent beach composed of crushed stone from the mines.

Continue south on R 575; after 2.5mi/4.2km turn right onto R 572.

Garnish Bay – At low tide one can walk from the tiny hamlet of six houses and a post office to **Garnish Island**, a good vantage-point for **views★** *(north)* of the Iveragh Peninsula and *(northwest)* of the Skellig Islands.

Continue west to Dursey Island.

Dursey Island ⊘ – *Access by cable-car. Limited tourist accommodation.* There is one village, Kilmichael (population 50), and one road; from the western end one can see the old and new Bull Rock lighthouses.

Return east; after 1.5mi/2.4km turn right to Crow Head.

Crow Head – The bleak headland provides a good view of Mizen Head *(south)* and the Skellig Islands *(north)*. On 23 July 1943 a Luftwaffe Junkers plane crashed in fog killing all four crew *(plaque)*.

Continue east on R 572; after 6mi/9.7km turn left.

Slieve Miskish Mountains – *After 2mi/3km the road becomes a track suitable only for climbers.* The high climb into the mountains is rewarded with splendid **views★**; the summit commands the entire length of Bantry Bay.

Return to R 572 and continue east; after 1mi/1.6km turn right (sign) to Dunboy Castle (0.5mi/0.8km).

Dunboy Castle – Surrounded by Dunboy woods *(walks and picnic areas)* are the remains of O'Sullivan Bere Castle, which was destroyed during a siege in 1602, and the vast shell of the 19C Dunboy Castle, part French château, part Italian villa, which was burned down in 1921 during the War of Independence. It was built by the Puxley family, the local landlords, with the huge royalties produced by the Beara copper mines. The history of the family and the mines inspired Daphne du Maurier to write *Hungry Hill.*

Continue east on R 572 to Castletownbere.

Castletownbere – Population 921. This town was developed in the early 19C when rich copper deposits were discovered at Allihies. The area was particularly badly hit by the 19C potato famine. Later in the century Castletownbere became an important fishing port; fish processing is now a substantial industry.

Bere Island ⊘ – *No tourist accommodation.* The island, once an important base for the Royal Navy, is home to a dozen families and the headquarters of a sailing school.

Take R 572 east to return to Glengarriff and N 71 north to return to Kenmare.

KILDARE★

The small cathedral town, which has the same name as the county, developed from a 5C religious community, founded by St Brigid and St Conleth; it was one of the few convents for women in the Celtic period. Kildare is located on the edge of **The Curragh**, an extensive plain of short springy turf dotted with clumps of yellow gorse and the headquarters of Irish horse racing. The area was also used for military manoeuvres; the barracks at the Curragh Camp were built in 1855 to train soldiers for the Crimean War.

★★**Cathedral** ⊘ – The present cathedral building is a late-19C reconstruction, incorporating portions of a 13C structure. The plain unplastered interior is relieved by ancient tombs with effigies, a medieval stone font and stained-glass windows.

The **round tower** (108ft/30m high) has been substantially restored in recent years; from the top there are **views** over the Curragh and the surrounding Midland counties.

A minor road opposite the cathedral leads to **St Brigid's shrine** and **well**.

Out and About

Horse Racing – The **Curragh Racecourse** ⊘ hosts all five Classic races including The Budweiser Irish Derby and 14 other race-days.

Canal Trips – Barge trips in summer from the **Old Canal Hotel** ⊘, Robertstown; cruisers for hire from Lowtown Marina *(see below)*.

Adjacent Sights – See Abbeyleix, Athy, Maynooth, Mullingar, Roscrea, Russborough, Tullamore, Wicklow Mountains.

EXCURSIONS

The Curragh

The name is derived from the old Irish word *(cuirrech)* meaning racecourse and the area has been associated with horse racing since the pre-Christian era. The first recorded prize is the Plate donated in 1640 by the Trustees of the Duke of Leinster. By the mid 19C there were some 25 courses at the Curragh ranging from a short course (2 furlongs/440yd/402m) for yearlings to "Over the Course" (4mi/6km).

★★**Irish National Stud** ⊘ – *Tully; 1mi/1.5km southeast of Kildare (sign)*. Lord Wavertree, a wealthy Scotsman from a brewing family, began breeding horses at Tully in 1900; in 1915 he gave his stud to the British Crown and it continued as the British National Stud until it was handed over to the Irish Government in 1943. The stallion boxes, with their lantern roofs, were built in the 1960s. In the Sun Chariot yard, finished in 1975, pregnant mares are stabled during the stud season and yearlings are housed from July to October. Mares and foals can be seen in the paddocks from the Tully Walk *(2mi/3km long)*.

Flat Racing at the Curragh (1987)

Slide File, Dublin

The most outstanding exhibit in the **Irish Horse Museum** is the skeleton of Arkle, the Irish racehorse with an outstanding record of wins whose career ended in a fall at Kempton Park in England on 27 December 1966. The other exhibits, which include a 13C horse skull found at Christchurch Place in Dublin and harness made in Dublin between the 13C and 15C, trace the history of the horse, horse racing and steeplechasing *(see p 250)*.

The grounds of the stud contain an extensive lake, created by Eida *(see below)*, and the ruins of the **Black Abbey**, founded as a preceptory of the Knights Hospitaller of St John after the Anglo-Norman invasion of Ireland in 1169. According to tradition it is connected by a tunnel (1mi/1.5km) to Kildare Cathedral. When the abbey was suppressed in the mid 16C, it passed into the possession of the Sarsfield family and it was here c 1650 that **Patrick Sarsfield** *(see p 240)*, leader of the Irish at the Siege of Limerick, was born.

★★**Japanese Gardens** ⓥ – *In the grounds of the National Stud (see above)*. The gardens were created for Lord Wavertree between 1906 and 1910 by the Japanese gardener Eida and his son Minoru. The main garden depicts the story of the life of man, beginning with the **Gate of Oblivion** and the **Cave of Birth**, continuing across the bridges of engagement and marriage to the **Hill of Ambition** and the **Well of Wisdom**. The garden used to conclude with the **Gateway to Eternity**. The **Garden of Eternity** (1974) depicts the conflict of human nature. The **Zen meditation garden** (1976) is not designed to suggest any particular thought; visitors are encouraged to generate their own concepts.

Peatland World ⓥ – *Lullymore; 12mi/19km north by R 401 and R 414*. The Centre, housed in the stables of an old estate, presents the history of the estate and of the Midland bogs. The display explains peat cutting by hand for the home, and by machine to fuel the peat-powered electricity generating stations. Among the exhibits are bog wood and bog butter and a pre-Christian bog-oak canoe, turf cutting spades, cloth made from peat fibres, products derived from peat such as oil, wax, candles, toilet articles such as shampoo, toothpaste and soap from Germany. Upstairs the display illustrates the flora and fauna of the peat bogs and their conservation.

Hill of Allen – *6mi/10km north by R 415*. The summit of the 19C tower (676ft/206m) provides **views** of the Bog of Allen *(northwest)*.

Robertstown (Inis Robertaig) – *10mi/16km north by R 415*. Population 235. The village consists of the waterfront buildings facing the Grand Canal, which reached Robertstown in 1785. Near Binns Bridge stands the **Old Canal Hotel** ⓥ, built in 1803 to serve the passengers on the flyboats *(see p 51)*; it now houses an exhibition.

Punchestown Standing Stone – *15mi/24km east by N 7 to Naas and R 411*. North of the racecourse *(Woolpack Road)* stands a granite long stone (20ft/6m high) which is thought to date from the early Bronze Age.

Kilcullen – *7mi/11km east by R 413*. Population 1 664. The **Hide Out Bar**, designed in the style of a jungle hut, preserves the black and withered right arm of prizefighter Dan Donnelly (1786–1820), who won a spectacular bout on The Curragh on 13 December 1815. The pub also displays a collection of old maps, deer heads, hunting guns and knives.

Grand Canal, Robertstown

KILKENNY★★

CILL CHAINNIGH – Co Kilkenny – Population 8 507
Michelin Atlas p 80 and Map 923 – K 10

Kilkenny, the county town, is Ireland's most outstanding medieval city, set on the banks of the River Nore and dominated by its castle and its cathedral, which face each other across the city centre. Narrow alleys, known locally as slips, recall the medieval street pattern.

The city's historical legacy, which is keenly preserved in several ancient buildings, all admirably restored, is matched by a strong artistic tradition.

The most famous pupil of Kilkenny College, a boarding school founded in 1666 by the first Duke of Ormond, was Dean Swift.

Capital of the Kingdom of Ossory – The city is named after St Canice, who founded a church here in the 6C. From the 2C to the 12C Kilkenny was the capital of the Gaelic Kingdom of Ossory; the ruling MacGiolla Phadruig family was engaged in a constant struggle for the kingship of Leinster.

Statutes of Kilkenny – Following the Anglo-Norman invasion in the 12C Kilkenny quickly became strategically and politically important; it was a major venue for Anglo-Irish parliaments. Under Anglo-Norman rule the native clans and the invaders lived

Out and About

Walking Tour ⊘ – Guided tour of medieval town from the Tourist Information Office.

Festivals – The **Kilkenny Arts Festival** (late Aug), one of the most important arts events in Ireland, based on classical music with a broad selection of other arts.

Crafts – The **Kilkenny Design Centre** ⊘ *(Castle Stables)*, housed in the monumental 18C stable buildings of the Castle, is a major retail outlet for high-quality souvenirs and provides accommodation for a variety of craftspeople; it was set up in the 1960s as a focal point for improvement in the design of ceramics, textiles, furniture and jewellery.

A number of craft studios are grouped in **Bennetsbridge** *(7mi/11km south)*, including **Nicholas Mosse**, housed in an old flour mill, which offers a variety of craft work, including pottery made on the premises.

For hand-blown glass, where the craftsmen can be seen at work, visit **Jerpoint Glass Studio** *(south of Stoneyford on the Thomastown road)*.

Sports – The magnificent estate of **Mount Juliet** ⊘ (1 400 acres/567ha) offers many sporting facilities including a golf course designed by Jack Nicklaus; the house (c 1780) is a luxury hotel, open only to residents.

Adjacent Sights – See Abbeyleix, Caher, Carlow, Cashel, Clonmel, Enniscorthy, New Ross, Roscrea.

Where to Eat or Drink

Kyteler's Inn (Y) – The half-timbered building, where Dame Alice Kyteler is said to have been born in 1280, became an inn in 1324.

Tynan's Bridge House Bar (Y) – The pub has a distinctive Victorian exterior and has retained its marble counter and low wooden ceiling painted red.

Where to Stay

Shillogher House, Callan Rd. *1mi/1.6km SW by N 76.* ☎ 056 63249; Fax 056 64865. Modern, purpose built, typical Irish guesthouse (6 rm); comfortable and good value.

Blanchville House, Dundell, Maddoxtown. ☎ 056 27197; Fax 056 27636. Georgian country house guesthouse (6 rm) in rural location; good value.

Berryhill, Inistioge. *15mi24km S by R 700.* ☎/Fax 056 58434. Ivy-clad farmhouse, a working farm on outskirts of the village; 3 rooms individual in style; good comfort.

Langton's House, 69 St John St. ☎ 056 65133; Fax 056 63693. Hotel (26 rm), in town centre, with distinctive decor, ample bar and eating facilities, comfortable rooms.

Kilgraney Country House, Bagenalstown. *4mi/6.4km S of Bagenalstown by R 705 Borris Rd.* ☎ 0503 75283; Fax 0503 75595. Georgian house (6 rm) with a collection of Far Eastern furniture and artefacts; very individual in style; rural location.

Hunters Yard at Mount Juliet, Thomastown. ☎ 056 73000. Small hotel (25 rm) in converted 18C stables; excellent facilities.

side-by-side in reasonable co-existence despite frequent incomprehension. Over the centuries many of the Anglo-Norman families, led by the dominant Butler family, tended to become absorbed into the native Gaelic culture. In 1366 a parliament in Kilkenny passed the **Statutes of Kilkenny** to prohibit the Anglo-Normans from intermingling with the Irish but the process was so far advanced that observance of the new laws was most impractical.

Confederation of Kilkenny – Kilkenny's most outstanding period was from 1642 to 1648, when the Confederation of Kilkenny functioned as an independent Irish parliament, representing both the old Irish and the Anglo-Irish Roman Catholics. Later the Confederation split and the Anglo-Irish side supported the English Viceroy, while the Old Irish relied on the military support of Pope Innocent X. The Old Irish, led by Owen Roe O'Neill, were eventually defeated; following Cromwell's siege of Kilkenny in 1650 the Irish army was permitted to march out of the city.

Nationalist Tradition – Kilkenny has always had a strongly nationalistic tradition and played a key role in the movement for independence earlier in the 20C. **William T Cosgrave**, first president of the Executive Council of the Irish Free State, was Sinn Féin member for Kilkenny, first at Westminster and then in the Irish Parliament *(Dáil)*.

★★KILKENNY CASTLE AND PARK ⊙ (Z)

The castle was built by William the Earl Marshal between 1192 and 1207 on a most imposing site overlooking the River Nore. Uniquely among Irish castles, it was a nobleman's residence, the main seat of the Butler family, Earls and Dukes of Ormond, for over five centuries from the 14C until 1935. It was extensively modernised in the 19C but was in a derelict state in 1967, when it was handed over by the 6th Marquess of Ormond to the people of Kilkenny.

KILKENNY

Kilkenny Castle

Interior – From the hall, paved with Kilkenny marble and hung with portraits, mahogany stairs installed in 1838 lead up to the Library and Drawing Room, restored to their Victorian appearance with some of the original furniture. The Dining Room is furnished in the style of the 18C.

The Long Gallery was designed in the 19C by John Pollen with a double fireplace in Carrara marble; the hammerbeam roof of Norwegian timber is decorated in the pre-Raphaelite style with neo-Celtic motifs. It is hung with 17C-to-19C portraits (on loan) and four Gobelin tapestries (1660) designed by Rubens. The bedrooms display hand-painted Chinese silk wallpaper and a mahogany bed with a horsehair mattress. In the 19C the castle was staffed by 93 servants who came and went through a tunnel under the road to the stables.

Butler Gallery ⊘ – *Basement.* These rooms house a collection of 19C and 20C Irish art and visiting exhibitions of contemporary art.

Park ⊘ – The extensive park (50 acres/20ha) provides many beautiful walks.

★★ST CANICE'S CATHEDRAL ⊘ (Y)

The cathedral stands upon a small hill, which may be the site of St Canice's 6C church, and is best approached by St Canice's Steps *(SE)* which date from the early 17C. It was built in the 13C in the early English Gothic style and has been periodically restored, first after 1650 when Cromwell damaged the monuments, destroyed the roof and stabled horses in the nave, second in the mid 18C and 19C, and again from 1959 to 1961 when the roof and organ were renovated.

Interior – The many architectural features of the cathedral, the second-longest in Ireland, are best appreciated from the west end of the nave. Among the many fine tombs the best-known *(south transept)* is that of Piers Butler, Earl of Ormond and Ossory, who owned the town and died in 1539, and his wife Margaret Fitzgerald; her effigy has a finely jewelled and embroidered girdle.

The oldest tomb (13C) *(north transept)* bears part of the original dog-tooth ornament. The oldest slab, found under the High Street in 1894, is the **Kyteler slab** *(north aisle)*, inscribed in Norman French in memory of Jose Kyteler, probably the father of Dame Alice Kyteler, who was tried for witchcraft in 1323.

Round Tower – The **round tower** (100ft/30m high), built between 700 and 1000, gives an overall view of Kilkenny and its surrounding countryside.

St Canice's Library – The library *(northwest)* contains some 3 000 books dating from the 16C and 17C.

TOWN CENTRE

Shee Alms House ⊘ (Z) – The 16C building houses the tourist information office.

★**Black Abbey** ⊘ (Y) – The church, one of the few **medieval churches** in Ireland still in use, was founded soon after 1226 for the Dominicans. The interior is decorated with fine early-14C window tracery in the south transept, particularly the five-light Rosary window. Although inscribed 1264, the alabaster carving of the Most Holy Trinity beside the altar is thought to date from c 1400. In the graveyard are 10 stone coffins dating from the 13C and 14C.
Near the abbey is the medieval **Black Freren Gate**.

★**Rothe House** ⊘ (Y) – The only surviving town house of the Renaissance period in Ireland was built in 1594 by a local merchant, John Rothe. In the 17C it was used as a meeting place by religious and political leaders during the Kilkenny Confederation. It now houses the local museum, which presents many historical curiosities, including letters written by Daniel O'Connell when he was MP for Kilkenny City in 1836–37, an 18C penal cross and the Carlingford Screw, all that remains of the first Irish aeronautical patent, taken out in 1856 by Viscount Carlingford, a local landowner. There is a small costume collection on the top floor.

Tholsel ⊘ (Y) – The Tholsel *(see p 84)*, built in 1761 (restored), contains examples of mayoral regalia dating back two centuries. The first tholsel was constructed around 1400, when the city walls were built.

Courthouse (Y) – The courthouse was built above Grace's Castle (1210) which was converted into a prison in 1568.

St Mary's Cathedral (Y) – The Roman Catholic cathedral was built in the 19C of limestone with a high tower (200ft/61m).

EXCURSIONS

Thomastown – *11mi/18km south of Kilkenny by R 700*. Little twisting streets focus on the market-like main street close to the old bridge over the Nore, half-obliterated by its modern concrete deck. There are remains of the medieval town walls and castle. **Ladywell Water Garden** ⊘ is an intricate mixture of trees, shrubs and aquatic plants.

★**Kilfane Glen and Waterfall** ⊘ – *14mi/23km south of Kilkenny by R 700 and N 9 north from Thomastown*. This is an unusual and fascinating garden, a romantic creation from the late 18C. Lost in its wooded ravine, it has been restored and linked in poetic counterpoint to more formal contemporary gardens and modern sculpture placed in the woodland. A barn-like structure among outbuildings, the work of the American artist, James Turrell *(see p 264)*, invites visitors to look anew at the heavens; modern sensibility is left far behind among the rock outcrops, deep shade and rushing stream of the ravine. Precipitous walks, steps and bridges, a winding stairway, a waterfall and, above all, a delightful thatched cottage orné, set in a grassy glen, all testify to the advanced taste of the Power family, in touch in this seemingly remote place with the latest trends in landscaping of the 1790s.

The ruined church in the village contains a famous effigy, the **Cantwell Knight★**, a fine carving of a Norman nobleman, placed upright in the roofless nave; he makes an awesome presence in this lonely spot.

★★**Jerpoint Abbey** ⊘ – *12mi/19km south of Kilkenny by R 700 and N 9 south from Thomastown*. The ruins on the banks of the Little Arrigle River, near its confluence with the Nore, are probably the most interesting and least ruined Cistercian remains in Ireland. Jerpoint was founded, probably as a Benedictine house, between 1160 and 1170 by one of the Kings of Ossory. In 1180 it became a daughter house of the Cistercian monastery at Baltinglass *(see ATHY)*.

In 1228 the community numbered 36 monks and 50 lay-brothers. After the Dissolution in 1540 the abbey was leased to the Earl of Ormond until the mid 17C.

B Lynch /Bord Fáilte, Dublin

Jerpoint Abbey Cloisters

The **Visitor Centre** presents an explanatory model of the abbey buildings.

The cruciform **church** has an aisled nave supported on stout Romanesque pillars; the transepts, which belong to the original late-12C construction, have two chapels each. In the **chancel** are the effigies of two bishops, one believed to be Felix O'Dulany, first abbot of Jerpoint and bishop of Ossory (1178–1202). On the north wall are remains of a 15C–16C wall painting showing the heraldic shields of some of Jerpoint's main benefactors. From the south transept a flight of wooden steps, on the site of the night stairs, leads to the roof of the east range of the monastic buildings. The tower with its stepped Irish battlements dates from the 15C.

The columns of the 14C or 15C **cloisters** (restored) bear remarkable carvings of animals, saints and secular figures showing the clothing and armour worn in Ireland at that period.

★**Kells Priory** – *8mi/13km south of Kilkenny by R 697.* Beside the Kings River are the extensive ruins (5 acres/2ha) of a 14C–15C priory with a fortified enclosure. Little remains of the original monastery founded in 1193 by Geoffrey de Marisco with four Augustinian canons from Bodmin in Cornwall.

Edmund Rice Centre ⊙ – *Callan; 10mi/16km southwest of Kilkenny by N 76.* A museum is now housed in the cottage **birthplace** of Edmund Ignatius Rice (1762–1844), founder of the Christian Brothers, a teaching order which has played an important role in Irish education. The kitchen has a stone-flagged floor, open hearth and spinning wheel, as in Rice's day: the other rooms are similarly preserved with furniture of the period.

In the town of Callan (population 1 246) there are substantial remains of a 15C Augustinian priory.

Bród Tullaroan ⊙ – *10mi/16km west of Kilkenny by a minor road.* This heritage centre, the "Pride of Tullaroan", set in deep countryside, is devoted to the memory of **Lory Meagher**, the "prince of hurlers" who dominated the sport in Co Kilkenny in the 1920s and 1930s. The thatched farmhouse where he was born and lived has been restored and furnished to evoke the period around 1884, the year in which the Gaelic Athletic Association *(see p 59)* was founded, by Lory's father among others. The adjoining **Museum of Hurling** presents the regional history of the sport in fascinating detail.

Kilcooly Abbey – *21mi/32km northwest of Kilkenny by R 693; from Urlingford take R 689 south for 3.5mi/5.5km; 500yd/0.5km on foot from parish church car park.* The substantial ruins of this Cistercian abbey, which was founded around 1200, include a massive tower over the crossing and a cloister. Among a number of fine monuments is the carved effigy of a knight. The abbey is protected by a ha-ha and formidably buttressed. In the field stands a large dovecot.

★**Dunmore Cave** ⊙ – *7mi/11km north of Kilkenny by N 77 and N 78.* One of the few large caves in Ireland, it has fascinating formations, including stalagmites and stalactites. The visitor centre explains its geology and history. In 928 the Vikings massacred 1 000 people in the cave, which is known in legend as one of the three darkest places in Ireland.

Castlecomer – *11.5mi/19km north of Kilkenny by N 77 and N 78.* Population 1 396. The village was laid out in the Italian-village style in 1635 by Sir Christopher Wandesforde, whose family mined the coal in this region for three centuries. The coalmining industry is now defunct but in Reddy's Coalmine Lounge, where the main bar is decorated like a mine, lumps of Castlecomer coal are on show, together with items of mining equipment such as lamps, picks and shovels.

KILLALA ★

CILL ALA – Co Mayo – Population 713
Michelin Atlas pp 94–95 and Map 923 – E 5

Killala is a quiet seaside resort overlooking Killala Bay at the mouth of the River Moy, which is partially blocked by Bartragh Island, a narrow sandbank. It has a sandy beach, and land and water sports facilities; the harbour **warehouses** show that it was once a busy port. The remote little town enjoys a place of disproportionate importance in the history of Ireland, as it was here that the French first halted when they invaded in 1798.

To the west lies North Mayo, one of the most remote and least inhabited regions of Ireland. The north coast confronts the Atlantic with a line of dramatic sea cliffs broken only by **Broad Haven**, a broad bay of sandy coves, narrow sea-inlets and tiny habitations, flanked by **Benwee Head** (829ft/253m – *east*) and **Erris Head** (285ft/87m – *west on the Belmullet Peninsula*). Inland the country is largely covered in Atlantic blanket bog (400sq mi/1 036km²), which is extensively exploited to generate electricity; the turf is harvested by machine to fuel the power station at Bellacorick, which is supplemented by wind turbines. In fine weather the bog gleams gold in the sun but when the sky is overcast the prospect is bleak like the entrance to the underworld.

St Patrick's Cathedral ⊙ – The present Anglican **cathedral** *(floodlit at night)* was erected in 1670 by Thomas Ottway, Bishop of Killala, using rubble and stones from the ruined medieval cathedral – south doorway and Gothic east window – and is furnished with box pews. In the graveyard stands a 12C **round tower**, which is built of limestone (84ft/25m high); the cap is a 19C reconstruction; it is all that remains of the monastery founded by Muiredach, the first bishop of Killala, who was appointed by St Patrick in the 5C. There is also a 9C **souterrain** with many chambers *(unfenced)*.

EXCURSIONS

North Mayo Coast

Rathfran Abbey – *3mi/4.8km N of Killala by R 314; after crossing the river turn right; at the crossroads turn right.* The ruins of a Dominican friary, which was founded in 1274, lie close to the shore. The long rectangular church, which has a panel depicting the Crucifixion over the west door, was lit by lancet windows. In the 15C some of the south windows were built up, an aisle was added and part of the nave was rebuilt. Little remains of the two cloisters and the 16C conventual buildings. Although the friary was suppressed and the buildings burned by Sir Richard Bingham, the English Governor of Connaught in 1590, the friars remained in the neighbourhood until the 18C.

Breastagh Ogham Stone – *5mi/8km N of Killala by R 314. After crossing the river turn right. Climb the stile into the field (left).* The stone (8ft/2.5m high), probably a Bronze Age standing stone, is marked with the linear Ogham script but the inscription is only partially legible.

★**Downpatrick Head** – *25mi/40km N of Killala by R 314; after crossing the river turn right; continue via Carrowmore, Killogeary and Rathlackan.* North of Killogeary the road follows the coast providing a fine view of the broad sands of Lackan Bay and then of Downpatrick Head projecting flat-topped and blunt into the sea against the backdrop of Benwee Head.

Turn right to Downpatrick Head; 20min there and back on foot from car park to cliff.

The projecting headland is undermined by the sea which appears at the bottom of a **blow hole** *(fenced off)*. Just offshore stands Dunbriste, a rock stack surmounted by a prehistoric earthwork, which was probably detached from the mainland in 1393. The view

Slide File, Dublin

Killala Harbour

includes *(E)* Benbulben and the Dartry Mountains north of Sligo, *(SE)* the Ox Mountains (Slieve Gamph), *(SW)* the Nephin Beg Mountains, *(W)* the cliffs to Benwee Head and the Stags of Broadhaven offshore.

Céide Fields ⊘ – *22mi/36km N of Ballina by R 314 via Ballycastle.* Under the blanket bog, which covers most of North Mayo, lies an extensive Stone Age monument – the stones of the houses and the walls which divided the gardens and fields of people who lived near the Céide Cliffs over 50 centuries ago and were contemporaries of the people who built the tombs in the Boyne Valley *(see BOYNE VALLEY)*. Using iron probes and bamboo markers the fields have been mapped over a wide area (4sq mi/10km²) although they extend even further.

The **Visitor Centre** explains the geological structure of the terrain, the development of the bog which now covers the site to a depth of 13ft/4m and the archaeological interpretation of the site. From the evidence found on the site – a primitive type of plough, postholes – deductions can be made about the lifestyle of the Stone Age farmers, who cleared the land of primeval forest and piled up the stones to create enclosed fields and houses. From the roof gallery there is a good view of the site.

Belderrig Prehistoric Farm ⊘ – *W of Belderrig by the coast road (sign).* The centrepiece of the **visitor centre** is a large and twisted Scots pine 4 400 years old, which was found in the vicinity. In the prehistoric era this site was a farming estate; it is now reduced to a circle of earth marked with post-stones and hearth-stones.

Moy Estuary

★**Moyne Abbey** – *1mi/1.6km SE of Killala by the coast road; 10min there and back on foot across the fields.* The ruins, which stand near the water, are those of a Franciscan friary, founded in the mid 15C. Although part of the original plan, the six-storey tower was added later. The church has been considerably enlarged on the south side. The cloisters date from the end of the 15C; the east range consists of the sacristy and the chapter-house; the kitchen and refectory on the north side are built over a stream. Although the buildings were burned by Sir Richard Bingham, the English Governor of Connaught in 1590, some friars continued in residence until the 17C; the last one died in about 1800.

★**Rosserk Abbey** – *4mi/6.4km S. of Killala by R 314; after 1.5mi/2.4km bear left.* The well-preserved ruins on the Rosserk River, a tributary of the Moy, belong to the first Franciscan house (mid-15C) to be built in Ireland. The decorative features of the church include the carved west door, the east window, the south transept window and the carved piscina in the chancel, which shows a round tower, angels and the instruments of the Passion. From the cloisters, stairs lead up to the dormitories and refectory above the vaulted rooms on the ground floor. In the 16C the friary was burned by Sir Richard Bingham, the English Governor of Connaught.

Ballina – *7.5mi/13km S of Killala by R 314.* Population 6 563. Ballina, the largest town in North Mayo and the seat of the bishop of the Roman Catholic diocese of Killala, straddles the River Moy. The **Cathedral of St Muredach** ⊙ on the east bank between the bridges was built in the 19C next to the ruins of a late-14C Augustinian **friary** founded by the O'Dowd family; the decorated west door and window of the friary church date from the 15C.

Inishcrone (Enniscrone) – *9mi/14km NE of Ballina by the coast road.* This is a popular family seaside resort on the east coast of Killala Bay, with indoor water facilities at **Waterpoint** ⊙. The local speciality is a traditional Irish **seaweed bath** ⊙ in the elegant Edwardian bath house; the deliciously silky warm seawater is not only a fine medium for relaxing but may also relieve the symptoms of rheumatism and arthritis.

KILLALOE★

CILL DALUA – Co.Clare – Population 972
Michelin Atlas p 84 and Map 923 – G 9

The village, an international watersports centre, is delightfully situated at the lower end of Lough Derg, the southern limit for navigation on the Shannon.

★**St Flannan's Cathedral** ⊙ – The **cathedral**, which stands on the site of a monastery founded in the 6C by St Molua and dedicated to his successor, was begun by Dónall Mór O'Brien in 1185. By 1225 it had been rebuilt in the present mixture of Romanesque and Gothic. It contains a 12C **Romanesque doorway**, a 12C High Cross from Kilfenora in the Burren *(see p 124)*, a cross shaft carved c 1000 bearing a dual inscription in both **Ogham** and **Viking Runic script** asking for a prayer for Thorgrim, and an oak screen erected in 1885.

> **Facilities** – Sailing, cruising and fishing.
>
> **Adjacent Sights** – See Birr, Cashel, Ennis, Limerick, Roscrea, Tipperary.

St Flannan's Oratory – Beside the cathedral stands the vaulted nave of a 12C Romanesque church incorporating a loft beneath the stone roof.

St Molua's Oratory – The oratory, which stands beside the Roman Catholic church at the top of the hill, was built c 1000 on Friar's Island in the Shannon; it was transferred stone by stone when its original location was submerged by the hydroelectric scheme in the 1920s.

Killaloe Heritage Centre ⊙ – The display traces in pictures and text the history of Killaloe from the birth of Brian Ború, through many years of fishing and cruising to the Civil War and the building of the Ardnacrushna dam to provide electricity.

EXCURSIONS

Béal Ború Earthwork – *1mi/1.6km N by R 463; turn right (sign) into a track (0.5mi/0.8km); cross the fields.* This large circular earthwork surrounded by a deep ditch and a grove of beech and pine trees is set immediately above the Lough Derg shoreline. From its name, which means "Pass of the Tributes", Brian Ború took his title.

Tuamgraney – *10mi/16km N by R 463.* The village is known as the birthplace of the novelist, Edna O'Brien *(see p 72)*. The **East Clare Heritage Centre** ⊙, which documents the local history, is housed in St Cronan's Church (Anglican), which is believed to be the oldest church in continuous use in Ireland or Great Britain. The west portion with its lintelled doorway dates from c 969; the east end of the building is 12C; note the Romanesque windows. Beside it stands a 15C tower house *(restoration in progress)*.

The **Memorial Park** *(300m W of the village)*, is planted with the indigenous trees and shrubs of Co Clare to commemorate the victims of the Great Famine of 1845-52.

★**Holy Island** ⊙ – *16mi/26km N by R 463. Accessible by boat from Mountshannon.* The **round tower** (80ft/24m high) and the extensive remains of six churches mark the site of a monastic settlement founded by St Caimin in the 7C. The **bargaining stone** has a hollow channel through which men would apparently shake hands to seal an agreement.

Graves of the Leinstermen – *4mi/6.4km NE of Ballina by R 494 and a minor road (sign); car park*. The group of prehistoric stones on the west face of Tountinna (1 512ft/461m) is probably one of the first inhabited places in Ireland. There are commanding **views**★ over much of Lough Derg to Slieve Bernagh.

★**Nenagh** – *15mi/24km NE of Ballina by R 494*. Nenagh, the administrative centre of Tipperary North Riding, is located between Lough Derg and the Silvermine and Arra Mountains. The town was first settled by the Anglo-Normans in the 12C; in the 19C it became a substantial garrison town. The 13C Franciscan friary, one of the most important in Ireland, was dissolved during the reign of Queen Elizabeth I; only the church walls still stand.

★**Nenagh District Heritage Centre** ○ – The Centre, which also operates the Tipperary North Genealogical Service, is housed in the old prison (1842). The **Gatehouse** contains the condemned cells and the execution room, which displays tableaux and biographical notes of the 17 men executed between 1842 and 1858. The octagonal **Governor's House** has been converted into a local museum.

★**Nenagh Castle** – The circular keep (100ft/30m high), once part of the curtain walls, and the 13C hall (restored) recall the fine Anglo-Norman castle built c 1200.

KILLARNEY★★

CILL AIRNE – Co Kerry – Population 8 809
Michelin Atlas p 77 and Map 923 – D 11

Killarney is set on the east shore of Lough Leane in Killarney National Park. The site is dominated by the Macgillycuddy's Reeks which include the **Gap of Dunloe** and culminate in the highest peak in Ireland, Carrauntoohill (3 414ft/1 041m). The town is an ideal touring centre, with many hotels and restaurants, not far from Farranfore airport *(north by N 22)*.

Founding of Killarney – Early in the 17C Sir Valentine Browne (1591–1633) moved from Molahiffe *(N)*, acquired in 1584 by his English grandfather, to Ross Castle and began to develop a village round Killarney church. By the 1620s the village was described as having 40 "good English houses"; 20 years later the Cromwellian wars brought destruction. Thomas Browne (1726–95), the 4th Viscount Kenmare, laid out the present street plan and created a neat town of slated houses and shops. He also introduced linen and woollen manufacturing. Tourism began in the 19C.

Cinematic History

The Dawn, a famous Irish film set in the War of Independence, was shot in Killarney between 1933 and 1934, with a cast of 250, mainly local amateurs; its initiator was Tom Cooper, a local cinema owner. Shooting usually took place on Thursdays, early closing day. Photographs of this production, of *The Quiet Man*, filmed in 1952 at Cong, and of *Ryan's Daughter*, shot at Banna Strand in 1968, can be seen in the bar of the Three Lakes Hotel.

SIGHTS

★**St Mary's Cathedral** ○ (CX) – The Roman Catholic cathedral with its prominent spire (285ft/87m high) was designed by Augustus Pugin; the austere unplastered interior reveals the various hues of the limestone. Although the foundation stone was laid in 1842, work was discontinued between 1848 and 1853 and the building used as a shelter for famine victims. The cathedral was consecrated in 1855 and adapted for the new liturgy in 1972–73.

Museum of Irish Transport ○ (DX M) – The many veteran and vintage cars, posters and magazines on display make this museum a Mecca for motor enthusiasts. The Silver Stream, designed in 1907–09, is the only car of its type ever built; the 1910 Wolseley which belonged to Sir Jocelyn Gore Booth *(see p 269)* was driven by Countess Markievicz and William Butler Yeats. Mercedes produced the 540K (1938) and the 300SL (1955) gullwing models.

St Mary's Church ○ (DX) – The Anglican church, built in 1870 in the Early-English style on the site of an earlier 17C church, contains a stained-glass window, which reproduces Holman Hunt's *Light of the World*. Among the several interesting memorials is one *(north side of the nave)* to the Revd Arthur Hyde, great-grandfather of Douglas Hyde *(see BOYLE)*, first president of Ireland.

Franciscan Friary (DX) – The friary, built in 1860 in a style similar to Muckross Friary *(see below)*, contains a stained-glass window *(entrance hall)* by Harry Clarke.

Out and About

National Park – There are **information centres** at Muckross House and at Torc Waterfall *(summer only)*. The **National Park** may be explored on land or by water. There are many miles of **walks** to suit all tastes at Ross Castle, Muckross House and through the Gap of Dunloe.

There are **boat trips** ⊙ on Lough Leane from Ross Castle or as part of the trip through the Gap of Dunloe.

Trips in a **jaunting car** ⊙ are available from the southern end of the Main Street or at Muckross House.

Gap of Dunloe – There are **organised round trips** ⊙ (6–7hr) from Killarney by bus to Kate Kearney's Cottage, by pony or pony and trap through the Gap of Dunloe *(see below)* to Lord Brandon's Cottage, by boat across the three lakes and by bus back to Killarney. Alternatively park at the north end of the Gap near Kate Kerney's Cottage and hire a pony or pony and trap or continue on foot to explore the Gap before returning to the car park.

Crafts – For woollen goods visit **Avoca Weavers** *(15mi/18km S by N 71 at Moll's Gap)* and the **Kerry Woollen Mills** ⊙ *(5mi/8km W by N 72; 4mi/6km turn right at sign; after 1mi/1.6km turn left and then right)*, where woollen goods have been produced for over 200 years; showroom and retail shop – rugs and blankets for people and horses, tweeds for clothes and furnishings, scarves and shawls, knitwear and knitting yarn.

Adjacent Sights – See Dingle Peninsula, Kenmare, Tralee.

Where to Eat

Coopers, Old Market Lane. ☎ 064 37716. Striking modern restaurant serving all day; mainly modern and eclectic food; light snacks available.

Gaby's, 27 High St. ☎ 064 32519; Fax 064 32747. Well known but quite expensive restaurant with distinctive interior providing good quality fresh seafood.

Killarney Manor, Loreto Road, Killarney. ☎ 064 31551; Fax 064 33366. For a medieval banquet accompanied by Irish music.

Where to Stay

Hussey's Townhouse, 43 High St. ☎ 064 37454; Fax 064 33144. Cosy little bar in the town centre, with small yet pleasantly furnished bedrooms (5 rm) above.

Naughton's Villa, Muckross Rd. ☎ 064 36025. Interesting house (5 rm) within walking distance of the town; up-to-date accommodation at a sensible price.

Lohan's Lodge. *4mi/6.4km N on N 22*. ☎ /Fax 064 33871. Traditional well kept out of town guesthouse (5 rm) with beautiful garden.

Redwood, Rockfield, Tralee Rd. *3mi/4.8km N on N 22*. ☎ 064 34754; Fax 064 34178. Modern spacious guesthouse (6 rm); well equipped with up-to-date facilities.

Kathleen's Country House, Tralee Rd. *2mi/3,2km N on N 22*. ☎ 064 32810; Fax 064 32340. Well known pleasantly furnished house (16 rm) providing good out of town accommodation.

Rivermere. Muckross Rd. *0.5mi/0,8km S on N 71*. ☎ 064 37933; Fax 064 37944. Modern house (8 rm) providing a high standard of comfort and facililties.

Killarney Lodge, Countess Rd. ☎ 064 36499; Fax 064 31070. Modern guest house (16 rm) offering a high standard of comfort and hospitality.

Gleann Fia Country House, Deerpark. *1.25mi/2km N by Emmett's Rd*. ☎ 064 ; Fax 064 . Out of town hotel (17 rm) in woodland setting providing peaceful comfortable accommodation.

Earls Court House, Woodlawn Junction, Muckross Rd. ☎ 064 34009; Fax 064 34366. Spacious purpose built guesthouse (11 rm) with large, comfortable, well equipped bedrooms.

Fuchsia House, Muckross Rd. ☎ 064 33743; Fax 064 36588. Modern house (10 rm) with elegant designer furnishings and spacious well equipped bedrooms.

KILLARNEY

Bohereen Na Goun...............CX 3
Bohereencael ....DX 4
Brewery Lane ....DX 6
College Square....................DX 7

College Street ....DX 9
Green Lawn ....CX 10
Hillard's Lane......................DX 12
Mangerton ....DX 13
Marian Terrace ....DX 15
O'Connell's Terrace.............DX 18

O'Sullivan's Place...............DX 19
Plunkett Street ....DX 21
St Anthony's Place..............DX 22

Kerry Poets' Memorial........DX **A**
Museum of Irish Transport..DX **M**

Kerry Poets' Memorial (DX **A**) – The memorial, a personification of Ireland in the form of a beautiful woman *(speir bhean)*, was created in 1940 by Seamus Murphy to commemorate Co Kerry's four best-known Gaelic poets – **Pierce Ferriter**, a poet, soldier and musician from the Dingle Peninsula, who refused to submit to the Cromwellians in 1652 and was hanged in 1653 in Killarney; **Geoffrey O'Donoghue of the Glens** (1620-78), who was Chieftain of Glenflesk and lived in Killaha Castle, southeast of Killarney; **Egan O'Rahilly** (1670-1728), the greatest of the four poets, who was educated in the bardic tradition and gave his allegiance to the Brownes, as the McCarthys were unable to act as his patrons; **Owen Roe O'Sullivan** (1748-84), who led a roving life as a hedge schoolmaster in winter and an itinerant labourer in summer, as well as serving in the British army and navy; to the delight of Admiral Rodney he wrote a poem in English about the Admiral's victory over the French at Dominica in 1782.

EXCURSIONS

★★★ 1 Killarney National Park ◎

Tour of 30mi/48km. S of Killarney by N 71.

The park (39sq mi/101km²) embraces the three lakes – Lower (Lough Leane), Middle (Muckross Lake) and Upper, which are linked by the Long Range River – the foreshore and the mountain slopes south and west. The nucleus of the National Park was the Muckross Estate, presented to the Irish State in 1932 as the Bourn Vincent Memorial Park (9 984 acres/4 000ha), to which have been added Knockreer, Ross Island and Innisfallen, formerly part of the Kenmare Estate. In 1981 the park was designated a Biosphere Reserve by UNESCO.

Knockreer Demesne ◎ – *Footpath to Ross Castle (see below).* The grounds of Knockreer House extend westwards from Killarney to the shore of Lough Leane; the entrance from the town is marked by a thatched cottage, **Deenagh Lodge** (CX **B**).

★ Ross Castle ◎ – *1mi/1.6km S by N 71 and a minor road W (sign). Boat trips to Innisfallen Island. Footpath to Knockreer Demesne (see above).* The castle, the last in Munster to hold out against Cromwellian forces (1652), who captured it only by attacking it from armed boats, was built on the shore of Lough Leane in the 15C by one of the O'Donoghue Ross chieftains. A fortified bawn reinforced by circular flanking towers surrounded the rectangular keep. The four floors, containing the parlour, the bedchamber and the Great Hall, have been restored using medieval building techniques and furnished in the style appropriate to the early-15C to late-16C period.

	Fishing		Nature reserve		Waymarked footpath
	Camping		Garden		Picnic area

Ross Island – The promontory, where there were active copper mines in the early 19C, extends into Lough Leane and is traversed by a profusion of tree- and flower-lined alleys. Shelley was particularly impressed by the arbutus (strawberry tree) during his visit in 1813. There are fine views of Lough Leane in its mountain setting and of the islands.

On **Innisfallen** *(access by boat from Ross Castle)* are the ruins of an abbey on the site of a 7C monastery.

★**Muckross Friary** ⊙ – *5min on foot from car park; footpath to Muckross House.* The friary, also called Muckross Abbey, was founded for the Franciscans in 1448 and constructed over a period of 59 years; it features a mid-15C nave and choir – the latter lit by a widely splayed window of four lights crowned by intersecting bar tracery – a broad central tower and a south transept built about 1500. The 22-arch cloisters and the domestic buildings were built in four different phases. The three-storey building north of the choir probably contained the Sacristy and the Sacristan's lodging.

★**Muckross House and Farms** ⊙ – *Car park; footpath to Muckross Friary.* Many of the rooms in the Elizabethan-style mansion (1840–43) are furnished in the style of the early 20C: the **drawing room**, **library** and **dining room**, with their lavish decorations; the nursery containing dolls made c 1870, an old-fashioned bathroom and a bedroom with a four-poster bed. The basement is devoted to regional crafts.

The beautiful **gardens** extend down to the lakeside.

The **Muckross Peninsula**, which divides Lough Leane from Muckross (Middle) Lake, contains one of the finest yew woods in Europe *(nature trails)*.

The **traditional farms** *(1hr on foot)* are worked in the manner which prevailed in Ireland in the early 20C. Live animals inhabit the yards and fields. The buildings, from the large farmhouse to the labourer's cottage, are appropriately furnished

Muckross Gardens

with dressers, presses and settle-beds. Indoors turf fires burn in the hearths and the staff, in period costume, demonstrate the work of a country housewife in those days.

★**Torc Waterfall** – *Car park*. The **cascade** (60ft/18m) is one of the highest in Ireland. The adjacent viewpoint *(173 steps)* provides a fine view of the lakes.

★★**Ladies View** – *Car park*. The panoramic views of Macgillycuddy's Reeks and of the Upper Lake dotted with islands appealed greatly to Queen Victoria and her entourage when they visited Killarney in 1861.

★**Moll's Gap** – *Car park*. The pass (863ft/263m) provides *(north)* a striking view of the Gap of Dunloe in Macgillycuddy's Reeks and *(south)* a glimpse of the Kenmare River.

Torc Waterfall

★★② Gap of Dunloe

Return trip of 24mi/38km. From Killarney take N 72 W; after 4mi/6km turn left. The narrow unsurfaced road through the gorge is unsuitable for vehicular traffic.

The jarvies plying for hire with their carriages throng the roadsides and the forecourt of **Kate Kearney's Cottage** ⊙, originally an old coaching inn kept by the beautiful Kate, who served *poteen* to 19C tourists.

The road through the narrow rock-strewn gorge, a U-shaped glacial breach (1 500ft/457m deep), leads up past three lakes to the Head of the Gap (794ft/242m). As the track descends into the Gearhameen Valley, where red deer graze, there is a fine view of the Upper Lake, bordered by native oakwoods and backed by Mangerton Mountain (2 756ft/838m).

★★RING OF KERRY

126mi/203km – 1 day

The Iveragh peninsula, also known as the Waterville promontory, rises to some of the highest peaks in Ireland. **The Ring of Kerry**, the road (N 70) which skirts the entire coastline between Killorglin in the north and Kenmare in the south, presents a succession of picturesque land- and seascapes.

From Killarney taken N 72 NW. Most coach tours on this route travel from north to south; passing is difficult as the coast road is narrow.

Dunloe Castle Hotel Gardens ⊙ – *After 4mi/6km turn left.* From the modern hotel the luxuriant gardens, partly enclosed by grey stone walls, extend to the 13C tower house overlooking the River Laune and the River Loe with a clear view of the Dunloe Gap. The botanic collection consists of exotic specimens from all parts of the world – the Killarney Strawberry tree, South African lilies, Australian gums, New Zealand cabbage trees and cherries, Japanese maples, North American dogwood, Chilean fir trees, South American fuchsias and such rare specimens as the Chinese swamp cypress and the "Headache" tree with its aromatic leaves.

Return to N 72 and continue NW to Killorglin.

Killorglin (Cill Orglan) – Population 1 229. The town is best known for the **Puck Fair** *(August)*; a large local billy-goat is enthroned on a chair in the town square during three days and nights of revelry.

The **Puck Fair Exhibition** ⊙, displayed in the basement room of a private house *(turn left before crossing the bridge at the foot of the hill)*, consists of souvenirs, photos, press cuttings etc.

Continue W on N 70; turn left to Caragh Lake, then right and left to Lickeen.

★**Lough Caragh** – The road along the west shore affords attractive views of the lake, which provides good salmon and trout fishing; southeast rise the Macgillycuddy's Reeks (3 414ft/1 038m).

Return to N 70 and continue W; in Caragh Bridge turn right.

Cromane Strand – The long spit of sand provides a good view of Castlemaine Harbour.

Continue W on N 70; on the far side of Glenbeigh take the minor road W across the bridge to Rossbeigh Strand.

Rossbeigh Strand – The long strand (3mi/5km) is backed by a small hamlet with a pub and a shop; there are extended walks in Rossbeigh Woods.

Continue W on N 70; in Kells turn right onto the minor road to Kells Bay (1mi/1.6km).

Kells Bay – This small secluded beach is a popular bathing place.

Continue W on N 70.

Beside the road *(right)* stand the gaunt ruins of **Daniel O'Connell's Birthplace**, Carhan House.

Cahersiveen (Cathair Saidhbhín) – Population 1 213. The native town of Daniel O'Connell dates from the early 19C. The **O'Connell Memorial Church**, built in 1888 of Newry granite with dressings of local black limestone, lacks the intended tower. Although rejected at first by the church authorities as too elaborate, the plans were approved by Pope Leo XIII.

The old police barracks by the bridge, burnt out in 1922, have been restored to house the Tourist Information Centre.

Take the minor road N towards Cooncrome harbour; after crossing the river turn left (2mi/3.2km).

Cahergall Fort – The walls of this large stone fort are stepped on the inside as at Staigue *(see below)*. They enclose two drystone buildings, a beehive hut and a rectangular house.

On foot continue W; turn right into a private road.

Leacanabuaile Fort – This partly reconstructed prehistoric drystone fort was inhabited during the Bronze and Iron Ages; from the top of the ramparts there are excellent **views★★** of the coast.

Return to Cahersiveen and continue W on N 70.

To visit Valencia Island EITHER turn right to Renard Point and take the ferry to Knight's Town OR continue on N 70, turn right onto R 657 to Portmagee and cross the bridge over the Portmagee Channel.

Valencia Island ⊘ – Although the island is small (7mi/11.3km x 2mi/3.2km), its name is well known to all who listen to the shipping forecasts relayed by the British Broadcasting Corporation.

Knight's Town (population 204), the main village, named after the Knight of Kerry, a former landowner, consists of a single street ending at the weather-boarded clock tower by the harbour. A steep narrow road north of the church leads *(2.5mi/4km)* up to a grotto created in the mouth of a disused slate quarry; from the headland there is a view of Beginish Island and Doulus Head.

Skellig Experience ⊘ brings to life the history of the Skellig Islands – its monastery, wildlife and lighthouses – through an exhibition and an audio-visual presentation *(16min)*. In the 7C St Finian founded a monastery which survived for 500-600 years on Skellig Michael; the ruins – the church, two oratories and six beehive cells – are perched on a narrow natural platform at the top of a flight of several hundred steps. In 1996 Skellig Michael was designated a World Heritage Site.

The western extremity of Valencia Island, Bray Head, is marked by **Bray Tower** *(30min on foot up a track from the end of the road)*, a 16C stone watchtower, which gives views (south) to the Skellig Islands and *(north)* to the Dingle Peninsula.

Beehive Huts on Skellig Michael

Take the bridge over the Portmagee Channel to Portmagee (An Caladh); turn right to take the coast road S.

The road climbs behind Glane“aragh (1 044ft/318m) and then plunges in steep narrow zigzags down to St Finan's Bay; in fine weather there is a view of the **Skellig Islands★★** – **Great Skellig**, also known as **Skellig Michael**, and **Little Skellig**, its smaller neighbour – two steep barren islands, outcrops of rock rising sheer from the sea west of Bolus Head.

Continue S on R 567.

Ballinskelligs (Baile an Sceilg) – This very small Irish-speaking village is noted for its minute harbour and long golden strand (4mi/6km).

Continue E on R 567; at the junction turn right onto N 70.

Waterville (An Coireán) – Population 475. The little resort is built on an isthmus between **Lough Currane** and the sea; it boasts a long promenade (0.5mi/0.8km). Many photographs of Charlie Chaplin's frequent visits are to be found in the foyer of the Butler Arms Hotel, redolent of the 1950s in its decor.

Coomakesta Pass – The winding pass (700ft/213m) offers striking views of the coast.

★★**Derrynane National Historic Park** ⊘ – The house and surrounding parkland formerly belonged to Daniel O'Connell (1775–1847), the Great Liberator.

The **park** (298 acres/121ha) which borders Derrynane Bay includes a bathing beach, a bird sanctuary and Abbey Island which is accessible at low tide. Near the house there are walks through flower gardens and woodlands.

The south and east wings of the slate-fronted **house** are presented as they were when built by O'Connell in 1825 – family portraits, original furniture and mementoes of O'Connell.

The centrepiece of the drawing room *(first floor)* is the elaborate **table** presented to O'Connell when he was an alderman of Dublin Corporation; the top is made of walnut and the base, made from Irish oak, features Irish wolfhounds and a harp; the carving took four years to complete. The chapel adjoining the house was built by O'Connell in 1844 in thanksgiving for his release from prison; the huge triumphal chariot, in which O'Connell was paraded through Dublin, has been restored to its full gilded magnificence.

From Derrynane take N 70 E; in Castlecove turn left at the Staigue Fort House hotel.

★**Staigue Fort** – *Narrow approach road; 20p donation "for trespass".* This 2 000-year-old drystone fort (restored) is one of the finest in Ireland. It was built as a centre of communal refuge probably before the 5C. The walls (18ft/5m high and up to 13ft/4m thick) are stepped on their interior face to provide access to the parapets. The entire fort is surrounded by a bank and ditch.

Continue E on N 70.

★**Sneem (An Snaidhm)** – Population 292. This attractive village is set at the head of the Sneem Estuary. Monuments to Cearbhall O'Dálaigh (1899–1976), former President of Ireland, who lived in Sneem, have been erected in the two large grass-covered squares, which are linked by a narrow bridge.

The **Anglican Church** ⊘ is a charming small building dating from 1810 with a tower and a small spire supporting a salmon-shaped weathervane. Among the few ornaments in the white-painted interior are a number of brass pew plates, bearing the names of former parishioners.

Continue E on N 70 to Kenmare (see p 62) and then on N 71 N to return to Killarney.

KILMALLOCK★

CILL MOCHEALLÓG – Co Limerick – Population 1 311
Michelin Atlas p 84 and Map 923 – G 10

This small town on the River Loobagh in the Golden Vale, which grew up round an abbey founded by St Mocheallog in the 7C, has preserved many of its historic buildings; from the 14C to the 17C it was the seat of the Fitzgeralds, Earls of Desmond, and one of the most important towns in the province of Munster. In 1568 James Fitzmaurice set fire to Kilmallock to prevent it from being taken by the English. During the Cromwellian wars in the 1640s it surrendered to Cromwell's forces; the extensive walls were later restored but large sections were finally destroyed in the 1690 Williamite wars.

Crafts – For porcelain figures visit **Irish Dresden** *(see below).*

Adjacent Sights – See Adare, Limerick, Mallow, Tipperary.

SIGHTS

★**Kilmallock Abbey** – The 13C Dominican foundation was lavishly endowed and was given to the Corporation of Kilmallock by Queen Elizabeth I following the Dissolution of the Monasteries (1540). A fine transept window survives; the tower (90ft/27m high) is gracefully supported by narrow arches but a substantial part of one corner has collapsed. At the entrance to the abbey is a small town **museum**.

★**Collegiate Church** (Roman Catholic) – In the 13C church, dedicated to St Peter and St Paul, the walls and arches of the nave and south transept are largely intact; the tower is part of an ancient round tower.

Blossom's Gate – The sole survivor of the five gates, which pierced the walls of the medieval town, spans the entrance to the town from the west.

Town Walls – A substantial portion of wall survives intact between Blossom's Gate and the vicinity of the Collegiate Church.

King's Castle – The 15C tower house occupies the site of an earlier fortress built to guard the Loobagh valley. During the Parliamentary Wars (1645–51) it was used as an arsenal by the Irish and later as a hospital by the Cromwellians.

15C House – *Wolfe Tone Street.* In this building next to the river bridge in 1795 there died a Gaelic poet of great renown, Aindrias Mac Craith, who composed *An Mangaire Súgach*; he was buried in the graveyard of the Collegiate Church *(see above).*

EXCURSIONS

★**Monasteranenagh Abbey** – *14mi/22.5km N of Kilmallock by R 512; in Holycross turn left.* The impressive ruins, parts of which survive to roof level, lie beside the River Camoge. The Cistercian monastery, colonised by monks from Mellifont, was founded in the 12C by Turlough O'Brien, King of Thomond, as a mark of thanksgiving for defeating the Danes in the Battle of Rathmore in 1148.

★**Lough Gur Interpretive Centre** ⊘ – *10mi/16km N of Kilmallock by R 512; in Holycross turn right.* The area around the lake is one of the longest-inhabited districts in Ireland; excavations have contributed information about life in the Stone Age. Many Stone and Bronze Age relics, as well as models of stone circles and burial chambers, are on display in the **visitor centre**, which also provides an audio-visual film illustrating the life of Neolithic man in this region.

Irish Dresden ⊘ – *15mi/24km W of Kilmallock by R 515.* The delicate and elaborate porcelain figures represent musicians and dancers, ladies in flounced skirts made of layers of simulated net, angels and figures for the Christmas crib, and birds and animals. The inspiration for such delicate craftsmanship originated in Vollestedt in Germany. After the Second World War, the business struggled on until 1960, when Johanna, great-niece of the founder, and her husband, Oscar Saar, moved to Dromcolliher, where they trained a new workforce, who use the old German master moulds and have also created new ones reflecting the factory's new surroundings.

De Valera Museum ⊘ – *Bruree; 6.5mi/10km NW of Kilmallock by R 518.* The museum and heritage centre, which celebrates Eamon de Valera, former President of the Republic, is housed in the old national school in **Bruree** (population 265) between the ancient six-arch bridge over the River Maigue and the old mill with

---

Eamon de Valera (1882–1975)

As a young boy Eamon de Valera (1882-1975) lived with his uncle near Bruree, where he attended the village school, which has been converted into a museum in his memory. He played a leading part in the Easter Rising in 1916, for which he was condemned to death, but was saved from execution because of his American birth. He was first elected to Parliament for Ennis in 1917. Later he became Prime Minister *(Taoiseach)* and then President of the Republic.

---

its perfectly preserved mill wheel. On display are de Valera's school copy-books and his desk with his initials carved into the top. Among the other relics are many 19C artefacts and tools, such as a thatcher's comb and querns for grinding corn. De Valera walked to school from the **cottage** where he lived with his uncle (*1.5mi/2.4km N on the road to Athlacca*).

KILRUSH★
CILL ROIS – Co Clare – Population 2 740
Michelin Atlas p 83 and Map 923 – D 10

Kilrush, the second-largest town in the county and the trading centre of southwest Clare, is situated on the north bank of the Shannon Estuary. Lively horse fairs are often held in the main square. In the 19C the area became popular with the people of Limerick as a holiday resort. In summer families of bottle-nosed dolphins can be seen sporting in the Shannon Estuary.

Out and About

Boat Trips – To Scattery Island as well as cruises and deep-sea fishing expeditions; **Dolphin watch trips** ⊘ depart from Kilrush Marina and from Carrigaholt. The marina at Merchant's Quay provides 120 berths, a boatyard and yacht hire.

Beaches – At Cappa and Brew's Bridge.

Shannon Car Ferry ⊘ – *(from Killimer; 5.5mi/8.8km E of Kilrush)* carries vehicles and passengers to Tarbert on the south shore of the Shannon Estuary.

Adjacent Sights - See Adare, Ennis, Limerick, Tralee.

Kilkee Beach

Slide File, Dublin

Kilrush Heritage Centre ☉ – *Main Square.* The Market House (1808) now presents a display explaining the role of the local landlord, the Vandeleur family, from the building of Kilrush in the 18C, through the Napoleonic Wars and the Great Famine, to the evictions of 1888.

Vandeleur Walled Garden ☉ – *Ferry Road.* The magnificent woodlands (420 acres/168ha) of the Vandeleur demesne remain but the family mansion (1803) was destroyed by fire in 1897. The stables and old walled garden are being restored.

Scattery Island Visitor Centre ☉ – *W of Merchant's Quay.* The centre provides information about the history and wildlife of Scattery Island *(see below).*

EXCURSIONS

★**Scattery Island** ☉ – *Accessible by boat from Kilrush.* Its 6C monastery, founded by St Senan, whose most famous pupil was St Ciaran of Clonmacnoise, and the remains of five medieval churches are dominated by the **round tower** (115ft/33m high), which has its doorway at ground level.

West Clare Railway ☉ – *Moyasta; 4mi/6.4km NW of Kilrush by N 67 opposite Clancy's pub.* Visitors may take a short ride on a restored section of the West Clare Railway, which originally ran between Ennis *(see ENNIS)* and Kilkee. There are plans to restore more of the line.

Kilkee (Cill Chaoi) – *8.5mi/13.5km NW of Kilrush by N 67.* This seaside resort is set deep in Moore Bay with a long promenade embracing a wide horseshoe-shaped sandy beach, where horse races at held at low tide *(last weekend in August).* The Duggerna rocks at the entrance to the bay are accessible at low tide.

Loop Head Peninsula – *Poor road surface in places.* West of Kilrush and Kilkee the land forms a peninsula, terminating in Loop Head. The treeless landscape is divided into fields by earthbanks rather than the hedges or flagstones found further inland.

On the south coast **Carrigaholt Tower House** stands beside the pier. It was built in the 16C by the McMahon family, who once controlled the peninsula, and was last besieged in 1649. From the top of the tower there are fine **views** south to the north Kerry coast *(3mi/5km).*

Off the north coast near Moneen a huge natural arch, the **Bridge of Ross★** *(sign),* formed by the action of the sea, is visible from the edge of the cliffs.

Loop Head is surmounted by the lighthouse (277ft/84m above sea-level) which was built on the headland in 1854; in 1869 the light was changed from fixed to intermittent. It is the third light on the site; the first, built in about 1670, was one of four stone-vaulted cottage lights which had a coal-burning brazier on a platform on the roof.

KINSALE★★

CIONN TSÁILE – Co Cork – Population 2 007
Michelin Atlas p 78 and Map 923 – G 12

Kinsale is a most attractive town with narrow lanes and slate-hung houses overlooking the broad estuary of the River Bandon. It is also the gourmet capital of Ireland with many excellent restaurants; a **gourmet festival** is held in October.

There are attractive views of the town from the tree-lined walk up to the **Carmelite Church**.

HISTORICAL NOTES

In 1223, soon after the Anglo-Norman invasion of Ireland, Kinsale passed by marriage to the de Courcy family. In 1333 the town received its first charter from Edward III. The most outstanding event in the town's history was the **Siege of Kinsale** in 1601–02, when a Spanish force occupied Kinsale and was besieged by English armies; an Irish attempt to raise the siege was defeated. The defeat at Kinsale meant the beginning of the end of the old Gaelic order and clan system. In 1641 the town declared for Cromwell and so was spared much damage. Until the end of the 18C no native Irish were to settle within its walls.

Similar lack of success attended James II who landed at Kinsale in March 1689 in an attempt to regain his kingdom; after the Battle of the Boyne *(see p 116)* he returned to exile in France from Duncannon in Waterford Harbour.

During the 17C Kinsale flourished as a shipbuilding port for the Royal Navy, which constructed *HMS Kinsale* here in 1700. The 18C trend towards larger ships rendered the docks obsolete. The closure of the railway line from Cork in 1931 also caused a decline in the economy, but since the 1960s Kinsale has enjoyed a considerable revival as a centre for tourism, yachting and deep-sea fishing.

SIGHTS

★**St Multose Church** (Anglican) ⊘ – The original church was built about 1190 and dedicated to St Multose or Eltin, the patron saint of Kinsale, who lived in the 6C. The tower doorway is 12C Irish Romanesque; the west doorway was built at a slightly later date. A statue of St Multose stands in a niche over the west door. The interior contains some interesting 16C gravestones.

★**Kinsale Regional Museum** ⊘ – Housed in the late-17C town hall, which is surmounted by distinctive Dutch gables, the museum has many relics of old Kinsale, including several royal charters. In the loggia is the Toll Board listing charges on goods coming to market, and a gun from *HMS St Albans*, which foundered in Kinsale harbour on 8 December 1693. The great hall is associated with the famous inquest on the victims of the *Lusitania (see below)*. The exhibition room displays a variety of items: Kinsale-made lace which, like the Kinsale cloak, was popular for over a century; footwear and cutlery belonging to the Kinsale giant, **Patrick Cotter O'Brien** (1706–1806), who made a lucrative career on the English stage. There are additional displays at Desmond Castle and at Charles Fort *(see below)*.

Kinsale

235

Desmond Castle ⊙ – The three-storey tower house was built in the late 15C or early 16C by the Earls of Desmond as a custom-house, as the site was then close to the harbour. During the siege of Kinsale it was used as a magazine and then reverted to being a custom-house until 1641. Subsequently it was used as a gaol for French and other foreign prisoners, hence its other name – the "French Prison". It now houses a **Museum of Wine** reflecting the days when Kinsale was a port, and traces the number of Irish families connected with winemaking in France, Spain, Australia and the USA.

EXCURSIONS

★Kinsale Harbour

There is a pleasant walk *(1.5mi/2.4km)* along the east bank of the Bandon estuary to **Summercove**; the single village street dips down to a minute harbour where English ships landed guns and supplies for their army during the siege of Kinsale (1601–02). From the graveyard of St Catherine's Anglican Church there are extensive **views★** across the harbour.

The star-shaped fortress, **Charles Fort★** ⊙ *(up the hill; car park)*, was begun about 1670 and in use until 1922. Many of the buildings surrounding the quadrangle of greensward are derelict but the old ordnance-store houses a good interpretive exhibition. From the fort there are extensive **views** of Kinsale harbour.

The harbour was guarded on the west side by **James Fort** *(cross the bridge over the Bandon River and turn left; after 0.5mi/0.8km park; 0.5mi/0.8km on foot)* which was built in 1604 but is less well preserved than Charles Fort; only the central tower, blockhouse and portions of the defensive walls are still partially intact.

The harbour entrance is protected by the **Old Head of Kinsale** *(from the river bridge take R 600 W and R 604 S)*. On the top of the headland stand the ruins of a 15C de Courcy fort. The road stops just short of the modern lighthouse, which replaced one built in 1683.

Lusitania

On the seabed *(12mi/19km S)* lies the wreck of the *Lusitania*, torpedoed on 7 May 1915; its sinking precipitated the entry of the United States into the First World War. Among the 1 500 who lost their lives was Sir Hugh Lane, who established the Municipal Gallery of Modern Art in Dublin.

★Carbery Coast *38mi/61km W of Kinsale by R 600*

The south coast of Co Cork is penetrated by a number of sea-inlets, some framed by woodland, and offers many attractive views of land and sea.

★**Timoleague** – The village on the Argideen estuary is dominated by a ruined **Franciscan friary★**, founded in 1320 and plundered by Oliver Cromwell in 1642. The extensive ruins include the cloisters and the outer yard, and *(0.5mi/0.8km S)* the ruins of a 12C leper hospital.

★**Courtmacsherry** – *3mi/5km detour E by R 601.* The railway line serving this attractive village, overlooking the estuary, closed in 1961 but there are walks in the woods leading to Wood Point, and a pebble beach at Broadstrand Bay.

From Timoleague take R 600 W. Before the junction with the main road (N 71) turn left (sign).

Lios na gCon ⊙ – The 10C ringfort has been restored according to the evidence uncovered by a team of archaeologists who conducted an excavation in 1987–88. The souterrain is still intact and the enclosing ditch and bank are well preserved and give a wide **view** of the surrounding country.

Clonakilty (Cloich na Coillte) – Population 2 576. The market town, founded in 1598, is renowned for its **black puddings**, which were first produced in the 1880s by Philip Harrington at 16 Sovereign Street (now Pearse Street). The celebrated water pump, known as the Wheel of Fortune *(at the junction of Connolly Street and Lamb Street Lower)*, was provided by the Earl of Shannon in 1890.

The town centre is distinguished by **Emmet Square**, an 18C Georgian square with a central garden, and by the use of Gaelic on many of the renovated shopfronts. The **West Cork Regional Museum★** ⊙, in the converted schoolhouse, traces the local history – minute-books of Clonakilty Corporation dating from 1675, photographs of *St Maloga*, the extraordinary steam engine that once worked the railway line to Courtmacsherry, extensive material on the War of Independence and on Michael Collins, who was born at Sam's Cross *(3mi/5km west)*.

The **West Cork Model Railway Village** ⊙, which is set in the 1940s, is a delight for young children, who should enjoy following the trains round the track and reading the historical and environmental captions at each station and halt.

The peninsula, Inchydoney Island *(3mi/5km S by the causeway road)*, is renowned for its sandy beaches; the large grass-covered spit of land jutting south into the sea is known as the "Virgin's Bank".

From Clonakilty take N 71 W.

Rosscarbery – This small village is built round an enormous quadrangular square. **St Fachtna's Cathedral** (Anglican) ⊙ is a 12C Romanesque building, restored in 1612, with an elaborately-carved west doorway. In AD 590 St Fachtna, bishop and abbot, founded a monastic school at Rosscarbery. It was here that St Kilian *(see p 211)* was educated before setting out as a missionary to Würzburg in Germany. Two centuries later, in the 8C, St James, a monk from Würzburg, established a Benedictine community in Rosscarbery.

From Rosscarbery take R 597 W towards Glandore; after 4mi/6.4km turn left to the Drombeg Circle (sign).

★**Drombeg Stone Circle** – This is probably the most impressive of the 60 stone circles built in prehistoric times in west Cork. It has 14 evenly-spaced stones which form an enclosed circle (30ft/9m in diameter); usually the number of stones was uneven. Of similar antiquity is the nearby cooking pit *(see p 83)*.

Continue W on R 597 to Glandore.

★**Glandore** – The original Irish name for this small village, Cuan Dor meaning the "harbour of the oaks", recalls the extensive woods that covered much of west Cork 300 years ago.

The semicircular harbour faces two minute islands in the estuary called Adam and Eve; old sailing directions told sailors to "avoid Adam and hug Eve". A walk up the hill *(300yd/274m)* leads to Glandore's upper level.

KNOCK

Until the end of the last century Knock was a quiet little village set on a wind-swept ridge in the middle of a blanket bog. Now it is usually thronged with pilgrims visiting the Shrine and the Basilica, especially during Knock Novena week in August, when the Statue of the Virgin is carried in procession in the grounds to celebrate the anniversary of the Apparition.

Crafts – For woollen goods visit the Foxford Woollen Mill *(see below)*.

Adjacent Sights – See Boyle, Sligo, Strokestown, Tuam, Westport.

Apparition at Knock

On a wet August evening in 1879 two of the village women reported seeing three figures – Mary, Joseph and St John – bathed in light against the south gable of the church. They called others to share the vision. A church commission examined the witnesses and accepted their account. Pilgrimages began the following year and many miraculous cures were reported. A second commission in 1936 confirmed the earlier finding. In 1957 the church was affiliated to the Basilica of St Mary Major in Rome and special indulgences are granted to pilgrims. In 1979, on the centenary of the apparition, Pope John Paul II visited Knock.

SIGHTS

Apparition Church – The south gable of the church where the apparition was seen has been glassed in to provide protection against the weather. Early pilgrims used to take away pieces of the wall plaster, believing it to have miraculous powers.

Basilica of Our Lady, Queen of Ireland – The huge hexagonal church (48 687sq ft/4 524m²), which can hold 12 000 people, was consecrated in 1976 and designed by Dáithí P Hanly. A slender spire surmounts the tower which contains the Blessed Sacrament Chapel.

The external covered ambulatory is supported on 12 pillars of red Mayo granite, and 32 pillars of stone from each of the 32 counties of Ireland.

Inside above the chapel entrance hangs a large tapestry depicting the apparition, designed by Ray Carroll in the form of a hand-woven Donegal carpet. The centre of the church is occupied by the high altar.

The rest is divided into five chapels dedicated to the Sacred Heart, St John the Evangelist, Our Lady of Knock, St Joseph and St Columba, each represented by a statue. Each partition wall contains a replica of a church window from one of the four provinces of Ireland.

Folk Museum ⊙ – A modern building, bearing the shields of the four provinces of Ireland – Ulster, Connaught, Leinster, Munster – houses a well-presented display illustrating life in the west of Ireland in the 19C; the development of Knock shrine; the Papal visit in 1979 and the life and achievements of Mgr James Horan, parish priest (1963–87).

Connaught Airport

The airport *(9mi/14.5km N. of Knock by N 17)* is also known as Horan International after the man whose foresight and perseverance brought it into being. The first scheme (1950s) for an airport at Knock proposed a grass airstrip for domestic flights. Convinced that the Pope's visit to Knock in 1979 would attract even greater numbers of pilgrims, the parish priest, Mgr James Horan, launched a more ambitious project. Despite great public scepticism and government refusal to provide financial assistance, the airport opened in 1985 with a runway long enough (8 000ft/2 438m) to accommodate jumbo jets; the airport is also used for pilot training. Since its inauguration it has been in constant use not only by pilgrims to Knock but by tourists to the west of Ireland.

EXCURSION

Lough Conn *Round trip of 86mi/139km*

From Knock take R 323 N via Kiltimagh; in Bohola turn left into N 5 and then right to Strade.

Strade – An annexe to the modern church houses the **Michael Davitt Memorial Museum** ⊘, devoted to the life of Michael Davitt (1846–1906), the founder of the Land League, who was born in Strade and is buried in the churchyard: letters, photographs, Land League sash, books by and about Davitt.

Michael Davitt (1846–1906)

Davitt was born in the middle of the Great Famine. When he was four years old his family was evicted for non-payment of rent and emigrated to Lancashire in England. At the age of nine he was employed in a woollen mill but three years later his right arm was amputated following an accident at work. The loss gave him time to attend a Wesleyan School and at 16, when he took up work in a printing business, he began to attend evening classes at the Mechanics' Institute and studied Irish history. He joined the Fenian movement and became organising secretary in Northern England and Scotland but was arrested and imprisoned for seven years for smuggling arms.

On his release in 1878 he returned to Co Mayo and helped to organise the tenants to obtain improvements from the landlords. Davitt persuaded Parnell to join the movement, and the Mayo Land League was formed in Daly's Hotel in Castlebar on 16 August 1879. The Irish National Land League was formed in October. During the ensuing Land War Davitt and others were arrested under the Coercion Act (1881). When the Land War ended in 1882 Davitt moved out of the limelight but continued to work as a reformer, teacher, writer and social thinker, with particular interest in the lot of the agricultural labourer and trade unionism; he was also involved in the formation of the GAA. He travelled widely and wrote several books – *Leaves from a Prison Diary* (1885), *The Fall of Feudalism in Ireland* (1904) and titles on working conditions in Australia and South Africa. He was elected to Parliament four times and used his position to advocate prison reform.

The ruined **friary** was founded in the 13C for the Franciscans but transferred to the Dominicans in 1252. Although most of the building seems to be 15C, the chancel is 13C; there are several cross-slabs against the south wall and a beautifully sculpted tomb in the north wall.

Take N 58 N to Foxford.

Foxford Woollen Mills ⊘ – The Woollen Mills were set up by Mother Arsenius, of the Irish Sisters of Charity, who came to Foxford (population 974) with a group of nuns in 1890 and established the thriving mill which has been independent of the nuns since 1987.

An audio-visual presentation about the history of the mill is followed by a tour of the obsolete machinery (1930s) and a view of the various processes – carding, spinning, weaving, mending, washing and drying – involved in the production of the famous Foxford blankets, rugs and tweeds, which are on sale in the shop.

From Foxford take R 318 W; at the T-junction turn left into R 310.

★**Pontoon Bridge View** – From the bridge there is an extensive **view**★ of Lough Cullin *(S)* and of Lough Conn *(N)*, both known for angling (brown and white trout); Lough Cullin has safer sandy beaches for swimming.

From Pontoon take R 315 N via Lahardaun; after 13mi/21km turn right to the lake shore.

★**Errew Abbey** – *20min there and back on foot across the fields.* The abbey ruins stand on a lonely and picturesque site on the very end of a spit of land extending into Lough Conn. Little remains of the abbey, which was founded in 1413 for the Augustinian canons; the 13C church with its piscina and trefoil windows pre-dates the cloister buildings.

Return S on R 315; in Lahardaun bear right up Glen Nephin via Bofeenaun and Burren towards Castlebar.

Windy Gap – The steep and narrow road through the pass provides **views** of Lough Conn and Castlebar.

Castlebar – The county town and commercial centre of Mayo, is pleasantly sited on the Castlebar River. In **The Mall**, which was once Lord Lucan's cricket pitch, stands a monument commemorating the 1798 rebellion of the **United Irishmen** *(see p 92)*; John Moore, who was then appointed President of the Provisional Government of Connaught, is buried beside it. Great flax markets used to be held in the Town Hall.

Take N 60 S to Claremorris and N 17 W to return to Knock.

LIMERICK★★

LUIMNEACH – Co Limerick – Population 52 039
Michelin Atlas p 84 and Map 923 – G 9, 10

Set astride the River Shannon, Limerick, the main administrative and commercial centre of the mid-west region, is the fourth largest city in Ireland. The historic centre, known as English Town or King's Island, which contains many examples of medieval architecture, is set on the north bank of the Abbey River, an eastern tributary of the Shannon; Irish Town developed on the south bank; in the 18C the city extended further south with the construction of Newtown Pery (1769). In 1848 the city was linked to Dublin by rail.

Many of Limerick's characteristic industries, such as bacon curing and grain milling, were developed during the last four decades of the 19C. After the foundation of the Irish Free State in 1922 the city suffered economic decline and heavy emigration, which have since been reversed owing to the construction of the hydro-electric scheme on the Shannon at Ardnacrushna *(east)*, which was completed in the 1920s, the opening of Shannon Airport in 1945, and the arrival since the 1960s of many new industries, notably computer manufacture and electronic engineering.

HISTORICAL NOTES

City of Sieges – Limerick takes its name from the Norse word *Laemrich* meaning "rich land". In 922 the Danish Vikings established a settlement from which they plundered the rich agricultural hinterland. For over a century the town was repeatedly attacked by Irish forces until Brian Ború, High King of Ireland, sacked it and banished the settlers.

The Normans, who captured Limerick in 1194 following the death of Dónall Mór O'Brien, King of Munster, built 400 castles in the city and in the countryside and raised extensive city walls, some of which survive (**YZ**). During the relative calm of Norman rule Limerick gave strong allegiance to the English throne. Under King Henry II the kingdom of Thomond (North Munster) was split between the Normans, who were allocated the land south of the River Shannon in Co Limerick, and the O'Briens who had the land to the north in Co Clare.

In Tudor times the city had rich trading links with France and Spain but in 1571 James Fitzmaurice Fitzgerald led the Geraldine revolt against English rule.

In 1642 confederate forces occupied the city; in 1651 Ireton, a Cromwellian commander, laid siege to Limerick for six months until it was betrayed by some of its garrison officers. After the Battle of the Boyne in 1690 the defeated Irish forces retreated to Limerick pursued by William of Orange who laid siege to Irish Town, but he was unsuccessful in his several attempts to capture the city.

Sarsfield's Ride

During the Siege of Limerick by William of Orange in 1691, Patrick Sarsfield, the Irish leader, acting on information from a deserter, slipped out of the city with 600 cavalry. They headed north and then east; they forded the Shannon upstream of Killaloe Bridge, which was held by the Williamites, and travelled south through the Silvermine Mountains to Glencar where they camped while scouts went out on reconnaissance. At midnight Sarsfield's troop set out via Cullen to Ballyneety *(18mi/30km south of Limerick)* where they intercepted the Williamite siege train – eight heavy cannon, five mortars and 200 wagons of ammunition and supplies. The noise of its destruction was heard in the city.

Treaty of Limerick – In 1691 after a two-month bombardment from the north and south by another Williamite army led by General Ginkel while an English fleet blockaded the river, Sarsfield sued for peace and signed the Treaty of Limerick. He then became a soldier in the French army and was killed in battle at the age of 43.

18C to 20C – Despite considerable agrarian revolt in the region in the 18C, the City Corporation decided that Limerick no longer needed to be fortified and in 1760 most of the city walls were demolished.

The 18C was also marked by the last flowering of the old Irish culture; after the severe 19C famine and subsequent emigration Gaelic ceased to be the vernacular language of Limerick. Gerald Griffin (1803–40), who was born in Limerick *(plaque in St Augustine's Place)*, made his name as a novelist and poet in English.

During the struggle for independence, Limerick and its county provided three leaders for the 1916 Easter Rising. The most famous was **Eamon de Valera** (1882-1975), later Prime Minister *(Taoiseach)* and then President of the Republic.

In 1919 at the start of the three-year War of Independence a general strike took place in Limerick in protest against British military rule in Ireland. In the same year a soviet was set up in the city.

Out and About

Sightseeing – Guided **walking tours** ⊘ – historical tour or the *Angela's Ashes* tour – depart from St Mary's Action Centre, 44 Nicholas Street.

Shopping – The main shopping areas are **O'Connell Street** and **William Street**. The **Arthur's Quay Centre** is a shopping complex, housing more than 30 stores. Market-lovers should visit the **Milk Market**, Limerick's market quarter; the Saturday morning market offers a range of fresh produce, and every Friday there is an Arts and Crafts Market.

Entertainment – The **Belltable Arts Centre** is host to various theatre productions; for details of events ☎ 061 319 866. The **Theatre Royal** in Upper Cecil Street is popular for music and other forms of entertainment; for full listings ☎ 061 414 224. The **Savoy Cinema**, Bedford Row, boasts five screens – ☎ 061 311 900. The **Irish Chamber Orchestra** is now based in Limerick, although it does also tour; for a full programme ☎ 061 202 620. The **University Concert Hall** has a regular and varied programme of music; for bookings ☎ 061 331 549. There are several art galleries which mount temporary exhibitions – **Belltable Arts Centre** *(see above)*; The **Dolmen Gallery**, Honan's Quay, ☎ 061 417 929; The **Bourne Vincent Gallery**, Foundation Building, University of Limerick ☎ 061 202 700; **Angela Woulfe Gallery**, 16 Pery Square ☎ 061 310 164.

Adjacent Sights – See Adare, Ennis, Killaloe, Kilmallock, Kilrush, Tipperary.

Where to Eat

Cherry Tree, Killaloe. ☎ 061 375 688; Fax 061 375 689. Modern restaurant offering original Irish themed dishes; views of the Shannon.

Bunratty Castle *(see below)* – For a medieval banquet accompanied by traditional Irish music.

Where to Stay

Bunratty Manor, Bunratty. ☎ 061 707 984; Fax 061 360 588. Comfortable guesthouse (14 rm), purpose built, in the centre of this historic village.

Clonmacken House, Clonmacken Rd (off Ennis Rd), Limerick. *2mi/3.2km NW by R 587.* ☎ 061 327 007; Fax 061 327 785. Friendly, spacious guest house (10 rm), offering well appointed, good value accommodation.

Limerick Inn, Ennis Rd, Limerick. *4mi/6.4km NW on N 18.* ☎ 061 326 666; Fax 061 326 281. Large modern commercial hotel (150 rm) on the River Shannon; ample parking; 2min on foot from city centre.

KING'S ISLAND

★★St Mary's Cathedral ⊘ **(Y)** – Limerick's oldest-surviving building, the Anglican cathedral, was founded on King's Island in the River Shannon in 1168 by Dónall Mór O'Brien, King of Munster.
Parts of the king's palace were incorporated in the original cruciform church, which was built in the transitional Romanesque style; the Romanesque west doorway may have been the palace entrance.

Interior – The black oak choir stalls and their misericords in the Jebb Chapel, both dating from the 15C, are the only surviving examples of their kind in Ireland. The reredos of the high altar was carved by the father of Patrick Pearse. The north transept contains fine 15C carvings on the **Arthur Memorial** *(below the window)*, which commemorates Geoffrey Arthur (d 1519), the cathedral Treasurer, and a small rectangular lepers' squint *(right)*. In the south transept is the 15C Galway-Bultingfort tomb.

★Limerick Museum ⊘ **(Z M²)** – The museum depicts the history of the city, particularly during the later 19C and early 20C. An extensive collection of 18C silverware recalls a now-defunct Limerick craft. The examples of Limerick **lace** include tambour, needlepoint and tape lace. The **Nail** from the Old Exchange *(see below)*, on which commercial transactions were settled, is made of limestone with a brass top; "paying on the Nail" was a common feature of English trading centres.

King John's Castle, Limerick

★King John's Castle ⊙ (Y) – The castle, a fine example of fortified Norman architecture, stands on the east bank of the River Shannon guarding Thomond Bridge. It was built between 1200 and 1216 without a keep; massive round towers reinforce the gateway and the curtain walls, which were higher in those days to withstand the contemporary siege machines. After 1216, when it was extensively repaired after siege damage, the castle featured frequently in Irish annals and English State papers as an important stronghold.

In the 17C a diamond-shaped gun bastion (1611) was built by Josias Bodley at the southeast corner, and the other towers and the wall-walks were lowered to accommodate cannon. The repairs carried out after the structure was bombarded by General Ginkel in 1691 can still be seen from Thomond Bridge. In the mid 18C barracks (demolished) were built within the castle walls and c 1793 the east wall and part of the southeast bastion were dismantled to enlarge the parade ground. The history of the castle and the city is traced through multi-media displays, including an audio-visual presentation, in the modern **Visitor Centre**, which is supported on piles to reveal the archaeological excavations below – pre-Norman fortifications and three houses.

In the courtyard are reproductions of war engines – mangonel, trebuchet and battering-ram. The sentry walk on the battlements between the Gate Tower and the Northwest Tower provides good views of the Shannon, the city and its surroundings.

Old Bishop's Palace ⊙ (Y) – The house, the oldest-surviving dwelling in Limerick, was designed in the Palladian style by Francis Bindon (c 1690–1765), who was a native of Limerick. It now houses the Limerick Civil Trust.

Old Exchange (Y B) – All that remains of the Limerick Exchange *(see above)*, built in 1673, is seven Tuscan columns, bricked up to form a wall.

Toll House (Y) – The Gothic-style building with castellated parapets by the eastern bridgefoot was built in 1839 at the same time as the Thomond Bridge, which is by James Pain.

Treaty Stone (Y) – *By the Thomond Bridge on the west bank of the river.* The 1691 Treaty of Limerick *(see above)* was said to have been signed on this block of limestone, which used to stand on the opposite side of the road, in front of the Black Bull public house, where it was used as a mounting-block and despoiled by souvenir hunters. In 1865 it was mounted on a pedestal and moved to the riverside.

Almshouses

Limerick is unusual among Irish towns in possessing two sets of almshouses north and south of the castle. The **Villiers Almshouses** *(north)*, founded in 1826 for 12 poor Protestant widows, each to receive £24 per annum, were designed by James Pain to form three sides of a courtyard built in the Bishop's garden. The **Corporation Almshouses** (**A**), also known as the 40-shilling (£2) Almshouses or the Widows' Almshouses, were built for the use of 20 widows by Limerick Corporation in 1691.

LIMERICK

CITY CENTRE

The old Irish town which grew up on the south bank of Abbey River, outside the walls of the English town, now forms the centre of modern Limerick.

The district south of Irish town is a fine example of 18C town planning – broad parallel streets lined with red-brick terraces – and named Newtown Pery after Edmond Sexton Pery (1719–1806), Speaker of the Irish House of Commons from 1771 to 1785.

** Hunt Museum ⊙ (Y) – The 18C Custom House designed by Italian architect Davis Duchart provides a fitting home for this outstanding collection of art and antiquities, the life's work of John and Gertrude Hunt, acknowledged experts in the field of Medieval and Religious Art. The exhibits are sensitively displayed so that visitors may explore the collection and the lives of the collectors. They span every age and include works from the immense to the miniature. Highlights on the First Floor include the wooden carved Apollo – Genius of the Arts, a small bronze Horse, attributed to Leonardo da Vinci, and a startling self-portrait by Robert Fagan (c 1745–1816), a painter of the English school and dealer in antiquities in Rome. The Second Floor is dedicated to the archaeological collection, embracing the ancient civilisations of Egypt, Greece and Rome, together with Irish treasures such as the Cashel Bell *(see CASHEL)* and Antrim Cross and a Jewellery Gallery where the Mary Queen of Scots Cross is exhibited. Religious Art on the **Ground Floor** is dramatically displayed in the Treasury; here among the gleam of silver and precious stones is a Greek coin, traditionally thought to be one of the "Thirty Pieces of Silver".

★**Georgian House** ⊘ – *2 Pery Square*. The terrace of six Georgian town houses facing People's Park, the epitome of the Newtown Pery district, was built by the Pery Tontine Company in 1838. One of the houses has been restored as a splendid example of Georgian architecture and décor; a unique feature is the basement mazzanine floor. The garden also has been faithfully re-instated. The **Ashes Exhibition** ⊘ in the coach house at the rear reflects the filming of the novel *Angela's Ashes* by Frank McCourt and life in the Limerick of his childhood.

★**John Square** (Z 20) – Started in 1751, the square is bordered on three sides by terraces of three-storey houses, plain limestone buildings with shouldered architraves above the main doorways and plain architraves surrounding the red-brick niches. Originally the houses were occupied by the wealthy citizens of Limerick, who spent the summer in Kilkee *(see KILRUSH)*; now restored, they are mainly used by the legal and medical professions.
The fourth side of the square is closed by **St John's Church** (deconsecrated), built of limestone in 1843.

★**St John's Cathedral** ⊘ (Z) – The Roman Catholic cathedral on the southern fringe of what was the old Irish town was built in the neo-Gothic style in 1861. The spire (280ft/85m high) was completed in 1883 and is the tallest in Ireland. The earliest reference to a church on this site was in 1205 when the Cathedral Chapter of the Diocese of Limerick was founded by Bishop Donatus O'Brien.

> ### Limerick Lace
>
> The traditional craft of lacemaking was introduced to Limerick in the 1820s by English lacemakers. At its 19C peak the local lace factory employed 900 girls. The elaborate Celtic patterns were outlined on machine-made cotton net in thin or thick thread and filled in with decorative stitches. The craft is still practised at the Convent of the Good Shepherd *(for visiting apply to the TIC)*.

Limerick City Gallery of Art ⊘ (Z M¹) – This two-storey building, once the Carnegie Library, set in a corner of the People's Park, now houses a permanent collection of leading Irish artists, such as Sean Keating, Jack B Yeats and Evie Hone. There are frequent visiting exhibitions.

EXCURSIONS

Cratloe Woods House ⊘ – *5mi/8km W by N 18*. A red gate-lodge marks the entrance to the estate, which provided the oak timber for the roof of Westminster Hall in London.
The house (1600) is a rare example of the Irish long house *(see p 86)*. In the early 1700s, in order to provide more privacy, a passage was added on the north side, together with a new staircase fashioned by a ship's carpenter; in 1884 the rear entrance was enclosed in a porch and became the front door. The interior displays furniture and souvenirs of the owners, direct descendants of Brian Ború and the O'Briens, the leading family of the region.
On the north side of the road covering the lower slopes of Woodcock Hill is **Cratloe Wood**; as well as the lake and forest walks there is a fine **view**★ of the Shannon Estuary from the car park *(0.75mi/1.2km from the entrance)*.

★★**Bunratty Castle** ⊘ – *7mi/11km W by N 18*. On the banks of the Bunratty River where it flows into the Shannon Estuary stands Bunratty Castle guarding the main road from Limerick to Ennis.
The **tower house**, built in 1460, was restored in the 1950s to its 16C state and now displays the Gort collection of furniture and tapestries dating from the 14C to the 17C. In the evenings medieval-style banquets are held in the Great Hall which has a fine **oak roof**.

Folk Park – The park illustrates country life in Ireland at the turn of the century when the old agricultural practices were giving way to the modern era. Some of the buildings in the park were transferred from their original sites and some are replicas: the blacksmith's forge, complete with bellows and iron-working tools; the flour mill with its river-driven horizontal wheel; the houses of many regional types including the mountain farmhouse, with its settle bed and flagstone floor, and the more elaborate thatched Golden Vale farmhouse.
The **village** contains typical 19C shops, such as a pawnshop, with its three balls symbol, a pub, a post office, a hardware shop, a grocery store, a draper's shop and a printer's workshop complete with hand-set type and a hand-operated printing press.

Bunratty Castle

Bunratty House – The house, built in 1804, is a local adaptation of the Georgian box house so common in Ireland. The **Talbot Collection of agricultural machinery** is displayed in the farmyard.

★**Castleconnell** – *7mi/11km E by N 7; bear left (sign) to Castleconnell.* Population 1 391.
The well-kept small village by the Shannon offers excellent salmon fishing and riverside walks under the trees.

★**Clare Glens** – *13mi/21km E by N 7 and R 503; E of Newport turn right (sign). Car parks both sides of the river.*
The Clare River descends from the Slievefelim Mountains in a series of **waterfalls** cascading through wooded glens.

Glenstal Abbey – *12mi/19km E by N 7 and R 506; on the N side of Murroe turn right through the park gates.*
Impressive grounds and lakes surround the castle which is now a Benedictine monastery and school *(private)*.
The modern **church** ⊘ is known for its surrealistic decor and for the Ikon Chapel in the crypt.

LISMORE★

LIOS MÓR – Co Waterford – Population 715
Michelin Atlas p 79 and Map 923 – I 11

Lismore is set on the south bank of the River Blackwater at its confluence with its tributary, the Owennashad. The small but attractive town in the shadow of Lismore Castle has one of Ireland's oldest cathedrals and some interesting domestic architecture, created during the 19C in an old-English Tudor style. The River Blackwater offers salmon, sea and brown trout fishing in idyllic rural surroundings; there is a picturesque walk along its south bank east of the bridge, which was designed in 1775 by Thomas Ivory (c 1720–86) of Cork.

HISTORICAL NOTES

The monastery founded by St Carthach in the 7C became one of Europe's most distinguished universities. In the 8C Lismore reached its academic peak, when it had 20 seats of religion or learning within its walls. In 978 the Danish Vikings raided the town and burned the monasteries.
In 1171 Henry II of England came to Lismore to receive the submission of many chiefs from Munster and Leinster, as well as those of the bishops and abbots of Ireland. Two years later Raymond le Gros completed the destruction of the monastic city. King John built a castle at Lismore in 1185 and a prosperous town grew up around its walls. In 1589 the castle passed into the hands of Sir Walter Raleigh, who sold it to Richard Boyle, the "Great" Earl of Cork. Like most of the town, it was destroyed by Cromwellian forces.

Adjacent Sights – See Caher, Clonmel, Cobh, Cork, Dungarvan, Mallow, Midleton, Youghal.

It was eventually rebuilt in the mid 19C in spectacular style by Sir Joseph Paxton, who had designed the Crystal Palace in London and was also the gardener of the Duke of Devonshire, the new owner of the castle. It rises dramatically, a magnificent neo-Tudor fantasy, over the park-like valley of the River Blackwater with its elegant bridge by the Dublin architect Thomas Ivory.

SIGHTS

★**Lismore Castle Gardens** ⊘ – The gardens, where Spenser is said to have composed part of *The Faerie Queene*, straddle the Riding Gate entrance to the castle. The lower garden, known as the Pleasure Grounds, dates from c 1850 although the Yew Walk is much earlier; it is at its best in spring – camellias, rhododendrons and magnolias. The terraced upper garden was laid out in the 17C. The central grass walk is aligned on the spire of the cathedral, and flowers and vegetables grow in the plots screened by yew, beech and box hedges. Against the north wall are greenhouses (1858) designed by Sir Joseph Paxton. The Broghill Tower *(SW corner)* provides a fine view.

★**St Carthage's Cathedral** (Anglican) ⊘ – Much of the present structure dates from the early 17C although three other religious edifices previously occupied the site. Stone fragments at the front of the west wall are all that remains of the Great Church of Lismore, mentioned in 1173. A new cathedral built in 1207 was razed during the Desmond rebellion in 1579. In 1633 Sir Richard Boyle decided to have the ruined church repaired. In 1679 Sir William Robinson was called in to complete the rebuilding. Two of the south transept windows date from this period, while the **ribbed ceilings** were built by Sir Richard Morrison about 1820 and the fine **tower** and **ribbed spire** were added in 1826 by the Payne brothers, architects in Cork. At the west end of the church there are fragments of 9C tombstones; the enormous Macgrath family **table-tomb** dates from 1548. Beside the 19C Gothic monument in the south transept is a **stained-glass window** by the pre-Raphaelite artist Sir Edward Burne-Jones. Pebbles from the Isle of Iona in Scotland are set into the floor of St Columba's Chapel.

St Carthach's Church (Roman Catholic) ⊘ – Designed by WG Doolin in 1881, it is one of the most outstanding Lombardo-Romanesque churches in Ireland, richly detailed and built of red sandstone with white limestone dressings. The square tower, adjacent to the main buildings, is in a campanile style. Over the main west door is a mosaic of Christ. The **interior** of the church features a wooden beam ceiling and a spacious gallery.

Facing the west entrance to the church is a fine row of 19C artisans' cottages.

Lismore Heritage Centre ⊘ – The Old Courthouse provides an introduction to the history of Lismore through models and an audio-visual presentation.

EXCURSIONS

★**The Gap** – *10mi/16km N by R 688*. The road through the V Gap in the Knockmealdown mountains offers fine **views**★. On the north slopes of Sugar Loaf mountain (2 144ft/653m) stands **Grubb's Grave**, the burial cairn of Samuel Grubb, a local Quaker who died in the 1920s. The sugar-loaf construction enabled him to be buried upright overlooking his estates.

★**Mount Melleray Abbey** ⊘ – *8mi/13km NE by N 72, R 669 and a minor road right*. As this abbey is a Cistercian monastery only the public church and part of the Community **church** are open to the public.

The monastery was founded in 1832 and derived its original monks from Melleray in France, where the community was threatened with suppression unless the foreign monks, who were mostly Irish, left. The monks are devoted to prayer but they also pursue a number of crafts, such as baking their own bread.

There are impressive views south from the slopes of the Knockmealdown Mountains across the Blackwater Valley.

In 1980 an extensive grotto was built in a quarry south of the monastery by the bridge. From the bridge there is an attractive walk beside the Glenshelane River.

On all town plans north is at the top of the page.

LONGFORD

AN LONGFORT – Co Longford – Population 6 393
Michelin Atlas p 91 and Map 923 – I 6

The county town of Longford lies on the Camlin River a few miles east of its confluence with the Shannon. Longford derived its name and its existence from a fortress *(longphort)*, built by the O'Farrells, but neither it nor the priory, which they founded in 1400, has survived.

The last engagement of the 1798 rebellion *(see p 222)* was fought at Ballinamuck *(10mi/ 16km north)*, where General Humbert's French and Irish volunteers were defeated by the English forces under General Lake.

> **Adjacent Sights** – See Athlone, Carrick-on-Shannon, Mullingar, Strokestown.

SIGHTS

St Mel's Cathedral ⊙ – *Dublin Street*. The cathedral, designed by Joseph Keane in 1840 in the Italian Renaissance style, resembles a Greek temple surmounted by a tall domed belfry. The interior is supported on a double row of Ionic columns. The **Diocesan Museum** *(right transept)* ⊙ houses **St Mel's Crozier** (10C), a stick of yew encased in bronze, inset with studs and decorated with animal motifs, foliage and interlacing; it was found at old St Mel's Church in Ardagh *(see below)* in 1860 and may originally have consisted of four sections. Among the other exhibits of local provenance are a number of Penal Crosses and the Ballinderry gaming board with 49 peg holes in seven rows of seven.

Town Centre – From the **Courthouse**, designed in 1791 in the Renaissance style with a pedimented central door surmounted by a Venetian window, the main street descends to the river and then climbs the north bank past the barracks adjoining the present castle (1627) and the 18C Anglican **Church of St John** *(right)*.

Maria Edgeworth (1767–1849)

She is best known for her novels on Irish life – *Castle Rackrent* (1800), *The Absentee* (1812) and *Ormond* (1817) – in which she developed the regional and historical novel; she also wrote English novels and stories for children. In her day her influence was acknowledged by Jane Austen, Macaulay, Ruskin, Thackeray, Turgenev and Sir Walter Scott, who described her as "the great Maria" and visited her in 1825. Apart from some time in England at school, she lived all her life (1767–1849) at the family home in Mostrim, also known as Edgeworthstown (8.5mi/14km east), where her circle included the Pakenhams of Tullynally and the Lefroys of Carrigglas. She was the eldest daughter of Richard Lovell Edgeworth, a wealthy landlord, who had four wives and 22 children. He was an eccentric man with an interest in science, who installed a central heating system at Tullynally Castle.

EXCURSIONS

Carrigglas Manor ⊙ – *3mi/5km E of Longford by R 194*. The castellated mansion is the home of the Lefroys, a family of Huguenot descent. It was designed in 1837 by Daniel Robertson of Kilkenny in the neo-Gothic style for Thomas Lefroy, Lord Chief Justice of Ireland and youthful inamorato of Jane Austen.

The outstanding feature of the interior (restored) is the **corniced and moulded ceilings** in the reception rooms. The house contains some fine early Dutch furniture, artefacts and pictures including many family portraits.

The **Costume Museum** *(stable buildings)* displays costumes worn by past generations of Lefroys and a collection of **lace**, some made by the ladies of Carrigglas.

The magnificent **double stable and farm yard** *(restoration in progress)* was designed by James Gandon in 1790; the stable yard is enclosed by four ranges of two storeys, with pedimented and rusticated arches, adjoining the farm yard where the lower storey is gradually absorbed into the rising ground.

The woodland garden, which contains an interesting collection of plants, was inspired by the great Victorian designer, William Robinson.

Ardagh – *20mi/32km SE of Longford by N 4 and R 393*. The charming little estate village was largely rebuilt in the 1860s by Lady Fetherstone, who lived at Ardagh House.

The ruins of a simple stone church, St Mel's Cathedral, are said to stand on the site where the saint was buried. He was appointed bishop by St Patrick, his uncle, who founded a church in Ardagh in the 5C.

Corlea Trackway

The **Ardagh Heritage Centre** ○ in the old schoolhouse traces the history of the locality from the pre-Christian era of folk tales, through the arrival of Christianity, the internal rivalries of the local O'Farrell tribe and the 1619 Plantation to the present.

Corlea Trackway ○ – *10mi/16km S of Longford by N 63 and R 397; in Keen turn right (sign).* The ancient trackway *(togher)*, discovered in the 1980s, dates from 147-8 BC. It consisted of oak planks secured by pegs and was wide enough to carry wheeled vehicles for the transport of animals and personal effects across the bog, although it lasted for only about 10 years as its weight caused it to sink below the surface. A section of it has been preserved and relaid under cover on its original site. Its excavation by an international team of archaeologists and its preservation are described in an audio-visual film; it is set in its Iron-Age context by the accompanying exhibition.

Goldsmith Country

The country around Lough Ree is where Oliver Goldsmith (c 1731–74), poet, playwright, historian and naturalist, spent the first 20 or so years of his life, visiting relatives and going to school in Elphin, Mostrim, Athlone and Lissoy.

The road from Ardagh to Athlone (N 55) links a number of sites connected with his life and work.

In **Ardagh** he himself experienced the plot of his play *She Stoops to Conquer*, by mistaking the big house for the village inn.

The site of his first boyhood home at **Pallas** is marked by a statue by Foley.

Until 1731 Goldsmith's father was Rector of **Forgney** church, which contains a stained-glass window depicting "sweet Auburn".

After her husband's death in 1747, Goldsmith's mother lived in **Ballymahon** on the Inny River.

It was in **Tang** that Goldsmith first went to school near the mill.

The pub, known as **The Three Jolly Pigeons**, preserves the name of the inn in Goldsmith's play *She Stoops to Conquer*.

Lissoy Parsonage, now in ruins, was the house where the Goldsmith family lived from 1731 to 1747; **Lissoy** village is recalled as "sweet Auburn" in his poem *The Deserted Village*.

For a clear understanding of the town maps, consult the key at the beginning of this guide.

MALLOW★

MALA – Co Cork – Population 6 434
Michelin Atlas p 78 and Map 923 – G 11

Mallow is attractively sited above the River Blackwater, sometimes described as the "Irish Rhine". It is a busy market town, noted for agricultural processing. Rathduff *(10mi/16km south)* is known for its cheese. The Duhallow Hunt was founded in Mallow in 1745.

Mallow Spa

From 1730 to 1810 Mallow was a popular spa with a fast reputation; its male patrons were known as the **Rakes of Mallow.** During the season, which lasted from April to October, visitors would take the waters before breakfast and during the afternoon; the evenings were spent in dancing and playing cards. Balls, music meetings and other diversions were held in the Long Room in emulation of the entertainment available in Bath, Tunbridge and Scarborough in England. By 1828, when the Spa House was built in the Tudor style with a pump-room, a reading room and baths, the popularity of Mallow was in decline.

The curative properties of the local water – it was reputed to be efficacious in purifying the blood – were discovered in 1724; the temperature varies from 66°F to 72°F according to the season.

HISTORICAL NOTES

The castle, built in the late 12C, had by the 16C become the seat of Sir John Norreys, Lord President of Munster. The town, which dates from 1298, was granted a charter in 1688 by King James II.

As the spa declined the town became a centre of considerable nationalistic political activity, helped by the fact that **Thomas Davis**, the mid-century political writer, was born *(no 73 Main Street)* and brought up in Mallow; so too was **William O'Brien** (1852–1928), a noted nationalist MP, who was born in what is now known as William O'Brien's House.

Adjacent Sights – See Cobh, Cork, Kilmallock, Lismore, Midleton.

Mallow has literary connections with **Anthony Trollope**, who was a resident for some years; with **Canon Sheehan**, one of Ireland's most prolific and popular authors in the late 19C and early 20C, who was born in 1852 in Mallow *(no 29 O'Brien Street)* and went to school in the town; and with Elizabeth Bowen.

Elizabeth Bowen (1899–1973)

For the first seven years of her life, Elizabeth Bowen used to spend the winter in Dublin, where she was born, and the summer at Bowen's Court (demolished), the family seat, built by Henry Bowen c 1775 near Kildorrery *(northeast of Mallow)*. Although she spent her later childhood and married life in England, she entertained many guests at Bowen's Court during the summer months until 1959 when the expense of maintaining such a large house obliged her to sell. She wrote of her early childhood days in *Seven Winters* (1942) and told her family history in *Bowen's Court* (1942). In *The Last September* (1929) she drew on her experience of country house life in Ireland. Her most widely read and best known works are *The Death of the Heart* (1947) and *The Heat of the Day* (1949).

SIGHTS

★**St James' Church** ⊘ – The modern Anglican church dates from 1824 but in its grounds are the substantial ruins of a much older building, St Anne's, for which the foundations were laid in 1291. In this older church Thomas Davis, the Protestant patriot, was baptized in 1814.

Fitzgerald Statue – JJ Fitzgerald (1872–1906) was described as a scholar, patriot and champion of all oppressed. The quotation on the statue – "Ireland has not in our time lost a more able or unselfish young patriot" – is by William O'Brien.

Clock House – *Main Street*. The curiously out-of-place half-timbered Tudor-style building (1855) consists of four storeys with an adjacent clock tower.

Mallow Castle Grounds – The castle *(private)* stands in **extensive** grounds, including a deer park, which extend to the River Blackwater with its impressive weir. At the entrance to the demesne stands the ruin of a 17C four-storey castle.

EXCURSIONS

★**Buttevant Friary** – *7mi/11km north of Mallow by N 20*. The ruins of a Franciscan friary, built in 1251, stand beside the River Awbeg next to St Mary's Roman Catholic Church. The building, which was used until recently as a place of burial, has two crypts, one above the other; the chancel walls are still largely intact.

★**Doneraile Wildlife Park** ⊘ – *6mi/10km northeast of Mallow by N 20 and R 581*. The walled demesne (395 acres/160ha) is noted for its herds of red, fallow and sika deer. Clumps of trees in this rolling parkland are broken by ornamental lakes. Doneraile Court was built c 1700 and remodelled in its present form in the early 19C; its lawn is complemented by fine old larch trees. A stone arched vault and spiral staircase are all that remains of **Kilcolman Castle**, once the residence of Edmund Spenser.

> ### Steeplechasing
>
> The first recorded **steeplechase** took place from Buttevant in 1752, using the steeple of the Anglican Church as the starting point of a race to St Leger Church near Doneraile (4.5mi/7km).

Outside the Roman Catholic church in Doneraile (population 815) stands a **statue** to Canon Sheehan, author of *My New Curate*, who was the parish priest from 1895 to 1913.

★**Annes Grove Gardens** ⊘ – *11mi/18km east of Mallow by N 72; in Castletownroche turn left onto the minor road*. The woodland gardens surrounding an 18C house and lawns overlooking the River Awbeg include a fine collection of rhododendrons and magnolias, as well as many rare trees and shrubs. Winding paths lead to the cliff garden overlooking the lily pond and the extensive river garden; in the walled garden with its 19C hedges there are herbaceous borders and water gardens.

Longueville House – *3mi/5km west of Mallow by N 72; turn right at sign*. This magnificent house (1720), now a hotel open to non-residents, features a dual staircase. The interior is hung with 18C and 19C political portraits: **Henry Grattan** and **Daniel O'Connell** in the anteroom; the presidents of Ireland, Douglas Hyde, Sean T O'Kelly, Eamon de Valera, Erskine Childers, Cearbhall ó Dálaigh and Patrick Hillery in the **Presidents' Room** restaurant.

In the courtyard at the back of the house there is a 150-year-old **maze**; the estate (500 acres/202ha) includes a **vineyard** (3 acres/1.2ha), the only one in Ireland; in a good year its grapes produce a Riesling-type wine.

★**Kanturk (Ceann Toirc)** – *13mi/21km west of Mallow by N 72 and R 576*. Population 1 870. This small market town has three interesting **bridges:** the six-arch humpback structure (1760) spanning the River Dalua; the nearby six-arch Greenane bridge (1745) over the River Allua; the four-arch Metal Bridge built in 1848 by Sir Edward Tierney over the River Dalua, at the western end of the town, near the Church of the Immaculate Conception built in the French Gothic style.

The **castle★** ruin *(south by R 579)* is still substantial. According to legend, in about 1609 the local chieftain, MacDonagh MacCarthy, built the biggest mansion to belong to an Irish chief; the English Privy Council ordered the work to stop on the grounds that "it was much too large for a subject"; when MacCarthy heard the news, he was so enraged that he threw away the blue glass tiles destined for the roof.

> ### Kilcolman Castle
>
> In 1586 a perpetual lease of the lands (3 028 acres) and castle of Kilcolman, a four-storey tower house near Doneraile, probably built by the 6th Earl of Desmond, was granted to Edmund Spenser, who held a post in the Dublin Court of Chancery which he resigned in 1588. It was at that time that he probably took up residence at Kilcolman Castle, where he lived, apart from visits to England, until 1598 and where he was visited, in the summer of 1589 by Sir Walter Raleigh. During his years at Kilcolman Spenser wrote poetry – the fourth, fifth and sixth books of *The Faerie Queen*, the *Amoretti* (love sonnets of his courtship of his second wife Elizabeth Boyle) and the *Epithalamion*, commemorating their marriage on Midsummer's Day in 1594, as well as his *Veue of the State of Ireland* (1596) and memoranda on the Irish situation. Although he had little sympathy for the Irish, Spenser's work reflects his sensitivity to the beauty of the landscape. During the Rising in 1598 Kilcolman Castle was attacked and burned by insurgents; some of Spenser's MSS may have perished, including a seventh book of *The Faerie Queen* of which only fragments are known; the poet and his family fled to England.

MAYNOOTH

Maynooth is a small town on the Royal Canal, which for centuries was the seat of the Fitzgeralds, who were made Earls of Kildare in 1316 and Dukes of Leinster in 1766; they were descendants of a Norman-Welsh adventurer who arrived in Ireland in 1169. They became one of the most powerful families in Ireland, holding the position of Lord Deputy from 1471 to 1534. The most famous was Garret Mór, the Great Earl of Kildare (d 1513). Maynooth is also famous as the site of the best-known seminary in Ireland.

> **Adjacent Sights** – See Dublin, Fingal, Kildare, Mullingar, Russborough, Trim.

SIGHTS

Maynooth Castle – At the west end of the main street stand the ruins of a castle, consisting of a massive keep surrounded by fragments of towers, walls and the entrance gate. It was built at the end of the 12C by the Fitzgeralds, who occupied it, except for 17 years following the rebellion of Silken Thomas in 1535, until 1656, when it was abandoned in favour of a new house at the east end of the main street. This house, known as Carton *(private)*, was rebuilt c 1739 by Richard Castle and remodelled c 1815 by Sir Richard Morrison.

Maynooth College ⊘ – The college, now part of the National University, was founded in 1795 as St Patrick's College, a seminary for the Irish priesthood on property offered on advantageous terms by the Duke of Leinster; an earlier college, founded by the Fitzgeralds in Maynooth in 1521, was suppressed in 1538.

A second court, added in 1845, was designed in the neo-Gothic style by Pugin. It contains the chapel which was designed in 1875 by Pugin's pupil, JJ McCarthy. The history of the college and of the town and district is presented in the **Visitor Centre**, which organises guided tours of the Chapel, Stoyte House, the Pugin building and the gardens.

EXCURSION

★★Castletown House ⊘

Celbridge; 4mi/6.4km SE of Maynooth by a minor road

The first great Palladian mansion to be built (1722) in Ireland faces south over the Liffey Valley to the Wicklow Mountains. The central block (13 bays), designed by Alessandro Galilei (1691–1737) of Florence, is linked by curved colonnades to two pavilions, designed by Sir Edward Lovett Pearce, who supervised the construction work. The house was commissioned by 'Speaker' Conolly and inherited by his great-nephew, Tom Conolly, who in 1758 married Lady Louisa Lennox (15 years old); she completed the interior decoration and replaced the formal gardens with serpentine walks and garden buildings.

Interior – A portrait of Galilei, the architect, hangs in the **hall**. The stairwell was empty until the cantilevered staircase of Portland stone was installed in 1760; its brass banisters were a novelty which started a fashion. The Baroque plasterwork (1759) is by the Lafranchini brothers.

The original 1722 scheme of interior decoration, using only local wood and stone, is preserved in the **Brown Study** – coved ceiling, tall narrow oak doors and pine panelling stained to resemble oak.

During the 1760s the ground-floor reception

> ### "Speaker" Conolly
>
> William Conolly (1662–1729) was a lawyer from Ballyshannon *(see p 158)*, who made a fortune dealing in forfeited estates after the Battle of the Boyne. He became Member of Parliament for Donegal in 1692, Commissioner of the Revenue in 1709, and in 1715 was elected Speaker of the Irish House of Commons.

rooms were remodelled to the designs of Sir William Chambers and decorated in the neo-Classical style; on display are original chairs and wallpaper, also a japanned lacquer cabinet (1740) with Italianate panels painted by Katherine, William Conolly's wife. The **print room** was decorated by Lady Louisa, who began to collect the prints of old masters' work in 1762; she started work in 1768 and finished in the 1770s.

Long Gallery, Castletown House

Irish Picture Library

The most impressive room is the **Long Gallery**. The Pompeian decor dates from the mid 1770s and was carried out by two English artists, Charles Reuben Riley and Thomas Ryder, who used vivid blue, red and green in the scheme. The chandeliers are of hand-blown glass from Murano near Venice. The portrait of Tom Conolly is a copy of the one painted in Rome in 1758 by Mengs. In Louisa's day the room was furnished with books, musical instruments and a billiard table, and was used by the family in winter as an all-purpose living room where they also took their meals.

Castletown Follies – Closing the vista to the north of the house stands the **Castletown Obelisk**, also known as the **Conolly Folly** *(visible from the windows of the Long Gallery and from the Maynooth–Castletown road);* the obelisk, mounted on two tiers of arches, was designed by Richard Castle and erected in memory of Speaker Conolly, by his wife, Katherine, to create employment during the severe winter of 1739.
The **Wonderful Barn** *(private)* which closes the north-east vista *(3mi/5km east by R 403 and R 404)* was built for Katharine Conolly in 1743 by John Glinn; it is a conical structure, with an external spiral staircase, containing four diminishing brick domes, used for drying and storing grain.

Steam Museum ⊘ *5mi/8km S of Maynooth by R 406*

The museum is housed in the old railway engineers' Gothic church, transferred from its original site in Inchicore. The Model Hall contains the Richard Guinness Collection of over 20 prototype locomotive models, dating from the late 18C. The hall is hung with the portraits of inventors and famous engineers. The Power Hall contains four live steam stationary engines and one marine engine – a six-pillar independent type beam engine from the Midleton Distillery, an architectural single-column beam engine purchased at the Manchester Exhibition in 1847 for Smithwick's Brewery in Kilkenny, a duplex steam pump from the Jameson Brewery in Dublin, a Victor Coates Mill engine used in the Frazer & Haughton bleaching and dyeing factory in Northern Ireland, and a triple-expansion marine engine from SS Divis of Belfast made by Workman Clark in 1920. Children usually enjoy working the hand pump in the courtyard.

Coolcarrigan Gardens ⊘

10mi/16km SW of Maynooth by R 408 via Donadea to Timahoe; 1mi/1.6km south of Timahoe turn right (sign).

The parkland laid out in the 19C has been much embellished by extensive planting of **shrubs** and **trees**, all clearly labelled: pine trees, clipped Irish yews, a tulip tree, acers, elaeagnus, *cedrus Atlantica*, *pinus silvestris*, buddleia, philadelphus, camellia, syringa, fuchsia, daphne and box. Roses and herbaceous borders are arranged in the formal gardens near the house. The **glasshouse** contains a vine, a passion flower, peaches and nectarines. At the end of the **woodland walk** *(30min)* through the forest there is a fine view across the Bog of Allen. The **church** (1881), which is surrounded by a moat and approached through a lych gate, is in the Hiberno-Romanesque revival style and decorated with stained glass.

MIDLETON

MAINISTIR AN CORANN – Co Cork – Population 3 266
Michelin Atlas p 79 and Map 923 – H 12

Midleton is a pleasant market town, dating from 1180, set in the rich fertile plain of East Cork on the main road from Youghal west to Cork city. It is now the centre of Irish whiskey production, where all the famous brands – except Bushmills *(see p 363)* – are distilled.

Old Midleton Distillery ⊙ – The home of Jameson Irish Whiskey is a modern distillery, built by Irish Distillers in 1975, beside the 19C buildings, which were used as a woollen mill and barracks before becoming a distillery in 1825. The tour begins with an audio-visual

Crafts – At the famous **Stephen Pearce Pottery** ⊙ *(9mi/14.5km southeast by R 630 and R 629)* visitors may watch the production process and buy the finished article.

Adjacent Sights – See Cobh, Cork, Kinsale, Youghal.

presentation on the history of the distillery and ends with a whiskey tasting; Irish whiskey, which is distilled three times, is smooth to the palate without the distinctive smokey flavour of Scotch. In between there is a guided tour of the old buildings and equipment – kiln where the malted barley was dried, five-storey storehouse where the grain was stored and turned, the water-wheel (1852) which operated five pairs of millstones, the **largest copper pot still** (1825) in the world (capacity 33 000 gallons/1 485hl), oak casks in which the spirit was matured to add tannin and vanillin for colour and taste, office where records were kept and payments made through a small window.

Midleton Distillery

Slide File, Dublin

EXCURSIONS

★**Cloyne Cathedral** ⊙ – 5mi/8km S by R 630 and R 629. The first church at Cloyne (population 731) was founded by St Colman (522–604). The **round tower** (100ft/30m high) dates from the 10C and may be climbed by visitors. The 14C cathedral (restored) contains a memorial in the north transept to its most famous bishop, **George Berkeley** (1684–1753), the distinguished philosopher, who was born at Thomastown *(see p 220)* and was bishop of Cloyne for 19 years from 1734; his line "Westward the course of empire takes its way" inspired the naming of Berkeley in California. Several interesting late-medieval tombs adorn the austere nave. A notice records that the cathedral's Coat of Arms was erected in 1722 and that the carver, Mr Maguire, was asked to complete the job for not more than £10. A small building near the cathedral is believed to be a reconstruction of St Colman's oratory.

Out and About

There are beaches and coves for bathing from Roche's Point eastwards to Knockadoon Head. Trabolgan recreation complex *(at Roche's Point)* offers an indoor swimming pool, plunge pool, sauna, solarium, fitness centre, tennis, 10-pin bowling and an indoor sports hall.

Sailing enthusiasts will find plenty of activity in Ballycotton Bay, at Roche's Point and in Cork Harbour. Anglers may choose between shore and lake fishing.

For those who prefer dry land there are many golf courses and pleasant walks, particularly along the cliffs from Roche's Point to Ballycotton.

Ballycotton – *11mi/18km SE by R 630 and R 629*. Population 444. The fishing village with its small harbour offers cliff walks overlooking Ballycotton Bay and the lighthouse on Ballycotton Island.

Rostellan Wood – *6mi/9.7km SE by R 630*. There are pleasant forest walks on the shore of Cork Harbour in what was once the demesne of Rostellan House (demolished).

Barryscourt Castle ⊙ – *4mi/6.4km W by N 25 and R 624. Restoration in progress.* The ruined castle occupies a strategic site on the main route from Cork to Waterford. The keep, which dates from 1420, is surrounded by a bawn, which incorporates the ruined wall of a 13C great hall. After an attack on the castle in 1580 by Sir Walter Raleigh *(see YOUGHAL)*, the keep was reinforced by the addition of the southwest and northeast towers. The castle takes its name from Philip de Barri of Manorbier in Wales, to whom the land was granted c 1180 by his uncle, Robert Fitzstephen, one of the first Norman adventurers in Ireland. Another member of the de Barri family was **Gerald of Wales** (c 1146–1233), also known as Giraldus Cambrensis or de Barri, an important Welsh cleric and a member of the Fitzgerald (Geraldine) family; he travelled in Ireland with Prince (later King) John and published two works – *Topographia Hibernica*, a description of the country and its people, and *Expugnatio Hibernica* (1188), an account of Henry II's conquest of Ireland.

MONAGHAN

MUINEACHÁN – Co Monaghan – Population 5 628
Michelin Atlas p 98 and Map 923 – L 5

Monaghan is the commercial centre and the county town of Co Monaghan, which was part of the original province of Ulster and projects deep into Northern Ireland as far as the Blackwater River. The town is a popular angling centre. In the 14C the McMahons established their headquarters on an artificial island *(crannóg)* in the lake and they dominated the area until the arrival of British settlers in the 17C.

Monaghan was granted a charter in 1613. Most of the grey limestone buildings lining the narrow streets date from the 18C when the town became an important centre for the linen industry; in the 19C the Ulster Canal and the Ulster Railway brought further prosperity.

Adjacent Sights – See Castle Coole, Cavan, Enniskillen, Newry.

SIGHTS

St Macartan's Cathedral ⊙ – *Dublin Road*. On a hill southeast of the town stands the Roman Catholic cathedral (1859-92) of the diocese of Clogher. It was designed by JJ McCarthy in the decorated French Gothic style and is built of local grey limestone. The exterior is dominated by the soaring spire (250ft/76m) and decorated with statues of saints and bishops. Beneath the splendid **hammerbeam roof** the interior was refurbished following Vatican II with three **tapestries** on the east wall, illustrating the Christian life and the life of St Macartan, and with a massive altar in the shape of a Tau cross, a lectern and an ambo in South Dublin granite.

Charles Gavan Duffy (1816–1903)

Duffy, who was born in Monaghan *(no 10 Dublin Street)*, became a journalist and co-founded *The Nation*. He worked through the Young Ireland movement to repeal the Act of Union, formed the Tenant Right League and was elected as MP for New Ross. Disillusioned by the lack of response from Westminster, he emigrated to Australia where he became Prime Minister of the State of Victoria (1871) and worked for federation of the states.

County Museum ⊘ – *Hill Street near the Tourist Office.* The modern museum displays the **Cross of Clogher** (14C) together with local crafts (lace) and historic and prehistoric items; art gallery.

Town Centre – The elegant **Market House** (1792), designed by Samuel Hayes, an amateur architect, in the local grey limestone with round-headed arches and decorative carved panels, now houses the Tourist Office.

Church Square *(east)* is marked by the **Courthouse** (1830) by Joseph Welland, a handsome Classical building of stone quarried in the north of the county, which bears the scars of the Civil War, and by **St Patrick's Anglican Church** (1831), designed by William Farrell in the Regency Gothic style; the east window (1862) is the work of Fred Settle Barff of Dublin.

East of Church Square is the **Diamond**, the original market place against the north wall of the 17C castle (demolished); the **Rossmore Memorial**, an elaborate neo-Gothic drinking fountain (1875) was erected to the 4th Baron Rossmore *(see below)*. At the south end of Dublin Street stands the 17C **Market Cross** in the form of a sundial; the head is upside down and the indicators are missing.

St Louis Convent – The history of the religious community from its foundation in France in 1842 is told in the **St Louis Heritage Centre** ⊘. There is a **crannóg** in Spark's Lake in the convent grounds.

EXCURSIONS

Rossmore Forest Park ⊘ – *2mi/3.5km S of Monaghan by N 54 and R 189.* The Forest Park, a delightful landscape of woods and water with rhododendron walks, was originally the demesne of the Earls of Rossmore.

Clones – *12mi/19km SW of Monaghan by N 54.* Population 2 094. Clones (pronounced as two syllables) is a pleasant market town and angling centre on the slope of a hill. In the central Diamond, below the Anglican church (1822), stands a **high cross** (c 10C) depicting *(west face)* Daniel in the Lions' Den, Cain and Abel and Adam and Eve, and *(east face)* the Crucifixion, the Last Supper and the Adoration of the Magi. It probably belonged to the monastery founded by St Tighernach in the 6C; the ruins *(bisected by Abbey Street)* include a **round tower**, a **monolithic shrine** and a **12C church.**

The **Ulster Canal Stores** ⊘ building has been converted to house a display of **Clones lace**, a crochet lace, in which individual motifs are connected by areas of Clones knot.

Clones Lace

B Lynch /Bord Fáilte, Dublin

Lough Muckno Leisure Park – *15mi/24km SE of Monaghan by N 2 to Castleblaney.* The island-studded waters of Muckno Lake are surrounded by a wooded park (91 acres/37ha) laid out with **nature trails.** It was formerly the grounds of Blaney Castle, also known as Hope Castle, as it was bought in the late 19C by Thomas Hope, a London banker; in 1830 he purchased a 45.5 carat diamond which was subsequently known as the Hope Diamond and is now in the Smithsonian Institution in the USA; it was apparently formed from the French Blue, which disappeared when the French crown jewels were stolen in 1792.

The first castle, round which Castleblaney (population 2 029) developed, was built on the orders of James I by Sir Edward Blaney, Governor of Monaghan. The 11th Lord Blaney (1784–1834) built the Georgian **Courthouse** and the Anglican church (1808).

On a town plan, the sights are indicated in orange. Some names appear on the map, others can be found by using the co-ordinates given in the caption below.

MULLINGAR

AN MUILEANN GCEARR – Co Westmeath – Population 8 040
Michelin Atlas p 91 and Map 923 – J, K 7

The county town of Westmeath is an important agricultural market in the middle of prime cattle country. It is a good centre for anglers as it lies in a loop of the Royal Canal on the west bank of the River Brosna between Lough Owel and Lough Ennell. During his student days **James Joyce** spent some time in Mullingar, where his father was reorganising the electoral rolls; he had already begun to write and the town provided him with settings for scenes in *Ulysses* and *Stephen Hero*.

HISTORICAL NOTES

In the 2C AD there was a royal residence on **Uisneach Hill** *(6mi/9.6km west by R 390)*, an ancient druidic sanctuary, where the Celts held ritual assemblies, particularly the Maytime festival. The **Catstone** marks the meeting point of the five provinces of ancient Ireland.

When the Normans arrived in the 12C, they constructed several mottes and baileys in the region as well as stone castles; a Corporation was established in Mullingar with a seal, discovered in 1880. In the 16C under Henry VIII Meath was divided in two and Mullingar became the county town of Westmeath.

> **Crafts** – At **Mullingar Bronze and Pewter** ⊘ *(5mi/8km east of Mullingar by N 4; after 4mi/6km bear left towards Killucan to The Downs)* visitors may watch the craftsmen at work, moulding, soldering, turning, polishing and blackening, and admire and purchase the finished articles in the showroom.
>
> **Sport** – Fishing and sailing on Lough Ennell.
>
> **Adjacent Sights** – See Athlone, Birr, Kells, Kildare, Longford, Trim, Tullamore.

SIGHTS

Cathedral of Christ the King ⊘ – *Mary Street*. At the end of the street, in parkland extending to the Royal Canal, rise the twin towers (140ft/43m), surmounted by crosses, of the Roman Catholic cathedral, which was dedicated in 1939. It was designed by Ralph Byrne with a Classical portico above the main door; the tympanum contains a **sculpture** in Portland stone by Albert Power. The **mosaics** in St Anne's and St Patrick's Chapels are by Boris Anrep, a Russian.

The **cathedral museum** *(upstairs – ask the Verger)* displays a letter written by Oliver Plunkett *(see p 167)*, his vestments; catechisms in Irish; a model of the earlier cathedral (1834–1936); penal crosses; chalices and monstrances.

Town Centre – In the market square stands the attractive 18C **market house**, now the local Tourist Information Office. The handsome **Courthouse** *(Mount Street)* dates from 1825. As the prison was erected opposite at the same time, public hangings took place in the intervening space.

All Saints' Church (Anglican) *(Church Avenue or Church Lane)* was built on the site of the Augustinian Priory founded in 1227 by Ralph le Petit, Bishop of Meath. The church, which incorporates some of the priory stonework, was reconstructed late in the 17C and again in 1814 when the transepts and spire were added and the rectory was built.

EXCURSIONS

★**Belvedere House and Gardens** ⊘ – *3.5mi/5.6km S of Mullingar by N 52 – half a day*. The beautiful site on the steep east bank of Lough Ennell is graced by an elegant villa (1740) which was probably designed by Richard Castle as a fishing lodge for Robert Rochfort, known locally as the Wicked Earl. From 1912 to 1960 the house became the property of Col Charles Howard-Bury.

The **Visitor Centre**, housed in the old stables, gives a detailed history of the estate, its owner and his wife.

The house has been restored to its original appearance and is furnished in period. The elegant **interior** is embellished with finely-carved wood work and ceilings of Rococo plasterwork.

The **gardens** include three terraces overlooking the lake, added by Charles Brinsley Marly, Robert's great-great-grandson. The **walled garden** was started by Marly and developed by Col Bury. The **woodland walk** *(2mi/3km)* on the north side of the house includes an **octagonal gazebo**, a **Gothic arch**,

> **Everest Expedition**
>
> In 1921 Col Charles Howard-Bury led an expedition to Everest. Dressed in Donegal tweed his party came within 2 000ft/609m of the summit, took the first photos of the mountain and brought back stories told by the local porters of "abominable snowmen" clad in their own hair.

The Wicked Earl

Robert Rochfort (1708–79), created 1st Earl of Belvedere in 1757, was a quarrelsome man. In 1736, following the death of his first wife, he married Mary Molesworth, aged 16; she was reluctant but her father was keen on the title and Robert's position at court; four children were born. As Robert spent more and more time at court, Mary turned in her need for company to her brother-in-law Arthur and his wife. Rumours of an affair between Mary and Arthur reached Robert. He brought an action against his brother for £20 000 damages; as Arthur was unable to pay, he went abroad. On his second visit to Ireland Robert had him arrested and he spent the rest of his life in prison. Mary was confined at Gaulstown, seeing no one but the servants. Once she escaped but her parents in Dublin sent her back to Gaulstown, where she stayed until Robert's death in 1774 when she was released by her son. Robert's rare visits to Gaulstown ceased completely once he had built Belvedere.

an **ice house** and two **stone bridges** over the stream. The 18C plantations of beech have been supplemented by exotic conifers and other rare and ornamental trees. The **jealous wall** (148ft/45m high), designed as a mock-Gothic ruin, was built in about 1760 by Robert either to hide the stables or to blot out the view of Tudenham House (now in ruins), the residence of his brother George, with whom he had quarrelled.

★**Multyfarnham Franciscan Friary** – *8mi/13km N of Mullingar by N 4; in Ballynafid turn right.* The outdoor Stations of the Cross are composed of life-size figures set in a grove of evergreens beside a swiftly flowing stream.

Taghmon Church – *7mi/11.5km N of Mullingar by N 4 and R 394; in Crookedwood turn right.* Between the stream and the foot of the slope on the site of a monastery founded by St Fintan Munna stands a fortified church, which probably dates from the 15C; the four-storey tower contains living accommodation and has two sculpted heads incorporated in the north and west walls.

★**Tullynally** ⊙ – *15mi/24km N of Mullingar by R 394 to Castlepollard and R 395 west; ramped drive (0.75mi/1.2km) from gateway to house.* Tullynally, the seat of the Pakenham family since 1655, is a great grey

The Children of Lir

Tullynally is the old Irish place name, which means the Hill of Swans, and Tullynally Castle is set on high ground sloping south to Lough Darravaragh, where, according to Irish legend, the Children of Lir spent 300 years after they were changed into swans by their jealous stepmother.

pile of turrets and crenellations, formerly known as Pakenham Hall. The original fortress with its masonry walls (10ft/3m thick) was converted early in the 18C into a country house. In the 19C Francis Johnston added a Gothic façade (1801–05); the central tower and the two wings (1840) – for the Dowager Countess and the servants – linking the house to the stable block were designed by Sir Richard Morrison. The tour of the castle includes the **drawing room**, designed by Francis Johnston in 1806; the **Great Hall**, designed in 1820 by James Shiel, which rises through two storeys to a vaulted ceiling and originally had red and blue painted woodwork; the octagonal **dining room**, with wallpaper designed by Pugin for the House of Lords and country-style Chippendale furniture; the extensive **library**. The Victorian service wings display the equipment required to run a large country house – butler's room; **kitchen** splendidly equipped with ovens, copper pans, a great pestle and mortar and an ice chest; **laundry** fitted with lead-lined sinks, washing boards and a huge box mangle; **ironing room**; **drying room** with vertical racks; **boiler room**. The family coach (restored) is on display in the courtyard.

By 1760 the early-18C formal layout with canals and cascades had been replaced by **gardens** designed in a more natural landscape style; the terraces were created in the Victorian era for tennis and croquet. The **woodland garden** contains a beech tree, that produces both cut-leaved and normal foliage. The **flower garden** dates from 1740; a "weeping pillar" embellishes the lily pond. Two sphinxes (1780) made of Coade stone flank the gate into the huge walled **kitchen garden**; its former glory is still appreciable in the fruit trees trained

A Literary Family

The talented Pakenham family includes Lord Longford, a Socialist peer, his wife Elizabeth who writes biographies, their son, Thomas Pakenham, an author, and their daughters Antonia Fraser, another biographer, and Rachel Billington, a novelist.

against the walls, in the Regency glasshouses, where grapes and peaches were grown, and in the avenue of Irish yews linked by a variegated hedge of box, yew and holly, so dense that moss can grow on its surface.

From the stretch of ornamental water a **forest walk** leads past a waterfall to the lower lake (herons, swans and wild duck) and a **view** of the castle.

★**Fore Abbey** – *15mi/24km N of Mullingar by R 394 to Castlepollard and R 195 east; turn right to Fore*. The ancient monastic site of Fore was inhabited from the 7C to the 16C. It was enclosed within a wall, under a charter of murage (1436), to protect it from attack by the Irish. The ruins of the south and west gates are visible beside the road. Various features have traditionally been known as the **"Seven Wonders of Fore"** and described in miraculous terms.

The "monastery in a bog" is the **abbey**, founded in 1200 by the de Lacys for a community of Benedictine monks from Normandy, which stands on an island of firm ground surrounded by a marsh. The 15C cloister arcade, part of which was re-erected in 1922, is bordered by the ruins of the 13C church, sacristy and chapter-house, and the 15C refectory and kitchen. Two towers were added when the abbey was walled. From the top of the west tower *(75 steps)* there is a good **view**; east stand the remains of a **columbarium** and of the **watergate**.

The "water that will not boil" refers to water from **St Fechin's Well** in the shade of a "tree that will not burn" with "no more or less than three branches", representing the Trinity; only one branch survives.

The "stream that flows uphill" appeared when St Fechin beat the ground with his crozier beside Lough Lene on the south side of the hill, to supply water power to the "mill without a race", which had been built at his command on dry ground; the mill ruins stand near the road beside a stream that flows from an underground source. The "hermit in the stone" was Patrick Beglen, the last anchorite in Ireland, who lived in the 17C in an old medieval watchtower, which was incorporated in 1680 into a **chapel mausoleum** for the Nugent family.

The "stone raised by St Fechin's prayers" is the huge lintel marked with a Greek cross over the west doorway of **St Fechin's Church** *(south)*, an 11C or 12C building named after the founder who died in 665. The figure of a seated monk is carved in the moulding *(north side)* of the chancel arch (1200).

NEW ROSS

ROS MHIC TREOIN – Co Wexford – Population 5 012
Michelin Atlas p 80 and Map 923 – L 10

Despite its late-19C appearance New Ross is one of the oldest settlements in Co Wexford and dates from the late 6C. Its narrow streets, many linked by footpaths incorporating flights of steps, rise steeply from the quays on the east bank of the wide River Barrow to Irishtown, an earlier monastic settlement, on the heights above. Rosbercon is a small suburb on the west bank of the river. New Ross is still an important inland port; its industries include the manufacture of fertiliser which began in the 1950s.

HISTORICAL NOTES

In the late 6C or early 7C St Abban founded a monastery on the heights near Irishtown. New Ross itself was founded in about 1200 by William le Marshall, Earl Marshal of Ireland, and his wife, Countess Isabelle de Clare, daughter of Strongbow. The first bridge across the River Barrow was built in 1211 and in 1265 the first town walls were constructed. By the 14C New Ross had become the principal port of Ireland but was overtaken in importance by Waterford by the end of the 17C. In 1649 the town was captured and devastated by Cromwell but in the 1798 rebellion it was successfully

> **Eating Afloat** – **Galley Cruising Restaurants** ⊘ organise gourmet and ecological boat trips on the local rivers.
>
> **Adjacent Sights** – See Clonmel, Enniscorthy, Kilkenny, Waterford, Wexford.

defended against the insurgents. During the mid 19C New Ross had a substantial maritime trade, its ships going as far afield as Newfoundland and the Baltic ports.

SIGHTS

★**St Mary's Church** ⊘ – The early-19C Anglican church was built on the site of the nave and crossing of what was probably the largest parish church in medieval Ireland, and belonged to an abbey founded by William le Marshall and his wife Isabelle between 1207 and 1220. The extensive abbey ruins are surrounded by a large unkempt graveyard. The south transept was restored in the 15C but the tower collapsed in 1763. The ruined chancel contains some striking late-13C and early-14C effigies.

Roman Catholic Parish Church – The design of the church with its high ceiling and Corinthian columns was inspired by that of St Mary's Church *(adjacent)*; the frieze and cornice above the altar were made by craftsmen from Bannow. Construction began in 1832 but was interrupted by the cholera epidemic in that year which killed 3 000 people in New Ross. The first building on the site was an Augustinian residence (1725); a chapel was erected in 1728. From the front of the church there are views over the town and river.

Medieval Gates – At Fair Green there are substantial remains of the 15C Maiden Gate; the Mural Tower and the Three Bullet Gate nearby date from the 14C. Cromwell entered the town in 1649 through the latter gate.

Tholsel ⊘ – This building, surmounted by a tower and a weather-vane, was built in 1749 and rebuilt in 1806, when the ground subsided. It houses the local council, which holds many volumes of corporation minutes dating from the 17C, as well as the mace of Charles II (1699) and the charter of James II (1688). Opposite the building is a statue of a **croppy boy**, a local term for the insurgents in the 1798 rebellion, owing to their short hair; it commemorates the uprising and the subsequent battle of New Ross.

Dunbrody Project ⊘ – *2mi/3.2km SE by N 25*. The project, inspired by the ideals and legacy of John Fitzgerald Kennedy, aims to record the achievement of Irish men and women at home and overseas. The main feature is the construction of a replica *Dunbrody*, a 3-masted bark which sailed to Canada for timber, to the States for cotton and to Peru for guano; during the Great Famine on the outward voyage, lasting 6-8 weeks, she carried 176 emigrants across the Atlantic.

EXCURSIONS *N of New Ross*

★**Graiguenamanagh** – *11mi/18km N of New Ross by N 30, R 700 and R 705*. Population 1 395. The riverside quays, once the site of much commercial activity, provide good walks beside the Barrow, a fine fishing river. The Duiske Inn (prounced Dooishka), near the bridge, displays many old photographs showing aspects of life in Graiguenamanagh in the earlier decades of this century.

★★**Duiske Abbey** ⊘ – The most outstanding feature of the restoration is the high-pitched church roof, constructed from unseasoned timbers of oak and elm with wooden pegs to secure the joints. The effigy of the Knight of Duiske, cross-legged, sword-seizing, dates from about 1300 and is one of the most impressive anywhere in Ireland; the knight's identity remains a mystery.

The Abbey Centre houses a museum, which displays some of the Abbey plate and other items relating to the abbey, and a gallery exhibiting the work of contemporary artists on Christian themes using a variety of media.

The abbey, which once covered most of the present town, was established early in the 13C by William le Marshall, Earl of Pembroke. Although it was suppressed in 1536, monks continued to occupy it for many years afterwards; the tower collapsed in 1774.

★**Inistioge** – *10mi/16km N of New Ross by N 30 and R 700*. Inistioge (pronounced Inisteeg), one of the most attractive villages in the locality, is set on the west bank of the Nore which is spanned by a 10-arch bridge; there are riverside walks *(picnic areas)*.

The ruins of a 1220 **castle**, once the borough courthouse, stand between the river and the **square**, which contains the remains of a cross erected in 1621 and damaged in 1798; on the west side next to the ruined Tholsel is the **Armillary Sphere**, a device said to have been invented by Eratosthenes in 250 BC to demonstrate the movements of the earth and moon. The 19C almshouse was built by Lady Louisa Tighe. The Roman Catholic church contains stone carvings *(near the entrance)* of uncertain date, said to illustrate the legend of the mermaid being taken from the River Nore in the village in 1118; up the lane is **St Colmcille's Well.**

Adjoining the Anglican Church are the tower, nave and Lady Chapel of an **Augustinian priory**, founded in 1210 and dedicated to St Mary and St Columba *(Colmcille)*. In the graveyard is the elaborate tomb erected in memory of Mrs Mary Tighe, a locally famous poet, who died in 1810.

Woodstock Forest Park *(1mi/1.6km SW of Inistioge)* is the former Tighe family demesne offering forest walks, an old tiled Japanese garden and a conical dove-cote; the house is largely ruined.

EXCURSIONS *S of New Ross*

★**Kennedy Arboretum** ⊘ – *7.5mi/12km S of New Ross by R 733 and R 734; turn right (sign)*. The arboretum (667 acres/252ha), opened in 1968 in memory of John F Kennedy, President of the USA, is divided into the plant collection, forest plots and mountain heathland. The many varieties of shrubs and trees are arranged in two circuits, one mainly conifers, the other broadleaf. When complete the collection should total 6 000 species. There are extensive walks through the arboretum, and a scenic road winds to the summit of Slieve Coillte. The views are superb, taking in the rich pattern of enclosed farmland, the Hook Peninsula and mountain ranges. Footpaths radiate from the car park, one of them leading to the **Mountain Viewpoint**, where a memorial stone commemorates the 1798 rebels who camped here.

Kennedy Homestead ⊙ – *Dunganstown; 4mi/6.4km S of New Ross by R 733 and the minor road W*. The birthplace in 1820 of the great-grandfather of John F Kennedy, President of the USA (1961–63) now displays photographs and mementoes of the President's visit in 1963, including the wreath he laid on the graves of the leaders of the 1916 Easter Rising at Arbour Hill in Dublin; family tree in Ireland and America.

Kilmokea Gardens ⊙ – *10mi/15km S of New Ross by R 733 and a minor road west*. In the 10C Hervey de Montmorency, Strongbow's uncle, established himself on Great Island, which was separate from the mainland until land reclamation took place in the 19C. A rectangular earthwork on the island probably represents the outline of his stronghold. Another enclosure within earthen ramparts (20 acres/8ha) was the site of an Early Christian monastic foundation. Within it stands a handsome Georgian glebe house; its gardens, developed over half a century, offer a delightful contrast between formal areas close to the house and a luxuriant, carefully created and maintained jungle extending along the narrow valley of a tiny stream.

★**Dunbrody Abbey** ⊙ – *10mi/15km S of New Ross by R 733. Key at Furlong's cottage by the main road entrance*. Close to the village of Clonmines, a deserted medieval borough with remains of tower houses, fortified church and Augustinian priory, are the handsome ruins of the abbey founded in 1170 by Hervey de Montmorency *(see Kilmokea above)*. The roofless but well-preserved cruciform abbey church, pleasantly set above an inlet of the river Barrow, has a low turreted tower and six transept chapels with slender single-light windows. Slight traces exist of some of the outlying buildings.

The abbey was built in 1182 by Cistercian monks from St Mary's Abbey in Dublin. It had the right of sanctuary and the abbot sat in the House of Lords. The last abbot was Alexander Devereux, elevated to the bishopric of Ferns in 1537.

After the Dissolution, the abbey passed into the hands of the Etchingham family; there are substantial remains of the fortified dwelling they erected around the Norman keep built to defend the abbey. In its grounds is a new-grown maze of yew.

Ballyhack Castle ⊙ – Overlooking the ferry crossing to Passage East on the west bank of Waterford Harbour is an imposing tower house (15C or 16C); steep stairs in the thickness of the wall link the five floors, of which the ground and first floor are vaulted and the others now open to the sky. The site originally belonged to the Knights Templar, from whom it passed to the Knights Hospitaller and then came into the possession of the Earl of Donegall.

★**Duncannon** – This small seaside village, partly built on a peninsula, has an attractive sandy beach. **Duncannon Fort** ⊙ (3 acres/1.2ha) was first selected for defensive purposes by the Anglo-Normans in the 12C. In 1588, as part of the precautions against the Spanish Armada, the fortress was strengthened and assumed its present star-shaped form with a dry moat. In 1690 both James II and William III took ship from Duncannon following the Battle of the Boyne.

★**Tintern Abbey** ⊙ – *5mi/8km E of Duncannon by R 737, R 733 and R 374 to Saltmills. Restoration in progress*. The ruined Cistercian abbey, a daughter house of Tintern Abbey in Monmouthshire, whence its name, was founded in 1200 by William the Earl Marshal in thanksgiving for his safe crossing from England in a violent storm. At the Dissolution of the Monasteries in the 16C the abbey was granted to the Colclough family, who took up residence in the nave and tower.

Hook Head Peninsula – A remote location, quiet beaches and distinctive landscapes have long drawn holiday-makers to the Hook Head Peninsula, bounded to the west by Waterford Harbour and to the east by Bannow Bay. In spring and autumn the peninsula is an important bird-watching location where over 200 species have been recorded.

Fethard, the largest town on the peninsula, was founded by the Anglo-Normans, whose first expedition to Ireland landed in 1169 at Bannow Island.

Slade is a minute fishing village, with a small double harbour, and is a popular scuba-diving centre because of the clear water and the range of interesting sea formations. On the pier are the remains of 18C salthouses where sea water was evaporated to make salt. Beside them stand the ruins of **Slade Castle**, consisting of a tower house (15C–16C) and a house (16C–17C), built by the Laffan family.

At the seaward end of the narrow limestone promontory stands **Hook Head Lighthouse** ⊙, one of the oldest lighthouses in Europe, where a light was maintained almost continuously for 1 500 years. The cylindrical keep (82ft/25m) with its vaulted chambers was built by the Normans in the early 13C to aid navigation up Waterford Harbour to their port at New Ross. It is topped by a more conventional structure erected early in the 19C.

PORTUMNA★

PORT OMNA – Co Galway – Population 984
Michelin Atlas p 90 and Map 923 – H 8

Portumna, meaning the port of the oak, is a major crossing point on the River Shannon where it enters Lough Derg, the lowest and most attractive of the Shannon lakes, which is a wildlife sanctuary.

★**Portumna Castle** ⊘ – The castle, which stands in the northeast corner of the park, was the seat of the Burke family. The approach passes through a series of formal gardens divided by an Adam Gate (partially ruined), a Gothic Gate and a Tuscan Gate *(nearest the house)*; the beds are planted

> **Portumna Lifting Bridge** ⊘ – The road bridge over the Shannon is raised at regular intervals to allow the passage of vessels on the river.
>
> **Facilities** – Coarse angling and game fishing and boating on the lake.
>
> **Adjacent Sights** – See Athenry, Birr, Clonmacnoise.

with rose trees. The handsome fortified house (restored) dates from 1518 and was accidentally destroyed by fire in 1826. The exhibition traces the history of the family, the house and its restoration. The castle caught fire in 1826 and was abandoned; a new house, designed by Sir Thomas Deane, was built but has left no trace.
The gate lodge *(opposite Reception)* displays a cannon, left by Patrick Sarsfield after the Battle of Aughrim *(see p 106)*.

Portumna Castle

Portumna Priory – South of the castle stand the ruins of a priory, originally a Cistercian chapel, which was granted to the Dominicans by O'Madden, the local chieftain. The north and south windows at the eastern end of the church, probably part of the Cistercian building, date from the 13C. The rest of the priory is 15C and contains some fine windows. The north transept seems to have been used as living accommodation. Parts of the cloisters were re-erected this century.

Portumna Forest Park – The park (1 400 acres/566ha), which extends west along the north shore of Lough Derg, combines a deer park with forest walks, nature trails, an observation tower, a marina and yacht club.

EXCURSIONS

★**Clonfert Cathedral** ⊘ – *17mi/27km NE of Portumna by N 65, R 355, R 356 via Eyrecourt and a minor road east; key available at the lodge.* The church was built in the 12C, probably for Conor O'Kelly, on the site of a monastery founded in 563 by St Brendan the Navigator *(see p 200)*. The **west doorway**★★ is a masterpiece of Hiberno-Romanesque decoration in red sandstone. It is surmounted by a triangular hood, containing alternating human heads and triangles above a row of arches,

---

De Burgo – de Burgh – Burke

The illustrious name of Burke derives from de Burgo, of Norman origin. In 1193 William de Burgo, who came to Ireland with Prince John in 1185, married the daughter of Donal Mor O'Brien, king of Thomond; his son was made Lord of Connaught; in 1265 Walter de Burgo was created Earl of Ulster. In the 14C the property passed to a descendant of Richard, Lord of Connaught, who adopted the name de Burgh by royal licence and was made Earl of Clanrickard in 1543. John, the 9th Earl, abandoned the family tradition of loyalty to the crown and fought with the Jacobites; he was taken prisoner at Aughrim (1691) and his lands confiscated but they were redeemed 12 years later for £25 000. On the death of Hubert de Burgh Canning (1832–1916), who was a bachelor recluse, the title passed to the Marquess of Sligo and the land to Henry Lascelles, 6th Lord Harewood who married the Princess Royal, daughter of George V and Queen Mary.

---

and is framed by six recessed orders decorated with a variety of motifs and animal heads. The sixth order was added in the 15C, at the same time as the tower, south transept and sacristy. The chancel arch, also 15C, is carved with angels, a rosette and a mermaid; the beautiful east windows are Romanesque. The Romanesque south transept is in ruins; the Gothic north transept has been demolished.

The grounds *(through the rear churchyard gate; turn left)* contain an ancient **yew walk**, now suffering from storm damage and exposure; it was probably planted by the monks in the shape of a cross over 400 years ago. The ruined Bishop's Palace belonged to Sir Oswald Mosley from 1951 to 1954 when it was destroyed by fire. The charming circular oratory serves the Emmanuel Retreat House.

Meelick Franciscan Friary – *7mi/11km NE of Portumna by N 65, R 355 and a minor road east.* The friary was built in the 15C on a slight rise overlooking the Shannon. In 1986 the ruins were restored and the church roofed and equipped for worship. Most of the walls, the west door and two arches in the south wall are original; between the arches is a small figure of St Francis, which was added later. During the restoration four quills were found in a chimney in the dwelling house, which dates from 1732.

A short walk *(0.5mi/1km east)* leads to Meelick Weir and Victoria Lock, the largest lock on the Shannon.

Lorrha – *6mi/10km E of Portumna by R 489 via Portumna Lifting Bridge and a minor road south.* The tiny village contains three ruined churches. Part of one is used for Anglican worship; on the west front there are antae and a 13C doorway framing a 15C doorway carved with a pelican vulning (pecking at her breast). It stands on the site of a monastery founded by St Ruadhán (d 845), a disciple of St Finian of Clonard. **St Ruadhan's Church** is a 15C building with an ornate west doorway, handsome east and west windows and a vaulted sacristy. On the south side of the village, next to the Roman Catholic church, are the remains of a church belonging to a Dominican priory founded by Walter de Burgo c 1269. The chancel was lit by a five-light east window and several lancets in the south wall.

ROSCREA★

ROS CRÉ – Co Tipperary – Population 4 170
Michelin Atlas p 85 and Map 923 – I 9

Roscrea is a prosperous agricultural town on the steep banks of the Bunnow River. It was founded in the 7C by St Cronan and developed into a medieval borough. The principal medieval relics are the castle and monastery.

SIGHTS

Roscrea Castle ⊙ – The 13C **castle** is an irregular polygonal enclosure surrounded by curtain walls and two D-shaped towers. It was originally entered through a gatetower (c 1280), topped by 17C gables and chimneys; the portcullis winding gear is visible in the Great Hall. The gatetower now houses the **Roscrea Heritage Centre**, which presents an exhibition on the history of Norman castles in Ireland, including Roscrea.

★ **Damer House** – Standing within the castle walls is an elegant 18C three-storeyed house containing a handsome pine staircase. It was started in 1715 by Joseph Damer, the richest man in the country when he died in 1720 and a member of a Plantation family which came to Ireland in 1661. The house was

Adjacent Sights – See Abbeyleix, Athy, Birr, Kilkenny.

completed in the 1720s and became the residence of the Anglican Bishop of Killaloe. In 1798 it was used as a military barrack. After remaining vacant for many years this century, it was saved from demolition to make way for a council car park. The rooms house exhibitions of local historical interest and a computerised genealogical service.

St Cronan's Church and Round Tower – *Church Street*. The site of a monastery, founded by St Cronan during the early 7C and destroyed four times during the 12C, is marked by the west façade of a 12C church; the carved figure above the doorway is probably St Cronan. North of the ruins stands a 12C **high cross** bearing two carved figures at the foot of the north and south faces of the shaft. The 8C **round tower** (60ft/18m high) lost its conical cap in 1135; another piece (20ft/6m) was destroyed in the fighting in 1798.

Franciscan Friary – The present Roman Catholic church of St Cronan, set on a slight incline, is approached through the bell-tower of the original 15C friary. The east and north walls of the earlier chancel and part of the nave arcade have been incorporated into the modern church.

EXCURSION

Monaincha Abbey – *1mi/1.6km W by N 7 and minor road from the roundabout*. The ruined abbey church stands on a raised site, once an island in a bog; it has a finely carved 12C west doorway and chancel arch, of sandstone. The sacristy dates from the 15C or 16C. The monastery was probably founded in the 6C by St Cainnech of Aghaboe in Co Laois but was also associated with St Cronán of Roscrea.

Devil's Bit Mountain – *15mi/24km S of Roscrea by N 62*. Legend has it that the gap at Devil's Bit Mountain was scooped out by the devil to form the Rock of Cashel. Reality is more prosaic; the hollow was created by glacial action. There is an easy climb to the summit of the mountain (1 577ft/479m), rewarding for the extensive views of the Golden Vale to the south and east.

RUSSBOROUGH★★★
Co Wicklow
Michelin Atlas p 87 and Map 923 – M 8

The magnificent Palladian mansion stands on slightly rising ground facing a stretch of water backed by the Wicklow Mountains. The grass terraces to the rear are part of the original landscaping. The short drive passes the old riding school before the full façade, consisting of a central block built of Wicklow granite, linked to two pavilions by curved colonnades, is revealed to view.

Adjacent Sights – See Athy, Dublin, Glendalough, Kildare, Maynooth, Powerscourt, Wicklow Mountains.

The house (1741–51) was designed by Richard Castle; following his death in 1757, the work was completed by Francis Bindon. It was commissioned by Joseph Leeson, made Earl of Milltown in 1763, who in 1740 had inherited a fortune from his father, a wealthy Dublin brewer. His caricature in stucco appears above the door from the staircase hall to the entrance hall.

TOUR ⊙ *1hr*

The ground floor is richly decorated with stucco ceilings, probably by the Lafranchini brothers, in the saloon, library and music room. The Dining Room and the barrel vault in the Tapestry Room are probably the work of pupils. An unknown and less accomplished hand created the very thick and ornate stucco on the staircase, depicting a hunting scene. The drawing room is probably the work of Francis Bindon; the decorative stucco panels on the walls were designed for the four Vernet seascapes, now back in their original places after being sold in 1926. Such

Bord Fáilte, Dublin

Drawing Room, Russborough

263

Beit Art Collection

The paintings, which are displayed in the main rooms, were collected in the late 19C by Alfred Beit (1853–1906). In 1875 he went to South Africa where he became a friend of Cecil Rhodes; together they founded the De Beers Diamond Mining Company. On his death he left his collection to his younger brother, whose son, Sir Alfred Beit, bought Russborough as a home for the collection in 1952. The collection has a strong emphasis on works from the Dutch, Flemish and Spanish schools but also contains Italian, French and English paintings, Italian bronzes, European porcelain, furniture, tapestries and carpets.

---

richness is complemented by ornate mantelpieces and extensive use of carved mahogany for the doors, dados, staircase and saloon floor, which is inlaid with satinwood.

The bedrooms on the upper floor contain maple and bamboo furniture and displays of porcelain and silver.

SKIBBEREEN

SCIOBAIRÍN – Co Cork – Population 1 926
Michelin Atlas p 77 and Map 923 – E 13

This busy market town owes its existence to Algerian pirates, who raided the neighbouring settlement of Baltimore in 1631. Some of the English settlers were captured but the remainder fled inland and set up two settlements, known as Bridgetown and Stapleton, which grew into Skibbereen.

The town suffered severely during the 19C famine but has regained a certain economic vitality in the last years of the 20C.

"Keeping an eye on the Czar of Russia"

In the 1890s a leader in the *Skibbereen Eagle* remarked that the paper was "keeping an eye on the Czar of Russia". The comment, outrageously bombastic for a small provincial newspaper, was picked up by the international wire services and went around the world. Still quoted today, it turned out to be the most famous line ever written in an Irish newspaper. The files of the old *Eagle* may be inspected by appointment at the offices of the *Southern Star* newspaper in Ilen Street.

EXCURSIONS

South of Skibbereen

★**Creagh Gardens** ⊙ – *3.5mi/5km W of Skibbereen by R 595.* The gardens (30 acres/12ha) were created in 1945 on gently sloping ground leading down to a sea-estuary. They are designed for the Romantic in the Robinsonian style with woodland glades. There are many rare and tender plants, traditional walled kitchen gardens and exotic farmyard fowl.

The Liss Ard Foundation ⊙ – *2mi/3km S of Skibbereen by R 596.* The estate is tended so as to enhance the natural flora and fauna. Each element is isolated from the rest to create a series of open-air "rooms" where visitors are invited to linger long in contemplation of the colours, shapes and sounds – the subtle colours in the wild flower meadow, the rustle of leaves in the woodland walk, the ripples on the surface of the lake, the chuckling of the waterfalls or the silence of the grass arena and oval of sky in the Crater, created by James Turrell *(see p 220)*.

Out and About

Events – The **West Cork Arts Centre** ⊙ *(North Street)* holds regular arts events.

Boat Trips ⊙ – In Roaring Water Bay and to **Sherkin Island** and **Cape Clear Island** from Baltimore and Skull *(see below)*.

Sailing – At Baltimore (temporary in summer) and Skull.

Adjacent Sights – See Bantry, Cork, Kinsale.

★**Castletownshend** – *5.5mi/8km SE of Skibbereen by R 596.* Population 147. The steep Main Street of this tiny village descends to the water's edge where a small pier offers views across the Castle Haven estuary.

St Barrahane's Church (Anglican) ⊙ is attractively set at the top of four flights of steps *(50)* at the foot of the Main Street; the Nativity Window was designed by Harry Clarke.

Somerville and Ross

The village of Castletownshend was once a stronghold of the Protestant Ascendancy, whose way of life in west Cork was comically portrayed by Edith Somerville and Violet Martin, second cousins, who wrote in partnership as **Somerville and Ross**. They are buried in the graveyard of St Barrahane's Church. Their most successful work, *Some Experiences of an Irish RM* (1899), led to *Further Experiences of an Irish RM* (1908) and *In Mr Knox's Country* (1915). Their novel *The Real Charlotte* (1894) is in a much less light-hearted vein. *The Big House at Inver* (1925) is the best of the novels written by Edith Somerville after Violet Martin's death.

Lough Hyne Nature Reserve – *6mi/10km southwest of Skibbereen by R 595 and a minor road south. Extensive observation facilities in preparation. The presence of sea urchins makes barefoot paddling dangerous.* Set among low hills, this marine nature reserve containing unpolluted salt water provides a unique ecosystem; over 60 species have been recorded, including the redmouth goby, otherwise found in Portugal. From the north side of the lough a track leads to a prominent viewpoint in the forest providing extensive panoramas of the area.

Baltimore – *8mi/13km SW of Skibbereen by R 595.* The fishing village offers some of the safest anchorages on the south-west coast. Overlooking the two piers – one old, one new – are the ruins of the early-17C fortified house built by Sir Fineen O'Driscoll. On the headland *(1mi/1.6km south)* stands **Lot's wife**, a medieval beacon, shaped like a rocket and painted white; from its immediate vicinity there are panoramic **views** of Sherkin Island.

★**Sherkin Island** – *A full day is needed to explore the island; if the weather turns stormy visitors may be marooned for a night or more.* Population 70. The **marine research station**, a privately owned undertaking, monitors the marine environment and organises courses on pollution.

Sherkin has three pubs, a number of guesthouses and four roads leading north and west from the harbour. The extensive ruins of a Franciscan **friary** near the harbour date from 1460.

Baltimore

Slide File, Dublin

Cape Clear Island – *At least two days, more in bad weather, are needed to visit the island. Basic accommodation for visitors is provided by the bird observatory.* The vast seabird colonies attract many ornithologists to Cape Clear Island. The north and south harbours are divided by an isthmus; the one tiny village is called **Cummer**. The island is one of the last bastions of the Irish language in west Cork. Many of the people living here are called O'Driscoll or Cadogan, which presents problems for the postman.

Mizen Peninsula

Tour of 35mi/56km W of Skibbereen – 1 day

From Skibbereen take N 71 W. After 10mi/16km turn left.

Ballydehob – Population 260. The steeply sloping Main Street is lined with many brightly painted houses. The 12-arch railway bridge, part of the Skull and Skibbereen light railway which closed in 1947, has been converted into a **walkway**.
Take the minor road north uphill bearing W and S to Mount Gabriel and Skull.

Mount Gabriel – This mountain (1 339ft/408m) offers a challenging climb. The traces of Bronze Age copper mining on the slopes contrast with the modern technology of the two globes near its summit which are aircraft tracking stations.
Take the road S to Skull.

Road Bowls

The ancient Irish sport of road bowling is still played on Sundays in Co Cork and Co Armagh. A heavy iron ball (28oz/794g; 7in/18cm) is hurled along a stretch of quiet winding country road in as few throws as possible; the ball may hurtle through the air at shoulder height. Betting is heavy.

★★View – Beyond the pass there is a fine view of Skull and Roaringwater Bay.

★Skull (Schull) – *Ferries to Baltimore and Cape Clear Island (see above).* Population 579. This small market town and commercial fishing centre is popular with yachtsmen. Skull can also claim two bookshops. The **planetarium** ⊘ presents an exhibition, regular astronomy shows *(60 seats)* and holds telescope viewing nights.
Continue W; in Toormore turn left into R 591 to Goleen and Crookhaven. Turn right (sign) at the entrance to the village of Goleen.

The Ewe Art Retreat ⊘ – This residential art centre welcomes visitors to its gallery and delightful sculpture garden overlooking the sea.

Crookhaven – This small hamlet set by the water's edge on the way to Streek Head can claim little more than two pubs, a few houses and the ruins of a 17C pilchard palace used for storing fish. From the harbour the extensive ruins of the late-19C copper mines are clearly visible on the north side of the inlet.
Take the minor road along the east side of Barley Cove.

Barley Cove – The deep inlet with its **sandy beach** between the cliffs makes a splendid holiday resort; the many chalets do not detract from the overall view.
After crossing the causeway at the head of Barley Cove turn left to Mizen Head.

Mizen Vision ⊘ – *10min steep descent on foot from car park.* A suspension bridge (150ft/46m above sea-level) spans the chasm between the mainland and Cloghane Island where a Fog Signal Station was built in 1910. It presents the work of the station and of lighthouse keepers, local marine life – dolphins, seals, basking sharks and whales and seabirds – and wrecks, the Fastnet Race and the building of the Fastnet Rock Lighthouse *(SE – 9mi/14km).*

SLIGO★★

SLIGEACH – Co Sligo – Population 17 786
Michelin Atlas p 96 and Map 923 – G 5

Sligo is a large and busy market town on the short River Garavogue which drains Lough Gill into the sea. It is surrounded by beautiful and varied scenery – green and wooded valleys, lofty mountains, sandy seashores. **Strandhill** (population 654) is good for wind-surfing but bathing can be dangerous. **Rosses Point** *(An Ros)* (population 707), a sandy peninsula projecting into Drumcliff Bay, provides a championship golf course and two beautiful sandy beaches for bathing and wind-surfing.

A Turbulent History – In 807 Sligo was plundered by the Vikings; following the Norman invasion in the 13C it was granted to Maurice Fitzgerald, who built a castle and the abbey; for 200 years its possession by the O'Conors was disputed by the

Yeats' Country

The beauty of the landscape is reflected in the poetry of William Butler Yeats and in the paintings of his brother, Jack B Yeats. They often spent the summer holidays with their Pollexfen cousins at Elsinore Lodge on Rosses Point, and would spend time watching their grandfather's ships in the bay from the top of his warehouse, now called the Yeats Watch Tower *(private property)*. William B Yeats, who is buried at Drumcliff *(see below)*, recorded in verse his visits to Lissadell House *(see below)* on Drumcliff Bay.

O'Donnells. A fort was built by the Cromwellians; Patrick Sarsfield reinforced the defences so that Sligo was one of the last places to capitulate after the Battle of the Boyne (1690). The Battle of Carrignagat (1798) was fought south of the town.

A Prosperous Port – In the 18C and 19C Sligo developed into a busy trading port which saw many emigrants set out for the New World. Several buildings date from that period: warehouses by the docks; the Courthouse (B), built in 1878; the City Hall (AB H), built in 1865 in the Italian Renaissance style. The stone building (A) with a roof-top look-out turret, now known as **Yeats Watch Tower**, once belonged to the Pollexfen family.

Out and About

Boat Trips – There are **waterbus trips** ⊙ on **Lough Gill**, particularly to the Isle of **Innisfree**, from Doorly Park and Parke's Castle.
There are also boat trips offshore to Inishmurray ⊙ from Rosses Point and from Mullaghmore *(north of Sligo)*.

Craftwork – **Sligo Crystal** *(10mi/16km north by N 15 at Grange)*, produces hand-cut crystal by the oldest known methods.

Theatre – The **Hawk's Well Theatre**

Adjacent Sights – See Boyle, Donegal, Enniskillen, Killala, Knock.

Where to Stay

Ard Quillinn Lodge, Drumiskabole. *3m SE by N 4 off R 284.* ☎ 071 63935. Out of town hotel (3 rm); good value.
Tree Tops, Cleveragh Rd. *025mi/1.5km S by Dublin rd.* ☎ 071 60160; Fax 071 62301. Very friendly personally run welcoming house (5 rm).

SIGHTS

★**Sligo Abbey** ⊙ – *South bank; Abbey Street.* The ruins standing on the south bank of the Garavogue River occupy the site of a Dominican friary, founded by Maurice Fitzgerald c 1252, which was accidentally damaged by fire in 1414; the refurbished buildings (1416), which were spared by Queen Elizabeth on condition that the friars became secular clergy, were deliberately set on fire in 1641 by Sir Frederick Hamilton. The nave, which contains an elaborate altar tomb *(north wall)* belonging to the O'Creans (1506), is separated by a 15C rood screen (partially restored) from the 13C chancel, which contains the 17C O'Conor monument. North of the church are the 13C sacristy and chapter-house and part of the carved 15C **cloisters**.

Model Arts and the Niland Gallery ⊙ – *The Mall.* The **Niland Collection**, displayed in rotation, contains some 200 works by Jack B Yeats, acquired by Norah Niland, former County Librarian. The **collection of modern Irish art** includes work by George Russell, Maurice McGonigal, Norah McGuiness, Estella Solomons, Paul Henry, Augustus John and Seán Keating.

County Museum ⊙ – *Stephen Street.* The old manse (1851) houses the **Yeats Memorial Collection** – manuscripts, photographs and letters connected with William Butler Yeats.

St John's Cathedral ⊙ – *South bank; John Street.* This unusual structure was designed in 1730 by Richard Castle; the apse and the windows were replaced during remodelling in the Gothic style in 1812. A brass tablet *(north transept)* commemorates the mother of William Butler Yeats, Susan, who was married in the church; the tomb of her father, William Pollexfen, is near the main gates.

Cathedral of the Immaculate Conception ⊙ – *South bank; John Street or Temple Street.* The Renaissance Romanesque building (1874) was designed by George Goldie. The lighting effect of the 69 stained-glass windows, made by Loblin of Tours in France, is best seen in the evening or early morning. By the main door is a small wooden statue of St Asicus.

EXCURSIONS

Sligo Peninsula

★**Carrowmore Megalithic Cemetery** ⊙ – *3mi/5km SW of Sligo by a minor road.* Carrowmore is the largest Stone Age cemetery in Ireland; it consists of over 60 passage graves – dolmens and stone circles and one cairn, which is the largest grave; the oldest dates from 3200 BC, 700 years earlier than Newgrange *(see BOYNE VALLEY)*. The Visitor Centre contains an exhibition about Stone Age man and the excavations.

★**Knocknarea** – *7mi/11km W of Sligo by R 292. After 6mi/10km bear left; after 1mi/1.6km park at the side of the road; 1hr 30min there and back on foot to the summit.*
The approach road climbs up "The Glen", a natural fault in the limestone creating a special habitat in which rare plants thrive. On the summit of **Knocknarea** (1 076ft/328m) is a massive **cairn** (197yd/180m round), visible for miles, which probably contains a passage grave. Tradition says it is the burial place of Maeve, Queen of Connaught in 1C AD (also known as Queen Mab) but it is more likely that she was buried at **Rathcroghan** *(see p 272)*. On a fine day the **view★★** from the top of the cairn is panoramic.

★★Lough Gill
Round tour of 30mi/48km E of Sligo – half a day

From Sligo take N 4 S; after 0.25mi/0.4km bear left (sign) to Lough Gill.

Tobernalt – *Car park (right) at the road junction.* The holy well shaded by trees marks an old Celtic assembly site where a festival was held in August (Lughnasa).
Continue on the shore road; at the T-junction turn left onto R 287.

Dooney Rock Forest – *Car park.* The top of Dooney Rock provides a view of the islands in Lough Gill and of Benbulben *(north)*.
At the crossroads turn left; after 2mi/3.2km turn left; 2mi/3.2km to car park.

Innisfree – The tiny lake isle of Innisfree, immortalised by Yeats' poem, lies a few yards from the jetty; view of Lough Gill and Parke's Castle *(see below)*.
Return to R 287 and continue E.

Dromahair – Population 329. This attractive riverside village lies between the shell of Villiers Castle (17C) and a ruined abbey.

Creevelea Abbey – *Park behind the Abbey Hotel (left); 6min there and back on foot across the bridge.* An avenue of evergreens beside the Bonet River leads to the ruins of a Franciscan friary which was founded by Owen O'Rourke in 1508. The church presents well-preserved east and west windows and west door. Carved pillars in the cloisters on the north side show St Francis with the stigmata and with birds perched on a tree. In the 17C the tower was turned into living quarters.
Continue on R 287 (car park and viewpoint).

★**Parke's Castle** ⊙ – The castle was built in 1609 by Capt Robert Parke, who became an MP in 1661; it was captured in 1647, surrendered to Coote in 1652 and soon abandoned. Extensive work has restored the stone slate roof, the mortice-and-tenon woodwork, the wainscoting and the window glazing. The bawn wall enclosing the yard supported the less substantial thatched outbuildings. There was a postern gate and a water gate to the lake; the water-level was higher (10ft/3m) in the 17C. The yard contains traces of an earlier tower house which probably belonged to the O'Rourkes. A limestone beehive **sweat house** stands by the shore.
Continue W on R 286 (car park and viewpoint); after 7mi/11.3km turn left.

Hazelwood – A nature trail explores the wooded peninsula which provides attractive views of the lake; the Palladian house *(private)* was designed by Richard Castle in 1731.
Continue W on R 286 to return to Sligo.

Benbulben
Round tour of 44mi/71km N of Sligo – 1 day

From Sligo take N 15 N.

★**Drumcliff** – *Car park.* In the churchyard at Drumcliff, where his great-grandfather had been rector, is **William Butler Yeats' grave** *(left)*. Although he died in Roquebrune in the south of France in 1939, his body was interred here in 1948, as he had wished, and he himself composed the epitaph inscribed on his tombstone.

Benbulben

The site under the square escarpment of Benbulben (1 730ft/526m) by the Drumcliff River was also chosen by St Columba for the foundation of a monastery in about 575; the **round tower** was damaged by lightning in 1396; the **high cross**, which was probably erected c 1000, shows Adam and Eve, Cain killing Abel, Daniel in the Lions' Den and Christ in Glory on the east face, and the Presentation in the Temple and the Crucifixion on the west.

Make a detour left via Carney.

Lissadell House ⊘ – The austere neo-Classical house, designed in 1830 by Francis Goodwin, stands on the north shore of Sligo Bay surrounded by woods. It is still the home of the Gore-Booth family, which settled in the district in the reign of Elizabeth I.

The oval gallery, which is hung with paintings collected on the Grand Tour, was designed as a music room and visitors may be invited to test the excellent acoustics at the grand piano. More paintings, by and of the family, hang in the rooms overlooking the garden. The influence of the Egyptian Revival is evident in the great marble chimney-pieces. The quaint mural portraits in the dining room were executed by Casimir de Markievicz. Souvenirs of the family are displayed in the billiard room.

Leave the grounds by the north gate; turn left; after 1mi/1.6km turn left to Raghly (sign – 3mi).

Ardtermon Castle – Standing within its bawn wall is an early-17C house (restored) built by Sir Nathaniel Gore. The entrance is flanked by two round towers; the staircase is contained in a semicircular projection at the rear facing the road.

Return to N 15 and continue N.

The road passes **Streedagh Point**, a sand bar (3mi/5km) lying parallel with the shore, where three ships from the Spanish Armada – *Juliana*, *La Levia* and *La Santa Maria de Vision* – were wrecked; over 1 300 men are thought to have died.

In Cliffony turn left to Mullaghmore.

Countess Markievicz

The most remarkable member of the Gore-Booth family was Constance (1868–1927), who was an artist like her Polish husband, Casimir de Markievicz; Constance was condemned to death in 1916 for her involvement in the Easter Rising but reprieved two years later; she was the first woman elected to the House of Commons in Westminster but never took her seat.

Mullaghmore – Population 124. Sandy beaches flank the approach to the rocky headland pointing north into Donegal Bay. The village on the sheltered east side is grouped round the stone-walled harbour, built in 1842 by Lord Palmerston, who also built **Classiebawn Castle** (1856) which rises on the exposed west shore. Several members of the Mountbatten family were murdered here in 1979 by the IRA.

Inishmurray – *11mi/18km offshore; access by boat from Mullaghmore pier and from Rosses Point near Sligo (see above).* St Molaise founded a settlement here in the 6C; remains of his monastery, which are surprisingly intact, include the Women's Church *(Teampall na mBan)*; rectangular and "beehive"-style dwellings; the main or Men's Church; underground passages and stone altars. Elsewhere on the island are pillar stones which may be pre-Christian, 57 inscribed stone slabs and 16 Stations of the Cross, spaced around the rocky perimeter. The island has a long history of human habitation – a decorated container found here dates back to 2000 BC – and not until 1948 did the last people leave, defeated by wartime fuel restrictions, which ended the regular supply-boat trips from Killybegs *(see p 159)*.

From Mullaghmore return inland bearing left at the first fork and right at the second. At the crossroads turn left onto N 15; car park opposite.

★**Creevykeel Court Cairn** – *Car park.* The well-preserved court tomb, which dates from the Late Stone Age (c 2500 BC), consists of an open court leading into a double burial chamber surrounded by a wedge-shaped mound of stones. Two other chambers, entered from the side, were probably made later.

At the crossroads turn left inland.

Gleniff Horseshoe Scenic Drive – The road makes a loop *(6mi/10km)* into the Dartry Mountains along the west face of **Truskmore** (2 120ft/644m), over the streams at the head of the valley behind **Benbulben** (1 730ft/526m).

Turn left onto the minor road. After 6mi/9.5km turn left onto N 15; before reaching Drumcliff turn left onto a minor road.

★**Glencar Waterfall** – *Car park left; access path right; 5min there and back on foot.* The waterfall, which is more impressive after rain, tumbles over layers of rock to a sheer drop (50ft/15m) into a round pool.

Continue E. At the junction turn right into N 16 to return to Sligo.

STROKESTOWN★

BÉAL NA MBUILLÍ – Co Roscommon – Population 568
Michelin Atlas p 90 and Map 923 – H 6

Strokestown is a fine example of an estate village. The broad main street, supposedly modelled on the Ringstrasse in Vienna, was laid out at the beginning of the 19C to complement the new Georgian Gothic entrance to Strokestown Park House; the site of the earlier village is marked by a ruined church (1236) in the park east of Strokestown Park House.

Adjacent Sights – See Athlone, Boyle, Carrick-on-Shannon, Knock, Longford, Tuam.

In 1635 the land at Strokestown was confiscated from O'Connor Roe, part of whose bawn survives in the building which now houses the restaurant. In 1659 approx 6 000 acres/2 828ha was granted to Capt Nicholas Mahon (d 1680) for his services as one of Cromwell's 49 militia officers; the estate was extended after the Restoration in 1660 by Charles II to guarantee Mahon's support.

Mahon Family

Nicholas Mahon's grandson, Thomas Mahon MP, incorporated parts of an earlier dwelling in a magnificent new mansion, which was enlarged by Thomas' son, Maurice. Unlike his father who had opposed the Act of Union, Maurice accepted a Union peerage in 1800, becoming Baron Hartland of Strokestown. In 1845 the property passed to Major Denis Mahon, who was shot dead in 1847 by some of his tenants, possibly in mistake for his over-zealous agent or for organising the assisted emigration to America of two-thirds of his destitute tenants during the Great Famine *(see below)*. Mrs Olive Hayes Pakenham Mahon, the last member of the family to live at Strokestown, left in 1979.

★**Famine Museum** ⊘ – The museum, which is housed in the stable yard, presents a comprehensive and detailed display, based on State archives and the Strokestown estate records for the famine years, which were used by Cecil Woodham-Smith in compiling her book *The Great Hunger*.

The detailed and balanced exhibition traces the history of the family and the estate, and explains the political, economic and natural events in the mid 19C which produced the Great Famine and Emigration, comparing conditions in 19C Ireland with those in the Third World in the 20C.

★**Strokestown Park House** ⊘ – The house, a fine Palladian mansion designed by Richard Castle in the 1730s, consists of a central three-storey block with a pillared portico, linked by curving corridors to the service wings, and incorporates parts of an earlier house.

From the **hall and staircase** with their cornice and expensive white panelling by **Castle** and a coffin table, the tour passes to the **drawing room**; the **library**, with its original brown and gold Paris wallpaper, added early in the 19C as a ballroom with a bowed wall to accommodate the musicians; the **dining room**, furnished with the original red damask wallpaper, plate buckets, a wine warmer and a wine cooler.

The **mistress's bedroom** and the **master's bedroom** share the first floor with a **schoolroom**, a child's bedroom and a **display of toys**.

The great **kitchen** *(north wing)* is fitted with a dresser displaying Belleek pottery *(see p 30)* and with spits and ovens for baking, roasting and smoking; it is overlooked by a **gallery**, which led to the housekeeper's room from a stair in the service corridor.

The splendid **vaulted stables** *(south wing)* were linked in the 19C by an underground passage to the yard on the north side of the house.

Both **Walled Gardens** have been fully restored to their original splendour. The larger pleasure garden (4 acres/1.6ha) is embellished with a magnificent Edwardian Pergola and herbaceous border; the smaller Georgian fruit and vegetable garden contains glasshouses (1780) for growing grapes, peaches and figs and an elegant gazebo with two Venetian windows providing fine views of the gardens and estate.

County Roscommon Heritage Centre ⊘ – At the north end of the village stands St John's Church (Anglican – deconsecrated), an octagonal structure designed in 1820 to resemble a medieval chapter-house; it now houses a genealogical research service and presents a historical interpretation of Strokestown.

EXCURSION

From Strokestown take R 368 and N 61 S.

★**Roscommon Castle** – *N of the town on N 61. From the car park 2min on foot over a stile and across a field.* On rising ground stands the impressive ruin of a Norman castle, built in 1269 by Robert de Ufford and originally protected by a lake or swamp. Its massive walls, which are defended by round bastions at each corner, enclose a large rectangular area. The mullion windows were inserted by Sir Nicholas Malby, Governor of Connaught, who probably occupied the castle in 1578. In 1645 it was captured by the Confederates under Preston but he surrendered in 1652 to the troops of Cromwell, who ordered its destruction.

Roscommon – The county town, an important market in the middle of rich cattle and sheep country, is named after St Comán, first Bishop of Roscommon and abbot of Clonmacnoise. He founded a monastery of Augustinian canons in Roscommon; traces of it may have been incorporated into the Anglican church. The history of the monastery, the town and the district is illustrated in the **Roscommon County Museum** ⊘.

Dominican Friary – *S of Roscommon off N 63.* The ruined friary was founded in 1253 by Felim O'Conor. In a recess in the north wall of the chancel is a late-13C carved effigy of Felim, his feet resting on a dog; below is a panel, probably 15C, which depicts eight soldiers, possibly gallowglasses, armed with swords although one carries a battle-axe; above them in the spandrels are angels.

★**Castlestrange Stone** – *7mi/11km S of Roscommon by N 63 and R 362 north. Turn right and left onto a private drive.* In a field *(right)* is a rounded granite boulder decorated with curvilinear designs in the Celtic style of ornament known as La Tène which dates from 250 BC.

Continue N on R 362; in Creggs bear right to Glinsk.

Glinsk Castle – The four-storey ruin is roofless and gutted but the windows and chimneys and projecting towers suggest a fine fortified house, built by the Burkes c 1618-1630.

Ballintober Castle – *From Glinsk continue N; turn right onto R 360; in Ballymoe turn right onto N 60 and left to Ballintober.* The ruined castle was inhabited as recently as the 19C. The high walls, fortified by a polygonal tower at each corner and originally surrounded by a moat, enclose a large rectangular courtyard. Two

Castlestrange Stone

projecting turrets guard the entrance gate. In 1652 the castle was captured by the Cromwellians but in 1677 it was returned to the O'Connor Don *(see below)*, by whose ancestors it was built c 1300.

Clonalis House ⊘ – *From Ballintober take the minor road and N 60 NW to Castlerea; west of the town centre turn right.*
Clonalis is a Clan House, the ancestral seat of the O'Connor Don (Don means king or leader), descendant of the High Kings of Ireland and head of the O'Connors of Connaught, whose possession of the land goes back over 1 500 years. The present house, which stands on rising ground beside the River Suck, was designed in 1878 by Pepys Cockerell in a Victorian Italianate style.
Beside the front door *(left)* stands the inauguration stone of the O'Connor clan which was formerly at **Rathcroghan** *(see above)*.
The house presents several mementoes of the O'Connors: the Standard of St Patrick which was carried by the O'Connor Don at the coronation of George V;. portraits of Hugh O'Connor, who founded Tucson in Arizona, and Maj Maurice of Ballintober *(see above)* whose lands were confiscated under Cromwell, returned by Charles II and mortgaged to raise troops for James II; a handsome collection of Meissen, Limoges and Minton porcelain figures; some 5 000 books, including the 18C diaries of Charles O'Connor (1710–90), written in Irish; facsimile of the *Book of Armagh*, the *Book of the Dun Cow*, the *Book of Fenagh* and the *Book of Hours of Anne de Bretagne*; O'Connor archives consisting of some 100 000 letters and documents; Irish Sheraton furniture; a Mason ironstone dinner service; recesses beside the dining room fireplace for logs; four-poster and tester beds; lace from Mount Mellick, Limerick, Brussels and Malta.
Two relics from the Penal Period are displayed in the **chapel**: the altar which comes from an earlier chapel concealed in the outbuildings; the chalice which unscrews into two separate pieces for easy concealment.
The **billiard room** now displays some of the O'Connor archives: facsimile of the death warrant of Charles I; a grant of O'Connor lands under James II; letters from Louis XIV about an officer's commission; famine documents; letters from Douglas Hyde, Daniel O'Connell, Samuel Johnson, William Gladstone, Charles Parnell, Laurence Sterne, Anthony Trollope, Napper Tandy; O'Carolan's **harp**, his concerto and his portrait.

Douglas Hyde Centre ⊘ – *From Castlerea take R 362 N; bear left to Tibohine; at juction with N 5 turn left.* The Anglican Church in Tibohine, where his father was Rector, is now devoted to the life of Douglas Hyde (1860–1949), first President of the Irish Republic (1938–45), who is buried at Tibohine. Unusually for one of Anglo-Irish origin, Dr Douglas Hyde was an Irish scholar and collected Irish poetry and folk tales. His aim was the preservation of Gaelic as the national language of Ireland, the study and publication of existing Irish literature and the cultivation of a modern Irish literature.

Rathcroghan – *From Tibohine take N 5 SE for 15mi/18km.* The hill, on which there are several earthworks, is claimed to be the inauguration place of the Kings of Connaught and the prehistoric capital of Ireland.

TIPPERARY

TIOBRAID ARANN – Co Tipperary – Population 4 772
Michelin Atlas p 84 and Map 923 – H 0

Tipperary is a pleasant country town on the River Ara in the Golden Vale, prime dairy farming country. The Normans built a motte and bailey, still visible northwest of the town. Its excellent modern sporting facilities contrast with its status as a heritage town and the conservation of its traditional 19C shop fronts. Tradition is also maintained by the **Genealogical Service**, housed in the old prison, and the clans office in James Street.
Tipperary is well-known, at least by name, from this refrain from a marching song which was popular during the First World War:

> It's a long way to Tipperary, it's a long way to go
> It's a long way to Tipperary, to the sweetest girl I know
> Goodbye Piccadilly, goodbye Leicester Square,
> It's a long, long way to Tipperary but my heart lies there.

New Tipperary

In the late 19C the town was a centre of Land League agitation. When the rents were raised in 1889 by Hugh Smith Barry, the local landlord, some tenants rebelled. West of the town centre, on land belonging to another landlord, they built a new town, assisted by tenants from all over Ireland who voluntarily gave a week's labour. The shopping arcade has been demolished but some of the properties still stand in Emmet Street and Dillon Street. In the former the buildings were designed so that, at a later date, the shop could be demolished leaving an ordinary house; Daltons (no 9) has been restored to its original state.

Tipperary Excel Heritage Centre ⊘ – *Market Square*. The centre comprises theatre and cinema, a gallery displaying art and crafts, and an interactive, multimedia exhibition on the major events in the life of Tipperary, past and present.

Old IRA Exhibition ⊘ – *Canon Hayes Sports Complex*. The display commemorates the exploits of the 3rd Tipperary brigade of the old IRA, which fought many battles during the War of Independence.

> **Adjacent Sights** – See Caher, Cashel, Kilmallock, Limerick.

EXCURSION

★**Glen of Aherlow** – *6mi/10km S. of Tipperary by R 664*. The road climbs through thick woodland over the Slievenamuck Ridge; gradually, as it descends the south face, the magnificent prospect is revealed. From the **viewpoint** *(parking)* one can see the beautiful glen (11mi/18km long), which follows the course of the River Aherlow as it flows east to join the River Suir. To the south rise the Galty Mountains, which provide delightful woodland trails in the forests on the lower slopes, and good climbing and hill walking among the corrie lakes and peaks of the upper slopes.

TRALEE

TRÁ LÍ – Co Kerry – Population 19 056
Michelin Atlas p 83 and Map 923 – C 11

Tralee, the county town of Kerry, is situated at the head of Tralee Bay on the northern approach to the Dingle peninsula. As the town was largely destroyed during the 17C wars, its architecture dates from the 18C. During the last three decades it has developed as the main commercial centre of north Kerry. Barnacle geese graze on the springy turf of Tralee Bay. The Vale of Tralee *(NE)*, which was thickly wooded in Tudor times, now provides rich pasture for the black Kerry cattle.

Rose of Tralee

Every August the town is host to the International Rose of Tralee Festival which attracts visitors, particularly emigrants, from many parts of the world; all girls of Irish descent are eligible for the title. In the Town Park stands a statue of William Mulchinock (1820–64), who wrote the song *The Rose of Tralee*, of which this is the refrain:

> "She was lovely and fair as the rose of the summer
> Yet t'was not her beauty alone that won me
> Oh no t'was the truth in her eye ever dawning
> That made me love Mary, the Rose of Tralee."

Out and About

National Folk Theatre of Ireland (Siamsa Tíre) ⊘ – The performances of this theatre, founded in 1974, draw on the rich local Gaelic tradition to evoke in music, song, dance and mime the seasonal festivals and rural way of life in past centuries. The past is also reflected in the ultra-modern theatre building which is shaped like a ringfort; a round tower gives access to the upper catwalks.

Beaches – West and north in Tralee Bay. There are indoor water facilities at the **Aqua Dome** ⊘.

Crafts – Visit the Blennerville craft workshops *(see below)*.

Adjacent Sights – See Adare, Dingle Peninsula, Kenmare, Killarney.

Desmond Stronghold and Denny Fief – Tralee grew up around the castle built by the Anglo-Norman, John Fitzgerald, in 1243; it became the principal seat of his descendants, who in 1355 received the title Earl of Desmond. Following the Desmond rebellion the town and neighbouring land (6 000 acres/2 428ha) were confiscated and granted to Sir Henry Denny, in recompense for his services to the English Crown at the massacre of Dun an Oir on Smerwick Bay in 1580 when the 15th Earl of Desmond was killed. For the next 300 years Tralee was controlled by the Dennys; the town became strongly nationalistic in outlook.

SIGHTS

Kerry – The Kingdom ⊘ – *Ashe Memorial Hall.* In **Geraldine Tralee** *(downstairs)* the sights, sounds and smells of the medieval town, the seat of power of the Anglo-Norman Fitzgeralds (1300–1500), are recreated for visitors who are carried through a partial reconstruction of Tralee in time cars equipped with multi-lingual commentary. In the **Kerry County Museum** *(upstairs)* the countryside north of Tralee and its history are illustrated by local artefacts and an audio-visual presentation – *Kerry in Colour*.

The surrounding **town park** contains the ruins of the **Geraldine castle** and a statue of William Mulchinock (1820–64) *(see above)*.

Town Centre – The commemorative figure of a Dominican *(Dominic Street)*, by local sculptor Noel Fitzgibbon, is backed by an arcade, carved by local apprentices in 1987–88 in the style of the original abbey, which was founded by John Fitzgerald in 1243 and destroyed by Cromwellian forces in 1652. The present Dominican Church *(Rock Street)* dates from 1861 when the Dominican order returned to Tralee. The **Courthouse** was designed in the mid 19C by Sir Richard Morrison in the Greek Revival style. The two lions gracing the entrance steps are dedicated to Irish soldiers who died in India and the Crimea.

Tralee–Blennerville Light Railway ⊘ – The Centenary Year of the old Tralee–Dingle Light Railway (1891–1953) was marked by the re-opening to passenger traffic of the first stretch *(1.5mi/2.4km)* of the narrow-gauge (3ft/1m) line between Tralee and Blennerville *(see below)*. The train is composed of three original carriages drawn by one of the original steam locomotives, no 5, a 2-6-2 built by Hunslett of Leeds.

EXCURSIONS

★Blennerville Windmill ⊘ – *2mi/3.2km S of Tralee by R 559.* The five-storey windmill (60ft/18m high), built by the local landlord, Sir Rowland Blennerhassett, c 1800 and derelict by 1880, is again in working order; an electric engine takes over when the wind fails.

The **Emigration Exhibition** in the adjoining building illustrates the experience of the many thousands who left Ireland for America in the 19C – embarkation, the sea voyage, food, medical matters, quarantine on arrival.

In the **craft workshops** visitors can see artists at work and buy the finished product – pottery, enamels etc.

★Crag Cave ⊘ – *11mi/18km E of Tralee by N 21 to Castleisland (Oileán Ciarraí); take the minor road N for 1mi/1.6km (sign).* The complex of limestone caves (4 170yd/3 813m), discovered in 1983, is thought to be over a million years old. A short descent *(62 steps)* leads to the tunnels and chambers of the show cave (383yd/350m); lighting enhances the natural beauty of the many calcite formations – stalactites, stalagmites, columns, curtains, drip stones and flow stones. The myriad shimmering white straw stalactites in the **Crystal Gallery** provide a magical climax.

★**Ardfert** – *5.5mi/9km N of Tralee by R 551*. Population 677. Ardfert was established as a missionary base as early as the 5C. The stone church, founded in the 6C by St Brendan the Navigator *(see p 200)* as part of a monastery, was destroyed by fire in 1089. Under the Normans Ardfert became an important borough; two major ecclesiastical ruins have survived from this period.

The **cathedral** ⊙ was built c 1150 and destroyed by fire in 1641 or during the Cromwellian wars. The south transept (15C) contains an exhibition on the history of the building and the two adjacent small churches, which are decorated with interesting sculptures.

Ardfert Friary, a Franciscan house, was founded in 1253 and substantially rebuilt in 1453; much of the tower and of the chancel with its nine lancets in the south wall and five-light lancet in the east wall are still intact.

Fenit Sea World ⊙ – *8mi/13km N of Tralee by R 551 and R 558; on the pier; parking*. Every few minutes a wave of water crashes into the **aquarium**. All the myriad species of fish displayed are named and identified. The touch-tank presents cockles, mussels, urchins, crabs, limpets and starfish.

★**Banna Strand** – *7.5mi/13km NW of Tralee by R 551*. The vast stretch of sandy beach (5mi/8km) was used for the filming of *Ryan's Daughter* in 1968. A memorial at the entrance commemorates Sir Roger Casement (1864–1916), who landed on the beach on 21 April 1916 from a German submarine with a consignment of arms for the Easter Rising.

★**Rattoo Round Tower** – *13mi/21km N of Tralee by R 556*. The round tower, which is very well preserved, and the ruined 15C church mark the site of an abbey founded in 1200 for the Knights Hospitaller of St John the Baptist. In 1202 it became an Augustinian house, which was burned in 1600.

The **Rattoo-North Kerry Museum** ⊙ at Ballyduff *(2mi/4km N)* displays relics illustrating the history of the locality – Bronze Age (2000 BC) ferry boat carved from a split oak trunk.

Listowel (Lios Tuathail) – *17mi/27km N of Tralee by N 69*. Population 3 347. The exceptional literary reputation of the market town of Listowel and of North Kerry is celebrated in **Writers' Week**, which is held annually in May and attracts world-wide participation. In the huge central square stands **St John's Art and Heritage Centre** ⊙, formerly the Anglican parish church, which offers live performances of music and theatre, film shows and various exhibitions about art, literature, history; the permanent display, consisting of collected texts, archive recordings and audio-visual presentations, covers the work of John B Keane, Brian McMahon, Brendan Kennelly and other local writers.

In the north-east corner of the square is the striking **plasterwork façade** of the Central Hotel.

Ballybunnion – *20mi/32km N of Tralee by R 556 and R 551*. Population 1 346. This seaside resort has many amusement arcades and several beaches; it is also noted for its outdoor baths, where seaweed is used for therapeutic purposes.

★**Carrigafoyle Castle** – *27mi/43km N of Tralee by N 69 to Listowel, R 552 to Ballylongford and a minor road north*. Once the principal seat of the O'Connor clan, who ruled most of north Kerry, the castle, originally on an island, was finally destroyed by Cromwellian forces in 1649. One of the flanker towers is fitted out as a dovecot. A spiral staircase leads to the top of the tower (80ft/29m high) for extensive **views** of the Shannon estuary.

Lislaughtin Abbey – *26mi/42km N of Tralee by N 69 to Listowel and R 552 via Ballylongford*. This Franciscan foundation dates from the 15C; the church has an attractive west window and three well-preserved sedilia; traces of the refectory and dormitory remain on the east side of the cloisters; the lavatories were housed in the tower at the north end.

Tarbert – *28mi/45km N of Tralee by N 56 via Listowel*. Population 679. **Tarbert Bridewell** ⊙, built 1828–31, has been converted into a museum describing, through wax tableaux in the courtroom and cells, the legal and penal systems in force in Ireland at that time.

The **woodland walk** *(starting from the car park)* leads through the grounds of **Tarbert House** ⊙ (17C), which has seen such notable guests as Benjamin Franklin, Charlotte Brontë and Daniel O'Connell, and continues along the wooded shore to Tarbert Old Pier. The new pier is the departure point for the **Shannon Car Ferry** *(see p 275)*.

TRIM★

BAILE ÁTHA TROIM – Co Meath – Population 1 740
Michelin Atlas p 92 and Map 923 – L 7

Trim straddles the River Boyne by an ancient ford. In the 12C Hugh de Lacy, appointed Lord of Meath by Henry II in 1172, chose the town as his headquarters, where Parliament sometimes met. He controlled his territory, which stretched from the Irish Sea to the Shannon, by dividing it into baronies which he granted to his knights.

> **Adjacent Sights** – See Boyne Valley, Fingal, Kells, Maynooth, Mullingar.

SIGHTS

★★**Trim Castle** ⊘ – *South bank; access through the Town Gate or along the river bank from the bridge.* The magnificent ruins of this medieval castle stand on the south bank of the River Boyne. The central **keep**, which was built between 1220 and 1225, consists of two great halls with sleeping accommodation above; the entrance in the east tower faces the Dublin Gate. The castle walls date from c 1250; the holes for the beams, which supported a wooden sentry walk, are best seen in the east section near the river.

The Pale

In the Middle Ages the Irish who lived outside the Anglo-Norman jurisdiction were said to be beyond the Pale. The term derives from the Latin word *palus* for a stake. Its use to describe the part of Ireland under effective English rule dates from 1446. The settlement made under Henry II (1154–89) comprised Louth, Meath, Trim, Dublin, Kilkenny, Tipperary, Waterford and Wexford, but by the late 15C the Pale had shrunk to only four counties, Louth, Meath, Dublin and Kildare.

The **Dublin Gate** was protected by two drawbridges and a barbican; the upper floors served as a prison where Henry IV was held by Richard II until he escaped and captured the English throne. Westwards along the wall are a 17C limekiln, two sally ports and a small square building where cannon balls were made in the Cromwellian period to be fired from a cannon mounted on the in-filled tower.

The west-facing **Town Gate** has a medieval flagstone floor, a portcullis groove and barrel-vaulted arches. The smaller breach in the river wall was caused by Cromwell's troops and the larger stretch collapsed in the Big Wind in 1839; in between is an underground chamber.

Across the river stands a stone arch, the medieval **Sheep Gate** where tolls were levied on flocks bought and sold at the great sheep fairs.

Yellow Steeple – *North bank; access from the High Street.* The ruined late-14C tower, which gleams in the sun, marks the site of **St Mary's Abbey**, an Augustinian community, founded by St Malachy of Armagh in the 12C near the point where St Patrick landed in the 5C and converted Foitchern, the son of the local chieftain and later first Bishop of Trim. Many pilgrims were attracted to the abbey by Our Lady of Trim, a wooden statue with a reputation for effecting miracles, which disappeared in the Cromwellian period.

In 1425 the west cloisters of the abbey were converted by Lord Lieutenant Talbot into a fortified house, **Talbot's Castle**, which bears the Talbot coat of arms on the north wall. After the Reformation the house became a Latin School, later attended by

Trim Castle

Sir Rowan Hamilton, the mathematician who discovered quaternions, and the Duke of Wellington, later MP for Trim, whose family home was at Dangan *(south-east)*.

Cathedral – *North bank; 1mi/1.6km E at Newtown Trim.* Among the graves of Newtown Cemetery is a **tomb** bearing the recumbent figures of Sir Luke Dillon, in his Renaissance armour, and his wife, Lady Jane Bathe, in an Elizabethan gown; people leave pins on the tomb in the belief that their warts will disappear.

Further west are the ruins of a **cathedral**, dedicated to St Peter and St Paul; it was built early in the 13C to replace the church at Clonard *(southwest)*, which was burned by the Irish at the end of the 12C. The founder, Simon de Rochfort, the first Anglo-Norman Bishop of Meath, was buried under the high altar. The foundations show that the original cathedral was very large with a long nave, aisles and transepts. The south wall collapsed in the Big Wind in 1839.

Southwest of the cathedral are the remains of a **priory**, also founded by Simon de Rochfort, for a community of canons regular of St Victor, who originated in Paris. The south and west walls of the refectory still stand, next to the 14C kitchen; the foundations of the chapter-house doorway are also visible.

Crutched Friary – *South bank; 1mi/1.6km E at Newtown Trim.* On the south bank of the Boyne are the ruins of a 13C hospital built by the Crutched Friars, an order of mendicant friars who wore a cross on their habits. The buildings consist of a keep with several fireplaces, a ruined chapel with a triple-light window and the hospital and stores beside the river.

EXCURSION

★Bective Abbey – *5mi/8km NE by R161 (T26); after 4mi/6.4km turn right. Park beyond the abbey near the bridge.* The impressive and extensive ruins stand in a field on the west bank of the Knightsbrook River. The abbey, one of the earliest Cistercian houses in Ireland, was founded in 1150 by the King of Meath, Murcha Ó Maolsheachlainn, and dedicated to the Blessed Virgin; its abbot was a member of the Parliament of the Pale and Hugh de Lacy was buried here in 1195. Little remains of the 12C buildings. The **cloisters**, the tower and the great hall in the south wing date from the 15C when the buildings were altered and fortified.

The film *Braveheart* (1996), about Robert Bruce, was shot among these ruins and also at nearby Dunsoghly Castle.

Dúchas, Dublin

TUAM

TUAIM – Co Galway – Population 3 446
Michelin Atlas p 89 and Map 923 – F 7

The small city of Tuam, with its two cathedrals, is the ecclesiastical capital of Connaught. In 1049 the O'Connor kings of Connaught made it their headquarters and in the 12C, when Turlough and Rory O'Connor were High Kings of Ireland, it was virtually the capital of the whole country.

In 1252 the right to hold markets was granted to the Archbishop by Henry III; in 1613 James I granted a charter and the city was laid out to its present plan, with all the streets converging on the central diamond.

> **Adjacent Sights** – See Athenry, Galway, Strokestown.

SIGHTS

★**St Mary's Cathedral** ⊘ – *West of the town centre.* The site, which is enclosed by a high wall, is that of a monastery founded late in the 5C by Jarlath, a follower of Benen of Kilbennan *(north)*. The original cathedral was founded in 1130 but most of the present Anglican church was designed by Sir Thomas Deane in 1860 in the neo-Gothic style, with a tower and a hexagonal spire (200ft/61m). In the north aisle by the west door stands the shaft of a 12C **high cross**; the inscription asks for prayers for the king, Turlough O'Connor, for the craftsman and for Jarlath's successor, Aodh Ó'hOisín, for whom the cross was made. The complete 12C cross, which formerly stood in the town square, is only partly composed of original pieces; one face depicts the Crucifixion and the other an abbot or bishop. All that remains of the original church is the red sandstone **chancel**; the two windows and the chancel arch with its five rows of moulding are fine examples of 12C Irish-Romanesque architecture. East of the cathedral is a 14C building, which was badly damaged by the Cromwellians and has been restored in its original castellated style to serve as a Synod Hall.

Cathedral of the Assumption ⊘ – *East of the town centre.* The foundation stone of the Roman Catholic cathedral was laid in 1827, a year before the Emancipation Act. Funds were subscribed by the local inhabitants regardless of denomination. The cruciform neo-Gothic structure was designed by Dominic Madden. The Stations of the Cross, thought to be by Eustache Le Sueur, a 17C portrait painter, were bought by Archbishop John McHale (1791–1881), an eminent Gaelic-speaking churchman, whose statue stands outside the entrance *(north)*. The east window (1832) by Michael O'Connor of Dublin depicts St Mary and the Evangelists; the fourth window in the north aisle (1961) shows Jarlath, who was advised by St Brendan of Clonfert to build where the wheel of his chariot broke. The four windows, depicting the Ascension, the Crucifixion, the Assumption and the Apparition at Lourdes, are from the Harry Clarke Studios.

Mill Museum ⊘ – *West of North Bridge.* The 17C corn mill on a tributary of the Clare River has been converted into a milling museum; three sets of mill-wheels are driven by an undershot spur wheel. There is an audio-visual presentation on the history of Tuam and its locality.

St Jarlath's Churchyard – *West of town centre.* Irish yews grow among the graves surrounding the ruins of the 13C parish church, which was dedicated to the patron saint of Tuam; the west tower contained a lodging for the priest, and after the Reformation Roman Catholic clergy were buried in a side chapel. Some of the tombstones are inscribed with symbols showing the occupation of the deceased.

EXCURSION

★**Knockmoy Abbey** – *12mi/19km SE of Tuam by R 332; after 9mi/14.5km turn right at the crossroads onto N 63. In Knockmoy village turn right. After crossing the river turn right and park by the cemetery. 15min there and back on foot by a path and four stiles.*

In the fields on the north bank of the River Abbert are the substantial ruins of an abbey which was founded in 1189 for the Cistercians of Boyle by Cathal O'Connor, king of Connaught, and dedicated to the Blessed Virgin Mary.

The church consists of the nave, a transept with two chapels and the **chancel**, which is decorated with some fine stone carving and a 13C tomb niche. Behind a protective grill is a rare **fresco** (1400) of the medieval legend of the Three Live Kings, who are dressed for hawking, and the Three Dead Kings, who bear the inscription "We have been as you are, you shall be as we are". Two partition walls, inserted in the 14C or 15C, have spoiled the east window of the chapter-house in the east wing of the conventual buildings; little remains of the refectory in the south wing and even less of the cloisters.

★**Ross Errilly Abbey** – *10mi/16km W of Tuam by N 17, R 333 and N 84 N for 2mi/3.2km.* Although in ruins, Ross Abbey on the south bank of the Black River is one of the best-preserved Franciscan friaries in Ireland. It was probably founded in 1351 and greatly extended in 1496. The gatehouse and enclosure date from 1572. After the Reformation, except for a period during the Commonwealth from 1698 to 1715, the friars continued in residence until 1753 largely owing to the protection of the 2nd Earl of Clanrickard.

The **church** was decorated with frescoes on the walls and ceilings; the windows are 15C. The **water spout**, by the pillar supporting the transept arches, channelled rainwater from the roof to an underground cistern, later used as a tomb. In the Lady Chapel is a wall plaque (1646) bearing the arms of the O'Donnells who invited the Franciscans of Ross to found a friary in Donegal *(see DONEGAL)*.

The buildings surrounding the **cloisters** *(entrance at the foot of the tower)* have survived in part to first-floor level.

Beyond is a second courtyard with a postern gate for entry to the friary after dark. The **kitchen** contained a round **fish tank**; the huge fireplace backed onto a large circular oven in the adjoining **bakery**; above were a dormitory and the Chapter House. The north range of the main cloister contained the east-facing **refectory** with a **wall lectern** and the **lavatorium**. Above the **sacristy** was the guesthouse or infirmary; guests or invalids could see the high altar through a **hagioscope** on the landing.

The **central tower** (70ft/21.5m), probably added in 1498, provides a fine **view**★ *(76 narrow wooden spiral steps).*

Annaghdown Church and Priory – *6mi/8km S of Ross Errilly by N 84; 5mi/7km S of Headford turn right to Annaghdown.*
St Brendan of Clonfert *(see p 200)* founded a convent for his sister at Annaghdown. The 15C building at the southern end of the graveyard is the Cathedral incorporating earlier decorated stonework – a fine doorway and window (c 1200). The middle church is the oldest on the site (11C or 12C). The other ruined building was a parish church. The ruined priory *(turn right into the lane beyond the graveyard)* is a good example of a fortified monastery (c 1195); there is some Romanesque carving in the church.

TULLAMORE

TULACH MHÓR – Co Offaly – Population 9 221
Michelin Atlas p 91 and Map 923 – J 8

The town of Tullamore has been the county town of Co Offaly since 1833. It is bisected by the Tullamore River and in 1798 was linked by the Grand Canal to Dublin and the River Shannon. To the south rise the Slieve Bloom Mountains.

Adjacent Sights – See Abbeyleix, Athlone, Athy, Birr, Kildare, Trim.

SIGHTS

Tullamore Distillery Heritage Centre ⊙ – A golden drop of *Tullamore Dew* or *Irish Mist* awaits in the bar but first it is worth discovering the history of Tullamore, particularly of the distillery, founded in 1829 by Michael Molloy. In 1887 Daniel E Williams, who had been steeped in whiskey production since joining the staff at the age of 15, became general manager and gradually acquired overall control of the business. He used his own initials to provide a brand name – *Tullamore Dew* – for the distillery's pot still whiskey and from that flowed the advertising slogan – *Give every man his Dew*. In the 1950s, when sales were low, the distillery began to produce *Irish Mist*, a whiskey-based liqueur, inspired by a traditional Irish recipe for heather wine made with pot still whiskey, herbs and heather honey.

Town Centre – The entrance to the **canal harbour** is spanned by Bury (Whitehall) Bridge, the last of the canal bridges to survive unaltered. The old warehouses have been demolished but the harbour-master's house still stands on the corner of St Brigid's Place. The **Roman Catholic church** (1985) is roofed with great lengths of timber and contains some stained glass by Harry Clarke. **St Catherine's Church** was designed by Francis Johnston and contains a memorial (1767) to the first Earl of Charleville by John van Nost.

EXCURSIONS

Durrow High Cross – *4mi/7km N of Tullamore by N 52; 10min there and back on foot along the drive.* The 10C **high cross** depicts the Sacrifice of Isaac on the east face together with Christ in Glory flanked by David with his harp *(left)* and David killing the Lion *(right)*; the west face shows the Crucifixion and associated events. There are fragments of two other crosses, 9C to 11C grave slabs, and the ruins of a small 18C church which may contain parts of earlier churches belonging to the monastery founded in 556 by St Columba.

The *Book of Durrow*, an illuminated manuscript, which is now in Trinity College Library in Dublin, was produced at Durrow c 650; it was rescued from a farmer who used to touch his sick cattle with it after dipping it in water.

Locke's Distillery ⊘ – *Kilbeggan; 7.5mi/12km N of Tullamore by N 52*. On the west bank of the River Brosna stand the extensive buildings of the distillery (1757–1953) established by John Locke, possibly the oldest licensed distillery. In the **cooperage** craftsmen make the oak casks in which whiskey, produced at Cooley, is matured. The process of distilling whiskey is explained and much of the original equipment is still in place: three sets of millstones for grinding barley; the mash tuns (known as kieves) for making wort; the huge wooden vats (washbacks) for fermentation; the hogsheads for maturing the whiskey; coopers' tools; the under-shot water-wheel, and the steam engine which replaced it when the water-level was too high or too low.

Clara Bog – *7mi/10km NW of Tullamore by N 80; in Clara take a minor road south; car park at the end of a short causeway; visitors should not stray from this causeway unless accompanied by a knowledgeable guide*. This raised bog (1 640 acres/665ha; 23ft/7km maximum depth) is one of the finest and largest raised bogs remaining in Ireland and is of international interest. In 1987 it was designated a National Nature Reserve. It has a diverse flora, including at least 10 different bog mosses; in wet areas carnivorous plants, like sundews and bladderworts, entrap unwary insects.

WATERFORD★

PORT LÁIRGE – Co Waterford – Population 42 540
Michelin Atlas p 80 and Map 923 – K 11

Waterford is a large seaport, with a strong industrial tradition, situated on the south bank of the River Suir, upstream of its confluence with the River Barrow in Waterford Harbour. The city is best known for its glassware, **Waterford Crystal**, which has been the main contributor to the economic prosperity of Waterford since the 1950s when the industry was revived.

Viking Settlement – The Danish Vikings established a settlement in 853 called *Vadrefjord*, which means weather haven. Despite constant warfare with the local Irish, the Danes retained control of their settlement until 1169 when the Anglo-Normans arrived. Under their rule Waterford became the second most important Anglo-Norman town in Ireland after Dublin. In 1649 Waterford was unsuccessfully besieged by Cromwell but it fell to his general, Ireton, the following year.

Famous Sons

Thomas Francis Meagher (1822–67) was a wealthy lawyer, who joined the Young Ireland Uprising. For his part in the rising at Ballingarry in Co Tipperary he received a death sentence, which was commuted to transportation to Tasmania. From there he escaped to the USA where he founded the Irish Brigade and fought in the American Civil War.
William Hobson (1783–1842), who was born in Lombard Street near The Mall, became the first Governor of New Zealand.

SIGHTS

★**Waterford Crystal** ⊘ – *1.5mi/2.5km south by N 25*. Waterford Glass in the original style was first produced in 1783; the factory is now the largest glassworks in the world.
The factory tours take in all aspects of production, starting with the moulding of the molten glass and concluding with the delicate polishing. A collection of crystal is on display; there are videos of the production process for sale.

★**City Walls** (YZ) – The watchtower (35ft/10m high) surveys a well-preserved section of the very extensive city walls. As well as the Norman extensions, which are mostly 13C, there are traces of the 9C and 10C Danish walls, including the sallyports in Reginald's Bar near Reginald's Tower.

Waterford Treasures ⊘ (Y F) – *The Granary*. The old grain store houses a display of Viking and medieval finds from local excavations – coins, leather-work, jewellery, woven cloth, pottery, bone needles, wooden bowls and spoons and a plan of a Viking house. Also on display are the city charters and regalia.

Reginald's Tower Museum ⊘ (Z) – This stone fortress, in a commanding location overlooking the River Suir, was built by the Vikings in 1013 as part of the town's defences. Its three floors, linked by a stair built within the thickness of the walls, contain displays on towers and fortifications.

Out and About

Waterford Light Opera Festival – The festival is held annually in September in the Theatre Royal *(see below)*.

Garter Lane Arts Centre ⊘ (**Y E**) – Regular art exhibitions, recitals and theatrical productions are staged throughout the year.

Walking Tours ⊘ – Tours of the city are organised by the Tourist Board.

Car Ferry ⊘ – There is a ferry across Waterford Harbour from Passage East *(southeast of Waterford by R 683)* to Ballyhack.

Adjacent Sights – See Clonmel, New Ross, Wexford, Youghal.

Wher283e to Eat

Wine Vault, High St. ☎/Fax 051 853 444. Converted 15C bonded warehouse in city centre with emphasis on the wine list; cellars open to view; modern Irish themed food.

The Ship, Dock Rd, Dunmore East. ☎ 051 383 141. Well run dining pub with nautical theme; seafood oriented menu.

Where to Stay

Avondale, 2 Parnell St. ☎ 051 852 267. Modern townhouse style guesthouse (6 rm) in town centre; fairly priced.

The Anchorage, 9 The Quay. ☎ 051 854 302; Fax 051 856 979. Bright modern B&B (12 rm) beside the River Suir; good value.

Coach House, Butlerstown Castle, Cork Rd, Butlerstown. *5mi/8km S by R 675.* ☎ 051 384 656; Fax 051 384 751. Strong and comfortable Victorian house guesthouse (7 rm); quiet location; ruins of Butlerstown Castle in the grounds.

Kilmeaden House, Kilmeaden. *1mi/1.6km NW by N 25 on R 680.* ☎ 051 384 254; Fax 051 384 884. Old Victorian rectory (5 rm); well appointed, spacious and comfortable; reasonably priced.

Waterford Castle, The Island, Ballinakill. *2.25m E by R 583 Ballinakill Rd and private ferry.* ☎ 051 878 203; Fax 051 879 316. 15C-19C castle, set in spacious and quiet location on its own island; expensive but very pleasant.

City Hall (**Z H**) **and Theatre Royal** ⊘ (**Z T**) – The **City Hall**, originally the city exchange, was designed by John Roberts in 1788. The first-floor council chamber displays a complete dinner service of 18C Waterford crystal, a cut-glass chandelier of similar vintage and a painting of Waterford city in 1736 by a Flemish artist, William van der Hagen.

The building incorporates the **Theatre Royal** (1876); its Victorian decor is rare in Ireland. The three-tier horse-shoe design (seating capacity 650) rises to an impressive dome; the specially designed Waterford Crystal chandelier was presented by Waterford Crystal in 1958.

French Church ⊘ (**Z B**) – The tower and chancel walls belonged to a Franciscan foundation, built in 1240, which remained in the friars' possession until 1539. The Holy Ghost hospital occupied part of the building from 1545 to 1882 when it moved to the outskirts of the city. A Huguenot chapel was in use between 1693 and 1815. Many of the most distinguished families of Waterford are buried within the precincts.

Christ Church Cathedral ⊘ (**Z A**) – The present building was designed by John Roberts (1714–96) in the 18C English Classical style; it was completed in 1779. In 1891 the galleries and square pews were removed. Within is a model of the original Viking church,

Waterford Crystal

Terry Murphy Photography

WATERFORD

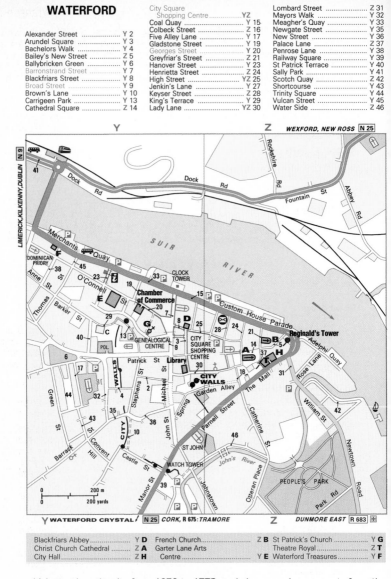

which stood on the site from 1050 to 1773, and also several monuments from the medieval church – the tomb of James Rice showing his body a year after his death with signs of decay and vermin; two monuments by John van Nost to the Fitzgeralds and to Susanna Mason.

Medieval Waterford – *First level below the City Square Shopping Centre.* During construction of the modern shopping centre 12 layers of housing were found resting on Viking foundations. Stones mark the site of St Peter's church (12C), the earliest example of an apsed church in Ireland. The mural depicts the area in c 1100.

St Patrick's Church (Y G) – The church, which dates from the Penal Period, was deliberately constructed to resemble a house from the outside. The **Waterford Heritage Genealogical Service** ⊘ is housed in the section facing Jenkin's Lane.

Chamber of Commerce ⊘ **(Y)** – The fine Georgian building (1795) was designed by John Roberts, a noted 18C Waterford architect; over the door are the words Waterford Harbour Commissioners; the interior contains a well-preserved dome, staircase and carvings.

EXCURSIONS

Passage East – *8mi/13km E of Waterford by R 683 and L 157. Car ferry across Waterford Harbour to Ballyhack.* Population 542. Formerly a fort, the fishing village is built beneath a high escarpment with small squares and streets; there are no fewer than three quays: Boathouse Quay, Hackett's Quay and Middle Quay.

Geneva Barracks – *8mi/13km SE of Waterford by R 683 and R 685.* On the west shore of Waterford Harbour stands an impressive 18C ruin; its four walls (each 0.25mi/0.4km long) are still remarkably intact. It was part of a new town built in 1793 by the Government for Swiss metalworkers, who left soon after the project was completed. During the 1798 rebellion the buildings were infamous for the atrocities committed against the rebels held within.

★**Dunmore East** – *12mi/19km SE of Waterford by R 683 and R 684.* Population 1 038. The fishing village, built in the Breton style, has several thatched cottages and a number of coves, including Badger's Cove and Ladies' Cove. There are forest walks beside the Ballymacaw Road *(0.25mi/0.4km west).*

Tramore (Trá Mhór) – *9mi/14.5km S of Waterford by R 675.* Population 6 069. Tramore is one of Ireland's main holiday resorts, built on a steep slope descending to a large amusement park (50 acres/20ha) and a long sandy beach (3mi/5km) overlooking Tramore Bay.

There are fine walks, with extensive sea views, along the Doneraile cliffs *(south).* Great Newtown Head *(west)* across the bay is crowned by three early-19C navigational pillars, one of which is surmounted by the **Tramore Metal Man**, a cast-iron figure (14ft/4m high), with pale blue jacket and white trousers, erected in 1823 as a warning to shipping.

WESTPORT★★

CATHAIR NA MART – Co Mayo – Population 4 253
Michelin Atlas p 94 and Map 923 – D 6

Westport occupies an attractive site on the meandering Carrowbeg River and is an excellent centre for touring the west coast of Mayo. Charming and elegant, it was planned and built c 1780 for the local landlord, John Denis Browne, of Westport House. Until the arrival of the railway in the 19C, Westport Quay on the estuary was a busy port lined with imposing 18C warehouses.

The Brownes of Westport

Twelve generations of Brownes have lived at Westport and their activities are recorded in the family archives which cover 400 years. The family is descended from Sir Anthony Browne of Cowdray Castle in Sussex, whose younger son John came to Mayo in the reign of Elizabeth I. The first house was built by his great-grandson, Col John Browne (1638–1711), a Jacobite, who was made bankrupt by the Williamite victory; his wife was the great-great-granddaughter of Grace O'Malley *(see below).* His grandson, John Browne (1709–76), was brought up as a Protestant to avoid the sanctions of the Penal Laws and ennobled as Earl of Altamont. Two generations later, John Denis (1756–1809) was made Marquess of Sligo at the time of the Act of Union in 1800. The 2nd Marquess, Howe Peter (1788–1845), a friend of Lord Byron, returned from a tour of Greece in 1812 with the two columns from the doorway of the Treasury of Atreus in Mycenae; in 1906 they were discovered in the basement, identified and presented to the British Museum.

★★WESTPORT HOUSE ⏱ *1hr 30min*

The house is the work of several architects: Richard Castle who designed the east front in 1730, Thomas Ivory who was responsible for the south elevation (1778), and James Wyatt who added the west front c 1780; the Greek columns on the south front are replicas *(see above)* erected in 1943. It replaces an earlier house built in 1650 on the site of an O'Malley castle. Originally the sea came right up to the house; the lake was created in the 18C by damming the Carrowbeg River. The garden terraces were built in the early 1900s.

The **tour** of the main rooms and bedrooms reveals the elegant decor and a number of distinctive items – the Pompeian frieze and cloud-painted ceiling in the drawing room *(restaurant)* commissioned by the 2nd Marquess in about 1825; a collection of **family portraits** in the Long Gallery; mahogany from the family estates in Jamaica for the dining room doors; the sideboards and wine coolers made for the 2nd Marquess; Waterford glass

Boat trips – Ferry from Roonagh Quay to **Clare Island** ⏱ *(see below)* in Clew Bay.

Facilities – For sailing, fishing, walking and horse riding; sandy beaches to the southwest.

Adjacent Sights – See Connemara, Knock.

Westport House

finger bowls; 18C silver dish rings and a unique **centrepiece** of bog oak and beaten silver; the **Mayo Legion Flag** brought to Mayo in 1798 by General Humbert *(see p 222)*; the **oak staircase** by James Wyatt; the **marble staircase** installed for the 3rd Marquess by Italian workmen; chalk drawings of the children of the 2nd Marquess by F Wilkin and *The Holy Family* by Rubens on the landing; 200-year-old wallpaper in the **Chinese Room**. The **basement** includes the dungeons of the O'Malley castle, now furnished with attractions for children.

Grounds – The old walled garden, containing a mulberry tree planted in 1690, now houses a small zoo. A **craft shop** is located in the Farmyard Buildings Holiday Centre and there are fishing and rowing boats on the lake.

WESTPORT TOWN

★**Town Centre** – From the **Octagon**, where the weekly market is held round a Doric pillar once crowned by a statue of George Glendinning, a local banker and benefactor, the main street descends to the **Mall**, a tree-lined stretch of the Carrowbeg River spanned by a narrow hump-backed bridge.

Holy Trinity Church ⓥ – The church, consecrated in 1872, is in the neo-Gothic style with a pencil spire over the east door. Under the hammer roof the interior is richly decorated with murals in marble mosaic by Italian craftsmen depicting scenes from the Gospels. From 1892 to 1913 the rector was Canon James Owen Hannay, whose pen-name was George A Bermingham.

Clew Bay Heritage Centre ⓥ – *Westport Quay*. The small museum gives an insight into the history of the area – the capture of the town in 1798 and pilgrimages to the top of Croagh Patrick – and of some local figures – Grace O'Malley *(see below)*; John MacBride (1868–1916), born in Westport and executed in Kilmainham Gaol for his part in the Easter Rising; William Joyce, who lived near Ballinrobe (1909–21) and broadcast from Germany as Lord Haw-Haw during the Second World War; the grandfather of Grace Kelly, wife of Prince Rainier of Monaco, who emigrated to America from a homestead near the road to Castlebar.

EXCURSIONS

★★Murrisk Peninsula

Drive of 51mi/82km S of Westport – 1 day

From Westport take R 335 W.

On leaving Westport Quay the road skirts the wooded shore, crossing the Owenee River at Belclare where the O'Malley chiefs *(see below)* had their seat.
After 5.5mi/9km turn right.

Murrisk Abbey – By the shore are the ruins of an Augustinian Friary founded by the O'Malleys in 1457 and suppressed in 1574, although a chalice was made for the monastery by Grace O'Malley's son Theobald in 1635.
Return to R 335.

★**Croagh Patrick** – *Car park; 2hr on foot to the summit.* According to legend all the snakes in Ireland plunged to their death when St Patrick rang his bell above the south precipice of Croagh Patrick (2 503ft/763m). A procession of pilgrims, some barefoot, climbs the stony slopes to the church on the summit on the last Sunday in July (Garland Sunday); they used to climb by torchlight, possibly an echo of the old Celtic festival of Lughnasa. On a fine day the **view** from the top embraces *(N)* Clew Bay with its many islands, *(W)* Clare Island, and *(S)* the Sheeffry Hills flanked by the Mweelrea (Muilrea) Mountains *(W)* and the Partry Mountains *(E)* and backed by the Twelve Pins of Connemara.
Continue W on R 335.

Louisburgh – Population 177. The central octagon of this charming little 18C town on the Bunowen River was laid out by the 1st Marquess of Sligo, whose uncle Henry had fought against the French at the Battle of Louisburgh in Canada.
Turn right at the central crossroads.

Granuaile

Granuaile is the Irish name of **Grace O'Malley** (1530–1603), who for many years resisted English domination while elsewhere in Ireland the Gaelic system succumbed to English rule. From her strongholds in Clew Bay, where the many islands made pursuit difficult, she commanded a fleet of privateers which preyed upon the shipping in Galway Bay, imposing pilot charges or confiscating cargoes. She was imprisoned by the English from 1577 to 1578. She had two sons and a daughter from her first marriage (c 1546–c 1564) to Donal O'Flaherty, who owned castles at Ballynahinch and Bunowen in Connemara; in 1566 she married Iron Richard Burke and, although she divorced him the following year, she retained possession of Carrigahowley Castle *(see below)*, where she spent the majority of her time and brought up her youngest son, Theobald Burke. She repulsed an English expedition from Galway which in 1574 attempted to besiege the castle. In the autumn of 1593 she sailed to Greenwich to present a successful petition to Elizabeth I for the release of her brother and her son Theobald Burke, who was made Viscount Mayo *(see p 286)* by Charles I in 1627.

Folk and Heritage Centre ⓥ – *Louisburgh*. The centre traces the family tree of the O'Malleys, the history of the clan and their territory, and the life of Grace (1530–1603), the most famous member of the family.

Take the road south to Killadoon; make a detour W to Roonagh Quay for the ferry to Clare Island.

Clare Island – *Bicycles for hire at the island harbour; bus tour and accommodation available.* The hilly bulk of Clare Island commands the entrance to Clew Bay. Grace O'Malley spent her childhood in the castle by the quay; she may be buried in the Carmelite friary which was founded on the island by the O'Malleys in 1224, although the ruins are of later date. The sandy beach near the harbour is safe for bathing and waters sports. Traditional Irish music is played in the island pubs.

Return to the road to Killadoon and continue S.

Killeen – A cross-inscribed stone stands in the northwest corner of the graveyard.

Turn right at the crossroads; after 0.5mi/0.8km turn right and park.

★**Bunlahinch Clapper Bridge** – Beside a ford stands an ancient stone footbridge of 37 arches constructed by laying flat slabs on stone piles.

Return to the crossroads. EITHER go straight across OR turn right to make a detour (10mi/16km there and back) to Silver Strand.

Beside the road *(left)* stands a **cross-inscribed stone.**

Silver Strand – The vast sandy beach (2mi/3.2km) is sheltered by dunes.

Return to the crossroads and turn right.

Bunlahinch Clapper Bridge

Altore Megalithic Tomb – Beside the road *(left)* overlooking Lough Nahaltora are the remains of a wedge-shaped gallery grave.

At the T-junction turn right onto R 335.

★**Doo Lough Pass** – The road, which was constructed in 1896 by the Congested Districts Board, descends from the pass to Doo Lough (2mi/3.2km long), which is enclosed by the Mweelrea (Muilrea) Mountains (2 668ft/817m) *(W)* and the Sheeffry Hills (2 504ft/761m) *(E)*; at the southern end of the lake rises Ben Gorm (2 302ft/700m).

Delphi – The 2nd Marquess of Sligo renamed his fisheries on the Bundorragha River near Fin Lough after visiting Delphi in Greece.

★**Aasleagh Falls** – *Car park left and right.* At the narrow head of the fjord the Erriff River gushes over a broad sill of rock. The fight in *The Field* was filmed at Aasleagh.

Turn right onto N 59.

★**Killary Harbour** – The harbour is a magnificent fjord, a narrow arm of the sea (13 fathoms deep) extending inland (8mi/13km) between high rock faces; it broadens out opposite Leenane on the south shore. *(See also p 144).*

Inland *Round trip of 70mi/113km*

From Westport take R 330 SE; after 11mi/18km turn left.

★★**Ballintubber Abbey** ⊙ – The abbey, one of the few medieval churches where mass has been celebrated continually for over 750 years, is a fine example of the Romanesque school of the West of Ireland.

It was founded in 1216 by Cathal O'Conor, king of Connaught, as the Monastery of the Holy Trinity in the town of St Patrick's Well *(Baile Tobair Pádraig)* for a community of Augustinian canons. Although suppressed by Henry VIII in 1536, the abbey was reclaimed by the Augustinian friars in 1635. In 1653 the Cromwellians destroyed the conventual buildings and burned the timber roof of the church.

The nave of the **church** was rebuilt following a fire in 1265. The 13C west door and window, removed in the 19C, were restored by the Church of Ireland in 1964. The windows in the north transept depict St Patrick and St Bridget; there is a 13C piscina with a carved head in the Lady Chapel and two tomb slabs (15C and 16C) in the adjacent chapel. The modern altar bears a 17C figure of Christ. The de Burgo chapel (now the Sacristy) contains the tomb of Theobald Burke, Viscount Mayo *(see p 285)*, who was murdered in the locality in 1629. The font, possibly a relic of the earlier church, dates from about 1200; the west window depicts St Columba. The **Cloisters** are in ruins but elements have survived of the 13C Treasury and Chapter House (east range) and of the warming room (early 15C) with under-floor heating ducts and an external fireplace (south range).

Continue S by N 84, R 334 and R 345.

★**Cong** – Cong, once the seat of the kings of Connaught, is an attractive village next to a ruined abbey. The base of the cross erected in the 12C to mark the completion of the abbey stands in the town centre. The cross it supports bears an inscription soliciting prayers for Niahol and Gillibard O'Duffy, Abbots of Cong in the 13C. The village takes its name from its position on a narrow neck of land (*conga* in Irish) dividing Lough Mask from Lough Corrib. The lakes are linked by the River Cong, which descends steeply (36ft/11m in 4mi/6.5km), mainly underground, creating caves in the porous limestone.

Cong Abbey ⊙ – *Car park.* The Augustinian abbey, which stands beside the river, was founded in the 12C, probably by Turlough O'Conor, King of Connaught and High King of Ireland, on the site of an earlier monastic foundation (6C or 7C). After the Dissolution of the Monasteries in 1542 the buildings fell into ruin. Among the remains are the chancel, a Romanesque doorway and traces of the night stairs in the churh; part of the **cloisters** (c 1200; the carved capitals are 19C); fine carved stonework in the **chapter house**; the Guest Refectory with a twisted chimney stack. West of the abbey grounds on an island in the river is the **monks' fishing house** (12C); when a fish was caught in the net which was lowered through a hole in the floor, a bell rang in the kitchen.

Dry Canal

The dry channel which runs east of the village parallel with the river between Lough Mask and Lough Corrib has never carried a boat. A canal with three locks was proposed; for six years men doing relief work during the famine laboured on piece rates, some earning only 3p a day. In March 1854 work was suspended owing to rising costs, competition from the railways and the uncertainty of being able to seal the channel in the porous limestone rock.

The Quiet Man

The Quiet Man was written by Maurice Walsh (1879–1964), a native of Listowel who was employed in Customs and Excise. In 1952 his novel was made into a film, in which **John Wayne** played the part of Sean Thornton, an Irish prize fighter, who returns to his native Ireland after making his name in the USA. Many of Wayne's fans think it was his best role and in recent years they have made their way to Cong in such large numbers that there is now a **Quiet Man Festival** held in June with a John Wayne lookalike contest and a costume ball.

Quiet Man Heritage Centre ⊘ – The interior is furnished as a replica of the cottage used in the film. Above is an exhibition on the local archaeological history.

Ashford Castle ⊘ – *Pedestrian entrance south of the Abbey; vehicle entrance on R 346 east of Cong.* The superb **site** between the river and Lough Corrib is occupied by a castle, now a hotel, designed in the Victorian baronial style by James Franklin Fuller for Arthur Edward Guinness, Lord Ardilaun; it incorporates Ashford House, built in the style of a French château, and part of a 13C castle, built by the de Burgos *(see PORTUMNA)*. The grounds include a stone bridge leading to the castle, formal gardens with a terraced walk *(north)*, the Joyces Tower in a woodland setting *(east)* and a series of underground caves known as the Pigeon Hole *(northeast)*.

From Cong take R 345 W; in Clonbur bear right.

Lough Mask – From the Ferry Bridge fine view of the lake stretching north at the foot of the Partry Mountains *(west)* towards the Plains of Mayo.

At the junction turn right into the minor road which follows the west shore of the lake. North of Srah take R 330 to return to Westport.

Clew Bay *Drive of 25mi/40km – half a day*
From Westport take N 59 N.

Newport – Population 521. This charming little angling resort is dominated by the disused railway viaduct (1892), which has been converted into an unusual walk spanning the Newport River. The broad main street climbs the north bank of the river to St Patrick's Church, built in the Irish-Romanesque style in pink granite (1914) and containing a fine **stained-glass window** by Harry Clarke.

Continue N on N 59; after 1mi/2.4km turn left.

★**Burrishoole Abbey** – By a narrow inlet where the waters of Lough Furnace drain into the sea lie the ruins of a Dominican Friary, founded in 1486. A squat tower rises above the church, which consists of a nave, chancel and south transept. The east wall is all that remains of the cloisters. In 1580 the friary was fortified and garrisoned by the English under Sir Nicholas Malby.

Burrishoole was an important port even before the arrival of the Normans but was abandoned as Westport harbour was developed.

Continue N on N 59; after 2.5mi/4km turn left.

Carrigahowley (Rockfleet) Castle – The 15C or 16C four-storey tower house is built on a most attractive site on flat rocks beside a sea-inlet commanding Clew Bay. The living room was on the fourth floor separated from the lower storeys by a stone vault. In 1566 the owner, Richard Burke, became the second husband of Grace O'Malley *(see above)*.

Take N 59 E; after 1mi/1.6km turn left.

★**Furnace Lough** – A narrow switchback road loops north between Lough Furnace and Lough Feeagh. At the salmon leap where the waters of Lough Feeagh tumble, golden and foaming, over the rocks into Furnace Lough, census work on the numbers of fish moving up- and down-stream is conducted by the Salmon Research Trust of Ireland. **View** north to Nephin Beg (2 065ft/628m).

Continue W on N 59 and R 319.

★**Achill Island** (36 223 acres/14 659ha) is approached by a bridge across Achill Sound from Corraun Hill (1 715ft/521m), itself a peninsula joined to the mainland by a narrow isthmus at Mulrany. The magnificent cliff scenery, the sandy bays, the surfing and boating and the sea angling attract many summer visitors.

The island is dominated by two peaks – Slievemore (2 204ft/671m) and Croaghaun (2 192ft/667m); the latter ends in the dramatic sea cliffs of Achill Head, accessible only by boat.

Doogort is a small resort with sandy beaches on the north coast. There are longer sandy beaches at **Trawmore Strand** and **Keem Strand** on the west coast.

The **Atlantic Drive** runs parallel with the rocky shore between Dooega Head and the mouth of Achill Sound.

On the shore of the Sound south of the bridge to the mainland stand the ruins (restored) of **Kildavnet** (Kildownet) **Church** (c 1700), which contains Stations of the Cross in Gaelic. The name means the church of Dympna, an Irish saint who sought shelter on Achill in the 7C.

Kildavnet (Kildownet) **Castle**, a square four-storey 15C **tower house**, commanding the southern entrance to Achill Sound, is chiefly associated with Grace O'Malley *(see p 285)*; there are traces of a boat slip and the original bawn.

WEXFORD★

LOCH GARMAN – Co Wexford – Population 9 533
Michelin Atlas p 81 and Map 923 – M 10

Wexford is the county town and the commercial centre of the southeast region. It is a town of great antiquity – it was first granted a charter in 1317 – with narrow streets and alleyways, set on the south bank of the River Slaney where it enters Wexford Harbour. The town has a strong cultural tradition and is known internationally for its annual **opera festival.**

HISTORICAL NOTES

In his 2C AD map of Ireland Ptolemy named the site of Wexford Menapia after a Belgic tribe which settled in the region in prehistoric times.

The name Wexford is derived from *Waesfjord* (the harbour of the mud-flats), the name the Vikings gave to the settlement which they established in 950.

When the Anglo-Normans invaded in 1169 Wexford was captured and the first Anglo-Irish treaty was signed at Selskar Abbey. In the 13C the earthen ramparts of the Norse town were replaced by a stone wall.

In 1649 Cromwell entered Wexford; Selskar Abbey was destroyed and 200 citizens were massacred in the market place by Cromwell's forces.

During the rebellion of the United Irishmen in 1798 Wexford was a stronghold of the insurgents, who held it for a month until it was recaptured with much bloodshed by the Crown forces.

In the 19C, led by local shipping companies, Wexford built up a strong maritime trade but it went into decline early in the 20C.

A native of Ballysampson in Co Wexford, **John Barry**, who became senior commodore of the US navy (1794–1803), is commemorated by a statue (Z) presented to the town by the American government in 1956.

Out and About

Wexford Festival Opera – The **Opera Festival** is an annual event, lasting 18 days in late October; during this time it puts on three productions and over 50 events. It has gained an international reputation for the quality of its performances and for its policy of specialising in rare or unjustly neglected operas. The company of artists and the audiences are truly international, being drawn from all over the world. The productions are staged in the **Theatre Royal** ⊙ (Z **T**).

Wexford Arts Centre ⊙ (Y) – Concerts, plays and art exhibitions are held throughout the year.

Walking Tours – Enquire at the Tourist Information Office.

Adjacent Sights – See Enniscorthy, New Ross, Waterford, Wicklow Mountains.

Where to Eat

Lobster Post, Carne. *15mi/24km S by a minor road.* ☎ 053 31110; Fax 053 31401. Busy, bustling pub, decorated in bright colours; menu predominantly seafood.

Where to Stay

Rathaspeck Manor, Rathaspeck. *4mi/6.4km SW by Rosslare Rd off Bridgetown rd.* ☎ 053 42661. Georgian country house (6 rm) in quiet rural setting.

Churchtown House, Tagoat, Rosslare. ☎ 053 32555; Fax 053 32577. Part 19C family owned guesthouse (12 rm) with garden.

Kelly's Resort, Rosslare. ☎ 053 32114; Fax 053 32222. Large, purpose built, family oriented hotel (99 rm) with many leisure facilities; rooms with sea view; formal or informal dining.

Ferrycarrig, Ferrycarrig Bridge. *2.75mi/4km NW by N 11.* ☎ 053 20999. Modern, purpose built hotel (86 rm) with good leisure facilities and pleasant views of River Slaney and estuary.

SIGHTS

★**Main Street** (YZ) – The commercial centre of Wexford is a narrow street, mainly pedestrianised, so narrow that the shops and houses on each side, fronted in the grey slate characteristic of the area, almost seem to touch. Many of the small shops retain the traditional 19C design and style of country town establishments; the once-proud boast of O'Connor's bakery (Y **A**) – "Bread is still the Staff of Life" – appears above the premises. Kelly's bakery (Z **B**) features window displays of traditional Irish loaves, such as wheatsheaves and ducks. The **Bull Ring** (Y) was originally used for bull baiting, a popular sport among the Norman nobles of 12C and 13C Wexford. The 1798 **memorial** shows the bronze figure of a pikeman, created by Oliver Sheppard.

★**Franciscan Friary** ⊙ (Z) – The church founded by the Franciscans in 1230 was confiscated in 1540 at the Dissolution of the Monasteries but returned in 1622. The present church (restored) contains an attractive stucco ceiling and works by contemporary Irish artists, including a striking modern sculpture – **The Burning Bush Tabernacle** – created by Brother Benedict Tutty of Glenstal Abbey (see p 245).
The adjacent convent claims to hold the remains of St Adjutor, a boy martyr of ancient Rome, together with a phial of his blood.

★**St Iberius' Church** ⊙ (Y D) – The Anglican church stands on an ancient Christian site dating back 1 500 years, at that time at the water's edge. The present church was built in 1760 in the Georgian style, with an Ionic reredos and two Corinthian columns screening the sanctuary. The Venetian-style façade was added in the mid 19C.

Selskar Abbey (Y) – The abbey, which was founded c 1190 by Sir Alexander de la Roche on his return from the Crusades, was dissolved in 1538. The outer walls and the square tower are well preserved. During Lent in 1172 Henry II, king of England, did penance at Selskar for the murder of Thomas à Becket.

West Gate Heritage Centre ⊙ (Y) – The West Gate is the only one of the five original fortified gates still standing; it was built by Sir Stephen Devereux c 1200 and closed to traffic in the late 16C. The Norman rooms in the tower give access to a battlement walk to Selskar Abbey; the cosmopolitan history of Wexford is traced in an audio-visual presentation.

★**Twin Churches** (Z) – The foundation stones of the **Church of the Assumption** in Bride Street and the **Church of the Immaculate Conception** in Rowe Street were laid on the same day in 1851. Both churches were designed by Augustus Welby Pugin in an almost identical Gothic style and their towers are the same height (230ft/70m).

EXCURSIONS

Wexford Wildfowl Reserve ⊙ – *3mi/4.8km N of Wexford by R 741; turn right along the coast.* For eight months of the year most of the world's population of Greenland White-fronted Geese winters on the north shore of Wexford Harbour.

★**Curracloe** – *6mi/9km N of Wexford by R 741 and R 742.* Thatched cottages, sand dunes and sandy beaches (7mi/12km) overlook Wexford Bay.

Rosslare (Ros Láir) – *10mi/16km S of Wexford by N 25 and R 740.* Population 847. The pleasant and popular seaside resort of Rosslare boasts a most attractive long beach (6mi/9.5km) and various sporting facilities.
The **ferry terminal** at Rosslare Harbour *(5mi/8km SE)* provides passenger services from Ireland to South Wales and the ports of northern France.

Lady's Island – *11mi/18km S of Wexford by N 25 and minor road from Killinick.* A place of pilgrimage, the island has the ruins of an Augustinian friary and a Norman castle; the tower of the latter leans at a greater angle than that at Pisa.

Tacumshane Windmill ⊙ – *11mi/18km S of Wexford by N 25 and minor road from Killinick.* The windmill, which was built in 1846, was restored complete with sails in the 1950s.

★★**Irish Agricultural Museum, Johnstown Castle** ⊙ – *5mi/8km SW of Wexford by N 25; after 4mi/6.4km turn right (sign).* The Johnstown estate was donated to the Irish State in 1945. **Johnstown Castle** *(not open)*, designed by Daniel Robertson, now houses an agricultural research centre.
The park (50 acres/20ha) contains **ornamental grounds** with over 200 species of trees and shrubs, three ornamental lakes, walled gardens, hothouses and a picnic area. The old farmyard buildings now house a well-presented museum displaying many examples of obsolete agricultural machinery. The transport section includes tub traps, widely used in rural Ireland until the arrival of the motor car in the 1920s, a jaunting car made in Gorey, Co Wexford, about 1880, carts, traps and harness; corn winnowing machines and old tractors, which heralded the revolution in farming. There are sections on dairying, haymaking and poultry keeping; reconstructions of a cooperage, a harness-maker's workshop, a blacksmith's forge and a carpenter's shop; a re-creation of 19C Irish rural living and a display of fine Irish country furniture.
The **Famine Exhibition** is a thorough science-based interpretation of the causes, effects and aftermath of the Great Famine (1845–49), with re-creations of a rural home and the lazy-beds in which potatoes were grown, as well as explanations of how life could be surprisingly well sustained on a monotonous diet of potatoes and dairy products and how the disaster affected different regions of the country. A reconstruction of a soup kitchen evokes relief work, and a reconstruction of a field laboratory demonstrates how the fight against disease was conducted.

★**Kilmore Quay** – *15mi/24km SW of Wexford by N 25 and R 739; boat trips.*⊙ Population 424. This fishing village retains much of its 19C atmosphere, as about 15 houses still have thatched roofs. The *Wooden House* pub has an extensive collection of historic photographs.
The **maritime museum** ⊙ in the former *Guillemot* lightship, moored in the harbour, contains many relics of the Wexford seafaring tradition, including old maps and a 200-year-old compass and binnacle, a whale's backbone and a large-scale model of *HMS Africa*, sister ship to Nelson's *Victory*.

★**Saltee Islands** ⊙ – *Boat trips from Kilmore Quay; 3mi/4.8km offshore.* The Great and Little Saltee Islands (each about 0.5mi/0.8km long), normally uninhabited, form Ireland's largest bird sanctuary, home for many thousands of gannets, guillemots and puffins (200 000 birds) as well as seals and dolphins.

★**Irish National Heritage Park** ⊙ – *Ferrycarrig; 2.5mi/4km NW of Wexford by N 11 going N across the River Slaney.* Nine thousand years of Irish history are brought to life by 16 separate sites, mostly reconstructed, linked by a visitors' trail and a nature trail. The **Stone Age**, 7000–2000 BC, is represented by a Mesolithic camp site, an early Irish farmstead and a portal dolmen. The **Bronze Age** is illustrated by a cist burial chamber and a stone circle. The Celtic and early-Christian ages, the most extensively reconstructed, are represented by an early-Christian monastery, an **Ogham stone** showing the earliest form of writing in Ireland, and a **crannóg**, an artificial island protected by a palisade. The horizontal watermill is a reconstruction of one dating from 833 in Co Cork. The round tower is a replica, built in 1857 to commemorate Wexford men killed in the Crimean War (1854–56).

The only real historic relic is the Norman earthworks and fortifications, built by Robert FitzStephen in 1169.

WICKLOW MOUNTAINS★★

Co Wicklow

Michelin Atlas p 87 and Map 923 – M, N 8, 9

The Wicklow Mountains south of Dublin provide high peaks and spectacular views, lakes, reservoirs and waterfalls, open moorland and verdant valleys, some landscaped into elegant gardens. The rolling heights are covered in peat bog where the rivers form broad shallow treeless corridors; on the harder schist they create deep and narrow wooded gorges, like Dargle Glen, Glen of the Downs and Devil's Glen.

There are electricity generating stations in the Wicklow Gap (Turlough Hill) and on the **Poulaphouca Reservoir**; the Vartry Reservoir supplies water to Dublin.

Along the coast, which is formed by a shingle ridge covered by sand dunes liable to severe erosion, is a string of seaside resorts and strands: Bray, Greystones, Wicklow and Arklow.

INLAND *North to south*

★★**Powerscourt** ⊘ – The estate takes its name from Eustace le Poer, a Norman knight. In 1609 the land was granted to Sir Richard Wingfield by James I, who made him Viscount Powerscourt. In 1961 the estate was sold to Mr and Mrs Slazenger.

The **gardens** were created on a steep south slope facing the Sugar Loaf Mountain (1 654ft/503m); they are well known for roses and flowering shrubs, an extensive range of conifers, a stand of Eucalyptus trees planted in 1897 and an avenue of beech trees which leads up to the front of the house.

Out and About

Tourist Information – There is an **Information Point** ⊘ for the Wicklow Mountains at the Upper Lake in Glendalough.

Outdoor Activities – **Boat trips** and other water sports are available at the Blessington Lakes Leisure Centre on the **Poulaphouca Reservoir** ⊘.

The **Tiglin Adventure Centre** in the Devil's Glen offers courses in caving, canoeing, hang gliding, hiking, mountaineering, orienteering, rock climbing, snorkelling and surfing.

The **Clara Lara Fun Park** ⊘ *(Vale of Clara)* offers a variety of activities for children – assault course, adventure playgrounds, radio-controlled boats, bathing, boating and fishing, picnic meadows.

Walking – The **Wicklow Way** is a long-distance footpath which starts in Rathfarnham, south of Dublin and ends in Clonegal in Co Carlow (access at Moyne, Bridgeland and Kilquiggin); the trail crosses mountains, switches back and forth through river valleys and presents glorious views.

Crafts – For woollen goods visit Avoca Weavers in Avoca or at Kilmacanogue *(see below)*.

Adjacent Sights – See Athy, Carlow, Dublin, Enniscorthy, Kildare, Maynooth.

Where to Eat

The Bakery, Church St. ☎ 0404 66770; Fax 0404 66717. Unusual restaurant in old bakery in town centre; interesting modern Irish menu.

Where to Stay

Hunters, Newrath Bridge, Rathnew. *0.75mi1.2km N by N 11 on R 761.* ☎ 0404 40106; Fax 0404 40338. Converted 18C coaching inn (16 rm), family owned since 19C, in pleasant spacious gardens.

Tinakilly House, Rathnew. *On R 50.* ☎ 0404 69274. Part Victorian country house (53 rm) in pleasant grounds; very comfortable but expensive.

The house, designed by Richard Castle in 1730 to incorporate an earlier castle, was accidentally burned out in 1974. The ground floor has been restored and now houses a terrace café overlooking the gardens and an **exhibition** with video on the history of the estate and its owners.

Turn right along the terrace.

At the west end of the terrace is the entrance to the memorial garden, created in 1931 in memory of Julia, widow of the 7th Viscount, by her son; the four busts of Michelangelo, Cellini, da Vinci and Raphael are copies of the Vatican originals. The Bamberg Gate is a fine example of Viennese ironwork (1770). Several walled gardens descend the hillside to the pets' corner and the rhododendron grove.

The **terraces** were begun in 1843 by the 7th Viscount and designed by Daniel Robertson, a gouty eccentric, who directed the work from a wheelbarrow. The beach at Bray provided the black and white stones for the mosaic. Many of the statues were collected by the 6th Viscount (1815–44) who travelled extensively in Europe. Children take great delight in rolling down the steep grass banks, which descend to a lake where a Triton spews a jet of water (100ft/30m high) into the air; in summer the water lilies are in flower.

From the east bank the paths plunge into the jungle-like profusion of the **Japanese Garden** which was created in 1908 on reclaimed bogland. The stone **tower** *(54 steps)* provides an interesting view of the house and terrace and of the surrounding tree-tops.

Take R 760 south; after 2mi/3.2km turn right (sign); at the crossroads drive straight on for 2mi/3.2km to Valclusa.

Powerscourt Gardens

★★**Powerscourt Waterfall** ⊘ – *5min on foot from car park to foot of waterfall; climbing the rock face is dangerous.* The waterfall is formed by the Dargle River which plunges (400ft/122m) in a spray of thick white spume down a jagged grey rock face in a horseshoe of hills. There are pleasant walks and nature trails by the river, and swings and slides for children at the visitor centre.

★**Killruddery** ⊘ – The **formal gardens** at Killruddery were designed by a Frenchman in 1682. The major features are a pair of parallel canals (550ft/168m long), the **Long Ponds**, prolonged by the **Lime Avenue** leading uphill to the 18C park. The **Angles** consists of a number of intersecting walks lined with high hedges; the wilderness of trees is bisected by broad walks; a bay hedge encloses the **sylvan theatre**; the **beech hedge pond** consists of two concentric circular beech hedges, surrounding a round pond (60ft/18m in diameter) and a fountain; the four 19C statues represent the four seasons. Two 19C ornamental gardens are bordered by box hedges. The octagonal ornamental building was originally a dairy.

The **house**, which dates from the 1650s, was considerably remodelled in the 1820s by Richard and William Morrison and the statue gallery was added in 1852. Above the stableyard entrance is a clock and striking mechanism, both operated by water power and built by members of the family in 1906–09.

The estate was granted in 1618 to Sir William Brabazon, created Earl of Meath in 1627, whose ancestors arrived in England with William the Conqueror and whose descendants still live at Killruddery.

Kilmacanogue – Population 763. The shop and factory of **Avoca Weavers** ⊘ stand on the site of a house, Glencormac, built in 1864

by James Jameson of the famous whiskey family. The grounds contain many rare species – a weeping cypress, Blue Atlantic cedars, 13 yew trees which are said to be 700 to 800 years old and originally formed part of an avenue leading to Holybrook Abbey, several Wellingtonias and various types of eucalyptus and pine.

★★**Sally Gap** – The crossroads on the Military Road gives splendid views of the surrounding blanket bog on the Wicklow Mountains.

★**Loughs Tay and Dan** – The two lakes are linked by the Cloghgoge River.

Roundwood – Population 437. The village (780ft/238m above sea-level) consists of little more than a broad main street with several pubs and craft shops; a pub and a café both claim the honour of being the highest in Ireland.

Annamoe – There are pleasant walks beside the Annamoe River. It was here at the age of seven that Laurence Sterne *(see CLONMEL)* fell into the mill race and emerged unscathed.

★**Glenmacnass Waterfall** – *Car park.* The mountain river streams down an inclined rock face.

★★**Wicklow Gap** – The road west from Glendalough to Hollywood follows the course of the medieval pilgrims' path, **St Kevin's Road**, through the Vale of Glendasan. Where the modern road loops northeast, hikers may follow the old direct route *(2mi/3km)* closer to Lough Nahanagan. The motor road rejoins the old route to pass through the Wicklow Gap between Tonelagee (2 686ft/816m *north*) and Table Mountain (2 302ft/700m *west*).

★**Devil's Glen** – The Vartry River makes a spectacular **waterfall** (100ft/30m) by cascading into the Devil's Punchbowl, a deep basin in the rock. There are **walks** in the immediate vicinity and good views of the coastline.

★**Mount Usher Gardens** ⊘ – Set on the outskirts of Ashford village (population 878), the natural-style gardens (20 acres/8ha), which are planted with over 5 000 species, many sub-tropical, are renowned for the collections of eucryphia and eucalyptus. They were laid out in 1868 by Edward Walpole, a member of a Dublin

Slide File, Dublin

Glenmacnass Waterfall

linen-manufacturing family, and totally restored following severe flood damage in 1986. Two suspension bridges lead to the woodland walks on the east bank of the River Vartry, which has been attractively developed with the addition of weirs.

Vale of Clara – The road, which follows the course of the Avonmore River, a trout stream, links Laragh (population 249), a meeting point of many roads and glens, to the attractive village of Rathdrum (population 1 175).

★**Glenmalur** – The road beside the upper reaches of the Avonbeg River ends in a remote and desolate spot at the northeast foot of Lugnaquilla, Ireland's second-highest mountain (3 039ft/926m high).

★**Avondale** ⊙ – The Avondale estate was the birthplace and family home of **Charles Stewart Parnell**, the 19C Nationalist leader (1846–91). The two-storey neo-Classical **house** has been restored to its appearance during Parnell's lifetime when it was much used for social occasions. It was designed in 1759 by Samuel Hayes; there is Coade stone ornamentation by the **Lafranchini brothers** in the dining room. The life of Charles Parnell, the history of his family in Ireland, his role in 19C Irish politics, are traced by a video. Among the furniture and memorabilia are Parnell's stick and chair (he was 6ft 3in/1.9m tall), photos of Parnell and Kitty O'Shea, her wedding ring of Avonmore gold mined by Parnell, a set of folding library steps made of Irish bog oak.

The **forest park** (512 acres/207ha) covers a steep slope facing east across the Avondale River. The oldest surviving trees – two gigantic silver firs by the river as well as oaks, beeches and larches – were planted by Samuel Hayes in the 18C. The stump of a beech tree, planted nearly 250 years ago, has its rings delineated in relation to subsequent historical events. There are several trails and woodland walks ranging from the **Pine Trail** (0.5mi/0.8km), which is suitable for disabled people, to the **River Walk** (4mi/6.4km), which passes through the massed conifers on the banks of the Avonmore River and along the Great Ride.

★**Meeting of the Waters** – The confluence of the rivers Avonbeg and Avonmore is set amid the forests of south Co Wicklow; nearby stands the tree beneath which the poet Thomas Moore (1779–1852) is said to have composed *The Meeting of the Waters* in 1807.

Motte Stone – The name of the large glacial boulder is derived from the French for half *(moitié)*, as it used to mark the half-way point on the Dublin–Wexford road before the advent of mileposts.

Vale of Avoca – There are forest walks in the wooded river valley. At the **Avoca Weavers Mill** ⊙, founded in 1723 and therefore the oldest surviving business in Ireland, visitors may watch the production of textiles by traditional methods.

The village of Avoca has attracted visitors in great numbers, since it was chosen as the setting for the hugely popular television series, *Ballykissangel*.

ON THE COAST *North to south*

Bray – Population 25 096. Bray is an old-established resort with a sand and shingle beach at the south end of Killiney Bay; in recent years it has become a dormitory town for Dublin. The public park on Bray Head provides a fine **view** of the coastline. The **Heritage Centre** ⏱ in the Town Hall traces the local history through photographs, maps and artefacts. The **National Sea-Life Centre** ⏱, on the sea-front, presents more than 30 displays populated by an array of marine and freshwater creatures.

Charles Stewart Parnell (1846–91)

After an unpromising school career Parnell entered Parliament in 1875 and soon attracted the attention of the Nationalists. He became Vice-President of the Home Rule Confederation of Great Britain. As President of the Land League he campaigned for the tenants to keep a firm grip on their home-steads and went on a fund-raising trip to America and Canada; he was so well received that he was dubbed the "uncrowned king of Ireland". In September 1880 he proposed the policy of "moral Coventry" which advo-cated what came to be known as boycotting, after Capt Boycott who was the first to feel its effect. Parnell used his own newspaper *United Ireland* to attack government policy. In 1882 he founded the National League to cam-paign for Home Rule. In 1886 he took up residence with Mrs Kitty O'Shea, whom he had met in 1880, and in 1889 Captain O'Shea won an uncon-tested case for divorce, citing Parnell as co-respondent. Parnell was called upon to resign but he refused and his party split. He died in October 1891 four months after marrying Kitty O'Shea.

Greystones – Population 9 649. The resort has developed from a fishing village with a harbour flanked by shingle beaches.

The Murrough – *0.5mi/0.8km north of Wicklow on the east bank of the estuary.* A long shingle beach (3mi/5km) backed by a broad grass bank is flanked by the sea and the **Broad Lough**, a lagoon noted for its wildfowl and golden plover.

Wicklow – Population 6 416. Wicklow is the county town and the main commer-cial centre for the northern part of Co Wicklow. It is also an attractive seaside town set at the eastern foot of the Wicklow Mountains.

The Irish name of the town *(Cill Mhantáin)* recalls St Mantan, a missionary who established a church in the 5C. In the 9C the Danish Vikings set up a port, which developed into an important trading centre. The English name of the town is derived from the Danish words for Viking meadow *(Wyking-alo)*.

The statue of a pikeman in the Market Square represents all those who fought in nationalist uprisings. The **Halpin Memorial**, an obelisk of polished granite, commem-orates Captain Robert C Halpin (1836–94), a native of the town, who commanded the *Great Eastern*, the ship built by Brunel that laid the first transatlantic telegraph cable; mementoes are displayed at his residence, Tinakilly House, now a hotel *(2mi/3km northwest by N 11)*.

Black Castle, which stands on a rocky promontory immediately south of the harbour, was built in 1176 by Maurice Fitzgerald, to whom the district had been granted after the 12C Anglo-Norman invasion, and was the subject of frequent attacks by local clansmen, the O'Byrnes and the O'Tooles, until the 16C. The ruins form a fine vantage point for **views** over the town and the coast of north Co Wicklow.

The 18C **Anglican Church** ⊙ has an onion-shaped copper cupola, donated in 1777, and incorporates a 12C Irish-Romanesque doorway. The interior contains a fine king-post roof, a 12C font, an organ, transferred in the late 18C from the Anglican cathedral in Cashel, and a memorial tablet to Captain Halpin *(see above)*. The title "the Church of the Vineyard" recalls the vines planted by the Normans on the "Vineyard Banks" which descend to the River Vartry.

The extensive ruins of the **Franciscan friary**, founded by the Fitzgerald family in the 13C, stand in the grounds of the parish priest's house. After the 16C Dissolution of the Monasteries, the building became a courthouse. In 1812 the buildings were given to the local parish priest, as a reward for his services in the Battle of Salamanca in Spain.

Wicklow's Historic Gaol ⊙ – The formidable stone-built prison dates from 1702, the time of the Penal Laws, and was used as a prison until 1924. It now houses elab-orate exhibits which bring to life some of the more dramatic aspects of Ireland's history. A warder inducts visitors into the ghastly conditions suffered by prisoners in the 18C; British soldiers ponder how to crush the 1798 Rebellion (many of the participants were tried in this building); local gentleman-rebel Billy Byrne awaits his execution; the life of convicts in the 19C, both here and in Australia, is evoked; stern Captain Betts shows how to deal with recalcitrant prisoners on board the transportation vessel Hercules.

Samuel Hayes

Avondale was inherited by the Parnell family from Samuel Hayes, a plantsman, whose Chippendale bureau is on display in the house. In 1788 Hayes presented a bill to Parliament "for encouraging the cultivation of trees" and in 1904 Avondale became the national forestry training centre.

Brittas Bay – The long sandy beach (3mi/5km), backed by dunes, is one of the most popular resorts on the east coast.

Arklow – Population 7 987. The seaside resort, founded by the Vikings on the south bank of the Avoca estuary, is also an important east-coast fishing harbour and a base for Ireland's main fleet of coastal trading ships. The most famous product of the local boatyards is **Gypsy Moth III**, the yacht in which Sir Francis Chichester sailed around the world in 1967. There are attractive walks by the harbour and along the south bank of the river.

The **Maritime Museum** ⊙ displays about 200 exhibits connected with Ireland's maritime history and traces the development of local commercial shipping since the 1850s; a video *Eyes to the Sea* tells the maritime history of Arklow.

Arklow Rock *(2mi/3.2km south)* provides a fine **view** of the coastline.

YOUGHAL★

EOCHAILL – Co Cork – Population 5 630
Michelin Atlas p 79 and Map 923 – I 12

Youghal (pronounced yawl) occupies an attractive **site** on the west bank of the Blackwater estuary. It derives its name from the Irish for yew wood, a reference to the great forests that surrounded the town in medieval times.

Strategically placed for the landing of forces from England and always vulnerable to the threat of invasion from France and Spain, Youghal became one of England's most strongly defended Irish seaports, enclosed by impressive town walls.

Several buildings of historical interest have survived, although the **North Abbey**, a Dominican establishment dating from 1268, is reduced to the west chancel wall standing in the main town graveyard.

HISTORICAL NOTES

First occupied by the Danish Vikings in the 9C, Youghal was later settled by the Anglo-Normans at the end of the 12C. The town supplied King John with three fighting ships and received its first charter in return. In the 13C it was completely enclosed on three sides by elaborate walls, the fourth side being protected by the River Blackwater.

In the late 16C, while mayor of Youghal, **Sir Walter Raleigh** introduced the tobacco and potato plants into Ireland. Following the Cromwellian invasion of 1649 Youghal passed through a particularly difficult period. In the 18C the closed borough was totally dominated by members of the Protestant minorities; Roman Catholics were utterly deprived of religious, political and civil rights, the cause of successive rebellions.

During the 19C Youghal developed a commercial tradition – in brick-making, now extinct, and lace-making, a nearly vanished craft. In the latter part of the 19C some 150 sail-powered schooners traded from the port; sailors from Youghal could recognise one another throughout the ports of the world by their distinctive whistle. This once-strong tradition began to decline early in the 20C with the silting-up of the estuary and the building of steam-powered freight ships.

YOUGHAL

Moby Dick's Pub.................. **A**

Out and About

Walking Tour ⏱ – Guided walking tour of Youghal organised in summer.

Adjacent Sights – See Cobh, Cork, Clonmel, Lismore, Midleton, Waterford.

Where to Eat

The Tannery, Quay St, Dungarvan. ☎ 058 45420; Fax 058 45518. Seaside restaurant with original and imaginative menu.

Where to Stay

Aherne's Seafood Restaurant and Bar (at Aherne's Hotel), 163 North Main St. ☎ 024 92424; Fax 024 93633. Renowned family run restaurant providing both formal and informal eating based on very fresh seafood; 12 very comfortable well furnished bedrooms.

SIGHTS

★★ St Mary's Collegiate Church ⏱ – It is probable that the first church on the site, a wooden building, was erected by followers of St Declan of Ardmore in c 400. The present early-13C edifice was pronounced "one of Ireland's most impressive churches" by the late Claud Cockburn, writer and long-time Youghal resident; it replaced an 11C Danish-built church destroyed in a great storm soon after its construction. During the late-15C wars, the forces of the Earl of Desmond occupied the building and removed the roof of the chancel. Large-scale restoration, including the re-modelling of the chancel, took place between 1851 and 1858.

The east window dates from 1498; the font in the nave is also from this period. The church contains a large collection of **grave slabs** and **effigies,** including some from the 13C and 14C with Norman-French inscriptions.

In the south transept stands a vast monument to the first Earl of Cork, his three wives and 16 children. He arrived in Ireland nearly penniless towards the end of the reign of Elizabeth I and became so rich that he is often described as one of Europe's first capitalists.

★ Town Walls – Youghal has the best-preserved town walls in Ireland, more extensive even than the city walls of Londonderry. They were built in the 13C and extended in the 17C; large sections are still in excellent condition, although only three of the 13 medieval towers remain. The portion restored in the 19C with a turret and a cannon is accessible from the churchyard; the sentry walk provides a fine **view** of the town and the harbour. The full length of the walls is best seen from the road at the rear *(Raheen Road).*

★ Clock Gate – The unusual four-storey building straddling the Main Street was constructed by the corporation in 1777 to replace the Iron Gate, also known as Trinity Castle, part of the walls. The new tower was used as the town gaol until 1837; such was the state of insurrection in the late 18C that it soon became overcrowded; rebels were hanged from the windows as an example to the rest of the populace.

The Red House – This fine example of early-18C Dutch domestic architecture creates a marked contrast with its neighbours. The red brick façade with white stone quoins is surmounted by a triangular gable and a steep mansard roof. It was designed in 1710 for the Uniacke family by a Dutch architect-builder Claud Leuvethen.

Youghal Heritage Centre ⏱ – The old Market House now houses the Tourist Information Office and an exhibition on the history of the walled port of Youghal. In the Market Square stands a memorial commemorating the *Nellie Fleming*, the last of the old Youghal sailing vessels.

In the pub on the corner, **Moby Dick's** (**A**), are many photographs taken during the filming of *Moby Dick* on location in Youghal during the summer of 1954.

Benedictine Abbey – All that remains of the abbey is the east gable wall pierced by a moulded Gothic doorway with ornamental spandrels; in the passageway are the arched piscina and square aumbry from the original church. The abbey was founded in 1350 and used by Cromwell as his winter headquarters in 1649–50.

Almshouses – The Elizabethan almshouses were erected in 1610 by the Earl of Cork, who provided "five pounds apiece for each of ye six old decayed soldiers or Alms Men for ever". They are still used for residential purposes, as is the neighbouring former Protestant asylum, dated 1838 and now called **Shalom House.**

Tynte's Castle – This 15C battlemented building has a device over the front door for pouring boiling oil on rebels and other unwelcome visitors. Once on the waterfront, it is now some distance (200yd/182m) from the river.

EXCURSION

From Youghal take N 25 E; turn right into a minor road to Moord and Ardmore.

★**Whiting Bay** – The bay, which is flanked by Cabin Point and Ardoginna Head, is very isolated but offers fine **views** *(SW)* across Youghal Bay to Knockadoon Head.

★**Ardmore** – Ardmore is renowned as a holiday resort with a small pier, a large amusement park and an extensive sandy beach which is safe for bathing. From the hotel in the village there is a steep climb to the well-defined footpath that leads past ruined Dysert church to Ram Head (2mi/3km) for a view of the coast. Nearby is St Declan's Holy Well. On the beach below is St Declan's Stone, a glacial boulder said to have carried the saint's bell across St George's Channel from Wales.

The **Round Tower**★ (97ft/29m), which probably dates from the 12C, is crowned by a conical cap. It is built of regular masonry and has roll moulding round the doorway, projecting string courses marking each of the four storeys and projecting corbels carved with human and other ornaments.

The adjoining "**cathedral**"★, which dates from the 10C to 14C, has an interior arcade and a pointed arch dividing the nave and chancel. The outstanding feature is the exterior **arcade**★ of sunken panels placed on the west gable, probably during 12C restoration work; there are 13 recesses above and two larger ones below. All but three of the upper panels are filled with sculptures similar in style to those found on high crosses dating from the 10C; this suggests that they were brought to Ardmore from elsewhere; the best-known panel *(no 10)* depicts the Weighing of Souls. The original building, also known as **St Declan's Oratory**, probably dates from the 5C settlement of Ardmore by St Declan; the eastern part of the church appears to be 14C.

Take the coast road E to Mine Head.

Mine Head – Mine Head provides impressive **views** of the cliffs.

Take the coast road E to Helvick Head.

Ringville (An Rinn) – This small village is the centre of an Irish-speaking area, the **West Waterford Gaeltacht**; excellent **views**★ across Dungarvan harbour.

★**Helvick Head** – *1mi/1.3km E of Ringville.* Helvick Harbour, a small but busy port backed by a row of fishermen's cottages, shelters below the headland which, despite its modest height (230ft/82m), provides outstanding **views**★ of the coastline.

Cunnigar Peninsula – *1mi/1.3m W of Ringville.* The sandy spit of land extending into Dungarvan harbour may be walked from end to end *(1.5mi/3km)*.

Dungarvan – *18mi/30km E by N 25.* The thriving seaside resort occupies an attractive **site** astride the Colligan estuary overlooking Dungarvan Harbour flanked by the Drum Hills *(S)* and the Monavullagh and Comeragh Mountains *(N)*.

King John's Castle, built by the king in 1185 not long after the Anglo-Norman invasion, consists of a large circular **keep** surrounded by fortified walls, much modified in subsequent centuries.

The **Dungarvan Museum** ⊙, housed in the Municipal Library, has a nautical theme; local shipwrecks are well documented, especially the *Moresby* which went down in Dungarvan Bay on 24 December 1895 with the loss of 20 lives.

On the east bank of the river are the ruins of a 13C **Augustinian priory** which was founded by the McGraths, who also built the 12C or 13C **castle**, of which only the west wall still stands. The walk on the seaward side of the graveyard provides fine **views**★ across Dungarvan Harbour south to Helvick Head.

Master McGrath Monument

In a career of 37 races, Master McGrath, a locally-bred greyhound, was beaten only once. Between 1868 and 1871 he won the Waterloo Cup in England three times and is commemorated in the only monument in Ireland to a dog *(2mi/3.2km NW of Dungarvan by R 672)*.

Giant's Causeway

S Chirol

Northern Ireland

ANTRIM

AONTROIM – Co Antrim – Population 20 878
Michelin Atlas p 103 and Map 923 – N 3

Antrim, a linen-spinning centre, was once the county town of the administrative area which bears its name. It lies on the Six Mile Water, a good trout stream, beside Lough Neagh. On the lake shore there is a championship golf course and a marina which provides cruises on Lough Neagh (see p 359). The town was burned by General Monro in 1649 and attacked during the 1798 Rebellion by a force of 3 500 United Irishmen under Henry Joy McCracken, a Belfast cotton manufacturer, who was defeated.

Out and About

Clotworthy Arts Centre ⊙ – Theatrical and musical performances, exhibitions of painting, photography and sculpture. Talks and lectures. Courses and workshops; located in Antrim Castle Grounds (see below). Open Mon–Fri, 9.30am–9.30pm, Sat, 10am–5pm, Sun, 2pm–5pm (July and Aug only).

Adjacent Sights – See Antrim Glens, Belfast, Carrickfergus, Lough Neagh.

SIGHTS

★**Round Tower** – Steeple Park. Among the trees stands a well-preserved round tower (90ft/27m); the conical cap has been restored. It was probably built c 900 and is all that remains of an important 6C monastery, abandoned in 1147.

Pogue's Entry ⊙ – East end of the main street. In a narrow alley stands the simple cabin where Alexander Irvine (1863–1941) spent his childhood. The front room served as kitchen, living room and workshop where his father made and repaired shoes; there was a bedroom at the back and the children slept in the loft. Irvine became a missionary in the Bowery in New York; his book, My Lady of the Chimney Corner, is about his mother's struggle against poverty.

Antrim Castle Gardens ⊙ – West end of the main street. Beyond the Market Place and the Court House (1726) stands a magnificent Tudor gate, the entrance to the former seat (the castle burned down accidentally in 1922) of the Clotworthy family, ennobled in the 17C as Lords Massereene. The top of the Norman motte is the best place from which to view this rare late-17C Anglo-Dutch water garden; the ornamental canals, connected by a cascade, are flanked by geometric parterres containing 17C culinary or medicinal plants and screened by high pleached hedges of lime and hornbeam.

Finishing Shop, Patterson's Spade Mill

Shane's Castle Grounds ⊙ – *0.25mi/0.4km west by A 6*. On the shore of Lough Neagh stand the ruins of **Shane's Castle**, the seat of the O'Neill family since 1607 when James I settled the estate on Shane McBrian O'Neill. A burial vault (1722) is linked by a tunnel to the ruins of the castle which burned down in 1816. A superb collection of camellias over 100 years old is housed in the surviving conservatory, designed by John Nash and an exact copy of his own on the Isle of Wight. He also designed the **terrace** overlooking Lough Neagh; the cannons are from a British man o'war which sank in Lough Foyle. In the **Nature Reserve** (80 acres/32ha) are rare breeds of cattle – Irish moiled (hornless), Highland and Belted Galloway, and a herd of feral fallow deer *(viewing area)*; a nature trail skirts the lake shore.

EXCURSIONS

Patterson's Spade Mill ⊙ – *5mi/8km SE by A 6 via Templepatrick*. The only surviving water-powered spade mill in Ireland was founded in 1919; five generations of Pattersons worked at the mill until 1990. The tour includes all the stages involved in producing spades in the traditional way – the forge for heating the metal billet, the huge tilt hammer for shaping the blade which is then sharpened and tempered, the riveting of the blade to the shaft, and the painting – all done by two men. Beside the mill are the ruins of associated industrial buildings.

Ballance House ⊙ – *11mi/17km S by B 101, A 26 and A 30 via Glenavy*. The house was the birthplace of John Ballance (1839–93), who emigrated to Birmingham and thence to New Zealand, where he became a journalist and then entered politics, becoming the first Liberal Prime Minister. The parlour is furnished in the style of 1850 as it was during John Ballance's childhood. The upper floor is devoted to the Ulster–New Zealand connection, particularly the continuing link between the Royal School in Dungannon and Dilworth School in New Zealand, and to Maori culture.

Templetown Mausoleum ⊙ – *Templepatrick; 5mi/8km E of Antrim by A 6. Park at the end of the drive*. A walled graveyard encloses the mausoleum, which was designed by Robert Adam in the Palladian style c 1770 for Sarah Upton in memory of her husband Arthur. It contains tablets to later generations of Uptons who received the title Viscount Templetown.
The name Templepatrick derives from an earlier church dedicated to St Patrick who is supposed to have baptised converts at a nearby Holy Well in about 450.

Slemish – *16mi/26km NE by A 26 to Ballymena, A 42 east and B 94; after 1mi/1.6km turn left; after 3mi/4.8km turn right (Carnstroan Road); after 0.25mi/0.4km turn right. From the car park 1hr there and back on foot*. The distinctive bare silhouette of Slemish (1 437ft/438m), an extinct volcano, rises abruptly from the flat landscape. On St Patrick's Day (17 March) it is a place of pilgrimage since tradition has it that **St Patrick** spent six years here in captivity herding swine for the local chieftain Miluic. From the top there is a fine **view** including the ruins of Skerry Church *(northwest)*, the burial place of the O'Neills, supposed to be founded by St Patrick himself.

Arthur Cottage ⊙ – *17mi/27km NW by A 26 to Ballymena and B 62 to Cullybackey. Cross the river and turn sharp right onto a narrow lane*. At the end of the lane stands an isolated one-storey cottage with the traditional split door. The floor is of clay and the roof of flax-straw thatch. From here the father of Chester Alan Arthur, 21st President of the USA, emigrated in 1816 to Vermont where he became a Baptist clergyman. The furniture is in period; in summer there are demonstrations of traditional domestic crafts. The large outbuilding contains collections of local agricultural and domestic implements from the past, and a display on Chester Alan Arthur's family and 19C emigration from Ireland.

Gracehill – *11mi/18km NW by A 26 to Ballymena and A 42*. Population 449. The Georgian architecture and attractive layout of this village are the work of the Moravians, who came via London from Bohemia where their church was persecuted. Their settlement, started in 1759 and grouped round a central square, included a church, the minister's house and communal houses for single men and women. The boarding schools for girls and boys acquired an enviable reputation far outside their locality. Men and women sat on separate sides in church and were buried in separate sections of the graveyard.

Randalstown Presbyterian Church – *5mi/8km W by A 6*. The charming oval church was built of dark stone with pointed windows in 1790. The porch, containing curved flights of steps to the internal gallery, was added in 1829 and the row of oval oculi was inserted in 1929 when the height of the walls was raised.

Glens of ANTRIM★★★

Co Antrim

Michelin Atlas p 103 and Map 923 – N, O 2, 3

A drive up the **Antrim Coast** offers a great variety of scenery and a sense of expectancy at each approaching headland. Seaward are attractive villages, long flat strands, steep basalt or limestone cliffs, and a distant prospect of the Mull of Kintyre in Scotland. Inland are the glens created by the tumbling mountain streams which descend from the uplands of heath and bog, now punctuated by forestry plantations. In the glens, where the underlying sedimentary rocks are exposed, the farms are arranged like ladders climbing the valley sides so that each has a share of the good land near the river and of the poorer upland pasture.

For many years this was the most isolated and least anglicised part of the country owing to the difficult terrain. There had always been a track along the coast, which still makes a good walk, but the first coast road, passable to coaches in all weathers, dates from 1832 when the Grand Military Road from Carrickfergus to Portrush was built under the supervision of William Bald.

Two narrow-gauge railway lines (3ft/1m) were laid down in the 19C to carry the increasing output of the Glenariff mines, which opened in the late 1860s. One, the railway built by the Glenariff Iron Ore & Holding Co, ran from Inverglen down Glenariff to the southeast end of Red Bay, where the bed of the track is still visible. The other ran from Ballymena up the Clogh Valley to Retreat (1876) but was never extended further, owing to the steep gradient down Glenballyemon to the coast; it turned to carrying passengers and opened up the glens to the tourist trade before ceasing operations in 1930.

Out and About

Adjacent Sights – See Carrickfergus, Giant's Causeway, Portrush.

Where to Stay

Derrin House, 2 Prince's Gdns, Larne BT40 1RQ. *Off A 2 Glenarm Rd.* ☎ 028 2827 3762; Fax 028 2827 3269. Friendly, well run guesthouse (6 rm); good value.

Londonderry Arms, 20 Harbour Rd, Carnlough BT44 0ᴱU. ☎ 028 2888 5255; Fax 028 2888 5263. Traditionally appointed period hotel (35 rm); good bedrooms.

Marine, North St, Ballycastle BT64 6BN. ☎ 028 2076 2222; Fax 028 2076 9507. Spacious, good value hotel (32 rm; well located for exploring the coast.

Larne to Ballycastle *70mi/113km – 1 or 2 days*

Larne – *Larne Lough Ferry* ⏱ *to Island Magee (see p 329)*. Population 17 575. The town, the southern gateway to the Glens of Antrim, is a busy port with a regular ferry service to Stranraer and Cairnryan in Scotland. In the 9C and 10C, landings were made by the Vikings, who called the lough Wulfrichford.

South of the harbour on the spit of land called Curran Point stand the ruins of a square, four-storey 16C tower house, now called **Olderfleet Castle** although its original name was Coraine; it was one of three castles which protected the entrance to the lough in the early 17C.

The **Chaine Memorial Tower**, a modern replica of the traditional Irish round tower, erected in honour of James Chaine, a local MP and benefactor, stands on the shore at the northern entrance to the harbour.

From Larne take A 2 N.

Carnfunnock Country Park ⏱ – The Park (473 acres/190ha) was once a private demesne north of Drains Bay village. Set among the flowers and shrubs in the walled garden are 12 sundials showing GMT, Summer Time or local time. A viewing platform overlooks the interior of the **maze**, which echoes the shape of Northern Ireland. The **limekiln walk** *(1hr)* includes the old ice house and the Look Out; there is also a walk through the forest. Opposite the park entrance on the shore are a marine promenade and boat slip.

Continue N on A 2.

Ballygally Castle – The Ballygally hotel was originally a planter's castle, built in 1625 by James Shaw; the twin bartizans are original but the sash windows were introduced later. Inland rises a natural amphitheatre, Sallagh Braes; the fine walk above the Braes along the plateau edge *(access via Carncastle and Ballycoose Road)* forms part of the Ulster Way.

Continue N on A 2.

MA Boet/Jacana

Seal

Glenarm Village – Population 650. This attractive village, which wears a light coating of white dust from the local limestone quarries, is the oldest village in the Glens. The main street runs inland past the 19C barbican gateway of **Glenarm Castle** *(private)*, the seat of the Earl of Antrim, which was begun in 1606 and re-modelled in the Elizabethan style by William Vitruvius Morrison early in the 19C. The **Forest Park** at the top of the street *(car park)* provides a view of the castle, and pleasant walks by the stream in the upper woodlands beyond the belt of conifers.

Return to A 2; turn left onto B 97.

Glenarm – The road passes through open farmland on the west slope facing Glenarm Forest across the glen. At the top, Slemish *(see p 303)* is visible to the south.

At the T-junction turn right onto A 42.

Glencloy – The road descends through gently sloping pastures to the coast.

Turn left into A 2.

Carnlough – Population 1 493. The large sandy bay makes this an attractive resort. Until the 1960s, limestone from the quarries above the town was transported by rail to the tiny harbour which is now full of pleasure-boats. The line was carried across the main road by a low bridge *(plaque)* which, together with the adjoining clock tower and former courthouse, was built by the Marquess of Londonderry *(see p 352)* in 1854.

Red Bay – Beyond Garron Point, the beautiful expanse of Red Bay comes into view, backed by the distinctive steep-sided, flat-topped silhouette of Lurigethan (1 154ft/352m). The bay is called red because of the colour of the sandstone washed down by the mountain streams.

Glenariff (also **Waterfoot**) – Population 300. The village, which lies at the mouth of the Glenariff River, is the site of the **Glens of Antrim Feis**, an annual festival of Gaelic sport and culture. On the headland, above the road tunnel, stand the ruins of Red Bay Castle, built by the Norman Bisset family.

From Glenariff take A 43 inland.

★**Glenariff** – The "**Queen of the Glens**" is enclosed between steep hanging crags.

★★**Glenariff Forest Park** ⊘ – The forest (2 298 acres/930ha) consists of woodland, turbary areas and several small lakes and rivers. The visitor centre beside the garden and aviary has an excellent display on forestry, local wildlife, the 19C iron ore and bauxite mines and their railways.

The **waterfall**★★ known as Ess na Larach *(1hr there and back on foot from the north side of the car park)* tumbles through a wooded gorge created by the Glenariff River; from the Fog House the waterfall can be viewed through panels of tinted glass which impart a sunlit glow, a moonlit chill or a luminous green light.

Continue SW on A 43; at the junction turn right onto B 14.

Glenballyemon – After emerging from an evergreen forest into open moorland the road passes through Retreat on the north slopes of Lurigethan.

Cushendall – At the crossroads in the centre of this charming village stands a red sandstone tower, known locally as the Curfew Tower, which was built as a watch-house in 1809 by Francis Turnly of the East India Company.

Take Layde Road, the steep coast road going N to Cushendun.

Layd Old Church – The ruins of the church stand in a graveyard beside a swiftly flowing stream which plunges directly into the sea. The church is thought to have been founded by the Franciscans but from 1306 to 1790 it was a parish church. There are MacDonnell memorials in the graveyard.

As the coast road continues uphill there is a fine panoramic view – even to Scotland.

At the T-junction in Knocknacarry turn left onto B92 and left again onto A 2.

Glencorp – The name of this short glen translates as the glen of slaughter.

After 1.5mi/2.4km turn right onto Glenaan Road. Turn left onto a lane (sign "Ossian's Grave"); car park beyond the farmhouse; 20min there and back on foot.

Ossian's Grave – The original Neolithic court tomb, consisted of a semicircular forecourt opening into a bi-cameral burial gallery, enclosed in an oval cairn. Ossian was an early Christian warrior-bard, the son of Finn McCool, whose legendary feats are recounted in the Ossianic Cycle.

Continue W up the glen.

Glenaan – The Glenaan River flows down from the slopes of Tievebulliagh *(south)* where Neolithic men made axe heads from the hard porcellanite rock.

At the crossroads turn right onto Glendun Road to Cushendun.

★**Glendun** – The Brown Glen is the wildest of the nine glens; its river, which is noted for sea trout and salmon fishing, flows under the viaduct designed by Charles Lanyon in 1839 to carry the main coast road.

Cushendun – Population 50. The houses of this picturesque village, which is now preserved by the National Trust, cluster at the southern end of a sandy beach flanked by tall cliffs. The most distinctive architecture is the work of Sir Clough Williams-Ellis (1883–1977), who designed Portmeirion in North Wales and was employed here by Ronald McNeill, Lord Cushendun. Glenmona Lodge (1923), which stands in a pine grove on the north side of the village facing the sea, is in the neo-Georgian style with an arcade supported on Tuscan columns. The three terraces of small, white houses facing onto a square date from 1912; the row of slate-hung cottages was erected in 1925.

From Cushendun take the coast road, a winding, steep and narrow road N. After 5mi/8km fork right onto Torr Road.

Murlough Bay and Fair Head

Torr Head – *Car park.* The low promontory is crowned by a look-out post, which is the nearest point to the Scottish coast (12mi/19km).

Continue NW along the coast road; after 2.5mi/4km turn right.

★★★**Murlough Bay** – *1mi/1.6km to the upper car park; smaller car park lower down the cliff face.* This is the most beautiful bay on the Antrim coast, set in the lee of **Fair Head** (Benmore) at the foot of steep and towering cliffs. From the shore, grassy slopes dotted with birch and rowan trees climb steeply to the escarpment. The stone cross is a memorial to Sir Roger Casement. From the lower car park there are two paths *(waymarked)*: one leads north to some long-abandoned coal mines before returning along the shore past the remains of the miners' cottages and the ruins of Drumnakill Church; the other leads south past an old lime kiln, bears inland through the wood to avoid Murlough Cottage *(private)* and ends at Benvan farmhouse.

From the upper car park there is a path *(waymarked)* along the clifftop to **Fair Head** (Benmore), which provides a wide **view**★★★ of Rathlin Island *(north)* and the Mull of Kintyre *(northeast)*; to return to the car park the path swings inland across the rough and often wet ground of the plateau, past a **crannóg** in Lough na Cranagh *(right)*, the farm buildings *(car park)* at Coolanlough and Lough Fadden *(left)*.

Return to the coast road; turn right to Ballycastle.

Bonamargy Friary – Well-sited beside a stream stand the ruins of a Franciscan friary (c 1500), now surrounded by Ballycastle golf course. The first of the roofless buildings is the **gatehouse**. The **church** was lit by an impressive east window, grooved to receive glazing; the round-headed cross in the nave is thought to mark the grave of Julia McQuillan, a 17C recluse known as "the black nun". The **MacDonnell vault** was added south of the altar in 1621 but probably modified at a later date. The **east cloister range** consists of two storeys linked by a flight of steps built in the thickness of the wall.

On the edge of Ballycastle turn left onto B 15; after 0.25mi/0.4km bear right uphill onto Dunamallaght Road.

Glenshesk – The road overlooks the Glenshesk River and skirts the southern edge of Ballycastle Forest. From Breen Bridge, at the foot of the south face of Knocklayd Mountain, a waymarked footpath, the **Moyle Way**, a spur of the Ulster Way, leads north over the summit of Knocklayd (1 695ft/514m) to Ballycastle *(4mi/6.4km).*

From Breen Bridge take B 15 W.

Armoy Round Tower – In the graveyard of St Patrick's Church stands the base of a round tower (30ft/9m), which dates from 460 and was part of a monastery founded by Olcan, a disciple of St Patrick.

From the crossroads take the minor road N to Ballycastle.

Glentaisie – The glen skirts the west face of Knocklayd.

Turn right onto A 44 to Ballycastle.

Ballycastle – Population 4 005. The attractive resort is situated at the foot of Knocklayd Mountain with a view over Ballycastle Bay to Rathlin Island. It has a long sandy beach, salt- and fresh-water angling, golf links and other sports facilities.

An Irish Music and Dance Festival is held here in June; the Ould Lammas Fair in August combines livestock sales with street stalls selling two traditional sweet confections – **Yellowman**, a sort of toffee, and **Dulse**, a dried edible seaweed. A stone memorial, symbolising aerials and radio waves, standing at the west end of the harbour, recalls the wireless link between Ballycastle and Rathlin Island set up in 1898 by Marconi *(see p 152)* and his assistant George Kemp.

The town centre is graced by **Holy Trinity Church** ⊘, an elegant 18C building with a balustraded tower and steeple built in 1756 by Col Hugh Boyd and maintained by his family for many years.

On the cliffs east of the town is the **Corrymeela Centre**, which works for reconciliation between the two cultural traditions in Northern Ireland; it contains a semi-underground heart-shaped oratory.

From Ballycastle take B 15 W. After 5mi/8km turn right to Larry Bane Bay and Carrick-a-rede Rope Bridge.

★★★**Carrick-a-rede Rope Bridge** ⊘ – *From the car park 30min there and back on foot. People cross the rope bridge at their own risk; dangerous in a high wind; remember the return journey.* The rope bridge (66ft/20m long) bounces and sways as one ventures gingerly along the planks above the rock-strewn water (80ft/25m below). In the past there was only one handrail but accidents seem to have been few during the bridge's 200 years of existence. Good view of the coast.

The rope bridge is put up every spring for the fishermen who operate the island salmon fishery. As the migrating salmon swim west along the shore seeking their freshwater spawning grounds in the River Bush or River Bann, they are deflected north by the island *(Carrick-a-rede* means Rock-in-the-Road) straight into the nets which are always set in the same place.

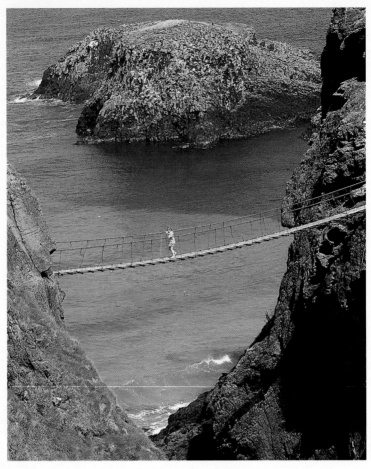

C. Boisvieux

Carrick-a-rede Rope Bridge

★ **Rathlin Island** ⊙ – *Access by boat from Ballycastle.* Population 100. The island lies north of Ballycastle across Rathlin Sound (5mi/8km), a rough and dangerous crossing except on a calm day. An additional hazard is the whirlpool off Rue Point which nearly claimed the life of St Columba (Colmcille) in the 6C. The traditional occupations are fishing and agriculture, supplemented in the past by smuggling and now by tourism. In the 17C the island passed from the MacDonnells to the Gages, whose memorials adorn St Thomas' Church.

From the sheltered harbour, where seals sometimes bask on the rocks, three roads radiate to the outlying homesteads and the lighthouses.

The L-shaped island is treeless, pitted with shallow lakes and almost entirely surrounded by high white cliffs, where in early summer the sea-birds congregate in their thousands; the fields are divided by dry white stone walls. Tradition has it that here in 1306 Robert the Bruce received his famous lesson in perseverance from a spider while taking refuge in one of the many caves *(accessible only by boat).*

ARMAGH★★

ARD MACHA – Co Armagh – Population 14 265
Michelin Atlas p 98 and Map 923 – L, M 4

Armagh lies in a fertile district of fruit orchards planted by 17C settlers from the Vale of Evesham in England. It has many fine Georgian buildings and two cathedrals, each set on a hill, the seats of the Anglican and Roman Catholic archbishops of Ireland. In July 1994 this county town was raised to city status by royal command.

Royal and Religious Centre – Armagh, derived from Ard Macha meaning Macha's Height, is named after a legendary pagan queen who built a fortress on the central hill of Armagh. Although the major pre-Christian power centre of Ulster was nearby Navan Fort *(see below)*, the settlement of Armagh grew in prominence after Navan's destruction in AD 332.

In his mission to convert Ireland to Christianity, c 445, St Patrick arrived in Armagh and chose it as the centre of the new religion; he declared that it should take precedence

Adjacent Sights – See Dungannon, Monaghan, Lough Neagh, Newry, Sperrin Mountains.

over all other churches in Ireland and from that time it has been the ecclesiastical capital of the whole country.

In the following centuries Armagh developed into an important centre of religion and learning under teachers such as St Malachy, St Celsus and St Concord; its reputation was such that in 1162 an ecclesiastical Synod decreed that only those who had studied at Armagh could teach theology elsewhere in Ireland. The school was suppressed at the Reformation under the Dissolution of the Monasteries but the scholastic tradition was revived in 1608, when James I founded the Royal School, which moved in 1773 from Abbey Street to new buildings designed by Thomas Cooley on College Hill.

Architectural Elegance

In the peaceful conditions of the 18C and early 19C, farming and commerce flourished; Armagh acquired some of its finest architecture under the benevolent patronage of two Anglican Primates: Richard Robinson, later Lord Rokeby, who became Archbishop in 1765 and attempted to establish a university in Armagh; and Lord John George Beresford, who was appointed Archbishop in 1822.

SIGHTS

★**St Patrick's Cathedral** ⊙ (Z) – The Anglican cathedral, which incorporates some medieval elements, was restored by Archbishop Robinson in 1765, and again by Archbishop Beresford between 1834 and 1837, when it was faced with a cladding of sandstone and the steeple demolished. It is now a plain building in the Perpendicular Gothic style with a squat crenellated central tower.

The **exterior** is decorated with a series of grotesque medieval stone heads and a sundial which dates from 1706. When King Brian Ború and his son, Murchard, were killed at the Battle of Clontarf (1014), on the north side of Dublin Bay, they were buried according to the king's wishes at Armagh *(plaque on west wall of north transept)*.

The **interior** contains a collection of 18C monuments by Roubiliac, Rysbrack, Nollekens and Chantrey, and pieces of an 11C market cross.

Cricket in the Mall, Armagh

Slide File, Dublin

★**St Patrick's Cathedral** ⊙ (Y) – The twin-spired Roman Catholic cathedral stands on a hill approached by a long flight of steps *(44 steps)*, flanked at the top by statues of Archbishop Crolly and Archbishop McGettigan, under whom it was built. Construction began in 1840 in the Perpendicular Gothic style of Thomas J Duff but the Great Famine brought work to a halt until 1854; the cathedral was completed in 1873 in the Decorated Gothic of JJ McCarthy. The statues in the niches on the west front represent the Apostles.

The **interior** is lavishly decorated with a painted vaulted roof, stained-glass windows and mosaics on the walls; the spandrels frame the heads of Irish saints. The sanctuary was renovated in 1981–82 under the architect, Liam McCormick.

★**The Mall** (YZ) – The Mall is a most attractive urban feature, a long stretch of grass with a pavilion and cricket pitch bordered by elegant terraces. In the 8C it was common grazing land, as its former name, The Commons, implies, and it was used for horse racing, bull-baiting and cock-fighting until these gambling activities were stopped by Archbishop Robinson in 1773 and the land converted to public walks. The Classical-style **Courthouse** was designed in 1809 by Francis Johnston.

The remaining stone was used to build the Sovereign's House (**M²**); the office of Sovereign was equivalent to that of Mayor but the title ceased to be used in 1850. It now houses the **Museum of the Royal Irish Fusiliers**★ ⊙ (Y **M²**); an excellent presentation of flags and standards, uniforms, medals, weapons, silver, portraits and paintings recalls the history of five regiments, which were raised in 1793 to fight the French and merged into one regiment with five battalions in 1881.

Beresford Row was designed by John Quinn between 1810 and 1827 and named after Lord John Beresford; the houses have elegant iron balconies.

Charlemont Place, one of the finest Georgian terraces, was designed by Francis Johnston in 1827.

★**Armagh County Museum** ⊙ (Y **M¹**) is housed in a building with an Ionic portico, set back from the street behind a lawn, designed by Francis Johnston in 1833 as the entrance to a school. The political and social history of the area is illustrated by a series of displays: prehistoric weapons and implements; early-Christian relics including illustrations of the three Tynan crosses; local buildings, both extant and demolished; 18C and 19C costumes and military uniforms; jewellery, clocks and watches; local crafts and woodcraft – bowls, cups, four-handled vessels (methers) for drinking.

A long tree-lined drive leads up to **St Mark's Church**, also designed by Francis Johnston in 1811.

His nephew, William Murray, designed the small **Savings Bank** building with an unpedimented portico in 1838. The old **Gaol** was erected in 1780 on the site of the barracks.

Palace Demesne (Z) – From the 17C to the 20C the estate was the residence of the Anglican Archbishop of Armagh.

The buildings surrounding the stable yard now house the **Palace Stables Heritage Centre** ⊙. A 19C town coach stands at the entrance. The display presents a typical day in the life of the stables and the palace, in fact 23 July 1776 when Arthur Young, the famous agricultural improver, and other guests were entertained by Archbishop Richard Robinson.

The **Primate's Chapel**, a superb example of Georgian neo-Classical architecture, was commissioned by Richard Robinson, begun in 1770 by Thomas Cooley but, owing to his death, completed in 1786 by Francis Johnston. It contains some very fine carved oak panelling and an ornamental plaster ceiling of rosettes surrounded by a frieze.

Nearby are the conservatory, an ice house and a tunnel providing access to the house for the servants. There is an eco-trail through the park.

The house, now the offices of Armagh District Council, was also begun by Cooley and completed in 1786 by Johnston, who later added a third storey for Lord John George Beresford.

Near the demesne entrance are the ruins of **Armagh Friary**. In accordance with Franciscan practice it was extremely long and narrow, the longest-known in Ireland (180ft/50m x 21ft/7.6m); a tower was added later at the junction of the nave and chancel. There are two tomb recesses in the north wall at the east end. The Franciscans were established in Armagh in 1263 or 1264. After the Dissolution the buildings fell into ruins; in 1618 the site became part of the archbishop's demesne.

St Patrick's Trian ⊙ (Y) – The Trian (pronounced Tree-an) was one of the administrative divisions of the city. The display traces the history of Armagh in association with the theme of religious belief through tableaux and an audio-visual presentation. The *Land of Lilliput* is an interpretation of *Gulliver's Travels*, whose author Jonathan Swift often visited the area.

The Trian also contains a Geneaological Research Centre, art exhibitions and the Tourist Information Centre.

ARMAGH

In Northern Ireland parking in the town centre may be restricted to attended vehicles only.

Armagh Planetarium ⊘ (Y) – The planetarium is housed under a dome (50ft/15m in diameter) which serves as a hemispherical screen for the projection of films of the sky at night. The Hall of Astronomy contains 12 computer stations presenting information on planets, constellations and space flight. The Planetarium was set up in 1968 by Dr Lindsay, Director of the Observatory (1937–74), who invited Patrick Moore to be its first director.

In the grounds stands the **Observatory**, founded and endowed in 1789 by Archbishop Robinson; it is one of the oldest meteorological stations in the British Isles.

Armagh (Robinson) Public Library ⊘ (Y A) – The library, which was founded by Archbishop Robinson in 1771, is housed in a building designed by Thomas Cooley; the Greek inscription on the façade means "the healing of the mind". The library contains a copy of *Gulliver's Travels* annotated by Swift and many other ancient books and manuscripts; it also contains the Rokeby Collection of 18C engravings as well as maps of historical interest, including a complete set of the 1838 edition Ordnance Survey Maps of the 32 counties of Ireland.

Infirmary (Y) – The infirmary, another of Archbishop Robinson's foundations, was designed by George Ensor *(see below)* and completed in 1774; it is still in use.

Vicar's Row (Y**Z**) – The terrace of small houses on the west side of the cathedral close was begun in about 1720 as accommodation for female clergy dependants.

Old Market House (**Z**) – A technical school now occupies the Market House, which was commissioned in 1815 by Archbishop Stuart from Francis Johnston, and originally consisted of only two storeys.

St Patrick's Fold (**Z**) – The house, which is thought to stand on the site of St Patrick's first church in Armagh, was designed in 1812 for Leonard Dobbin, MP for Armagh from 1833 to 1838, by Francis Johnston to whom the houses (1811) in nearby Dobbin Street are also attributed.

Road Bowls

The ancient Irish sport of road bowling is still played on Sundays in Co Cork and Co Armagh. A heavy iron ball (28oz/794g; 7in/18cm) is hurled along a stretch of quiet winding country road in as few throws as possible; the ball may hurtle through the air at shoulder height. Betting is heavy.

Shambles (Y) – As is written over the entrance, the building was erected in 1827 by Archbishop Beresford; it was designed by Francis Johnston and is still used as a meat market.

EXCURSIONS

★**The Argory** ☉ – *10mi/16km NE of Armagh by A 29 and a minor road right.* The Argory house on the Derrycaw estate beside the River Blackwater was built in about 1824 by Walter McGeough, who took his paternal grandmother's name of Bond. It passed to his second son, Ralph Shelton McGeough Bond, known after 1873 as Captain Shelton.

The house contains a number of family portraits. The cast-iron stove in the entrance hall has a descending flue which passes under the floor to the drawing-room chimney. The **drawing room** is elegantly furnished with many rare pieces. Each generation has contributed to the comfortable informality of the **study**. The dado in the **billiard** room is painted to resemble panelling and the shutters grained to imitate walnut veneer. The **dining room** is furnished with two round-topped tables in mahogany adjusted by a system of internal pulleys, two side tables, beneath which stand two plate buckets and a tea caddy; there is a warming cupboard beside the fireplace *(left)*.

The cabinet **barrel organ** (1820) is by James Bishop; Samuel Wesley was consulted over the selection of the original six barrels. The distinctive **light fittings** on the dressing tables in the bedrooms date from 1906 when an acetylene gas plant was installed to provide artificial light.

Staircase Hall, The Argory, Co Armagh

A von Einsiedel/National Trust Photographic Library

Ardress House Yard, Co Armagh

A von Einsiedel/National Trust Photographic Library

The **Gardens**, which extend to the Blackwater River, comprise old roses set in box-lined beds, a sundial dated 1820, yew tree arbours, a cedar of Lebanon and a tulip tree growing in the Pleasure Grounds, a Garden House and a Pump House, and a lime tree walk.

Ardress House ⊘ – *7mi/11km NE of Armagh by B 77.* Ardress is a simple 17C manor house, of five bays, enlarged and embellished in the 18C. It was inherited by the architect, George Ensor, on his marriage in 1760.

The house displays glass from Dublin, Cork and Belfast, and some fine furniture, including Irish Chippendale chairs. The front door has retained its original brass furnishings. The symmetry and proportions of the elegant **drawing room** are enhanced by the delightful stuccowork by Michael Stapleton on the walls and ceiling.

The cobbled **farmyard** with its central pump is alive with domestic animals. The surrounding farm buildings include a milking shed, a dairy with pottery and wooden skimming dishes, churns and measures, a forge, a threshing barn and a display of old farm implements including baskets and bee skeps.

Orange Order Museum ⊘ – *6mi/10km NE of Armagh by A 29 and B 77 to Loughgall; half way up the west side of the main street; caretaker's house on the right of the museum.* The museum is housed in a single narrow room overflowing with mementoes of the Orange Order: sashes, caps, waistcoats, banners, the table on which the first warrants were signed, guns and pikes used in 1795 at the Battle of the Diamond *(3mi/5km NE).* The room, formerly Jim Sloane's pub, was converted into a museum in 1961.

Tayto Potato Crisp Factory ⊘ – *11mi/18km E of Armagh by A 51; factory entrance next to the police station on entering Tandragee.* The factory is housed in Tandragee Castle, which dominates the town (population 2 871); it was built in 1837 by the 6th Duke of Manchester.

The tour *(1hr)* starts in the warehouse in which great cliffs of potatoes are stored; it then passes the washing, peeling and slicing machines to where the raw white wafers enter a tunnel of hot sunflower oil and emerge as wavy golden crisps. At the next stage the crisps acquire a flavour and are packed by ingenious machines, one of which swathes stacks of cardboard boxes in polythene film like mummies.

★**Gosford Forest Park** ⊘ – *7mi/11km SE of Armagh by A 28 to Markethill; two car parks: one near the entrance and the other between the Castle and the Walled Garden.* The Forest Park was formerly the demesne of the Earl of Gosford whose family name was Acheson. Contemporary with the building of the present castle, a huge pseudo-Norman pile designed by Thomas Hopper in 1819, are the **arboretum**, which contains many magnificent mature trees from all over the world, and the **walled gardens**, which are beautifully laid out with flowers and shrubs, and contain a brick **bee house** with niches to protect the straw skeps from the damp. A **nature trail** round the park includes various forestry plantations, two raths *(see p 83)* and a stretch of the Drumlack River with a waterfall at **Swift's Well.**

An interesting feature of the original gardens is the **Dean's Chair**, an artificial sun trap created by making a semicircular hollow protected by a yew hedge in a south-facing bank; it is named after Jonathan Swift who spent over a year at Gosford between 1728 and 1730 as a guest of Sir Arthur Acheson.

The **Gosford Heritage Poultry Collection** aims to conserve in their natural surroundings the native poultry breeds that would have been found in the 18C poultry yard of a large estate.

★**Navan Fort** ⊘ – *2mi/3.2km W of Armagh by A 28.* The fort is an impressive earthwork, surrounded by sacred places and settlement sites, which in the late Bronze Age was the most important place in Ulster. Navan is thought to be synonymous with Emain Macha, the capital of legendary Ulster, mentioned in the *Ulster Cycle (see p 57).*

The exhibition in the **Visitor Centre** traces the archaeological study of the fort and its associated sites and shows how they were used by their Neolothic builders. Two films provide further information – *The Dawning* evokes the pre-Christian and early-Christian era in Ireland with its tradition of storytelling; the second film recounts and illustrates the myths and legends associated with Navan.

The fort itself *(5min on foot from the Visitor Centre or by road; car park)* consists of a massive bank and inner ditch enclosing a circular area. Within is a high mound on the highest point of the hill, flanked by a low circular mound surrounded by an infilled ditch.

Navan Fort Excavations

Excavations carried out between 1961 and 1971 showed traces of human activity as early as 2000 BC; in c 400 BC a round wooden house and yard was built, which was replaced many times during the next 300 years. In c 100 BC a huge wooden structure (125ft/40m in diameter) was erected consisting of an outer timber wall and five concentric inner rings of large posts; the remains of a very large central post made it possible to date the structure, which was probably roofed. Soon after it was built it was filled with limestone boulders and set on fire and the remains covered with earth to form a mound, probably as part of a religious ritual. Navan Fort seems to have been part of a religious complex. The four Iron Age bronze trumpets (one is now in the National Museum in Dublin), which were found in the 18C in the water at the edge of Lough na Shade *(NW of the Fort beyond the quarries)*, may have been deposited in the lake as an offering to the gods. Excavations carried out in 1975 show that the King's Stables *(NW of the Fort)* was an artificial pool used for ritual deposits in the Late Bronze Age.

BANGOR

BEANNCHAR – Co Down – Population 52 437
Michelin Atlas p 99 and Map 923 – O P 4 – Local map Strangford Lough

Bangor, now partially a dormitory town for Belfast, lies on the south shore of Belfast Lough at the north end of the Ards Peninsula. Bangor developed from an early monastic settlement, via a 17C Plantation into a 19C seaside resort with safe sandy beaches, a sea-water swimming pool, several yacht clubs and a golf course.

HISTORICAL NOTES

Bangor Abbey – The abbey founded at Bangor by St Comgall in 558 became one of the most famous abbeys in western Christendom. Its monks founded other monasteries in Ireland and abroad *(see p 62).* In the 9C Comgall's tomb was desecrated in Viking raids; Malachy, appointed abbot in 1124, built a stone church and introduced the Augustinian Order. The 14C tower, the only structure to survive Dissolution in 1542, is now part of **Bangor Abbey Church** ⊘.

Scottish Settlement – On the accession of James I, Bangor was granted to Sir James Hamilton, later Viscount Clandeboye, who founded a town with settlers from his native Ayrshire. In 1710 his estates passed by marriage to the Ward family of Castle Ward on the south shore of Strangford Lough. Two generations later Col Robert Ward improved the harbour, promoted the textile industry and founded a boys' school. When the railway arrived in 1865 Bangor developed into a seaside resort with a pier (demolished 1981).

SIGHTS

★**North Down Heritage Centre** ⊘ – The Centre, housed in the service wing of Bangor Castle, traces the history of Bangor Abbey (9C Irish bronze hand bell), the Scottish settlement, the local landed families and Bangor's heyday as a seaside resort, as well as the Prehistoric Period, the Bronze Age and the Viking invasions with local archaeological exhibits. Almost all the items in the **Jordan Collection** of Far Eastern objets d'art are 19C and 20C Chinese.

Out and About

Waterfront – The whole of the waterfront was refurbished in the late 1980s in a multi-million-pound project which included a fun park and a popular marina (560 berths).

Boat Trips ⊘ – There are boat trips in Bangor Bay, cruises to the Copeland Islands in the afternoon and deep-sea fishing trips from Donaghadee *(see below)* in the morning or evening.

Adjacent Sights – See Belfast, Mount Stewart, Strangford Lough.

Where to Eat

Fontana, 61A High St, Holywood. ☎ 028 9080 9908; Fax 028 9080 9912. Modern vibrant decor; Californian influenced food; very good value.

Where to Stay

Cairn Bay Lodge, 278 Seacliffe Rd, BT20 5HS. *1.25mi/1km E by Quay St.* ☎ 028 9146 7636; Fax 028 9145 7728. Friendly welcoming seaside guest house (3 rm).

Royal, 26 Quay St, BT20 5ED. ☎ 028 9127 1866; Fax 028 9146 7810. Immaculately kept private hotel (50 rm); close to town centre and harbour

Clandeboye Lodge, 10 Estate Rd, Clandeboye, BT19 1UR. *3mi/4.8km SW by A 2 and B 170; sign Blackwood Golf Centre.* ☎ 028 9185 2500; Fax 028 9185 2772. Comfortable hotel (43 rm); conference facilities; adjacent to golf club.

Marine Court, The Marina, BT20 5ED. ☎ 028 9145 1100; Fax 028 9145 1200. Spacious very comfortable hotel (52 rm) by the harbour.

Bangor Castle, now the Town Hall, was built by Robert Edward Ward (1818–1904); 1852, the date of completion, is inscribed above the door. The Elizabethan–Jacobean revival style – mullioned windows, oriels crested with strapwork, steep gables with finials and a battlemented tower with a pyramidal clock turret – suggest that the architect may be William Burn; the stables may be the work of Anthony Salvin.

Old Custom House and Tower – In 1620 Sir James Hamilton was granted a warrant to establish a maritime port in Bangor including the nearby creeks. By 1637 with financial assistance from the Crown he was building a Custom House (now the Tourist Centre) in the Scottish Baronial style with flanking watchtowers, a crow-stepped gable and a quarter-round corbelled turret.

EXCURSIONS

Crawfordsburn Country Park ⊘ – *7mi/11km W of Bangor by B 20.* The country park, like the picturesque village, takes its name from the Crawford family from Scotland who were tenants of Sir James Hamilton in the early 17C. In 1674 they bought the estate, which they landscaped and planted with rare species.

The history and flora and fauna are illustrated in the **Park Centre**, which also has a 3-D show on bees and wasps, a colony of leaf-cutter ants, and an array of brightly coloured interactive exhibits.

The **glen walk** *(30min there and back on foot)* passes the old salmon pool and then under the viaduct, designed by Sir Charles Lanyon in 1865, which carries the railway across the glen on five arches (80ft/24m). Upstream is the waterfall, a rushing torrent after heavy rain, which formerly drove corn, flax and saw mills and in 1850 generated electricity to light the glen.

Grey Point Fort – *Accessible by footpath (1hr there and back) within the Country Park or by residential roads (Coastguard Avenue).* The fort (1907-63) commands the sea approaches to Belfast and was manned during both World Wars by the Royal Artillery. Panels outline its history and a solitary six-inch gun, a gift from the Government of the Republic of Ireland, is mounted in one of the massive reinforced concrete gun emplacements.

★★**Ulster Folk and Transport Museum** ⊘ – *8mi/13km W of Bangor by A 2.* The grounds of Cultra Manor have been converted into an extensive museum bisected by the coast road *(A 2)*; the folk section is on the south side inland, and the buildings housing the transport section are on the north side extending to the seashore.

Folk Museum – Since 1958 various buildings mostly from the Ulster countryside have been re-erected to form a vast open-air museum. **Demonstrations** of cooking, weaving, spinning and agricultural work are given in season.

Rectory and Church, Ulster Folk Museum

The dwellings, which are furnished as they would have been at the turn of the century, range from a one-room farmhouse, shared by the family with the cows, to a substantial 17C farmhouse with panelled walls. The working premises include a flax-scutching mill and a spade mill, a weaver's house and a bleach green watchman's hut to shelter the person protecting the webs of linen, spread out on the green to bleach, from theft or damage by animals. The village is composed of a school, a market-cum-courthouse, a church and a rectory, together with two terraces of urban cottages including a shoemaker's workshop and a bicycle repair shop.

In the **Gallery** *(three floors)* the traditional Ulster way of life is illustrated with original domestic, industrial and agricultural implements.

Transport Museum – Visitors may view the **Irish Railway Collection** from a first-floor viewing gallery or walk at track or platform level and enter some of the exhibits – *Maeve (Maebh)* (1939), a 4-6-0 800 Class; *Dunluce Castle*, a 4-4-0 Class U2. Printed wall panels provide information on the history of Irish Railways.

The **Road Transport Galleries**, richly furnished with all types of transport memorabilia, display two-wheelers of all kinds, from the draisiennes and velocipedes of early days to the stylish scooters of the 1960s or the massive mounts of tattooed ton-up bikers. Buses include a 1973 Daimler Fleetline, burnt out but lovingly restored, while the most extraordinary vehicle is perhaps No 2 of the Bessbrook and Newry Tramway Co, built in 1885 and still carrying passengers in the 1940s.

The final gallery is devoted to *The Car in Society* – from the 1898 Benz Velo Confortable, the oldest petrol vehicle in Ireland, to one of the glamorous cars produced in 1981 by the short-lived De Lorean company, with the emphasis as much on car culture as on the vehicles themselves; many tentative answers are provided as to why a nominally functional object should play such a dominant part in people's lives.

The **Dalchoolin Transport Galleries** present a miscellany of exhibits – shoulder creels and wooden sledges, carts and jaunting cars; horse-drawn vehicles from a dogcart to a dress chariot; A selection of cars and motorcycles spanning the century; a description of the internal combustion engine; ingenious machines designed by Rex McCandless which challenged conventional motorcycle design; ships and aircraft, including the Short SC1, a pioneering VTOL (Vertical Take-off and Landing). The **Titanic Gallery** describes how the great liner, built at the famous Harland and Wolff shipyard in Belfast, sank on her maiden voyage after being holed by an iceberg, and shows pictures of the wreck obtained by divers in 1985.

Somme Heritage Centre ⊘ – *3mi/5km S of Bangor by A 21.* The time tunnel carries the visitor back to the outbreak of the First World War in 1914 and to one of the bloodiest battles, the Somme offensive (1916), where nine Irish regiments drawn from all over the country fought side by side in a common cause.

The display recaptures through photos and exhibits the volunteers being issued with uniforms, kit and weapons and embarking for France; reconstruction of the trenches and the sights and sounds of war over noman's land.

Groomsport – *1.5mi/2.5km E by coast road.* Population 900. Groomsport is an attractive little seaside resort, flanked by sandy beaches and modern bungalows and caravan parks. In the harbour, yachts ride the water beside the fishing boats. Fishing is still an important activity but only two fishermen's cottages, one thatched, still stand beside the harbour; they now house an **art gallery**.

In 1689 the Duke of Schomberg landed at Groomsport; his army of 10 000 men probably came ashore at Ballyholme or Bangor where he spent the first night as a guest of Sir James Hamilton *(see above)*, before proceeding south to the Battle of the Boyne, where he was killed.

Donaghadee – *7mi/11km E of Bangor by B 21.* The picturesque, winding streets lead to the **parish church** which dates from 1641. The huge harbour, now full of pleasure boats, was built in 1820 to accommodate the mail ships, which were transferred to Larne in 1849. From the 16C to 19C Donaghadee–Portpatrick was the most popular route between Ireland and Scotland as it is the shortest crossing (21mi/34km). The Norman **motte** near the shore was probably raised by William Copeland, a retainer of John de Courcy; it is crowned by a stone building (1818) providing a fine **view** of the Copeland Islands and the coast of Galloway across the North Channel.

Copeland Islands – *Accessible by boat from Groomsport or Donaghadee.* The nearest and largest island was inhabited until the 1940s, when the last residents moved to the mainland and the island was left to the sheep and weekend cottages. A modern lighthouse was built on Mew Island in 1884. Lighthouse Island is now a wildlife sanctuary in the care of the National Trust – buzzards, golden eagles, resident seals, dolphins, porpoises, basking sharks, minky whales, killer whales.

Ballycopeland Windmill

★**Ballycopeland Windmill** – *10mi/ 16km SE of Bangor by B 21 and A 2; in Millisle turn right. Car park. The mill is not open to the public when the machinery is working owing to the risk of accident.* In the late 18C, when grain was grown extensively in the Ards Peninsula, the landscape was thickly dotted with windmills. The rare survivor at Ballycopeland was probably built in 1780 or 1790 and worked until 1915. It is again in working order; the neighbouring miller's house provides an explanatory display. Beside the mill is a dust-house and the kiln where the grain was dried before being milled.

Ards Peninsula – The peninsula is a long narrow tongue of land *(23mi/37km x 3–5mi/5–8km)* extending west and south of Bangor to Ballyquintin Point which marks the southern tip. Owing to its soil and climate the low-lying land is one of the best grain-producing regions of Ireland.

The east coast is swept by bracing sea breezes; the **coast road**, which follows the bare shoreline, skirting frequent sandy beaches and occasional rocky outcrops, is almost constantly in sight and sound of the sea. **Portavogie** is the home base for one of Northern Ireland's three fishing fleets, where fish is sold on the quayside when the fleet is in port. The southern end of the peninsula presents an austere landscape of marsh and heath.

BELFAST★

BÉAL FEIRSTE – Co Antrim – Population 279 237
Michelin Atlas p 99 and Map 923 – O 4

Belfast, since 1920 the capital of Northern Ireland, is an industrial and predominantly Victorian city which owes its rapid expansion during the 18C and 19C to the textile, engineering and shipbuilding industries.

It is also a large port on an ideal site where the River Lagan flows into Belfast Lough, a long arm *(12mi/19km)* of the North Sea, sheltered on both sides by hills.

Belfast is also a university city with a lively cultural life; the annual Belfast Arts Festival is held in November at Queen's University. The **Grand Opera House**, designed by Frank Matcham in 1894 with a gilt-and-red plush interior (restored in the 1980s); puts on regular performances and is also the venue for the Northern Ireland Opera spring and autumn seasons. The Ulster Orchestra gives concerts at the **Ulster Hall**, designed in 1860 by WJ Barre, which has a good organ.

HISTORICAL NOTES

Belfast takes its name from the ford by the sandbank (*bealfeirste* in Irish), where John de Courcy built a castle when he invaded Ulster in 1177. The castle was destroyed by Edward Bruce in 1315 and the town was held by the O'Neill clan until their possessions were forfeited following the Flight of the Earls in 1603. Belfast then passed to Sir Arthur Chichester and remained in the family until his descendant, the Marquess of Donegall, went bankrupt in the late 1840s.

Port of Belfast – The development of the port began with the construction of a quay under a royal charter (1613) and was promoted by the purchase from Carrickfergus in the 1630s of the monopoly of imported goods in the northeast of Ireland. A corporation for improving the port was established in 1784 and the Victoria Channel from the port to Belfast Lough was dredged in 1849. Shipbuilding, a significant element of the local economy, began in 1791. The Harland and Wolff shipyard, the largest shipbuilding and repair yard in the UK, bears the names of Edward James Harland, an engineer from Yorkshire, who came to Belfast in 1850, and Gustav Wilhelm Wolff, a marine draughtsman from Hamburg.

Short Brothers, the second-largest employer, produced the Sunderland flying boat and the first VTOL jet; their airstrip in the docks now doubles as Belfast City Airport.

Industrial Development – The local linen industry benefited greatly from the new methods, introduced by French Huguenot refugees in the 17C, and grew steadily in importance. Cotton spinning, introduced in 1777, also prospered, particularly during the American Civil War. The success of the textile and allied engineering industries promoted a revival in shipbuilding in 1833.

Religious and Political Dissent – Owing to the predominance of the Presbyterian Church, its cultural links with Scotland and its commercial wealth, Belfast early became a centre for intellectual activity and sometimes dissent. Belfast had the first printing press in Ireland (c 1690) and published the first Irish newspaper, the *Belfast News Letter*, in 1737; it is the oldest morning paper in the British Isles.

It was in Belfast in 1791 that Wolfe Tone helped to found the Society of United Irishmen; in 1792 they published the *Northern Star*, a newspaper which expressed radical opinion and first promoted the idea of the Irish nation.

UNIVERSITY DISTRICT

★★Ulster Museum ⊙ (AZ M¹) – The national museum and art gallery of Northern Ireland is housed in a modern building (1972), added to the previous premises built in 1929 in the Botanic Gardens. The nucleus of the present collections was first put on display in 1831 by the Belfast Natural History Society in a museum building in College Square North.

Visitors are advised to take the lift to the fourth floor and descend through the galleries which are linked by ramps.

Art Galleries – The small collection of pre-1900 British and Continental painting includes works by JMW Turner (1775–1851), portraits of local gentry by Sir Joshua Reynolds (1723–92), George Stubbs (1724–1806) and Pompeo Batoni (1708–87) and two views of the Giant's Causeway by Susanna Drury (c 1740), which brought it to the attention of the public.

Works by Irish artists – portraits, landscapes and watercolours – or on Irish subjects are periodically presented together with Irish furniture in the **Irish Gallery**: among the artists represented are Hugh Douglas Hamilton (1740–1808), Joseph Peacock (c 1783–1837), Sir John Lavery (1856–1941), Roderic O'Conor (1860–1940), Sir William Orpen (1878–1931), Andrew Nicholl and Richard Dunscombe Parker.

Craft Galleries – The collections cover glass (pieces commemorating personalities and incidents in Irish history), ceramics (Belleek *(see p 341)* pottery), the work of Irish silversmiths (17C to 19C), jewellery (16C to 20C), costume and textile collection (18C to 20C) as well as lace, embroidery and household linen.

Geology of Ireland – A skeleton of the extinct Giant Irish Deer dominates this excellent gallery – sections on Irish Flora and Fauna and the Living Sea giving a comprehensive view of the landscape of Ireland.

Antiquities – Human activity from the Prehistoric Era to the Middle Ages is traced through artefacts excavated from archaeological sites: the **Shrine of St Patrick's Hand★**, a 14C or 15C silver-gilt hand studded with glass and rock crystal and stamped with animal figures; a Bronze Age cauldron and a pair of horns which still produce a musical note; early Iron Age sword scabbards decorated in the "Celtic" style; an early Christian brooch. Pride of place goes to the **Spanish Armada treasure★★**, excavated from shipwrecks on the Irish coast: cannon and shot, a gold salamander set with rubies, gold chains, rings and crosses and coins.

Local History (16C-20C) – The "Made in Belfast" gallery is devoted to the history of industry in the city and the northeast of Ireland.There is also a section on coins minted in Ireland up to 1690 and another on the Post Office displaying the portable desk used by **Anthony Trollope** *(see p 129)* to write his novels.

Textile Gallery – Here the process of turning flax into linen is explained by means of texts and diagrams and 11 of the original machines.

Botanic Gardens ⊙ (AZ) – At the entrance to the Botanic Gardens stands a statue of Lord Kelvin (1824–1907), a native of Belfast, who invented the absolute scale of thermodynamics, the Kelvin Scale.

Out and About

Tourist Information Centre – Northern Ireland Tourist Board, *St Anne's Court, 59 North Street, BT1 1NB* ☎ 028 9024 6609; www.belfastcit.gov.uk
– Belfast City Airport ☎ 028 9045 7745
– Belfast International Airport ☎ 028 9442 2888

Public Transport – For travel within the city of Belfast apply to **Citybus** ☎ 028 9024 6485 (24hr information) or call at the Citybus kiosk, *Donegall Square West (Open Mon-Sat, 8am-6pm)*.
There is a bus service between Belfast International Airport and the Europa Bus Centre (Glengall Street).
For travel outside Belfast apply to **Ulsterbus** ☎ 028 9033 3000 (enquiries); 028 9032 0011 (Europa Bus Centre, Glengall Street, Belfast BT12 5AH).

Guided Tours – Various **Citybus tours** ☉ are organised between June and September from Castle Place.
The **Black Taxi Service** ☉ offers guided tours with commentary in a black taxi cab of central Belfast, including the murals in the Shankhill Road and the Falls Road.

There are various **themed walking tours** of the city, including:
Belfast – The Old Town of 1660–1685 – Easter to October, Saturday, 2pm from the Tourist Information Centre, NITB, *59 North Street* ☎ 028 9024 6609.
Bailey's Historical Pub Tour of Belfast – Saturday, 4pm and Tuesday, 7pm from Flannigan's (upstairs in the Crown Bar), *Great Victoria Street* ☎ 028 92 68 3665 (Judy Crawford) or ☎ 028 9088 2596.
Belfast Town and Gown Tour – June to September, Saturday, 10.30am from the Wellington Park Hotel ☎ 028 9049 1469 (Kathleen Chandler) for group bookings.
Belfast City Centre and Laganside Walk – June to September, Friday, 2pm from the front gates of City Hall ☎ 028 9049 1469 (Kathleen Chandler) for group bookings.
Laganside Walk – From the **Lagan Lookout** there is a tow-path walk beside the river extending upstream to Lisburn *(7mi/12km)*.

Shopping – Shops are generally open from 9am to 5.30pm, Monday to Saturday, with late-night shopping until 9pm on Thursday. Shops in the city centre are also open from 1pm to 6pm on Sunday.
Modern Belfast is a good centre for buying linen and woollen goods, glassware and pottery and other crafts. The main shopping area is around **Donegall Place**, with many High Street stores and a selection of local shops. Through Queen's Arcade to the left of Donegall Place you will find the **Fountain Area**, a number of streets with a diverse range of shops and produce. The **Castlecourt Centre** in Royal Avenue boasts over 70 shops, including many High Street brands, all under one roof, as well as several food shops.
Lovers of markets and antiques should head for the **Donegall Pass**, located off Shaftesbury Square, home to several antique shops and a weekly bric-a-brac market. Other markets worth visiting include **St George's Market** (Friday mornings), for fresh produce, and the **Variety Market** next door, where you can find just about anything you are looking for.

Adjacent Sights – See Antrim, Bangor, Carrickfergus, Lisburn.

Entertainment

Lovers of the arts can choose from several venues and art forms including:
Belfast Waterfront Hall ☎ 028 9033 4455 (Box Office); ☎ 028 9033 4400 (Information and reservations) – A wide and varied programme of entertainment, offering something for lovers of contemporary and classical music alike.
The Grand Opera House, *Great Victoria Street* ☎ 028 9024 9129 (24hr information).
The Lyric Theatre, *Ridgeway Street* ☎ 028 9038 1081.
Belfast Civic Arts Theatre, *Botanic Avenue* ☎ 028 9031 6900 – Musicals, contemporary drama and concerts.
Old Museum Arts Centre, *College Square North* ☎ 028 9023 3332 (Ticket Line) – Drama, poetry, dance and workshops.
The Crescent Arts Centre, *University Road* ☎ 028 9024 2338 – Various workshops in what was originally a Victorian school.
Cultúrlann Macadam Ó Fiaich, *Falls Road* ☎ 028 9023 9303 – Irish Language arts centre featuring concerts and exhibitions.

Ulster Hall, *Bedford Street* ☎ 028 9032 3900 – Pop concerts, sporting events and a regular venue for the Ulster Orchestra.

King's Hall, *Balmoral* ☎ 028 9066 5225 – A major venue which can accommodate up to 7 000 people.

Cinema-goers can choose from several cinemas including:

Queen's Film Theatre, *University Square Mews* ☎ 028 9024 4857 – A 2-screen arthouse cinema.

Virgin Cinema, *Dublin Road* ☎ 0541 555 176 – A 10-screen complex.

The Movie House, *Yorkgate, York Street* ☎ 028 9075 5000.

The Curzon Cinema, *Ormeau Road* ☎ 028 9064 1373.

The Strand Cinema, *Holywood Road* ☎ 028 967 3500.

Pubs

In Belfast the **public houses** are generally open from 11.30am to 11pm, Monday to Saturday, and noon to 10pm on Sunday. A selection of pubs worth a visit includes:

Robinson's Bar, *Great Victoria Street*.

The Duke of York, *Commercial Court*.

The Empire, *Botanic Avenue* – Different types of music plus a comedy club.

Kitchen Bar, *Victoria Square, Belfast 1* – Opened in 1859 and renowned for its music – traditional live music Friday and Saturday nights.

Maddens, *Berry Street* – Musical instruments adorning the walls give some idea of the role that music plays in this pub, where there is traditional live music Wednesday and Sunday nights.

The Liverpool – Traditional live music Wednesday and Sunday nights.

The Blackthorn, *Skipper Street* – Traditional live music Thursday nights.

Katy Daly's, *Ormeau Avenue* – All types of live music.

Pat's Bar, *Princes Dock Street* – Traditional live music.

Bittles Bar, *Victoria Square* – A whimsical triangular building dating from 1861 (formerly *The Shakespeare*).

The Garrick, *Chichester Street* – Portraits of golfing heroes now adorn the walls of this recently restored pub which lies in the heart of Belfast's commercial area.

Kelly's Cellars, *Bank Street* – Established in 1720 and recognisable by its attractive red-and-cream exterior.

Where to Eat

Morning Star, 17-19 Pottinger's Entry, off High St, BT1 4DT. ☎ 028 90 23 5986; Fax 028 9043 8696. Very busy pub offering traditional hearty home-cooked food.

La Belle Epoque, 61-63 Dublin Rd, BT2 7HE. ☎ 028 9032 3244; Fax 028 90 20 3111. Personally run, busy French style bistro in a popular location.

Nick's Warehouse, 37-39 Hill St, BT1 2LB. ☎ 028 9043 9690; Fax 028 90 23 0514. Bustling brasserie with wide ranging eclectic menus.

Deanes Brasserie, 38-40 Howard St, BT1 6PD. ☎ 028 9033 1134; Fax 028 90 56 0001. Very busy brasserie serving modern Irish food with strong traditional base.

Cayenne, 7 Lesley House, Shaftesbury Sq, BT2 7DB. ☎ 028 9033 1532; Fax 028 9026 1575. Modern vibrant restaurant with Californian influenced menu.

Where to Stay

Malone, 79 Malone Rd, Belfast BT9 6SH. ☎/Fax 028 9066 9565. Clean, friendly and personally run hotel (8 rm); good value.

Ash Rowan, 12 Windsor Ave, BT9 6ᴱE. ☎ 028 9066 1758; Fax 028 0966 3227. Friendly, personally run guesthouse (5 rm) in residential area.

Benedict's, 7-21 Bradbury Pl, Shaftesbury Sq, BT7 1RQ. ☎ 028 9059 1999; Fax 028 9059 1990. Comfortable modern minimalistic hotel (32 rm) with well appointed bedrooms.

The Crescent Town House, 13 Lower Cres, BT7 1NR. ☎ 028 9032 3349; Fax 028 9032 0646. Regency period town house (11 rm) with original fittings in busy residential area.

Belfast City

Slide File, Dublin

The gardens (28 acres/11ha), consisting of a bowling green, sweeping lawns, shrubberies, flower beds and a rose garden with pergola, slope gently to the River Lagan. Although the gardens were originally laid out for the study of plants by the Botanic and Horticultural Society, founded in 1827, many other activities and entertainments were organised to meet the constant need for funds. In 1895 the Gardens became a public park.

★ **Palm House** – This beautiful cast-iron and curvilinear glass structure, one of the earliest of its type, was designed by Charles Lanyon and completed in 1840. It was constructed by Richard Turner, who later collaborated with Decimus Burton on the construction of the Great Palm House at Kew. The dome was added in 1852.

Tropical Ravine House – The present house is an extension of the older Fernery established in 1887 by the curator, Charles McKimm. In 1900 a stove section was added; two years later the lily pond was created over the boiler house. An internal gallery enables the plants to be viewed from both above and below.

Queen's University (**AZ U**) – Queen's College, Belfast, was incorporated in 1845 and established as a university in 1908. The red-brick Tudor-style building by Charles Lanyon is reminiscent of Magdalen College in Oxford.
Opposite stands **Elmwood Hall**, now an examination hall, an Italianate building with an arcaded façade in polychromatic freestone which was designed in 1862 by John Corry as a Presbyterian Church.

University Square (**52**) is an attractive mid-Victorian terrace, now occupied by the Faculty of Arts, with fanlights over the front doors and magnolia trees in the gardens.

CITY CENTRE

★ **City Hall** ⊘ (**BZ**) – The City Hall was begun in 1898 and completed in 1906 to celebrate Belfast's new city status, which was granted by Queen Victoria in 1888. The Portland stone building, which stands on the site of the old White Linen Hall (1784), was designed by Sir Brumwell Thomas in the Classical Renaissance style round a courtyard. The great copper-covered dome, capped by a stone lantern (173ft/53m), dominates not only the building but the whole square.
The guided tour of the **interior** includes the grand staircase; a mural of the founding of the city and its principal industries painted by John Luke, a Belfast artist; a sculpture by Patrick MacDowell (1790–1870), a native of Belfast, of the Marquess of Donegall (1827–53), who devoted the proceeds of his music and poetry to good works; the Council Chamber, panelled in hand-carved Austrian oak; the Reception Hall displaying the original Charter of Belfast granted by James I on 27 April 1613; the Banqueting Hall; portraits of sovereigns who have visited Belfast and the shields of the Provinces of Ireland in the stained glass in the Great Hall.

BELFAST

0 ———— 1 km
0 ———— 1/2 mile

★**Donegall Square** (BZ 20) – The hub of Belfast is Donegall Square, a vast rectangle of grass and flower beds formally laid out round the City Hall; here all the buses converge on the edge of the pedestrian shopping precinct.

The gardens at the centre of the square contain several statues: Queen Victoria is flanked by two bronze figures representing shipbuilding and spinning; a group commemorates the *Titanic*, which was built in Belfast by Harland and Wolff and sank on her maiden voyage in 1912 after colliding with an iceberg; in front stands Sir Edward Harland.

Bordering the square are *(north side)* the **Linen Hall Library** ⊘ (**F**), which was founded in 1788 as the Belfast Library and Society for Promoting Knowledge and has retained its old-fashioned interior; an old linen warehouse (**E**) (1869) built of pink

BELFAST

In Northern Ireland parking in the town centre may be restricted to attended vehicles only.

stone in the Venetian style; *(south side)* **Yorkshire House**, which is decorated with roundels containing low-relief heads of famous men and gods and goddesses; *(west side)* an office block (**G**) (1899–1902), designed by the Belfast architects, Young and Mackenzie, for Scottish Provident.

★**St Anne's Cathedral** ⊙ (**BY**) – Belfast's Anglican Cathedral is built of white stone on the basilical plan in an adapted Romanesque style designed by Sir Thomas Drew and followed by Sir Charles Nicholson. Although begun in 1899 it was not completed until 1981.

The West Front is pierced by three doors surmounted by carving: Christ in Glory *(centre)*, the Crucifixion *(north)* and the Resurrection *(south)*. The north transept incorporates a huge Celtic cross, the key to reconciliation.

Crown Liquor Saloon

The Baptistery *(north aisle)* was the first part of the cathedral to be completed; the windows illustrate the Sacrament of Baptism, and the mosaic vault the Creation. The Chapel of the Holy Spirit *(south aisle)* commemorates St Patrick's mission to Ireland, shown in the mosaic above the entrance; the altar of inlaid wood is a replica of an early-Christian style. The capitals of the columns supporting the nave depict different aspects of Belfast life. The **north transept chapel** is dedicated to the Royal Irish Rangers, the stained-glass window being a memorial to those who died in war. The **East Window**, depicting the story of the Good Samaritan, comes from the earlier church, which was finally demolished in 1903.

★**Crown Liquor Saloon** ⊘ (BZ) – The Victorian interior is richly decorated with coloured glass and brightly coloured and moulded tiles, reflected in the arcaded mirrors behind the long curved marble bar. Carved animals top the doorposts of the panelled snugs. The ornate ceiling is supported on hexagonal wooden columns with feathered ornament. Inspired by his travels in Spain and Italy, Patrick Flanagan built the public house as a railway hotel in 1885; it is now owned by the National Trust.

★**Sinclair Seamen's Church** ⊘ (BY) – The church's service to the maritime community is reflected in its position near Belfast docks and its interior decoration. The ship's bell from *HMS Hood* is rung at the beginning of the evening service; the collection is taken up in model life-boats instead of the pole boxes which now hang on the walls; a ship's wheel and a capstan stand in front of the pews; a ship's binnacle once served as a font; the reading desk is shaped like the prow of a ship; the pulpit and organ are adorned with port and starboard lights, a mast-head light, a ship's clock and a barometer.

★**St Malachy's Church** ⊘ (BZ) – The austere fortified exterior of this red-brick crenellated Roman Catholic church (1844) gives no hint of the ornate interior, which is dominated by a white stucco Rococo ceiling of roundels and pendants.

Oval Church ⊘ (BZ) – The First Presbyterian Church, the oldest church in Belfast, opened in 1783. Its elliptical plan was designed by Roger Mulholland. The line of the box pews echoes the curve of the galleries, which are supported on columns with Corinthian capitals. The Lewis organ (1907) retains its tubular pneumatic action and is of special interest to visiting musicians.

ADDITIONAL SIGHTS

Lagan Look-out ⊘ (BY K) – The display in the glass look-out describes the history of the River Lagan, its history as a major shipbuilding centre, its flora and fauna, the modern weir which controls the tides and creates a lagoon in the heart of the city.

Church House (BZ) – The headquarters of the Presbyterian Church in Ireland was designed by Young and Mackenzie (1905), Belfast architects, in the 15C Gothic style. The massive corner tower, which derives from St Giles' Cathedral in Edinburgh, contains a peal of bells. The semicircular Assembly Hall with its two galleries (refurbished in 1991) can seat about 1 500 people.

The **Presbyterian Historical Society Museum** ⊙ contains old communion plate, pitch pipes and communion tokens, originally lead, now card. The Society keeps records and information about the Presbyterian Church in Northern Ireland but has little information from the 17C and 18C.

Royal Ulster Rifles Museum ⊙ (BY) – The small museum celebrates the military exploits of the regiment through weapons, sporting and shooting trophies, medals, 19C uniforms and a collection of drums including the Lambeg (see p 348).

Royal Belfast Academical Institute (BZ) – The inter-denominational boys' school, commonly known as "Inst", is set back from the street behind pleasant gardens. The main block – a long three-storey brick façade relieved by four pairs of plain pilasters and a recessed doorcase at the back of a Doric porch – was probably designed by Sir John Soane and completed in 1814.

Clifton House (BY) – The wrought-iron entrance gate opens into a pleasant garden in front of a red-brick building with stone dressings set on a half-basement. It was designed by Robert Joy and opened as the Belfast Poorhouse in 1774, the date on the weather-vane which tops the octagonal stone spire.

Custom House (BY) – The building was designed by Charles Lanyon and erected in 1857 on the west bank of the River Lagan overlooking the docks; the two wings and central porch make an E-shape facing the city.

Royal Courts of Justice (BZ) – The massive building of Portland stone was designed by JG West and built between 1929 and 1933.

Albert Memorial Clock (BY B) – Owing to subsidence the tower has inclined slightly from the vertical since it was built in 1865 by WJ Barre; a statue of the Prince Consort stands in a niche facing up the High Street.

St George's Church (BYZ D) – The church was designed by John Bowden in 1816; the Classical portico comes from the palace which the Earl Bishop (see p 364) started to build at Ballyscullion after 1787.

EXCURSIONS

★★**Belfast Zoological Gardens** ⊙ – 5mi/8km N of Belfast by A 6. Car park; footpath to McArts Fort (see below). The Zoo, which opened in 1934, lives up to its full name since the animal enclosures are set in the former Hazlewood Gardens, surrounded, where possible, by dry ditches or water-filled moats. There are spacious green areas for the big cats, the various types of deer and kangaroos; an aquatic complex is subdivided to house penguins, sea-lions and polar bears; water fowl and flamingoes congregate round the large lake. A large walk-through aviary enables visitors to see free-flying birds at close quarters. The zoo is in a state of continuous development; recent additions include an otter park and buildings housing groups of chimpanzees and gorillas.

Belfast Castle ⊙ (AY) – 4mi/6.4km N of Belfast by A 6. Turn left into Innisfayle Park to Belfast Castle. In a superb location on the lower slopes of Cave Hill, this great mansion in Scottish Baronial style was built for the Donegall family in 1867–70 by WH Lynn; the external Baroque staircase was added to the east front in 1894. The interior now houses a restaurant and reception rooms, as well as a **Heritage Centre** on the top floor, with displays on the history of the castle and its surroundings. The commanding views over the city in its setting can be enjoyed by use of a remote camera with a powerful zoom lens. The castle has formal gardens and is one of a number of starting points for the waymarked trails through **Cave Hill Country Park**.

Cave Hill (AY) – 4mi/6.4km N of Belfast by A 6. Accessible on foot from several car parks, including those at Belfast Castle and at the Zoological Gardens; various waymarked paths lead to the summit.

North of Belfast rears the black basalt cliff, known as Cave Hill (1 182ft/360m), which marks the southern end of the Antrim plateau and is said to resemble the profile of Napoleon. The headland, which is separated by a deep ditch from the rest of Cave Hill, is marked by an ancient earthwork, known as **McArts Fort**, after a local 16C-to-17C chieftain who was probably killed by the Elizabethans; it has served as a watchtower and place of refuge for the native Irish against Vikings and Anglo-Normans. In 1795 Wolfe Tone and his fellow United Irishmen (see p 92) spent two days and nights in the fort planning the independence of Ireland. Fine view of Belfast city and Belfast Lough and, on a clear day, of County Down and Strangford Lough (southeast), Lough Neagh and the Sperrin Mountains (west), and Scotland (northeast).

Stormont ⊘ – *4mi/6.4km E of Belfast by A 20.* The Northern Ireland Parliament, a plain white Classical building with a central portico, which was designed by A Thornley, stands prominently on a hill approached by a broad avenue (1mi/1.6km long) through rolling parkland. A statue of Sir Edward Carson (1854–1935) stands at the centre of the roundabout. Parliament met regularly from 1932, when the building was opened, until 1972 when direct rule from Westminster was imposed. Stormont Castle, in the Scottish baronial style *(right)*, houses other government offices. In 1999 it became the meeting place of the new Northern Ireland Assembly.

Glencairn People's Museum ⊘ – *Fernhill House; 4mi/6.4km W of city centre by Shankhill Road, Woodvale Road, Ballygomartin Road, Forthriver Road and Glencairn Road to Glencairn Park.* Set in a mid-Victorian butter-merchant's mansion, with wide views across Glencairn Park to the city centre, this museum includes an exhibition on the social history of the Shankhill area, with fascinating photographs of residents and their houses, and *(upstairs)* a history of Unionism.

CARRICKFERGUS

CARRAIG FHEARGHAIS – Co Antrim – Population 22 786
Michelin Atlas p 103 and Map 923 – O 3

The largest and best-preserved Norman castle in Ireland dominates this pleasant seaside town on the north shore of Belfast Lough. A broad promenade runs along the front, between the bathing beach and the Marine Gardens; and a marina packed with yachts and fishing boats now occupies the harbour where, until the development of Belfast, there was a thriving port.

The district has nurtured three literary figures: Jonathan Swift wrote his first book at Kilroot; William Congreve and Louis MacNeice lived in Carrickfergus as children.

HISTORICAL NOTES

The name Carrickfergus, meaning the Rock of Fergus, recalls the ruler of the ancient kingdom of Dalriada, Fergus Mór, who was drowned in a shipwreck off the coast c 531.

The town grew up in the shadow of the castle and shared its history. The castle was built late in the 12C by the Anglo-Norman, John de Courcy, and completed by Hugh de Lacy c 1240. In 1315 it was captured after a year-long siege by Lord Edward Bruce from Scotland. The English recaptured it and held it for the next 300 years, withstanding many attacks by the local Irish and by invading Scots troops.

In 1688 the castle and the town were held for James II by Lord Iveagh but were captured in 1689 by Schomberg. On 14 June the following year William of Orange landed in Carrickfergus harbour *(plaque)* on his way to the Battle of the Boyne *(see p 116)*.

A bronze statue of William III was unveiled in 1990 to commemorate the tercentenary of his landing.

In February 1760 the town was held briefly by a French squadron under Thurot. In 1778 the American privateer John Paul Jones in his vessel *Ranger* attacked HMS *Drake* in an offshore engagement.

Events – Medieval banquets and the annual Lughnasa Fair *(August)* are held in the castle.
Boat Trips – Rowing boats for hire at the harbour
Adjacent Sights – See Antrim, Antrim Glens, Belfast.

★★CASTLE ⊘

The castle stands on a basalt promontory, originally protected by the sea on all but the landward side. Its position commands the entrance to Belfast Lough. It was begun soon after the Anglo-Norman invasion in 1177 and twice extended to secure the whole promontory by the middle of the 13C.

Life-size figures of the castle's inhabitants and garrison illustrate its 800 years of active use.

The oldest part of the castle, built by John de Courcy between 1180 and 1200, is the **inner ward**, which is enclosed by a high curtain wall; there was a hall against the east wall. The brick-built gunports were introduced in the 16C; the 19C gun platforms at the southern end provide a view of the castle and its surroundings. The **keep** provided living accommodation for the lord of the castle. The life led here is evoked in a variety of ways; there is a large model of the castle at the time of Schomberg's siege in 1689; an audio-visual show, *Feasts and Fasts*, in the Banqueting Hall, and, on the banner-hung top floor, the opportunity to dress up in period costume.

CARRICKFERGUS CASTLE

0   30 m
0   100 feet

The wall enclosing the **middle ward**, now partly reduced to its foundations, was built to improve the castle's defences soon after it had been successfully besieged by King John in 1210. The northeast angle tower is a fine example of 13C defensive work with an impressive array of arrow slits. There is a postern gate in the southeast corner.

The **outer ward** was probably built by Hugh de Lacy, between 1228 and 1242, to enclose the whole promontory and make the castle less vulnerable to attack from the land. Originally it probably contained living quarters but these were replaced in the 19C by ordnance stores supporting gun platforms.

The **gatehouse towers**, which were completely circular when they were built at the same time as the Outer Ward, were cut back some time after the Elizabethan period. The room over the entrance passage contains the portcullis winding-gear and a "murder hole". The Chapel on the first floor of the east tower is so called because of its elaborate east window.

TOWN CENTRE

★St Nicholas' Church ⊘ – The late-12C pillars in the nave are part of the original structure which was built by John de Courcy. After several centuries of turbulence the church was heavily restored in 1614. The west tower, the bell-tower, which was begun in 1778, was completed in 1962 as a memorial to both World Wars. In the north transept is a marble and alabaster monument to Sir Arthur Chichester (1563–1625), Governor of Carrickfergus, and his wife and son. The stained glass in the south side and west end of the nave is 16C from Co Meath.

North Gate and Town Walls – Carrickfergus was enclosed with defensive walls and ditches between 1607 and 1610 by Lord Deputy Arthur Chichester. The big arch of the North Gate is still largely 17C work but the structure has been repaired and altered many times; the pedestrian arch and crenellations are a 19C addition. A good stretch of wall survives to the east in Shaftesbury Park.

Knight Ride ⊘ – Visitors are carried in knights' helms on a monorail above the shopping precinct and into the dark ride, where the history of Carrickfergus is recalled in a strong local accent, from the legendary shipwreck of Fergus, through the invasions of Vikings, Normans and Williamites, to the present day. The static exhibition includes a scale-model of the town.

EXCURSIONS

Andrew Jackson Centre ⊘ – *2mi/3.2km N of Carrickfergus by A 2; turn right onto Donaldsons Avenue.* Between the road and the sea stands a 17C single-storey cottage near the site of the Jackson family homestead. The property has been restored to its original condition: earthen floor, wattle-and-daub canopy over the open hearth, hanging crane; the furniture dates from the 1850s.
The gallery traces the Ulster-American connection, in particular the life of Andrew Jackson, whose parents emigrated in 1765 to South Carolina, where Andrew was born in 1767. In 1829 he was elected 7th President of the USA and served two terms of office.
The adjoining **US Rangers Centre** presents the story of this American force which was formed in Northern Ireland in June 1942, with the task of acting as a Spearhead for the invasions of the Second World War.

Dalway's Bawn – *6mi/10km N of Carrickfergus by A 2, B 149 and B 90.* South of Ballycarry beside the road *(left)* stand the remains of a bawn, with three flanker towers built by John Dalway c 1609 and now part of a farm.

Whitehead – *5.5mi/9km NE of Carrickfergus by A 2.* Population 3 761. This seaside resort is sheltered between the cliffs of White Head and Black Head. It has a pebble beach backed by a promenade and two golf courses.

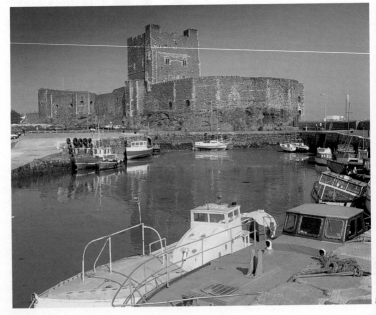

Carrickfergus Castle

The town is also one of the bases of the **Railway Preservation Society of Ireland** ⊘ which owns a unique collection of steam locomotives and coaches, and operates steam rail tours to all parts of Ireland during the summer season.

Island Magee – *6mi/10km N of Carrickfergus by A 2. Ferry from Larne (see p 304).* Although not an island, the peninsula (7mi/11km long), which separates Larne Lough from the North Channel, feels quite detached. The road *(B 90)* along the west side of the peninsula provides a good view across Larne Lough. At its north end in the front garden of a private house *(right)* stands the **Ballylumford Dolmen★**, a Neolithic burial monument, consisting of four stones supporting a capstone. From **Brown's Bay**, a sandy beach sheltered between low headlands on the north coast, there is a view of the shipping entering and leaving the port of Larne, and in clear weather the coast of Scotland *(north)*. **Portmuck** is a small bay and harbour. Further south are **The Gobbins**, precipitous cliffs (2mi/3.2km) from which the local inhabitants were flung into the sea in 1641 by the soldiers from the garrison in Carrickfergus.

Glenoe Waterfall – *12mi/20km N of Carrickfergus by B 58 and B 99; car park (right) in Waterfall Road half way down the hill.* The gorge is so deep and so well screened by trees that the waterfall is audible before it is visible. The river falls in a double cascade into a deep pool before flowing on under an old stone bridge through the village, which is now preserved by the National Trust.

CASTLE COOLE★★★

Co Fermanagh
Michelin Atlas p 97 and Map 923 – J 4
1.5mi/2.4km SE of Enniskillen by A 4

Probably the finest neo-Classical house in Ireland, Castle Coole was designed by James Wyatt and completed in 1798. The house, which is set on a rise sloping to the lake, consists of a central block containing the formal rooms, flanked by two single-storey wings containing the family rooms.

In the 1980s it was restored to something like its early-19C appearance by the recladding of the exterior and the redecoration of the interior, in accordance with the original intentions of Wyatt or of Preston, one of the leading Dublin upholsterers of the period, who refurbished the interior between 1807 and 1825.

The stable yards (restored), built out of sight below the level of the house and linked to it by a tunnel, were designed in 1817 by Richard Morrison. On display is Lord Belmore's coach, built in 1863 and still used in the 1940s to fetch guests from the station.

The Corrys of Coole

John Corry, a Belfast merchant, originally from Dumfriesshire, purchased the manor of Coole in 1656 and in 1709 built a new house near the lake incorporating parts of an early-17C castle. In 1741 the estate passed to Armar Lowry-Corry, created 1st Earl of Belmore in 1797, who commissioned Wyatt to design the present house; his son, the 2nd Earl of Belmore, was responsible for the interior decoration and the Regency furnishings.

Adjacent Sights – See Enniskillen, Sperrin Mountains.

TOUR *1hr*

The spaciousness and sense of proportion experienced in the **entrance hall** are repeated throughout the house. Family portraits are hung in some of the main rooms; the Breakfast Room contains many important pictures.

James Wyatt's scheme of decoration and furnishings is best seen in the **library** and in the **dining room**, where the decoration and the furniture have altered little since Wyatt's day. The **oval Saloon**, the most important room in the house, is decorated with elaborate plasterwork; the curved doors, which are made of mahogany veneered with satinwood, are hung on pivots. Wyatt specified the ceramic stoves which have the same decorative motif as the friezes.

Preston's more flamboyant style is evident in the porphyry colour used in the hall, on the staircase and in the lobby on the first-floor landing. He provided the hangings and furniture in the drawing room and the saloon, and substituted a larger table in the dining room.

The **Bow Room** on the first floor, is also by Preston; it was known as the Work Room and used by the ladies of the house for sewing, talking, reading or playing the piano. The gold and scarlet decoration and furnishing of the **State Bedroom** by Preston were in anticipation of George IV's visit to Ireland in 1821.

State Bedroom, Castle Coole

Christopher Hill/National Trust Photographic Library

DOWNPATRICK

DÚN PÁDRAIG – Co Down – Population 10 113
Michelin Atlas p 99 and Map 923 – O 4 5 – Local map Strangford Lough

The name Downpatrick recalls an early pre-Christian fort (*dún* in Irish) and St Patrick, the patron saint of Ireland. The fort developed into an ecclesiastical city with many religious foundations clustered round the cathedral which still dominates the region. Downpatrick is an important historical town, which until recently was almost entirely surrounded by water; its narrow medieval streets – English, Irish and Scotch Street – converged on the town centre where the market house once stood. Despite losing its status as a county town in 1973, Downpatrick is still a busy market town serving the surrounding agricultural area, which to the south is known as the Lecale Peninsula.

SIGHTS

★**Down Cathedral** ⊘ – There is no trace of the monastery which grew up over the centuries since the time of St Patrick, although a round tower survived until 1780. In the 12C John de Courcy replaced the incumbent Augustinians with a community of Benedictine monks from Chester, rebuilt the abbey church, changed the dedication to St Patrick, to please the native Irish, and renamed the town Downpatrick. He claimed he had found the bodies of Patrick, Colmcille and Brigid and reburied them in his new church. This building was destroyed in 1316 by Edward Bruce and in 1538 its successor was set on fire by the English Lord Deputy Lord Grey.

Out and About

Adjacent Sights – See Lisburn, Mourne Mountains, Strangford Lough.

Where to Eat

The Restaurant (at The Narrows Hotel), 8 Shore Rd, Portaferry BT22 1JY. ☎ 028 4272 8148; Fax 028 4272 8105. Modern brasserie with daily changing blackboard menu with strong seafood base.

Where to Stay

The Narrows, 8 Shore Rd, Portaferry BT22 1JY. ☎ 028 4272 8148; Fax 028 4272 8105. Modern stylish minimalistic hotel (13 rm) by the water.

The Mill, Ballydugan, BT30 8HZ. ☎ 028 4461 3654; Fax 028 4461 7608. Fully restored impressive period mill (11 rm) with distinctive interior.

Portaferry, 10 The Strand, Portaferry BT22 1PE. ☎ 028 4272 8231; Fax 028 4272 8999. Personally run part 18C house (13 rm) by the water.

St Patrick

When St Patrick returned to Ireland in 432 to convert the population to Christianity, his ship was carried by the wind and tide into Strangford Lough and he landed near Saul after sailing up the River Slaney, now a mere stream. He converted the local chief, Dichu, who gave him a barn (*sabhal* in Irish, pronounced Saul) to use as a church. St Patrick was very attached to Saul and returned there to die in 461. Some records state that he was also buried in Saul, rather than in Downpatrick.

In 1790 the building was restored and the west tower was built using the stones of the round tower. The cathedral now consists of the chancel of the abbey church. The original dedication to the Holy and Undivided Trinity was restored by James I in 1609. At the east end stands a granite High Cross, dating from the 10C or 11C, which until 1897 stood in the town centre. It is badly worn but the top panel represents the Crucifixion.

A stone bearing the names of the three most famous Irish saints – Patrick, Brigid and Columba (Colmcille) – stood in the graveyard south of the cathedral until early this century, when it was replaced by the present slab of granite marking the traditional site of **St Patrick's Grave.**

The granite font in the narthex was previously used as a watering trough and originally was probably the base of a cross.

Beside the Chapter Room door are two figures in ecclesiastical robes, which date from 1150 and are unique in Ireland.

The **organ**, which is mounted on the choir screen in a unique Georgian Gothic case, was built in the late 18C by Samuel Green for George III who presented it to the Cathedral in 1802.

The **choir screen** over the eight canons' **stalls** is the only one of its kind remaining in Ireland. Opposite the **bishop's throne** stands the Judge's Stall, a reminder of the importance of Downpatrick as an assize town; it may have been used by the judge when courts of law were held in churches.

★**Down County Museum** ⊘ – *The Mall.* The museum is housed in the old Down County prison, which was built between 1789 and 1796; Thomas Russell, the United Irishman, was hanged in the gateway in 1803. When a new prison was built in the 1830s the old buildings were occupied by the South Down Militia and then by the army until the mid 20C. Surviving **cells** form part of the museum display.

The **gatehouse** contains the **St Patrick Heritage Centre** which tells the saint's history in words and pictures, and illustrates *(video)* the many local sites connected with St Patrick.

The display in the former **Governor's House** in the centre of the courtyard traces the history of Co Down from 7000 BC and describes the local wildlife.

The Mall – To avoid the deep dip between the Cathedral and English Street the road was raised (15ft/5m) in 1790.

St Patrick's Gravestone

Well below the level of the road stands the **Southwell Charity**, which was founded in 1733 as a school and almshouses by Edward Southwell, the Secretary of State for Ireland, who by his marriage in 1703 became Lord of the Manor of Down. The two teachers' houses are set well forward and linked to the main block by low quadrant walls. Opposite are the **Judges' Lodgings** *(nos 25 and 27)*, two late Regency-style houses built soon after 1835.

English Street – East of the Museum stands the Courthouse (1834), the sole relic of a new prison constructed behind the courthouse in 1835. East of the court-house is a low two-storey building, originally designed with vaulted cells on the ground floor to hold prisoners but converted in 1798 into the **Downe Hunt Rooms**; the Hunt has unbroken records dating from 1757. The Clergy Widows' Houses *(nos 34–40)* date from 1730 and 1750 although their appearance was altered early in the 19C. The **Customs House** *(no 26)* was built in 1745 by Edward Southwell. Closing the lower end of the street are the red-brick Assembly Rooms designed in the Venetian Gothic style in 1882 by William Batt of Belfast.

Mound of Down – A second great Iron Age earthwork rises from the marshy levels around the town. The tree-covered mound sheltered an urban settlement destroyed by the Norman knight de Courcy in 1177.

EXCURSIONS

Saul – *2mi/3.2km E of Downpatrick*. The hilltop site, where St Patrick is said to have made his first Irish convert, is now crowned by **St Patrick's Memorial Church** ☉ which was built in 1932 to commemorate the 1500th anniversary of St Patrick's landing near Saul in 432. It was designed by Henry Seaver of Belfast and is built of Mourne granite, with a characteristic Irish round tower incorporated as the vestry. The medieval abbey was occupied by Augustinian canons from the 12C until the Dissolution in 1540. In the graveyard there are two cross-carved stones and two small **mortuary houses**.

Slieve Patrick – *3mi/4.8km E of Downpatrick. Car park. 15min there and back on foot to the top of the hill.* A statue of St Patrick was erected on the top of the hill in 1932 to commemorate the 1500th anniversary of St Patrick's landing near Saul in 432. The path up to an open-air altar is marked by the Stations of the Cross. From the top there is a **view**.

St Tassach's (Raholp) Church – *4mi/6.4km E of Downpatrick*. In a field are the ruins of St Tassach's Church, also known as Templemoyle. It dates from the 10C or 11C and was in ruins by 1622; some restoration took place in 1915. The east window lintel is inscribed with crosses and the altar is flanked by recesses. It is here that Bishop Tassach is said to have administered the last sacrament to St Patrick.

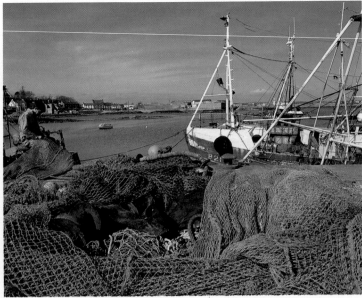

Ardglass Harbour

★**Struell Wells** – *2mi/3.2km SE of Downpatrick.* The site, in a secluded rocky hollow by a fast-flowing stream, comprises five buildings: an unfinished 18C church; a circular Drinking Well with a domed roof built on a wicker supporting arch; a rectangular Eye Well with a pyramidal corbelled roof; a Men's Bath-house, with a stone roof and a dressing room with seats next to the bath; and a Women's Bath-house without a roof – its dressing room is in the men's bath-house.

Although the oldest of these buildings dates only from c 1600, there is written reference to a chapel on the site in 1306. A strong tradition associates the site with St Patrick. Struell has probably attracted pilgrims since the pre-Christian period, since streams and springs were important in Celtic pagan religion, but it was most popular from the 16C to 19C.

★**Ardglass** – *7mi/11km S of Downpatrick by B 1.* Ardglass stands on the south side of a natural harbour and has an active fishing fleet. In the 15C it was the busiest harbour in Ulster. Its importance as a fishing and commercial port in the medieval period is evident from the number of fortified buildings that were erected to protect this Anglo-Norman enclave from the native Irish.

Jordan's Castle ⊙, an early-15C tower house in the middle of the town overlooking the harbour, houses a collection of antiquities made by FJ Bigger, a solicitor and antiquarian from Belfast, who restored the building in 1911. The entrance is protected by two machicolations between the projections. In the Elizabethan period it withstood a three-year siege under its owner, Simon Jordan, until relieved by Mountjoy *(see p 91)* in June 1601.

Two other castles, King's Castle and Isabella's Tower, are mainly 19C structures. A row of fortified warehouses on the south side of the harbour has been converted into the clubhouse of the local golf course.

Killough – *7mi/11km S of Downpatrick by B 176.* Population 500. A broad central avenue runs through this quiet but attractive village on the south side of a deep sea-inlet. In the 17C it was known as Port St Anne after Anne Hamilton, whose husband, Michael Ward of Castle Ward, developed the port to facilitate the export of lead and agricultural products from his estates.

St John's Point – *10mi/16km S of Downpatrick by B 176, A 2 and a minor road.* Near the point are the ruins of a 10C or 11C church built on the site of an early monastery. It is a pre-Romanesque building; the west door has sloping jambs and a lintel; the high gable carried a roof supported on antae. The lighthouse stands on the southernmost point of the Lecale Peninsula; there is a fine **view** across Dundrum Bay.

Ballynoe Stone Circle – *3mi/5km S of Downpatrick. Park opposite the old railway station (east); 6min there and back on foot by the track (west) between the fields.* The large circle is composed of low close-set stones round an oval mound which contained a stone cist at either end in which cremated bones were found during excavations in 1937–38. Nothing certain is known about its date but it was probably built by the late-Neolithic Beaker people c 2000 BC.

Clough – *6mi/10km SW of Downpatrick by A 25.* Population 269. North of the crossroads stands a stone tower (13C with later medieval additions) surmounting an Anglo-Norman earthwork castle, which in the late 12C or early 13C was surrounded by a wooden palisade.

Seaforde Garden ⊙ – *9mi/14.5km W of Downpatrick by A 25 and A 2 north.* The old walled garden at Seaforde has been revived with a large hornbeam **maze**. Beyond is the Pheasantry, a deep dell dominated by great rhododendrons and exotic trees. Even more exotic is the **tropical butterfly house**, where brilliantly coloured specimens flutter among the vegetation and other creatures lurk in the lush undergrowth.

Loughinisland Churches – *5mi/8km W of Downpatrick by A 2 and a minor road north.* Three ruined churches stand on what was originally an island overlooking the lake. The oldest church (13C) stands in the middle. The larger church dates from the 15C and was in use until 1720. The smaller church bears the date 1636 over the door but it may be earlier; the initials PMC stand for Phelim MacCartan, whose family held land in the district and probably used the graveyard for their burials.

DUNGANNON

Dungannon, which is the administrative centre of the district, is set on a hill surrounded by rich farmland. The chief industry is agriculture: dairy farming and fruit growing with their attendant processing and packing activities and a weekly livestock market. There are many manufacturing industries; one of the oldest, textiles, has brought international fame to the name of Moygashel (founded in 1875).

Victorious O'Neill

Two important military engagements took place south of Dungannon. At the **Battle of the Yellow Ford** on the River Callan in 1598 Hugh O'Neill defeated the English forces under Sir Henry Bagnall; only about 1 500 Englishmen out of over 4 000 survived. In 1646 at the **Battle of Benburb**, fought at Derrycreevy west of Benburb on the north bank of the River Blackwater, the Scottish army of General Monroe was outmanoeuvred by Owen Roe O'Neill and 3 000 Scots were killed.

Plantation Town – Under the O'Neill clan Dungannon was little more than a collection of huts grouped round Castle Hill but early in the 17C the English and Scottish settlers began to build a modern town. A charter was granted in 1612; in 1614 the Royal School was founded. When the native Irish rebelled in 1641 they were at first successful; the settlers' buildings were burned and their farms and orchards destroyed; the population dropped to 130. A new plantation followed the restoration of peace in 1653. After the Battle of the Boyne (1690) Dungannon expanded rapidly; in 1692 the town was purchased by Thomas Knox, whose expansionary regime coincided with the development of the coalfields at Drumglass and the digging of the local canal.

Adjacent Sights – See Armagh, Lough Neagh, Sperrin Mountains.

SIGHTS

Tyrone Crystal ⊘ – *NE in Killybrackey Road (A 45)*. Tyrone Crystal opened in 1971, exactly 200 years after an earlier glasshouse had started production under Benjamin Edwards at Drumreagh, Newmills *(north)*. The nascent enterprise faced closure in the late 1970s' recession but local financial support was found and the factory moved into its present premises in 1990.
The **tour** covers the various stages in the process of producing hand-blown glass: preparing the molten glass, shaping the pieces by blowing, cooling, inspection for faults, bevelling, marking, cutting and polishing.

Heritage World ⊘ – *Main Street*. The stone building at the head of the sloping main street houses a genealogical research centre, with extensive computerised archives enabling people to "discover the path to their Irish roots".

EXCURSIONS

Cornmill Heritage Centre ⊘ – *Coalisland; 4mi/7km NE of Dungannon by A 45*. The landscape around Coalisland is still marked by the extractive and other industries which once flourished here. Coal was being dug from bellpits as early as the 17C but severe faulting problems led to the closure of the last mine in 1970. Other industries included weaving, milling and a fireclay works; the Coalisland Canal had the first inclined plane to be built in the British Isles. The big brick cornmill, which dominates the centre of the town, was built in 1907 and has been extensively refurbished to serve as a community and heritage centre. The "Coalisland Experience" brings to life the past of this industrial area, unique in Ireland.

Donaghmore – *Donaghamore; 5mi/8km N of Dungannon by B 43*. In the centre of this quiet village stands an ancient sandstone cross (AD c 700–1000), associated with a former abbey; it is composed of the base and shaft of one cross and the shaft and head of another, which is decorated with motifs and biblical scenes: New Testament on the east face and Old Testament on the west. Originally it belonged to a nearby monastery said to have been founded by St Patrick. Its history is traced with cuttings and pictures in the nearby **Donaghmore Heritage Centre** ⊘, housed in the former primary school.

Donaghmore Clergy

The Revd **George Walker**, Rector of Donaghmore in 1674, was governor of Derry during the siege and died at the Battle of the Boyne.

Charles Wolfe *(blue plaque)* was curate of Donaghmore when he wrote his poem about the Burial of Sir John Moore at Corunna, which appeared in the *Newry Telegraph* in 1817.

Castlecaulfield – *5mi/8km NW of Dungannon by A 4 and a minor road N.* Population 350. On the southeast edge of the village stand the stark ruins of a Jacobean **mansion** built (1611–19) by an ancestor of the Earls of Charlemont, Sir Toby Caulfield, who commanded Charlemont Fort *(see below)* and whose arms appear over the gatehouse, an earlier structure defended with murder holes above the main door. The house was burned by the O'Donnells in 1641 but occupied for another 20 years by the Caulfields.

Moy – *5.5mi/9km S of Dungannon by A 29.* Population 850. "The Moy" is an attractive Plantation town which was laid out in the 1760s by James Caulfield, Earl of Charlemont *(see p 187)*, on the model of Marengo in Lombardy, which he had seen while making the Grand Tour.

Horse chestnut trees line the main road where it passes through the broad central green, once the site of the great monthly horse fairs which lasted a whole week. The road slopes down to the Blackwater River past the screen and entrance gates to Roxborough Castle (destroyed by fire in 1921), the 19C seat of the Earl of Charlemont.

On rising ground on the south bank stand the ruins of Charlemont Fort which was built in 1602 by Lord Mountjoy. Most of the fort was burned down in 1922; the gatehouse still stands at the end of a short avenue of trees; star-shaped ramparts are visible near the river.

Benburb – *7mi/11km S of Dungannon by A 29 to Moy and W by B 106.* The ruins of **Benburb Castle** *(access on foot from priory grounds or just inside priory entrance)* occupy a dramatic site, a rocky ledge above the River Blackwater, which tumbles through the tree-lined gorge (120ft/37m below). The castle, which was built by Sir Richard Wingfield in 1611, replaces an earlier O'Neill stronghold. The entrance is flanked by two rectangular towers containing rooms with fireplaces; the walls, which are pierced by musket-loops, enclose an irregular rectangular bawn containing a 19C house *(private)*; the round tower overlooking the river contains a stair leading to a postern gate.

★**Parkanaur Forest Park** ⊘ – *7mi/11km W of Dungannon by A 4. Car park.* The herd of **white fallow deer** at Parkanaur are direct descendants of a white hart and doe given by Elizabeth I in 1595 to her goddaughter, Elizabeth Norreys, who married Sir John Jephson of Mallow Castle *(see p 250)*. In 1978 five white fallow deer – a mature buck, a pricket and three does – were purchased from Mallow and established at Parkanaur. Fallow deer vary greatly in colour, from almost black through dark chestnut to light fawn with prominent white spots, and even pure white; the winter coat is usually much darker than the summer.

Formerly the property of the Burgess family, Parkanaur is an old estate with several unusual specimen trees; two parasol beeches with branches like corkscrews grow beside the front drive. The woodland is being developed as an oak forest. The

Fallow deer

Christopher Hill, Belfast

walks and nature trail include the formal Victorian Garden, the stone archway, the wishing well and the stone bridge and weir on the Torrent River. The farm buildings (1843, later restored) contain a display of forestry machinery.

Simpson-Grant Homestead ⊙ – *11mi/18km W of Dungannon by A 4; just before Ballygawley turn left to Dergenagh. Car park.* On the west side of the road stands the 17C homestead of the ancestors of Ulysses S Grant, President of the USA (1869–77).

The **Visitor Centre** tells the story of the Ulster-Scots Plantation, the Simpson family and the Ulster-American connection through an audio-visual film.

The house, restored in 1978 to its mid-19C state, has an ashpit for cooking potatoes before the hearth. The shed contains the appropriate farm implements; hens range in the yard and ducks dabble in the pond.

Across the road are the eight fields of the smallholding (10 acres/4ha): three for grazing a horse, a goat and two "mountainy" cattle; one for root crops (potatoes, turnips); one for a grain crop with the straw for bedding and thatching; three for a cash crop such as flax for the linen industry; there was also a flax hole or dam for "retting" the flax.

Errigal Keerogue Cross – *16mi/25km W of Dungannon by A 4; 1mi/1.6km W of the Ballygawley roundabout turn right to Errigal Keerogue (sign); at the crossroads in Ballynasaggart continue W; after 2mi/3.2km turn right.* In the graveyard stands a **high cross**; the carving is unfinished, probably owing to a fault in the stone. Two yew trees grow in the ruins of the medieval church, thought to be a Franciscan foundation (1489) which replaced an earlier monastery associated with St Kieran.

Augher – *18mi/29km W of Dungannon by A 4.* Population 400. The village is set on one of the most beautiful stretches of the Blackwater River which provides good fishing. On the north side of the lake stands Spur Royal, now a hotel; it began as a bawn on the site of an earlier stronghold in 1615, was restored after a fire in 1689 and enlarged in 1832 by William Warren, an architect from Sligo.

★**Clogher Cathedral** ⊙ – *20mi/32km W of Dungannon by A 4.* The cathedral, which dominates the village (population 550) from its hilltop site, was built from 1740 to 1745, in the austere Classical style with a squat tower topped by a balustrade and four pinnacles. Two **stone crosses** dating from the 9C and 10C stand in the graveyard outside the west door. A 7C **stone cross** *(outer porch)*, which is also thought to be a sundial for timing the services of the Celtic church, has a fish, an early Christian symbol, carved on the base. The **Golden Stone** *(inner porch)*, which was a famous oracle in pagan times, is known in Irish as **Clogh-Oir**, which may be the origin of the name Clogher. Clogher claims to be the oldest bishopric in Ireland, founded in the 5C. According to legend, its first bishop, to whom the cathedral is dedicated, was St Macartan or Macartin, a disciple of St Patrick.

Southwest of the cathedral stands Park House (1819), formerly the Bishop's Palace.

★**Knockmany Passage Grave** – *21mi/34km W of Dungannon by A 4 and N by B 83; 1.5mi/2.4km N of the crossroads turn right onto a track. Car park; 20min there and back on foot.* The hilltop site commands a superb view south over Knockmany Forest into the Clogher Valley. In 1959 a concrete bunker and skylight were built to protect the cairn from the weather but the stones of the burial chamber are visible through the grill: the decoration of circles, spirals and zigzags is typical of passage grave art.

ENNISKILLEN

INIS CEITHLEANN – Co Fermanagh – Population 11 436
Michelin Atlas p 97 and Map 923 – J 4

Enniskillen is a lively commercial town, which occupies an attractive island site between Lower and Upper Lough Erne. It makes an ideal base for exploring Lough Erne, for embarking on the Shannon–Erne Waterway *(see p 128)*, for fishing the Fermanagh lakes or for touring the Sperrin Mountains.

SIGHTS

Town Centre – In 1688 the **East Bridge**, which has almost disappeared under later alterations, replaced the drawbridge built by the planters on the site of an old ford in 1614. From the bridge the street passes the **Courthouse** *(left)*, radically remodelled in 1821–22 by William Farrell of Dublin. At the top of the hill in The Diamond stands the **Town Hall** *(right)*, designed by William Scott in 1898.

The **Buttermarket**, which is further along in Down Street *(turn right at the junction of High Street and Church Street)*, has been converted into a craft and design centre.

Out and About

Tourist Information – **Lakeland Visitor Centre** *(Shore Road on the west side of the town centre)* for information about activities on or around the lake.

Boat Trips – **Lough Erne Waterbus Cruises** ⏱ depart from the **Round 'O' Jetty** in Brook Park on the west bank of the River Erne *(northwest of the town centre)*.

Upper Lough Erne Cruises ⏱ *(1hr 30min)* in replicas of a Viking longship depart from the Share Centre in Lisnakea *(east shore of Upper Lough Erne)*.
The principal marinas are on Lower Lough Erne at **Kesh** *(east shore)* and on Upper Lough Erne at **Bellanaleck** *(west shore)* and **Carrybridge** *(east shore)*.

Fishing – **Day boats** ⏱ for fishing are available in Enniskillen, Killadeas, Kesh, Belleek, Garrison, Bellanaleck, Teemore and Newtownbutler.

Sports – There is a **Lakeland Canoe Centre** on Castle Island, Enniskillen.
The **Lakeland Forum** offers facilities for swimming, squash, volley-ball, basketball, badminton, table tennis, bowls, archery, soccer, judo and keep-fit.

Events – The **Lady of the Lake** festival takes place in Irvinestown in July.

Crafts – For pottery visit the **Belleek Pottery** *(see below)*.

Adjacent Sights – See Castle Coole, Cavan, Donegal, Sligo, Sperrin Mountains.

Where to Stay

Manor House Country, Enniskillen. ☎ 028 6862 2211; Fax 028 6862 1545. Hotel (46 rm) for business and tourist visitors; good leisure complex; views over Lough Erne and the Fermanagh countryside.

Carlton, Belleek. ☎ 028 6865 8282; Fax 028 6865 9005. Commercial style hotel (19 rm) with modern amenities, located on the banks of the River Erne.

The main street *(Church Street)* continues to **St Macartin's Anglican Cathedral** standing in its graveyard *(right)*; it was completed in 1842 although the tower was part of the earlier 17C church. Opposite is **St Michael's Roman Catholic Church**, completed in 1875; the façade of this French Gothic Revival building by John O'Neill lacks the spire which was intended to crown the tower; more impressive is the external view of the apse rising above the sub-structure, supported by flying buttresses (1921).

The street descends towards the **West Bridge** (completed in 1892); to the right are the Old Militia Barracks (1790), now occupied by the Royal Ulster Constabulary and to the left is Enniskillen Castle.

Enniskillen Castle ⏱ – Until the 18C the castle stood on its own island protected by a deep ditch spanned by a drawbridge. The central **keep** incorporates part of the first castle, built in the 15C by Hugh Maguire. In 1607 Captain William Cole rebuilt the castle, which had been damaged in war, and c 1615 he erected on the outer walls a turreted building, known today as the **Watergate**, which is best seen from the lake. There is no

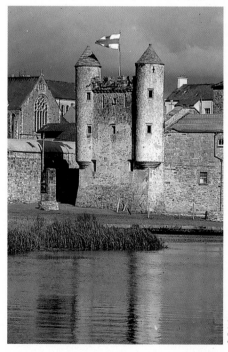

Watergate, Enniskillen Castle

C. Boisvieux

337

sign of its ever having contained an entrance but it may have been built near an earlier gate giving access to the lake. In the 18C the Cole family moved from Enniskillen Castle to their property at Portora *(northwest of the town centre where the river enters the lough)* and thence to Florence Court. Under the threat of French invasions new buildings were erected against the curtain wall west of the Watergate (1796) and along the north moat (c 1825). Exhibitions in the Watergate cover the ancient monuments and castles of Fermanagh, and the pilgrim's trail to Devenish Island *(see p 339).*

In the courtyard stands a German 8in/21cm mortar captured in 1914.

The **Heritage Centre** illustrates the history of Fermanagh and its rural landscapes and wildlife using audio-visual presentations and local artefacts – yew horn (8C–10C) with bronze mounts.

The **keep** houses *(ground floor)* an exhibition on the history of the castle and a video on the Maguire family. A 3-D representation of Enniskillen, based on an OS map of 1833, takes up the whole of one wall. Downstairs, the storage vaults, sole survivors of the earliest (15C) castle, house life-size figures in vignettes showing the cramped conditions of castle life in the 15C and 17C.

The **Regimental Museum of the Royal Inniskilling Fusiliers** ⊘ *(ground and first floors)* traces the history of this famous regiment, which was formed in the late 17C together with the Inniskilling Dragoons.

Portora Royal School

The school was founded in 1608 by James I at Lisnakea *(south)*. In 1643 it moved to Enniskillen and in 1777 to a site near **Portora Castle** (17C), which was partially destroyed by an explosion caused by schoolboys in 1859. Among its pupils were Oscar Wilde and Samuel Beckett.

Forthill Park – *SE of the town centre.* This conical-shaped hill, known formerly as Camomile Hill or Commons Hill or Cow Green, received its present name from a star-shaped fort with four bastions and cannon built in 1689 during the Williamite Wars. In 1836 the hill was enclosed and planted with trees. The delightful Victorian **bandstand** is an oriental-looking cast-iron structure with an octagonal canopy, supported on eight slender columns and surmounted by a clock. The centre of the fort is now occupied by **Cole's Monument** ⊘, erected between 1845 and 1857, in memory of General the Hon Sir Galbraith Lowry Cole (1772–1842), brother of the 2nd Earl of Enniskillen of Florence Court; he was a close friend of the Duke of Wellington and fought in the Peninsular Wars. Within the fluted Doric column a spiral stair *(108 steps)* climbs to a platform: extensive **view** of Enniskillen and the surrounding countryside.

EXCURSIONS

The Cole Family

The Coles came to Ireland from Devonshire, in the reign of Elizabeth I. They lived first at Enniskillen Castle and then at Portora Castle *(see p 338)*. It was Sir John Cole (1680–1726) who settled at Florence Court, named after his wife, Florence Wrey, a wealthy heiress from Cornwall. Their son, also John Cole (1709–67), made Lord Mount Florence in 1760, built the present central block; the wings were added by his son, William Willoughby Cole (1736–1803), later Viscount and then Earl of Enniskillen, who made the Grand Tour in 1756–57.

★★ Florence Court ⊘ – *8mi/13km S of Enniskillen by A 4, A 32 and W by a minor road.* This charming Palladian mansion stands in its own extensive parkland at the foot of Cuilcagh Mountain.

The original three-storey house, probably designed in the 1740s, is flanked by seven-arched colonnades and canted pavilions, which were probably designed in the 1770s by Davis Ducart, a Sardinian, who spent most of his working life in Ireland. The property was transferred, largely unaltered, to the National Trust in 1955.

House – *Tour 1hr 30min.* The glory of the house is the exuberant **Rococo plasterwork**, in the style of Robert West. Some of it, including the nursery ceiling which was adorned with drums and rocking horses and other toys, was destroyed by fire in 1956. The hall and most of the rooms are decorated with portraits, photographs, drawings and other memorabilia, returned from the family home in Scotland in 1997, after 25 years' absence.

The **Library** is lined with 18C pinewood bookshelves which complement the original plasterwork of the cornice, ceiling and door panel. The **Drawing Room** cornice of bucolic motifs is original but the centrepiece was destroyed in the fire. The **Dining Room** ceiling was saved from collapse during the fire by the drilling of small holes through which the water could drain. A surround of trailing foliage encloses the central panel where the four winds, represented by puffing cherubs, encircle an eagle.

The decorative plasterwork is at its most exuberant on the **staircase:** wall panels overflowing with scrolls of foliage between a horizontal band of scrolls and a cornice formed of pendants. Recesses on the landing are hung with a colourful collection of Japanese woodblock prints.

Grounds – The Pleasure Grounds were mostly planted by the 3rd Earl early in the 19C. In the walled garden the original ornamental section has been retained whereas the vegetable plot has been laid out as lawn with shrubs and ponds. An 18C summerhouse has been meticulously rebuilt and there is a fascinating brick-lined ovoid ice house as well as a working sawmill (restored).

Forest Park ⊙ – Since 1975 the estate grounds have been developed as a forest park. In the woodlands southeast of the house stands the famous **Florence Court Yew**, also known as the Irish Yew, a columnar-shaped freak, which can be reproduced only by cuttings as seedlings revert to the common type. There are several trails of different lengths signposted with coloured indicators; the longest extends to the moorland to the southwest and gives access *(9hr there and back on foot)* to the top of Cuilcagh Mountain (2 198ft/670m).

★★ **Marble Arch Caves and Forest Nature Reserve** ⊙ – *11mi/18km S of Enniskillen by A 4, A 32 and W by a minor road. .*

The cave system was formed in a bed of Dartry limestone by three streams on the northern slopes of Cuilcagh Mountain; they converge underground to form the Cladagh River which emerges at the Marble Arch and flows into Lough Macnean Lower.

The **reception centre** presents an exhibition on caving and a video *(20min)*, which covers the same ground as the tour and is a good substitute for those who cannot manage the many steep slopes and steps involved in the tour itself.

The **cave tour** includes a short boat trip on an underground lake which opens the way into a fantastic subterranean decor of stalactites, stalagmites, columns, flow stones, cascades, draperies and curtains, with picturesque names such as the Porridge Pot, Streaky Bacon, Cauliflowers, Tusks and Organ Pipes. The skilful illumination of these superb geological features is sometimes enhanced by reflection in pools of water. The longest stalactite (7ft/2m) is named after Edouard Martel, a famous French cave scientist who explored the caves in 1895.

The **nature reserve** *(car park at the cave entrance and on the Blacklion–Florence Court road)* consists of the wooded Cladagh gorge created by the collapse of caves eroded by the river. A path *(1hr there and back on foot)* along the east bank links the **Marble Arch**, a natural limestone arch, where the turbulent brown stream emerges from the ground, and the **Cascades**, where more water gushes forth. The forest is composed of ash, oak and beech and some conifers; in the spring the floor is a sea of bluebells.

★★LOUGH ERNE

Lough Erne is the largest stretch of water (50mi/80km long) in the Fermanagh Lakeland. It is fed by the River Erne, which rises at Lough Gowna south of the border and flows northwest until it reaches the sea at Ballyshannon, also in the Republic. Relics of ancient monasteries survive on some of the 154 islands; fortified houses and stately mansions were erected on the shore.

Owing to its extent and configuration Upper Lough Erne rarely feels crowded. Boats are available for hire and there are many jetties and quays along the shore. Fishing is popular and the lake is used for water sports of various kinds. The recreational attractiveness of the Lough as a cruising centre was greatly enhanced in 1994 by the re-opening of the **Shannon–Erne Waterway** *(see p 128)*.

Lower Lough Erne *Round tour of 66mi/106km – 1 day*
From Enniskillen take A 32 N; after 3mi/5km turn left to Trory Point.

★ **Devenish Island** ⊙ – *10min there and back by ferry.* The island monastery was founded in the 6C by St Molaise. It suffered from Viking raids and local feuds and in the 12C was occupied by a community of secular canons. In the 16C they and the neighbouring priory of Augustinian canons regular were suppressed. The **museum** traces the history of the monastery, with miniature models illustrating the seasonal activities of the monks.

The **round tower** dates from the 12C (81ft/25m high). The view from the top floor *(key from the Caretaker)* is limited by the narrowness of the four windows.

The **Lower Church** (Teampull Mór), nearest to the jetty, began as a short building c 1225 but was later extended. A dwelling for the canons was added to the north side and a mortuary chapel to the south for the Maguires of Tempo, whose arms are visible near the entrance and on the east wall. The oldest gravestone is a long flat slab with a two-armed cross in the southeast corner.

Devenish Island, Lough Erne

The smallest and oldest building, **St Molaise's House**, dates from the 12C although it is based on an earlier wooden church.

St Mary's Priory dates from the 15C although the tower is later. The two doorways at first-floor level gave access to a rood screen dividing the monks' chancel from the laymen's nave; bell ropes passed through the holes in the vault. A most unusual 15C **high cross** stands in the graveyard.

Continue N by B 82 along the east shore of the lake.

Killadeas – Ancient crosses stand in the churchyard.

★**Castle Archdale Country Park** ⓥ – The park on the lake shore includes extensive woodlands including over 20 kinds of trees and shrubs, which provide a habitat for fallow deer, red squirrels, badgers, otters, game birds and wildfowl. There are several relics of the Archdale family from East Anglia who were granted the land in 1612: an arboretum incorporating some fine specimens over 200 years old; a walled garden for flowers and fruit; the 19C pleasure grounds with a rockery and Irish yews; a cold plunge bath and sweathouse; the former outbuildings, now housing a Visitor Centre and a display of agricultural implements, adjacent to the site of the house (1773). Modern additions include a butterfly garden, a Japanese garden, a marina, and a camping and caravan site converted from a Second World War base for Sunderland and Catalina flying boats which patrolled the North Atlantic sea lanes. The ruins of the original dwelling, **Old Castle Archdale**, damaged in 1641 and abandoned in 1689, stand near the northeast entrance to the park *(car access from the road)*. The **bawn** still has its original gateway, a rare survival.

Festival of the Lady of the Lake

★**White Island** ⊘ – Within a large pre-Norman monastic enclosure stand the remains of a 12C church with a handsome Romanesque doorway. The eight **stone figures** set up against the north wall are definitely Christian but otherwise the subject of speculation; they probably date from the 9C or 10C and, as they have sockets in the heads and stumps on the feet, they may have been supportive members of a pulpit or shrine in an earlier church. In the 12C church they were used as building blocks.

Continue N by the scenic route; N of Kesh bear left onto A 47. Near the W end of Boa Island park beside the road and follow sign to cemetery (about 550yd/500m there and back on foot).

★**Janus Figure** – The squat and ancient stone figure with two faces probably dates from the Iron Age.

Continue W on A 47.

Janus Figure, Boa Island

Castle Caldwell Forest Park ⊘ – The forest covers two long fingers of land at the western end of Lough Erne and is managed with a threefold purpose: timber production, nature reserve and appropriate recreational activities such as shooting. The area is the main breeding ground of the Common Scoter duck and the islands are recognised bird sanctuaries. At the entrance stands the **Fiddler's Stone**, a memorial to a drunken fiddler who fell off a Caldwell boat in 1770 and was drowned. Beside the Visitor Centre is a **Fermanagh cot**, a flat-bottomed boat used until 1970 to transport cattle and sheep to and from the islands on the lake; the name originally applied to a boat made by hollowing out a large oak log. The castle, now in ruins, was built by Sir Edward Blennerhassett in 1612.

Continue W on A 47.

Belleek – The village stands at the point where the waters of the Erne flow swiftly westward in a narrow channel to enter the sea in Donegal Bay.

Belleek Pottery ⊘ – The pottery, which has an international reputation for its distinctive highly decorated Parian ware, takes its name from the small border village of Belleek.

Belleek Parian Ware

The pottery in its handsome building was founded in 1857 by John Caldwell Bloomfield, who had just inherited Castle Caldwell and needed to increase his income. He was a keen amateur mineralogist and realised that the estate contained the necessary ingredients to make pottery – feldspar, kaolin, flint, clay, shale, peat and water power. At first only earthenware was produced; the first Parian ware was the result of 10 years of experiment. Belleek won its first Gold Medal in Dublin in 1865.

The **tour** begins where the slip, a mixture of feldspar, china clay, frit (glass) and water, is moulded and trimmed. Gum arabic is added to produce the extruded raw material used to make the ornaments and the basketware which is woven by hand. By individual choice this is men's work; the women prefer to do the hand painting. All serve a five-year apprenticeship. The results of their craftsmanship are on show and for sale in the Visitor Centre.

ExplorErne ⊘ – The exhibition, which is housed in the purpose-built Tourist Information Centre, introduces visitors to the history, landscapes and ecology of the Lough, from legendary beginnings to the harnessing of its waters to generate hydroelectric power and control the capricious changes in level, which once meant that "in the summer Lough Erne is in Fermanagh, and in the winter Fermanagh is in Lough Erne".

Leave Belleek by A 46 going E.

The road skirts the southern shore of Lough Erne beneath the high Cliffs of Magho.

After 10mi/16km turn left to Tully Castle.

★**Tully Castle** ⊘ – The castle, a good example of a fortified planter's house, was built in 1613 by Sir John Hume from Berwickshire but captured and abandoned in 1641. The partially paved bawn is protected by walls and corner towers with musket loops; each corner tower was also a house. A 17C-style garden has been made inside the bawn. The three-storey house has a vaulted room on the ground floor containing the kitchen fireplace, an unusually large staircase leading to a reception room on the first floor and a turret stair to the floor above. The projecting turrets are best seen by walking round the outside.

Return to A 46 and immediately turn right onto B 81 and then second right to the Lough Navar Scenic Drive. After 3mi/5km turn right opposite Correl Glen.

★★★**Cliffs of Magho Viewpoint** – The Scenic Drive *(7mi/11km – one way)* through **Lough Navar Forest** ⊘ leads to a viewpoint *(car park)* on the top of the Cliffs of Magho. The view embraces the north end of Lower Lough Erne with the Blue Stack Mountains in Donegal visible on the horizon *(north)*.

Return to A 46 and continue S.

Ely Lodge Forest – There are trails along the shore through the mixed woodland.

Continue S on A 46; turn right to Monea Castle.

Monea Castle – *Proceed up the drive; after 0.25mi/0.3km turn right at the gates of the house.* The ruined castle, one of the largest and best-preserved of the 17C tower houses, was built on a rocky bluff in 1618 by Malcolm Hamilton. The bawn wall, added in 1622, has two flanker towers; the one in the northwest corner beside the entrance gate has internal compartments which suggest it served as a dovecote. The crow-stepped gables and the corbelling on the towers and turrets are characteristic of the late-medieval Scottish style. Inside the three-storey castle are vaulted kitchens on the ground floor and five chambers on the upper two floors.

On leaving turn left; in Monea turn left onto B 81 to return to Enniskillen.

Upper Lough Erne

Crom Estate ⊘ – *21mi/34km S of Enniskillen by A 4 and A 34; in Newtownbutler turn right onto a minor road.* The estate, a National Nature Reserve, which lies on the east shore of Lough Erne, consists of parkland, oak woodland (1 800 acres/728ha) and wetland and lake shore (12mi/19km), unimproved fen meadows with reed beds, and a large heronry.

The **Visitor Centre** presents an exhibition about the history of the estate, its owners, the Creighton family from Scotland, later ennobled as Earls of Erne, the 17C planter's castle and the present 19C castle *(private)* designed by Edward Blore in 1838, the yachting parties held in the 19C.

The **Culliaghs Trail** passes through the oak woodland which contains a hide for mammal- and bird-watching. The longer trail *(1hr)* follows the lake shore to the remains of Crom Old Castle (17C) and two ancient yew trees once part of a formal garden, to the Boat House, across the White Bridge to the old Garden Orchard and Walled Garden on Inisherk, back to the mainland to the Old Boat House, the summer house, the Turf House, the Riding School and Stable Yard, before crossing the main drive and skirting the deer park.

Crom boat-house

GIANT'S CAUSEWAY★★★

Co Antrim
Michelin Atlas p 102 and Map 923 – M 2

The Giant's Causeway painted c 1740 by Susanna Drury

The Giant's Causeway is the most famous natural wonder in Northern Ireland. According to legend it was built by the giant Finn McCool so that the Scottish giant could accept his invitation to Ireland for a trial of strength. When the latter had returned home defeated, the causeway sank beneath the sea. In fact the Causeway itself is the most spectacular of a series of similar geological features to be found all along the North Antrim Coast. These were caused by a volcanic eruption which took place some 60 million years ago and affected not only northeast Ireland but also western Scotland (similar rock formations are to be found in Fingal's Cave on Staffa) the Faroes, Iceland and Greenland. Several flows of lava exuded from fissures in the chalk and solidified into layers of hard basalt which cracked as they contracted, forming masses of adjoining columns; the majority are hexagonal in shape although some have four, five, seven, eight and even nine sides.
It was, however, little known until about 1740 when a local artist, Susanna Drury, painted two views of the Causeway, from the east and the west, which are now in the Ulster Museum in Belfast. Engravings of her work aroused great speculation among British and French geologists about the origins of the Causeway.

Access and Cliff Walks – From the Visitor Centre to the Causeway proper takes 10min on foot. In the summer there is a bus-shuttle service ⊘.
For a bird's-eye view of the Causeway itself continue eastwards into the middle of Port Noffer and take the Shepherd's Path (steps) up to the clifftop; return to the Visitor Centre along the cliff path.
There is a round tour between the Giant's Causeway and Benbane Head (5mi/8km – 2hr there and back on foot). From Port Noffer continue eastwards, before following the path (steep steps) up to Benbane Head and returning along the cliff top path. The path is liable to erosion; stout shoes are required and children should be accompanied by an adult.
From Benbane Head the path continues east along the cliffs (2hr); it is narrow and difficult in bad weather and may be closed owing to erosion; it rejoins the road (B 146) at Dunseverick Castle *(see below)*.

Adjacent Sights – See Antrim, Glens of Antrim, Lough Neagh, Portrush.

Visitor Centre ⊘ – This attractive modern building, which echoes the roofline of the Bushmills Distillery *(see p 363)*, contains a restaurant and a shop and an excellent video and exhibition about the Causeway Coast: geological formation, flora and fauna, mining and kelping, and various other local activities such as the Ballycastle Lammas Fair.

Early Tourism

In the early days visitors to the Causeway travelled by boat or on horseback. Numbers greatly increased with the advent of the railway line from Belfast to Portrush. In 1883 a hydroelectric narrow-gauge tramway, powered by the River Bushmills, was built from Portrush to Bushmills and extended to the Causeway in 1887; it closed in 1949 unable to compete with road transport. Some people came on day trips from Belfast; others stayed in one of the two hotels or the nearby boarding-houses.
The Causeway swarmed with souvenir sellers and unofficial guides who repeated fantastic legends about the formation of the Causeway and invented fanciful names for the different features.

★★★**Giant's Causeway** 1 – The Causeway proper extends from the foot of the cliffs into the sea like a sloping pavement. It consists of about 40 000 hexagonal columns, resembling stacks of old threepenny bits, and has been divided by the action of the waves into three sections: the Little Causeway, the Middle Causeway and the Grand Causeway. The columns themselves are split horizontally, forming concave and convex surfaces. The individual features are not easily recognisable by their local names: the **Wishing Well** (1) was a natural freshwater spring in the Little Causeway; the **Wishing Chair** (2) on the Middle Causeway is formed by a single column, the seat, backed by a semicircle of taller columns; the **Giant's Gate** is the natural gap carrying the coastal path through the **Tilted Columns** (3).

East across Port Noffer the columns (40ft/12m) of the **Organ** (4) are visible in the cliff face; the **Chimney Tops** (6) are silhouetted against the skyline.

Benvarden Garden

Bird's-eye View – The headland, Aird Snout, gives an excellent view of the Causeway from above. From the next headland, Weir's Snout, there is a view across Port Ganny *(east)* to the Causeway and down into Portnaboe *(west)* where a volcanic dyke, known as the Camel's Back, is visible in the sea beyond the slipway where early visitors to the Causeway used to land.

Benbane Head 2 – The walk to this headland from the Causeway includes many of the associated volcanic formations along the Causeway Coast.

After Port Noffer comes Port Reostan, where the curved columns of the **Harp** (5), a product of the first lava flow, are set in a natural **amphitheatre**. The next headland is distinguished by the **Chimney Tops** (6), three rock stacks formed by the second lava flow. Through a passage in the rocks the path enters Port Na Spaniagh where the *Gerona*, a galleass of the Spanish Armada, was wrecked in 1588 with no survivors; the treasures recovered by diving on the wreck in 1968 are now in the Ulster Museum in Belfast. Beyond the next headland, the Horse Back, lies Port na Callian; the further promontory consists of the **King and his Nobles** (7), a file of figures apparently riding in from the sea. After skirting the next two bays the path climbs up past the **Horseshoe** (8) in the rocks *(left)* to **Hamilton's Seat** on Benbane Head. It is named after Dr William Hamilton who published his *Letters concerning the Northern Coast of Antrim* in 1786, and is a perfect place from which to survey the geological formations and admire the **view★★**, which on a clear day reaches to the mountains of Donegal *(west)*, and Rathlin Island and in Scotland the Mull of Kintyre *(east)*.

The clifftop path back to the Causeway Centre provides a bird's-eye view of the volcanic formations.

Dunseverick Castle – *Accessible by road (B 146) from Bushmills.* The importance accorded to this castle in the written records is supported less by the scanty ruins than by the impressive site, a promontory separated from the mainland by two defiles. Dunseverick, which means the royal fort of Sobhairce, was visited by St Patrick in the 5C and was linked to Tara in Co Meath by the road through the Moyry Gap *(see p 360)*.

LISBURN

LIOS NA GCEARRBHACH – Co Antrim – Population 42 110
Michelin Atlas p 99 and Map 923 – O N 4

The town is situated in the middle of the linen-producing district in Ulster, and throughout the 19C it produced half of the linen woven in Ulster. Louis Crommelin made it his headquarters when he was appointed Linen Overseer of Ireland by William III.

In 1707 most of the town was destroyed by fire, except for the Assembly Rooms at the top of the market square.

Irish Linen Tour ⊘ – Guided tour of various linen factories and the Linen Centre in Lisburn.

Walks – Lagan Canal towpath walk from Lisburn to Belfast *(9mi/14.5km)*.

Adjacent Sights – See Belfast, Newry, Downpatrick, Strangford Lough.

SIGHTS

★**Irish Linen Centre and Lisburn Museum** ⊘ – Lisburn's Assembly Rooms have been adapted and extended to house the town's museum as well as extensive and attractive displays, which tell the story of the area's linen industry from its origins in the 17C to the present. The emphasis is not only on technique, but on the beauty and adaptability of the product and on the lives of the people involved in its manufacture. There are reminders of the role of linen in the ancient world in the form of material from Tutankhamun's tomb. In the Middle Ages Irish flax was exported to England to be woven into cloth. Then in the 17C English and Scottish weavers helped establish the weaving industry, eventually under the direction of Crommelin, whose portrait hangs in the main hall of the Assembly Rooms. There are live demonstrations of spinning and weaving, a re-creation of a family at work in a late-18C–early-19C spinner's cottage, and a vivid reconstruction of the weavers' toil in "Webster's", a hypothetical 19C mill, where conditions, however harsh, were nevertheless preferable to life on the farm –

> *"I'll ne'er despise the weaving trade,*
> *The shuttle's lighter than the spade".*
>
> John Dicky (1818).

Exquisite traditional items in diaper and damask are contrasted with their contemporary equivalents, where the creative potential of the computer has been harnessed to produce designs of great appeal and originality.

Temporary exhibitions draw on the extensive local history and other collections from the town museum.

Christchurch Cathedral ⊘ – The town is dominated by the cathedral, a good example of Planters' Gothic (1623, reconstructed in 1708); in the graveyard *(south side)* is the Crommelin tomb.

Lisburn Castle Park – North of the cathedral is the site of the **castle**, now a small public park enclosed within the surviving walls; from the parapet there is a good view of the Lagan winding past below.

Sir Richard Wallace

From 1873 to 1885 the MP for Lisburn was Sir Richard Wallace, owner of the Wallace Collection in London, whose mansion, built in imitation of Hertford House in London, stands opposite the entrance to the Castle Park.

EXCURSIONS

★**Hillsborough** *2.5mi/5km S of Lisburn by minor roads*

This charming town acquired its Georgian aspect under Wills Hill (1718-92), created Marquess of Downshire in 1789.

At the top of the hill on the west side of the square is **Hillsborough Castle**, which was begun in 1760 by Wills Hill, later became the residence of the Governor of Northern Ireland and is now used for state functions. It stands behind an elegant wrought-iron screen with gates, erected in 1936 but originally designed in 1745 for Richill Castle in Co Armagh, probably by the Thornberry brothers.

Court House ⊘ – In the centre of the square stands a two-storey block pierced by an archway, which was built as a market house in 1760; two wings were added in about 1810 to contain the courthouse and a larger market hall.

The informative **exhibition on justice and law** begins with a summary of Brehon law tracing parallels with modern penal policy, reviews the origins of Common Law via written panels and an audio-visual presentation *(10min)*, and describes the traditions of legal dress with life-size mannequins.

★**Hillsborough Fort** ⊘ – The gates on the east side of the square open into a drive leading to the fort, which was begun c 1630 to command the chief roads in Co Down, and was completed in 1650 by Col Arthur Hill, who was appointed hereditary constable with 20 warders in 1650 by Charles II, who declared it a royal fort. It is laid out as a square (270ft/82m x 270ft/82m) with a spear-shaped bastion at each corner to provide flanking fire from heavy cannon.

In 1770 Wills Hill created another entrance in the northeast rampart, surmounted by a gazebo with tracery windows, and converted the gatehouse in the north-west rampart into a little fort in the Gothic style with pointed doors and windows and hood-mouldings supported on grotesquely-sculptured heads; large-scale entertainments were held on the first floor of the gatehouse or in the open enclosure.

The central ditch is part of a circular trench revealed by excavations (1966–69) which suggest that the site had been occupied since c 500–1000.

St Malachy's Church – The Anglican church, built in 1662 on the site of its predecessor (1636–41), was enlarged (1760–73) by Wills Hill, who added the main tower and spire and the two subsidiary towers, and furnished the interior with

Walled Garden, Rowallane

J Harpur/National Trust Photographic Library

Irish oak Gothic woodwork and box pews which are raised in the transepts. Sir Hamilton Harty (1879–1941), the conductor, whose father was church organist, is buried in the churchyard.

★Rowallane Gardens ⊘

10mi/16km E of Hillsborough by B 178 towards Carryduff, B 6 to Saintfield and A 7 south

The gardens (52 acres/21ha), which are famous for massed plantings of azaleas and rhododendrons, are the work of a plantsman, Hugh Armitage Moore, who inherited the estate in 1903. During the next half-century he turned the drumlins with their light acid soil into a natural garden: a rock garden on a natural outcrop of stone; patches of wild flowers to attract butterflies; a spring ground and a stream ground; walled garden with fuchsias and shrub roses. In the old wood the stone walls between the original fields are still standing. The pleasure grounds behind the house (National Trust headquarters) extend in a great grass sweep to a small pond.

Lagan Valley *9mi/14.5km – half a day*

The valley of the River Lagan, which flows north through Belfast and enters the sea in Belfast Lough, is one of the most fertile areas in Northern Ireland. It now forms a Regional Park, traversed by the **Lagan Canal**, which was built to bring coal from Coalisland via Lough Neagh to Belfast; ironically it was mostly used to carry coal imported through Belfast. Under the Lagan Navigation Company, founded in 1843, it became Ulster's most successful waterway but its use declined in the 1930s; it was closed in 1958 and its course west from Lisburn to Moira turned into a motorway.

From Lisburn take A 1 N; in Hilden turn right (sign).

Hilden Brewery Visitor Centre ⊘ – The brewery occupies a Georgian house, once visited by William Wordsworth, adjoining a pleasant courtyard. An exhibition in the

NITB, Belfast

Lambeg Drums

347

restaurant covers the history of beer-drinking and brewing, Hilden Village and the brewery building. The guided tours of the brewery take place before and after lunch.

Continue N on A 1 and turn right under the railway bridge onto B 103 to Lambeg.

Lambeg – This attractive village has given its name to the huge drums (over 30lb/14kg) with painted decoration which are played in the Orange Day parades; they were introduced to Ireland from the Netherlands by William III's army.

Continue on B 103 to Drumbeg. Car park (left) opposite the church.

Drumbeg Church ⊘ – From the magnificent Lych Gate (1878) the footpath passes through arches of yew up to the church which stands on a knoll. The present church (1870) is cruciform with a shallow apsidal chancel and an interesting wooden roof. The entrance porch contains a stone, marked "A Free Howse 1675", to which is attached a touching love story retold alongside. The earliest record of a church here dates from 1306 but the dedication to St Patrick and its position by a ford suggest that a church was in existence much earlier.

Continue N on B 103.

Dixon Park – *Car park.* The park is famous for the rose trial grounds (11 acres/4ha) which contain about 30 000 roses. The final judging of the trial roses takes place during **Belfast Rose Week** (mid July) which attracts breeders from many parts of the world. Originally the grounds of a private house on the River Lagan, the park was presented to Belfast Corporation by Lady Edith Stewart Dixon in 1959 so that its mature trees, woodland, copses and rhododendrons could be enjoyed by all.

Continue N on B 103. At the roundabout turn right onto the dual carriageway and right again.

Malone House ⊘ – *Car park.* In 1603 James I granted the Barnett demesne to the Chichester family, later to become Earls of Donegall. Since then three houses have occupied the hilltop overlooking the Lagan crossing. The present house, which was severely damaged by terrorist bombs in November 1976, was built in the late 1820s and probably also designed by William Wallace Legge, who later bought the lease of the whole demesne. Owing to the existence of accurate records it was possible to rebuild the house to its original design.

The plain and unpretentious exterior belies the elegant and spacious interior. The broad T-shaped hall leads to a stone staircase with crinoline-bowed iron balusters set in an apsidal stairwell, with sculpture niches flanking the tall arched window. The doorways are framed by Classical surrounds with decorative reliefs and console brackets supporting triangular pediments.

From the upper windows there is a magnificent view over the garden to the wooded grounds, which slope south down to the modern road bridge spanning the Lagan, beside the five stone arches of **Shaw's Bridge** (1711), which replaced an oak bridge built by Captain Shaw in 1655 so that Cromwell's cannon could cross the river.

On leaving the park turn right; after crossing the bridge turn right; take the road along the south bank to Edenderry (sign).

Edenderry – The road ends beside the river among five terraces of red-brick cottages and a chapel; the weaving mill which they served no longer exists.

Return to the last T-junction; turn right onto Ballynahatty Road; after 1mi/1.6km turn right (sign "Giant's Ring").

Giant's Ring – *Car park.* The Ring is a huge bank of gravel and boulders enclosing a circle (600ft/183m in diameter) with a megalithic chambered grave in the middle. Its purpose is unknown but it may have been a place of assembly or worship and its construction would have required large resources.

LONDONDERRY★

DOIRE – Co Londonderry – Population 72 334
Michelin Atlas p 101 and Map 923 – K 3

Londonderry is often known by its original name, Derry, meaning an oak grove; the prefix "London" was added in the 17C when large areas in the north of Ireland were granted to the London livery companies for development.

The old city, which stands on a hill on the west bank of the River Foyle, is still surrounded by its 17C walls.

Southeast rise the smooth rounded Sperrin Mountains; west and north lies the wild grandeur of the mountains of Donegal.

Monastic Foundation – According to tradition, the monastery of Derry was founded in 546 by St Columba (*Colmcille* in Irish). Derry was occupied by the English in 1565 and 1600. During the four-month rebellion of Sir Cahir O'Doherty in 1608, his forces attacked and captured Derry but could not sustain their momentum after his death at Kilmacrenan in Donegal.

Siege of Londonderry

In the uncertainty created by James II's flight to France and William of Orange's landing in Devon, 13 Derry apprentices locked the city gates against a Jacobite regiment under the Earl of Antrim sent to garrison the town in December 1688. The citizens declared for William and received an influx of supporters although food supplies were low. In March James II landed in Ireland with an army of 20 000 and in April besieged the city, erecting a boom across the river which held the relief ships at bay for seven weeks.

After the departure of Lundy, who had proposed surrender, Major Henry Baker and the Revd George Walker took command. On 10 July a shell bearing terms for surrender was fired into the town by the besiegers; the defenders raised a crimson flag on the Royal Bastion to signify "No surrender".

The siege lasted 15 weeks during which thousands of the 30 000 within the walls died of starvation. On 28 July 1689 the boom was broken and the relief ships sailed through to the quay. Three days later the Jacobite army retreated.

The Irish Society – Under the scheme for the colonisation of Ulster *(see p 64)* with settlers from Britain, The Honourable The Irish Society was consti-tuted by Royal Charter in 1613 to plant the County of Col-eraine, which was renamed County Londonderry. Most of the land was parcelled out to the 12 main livery companies of London but the towns of Derry and Coleraine were retained by the Society, which still uses its income from fisheries and property to sup-port projects of general benefit to the community.

Adjacent Sights – See Buncrana, Donegal Coast, Donegal Glens, Portrush, Sperrin Mountains.

THE WALLED CITY

★★**City Walls and Gates** ○ – The walls (1mi/1.6km long) enclosing the Plantation town were built from 1613 to 1618 by The Irish Society and originally pierced by four gates. **Ferryquay Gate** was closed by the 13 Apprentice Boys at the beginning of the siege in 1688; **Shipquay Gate** is surmounted by five of the cannon which defended the city during the Great Siege; southwest of **Butcher's Gate** stands the **Royal Bastion** on which Col Michelburn hoisted the crimson flag to signify "No sur-render"; **Bishop's Gate** was rebuilt in 1789 as a triumphal arch to commemorate William of Orange. The other three openings were created later.

★**St Columb's Cathedral** ○ (Z) – The decision to build was taken by The Irish Society in 1613 but the cathedral was not begun until 1628; it was consecrated in 1634, the first cathedral to be built in the British Isles since the Reformation. The original plans made provision for a chancel but it was not added until 1887. The cathedral is in the late-Perpendicular style with a fully embattled exterior. The tower houses a peal of 13 bells and is surmounted by an early-19C spire (191ft/58m).

The **mortar shell** containing terms for surrender which was fired into the city during the siege in 1689 is preserved in the porch.

The Baptistery *(left)* commemorates Mrs CF Alexander (1818–95), wife of the Bishop of Derry; she wrote several well-known hymns which are illustrated in one of the windows in the north wall.

The window in the Choir Vestry *(right)*, presented in 1913 by the descendants of the defenders of the city, depicts the Closing of the Gates in 1688 *(left)*, the Relief of the city in 1689 *(centre)*, and the Centenary celebrations in 1789 *(right)*. The superb open-timbered **nave roof** is supported on stone corbels carved to represent the Bishops of Derry from 1634 to 1867 and the Revd George Walker. The mahogany organ case dates from 1747. In the north aisle are several interesting wall tablets; the fourth one incorporates the mortuary symbols of the period.

The **bishop's throne**, unusually placed in the nave in 1861, is a splendid mahogany chair of Chinese Chippendale (18C), probably given by the Earl Bishop *(see p 364)*. On the chancel arch above the pulpit is a **Cross of Nails**, a gift from Coventry Cathedral, signifying peace and reconciliation. Below the east window of the Ascension is a reredos of Caen stone; the mosaics in the wings represent the four Evangelists and St Patrick and *(second from right)* St Columba. The coats of arms in the hand-made carpet are those of The Irish Society, the See of Derry and Raphoe, and the See of Derry. The two flags were captured from the French during the Siege in 1689; only the wire work and the poles are original.

The **chapter house** *(for access ask the Verger)* was built in 1910 and contains several items of interest: padlocks and keys of the original city gates; cannon balls;

LONDONDERRY

In Northern Ireland parking in the town centre may be restricted to attended vehicles only.

Governor Walker's sword; fragments of the crimson flag of Col Michelburn; silver plate, some of which dates from 1613; a pair of pistols and a kidney-shaped desk, thought to belong to the Earl Bishop; portraits of Mrs Alexander and her husband; a copy of her book *Hymns for Little Children*.

★**Tower Museum** ⊘ (Y) – The medieval-style modern building houses a comprehensive display about the history of the city of Derry using historical artefacts, wall panels and audio-visual and theatrical devices.

A brick-built tunnel, typical of the 17C houses, leads to the monastic origins of Derry in an oak grove, the 17C Plantation, the Siege of Derry and its aftermath, 19C emigration, the Partition of Ireland, the Second World War and post-war troubles.

Fifth Province ⊘ (Y) – *Butcher Street*. Embedded in the modern Calgach conference and office centre is this ambitious and imaginative evocation of the history and culture of the Celts. A wide variety of contemporary techniques, including exciting voyages by module and space shuttle, give magical life to the past and demonstrate its relevance to present-day people of Irish descent.

Craft Village (Y) – Neglected back yards have been artfully transformed into a web of picturesque alleyways, centred on a little square and lined with a variety of traditionally styled buildings housing cafés and specialist shops.

City Centre – *Shipquay Street* (Y), one of the steepest commercial streets in the British Isles, contains several imposing buildings and basement bars.
The **Diamond** (Y), where the Town Hall used to stand, is marked by a war memorial. The four main streets lead to the four main gates.
The **Apprentice Boys' Hall** (YZ) stands on the site of the original Shambles.

Bishop's Street Within (Z) contains several fine buildings. The offices of **The Irish Society** are housed in a dignified Georgian building (1764). Next door is **The Deanery**, an elegant Georgian house with a splendid doorway. The **courthouse** is a white sandstone building in the Greek revival style with an Ionic portico. Opposite stands the former **bishop's palace** (now the Freemasons' Hall), built of red brick by the Earl Bishop; it stands on the site of the house occupied by Col Henry Baker, who was in command of the defences of the city during the siege.

ADDITIONAL SIGHTS

★**Long Tower Church** ⊘ (X) – This is the oldest Roman Catholic church in Derry (1784–86). The present building has an interesting Rococo interior with extensive steeply sloping galleries. It stands on the site of Templemore, a great medieval church built in 1164, and its name recalls the Long Tower (10C), all that remained when the medieval church was destroyed by an explosion in 1567. From the churchyard there is a fine view of the Royal Bastion.

★**Guildhall** ⊘ (Y) – The Guildhall, which has twice been severely damaged – in 1908 by fire and in 1972 by bombs, was erected in 1890 in the late-Gothic style with a loan from the Irish Society. The river façade is richly ornamented; the corner tower contains a large four-faced clock. A reproduction of Follingby's painting of the Relief of Derry decorates the marble-faced vestibule. The stained-glass windows are the work of Ulster craftsmen: London scenes on the stairs, early views of Derry in the Great Hall, which is panelled in oak and has a richly decorated ceiling.

Harbour Museum ⊘ (Y) – The grandiose 19C building, which once housed the meetings of the Londonderry Port and Harbour Commissioners, is now a museum with paintings, models and all kinds of maritime memorabilia. The dominant exhibit is the largest curragh ever built, constructed in 1963 to recreate the legendary voyage of St Columba to Iona.

St Eugene's Cathedral ⊘ (X) – Northwest of the city centre, between a district of elegant Georgian terraces and the green peace of Brooke Park, stands the Roman Catholic Cathedral, which was dedicated to St Eugene in 1873 by Bishop Keely, to whom the great east window is a memorial. The building was designed in the Gothic revival style by JJ McCarthy in 1853 and finally completed with a cross on the top of the spire in 1903.

Foyle Valley Railway Centre ⊘ (X M) – Londonderry was once the focal point of no fewer than four railway companies, including the Londonderry and Enniskillen, "possibly the least efficient if not the most dangerous railway ever to operate in Ireland". Here too was the terminus of the County Donegal Railway, which was the most extensive of all the Irish narrow-gauge systems (125mi/200km). The Centre has steam engines, coaches, an old goods wagon, signals, signs and luggage. Excursion trains drawn by diesel car (1934) operate on a stretch of narrow-gauge line (2mi/3.2km) beside the Foyle. It is proposed to extend the line upstream to St Johnston (9mi/14.5km).

★**Workhouse Museum** ⊘ – *23 Glendermott Road, Waterside*. The city workhouse, designed by George Wilkinson and opened in 1840 with 800 inmates, now houses a library on the ground floor and a museum on the two floors above. The first stage has excellent displays and film footage about the role played by the city in the Second World War, and particularly in the Battle of the Atlantic. On the upper floor, the grim 19C workhouse conditions have been recreated; an original display compares the 1845–49 Irish famine with the modern famines of the Horn of Africa and especially Somalia.

Co Down

Michelin Atlas p 99 and Map 923 – P 4

5mi/8km SE of Newtownards by A 20

Adjacent Sights – See Bangor, Down-patrick, Strangford Lough.

A belt of trees on the east shore of Strangford Lough shelters the famous Mount Stewart **gardens** which complement the house, designed by George Dance and William Vitruvius Morrison. The banqueting house, an imitation of the Tower of the Winds in Athens, was designed by James "Athenian" Stuart.

Soldiers and Statesmen

The Mount Stewart estate was bought in 1774 by Alexander Stewart, whose Scottish forebears were granted land near Moville on the Inishowen Peninsula in the 17C. He built a house called Mount Pleasant, which was enlarged by his son Robert, made Marquess of Londonderry in 1816. The best-known member of the family is his elder son, Lord Castlereagh, who entered politics in 1790, aged 21, and rose to be Foreign Secretary and leader of the House of Commons at Westminster. His half-brother, the third Marquess, fought in the Peninsular Wars and became ambassador in Vienna. Later generations have followed in their footsteps as soldiers and as politicians at Westminster or Stormont.

TOUR ⊙

Gardens – The gardens were created by Edith, Lady Londonderry, in the 1920s to enhance the immediate surroundings of the house and to absorb some of the surplus labour after the First World War. The plants are drawn from all over the world; the more formal arrangements are closer to the house.

The huge Irish Yews near the house look down on the **Italian Garden** which contains mainly herbaceous plants; it is enclosed at the east end by the **Dodo Terrace**, which is decorated with stone animals, recalling the nicknames, not always complimentary, given by Lady Londonderry to some of her friends who were members of the Ark Club, which she founded in London during the First World War. To the south is the **Spanish Garden** designed after a ceiling pattern in the Temple of the Winds *(see below)*. The theme of the **Shamrock Garden**, named for its shape, is Ireland: a topiary harp and a bed in the shape and colour of the Red Hand of Ulster.

The hill which overlooks the **lake**, created in 1846–48, provides a superb **view** over Strangford Lough. A genuine but miniature Japanese pagoda stands beside the **Ladies' Walk**, an old path to the dairy and kitchen gardens.

House – The west wing was built in 1804–05 by George Dance. The major part of the house (1825–35) is the work of William Vitruvius Morrison, who produced a symmetrical design in the same dark stone with lighter dressings and added a balustrade at roof level to create a sense of unity. A giant Ionic portico wide enough to take a carriage screens the entrance.

The interior is richly decorated with portraits of the family and their racehorses, Irish and English furniture, collections of porcelain and Classical sculpture.

The portraits in the **Dining Room** include Lord Mountjoy (in armour; *see p 91*), William of Orange and Schomberg. Lining the wall are the 22 Empire chairs used by the delegates at the Congress of Vienna in 1815.

The next room displays **souvenirs of Lord Castlereagh**, who as Foreign Secretary attended the Congress of Vienna in 1814 and the Peace of Paris in 1815: his portrait after Lawrence over the fireplace, busts of contemporary political figures and a bust of Napoleon. The five 18C angle chairs made of padouk wood are Goanese. Much of the **woodwork** in the west wing is by John Ferguson: in the Music Room the inlaid wooden floor in oak, mahogany and bog-fir reflects the curved plaster ceiling.

The **Rome Bedroom** reflects the 1920s taste for strong colours and rich materials. The spacious **Drawing Room**, created by Morrison out of three smaller rooms, contains portraits of Viscount and Viscountess Castlereagh and many objects of virtue. The room is furnished with three Aubusson carpets, two 18C Italian pier-glasses at the ends, a large Austrian inlaid walnut writing-desk, a Boulle bracket clock in red tortoiseshell and brass. The lamps include several translucent alabaster and Carrara marble urns and vases, and a pair of tripod candlesticks carved with winged lions, all fitted with electricity.

Temple of the Winds – *30min there and back on foot from the house or 200yd/183m SE by road to the car park and 4min there and back on foot.*

J Cornish/National Trust Photographic Library

Italian Garden, Mount Stewart

The temple stands on a mound with a clear view across Strangford Lough to Scrabo Hill where the stone for it was quarried. It was designed as a banqueting house for the 1st Marquess of Londonderry by James "Athenian" Stuart in 1783 and is an accurate copy of the Temple of the Winds in Athens except for the balconies. A cantilevered spiral stair rises under an elegant coffered ceiling in the rear turret. The inlaid wooden floor of the first-floor room matches the coffers, scallops and scrolls of the plasterwork ceiling. The domestic offices where the meals were assembled are concealed underground and linked to the vaulted basement by a passage.

MOURNE MOUNTAINS★★

Co Down
Michelin Atlas p 99 and Map 923 – N O 5 – Local map below

The Mourne Mountains reach their highest point in Slieve Donard (2 796ft/852m) and extend westwards to Carlingford Lough and north into rolling foothills. The **Kingdom of Mourne** was the name given to the strip of land between the mountains and the sea, a region of small fields divided by drystone walls where for centuries a life of farming and fishing continued largely undisturbed by external events. The Anglo-Normans built castles at Newcastle and Greencastle but only the latter, once the capital of the kingdom, has survived. Newcastle is now a seaside resort on Dundrum Bay and the main town of the area.

DUNDRUM BAY

Newcastle – The town "where the mountains of Mourne sweep down to the sea", immortalised in verse by Percy French *(see p 134)*, is one of Ireland's foremost resorts, which began to develop in the early 19C when seaside holidays became fashionable. From the tiny harbour a long promenade of hotels, shops and amusement arcades extends northeast beside a long sandy beach overlooking Dundrum Bay. Beyond the red-brick bulk of the Slieve Donard Hotel, built by the railway company in 1898, lie the championship links of the Royal County Down Golf Club.

Our Lady of the Assumption ⊙, the Roman Catholic church, is a circular building (1967), decorated with bold and vivid stained-glass windows installed in 1969; the clerestory windows represent the 12 Apostles with their appropriate symbols; the windows in the side chapels bear a symbolic representation of the Birth, Life, Passion and Crucifixion of Jesus.

Donard Park on the banks of the Glen River was once the grounds of Donard Lodge (demolished), which was built in the 1830s as a summer house by Earl Annesley of Castlewellan *(see below)*. There is a path which leads up from the Donard Bridge through Donard Wood to **Slieve Donard** (2 796ft/850m). The highest peak in the

Mourne Mountains, originally known as Slieve Slanga, was renamed in honour of Donard, a local chief, who is supposed to have been converted by St Patrick. After his death in 506, pilgrims used to make an annual pilgrimage on 25 July to St Donard's cairn on the summit.

Murlough National Nature Reserve ⊘ – *2mi/3.2km E of Newcastle by A 2. Car park.* This reserve consists of a stretch of sand dunes, some at least 5 000 years old, between the Carrigs River and the northwest shore of Dundrum Bay. Many plants thrive on the soil, providing an environment attractive to a wide variety of birds. Archaeologists have discovered evidence of early human habitation as well as a tripod **dolmen** (8ft/2.5m high), which is about 4 000 years old.

★**Dundrum Castle** ⊘ – *4mi/6.4m E of Newcastle by A 2; in Dundrum turn left uphill to car park.* The ruins of the castle stand on an attractive grassed and wooded site on a hilltop north of the town. It is also known as the Magennis Castle after the Irish family of that name who held it in the later Middle Ages. The Lower Ward (13C to 15C) contains the ruins of a once-grand house built by the Blundell family in the 17C. The Upper Ward, the oldest part of the present ruins, was built on a previously occupied site, probably by John de Courcy c 1177 to defend the Lecale Peninsula. The natural defences have been supplemented by an impressively deep rock-cut ditch. The circular 13C keep was modified in the 15C; the original entrance at first-floor level was linked to the curtain wall by a bridge. In place of the usual well, a cistern, cut into the rock and fed by seepage, supplied the castle with water. From the parapet of the keep there is a splendid *view* (E) of the Lecale Peninsula, and (SE) of the Blackstaff estuary and the narrow channel leading into Dundrum Bay, which extends from the lighthouse on St John's Point *(east)* to Slieve Donard and the Mourne Mountains *(SW)*.

INLAND

★**Tollymore Forest Park** ⊘ – Tollymore (1 235 acres/500ha) straddles the Shimna, an excellent salmon river which rises in the northwest foothills of the Mourne Mountains.
There are many walks exploring the azalea walk, arboretum, wildfowl enclosure on the lake, cascade (30ft/9m), salmon leap, mill ponds and a weir on the river, Old Bridge (1726), Hermitage, Clanbrassil barn (c 1757) resembling a church, Gothic

Gate (1786) and Barbican Gate (1780) approached by an avenue of Himalayan cedars. The commercial forest area provides a habitat for foxes, otters, badgers, red squirrels and pine martens, moths, butterflies and many species of birds including woodcock.

It was James Hamilton, created Earl of Clanbrassil in 1756, who built the house (demolished) in 1730 and laid out the park in the naturalistic manner of William Kent; he planted many trees, particularly larch and some rare and exotic species. The follies were built by the second Earl. The estate then passed to the Earls of Roden who sold it to the State in 1939 and 1941.

★★Castlewellan Forest Park ⊙ – *4mi/6.4km N of Newcastle by A 50.* The park, which was sold to the Department of Agriculture in 1967, surrounds a lake providing excellent fishing. The

Boley Fair, Hilltown

Sculpture Trail *(3mi/5km)* along the lake shore presents pieces created since 1992 from natural materials, most of which were gathered in the park. There is an ice-house on the south shore and a pagan standing stone now covered with Christian symbols on the north bank. Higher up the hill behind the castle *(private)* are the **Annesley Gardens**, enclosed by a wall and embellished by two fountains; all the plants are labelled. The formal garden contains geometric beds and greenhouses; the informal **Arboretum** was planted between 1850 and 1900 and the surrounding parkland is thought to have been planted between 1740 and 1760. The rest of the estate, which rises to a central high point, Slievenaslat (896ft/273m), is covered in woodland.

The land at Castlewellan was purchased from the Magennises in 1742 by the Annesley family, originally of Breton origin, who moved to England during the Norman Conquest and thence to Ireland in the reign of Elizabeth I. They lived at The Grange, an

Castlewellan

355

18C farm beside the car park, or at Castlewellan Cottage (demolished) on the north shore of the lake, before building the present castle which was designed in the Scottish baronial style by William Burn in 1856.

Castlewellan – *4mi/6.4km N of Newcastle by A 50.* Population 2 133. The elegant town was laid out in 1750 by the Earl of Annesley. The buildings are pleasantly arranged round two squares; the market house (1764) stands in the centre of the western square; the eastern square is lined with trees.

Legananny Dolmen – *11mi/ 18km north of Newcastle by A 50 and side roads (signed) from north of Castlewellan.* The dolmen, which consists of a huge slanting capstone delicately balanced on three unusually low supporting stones, is a prehistoric burial monument. From its site on the south slope of Slieve Croob (1 745ft/ 532m) there is a magnificent view of the Mourne Mountains.

Brontë Centre ⊙ – *1.5mi/ 2.5km N of Rathfriland, off B 25 in Drumballyroney (sign).* The little white schoolhouse and church in this hamlet have been turned into an interpretative centre which makes the most of the area's connections with the Brontë family. The occasion of the first sermon preached by Patrick Brontë, father of the famous literary sisters, is recreated in the adjoining deconsecrated church.
A **tour** *(signed 10mi/16km)* leads to other sites associated with the family.

★**Drumena Cashel and Souterrain** – The cashel consists of an oval area enclosed by a drystone wall containing the foundations of a house and a T-shaped underground tunnel, called a souterrain. It was a farmstead enclosure and dates from the early-Christian period.

★**Silent Valley Reservoir** ⊙ – *Car park at the end of the drive.* The dam and reservoir (2.5mi/4km x 1.5mi/2.4km) were built between 1928 and 1933 to supply Belfast and Co Down with water (30 million gallons/136 million litres per day).

There is a pleasant walk *(2hr there and back on foot)* to the dam which provides a superb **view**★ of the still waters of the reservoir at the foot of the west face of Slieve Binnian (2 441ft/744m). The **Mourne Wall**, which encloses the catchment area of the dam, can be seen snaking its way up the slope. From the east end of the dam the path continues north to **Ben Crom Reservoir** (3mi/4.8km). From the west end of the dam the path returns down the valley past **Sally Lough**, an attract-

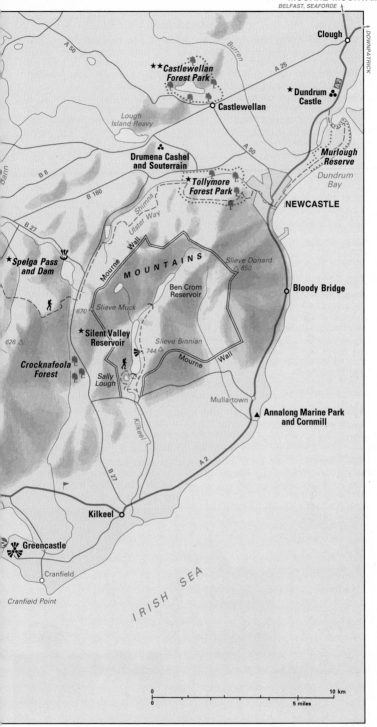

ive natural lake, through a grove of conifers and back over a wooden footbridge spanning the Kilkeel river.

★ **Spelga Pass and Dam** – From the dam there is a superb **view** north over the foothills of the Mourne Mountains to the rolling hills of Co Down.

The still waters of the reservoir, which provides fine angling for brown trout, cover the Deer's Meadow, formerly summer pasture which was inundated in 1959.

357

Brontë Country

Among the rolling northern foothills of the Mourne Mountains stands the ruined cottage *(plaque)* where Patrick Brontë, the father of the famous literary sisters, Charlotte, Emily and Anne, was born in 1777. In 1802 he went to study theology at St John's College, Cambridge. He was ordained in 1811 and moved to Haworth in Yorkshire in 1820.

He seems to have changed his name from Brunty (O'Pronitaigh), which is a local one, to Brontë before leaving Ireland; three years earlier in 1799 Lord Nelson had been made Duke of Brontë, a place in Sicily, by Ferdinand, King of Naples, in recognition of Nelson's assistance in recapturing Naples from the French.

Crocknafeola Forest – *Picnic areas.* The small coniferous forest stands beside the road which traverses the Mourne Mountains from north to south skirting the west face of Slieve Muck (2 198ft/670m).

ON THE COAST *East to west*

Bloody Bridge – In 1641 a group of prisoners, being conducted from Newry to Downpatrick to be exchanged for rebel prisoners, was murdered by the man in charge of them, an insurgent called Russell, who was afraid of being attacked.

★**Annalong Marine Park and Cornmill** ⊙ – *From A 2 turn S by the Police Station towards the shore.* On the banks of a stream stands an early-19C **cornmill** (restored), driven by a back-shot breast-shot water-wheel. It is typical of some 20 mills which existed in the Kingdom of Mourne in the late 17C and 18C for grinding wheat and oats or scutching flax. The Exhibition Room describes the history of milling.

The tour starts in the kiln house where the grain was dried overnight on perforated metal plates; anthracite was used to avoid tainting. The grain was then collected in hoppers and hoisted to the top storey where it was fed into one of three mill wheels: one of French burr for wheat, two of Mourne granite for dehusking and grinding oats. The water-wheel drives all the machinery in the mill and the teeth of the gear wheels are made of wood for easy replacement.

Kilkeel – Kilkeel is a small town, with stepped pavements and many changes of level, in an attractive setting at the mouth of the Kilkeel River.

The harbour is a lively place when the fishing fleet, the largest in Northern Ireland, is in port and the catch is being sold on the quay.

Greencastle ⊙ – The ruins of an Anglo-Norman stronghold, probably built in the mid 13C, are set on a low outcrop of rock extending into Carlingford Lough. The castle consisted of a large rectangular keep within a four-sided walled enclosure

Narrow Water Castle

Christopher Hill, Belfast

with D-shaped corner towers, which was surrounded by a moat cut in the rock. From the top of the keep there is a fine view. Cranfield Bay *(southeast)* has a sandy beach which is ideal for bathing.

Rostrevor Forest Park – *Forest Drive to car park.* The pine forest covers the south bank of the Kilbroney River and the steep northwest slopes of Slieve Martin (597ft/182m) beside a mountain stream. There are several walks – to the **Cloghmore**, a great glacial boulder, and to the **viewpoint★** high above Rostrevor Bay; on the opposite shore of Carlingford Lough rise the mountains of the Cooley Peninsula in the Republic.

Rostrevor – This is an attractive little town, which extends from the central square to the waterfront on Carlingford Lough. Even palm trees and mimosa thrive in its sheltered position at the foot of Slieve Martin.

Warrenpoint – Population 5 408. The town is both a port, equipped to take container traffic, and a pleasant resort, with a vast central square, used for markets and festivals, and a promenade facing south down Carlingford Lough between the Mourne Mountains and the Cooley Peninsula.

★**Narrow Water Castle** ⊙ – *2mi/3.2km N of Warrenpoint on A 2.* The castle occupies an attractive and strategic site on a promontory commanding the narrows at the mouth of the Newry River where it enters Carlingford Lough. It was built in the 1650s as an English garrison at the cost of £361 4s 2d. Although restored, it is an excellent example of a **tower house**, complete with its **bawn**. The entrance to the three-storeyed tower was defended by a murder-hole immediately above the door. On the first floor the wickerwork support, used in recent restoration of the windows, has been left in place to illustrate this peculiarly Irish technique. From the narrow windows there is a view of the river.

Lough NEAGH★

Co Antrim, Armagh, Tyrone and Londonderry
Michelin Atlas p 102 and Map 923 – M N 3 4

The largest lake in the British Isles (153sq mi/400km^2 and 40–50ft/12m–15m deep) is drained by the Lower Bann and fed by 10 rivers, which flow into it from the south, east and west.

The waters of Lough Neagh and its tributaries provide every kind of freshwater fish: rudd, roach, pike, eels as well as the rare dollaghan and pollan; giant pike in Lough Beg on the Lower Bann, bream in the Blackwater, trout and salmon in the Bann, Main, Six Mile Water, Blackwater, Ballinderry and Moyola rivers. At Toome, where the River Bann flows north out of the lake, there is an important eel fishery, which exports most of its catch.

Lough Neagh and its tiny northern neighbour, Lough Beg, are sites of international importance for wintering wildfowl; nature reserves have been established on many of the islands. Only in Antrim Bay is the shore lined with woodland; elsewhere it is low and marshy and sometimes infested with (non-biting) midges. As there is no shore road, the lake is best explored by boat.

Out and About

Cruising – Lake Cruises ⊙ are available from **Kinnego Marina** on the south shore and from **Sixmilewater Marina** in Antrim. Occasionally there is also a **Bann cruise** between Antrim and Castlerock *(35mi – 6/7hr)*.

Fishing Permits – Licences ⊙ for Lough Neagh are available from tackle shops and from the Fishery Conservancy Board in Portadown.

Permits ⊙ and **gillie services** for the Lower Bann are available from Bann Systems, Coleraine.

Adjacent Sights – See Antrim, Armagh, Belfast, Lisburn, Sperrin Mountains.

SIGHTS *In clockwise order starting from the south-east corner*

Lough Neagh Discovery Centre ⊙ – *South shore; Oxford Island; sign at Junction 10 on M 1.* This modern visitor centre, set among lakeside meadows and reached across a moat, is one of the best places to make the acquaintance of the lough. It presents an exhibition about the wildlife, history and management of the lake through audio-visual shows and touch-screen computers; there are five bird-watching hides and footpaths *(4mi/7km)* along the shoreline – reedbeds, wildflower meadows, woodland – and marina in Kinnego Bay.

Peatlands Park ⊙ – *South shore; sign at Junction 13 on M 1.* The park (618 acres/250ha), including Derryadd Lough, was used in the 19C for hunting and growing timber. About half the acreage has been designated a **National Nature**

Reserve with restricted access to protect the natural flora and fauna. The public park includes a **bog garden**, two small lakes, an orchard and woodland; **demonstrations of turf cutting** by hand and machine are given at the outdoor turbary station. The **narrow-gauge railway** installed by the previous owners, the Irish Peat Development Company, provides a scenic tour in trains hauled by the original diesel engines. General information on bogs and peat extraction is displayed in the **Visitor Centre**.

Maghery – *South shore*. Country park from which Coney Island, a densely wooded island, can be visited by boat.

Ballyronan – *West shore*. Small marina and beach enhanced by pleasant walks.

Mountjoy Castle – *West shore*. A ruined early-17C castle with gun loops, built of stone and well-weathered brick.

Kinturk Cultural Centre ⊘ – *West shore*. A lavish new community centre contains a fascinating exhibition dealing comprehensively with the long-established Lough Neagh eel fishery.

★**Ardboe Cross** – *West shore, E of Cookstown by B 73*. The cross, which stands at the entrance to a graveyard round the ruins of a 17C church, is the finest in Ulster and extensively carved with biblical scenes: Old Testament on the east side and New Testament on the west. The cross probably dates from the 10C and marked the site of Ardboe Abbey, probably a 6C foundation, which was associated with St Colman. From Ardboe Point there is an extensive **view**★ of Lough Neagh surrounded by mountains: Slieve Gallion and the Sperrin Mountains *(northwest)*, Slemish *(northeast)*, Divis Mountain *(east)*, the Mourne Mountains *(southeast)*.

Bellaghy Bawn ⊘ – *North shore; in Bellaghy, 4mi/7km N of A 6*. The 17C bawn (restored) in the village of Bellaghy was built by the Vintners' Company in 1619; its exhibits pay tribute to Seamus Heaney and his writing. As well as books and manuscripts, there is the opportunity to see a film introduced by Heaney and listen to recordings of his broadcasts.

Churchtown Point – *North shore*. A low promontory marked by a holy well and the ruins of Cranfield Church, which probably dates from the 13C and attracted many pilgrims in the past.

Shane's Castle Terrace – *North shore; see p 303*.

Seamus Heaney

The poet and Nobel Prize winner Seamus Heaney (b 1939) was born at his family's farm near Bellaghy. Much of his work, in particular his Lough Neagh cycle, reflects the influence of the landscapes and people of his youth. His feeling for the land of Ireland and his respect for those who, like his father, were bound to it by hard physical work, is carried over into his own physical act of writing:

> "Between my finger and my thumb
> The squat pen rests.
> I'll dig with it."
>
> *Digging* (1966)

NEWRY

Newry occupies a strategic position in the "Gap of the North", the Moyry Gap in the line of hills which separates Ulster from the plains of Meath.
The city has something of a split personality since it straddles the Clanrye River, which is the border between Co Down and Co Armagh, and the Town Hall (1893) is said to have been built over the river so that it should be in neither county. More recently a dual carriageway has separated the older east side of the city from the modern shopping centre.

16C Foundation – When Sir Nicholas Bagenal, Marshal of Ireland, came into possession of the lands of Newry in the 16C he took up residence in a former Cistercian Abbey, founded in 1157. He built a castle, which has not survived, and St Patrick's Church (1578), with his coat of arms in the porch, on the hill east of the city centre; it was the first Anglican church built in Ireland after the Reformation. He was succeeded by his son Henry who was killed at the Battle of Yellow Ford *(see p 334)* in 1598.

Adjacent Sights – See Armagh, Dundalk, Monaghan, Mourne Mountains.

> ### Newry Canal
>
> Newry was once a port of some importance, as is evident from the warehouses by the canal. The inland canal, from Newry to the River Bann, was begun in 1731, opened in 1742 and closed in 1956. The town stretch, which is now obstructed by low bridges, is used for fishing. The Ship Canal, from Newry to Carlingford Lough, which operated from 1761 to 1974 when the shipping trade moved downstream to Warrenpoint, was re-opened in 1987 for leisure use.

SIGHTS

Newry Cathedral ⊙ – *Town Centre*. Newry became the seat of the Roman Catholic diocese of Dromore in about 1750. The cathedral, which is dedicated to St Patrick and St Colman, was the first Roman Catholic cathedral to be built in Ireland at the time of the Act of Emancipation. Its Tudor-Gothic exterior was designed by Thomas Duff in 1825; the tower and transepts date from 1888. The interior decor of stained glass and mosaics was added later.

Newry Museum ⊙ – The museum is housed in the modern Arts Centre beside the Town Hall. Through its exhibits it traces the history of the area: the seal of the abbey – seated abbot flanked by yew trees – which has been adopted as the City seal; lace and linen from Bessbrook *(see below)*; a panelled room from the Old Coach House (early 18C) which stood in North Street; 18C Delft tiles from a Dutch house on the site of the abbey; photographs of old Newry and the canal.

EXCURSION

★**Slieve Gullion** *Round tour of 27mi/43.5km – 1 day*

From Newry take A 25 W; after 1.5mi/2.4km turn right onto B 133 to Bessbrook.

Bessbrook – The village consists of granite terrace cottages ranged round three sides of two grass squares (bowling green and children's playground) on the north side of the road; opposite with its attendant ponds stood the flax mill where the inhabitants worked. The settlement, which included churches, schools, a community hall and shops but no public houses, was founded in 1845 by John Richardson, a Quaker linen manufacturer. One of the first industrial model villages, Bessbrook later inspired the Cadbury family to build Bournville near Birmingham.

From Bessbrook take B 112; turn right onto A 25. W of Camlough village turn left onto B 30.

Cam Lough – From the road there is a fine view of the narrow lake extending south along the west foot of Camlough Mountain (1 417ft/423m).

At the crossroads turn left onto a narrow road along the west side of Cam Lough.

Killevy Churches – An ancient graveyard, overhung with beech trees, surrounds the ruins of two churches, standing end to end. The eastern church is medieval and its east window dates from the 15C. The western building is earlier (12C) although the west wall, which is pierced by a doorway below a massive lintel, may be 10C or 11C. A granite slab in the northern half of the graveyard is said to be the grave of St Monenna (also known as Darerca and Bline) who founded an important early nunnery at Killevy in the 5C; later it became a convent of Augustinian nuns until it was suppressed in 1542. A path north of the graveyard leads to a holy well.

Continue S for 1.5mi/2.4km; turn right onto B 113.

★**Slieve Gullion Forest Park** ⊙ – *Car park and picnic area. 8mi/13km Scenic Drive; steep gradients and difficult bends.* The forest, which consists of pines, larches, spruce and other conifers, covers the lower slopes of the southwest face of Slieve Gullion. The Visitor Centre, which contains an exhibition on forestry and a display of obsolete hand tools, is housed in old farm buildings adjoining a walled garden set out with lawns round a small pond.

After climbing through the wood, the Scenic Drive emerges on the open slopes of Slieve Gullion and runs northwest skirting the forest; on the left is an extensive view over the treetops; on the right is the path, waymarked in white, to the top of the south peak of Slieve Gullion (1 894ft/573m) where there is a cairn; another cairn crowns the lower north peak. The Drive swings left downhill and doubles back along the southwest slope, through the trees and rocks, to a **viewpoint**★ *(car park)* overlooking a section of the **Ring of Gullion**, a ring-dyke of smaller volcanic hills which encircle Slieve Gullion.

At the exit turn right onto B 113 and immediately turn left. After 1.5mi/2.4km turn right; after 1mi/1.6km park at the T-junction.

Kilnasaggart Stone – *6min there and back on foot across two fields and stiles.* In a hedged enclosure in the third field stands a tall granite pillar, which dates from about AD 700 and marks the site of an early-Christian cemetery. It bears 10 crosses on the northwest face and three on the southeast face, which also bears an inscription in Irish stating that the site was dedicated under the patronage of Peter the Apostle by the son of Ceran Bic, Ternohc, who died c 715.

Return to B 113; turn right towards Newry; after 5mi/8km turn left to Ballymacdermot Cairn (sign).

Ballymacdermot Cairn – Beside the road *(right)* on the south slope of Ballymacdermot Mountain are the remains of a Neolithic court grave, which consisted of two burial chambers preceded by an antechamber and a circular forecourt enclosed in a trapezoidal cairn. From the site there is a fine **view** southwest across the Meigh plain to Slieve Gullion and the Ring of Gullion.

Continue for 1mi/1.6km.

★★★ **Bernish Rock Viewpoint** – *Car park.* The view extends from Newry in the valley below to the Mourne Mountains on the horizon to the east.

Return downhill to Newry.

Cullyhanna

Cardinal O'Fiaich Centre – *Cullyhanna; 15mi/24km W of Newry by B30 and N by A29 and a minor road (left).* The centre is devoted to the life story of Tomás O'Fiaich, a local boy, who became Cardinal-Primate of all Ireland. It reviews his career as student, priest, professor, scholar, using audio-visual presentations of interviews and conversations, personal memorabilia. panels depicting life and times. archaeological models and artefacts.

PORTRUSH

Co Antrim – Population 5 703
Michelin Atlas p 102 and Map 923 – M 2

The town is a popular seaside resort set on a peninsula, which is flanked by several sandy beaches and ends in Ramore Head, a haunt of bird watchers.

West of Portrush the coast is broken by the estuary of the River Bann and ends in a long sand dune extending into Lough Foyle. Eastwards dramatic cliffs extend to the volcanic rock formations of the Giant's Causeway. The geological importance of the north Antrim Coast is recognised by its designation as a National Nature Reserve; it was at Portrush that the evidence was found which settled the long-standing controversy about the origin of such features as the Giant's Causeway.

Town Centre – The **Dunluce Centre** ⊘, in the same prominent pavilion as the Tourist Information Centre, contains such lavish revisions of traditional end-of-the-pier entertainments as Turbotours and Earthquest.

The **Countryside Centre** ⊘, located in an old Victorian bath-house, introduces the ecology and marine life of the locality; visitors can observe the denizens of the seabed from within the "wreck" of the Nautilus.

EAST OF PORTRUSH *7.5mi/12km*

From Portrush take A 2 E.

★★ **Dunluce Castle** ⊘ – *Car park.* The jagged silhouette of the ruins of Dunluce Castle rises from the cliff edge above the sea (100ft/30m). The site, an isolated rock stack separated from the mainland by a wide deep defile (20ft/7m), makes a perfect natural fortress. The castle was captured from the MacQuillans in the 16C by the MacDonnells from Scotland. In 1584 it was badly damaged by the English Lord Deputy but Sorley Boy MacDonnell restored the family position and he and his son James repaired and strengthened the castle to withstand artillery fire. The **pound**, the grassy area below the drawbridge, leads into a cave beneath the castle rock communicating with the sea; it was used as a retreat in the Early-Christian period.

The mainland courtyard was built in the 17C to provide store rooms, a forge and stabling. Contemporary structures in traditional style house ticket office and an audio-visual theatre. The converging walls create a funnel from which a drawbridge spanning the defile gave access to the late-16C **gatehouse**, built in the Scottish style with corbelled corner turrets. A stone in the wall *(left)* at the inner end of the gatehouse bears an etching of a **masted galley**. Vestiges of a late-16C **loggia** survive *(right)*. The oldest parts of the castle, the two east towers and the south wall, date from the 14C. The **great hall**, which now almost fills the upper yard, was added in the 17C by the Earls of Antrim; it is built in a grand style with bay windows on

Out and About

Excursions by bus ⊘ – Along the Causeway Coast by **open-top bus** between the Giant's Causeway and Portstewart.

Excursions by boat – To visit the caves in the limestone cliffs at **White Rock** *(east)*, and to **The Skerries** , a chain of offshore islands densely populated by sea birds.

Beaches – Sandy beaches at Portballintrae, Portrush, Portstewart, Castlerock and Magilligan Strand (Benone).

Adjacent Sights – See Giant's Causeway, Londonderry, Lough Neagh, Sperrin Mountains.

Where to Eat

The Harbour Bar, The Harbour, Portrush BT56 8BN. ☏ 028 7082 2430. Very good value, popular, with buzzy atmosphere.

Ramore Wine Bar, The Harbour, Portrush BT56 8BN. ☏ 028 7082 4313; Fax 028 7082 3194. By the main harbour; popular home cooked dishes.

Where to Stay

Greenhill House, 24 Greenhill Rd, Aghadowey, Coleraine BT51 4EU. *9mi/14.5km S by A 29 and B 66.* ☏ 028 7086 8241; Fax 028 7086 8365. Comfortable farmhouse offering good B&B.

Bushtown House, 283 Crumcroone Rd, Coleraine BT51 3QT. *2.5mi/4km S on A 29.* ☏ 028 7035 8367; Fax 028 7032 0909. Spacious friendly house (39 rm); good size traditional bedrooms.

Brown Trout Golf and Country Inn, 209 Agivey Rd, Aghadowey, Coleraine BT51 4AD. ☏ 028 7086 8209; Fax 028 7086 8878. Personally run hotel (17 rm); next to golf course.

Magherabuoy House, 41 Magheraboy Rd, Portrush BT56 8NX. ☏ 028 782 3507; Fax 028 7082 4687. Hotel (38 rm); good value.

the west front and two fireplaces. Northeast of the hall is the **kitchen** which has a vast fireplace, stone-built ovens, cupboard recesses and stone drainage. The cobbled **lower yard** is surrounded by service buildings including the bakery. In 1639 part of the castle, either here or near the kitchen, collapsed into the sea causing several deaths. From the lower yard there is a superb **view** of the Causeway Coast.
Continue E on A 2.

Bushmills Distillery ⊘ – *Car park.* The prominent feature of Bushmills (population 1 348) is the distinctive caps of the kilns in the **distillery**. The original licence to distil was granted to Sir Thomas Phillips in 1608, although the earliest mention of distilling on the site goes back to 1276. Using its own supply of water from St Columb's Rill, a tributary of the River Bush which rises in peaty ground, the distillery produces two blended whiskeys and one malt. The tour includes the main stages in the production of whiskey: mashing, fermentation, distillation, maturing in oak casks, blending and bottling. Tasting takes place in the Potstill Bar; a small museum has been created in the old malt kilns.

INLAND *15mi/24km*

From Portstewart take A 29 inland to Coleraine.

Coleraine – Coleraine, a university town since 1968, is an excellent shopping centre and market town at the head of the Bann estuary, with a bird sanctuary and a marina on the river, which is a good place from which to watch the local regattas. The town first became prosperous in 1613 when the land was granted by James I to the City of London Companies *(see p 365 and 369).*

From Coleraine take B 67 E via Ballybogy for 5.5mi/9km.

★**Benvarden** ⊘ – Benvarden House, home of the Montgomery family since 1798, opens its garden and grounds to the public every summer. A walled garden (2 acres/0.8ha), parts of which may date back to the original fortified enclosure, features rose beds, a formal hedged garden, a vinery and a pergola walk. Beyond are the kitchen gardens, with Victorian hothouses and the old gardener's bothy. A wild garden and azalea walk lead down to the River Bush, which is spanned by a Victorian stone and cast-iron bridge, rare of its type in Ireland.

Return to Ballybogy. Turn left onto B 62 towards Ballymoney; from the by-pass roundabout follow the sign.

Leslie Hill Open Farm ⊙ – This mixed-farming estate has been in the ownership of the same family since the mid 18C. The agricultural writer Arthur Young stayed at Leslie Hill in 1776 and devoted no fewer than 18 pages of his *Tour in Ireland* to a description of the progressive farming practised here. The array of buildings and implements dating from most periods of the farm's existence give a vivid picture of its evolution. The cathedral-like Bell Barn contrasts with the modest two-room cabin lived in by the coachman's family. A little museum contains a fascinating collection of farm and family memorabilia. A track, hidden from view from the imposing Georgian house by a ha-ha, leads to the walled garden with its pit-house, hot wall, and the remains of the heating arrangements for growing peaches.

WEST OF PORTRUSH *20mi/32km*

From Portrush take A 2 W.

Portstewart – Although quieter than its neighbour, Portstewart with its pictur-esque harbour was a fashionable watering-place in the 19C, dominated by O'Hara's Castle, a Gothic-style mansion (1834), which is now a Dominican college. From the promenade, paths lead west along the cliffs to Portstewart Strand *(2mi/3.2km)*. Regular exhibitions are held at the Flowerfield Arts Centre.

Continue W on A 2 via Coleraine (see above); 1mi/1.6km beyond Articlave at the Liffock crossroads turn left into the car park.

Hezlett House ⊙ – *Castlerock, on the NW corner of the crossroads.* Hezlett House, which was built in 1691 probably as a clergyman's residence, is a long, single-storey thatched cottage with battered, rough-cast walls, an attic and cruck truss roof. It was taken over by the Hezlett family in 1761 and acquired by the National Trust in 1976.

Visitors are led through the tiny kitchen, pantry, dining room, bed-sized bedrooms and parlour and up into the attic, where the servants slept. Furnishings date from the 19th century and include balloon chairs (with holes for women's bustles) and prayer chairs, allowing women to kneel in hoop skirts while retaining their dignity. The walls and roof have been stripped back in places to show the timbers, peat infill and plastering techniques. A small museum in the outbuildings shows Victorian farming implements.

Continue W on A 2.

Earl Bishop

The Earl Bishop was the eccentric Bishop of Derry, Frederick Hervey, who on the death of his elder brother became the 4th Earl of Bristol. He trav-elled extensively on the Continent and many a Hotel Bristol is named after him.

He commissioned the house at Downhill, known as **Downhill Castle**, in 1772 from Michael Shanahan, his favourite architect, to house the large collec-tion of sculpture and paintings which he collected during his Continental journeys; most of it was destroyed in a fire in 1851.

He began a second large house in Ireland after 1787 at Ballyscullion on the west shore of Lough Beg; the portico now stands at the entrance to St George's Church in Belfast. The Earl Bishop also created an eccentric house on the family estate in England, Ickworth Place in Suffolk, which was started in 1795.

★**Downhill** – A charming glen planted with flowers and shrubs, many presented by visitors, leads up to the cliff top.

By the **Bishop's Gate** stood a mausoleum *(left)*, by Michael Shanahan, supporting a statue by Van Nost of the 3rd Earl of Bristol, which was blown from its pedestal in a high wind.

The great house was destroyed in a fire in 1851, after which it was rebuilt, but since 1951 it has been a roofless shell.

The **Mussenden Temple** ⊙★, an elegant Classical rotunda, based on the Temple of Vesta at Tivoli, built of local basalt faced with sandstone from Ballycastle, perches precariously on the very edge of the high cliffs. It was erected in 1785 as a memor-ial to Mrs Mussenden, the Bishop's cousin; he used it as his library and allowed the local Roman Catholic priest to say Mass in the basement. From here there is a splendid **view** of the coast in both directions and of the railway entering a tunnel *(below)*.

Continue W on A 2.

Beyond the Lion Gate there is a fine view of the sea and the strand where the Bishop held horse races and the present generation indulges in surfing.

Bear left into the Bishop's Road.

★★**Gortmore Viewpoint** – *Car park.* The road climbs steeply up the northeast slope of Binenvenagh Mountain. There is a superb **view** of Magilligan Strand extending across the mouth of Lough Foyle towards the Inishowen Peninsula; in the last century it was used as the base line for the Ordnance Survey of Ireland.

Return downhill; turn left onto A 2.

★★**Magilligan Strand** – The long stretch of golden sand dunes (6mi/10km) is equipped with sports facilities at Benone. Much of the land is reserved for military purposes. The Point, where a Martello Tower (1812) was built during the Napoleonic Wars, is now a Nature Reserve.

SPERRIN MOUNTAINS★
Co Tyrone and Co Londonderry
Michelin Atlas p 101-102 and Map 923 – J K L 3 – Local map below

The Sperrin Mountain range, a curved ridge of schists and gneisses including rare but minute deposits of gold, rises to its highest point in Sawel Mountain (2 224ft/678m). The area was once covered in magnificent forests of Scots pines and other species. The extensive open moorland of the upper slopes, composed of blanket bog and purple heather, is used as sheep pasture; woodland and farmland alternate on the better-drained sand and gravel of the lower slopes and in the valleys, providing a suitable habitat for red grouse, pheasant and woodcock, and also the cloudberry which grows nowhere else in Ireland. The deep gorges created by the mountain streams are now thickly wooded. The land along the south shore of Lough Foyle (slob land) was reclaimed from the sea in the 19C and drained by pumps to grow flax but now produces good grain crops, and the mouth of the River Roe has been designated a nature reserve.

Plantation – In the 17C some of the area was granted to the London city livery companies – Drapers *(see below)*, Skinners, Grocers and Fishmongers – who brought in new settlers mainly from Scotland. Initially the land was let through local landlords on the rundale system *(see p 49)*; by the early 19C it was overpopulated. Traces remain of the direct management which was then adopted in some areas. Assisted emigration was introduced; the land was re-allocated in holdings of 20-30 acres/ 8-12ha of neatly-hedged fields; model farms were established to promote modern methods; roads and bridges, churches, schools and dispensaries were built.

Out and About

Angling – The many good angling streams drain southeast into Lough Neagh, or north and west down the River Roe and the Foyle tributaries into the Foyle estuary.
The Owenkillew and the Glenelly are both good trout streams.

Adjacent Sights – See Dungannon, Londonderry, Lough Neagh.

Where to Stay

Fir Trees, Melmount Rd, Strabane BT82 9JT. *1m/2km S by A 5.* ☎ 028 7138 2382; Fax 028 7138 3116. Busy, friendly hotel (24 rm); centrally located.

White Horse, 68 Clooney Rd, Londonderry BT47 3PA. *6.5m NE by A 2 Coleraine rd.* ☎ 028 7186 0606; Fax 028 7186 0371. Extended 18C merchant house (43 rm); good value.

Trinity, 22-24 Strand Rd, Londonderry BT48 7AB. ☎ 028 7127 1271; Fax 028 7127 1277. Distinctive well run hotel (37 rm) with individual style; good value.

Ardtara Country House, 8 Gorteade Rd, Upperlands, Maghera BT46 5SA. *3.75mi/6km N by A 29 off B 75.* ☎ 028 7964 4490; Fax 028 7964 5080. Spacious Victorian hotel (8 rm) with very comfortable bedrooms; rural setting.

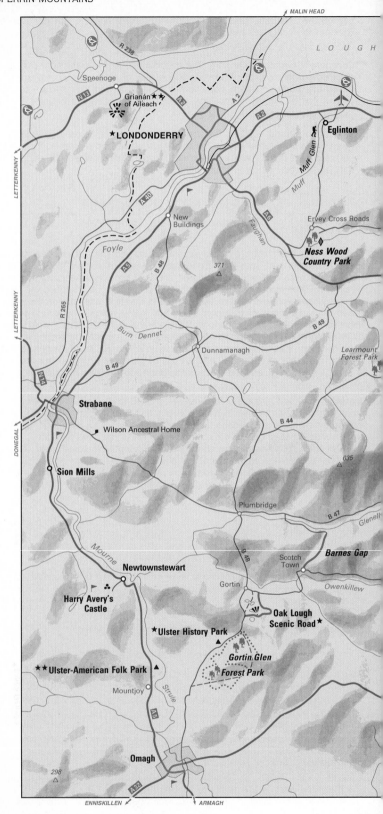

MALIN HEAD

R 238

Speenoge

N 13

Grianán ★★
of Aileach

★ LONDONDERRY

LETTERKENNY

LOUGH

A 2

A 2

Eglinton

Muff Glen

Muff

Ervey Cross Roads

Ness Wood
Country Park

New
Buildings

A 40

Foyle

A 5

LETTERKENNY

R 265

B 48

371

Faughan

A 6

Burn Dennet

Dunnamanagh

B 49

Learmount
Forest Park

N 14

DONEGAL

B 49

Strabane

Wilson Ancestral Home

B 44

635

Sion Mills

Plumbridge

B 47

Glenell

Mourne

B 48

Barnes Gap

Scotch
Town

Owenkillew

Newtownstewart

Gortin

Oak Lough
Scenic Road ★

Harry Avery's
Castle

★ Ulster History Park

Gortin Glen
Forest Park

★★ Ulster-American Folk Park

Mountjoy

Strule

A 5

Omagh

298

A 32

ENNISKILLEN

ARMAGH

COLERAINE

FOYLE

Limavady

Ballykelly

Roe Valley
Country Park ★

B 66

399

Bovevagh
Church

Burnfoot

Burntollet

Garvagh

Ulster Way

B 69

B 192

Roe

B 69

Dungiven

B 74

Priory

Banagher Church

Benady
Glen

Roe

★ Glenshane

Carntogher
462

B 44

Pass

Dreen

Mullaghmore
555 △

Ulster Way

A 6

Maghera
Old Church

Sawel Mountain
678 △

★ Sawel Mountain Drive ★

Mount Hamilton
or Sperrin

Tobermore

Draperstown

BELFAST

Sperrin
Heritage Centre

B 47

A 31

Davagh
Forest Park

Slieve Gallion
527 △

★ Beaghmore
Stone Circles

Moneymore

Springhill ★

★ Lough Neagh

Dunnamore

Wellbrook ★
▲ Beetling
Mill

A 29

A 505

Drum Manor
Forest Park

B 73

Cookstown

0   8 km
0   4 miles

Tullaghoge
☆

↓ Dungannon

CENTRAL HEIGHTS

Sperrin Heritage Centre ⊘ – The Centre, which is built in the vernacular style to resemble three adjoining cottages, is set in the beautiful Glenelly Valley surrounded by the natural beauty of the Sperrin scenery. The symbol of the centre is the Hen Harrier, an indigenous bird of prey which still survives in the Sperrin uplands. Videos, computers and exhibitions enable visitors to explore the local flora and fauna, history and culture, and consider future management options.

Scenic Routes – The **Sawel Mountain Drive★**, a narrow unfenced road along the east face of Sawel Mountain (2 229ft/678m), the highest peak, passes through the wild and austere beauty of the open moorland; the **views★★** are spectacular.
The **Oak Lough Scenic Road★** is a minor road which loops round a cluster of lakes, the delight of canoeists, and provides a fine **view** of Gortin (population 300) on the Owenkillew River.
The **Barnes Gap** carries the road through a narrow cleft in the hills between the valleys of the Owenkillew and Glenelly Rivers.

EASTERN FOOTHILLS

★Springhill ⊘ – This house was the family home of the Conynghams, who came to Ulster from Ayrshire early in the 17C. They were already extensive landowners when they acquired the Springhill estate (350 acres/141ha) for £200. The oldest part of the house seems to have been built c 1680 by William Conyngham for his bride Anne Upton of Templepatrick in Co Antrim. The property was altered by subsequent generations of Conynghams, who usually followed military careers, and was transferred to the National Trust in 1957.
The original 17C slate-roofed house was enlarged in the 18C by the addition of the bay window wings. There are family portraits throughout the house and much **fine 18C and 19C furniture** including a set of 18C "ladder-back" chairs, an oak press inscribed by its maker and an early-18C medicine chest. The oak **stairs** have a yew handrail with two balusters, one spiral and one plain, to each shallow tread. The **Dining Room** is furnished with an 18C mahogany plate bucket, a hexagonal wine-cooler and a set of marquetry walnut fiddle-back chairs (late-17C); the mantelpiece is made of marble brought from Herculaneum by the Earl Bishop *(see p 364)*. The **Gun Room** contains a "cock-fighting" chair and a collection of weapons: four flint-locks used during the Siege of Derry and later converted to muzzle-loaders, and two pikes from the Battle of Vinegar Hill *(see p 200)*.

The entrance court is flanked by low outbuildings which accommodated *(east)* the senior staff and *(west)* the junior staff, stables, laundry, brewhouse, slaughter-house and turf-shed which was kept stocked by the tenants. They now house a **costume collection** consisting of about 150 articles of men's and women's dress from the 18C, 19C and 20C, which are displayed in rotation and include several rare 18C men's costumes and a court mantua of Spitalfields silk (1759). The **barn**, built

Gun Room, Springhill

Beaghmore Stone Circles

of the same rough-hewn local oak for the timberwork as was used in the house, is surmounted by a bell which could be rung to warn of approaching danger; a circular **dovecot** stands between the house and the road.

★**Beaghmore Stone Circles** – The stone circles, seven in number, are formed of quite small stones set on, rather than in, the ground. Six of the circles are arranged in pairs, with a cairn and a row of stones near the point of intersection. The area enclosed in the seventh unattached circle is studded with close-set stones, known as "Dragons' Teeth".

Archaeological investigations suggest that the circles date from the Bronze Age, between 1500 and 800 BC; they may have been used to calculate the rising and setting of the sun and moon.

★**Wellbrook Beetling Mill** ⊘ – *5mi/8km west by A 505; after 3mi/5km turn right (sign).* Beetling is the last stage in the production of linen where the cloth is beaten to close up the weave and give it a smooth sheen. The first mill at Wellbrook came into operation in September 1767; eventually there were six and the present mill, known as no 6, dates from about 1830. It continued in operation until 1961 and is maintained in working order by the National Trust.

The **tour** starts with a display on the production of linen and the history of the Irish linen industry; it occupies the drying loft which was originally fitted with frames capable of holding 100 pieces of cloth (23yd/21m long).

On the lower floor are the seven **beetling machines** turned by an external wooden water-wheel, which is fed by water carried from the mill race in a wooden flume (restored). The amount of noise produced by two beetling engines operating for a few minutes explains why deafness was common among beetlers, who worked from early morning to nine at night.

Drum Manor Forest Park ⊘ – *2.5mi/4km west by A 505.* The Forest Park, which was formerly a private estate, consists of open parkland and three walled gardens surrounded by woodland. The Visitor Centre contains an exhibition on butterflies and forest habitats.

The **butterfly garden**, which is perfectly sheltered in one of the old walled gardens, presents butterflies living naturally without restraint. The centre of the garden is laid out with paths and planted with flowers and shrubs, such as buddleia, sweet rocket, single Michaelmas daisies, lavender and aubrietia, which provide nectar for the butterflies; the corners are allowed to grow wild to provide grass, docks, nettles and other wild plants as food for the caterpillars.

A most attractive **flower garden** has been created in the ruins of the manor house which was built between 1829 and 1869. Steps descend from the terrace to the south lawn which slopes to the pond where ducks and other wildfowl congregate.

Draperstown – The town is a pleasant and busy market centre in the heart of Sperrin Mountain country. In the **Ulster Plantation Centre** ⊘ visitors move through a series of different settings to watch videos of costumed actors relating the defeat and **Flight of the Earls** of Ulster *(see p 162)*, and Tudor and Stuart plans to settle the area with English and Scottish planters. An exhibition follows, tracing the history of the Plantation from the 17C to the present day, with interesting displays on the Great Famine and emigration, and the influence of the Drapers' Company on the life and architecture of Draperstown itself.

Cookstown – Population 9 842. Once an important linen centre, Cookstown now serves a predominantly agricultural community processing pork and dairy products.

Its most notable feature is the very broad main street which, under 10 different names, extends north from the River Ballinderry towards the silhouette of Slieve Gallion (1 732ft/528m). On the west side stands **Holy Trinity Church** (Roman Catholic) designed by JJ McCarthy in 1860. The neighbouring convent **chapel**, completed in 1965, is decorated with bronze panels and stained-glass windows. Opposite stands the 18C **courthouse**.

Tullaghoge Fort – *2mi/3.2km S of Cookstown by A 29 and B 520. Turn left on a blind corner into the car park; 10min there and back on foot.* This hillfort is unusual in that it is surrounded by a wide outer bank but no ditch; at the centre of the oval inner area is a shallow depression. It was the residence of the O'Hagans and the headquarters of the O'Neills, the kings of the *Cenél nEógaín*; their stone inauguration chair, which stood on the hillside nearby *(southeast)*, was broken up by Lord Mountjoy in 1602. The **view** from the tree-crowned earthworks is extensive: southwest to the circular walled graveyard at Donaghrisk where the O'Hagans, who were the guardians of the fort, were buried; east towards Lough Neagh; north to Slieve Gallion with the River Ballinderry in the foreground and Killymoon Castle in the trees by the river.

> ### Royal Charter
>
> Cookstown takes its name from Dr Allen Cooke who c 1620 obtained a Royal Charter to establish a market town; it was destroyed in the Rebellion (1641–43). A second project, in which every house possessed a garden, as most still do, was implemented in the early 1700s by James and William Stewart; they laid out a broad avenue extending south from Dr Cooke's settlement to their own property at Killymoon Castle *(private)*, which was redesigned by John Nash in 1803; the grounds are now a golf course.

WESTERN FOOTHILLS

★★**Ulster-American Folk Park** ◷ – The park is devoted to emigration from Ireland to America and has been developed with the generous assistance of the Mellon family of Pittsburg, Pennsylvania, round the ancestral cottage from which **Thomas Mellon** emigrated with his family at the age of five in 1818.

Conestoga Wagon, Ulster-American Folk Park

NITB, Belfast

Visitor Centre – The exhibition traces the Ulster connection with America. On display is a **Conestoga wagon**, in which the pioneers trekked into the Wild West; this sort of covered wagon originated in the 18C in Lane County, Pennsylvania and was drawn by four to six horses. The **Emigration Gallery** describes in detail the reasons for emigration at different times, the sort of people who left and how they travelled – initially by sailing ship and packhorse but later by steamship and rail – and their success or failure in the New World.

Outdoor Exhibition – In the **Old World** section a typical **18C Ulster village** has been created by erecting other buildings from the same period round the Mellon cottage. The **Ship and Dockside Gallery** contains a replica of part of an emigration ship; the voyage could take from 20 days to 12 weeks. The **New World** section of the park shows the way of life the emigrants adopted on arrival in America – log cabins.

In the workshops and cottages local people in **period costume** demonstrate the old crafts: cooking, spinning, weaving, basket weaving; making candles and soap; working in the forge and the carpenter's shop; turf fires burn on the hearths throughout the year filling the air with their sweet fragrance.

★**Ulster History Park** ◷ – *Development in progress.* The theme of the park (35 acres/14ha) is the history of settlement in Ireland, from the arrival of Mesolithic hunters to the 17C Plantation. The indoor display and film explain the origins of the full-scale reconstructions in the open-air park – a Mesolithic encampment (c 7000-4000 BC) and two Neolithic houses (c 4000-2000 BC), a court tomb and a wedge tomb, a standing stone and a stone circle, an early-Christian rath *(see p 83)* containing several round thatched huts, a cooking pit where the water was heated with hot stones *(fulacht fiadh)*, a crannóg, an early-Christian complex of round tower and church, a Norman motte and bailey, and a 17C Plantation house and bawn with a water mill.

Gortin Glen Forest Park ⊘ – The park, which was opened in 1967, is part of the larger Gortin Forest, a coniferous woodland planted to produce timber for commercial purposes. The forest drive *(5mi/8km – one direction only)* offers a number of beautiful vistas over the Sperrin Mountains. Detailed information is supplied in the Nature Centre and on the forest trails. The deer enclosure provides a close-up view of the Sika deer, and the pond attracts wildfowl.

Strabane – This small town has developed where the River Finn and the Mourne River flow into the Foyle, which forms the border between Co Londonderry and Co Donegal.

Behind the bowed Georgian shopfront of **Gray's Printery** ⊘ *(49 Main Street, Strabane)*, a 19C printing shop has been preserved with its 19C hand- and foot-operated presses.

In the 18C, **Strabane** was a lively publishing centre. Two local apprentices made their mark in the USA: John Dunlap (1747–1812), an apprentice in Gray's Printery, printed the American Declaration of Independence in his newspaper the *Pennsylvania Packet*; James Wilson became editor of a Philadelphia newspaper. The **Wilson Ancestral Home** ⊘ is a whitewashed thatched cottage, where James Wilson, grandfather of **President Woodrow Wilson**, lived until he left for America in 1807 at the age of 20. The house contains some of the original furniture: a cupboard bed by the kitchen fire and curtained beds in the main bedroom. The first-floor room is a later addition. Wilsons still live in the modern farmhouse behind the cottage.

Sion Mills – Broad grass verges, beech and chestnut trees line the main street of this model village, which was established by the three Herdman brothers, who in 1835 started a flax-spinning operation in an old flour mill on the Mourne. Twenty years later they built a bigger mill which is still working. The terraced cottages for the millworkers were built in the Gothic style. The black-and-white half-timbered buildings, in particular Sion House, were designed by James Herdman's son-in-law, William Unsworth, an English architect, who also designed the Church of the Good Shepherd in an Italianate Romanesque style, modelled on a church in Pistoia in Italy. St Teresa's Roman Catholic Church (1963) is a striking modern building by Patrick Haughey of Belfast; a slate mural of *The Last Supper* by Oisin Kelly adorns the façade.

Newtonstewart – The village is set near the confluence of the River Mourne and the River Strule. On a nearby hilltop stands **Harry Avery's Castle**, two D-shaped towers from a 14C Gaelic stone castle built by Henry Aimbreidh O'Neill who died in 1392. There is a clear view of the surrounding countryside.

Omagh – Omagh is a quiet market town built on a steep slope overlooking the point where two rivers, the Camowen and the Drumragh, join to form the Strule. The main street divides in front of the Courthouse (1820).

NORTHERN UPLANDS

★**Glenshane Pass** – The pass between Mullaghmore (1 818ft/555m – south) and Carntogher (1 516ft/462m – north) carries the main road through the Sperrin Mountains. The northern approach through dramatic mountain scenery overlooks Benady Glen on the River Roe; the southern approach *(viewing point)* provides a **panoramic view**★★ across Lough Neagh in the mid-Ulster plain to Slemish *(see p 303)*.

★**Roe Valley Country Park** ⊘ – The country park extends along a stretch *(3mi/4.8km)* of the wild thickly wooded valley, where the peaty red River Roe tumbles over rocks and through gorges on its way north to the sea at Lough Foyle. As well as great natural beauty and scenes of the O'Cahans' legendary exploits, the park preserves evidence of early industrial activity: bleach greens, weirs and mill races, and 18C water-powered mills for sawing wood, scutching flax, weaving and beetling linen. An unusual feature is the stone-built **Power House**, built in 1896 and the site of early success in generating hydroelectric power. The **Visitor Centre** at the Dogleap Bridge provides information on the local flora and fauna, old industries and on the 17C Plantation.

Ness Wood Country Park – *From the car park walk through the picnic area into the wood. The waterfall (30ft/9m) is unfenced; children should be accompanied. Woodland walk along both sides of the stream meeting at a bridge about 600yd/548m from the car park.*

The spectacular waterfall (*an eas* in Irish) was created, together with a series of gorges, potholes and rapids, by the River Burntollet eroding a channel through the metamorphic schist rock since the end of the last Ice Age. The wood (46 acres/19ha) was mostly oak trees until the 17C but now many species flourish.

Eglinton – This elegant little village with its **Courthouse** was developed by the Grocers' Company between 1823 and 1825 round a tree-shaded green beside the Muff River. Upstream the river tumbles through **Muff Glen**, a narrow tree-lined valley of pleasant walks.

Dungiven Priory ⊘ – The priory ruins stand on a natural strongpoint above the River Roe. A pre-Norman monastery, associated with St Nechtan, was replaced late in the 12C with a priory of Augustinian canons which flourished until the mid 16C. The **church** is an impressive example of medieval architecture. The nave, the oldest part of the church, probably dates from the early 12C and was originally shorter; two round-headed arches in the Romanesque style in the east wall are most likely the work of the Augustinians, who also added the chancel in the 13C. Against the south wall stands a magnificent **tomb** designed in the tradition of 15C western Scotland; beneath a traceried canopy lies an armed figure, said to be a chieftain of the O'Cahans, Cooey-na-Gal, who died in 1385; on the front of the tomb are six "gallowglasses", Scottish mercenaries in kilts.

In the 17C Sir Edward Doddington, who constructed the walls of Londonderry, built himself a house in the cloister; its foundations were excavated in 1982.

North of the path is a **bullaun**, a hollowed stone which was originally used for grinding grain but now collects rainwater; it is visited by people seeking cures for warts who tie rags on the overhanging tree.

Banagher Church – The ruined church dates from the late 11C or early 12C. In the graveyard stands a **mortuary house**, built of dressed stone early in the 12C, probably to house some relics disturbed by the addition of a chancel to the church. The panel on the west gable depicts a figure with a hand raised in blessing and bearing a crozier. According to tradition it is the tomb of St Muiredach O'Heney and sand from his tomb brings good luck.

Bovevagh Church – In the churchyard of a ruined medieval church stands a **mortuary house** similar to the one at Banagher *(see above)*; its ruined state reveals the cavity, which contained the body, and the hand hole in the east end through which the faithful could touch the relics.

Maghera Old Church ⊘ – *At the north end of the main street turn right into Bank Square, then left to the car park.* The nave of the ruined church probably dates from the 10C. The fine west door is probably mid-12C and similar in structure to the door of Banagher Church *(see above)*; the lintel bears a Crucifixion scene. The chancel was added c 1200 and the tower in the 17C. In the graveyard stands a rough pillar stone, carved with a ringed cross, which, according to tradition, is the grave of St Lurach, who founded an important monastery on this site in the 6C.

Ballykelly – The village was established early in the 17C by the Fishmongers' Company, who built a model farm which still stands on the north side of the road; a two-storey block is linked to two one-storey pavilions by curtain walls enclosing a farmyard. Opposite is the Presbyterian Church (1827). The Anglican Church, which stands on a slight hill screened by beech trees on the east side of the village, was built in 1795 by the Earl Bishop of Derry.

Limavady – The town takes its name from the Irish for Dogleap since the original settlement was further upstream (2mi/3.2km) by the 13C O'Cahan castle in the Roe Valley Country Park *(see above)*. It was re-founded as Newtown-Limavady in the 17C by Sir Thomas Phillips, Chief Agent of the City of London in Ulster. It is now a pleasant Georgian market town where the famous song, *Danny Boy*, also known as *The Londonderry Air*, was noted down in 1851 by Jane Ross (1810–79) who lived at 51 Main Street *(plaque)*.

STRANGFORD LOUGH★

Co Down

Strangford Lough is a landlocked sea-inlet (18mi/29km long with an 80mi/142km coastline). It is linked to the Irish Sea by a narrow channel through which 350 million tonnes of sea water races at about 10 knots when the tide changes. The Viking name Strangford (violent fjord) has prevailed over the old Irish name of Lough Cuan. The area invaded by the sea was composed of drumlins which now emerge from the water as smooth green hummocks, particularly along the sheltered western shore; those along the eastern shore have mostly been eroded by the prevailing westerly wind. By the water's edge are attractive lakeside villages.

The whole of the Lough is now a **Marine Nature Reserve**, the first to be designated in Northern Ireland. Some islands, stretches of the foreshore and neighbouring areas are protected as National Nature Reserves or as Areas of Special Scientific Interest. Most of the shore is managed by public bodies, the National Trust or the Royal Society for the Protection of Birds.

Out and About

The Tourist Information Centre in Portaferry presents an exhibition on things to see around Strangford Lough, flora and fauna, local history and a film about tower houses.

Wildlife – The many places where wild flowers, nesting birds, flocks of wild-fowl, seals and other marine animals can be seen include bird hides at Castle Espie, Delamont, Quoile Countryside Centre, Castle Ward and Mount Stewart. The marine life of the Lough can be viewed at **Exploris**, an aquarium in Portaferry.

Castle Ward Opera Festival ⊘ – The festival is held in June in the grounds of this beautiful country house *(see below)*.

Strangford Narrows Car Ferry ⊘ –The ferry carries vehicles between Strangford and Portaferry.

Adjacent Sights – See Bangor, Downpatrick, Lisburn, Mount Stewart.

SIGHTS *Clockwise from Strangford*

★**Strangford** – This charming little port, which dates from the Middle Ages, nestles on the west side of the Narrows. The **tower house** ⊘ was begun in the 15C but is chiefly 16C in style. An internal wooden stair climbs the three storeys to a very narrow roof walk which provides a fine **view** of the port, the Narrows, Portaferry and the southern end of the Ards Peninsula.

Kilclief Castle ⊘ – *2.5mi/4km S of Strangford by coast road (A 2)*. The **tower house**, which is in the gatehouse style, with two projections to protect the entrance, was built, probably by the bishop of Down between 1413 and 1441, to guard the entrance to the Strangford Narrows.

★★**Castle Ward** ⊘ – The house at Castle Ward is unique, an architectural compromise combining the conventional Classical idiom with the first example of Georgian Gothic in Ireland. It reflects the conflicting tastes of Bernard Ward and his wife, who married in 1747 but later separated. The three-storey rectangular block with a semi-octagonal bay at each end is built of Bath stone and was designed in the early 1760s. From the Gothic front there is a fine **view** of Strangford Lough.

The car park near the house is linked by a drive to another by the lake shore (Old Castle Ward).

House – The original entrance in the southwest Classical front opens into the **hall** which is highly decorated with stuccowork – partly the work of Dublin plasterers and partly in a more robust style by local workmen – and now in what is thought to be the original colour scheme.

Ward Family

Late in the 16C Bernard Ward from Capesthorne in Cheshire bought the Castle Ward estate from the Earls of Kildare. In 1610 Nicholas Ward built a tower house, Old Castle Ward, on the shore of Strangford Lough. No trace remains of the 18C house built in the sixth generation by Michael Ward, who promoted the linen trade, developed the lead mines on his estate and became a Justice of the Court of the King's Bench in Ireland. In 1812 the property passed to Robert Ward, who abandoned it in favour of his other house, Bangor Castle. In 1827 the 3rd Viscount Bangor (the title was bestowed in 1781) began to restore the house and estate. On the death of the 6th Viscount Bangor in 1950 the house was received by the state in lieu of death duties and presented to the National Trust.

Gothick Boudoir, Castle Ward

The rooms on the northeast side of the house are decorated in the Gothic style favoured by Lady Bangor – the boidoir with **fan vaulting** based on that in Henry VII's Chapel in Westminster Abbey; the **saloon** with glass window panels thought to be 17C Flemish; and the Gothic **morning room** containing a landscape of Castle Ward in 1785 by William Ashford. The **dining room** is on the Classical side of the house; in 1827 the 18C panelling was painted, grained and parcel-gilt; the dining chairs (c 1760) are in the Chippendale style.

A tunnel leads from the basement to the **stable yard** where the ground level was lowered to hide the buildings from the house. The **laundry** is an 18C building with 19C equipment: wash tubs, a copper boiler, a stone mangle.

Grounds – In 1902 the **Sunken Garden** near the stable yard consisted of 61 flat beds producing flowers, several beds of roses on the terrace and a collection of begonias. Beyond were the Yew Terraces, planted in 1720 with Florence Court yews, and a Pinetum.

When the new house was built in the 1760s, an informal landscape with broad sweeps of grass and clumps of trees and a deer park was substituted for the earlier formal landscape, of which the chief feature, the **Temple Water**, remains; it was created in 1724 and aligned on the tower of Audley's Castle *(see below)*. The Queen Anne house had stood on the east side of the Water near the **ice house**. Opposite on a hill stands the **Temple**, a Classical summer house with a Doric portico (1750), next to the Walled Garden, which originally produced flowers, fruit and vegetables for the house and now contains pens for the **Wildfowl Collection**, reflecting the wildfowl to be found on Strangford Lough.

The 17C **tower house**, known as Old Castle Ward, was the first dwelling built on the estate by a Ward. It is now surrounded by the farmyard buildings, most of which were built in a matching castellated style in the mid 19C. The original 18C mill, which was a tidal mill, was later driven by water from the Temple Water. Another building houses the **Strangford Lough Wildlife Centre**.⊘

★**Audley's Castle** – *Access via Castle Ward or by minor road W of Castle Ward estate. Drive through the gate to the car park.* The ruins of this 15C **tower house**, which was designed in the "gatehouse" style, stand on a spit of land projecting into Strangford Lough. It was built by the Audley family, who held land in the area in the 13C, and sold in 1646 to the Wards of Castle Ward. There is a fine view of the wooded shores. The hamlet of Audleystown was demolished in the 1850s and the inhabitants are thought to have emigrated to the USA.

Audleystown Cairn – *Walk across the fields.* The cairn, which is revetted with drystone walling, is a dual court tomb with a forecourt at each end opening into galleries. Excavations in 1952 discovered 34 partly burned skeletons, Neolithic pottery and flint implements.

★**Quoile Countryside Centre** ⊘ – In 1957 a barrage was built at Hare Island excluding the sea from the Quoile estuary, which had formerly been tidal, and turning the last few miles of the river into a freshwater lake with sluice gates to control flooding. This area (494 acres/200ha) is now a Nature Reserve with woodland, rushy grassland and reedbeds, providing a habitat for many woodland and wetland birds and several species of waterfowl, as well as otters.

From **Quoile Quay**, which was built in 1717 by Edward Southwell and served as a port for Downpatrick until 1940, the road reaches **Quoile Castle**, a late-16C tower house inhabited by the West family until the mid 18C; the south corner collapsed in 1977 revealing two vaulted rooms with gun loops on the ground floor. The **Visitor Centre** gives details of the local and natural history. The road ends at the Steamboat Quay, which was built in 1837 by David Ker as part of an unsuccessful attempt to establish a paddle-steamer service to Liverpool.

★**Inch Abbey** ⊘ – *2mi/3.2km NW of Downpatrick by A 7; after 1mi/1.6km turn left; car park.* The attractive site of the abbey ruins was originally an island in the marshes on the north bank of the Quoile River, approached by a causeway which carries the modern road. The abbey, a daughter house of the Cistercian abbey at Furness in Lancashire, was founded c 1180 by John de Courcy. The 13C church is quite well preserved. Only the foundations are left of the buildings which surrounded the cloisters. The detached buildings near the river were probably an infirmary *(southeast)*, a bakehouse and well *(southwest)* and a guesthouse.

Delamont Country Park ⊘ – *Spacious bird hide.* The park, which contains a walled garden laid out with formal beds of shrubs, extends to the shore of Strangford Lough. In spring the woodlands are bright with wildflowers, and young lambs gambol in the meadows. One can see foxes, stoats and badgers; by the water, otters and seals. The bird population includes herons, which nest and rear their young between February and midsummer, treecreepers, owls, wrens, finches, wildfowl, guillemots, curlews, oystercatchers and several sorts of terns.

Killyleagh – Killyleagh is an attractive sailing centre on the west shore of Strangford Lough, dominated by its turreted **castle**, which was redesigned in 1850 by Charles Lanyon, and incorporates two circular towers dating from the 13C and 17C. The original castle, which was built by de Courcy, came into the possession of the O'Neills, was destroyed by General Monk in 1648 and then rebuilt by the Hamiltons, Earls of Clanbrassil *(see p 355)* and Viscounts Clandeboye.

> Killyleagh was the birthplace of **Sir Hans Sloane**, whose collection of curios, books and manuscripts formed the nucleus of both the Natural History Museum and the British Museum in London.

Sketrick Castle – *Car park.* The four-storey tower house, which collapsed in a storm in 1896, was erected to command the approach to the island from the mainland, probably in the 15C before the causeway was built. The ground floor was divided into four rooms; the largest, which is vaulted, was probably the kitchen; the one in the centre may have been a boat bay. At the rear a tunnel leads to a spring covered by a corbelled vault.

★**Nendrum Monastery** ⊘ – *At the north end of Mahee Island; car park.* The causeway approach is commanded by the ruins *(dangerous)* of **Mahee Castle**, built in 1570 by Captain Browne, an English soldier.
The **Visitor Centre** presents the history of the site and of the missionaries of the early Celtic church. The early-Christian site, originally approached by boat or across fords, is composed of three concentric enclosures protected by drystone walls. The innermost enclosure contained the round tower and the church, which may date from the 10C or 11C at the west end, while the east end is 12C Benedictine; the surrounding area was the graveyard. The school stood on the west side of the intermediate enclosure, which also contained the monks' workshops. The outer enclosure was probably given over to the guesthouse, tenants' dwellings, gardens, orchards, pastures and arable fields. St Mochaoi (5C), from which Mahee is derived, appears to be connected with the monastery's origins but the written records and the archaeological evidence date from the 7C. The monastery suffered during the Viking invasions, and in the 12C John de Courcy established a Benedictine house at Nendrum but it seems to have closed by the early 14C. The site was identified in 1844 and excavated in 1922–24.

★**Wildfowl and Wetlands Trust (Castle Espie Centre)** ⊘ – The centre occupies an attractive site on the west shore of Strangford Lough. Its freshwater lakes, formerly clay and limestone workings belonging to a brick, tile and pottery factory, make ideal breeding grounds and wintering habitats for both wild birds and endangered species bred in captivity. From the Lance Turtle hide, one can observe some of the wildfowl which arrive each winter from the Arctic. Among the ducks, geese and swans from all over the world are Bufflehead, King Eider and Cinnamon Teal; Hawaiian Geese will feed from the hand; many small birds are attracted to the feeding stations in the woodland walk.

Scrabo Country Park ⊘ – *Car park at the top of the hill; 5min on foot to the tower. Second car park in Killynether Wood.* The dominant features of the park are Scrabo Hill, formed by a layer of volcanic lava covering and protecting the underlying sandstone, and **Scrabo Tower**, which was erected in 1857 to commemorate the 3rd Marquess of Londonderry (1778-1854) *(see p 352)* and his concern for his tenants during the Great Famine. The tower (135ft/41m high, walls 4ft/1.25m thick) was designed by

Lanyon and Lynn and constructed of **Scrabo stone**, dark dolerite for the walls and light sandstone for the roof, quoins and dressings. It now houses an exhibition about the country park – geology, early settlers, flora and fauna – and *The Story of Strangford Lough*, an audio-visual presentation *(12min; every 30min)*. The **view★★** from the top *(122 steps – viewing maps)* is panoramic extending as far as the Scottish coast *(north)* and the Isle of Man *(southeast)*.

Newtownards – The town is now a busy modern shopping centre a little way inland from the north shore of Strangford Lough.

The handsome **town hall**, built as a market house in 1765 of local Scrabo stone, stands in the town centre on the north side of Conway Square where a market is held on Saturdays. At the east end of the High Street stands the **market cross** which was severely damaged in 1653. In Court Street on the south side of the town are the ruins of the church of **Newtownards Priory** which was founded in the 13C by Walter de Burgh; it was built of Scrabo stone and contains the burial vault of the Londonderry family *(see p 352)*; the tower dates from the 17C. A fine collection of 13C **cross slabs★** inscribed with foliate crosses is built into the north wall of the ruined church of **Movilla Abbey** *(2mi/3.2km NE by A 48, B 172 and Old Movilla Road (right); entry through the graveyard)*; the abbey, one of the most important in Ulster, was founded c 540 by St Finian.

★Grey Abbey ⊘ – *Car park.* The ruins of the monastery stand in a quiet verdant hollow beside a stream. It was founded in 1193 by Affreca, the wife of John de Courcy, as a daughter house of Holm Cultram Abbey in Cumbria, a Cistercian foundation. It was burned during the Elizabethan wars but then re-roofed and equipped with a bell turret and used as the parish church until 1778. The little visitor centre has displays on monastic life and on the building of the abbey.

A magnificent **west door** (1220-30) is decorated with elaborate moulding and dog-tooth decoration. The monastic buildings were ranged round the cloisters according to the usual Cistercian practice. The herb garden contains over 50 different medicinal plants and herbs of the kinds the Cistercian monks may have used in practising medicine.

Portaferry – *Strangford Narrows car ferry.* A busy coastal town until the mid 19C, Portaferry is now a yachting and sea angling centre. The attractive long waterfront, facing Strangford across the narrow strait, includes two handsome Georgian houses, now the marine biology centre of Queen's University, Belfast. **Portaferry Castle**, a tower house with only one projection flanking the entrance, was probably built early in the 16C by the Savage family.

★Exploris ⊘ – Much more than just an aquarium, Exploris presents the marine life of Strangford Lough and the Irish Sea in all its richness and complexity, with convincing re-creations of many underwater and shoreline habitats. There are Touch Tanks, a Marine Discovery Lab, and an Open Sea Tank, one of the largest of its kind in the United Kingdom, which visitors can view from above or from the depths of an underwater cave.

Drumlins in Strangford Lough

Grey Point

Belfast Lough

Groomsport

Copeland Islands

Crawfordsburn
Country Park

BANGOR

BELFAST

A 2

A 2

NORTH

Donaghadee

A 48

Somme Heritage
Centre

A 21

★ Ballycopeland

Millisle

CHANNEL

Newtownards

A 20

A 2

Movilla Abbey

Ballyferis Point

Scrabo
Country Park

A 20

ARDS

Comber

A 21

MOUNT STEWART ★★★

▲ **Temple of the Winds**

Ballywalter

A 22

Wildfowl and
Wetlands Trust ★

B 5

Grey Abbey ★

Rowallane Gardens ★ *Hillsborough* ★

★ *STRANGFORD*

Mahee Castle

Mahee Island

PENINSULA

A 22

Nendrum Monastery ★

Kircubbin

Burr
Point

Sketrick Castle

A 2

LOUGH

Portavogie

A 20

Rowallane Gardens ⟍ *BELFAST*

Killyleagh

A 22

Delamont
Country Park

★ **Audley's
Castle**

A 7

Audleystown Cairn

Portaferry

★ Quoile Countryside
Centre

★★ **Castle Ward**

Strangford ★

B 2

Raholp

A 25

St Tassach's Church

★ **Inch
Abbey**

Saul

Quoile

Slieve Patrick

Kilclief Castle

Downpatrick

★ Struell Wells ★

Ballyquintin Point

A 25

LECALE   PENINSULA

IRISH

NEWCASTLE

Killard Point

Stone Circle

B 1

Ballynoe

A 2

Ardtole

SEA

Killough

Ardglass ★

A 2

*Dundrum
Bay*

Church

STRANGFORD LOUGH

St John's Point

0 ——— 5 km
0 ——— 3 miles

Admission Times and Charges

As admission times and charges are liable to alteration, the information printed below – valid for 2000 – is for guidance only. Where it has not been possible to obtain up-to-date information, the admission times and charges from the previous edition of the guide are printed in italics.

⊙ – Every sight for which times and charges are listed below is indicated by the symbol ⊙ after the title in the Sights section.

Order – *The information is listed in the same order as in the Sights section of the guide.*

Facilities for the disabled – ⅙ *(⅙) mean full or partial access for wheelchairs. As the range of possible facilities is great (for impaired mobility, sight and hearing), readers are advised to telephone in advance to check what is available.*

Dates – *Dates given are inclusive. The term weekend means Saturday and Sunday. The term holidays means bank and public holidays, when shops, museums and other monuments may be closed or may vary their times of admission. The term school holidays refers to the breaks between terms at Christmas, Easter and during the summer months and also to the short mid-term breaks (one week), which are usually in February and October. See PRACTICAL INFORMATION.*

Admission times – *Ticket offices usually shut 30min before closing time; only exceptions are mentioned below. Some places issue timed tickets owing to limited space and facilities.*

Charge – *The charge given is for an individual adult. Reductions may be available for families, children, students, senior citizens (old-age pensioners) and the unemployed; it may be necessary to provide proof of identity and status. Large parties should apply in advance as many places offer special rates for group bookings and some have special days for group visits.*

Prices – *Prices are given in Irish currency (punt) in the Republic of Ireland and in Sterling in Northern Ireland.*

Foreign languages – *Where foreign languages are mentioned, an English language version is also available.*

Abbreviations – *Dúchas = Department of Arts, Heritage, Gaeltacht and the Islands*
HM = Historic Monuments Branch, Department of the Environment, Northern Ireland
NT = National Trust, Nothern Ireland.

Churches – Many Church of Ireland (Anglican) and Presbyterian churches are locked when not in use for services.

Tourist Information Centres – *The addresses and telephone numbers are given for local Tourist Information Centres, which may provide information advice and booking services and information about local amenities, local market days, early closing days etc.*

A

ABBEYLEIX

Abbeyleix Heritage House – ⅙ Open Mar-Sep, daily, 10am (1pm, Sun and bank hols) to 6pm. £2, reductions available. Parking. Coffeeshop. ☎ 0502 31653; Fax 0502 30059; abbeyleix@ireland.com; www.laois.local.ie/abbeyleix

Abbey Sense Garden – ⅙ Open daily, 9am-4pm. Donation. ☎ 0502 31636, 31325; Fax 0502 31386.

Excursions

Emo Court – (Dúchas) Gardens: Open daily; guided tour (45min), July-Aug, Sun at 3pm. House: Guided tour (30min) mid-June to mid-Sep, daily, 10am-6pm (4.30pm last tour). £2, reductions available. Music recitals in winter. Parking. ☎ 0502 26573; Fax 0502 26573.

Coolbanagher Church – Services: First Sun of month, 9.30am (Matins), other Sundays, 12midday. ☎ 0502 24143 (Rector).

Stradbally Steam Museum – ⅙ Museum: Closed for renovation until 2001. Open usually Easter to Oct, bank hol Sun and Mon. Annual Steam Rally at Stradbally Hall: Aug bank hol Sun and Mon. ☎ 0502 25444.

Heywood Gardens – (Dúchas) Open daylight hours. Guided tour Jul-Aug, Sun, 3pm. ☎ 056 51863 or 0502 33563 (1pm-1.30pm).

ADARE

Adare Heritage Centre – ♿ Open May-Sep, daily, 9am-6pm; Oct-Apr, daily, 10am-5pm. Exhibition £3, reductions available. ☎ 061 396 666; Fax 061 396 932; adareheritage@eircom.net

Excursions

Croom Mills Waterwheel and Heritage Centre – Open daily, 9am-6pm (later in summer). No charge for waterwheel. Exhibition £3, reductions available. Guided tour available. Parking. Mill Race Restaurant. Corn Loft Bistro. Craft shop. Gift shop. ☎ 061 397 130; Fax 061 397 199 (Mary Hayes).

Castle Matrix – (♿) Guided tour mid June-Sep, daily, 9.30am-6.30pm. £2, reductions available. Poetry and musical evenings by appointment. Parking. Wheelchair access to ground floor. ☎ 069 64284; castlematrix@tinet.ie

Irish Palatine Heritage Centre – ♿ Open May-Sep, Mon-Sat, 10am-midday and 2-5pm, Sun, 2-6pm. £2, reductions available. Parking. Tearoom. ☎ 069 63511; Fax 069 63511; ipass@tinet.ie

Desmond Hall – (Dúchas) (♿) Guided tour (50min) mid-June to mid-Sept, daily, 9.30am-6.30pm (5.40pm last tour). £1.50, reductions available. ☎ 069 77408.

Foynes Flying Boat Museum – ♿ Open end-Mar to Oct, daily, 10am-6pm (5pm last admission); Nov-Apr, by appointment. £3.50, reductions available. Film and brochure (French, German, Italian). Parking. Refreshments. ☎/Fax 069 65416; famm@eircom.net; www.webforge.net

Glin Castle – ♿ Guided tour by appointment only. £3, reductions available. Parking. ☎ 068 34173, 34112; Fax 068 34364; knight@iol.ie; www.glincastle.com

Glin Heritage Centre – Open May-Sep, Tue-Sun, 10am-6pm. £2. ☎ 068 34001.

ARAN ISLANDS

Aran Islands Air Service – Operates from Connemara Airport, Inverin (west of Galway) daily, 8 flights (10min) per day (hourly in summer) to Inishmore, Inishmaan and Inisheer. ☎ 091 593 034, 593 054 (reservations); ☎ 099 61109; Fax 091 593 238 (Aer Arann); aerarann.@iol.ie; www.aerann.ie

Galway – Aran Islands Ferry – Operates (2hr) June-Sept, daily, at 10.30am (from Galway Docks), at 5pm (from Aran). ☎ 091 567 676, 091 567 283 (ticket reservations); Fax 091 567 672.

Rossaveal – Aran Islands Ferry – Operates (40min) from Rossaveal to Inishmore, Inishmaan and Inisheer, twice daily (Apr-Nov, 3 times to Inishmore, 4 times from Inishmore); also July-Aug, extra crossings. Return £15, reductions available. Inter-Island ferry service available. Reservation service for minibus, bike hire, walking tours, accommodation, lunch and dinner. Supervised parking at Rossaveal. Coach service from Galway city. ☎ 091 568 903, 561 767, 572 050, 572 273 (after hours); Fax 091 568 538 (Island Ferries Teo); island@iol.ie; www.aranislandferries.com

Doolin (Co Clare) – Aran Islands Ferry – Operates (weather permitting) June-Aug: to Inishmore (60min), 2 times daily; to Inishmaan (45min), 2 times daily; to Inisheer (30min), 6 times daily (additional sailing Fri only at 6.30pm); from Inishmore, 2 times daily; from Inishmaan, 2 times daily; from Inisheer, 5 times daily; Easter-May and Sept: telephone for details. Return £15-£20. ☎ 065 707 4455, 707 4466, 707 4189; Fax 065 707 4417 (Doolin Ferry Co); doolinferries@eircom.net; http://homepage.eircom.net/~doolinferries/

Aran Heritage Centre – (♿) Open Jun-Aug, daily, 10am-7pm; Apr-May and Sept-Oct, daily, 11am-5pm. £2.50, reductions available. Documentary film 'Man of Aran': daily. Café. Bookshop. Craft Shop. Bureau de change. Wheelchair access to ground floor. ☎ 099 61355; Fax 099 61454; ☎ 091 563 081 (Galway Tourist Office).

Dún Aonghasa – (Dúchas) Visitor Centre: Admission times and charges by telephone. 01 661 3111 (Dœchas Head Office).

ATHENRY

Athenry Heritage Centre – ♿ Open Apr-Sept, daily, 10am-6pm. £2.50, reductions available. A/v (45min) in 2/5min soundbites. Parking at Castle. ☎ 091 844 661; athenry heritage@oceanfree.net

Athenry Castle – (Dúchas) (♿) Open mid-Apr to May, Tues-Sun, 10am-5pm; Jun-Sep, daily, 9.30am-6.30pm (5.45pm last admission). £2, reductions available. A/v (20min). Guided tour (45min) by appointment. Parking. Wheelchair access to ground floor. ☎ 091 844 797.

ATHENRY

Athenry Dominican Friary – (Dúchas) Key available from Mrs Sheehan in Church Street (£5 deposit).

St Brendan's Cathedral – & Open daily, 9am-9pm. No charge. Audio tour (£2). Leaflet, guide book available. ☎ 091 841 212; Fax 091 847 367.

Diocesan Museum – & Open Jun-Aug; if closed, key available from the Cathedral Presbytery. Guided tour by appointment. Parking. ☎ 091 841 212.

Excursions

Battle of Aughrim Interpretive Centre – Open Easter-Sep, daily, 10am-6pm; Oct-Easter by appointment. £3, reductions available. Parking. Refreshments. ☎/Fax 0905 73939.

Thoor Ballylee – (&) Open Apr-Sep, daily, 10am-6pm. £3.50, reductions available. A/v presentation (17min). Audio-guide (Dutch, French, German, Irish, Italian, Spanish). Guided tour (30min) available. Parking. ☎ 091 631 436 (Easter-Sept), 091 563 081 (Oct-Easter); Fax 091 565201, 091 631 436.

Kiltartan National Museum – Open Jun-Aug, daily, 10am-6pm; Sep-May, Sun, 1-5pm. £1.50. ☎ 091 632 346, 091 631 069 (after 6pm and Sep-May).

Coole Park – (Dúchas) & Park: Open daily. Visitor Centre: Open mid-Apr to mid-Jun, Tue-Sun, 10am-5pm; mid-Jun to Aug, daily, 9.30am-6.30pm; Sep, daily, 10am-5pm. Last admission 1hr before closing. £2, reductions available. Guided tour (30min) of exhibition: every 30min. A/v presentations (25min; 30min). Nature trails. Parking. Coffee shop. ☎ 091 631 804; Fax 091 631 653.

Dunguaire Castle – Open mid-Apr to Oct, daily, 9.30am-5.30pm (4.30pm last admission). Medieval banquets: daily at 5.30pm and 8.45pm. Castle £2.90, reductions available; banquet £30, reductions available. Parking. Souvenir shop. ☎ 091 37108 (Castle); ☎ 061 361 511, 061 360 788 (Shannon Heritage); Fax 061 361 020.

ATHLONE   🄷 Athlone Castle Visitor Centre, St Peter's Square – ☎ 0902 94630

Shannon Boat Trips – Operate (90min) from Jolly Mariner Marina, Coosan, Jun-Aug, daily, 11am, 2.30pm (times subject to variation). £6, reductions available. Taped commentary; bar. Parking. Coffee shop. ☎ 0902 72892, 72113; Fax 0902 74386 (Athlone Cruises).

Athlone Castle – Open Apr-Oct, daily, 10am-5.30pm. A/v presentation (40min; French, German): last show 4.30pm. ☎ 0902 92912.

Athlone Castle Museum – Open May to early-Oct, daily, 10am-5.30pm. Visitor Centre and Museum £3.50, reductions available. Parking. ☎ 0902 92912 (Castle), 72107 (Urban District Council).

ATHY   🄷 Portlaoise – ☎ 0502 21178

Athy Heritage Centre – Open daily, 10am-6pm (5pm last admission). £2, reductions available. ☎ 0507 33075; Fax 0507 33076; athyheritage@eircom.net; www.kildare.ie

Quaker Meeting House – Open Jun-Sep, Wed-Sun, midday (2pm Sun) to 5pm (6pm Sun); Oct-May, Tues-Sat, midday-5pm. ☎ 0507 23344.

Crookstown Mill and Heritage Centre – (&) Open Apr-Sep, daily, 10am-7pm; Oct-Mar, daily, 11am-4pm. Closed Good Fri, 25 Dec. £2.50, reductions available. Parking. Tearoom. Gift shop. Wheelchair access to ground floor. ☎ 0507 23222.

Irish Pewter Mill and Crafts Centre, Timolin – (&) Open Mon-Fri, 9.30am-4.30pm. Closed Good Fri to Easter Sun, 25 Dec. No charge. Parking. Ramp. ☎ 0507 24162.

B

BANTRY   🄷 Old Courthouse – ☎ 027 50229 (Apr-Oct, Mon-Wed and Fri-Sat; also Jul-Aug, daily)

Whiddy Island Ferry – Operates in summer, daily, every hour.

Bantry House – (&) Open Mar-Oct, daily, 9am-6pm. House and garden £6, reductions available. Brochure (Dutch, French, German, Italian, Spanish). Parking. Tearoom; B&B accommodation. Wheelchair access to ground floor. ☎ 027 50047; Fax 027 50795.

1796 Armada – (&) Open Mar-Oct, daily, 9am-6pm. £3.50, reductions available. ☎ 027 50047; Fax 027 50795.

BIRR

Shannon Cruise – Cruise operates Jun-Sep, Sun, at 3.30pm; also Thur, at 3.30pm (according to demand); from Banagher Marina downstream to Victoria Lock, Meelick and return (1hr 30min). £4, reductions available. ☎ 0509 51112 (Silverline Cruisers).

Birr Castle Demesne – (♿) Open daily, 9am-6pm/sunset. Exhibition Gallery: Open daily, 9am-6pm (exhibitions change annually). £5, reductions available. Demonstration of the telescope: May-Aug, at 2.30pm (weather permitting). Brochure (French, German, Italian, Spanish). Horse-drawn carriage tour of the grounds. Concerts: mid June. Parking. Coffee shop; picnic areas. Wheelchair access to garden and gallery. ☎ 0509 20336; Fax 0509 21583; info@birrcastle.com

Excursions

Slieve Bloom Display Centre – Open Apr-Sept, daily. ☎ 0509 37299; 0509 37272.

Clonmacnoise and West Offaly Railway – ♿ Guided tour by train (50min) Apr-Sep, daily, 10am-5pm, on the hour. £4, reductions availiable. Machine Museum. Craft shop. Parking. Tearoom. ☎ 0905 74114, 74121; Fax 0905 74210.

Cloghan Castle – Guided tour Jul-Aug, Tue-Sun and bank hol Mon, 2-6pm. £4, reductions available. ☎ 0509 51650.

BOYLE

Boyle Abbey – (Dúchas) (♿) Open early-Apr to Oct, daily, 9.30am-6.30pm (5.45pm last admission). £1, reductions available. Guided tour (40min): 10am-5pm, every hour. Leaflet (French, German, Italian, Irish, Spanish). Parking. ☎ 079 62604.

King House – Open Apr to mid-Oct, daily, 10am-6pm (5pm last admission). £3, reductions available. Parking (footbridge over river from car park to house). Coffee shop. Craft shop. ☎ 079 63242; Fax 079 63243; kinghouseboyle@hotmail.com

Frybrook House – Open Jun-Aug, Wed-Sun, 2pm-5.30pm; Sep-May, by appointment. £3, reductions available. Parking. ☎ 079 63513.

Excursions

Lough Key Forest Park – Open daily. Admission charge (Easter to Sep), £3. Moylurgh Tower: Open Easter-Sep, daily, 8am (11am Sat-Sun) to 4pm (6pm Sat; 7pm Sun). Parking. Coffee shop. ☎ 079 62363 (Irish Forestry Board – Coillte Teoranta).

Sliabh An Iarainn Visitor Centre – Open Apr-Oct, daily, 10am (2pm Sun) to 6pm. A/v presentation (30min) £1, reductions available. ☎ 078 41522.

O'Carolan Harp Festival, Keadew – Late-Jul to early-Aug. Information from the Secretary, Keadew, Co Roscommon. ☎ 078 47204; Fax 078 47511.

O'Carolan Harp and Traditional Music Festival, Nobber – First Fri-Sun in Oct. Information from the Secretary, Keadew, Co Roscommon. ☎ 046 52115 or 52272.

BOYNE VALLEY

Brú na Bóinne Visitor Centre – (Dúchas) Access to tombs site via Visitor Centre only (south bank of the River Boyne). Footbridge from Visitor Centre to bus depot. Shuttle-bus service from bus depot to tombs site (3mi/5km) every 30min. In the high season it is advisable to arrive early at the Visitor Centre as guided tours are on first-come-first-served basis.

Visitor Centre: Open May-Sep, daily, 9am-6.30pm (7pm Jun-mid-Sep); Oct-Apr, daily, 9.30am-5.30pm (5pm Nov-Feb); last admission 45min before closing. Closed 25-26 Dec. A/v presentation (7min). Leaflet (French, German, Irish, Italian, Japanese, Spanish). Guided tour of Visitor Centre (45min).

Newgrange Passage Grave: (♿) Guided tour (45min) daily; last tour 90min before closing time of Visitor Centre.

Knowth Passage Grave: Guided tour (45min; no access to interior of tomb) May-Oct; last tour 1hr 30min before closing time of Visitor Centre. Centre (1hr) £2, reductions available; Centre and Newgrange (2hr) £4, reductions available; Centre and Knowth (2hr) £3, reductions available; Centre and Newgrange and Knowth (3hr) £7, reductions available. Parking. Tearooms. ☎ 041 988 0300, 041 982 4488; Fax 041 982 4798.

Hill of Tara – (Dúchas) (♿) Site: Open daily. Visitor Centre: Open mid-June to mid-Sept, daily, 9.30am-6.30pm; May to mid-June and mid-Sept to Oct, daily, 10am-5pm; last admission 45min before closing. £1.50, reductions available. A/v presentation (22min; French, German, Italian). Guided tour (40min) by appointment. Parking. Refreshments. Gift shop. ☎ 046 25903; Fax 046 25903; Nov-Apr ☎ 041 982 4488; Fax 042 982 4798.

Mellifont Old Abbey – (Dúchas) (♿) Open mid-June to mid-Sept, daily, 9.30am-6.30pm; May to mid-June and mid-Sep to Oct, daily, 10am-5pm; last admission 45min before closing. £1.50, reductions available. Guided tour (45min) by appointment. Exhibition centre. Parking. Access by stone steps. ☎ 041 982 6459, 041 982 4488 (Nov-Apr); Fax 041 982 4798.

Termonfeckin Tower House – (Dúchas) Key available from the cottage opposite.

Slane Castle – Castle and grounds closed until further notice.

Ledwidge Cottage Museum – ♿ Open daily, 10am-1pm and 2pm-5.30pm. £2, reductions available. Parking. ☎ 041 9822 4544; 041 982 4244.

BUNCRANA
🚹 ☎ 074 21160 (Jun-Oct, Mon-Sat)

Dunree Fort Military Museum – Open Jun-Sep, daily, 10.30am (12.30pm Sun) to 6pm. £3, reductions available. Guided tour (30min) available. Parking. Refreshments. ☎ 077 61817.

Grianán Ailigh Centre – ♿ Open daily, 10am (midday in winter) to 6pm. £1.50, reductions available. Restaurant: Open daily, 10am (midday in winter) to 10pm. ☎ 077 68000; Fax 077 68012; www.griananailigh.com

The BURREN
🚹 Cliffs of Moher, Liscannor – ☎ 065 708 1171 (Apr-Oct, daily)

Burren eXposure – ♿ Open Apr-Oct, daily, 10am-6pm. £3.50, reductions available. Parking. ☎ 065 7077 277; Fax 065 7077 278; douglasculligan@eircom.net

Newtown Castle and Trail – Open Easter-Sept, daily, 10am-6pm (7pm Jul-Aug). Last admission 1hr before closing. Castle and trail £3.50, castle or trail £2. Parking. ☎ 065 77200; Fax 065 77201.

Aillwee Cave – (♿) Guided tour (35min; French, German) mid-Mar to Nov, daily, 10am-6pm (7pm Jul-Aug); Nov to mid-Mar, daily, 3 tours. £4.75, reductions available. Brochure (French, German, Japanese, Spanish). Farm shop: cheese-making daily. Parking. Restaurant. Disabled by appointment. ☎ 065 707 7036, 707 7067; Fax 065 707 7107; aillwee@eircom.net; www.aillweecave.ie

Burren Perfumery – Open Mar-Jun and Sept-Oct, daily, 9.30am-5pm; Jun-Aug, daily, 9am-7pm; in winter by appointment. No charge. Parking. ☎ 065 89102; Fax 065 89200.

Leamaneh Castle – For permission to view ask at the modern house (left of the castle).

Poulnabrone, The Burren
Irish Picture Library

Burren Centre – ♿ Open Jun-Sep, daily, 9.30am-6pm; Mar-May and Oct, daily, 10am-5pm. £2.50. Guided tour (30min; French, German etc). Parking. Restaurant. Bookshop. Tourist information. Bureau de change. ☎ 065 708 8030; Fax 065 708 8102.

Cliffs of Moher Visitor Centre – ♿ Site: Open daily. Visitor Centre: Open Jun-Aug, daily, 9am-8pm; Sep-May, daily, 9.30am-5.30pm. O'Brien's Tower: (weather permitting) May-Sep, daily, 9.30am-5.30pm. Centre no charge; O'Brien's Tower £1.50, reductions available. Closed Good Fri, 24-26 Dec. Parking. Tearoom. ☎ 065 7081 565 (Centre); ☎ 061 361 511, 061 360 788 (Shannon Heritage); Fax 061 261 020.

C

CAHER
🚹 ☎ 052 41453 (Jun-Sep, Mon-Sat; also Sun Jul-Aug)

Cahir Castle – (Dúchas) (♿) Open mid-Jun to mid-Sep, daily, 9am-7.30pm; mid-Mar to mid-Jun and mid-Sep to mid-Oct, daily, 9.30am-5.30pm; mid-Oct to mid-Mar, daily, 9.30am-4.30pm. Last admission 45min before closing. Closed 24-30 Dec. £2, reductions available. A/v presentation (French, German, Italian). ☎ 052 41011; Fax 052 42324.

Swiss Cottage – (Dúchas) Guided tour (25min) May-Sep, daily, 10am-6pm; mid-Mar to Apr and Oct-Nov, Tues-Sun and bank hol Mon, 10am-1pm and 2-6pm. Last admission 45min before closing. £2, reductions available. Parking. Guide book (Irish, Italian, French, German). Access by stone steps. ☎ 052 41144.

Excursions

Mitchelstown Cave – Guided tour (35min; French, German) daily, 10am-6pm, every 15min (every 30min in winter). £3.50, reductions available. Parking. ☎ 052 67246.

Ronald Reagan Centre, Ballyporeen – By appointment only. ☎ 052 67105 (Parish Priest, Ballyporeen).

CARLOW
🚹 Kennedy Avenue – ☎ 0503 31554 (Mon-Fri; also Sat Apr-Oct)

Carlow Museum – Open Tue-Fri, 11am-4.45pm. £1, reductions available. Guided tour available. ☎ 0503 40730.

Excursions

Altamont Gardens – (Dúchas) (♿) Open Thur-Sun and bank hols, 10.30am-6.30pm. £2, reductions available. Parking. Plant sales. ☎/Fax 0503 59444.

CARRICK-ON-SHANNON
🚹 Old Barrel Store, The Marina – ☎ 078 20170

Costello Chapel – Open Mar-Oct, daily. No charge. Brochure (French, German). ☎ 078 20251.

Excursion

Lough Rynn Demesne – Open May-Aug, daily, 10am-7pm. Grounds £1.25min-£3.50 max (per car). Guided tour £1, reductions available. Restaurant. Craft shop. Plant sales. ☎ 078 31427; Fax 078 31518.

CASHEL
🚹 Town Hall, Main Street – ☎ 062 61333 (Apr-Sep, Mon-Sat; also Sun Jul-Aug)

Rock of Cashel (St Patrick's Rock) – (Dúchas) (♿) Open daily, 9am-7.30pm (5.30pm, mid-March to mid-June; 5pm mid-Sept to mid-Mar). Last admission 45min before closing. Closed 25-26 Dec. £3.50, reductions available. A/v presentation (French, German, Italian). Parking 50p. ☎ 062 61437; Fax 062 62988; www.heritageireland.ie

Brú Ború – ♿ Open May-Sep, daily, 9am-5pm. Craft shop: Open daily, 9am-5pm. Folk Theatre (music, song, dance): Open Jun-Sep, Tues-Sat, at 9pm. Theatre show £8; Theatre show and Banquet £25. Restaurant. ☎ 062 61122; Fax 062 62700; bruboru@comhaltas.com

Cashel Heritage Centre – Open Mar-Sep, daily, 9.30am-5.30pm; Oct-Feb, Mon-Fri, 9.30am-5.30pm. No charge. Commentary (10min; French, German, Italian, Spanish). Shop. ☎ 062 62511; Fax 062 62068; cashelhc@iol.ie; www.iol.ie/tipp

Cashel Palace Gardens – Open daily; Bishop's Walk closed Nov-Good Fri. Parking. Café. ☎ 062 61437.

GPA Bolton Library – Open Mar-Aug, Tue-Sun, 9.30am-5.30pm; Sep-Feb, Mon-Fri, 9.30am-5.30pm. £1.50, reductions available. Guided tour (30min) available. Parking. ☎ 062 61944 (Library), 62511 (Cashel Heritage Centre).

Cashel Anglican Cathedral – Open May-Sep, daily, 9.30am-5.30pm; if closed, key available from Bolton Library in Cathedral grounds. No charge. Parking. ☎ 062 61232.

Folk Village – ♿ Open daily, 10am-7.30pm (earlier mid-Oct to mid-Mar). £2, reductions available. Brochure (Dutch, French, German, Irish, Italian, Spanish). Guided tour (1hr) subject to demand. Parking. ☎ 062 62525.

Excursions

Holy Cross Abbey Church – Open daily, 10am-6pm. Guided tours, Jun-Sep. ☎ 0504 43241 or 43118.

Lár na Páirce – Open Mar-Oct, daily, 10am-1pm and 2pm-5.15pm. £2.50, reductions available. ☎ 0504 23579.

CAVAN
🚹 1 Farnham Street – ☎ 049 433 1942 (Apr-Sep, Mon-Sat)

Cavan Crystal – ♿ Open Mon-Fri, 9.30am-6pm; Sat-Sun and public hols, midday (10am Sat) to 5pm. Guided factory tour (advance booking). No charge. A/v presentation. Brochure. Parking. Restaurant. ☎ 049 433 1800; Fax 049 433 1198; cavancrystal@eircom.net

Life Force Mill – Open Mon-Sat, 9am-5pm, tours by appointment. £4, reductions available. ☎ 049 436 2722; Fax 049 436 2923; lifeforce.mill@oceanfree.net

Excursions

Cavan County Museum – Open Tues-Sat, 10am-5pm; also Jun-Sep, Sun, 2pm-6pm. £2, reductions available. ☎ 049 854 4070; Fax 049 854 4332; ccmuseum@tinet.ie

Carraig Craft Visitor Centre and Basketry Museum – Open Apr-Oct, Sun-Fri, 10am (2pm Sun) to 6pm; Nov-Mar, by appointment. £2, reductions available. Craft shop. Coffee shop. Tourist information. ☎ 049 854 0179.

Kilmore Cathedral – Open by appointment. Key available from the Deanery, Danesfort. No charge. Parking. ☎/Fax 049 433 1918; dean@kilmore.anglican.org

CLONMACNOISE

🅱 ☎ 0905 74134 (Apr-Sep)

Clonmacnoise Visitor Centre and Site – (Dúchas) &. Open Jun to early-Sep, daily, 9am-7pm; early-Sep to May, daily, 10am-6pm (5.30pm Nov to mid-Mar). Last admission 45min before closing. Closed 25 Dec. £3.50, reductions available. A/v presentation (22min; French, German, Italian). Parking. ☎ 0905 74195; Fax 0905 74273.

Temple Connor – Services: May-Aug, last Sun in the month.

CLONMEL

🅱 Community Office – ☎ 052 22960 (daily)
🅱 Heritage Centre, Carrick-on-Suir – ☎ 051 640 2000 (daily)
🅱 Tierry Centre, Fethard – ☎ 052 31000 (all year)

Tipperary Crystal – (&.) Open Mar-Oct, daily, 9am (9.30am Sat; 11am Sun) to 6pm (5pm Sat-Sun); Nov-Feb, daily, 10am-5.30pm. Guided tour (30min) May-Sep, from 10.30am. No charge. Parking. Refreshments. Access for the disabled (telephone in advance). ☎ 051 641 188; Fax 051 641 190; tippcrys@iol.ie; www.tipperary-crystal.com

County Museum – Open Tue-Sat, 10am-5pm. Closed public hols. ☎ 052 25399; Fax 052 80390; museum@southtippcoco.ie

St Mary's Church (Anglican) – Services: Sun, 10.45am. Key available from the shop of H J Morgan outside the West Gate. ☎ 052 26643 (Revd George Knowd), 087 284 2350 (mobile).

Museum of Transport – Open Mon-Sat, 10am-6pm; also Jun-Sep, Sun, 2.30-6pm. Coffee shop. ☎ 052 29727.

Excursions

Carrick-on-Suir Heritage Centre – (&.) Open May-Aug, daily, 10am-5pm; Sept-Apr, Mon-Fri, 10am-5pm. £2, £5 (family), £1.50 (student, child), £1.50 (senior citizen). Parking. Picnic area. Shop. ☎ 051 640 200; cosda@iol.ie; www.iol.ie/~cosda

Ormond Castle – (Dúchas) (&.) Guided tour (40min) mid-June to Sept, daily, 9.30am-6.30pm (5.45pm last admission). £2, reductions available. Leaflet (French, German, Irish, Italian, Spanish). Public parking nearby. ☎ 051 640 787.

Fethard Museum – &. Open Sun and bank hol Mon, 11.30-5pm; otherwise by appointment. Sunday £1; other days £2, reductions available. Guided tour (30min). Brochure (French). Collectors' market and car boot sale: Sun and bank hol Mon. Parking. Picnic area. Playground. ☎ 052 31516.

COBH

Cork Harbour Car Ferry (Carrigaloe/Glenbrook) – Operates daily, 7am-12.15am. Time 5min. Capacity 28 cars. Return £3.50 (car), £1 (pedestrian), reductions available. ☎ 021 811 223; Fax 021 812 645.

Cork Harbour Cruises from Kennedy Pier – Operate from Kennedy Pier (1hr – harbour forts, Spike Island, Naval base and major harbour industries) early-June to early-Sep, daily, 12midday, 2pm, 3pm, otherwise by appointment. £3, £2 (child). Parking (5-10min walk). Refreshments available ashore. ☎ 021 811 485 (Marine Transport Services Ltd).

Rail Service To Cork Via Fota Island – Operates between Cobh and Cork via Fota Island Wildlife Park, daily. ☎ 021 506 766 (Cork Railway Station). www.irishrail.ie

St Colman's Cathedral (Roman Catholic) – Open daily, 7.30am-9pm (8pm winter). No charge. Brochure (French, German, Irish, Italian, Spanish). Parking. ☎ 021 813 222; Fax 021 813 488.

Cobh Heritage Centre: The Queenstown Story – &. Open daily, 10am-6pm (5pm last admission). £3.50, £10 (family 2A+4C), £2 (child). Audio-visual presentation (5min). Brochure (French, German, Italian, Spanish). Café. Shop. ☎ 021 4813 591; Fax 021 4813 595; cobhher@indigo.ie; www.cobhheritage.com

Cobh Museum – Open Easter-Oct, Mon-Sat, daily, 11am-1pm and 2-6pm (5.30pm last admission); Sun, 3-6pm. £1, £2.50 (family), 50p (child). Brochure (French, German, Spanish). ☎ 021 4814 240; Fax 021 8411 018; cobhmuseum@hotmail.com

Excursions

Fota House – Due to open summer 2001. ☎ 021 812 555 (Administrator), 021 273 251 (Cork Tourist Office).

Fota Wildlife Park – ♿ Open mid-Mar to end-Sep, daily, 10am (11am Sun) to 6pm (5pm last admission); Oct to early-March, Sat-Sun. Time 90min. £4.80, £18 (family 2A+4C), £2.70 (child (3-16)/student). Train: single 50p, round trip £1. Parking £1. Children's playground. Restaurant. Gift shop. ☎ 021 4812 678, 4812 736; Fax 021 4812 744; info@fotawildlife.ie; www.fotawildlife.ie

Fota Arboretum – (Dúchas) (♿) Open 9am to 6pm (5pm Nov-Mar). Closed 25 Dec. Parking £1. Guided tours by arrangement. Self-service restaurant, picnic area. ☎/Fax 021 4812 728; Mob ☎ 087 279 9508.

CONNEMARA

🛈 Galway Road, Clifden – ☎ 095 21163

Inishbofin Ferry (1) – Operates (weather permitting) Apr-Oct, from Cleggan, at 11.30am, 6.45pm (also 10am, 2pm, 5.45pm July-Aug); from Inishbofin, at 9am, 5pm (also 10.45am, 1pm, 6.15pm July-Aug). ☎ 095 44642, 21520; Fax 095 44327 (Kings Ferries); conamara@indigo.ie; www.failte.com/cleggan

Inishbofin Ferry (2) – Dun Aengus operates Apr-Sept, daily, from Cleggan, at 11.30am and 6.45pm (also 2pm June-Aug), from Inishbofin at 9.15am and 5pm (also 12.30pm June-Aug). Time 40min. Return £10. Brochure (French, German, Irish, Italian, Spanish). ☎ 095 45806 (Patrick O'Halloran).

Connemara National Park – (Dúchas) ♿ Open daily. Visitor Centre: Open Apr-Oct, daily, 10am (9.30am July-Aug) to 5.30pm (6.30pm June-Aug); last admission 45min before closing. £2, £5 (family), £1 (child/student), £1.50 (senior citizen). Audio-visual presentation (15min). Leaflet (Dutch, French, German, Irish, Italian, Spanish). Self-guiding trails. Guided nature walks (2-3hr): July-Aug, Mon, Wed, Fri, 10.30am (rain-wear and boots required). Nature days for children: Tues and Thur from 10.30am. Parking. Tearoom; indoor and outdoor picnic areas. ☎ 095 41054, 41006; Fax 095 41005.

Kylemore Abbey – Visitor Centre – (♿) Abbey exhibition, Gothic Church, lake walk and video: Open all year, daily, 9am-6pm. Closed Good Friday and Christmas week. Garden: Easter to Oct, 10.30am-4.30pm. Closed Good Friday. Joint ticket £6, £12 (family 2A+children under 16), £4 (student/senior citizen); Garden only or Abbey exhibition, Gothic Church, lake walk and video £3.30, £7 (family 2A+children under 16), £2.30 (student/senior citizen). Audio-visual presentation (French, German, Italian). Leaflet (French, German, Italian, Spanish, Dutch). Parking. Restaurant. Wheelchair access to Craft shop, restaurant and video presentation. Limited access to Abbey. ☎ 095 41146; Fax 095 41145; enquiries@kylemoreabbey.ie; www.kylemore-abbey.com

Leenane Cultural Centre – Open Apr-Oct, daily, 9am-6pm; otherwise for groups only. £2, £5 (family), £1 (concession). Audio-visual presentation (13min; French, German, Irish, Italian). Brochure. Shop. Café. ☎ 095 42323, 42231; Fax 095 42337; noeot@eircom.net; www.leenane-connemara.com/shop.htm

St Macdara's Island Ferry – No regular sailings. Passage offered (weather permitting) by local fishermen on Festival Day (16 July) and other days.

Pearse's Cottage – (Dúchas) (♿) Open mid-June to mid-Sept, daily, 9.30am-6.30pm (5.45pm last admission). £1, £3 (family), 40p (child/student), 70p (senior citizen). Parking. ☎ 091 574 292.

CORK

🛈 Grand Parade – ☎ 021 427 3251
🛈 Airport – ☎ Freephone at Airport Terminal
🛈 Blarney – ☎ 021 438 1624 (daily)
🛈 Castle Gates, The Square, Macroom – ☎ 028 43280 (Jun-Sep, Mon-Sat)

Triskel Arts Centre – ♿ Open Mon-Sat, 10am-5.30pm. Doors open at 7pm for evening performances. Gallery no charge. Café. Bar. ☎ 021 427 2022; Fax 021 427 2592; triskel@iol.ie

Crawford Municipal Art Gallery – ♿ Open Mon-Sat, 10am-5pm. No charge. Guided tour by appointment. Restaurant. ☎ 021 427 3377; Fax 021 427 5680; www.synergy.ie/crawford

Cork Archives Institute – Open by appointment Tues-Fri, 10am-1pm and 2.30-5pm. Closed public hols. ☎ 021 427 7809.

Cork Vision Centre – Open Tue-Sat, 10am-5pm. No charge; donations welcome. ☎ 021 427 9925; visioncentre@eircom.net; www.homepage.tinet.ie/~visioncentre/

University College – Guided tour by prior arrangement for groups only. £15 per group. Walking Tour of Cork: Operates daily. ☎ 021 490 2371; Fax 021 427 7004; information@ucc.ie; www.ucc.ie

Cork Public Museum – Open Mon-Fri, 11am-1pm and 2.15-6pm (5pm Sep-May); Sun, 3-5pm. Closed public hols. Time 30min. Sun £1, reductions available. Parking. ☎ 021 427 0679; Fax 021 427 0931; museum@corkcorp.ie

St Fin Barre's Cathedral – ♿ Open Mon-Sat, 10am-5.30pm (5pm Oct-Apr). Services: Sun, 8am, 11.15am, 7pm. Closed public hols. Donation (£2). Guided tour available. Leaflets (French, German, Italian, Spanish, Dutch, Japanese). Parking. ☎ 021 496 3387, 496 4742 (Revd Michael Jackson); sfb@iol.ie; www.creativecom.net/stfinbarres

Cork Heritage Park – ♿ Open May-Sep, daily, 10.30am (midday Sat-Sun) to 5.30pm. £3.50, reductions available. Parking. Café, picnic areas. Bus routes 2 and 10 from Cork city centre. ☎ 021 435 7730; Fax 021 435 9395.

Shandon Bells – Open Mon-Sat and public hols, 9am-6pm (9.30am-4pm winter); Sun by appointment. £4, reductions available. Parking. ☎ 021 450 5906; shandonbells@yahoo.com; www.shandonsteeple.com

Cork Butter Museum – Open May-Sep, Sun-Fri, 10am-1pm and 2-5pm. £2.50, £2 (concession). ☎ 021 430 0600; Fax 021 430 9966.

Cork City Gaol – Open Mar-Oct, daily, 9.30am-6pm; Nov-Feb, 10am-5pm. Last admission 1hr before closing. £3.50, reductions available. Audio-guide (Dutch, French, German, Irish, Italian, Japanese, Spanish). ☎ 021 4305 022; Fax 021 4307 230.

Excursions

Blarney Castle – (♿) Open Mon-Sat, 9am-7pm (6.30pm May and Sep; 6pm/sunset, Oct-Apr); Sun, 9.30am-5.30pm/sunset. Closed 24-25 Dec. £3.50, reductions available. Brochure (French, German). Parking. Refreshments. ☎ 021 438 5252; Fax 021 438 1518; info@blarneyc.iol.ie

Blarney Woollen Mills – ♿ Open daily, 9am-6pm (8pm, Jun-Aug; 7pm, May; 8pm, Fri in December). Closed 1 Jan, 25-26 December. Restaurant. ☎ 021 385 280; Fax 021 381 547; info@blarney.ie; www.blarney.com

Dunkathel House – Open May to mid-Oct, Wed-Sun, 2pm-6pm. £2, reductions available. Brochure (French, German, Italian). Guided tour (30min) available. Parking. ☎ 021 482 1014; Fax 021 482 1023.

Riverstown House – Open May-Sept, Wed-Sat, 2pm-6pm; otherwise by appointment. £3. Guided tour available. Parking. ☎ 021 482 205.

Ballincollig Gunpowder Mills Heritage Centre – ♿ Guided tour (1hr) Apr-Sept, Sun-Fri, 10am-5pm. £3, reductions available. A/v presentation (15min). Guided tour (French, German). Parking. Coffee shop. Craft shop. ☎ 021 487 4430; Fax 021 487 4836; ballinco@indigo.ie; indigo.ie/~ballinco

D

DINGLE 🅿 The Quay – ☎ 066 915 1188 (Mar-Nov)

Craft Centre, Ceardlann Na Coille – Open daily, 10am-6pm (earlier in winter); Jan-Feb, phone for opening times. No charge. Parking. Café. ☎ 066 915 2039.

Oceanworld Aquarium – Open daily, from 10am. £4. ☎ 066 915 2111; Fax 066 915 2155.

Presentation Convent Chapel – Open June-Aug, Mon-Fri, 10am-noon and 2-4pm.

Dingle Library – Open Tues-Sat, 10.30am-1.30pm and 2.30-5pm. ☎ 066 915 1499; library.dingle@eircom.net

Great Blasket Centre – (Dúchas) ♿ Open Apr-Oct, daily, 10am-6pm (7pm July-Aug). Last admission 45min before closing. £2.50, £6 (family), £1 (child/student), £1.75 (senior citizen). Audio-visual presentation (22min; English, French, German, Irish, Italian). Guided tour (45min) by appointment. Parking. Coffee shop. ☎ 066 915 6444, 915 6371; Fax 066 915 6446.

Blasket Islands Ferry – An t-Oileánach and Oileán na n-óg operate cruises and tours from Dunquin to the Blasket Islands in calm weather. ☎ 066 9156422.

Corca Dhuibhne Regional Museum – Open May-Sep, daily, 10am-5pm; Oct-Apr, by request. £1.50. Refreshments in summer. Bureau de Change. Bookshop. ☎ 066 915 6100, 915 6333; Fax 066 915 6348.

DONEGAL 🅿 The Quay – ☎ 073 21148
🅿 Main Street, Bundoran – ☎ 072 41350 (Jun-Sep, Mon-Sat; also Sun Jul-Aug)

Hand-Loom Weaving – (♿) Open all year, demonstrations given on request (in the shop), Mon-Sat, 9am-6pm. Leaflet (French, German). ☎ 073 22660; Fax 073 23271; sales@mageeshop. com; www.mageeshop.com

Waterworld – Open Easter week and Jun-Aug, daily, 10am-2pm and 3pm-7pm; Apr-May and Sep, Sat-Sun, same times. £5, £3.50, (child under 16), £1.50 (child under 3). Sauna/steam bath. Restaurant. ☎ 072 41172/3; Fax 072 42168.

Donegal Castle – (Dúchas) Open mid-Mar to Oct, daily, 9.30am-6.30pm (5.45pm last admission). £3, £7.50 (family), £1.25 (child/student), £1.50 (senior citizen). Guided tour (30min) every hour. Leaflet (French, German, Irish, Italian, Spanish). ☎ 073 22405.

Donegal Railway Heritage Centre – Open Mon-Sat, 9am-5pm, Sun 2-5pm (closed Sun, Oct-May). £2, £5 (family 2A+2C), £1 (child 5-15/student/senior citizen). ☎ 073 22655; www.cdrrs.future.easyspace.com

Assaroe Abbey Waterwheels – Open Easter week, May-Aug, daily, 10.30am-6.30pm; otherwise, Sun, 1.30pm-6.30pm. No charge. Parking. Coffee shop, restaurant. Craft shop. ☎ 072 51580.

DONEGAL COAST
🛈 Dunglow – ☎ 075 21297 (Jun-Aug, daily)

Glencolumbkille Folk Village – ♿ Guided tour (20min) Apr-Sept, daily, 10am (noon Sun) to 6pm, every 30min. £2, £7 (family), £1.50 (child/reduction). Brochure (English only). Guided tour. Nature walk. Craft shop. Tearoom. Tourist information. Bureau de change. Parking. ☎ 073 30017, 39026; Fax 073 30334; folkmus@indigo.ie; www.infowing.ie/donegal/ad/fr.htm

Ulster Cultural Institute – ♿ Open Mon-Fri, 9.30am-5pm; also Sat-Sun in summer. No charge. Restaurant. ☎ 073 30248; Fax 073 30348; oidsgael@iol.ie; www.oidas-gael.com

Ardara Heritage Centre – Open Jun-Sep, daily, 10am-6pm, Oct-May, Mon-Fri, 10am-5pm. Audio-visual presentation (15min). Tearoom. ☎ 075 41704.

St Connell's Museum and Heritage Centre – Open Apr to late-Sept, Mon-Sat, 10am-5.30pm. £2, 50p (child). Parking.

Aranmore Island Ferry – Operates from Burtonport: Jun-Aug, Mon-Sat, 8 sailings daily (7 in Jun); Sun and church hols, 7 sailings daily (6 in Jun); from Aranmore: Jun-Aug, Mon-Sat, 8 sailings daily (6 in June); Sun and church hols, 7 sailings daily (6 in June). Fewer sailings out of season. Return: £7 (pedestrian; reductions available), £20 (car and driver), £28 (car and family). ☎ 075 20532; Fax 075 20750.

Tory Island Ferry from Bunbeg and Magheraroarty – Operates (weather permitting) Bunbeg – Tory Island (1hr 30min): June-Aug, daily, once; Oct, daily, once; Nov-May, 5 sailings per week; Tory Island – Bunbeg (1hr 30min): June-Aug, daily, once. Magheroarty – Tory Island (45min): June, twice daily; July-Aug, 3 times daily. Tory Island – Magheroarty (45min): June, 3 times daily; July-Aug, 4 times daily. Return fare £15, reductions available.

Coastal Cruises from Bunbeg: Operate on request. Coastal Cruises from Magheroarty (Meenlaragh): Operate on request.

☎ 074 35502 and 074 35920 (accommodation on Tory Island). ☎ 074 35061 (Magheroarty Pier Office). ☎ 075 31991 (Bunbeg Pier Office); 31320 and 31340; Fax 075 31665 (Donegal Coastal Cruises (Turasmara Teo), Strand Road, Middletown, Derrybeg, Co Donegal).

Dunfanaghy Workhouse – ♿ Open Easter-Sep, daily, 10am (12midday Sat-Sun) to 5pm. Admission charge. ☎ 074 36540.

Doe Castle – (Dúchas) Refurbishment in progress; scheduled to reopen during 2001. Parking. ☎ 074 38124 (Caretaker); 074 38445 (Castle).

Flight of the Earls Exhibition – (♿) Open Easter-Sep, daily, 10am (midday Sun and public hols) to 5pm. Closed Good Fri. £1.50, reductions available. Guided tour (45min) available. Parking. ☎ 074 58178; Fax 074 58458; infotheflightoftheearls.com

Donegal Ancestry – Open Mon-Thur, 9am-4.30pm (3.30pm Fri); also Sat-Sun, Mar-Oct. ☎ 074 51266; Fax 51702; donances@indigo.ie; www.indigo.ie/donances

DONEGAL GLENS
🛈 Derry Road, Letterkenny – ☎ 074 21160

Donegal County Museum – ♿ Open Mon-Fri, 10am-12.30pm and 1-4.30pm, Sat, 1-4.30pm. No charge. ☎ 074 24613; Fax 074 26522.

Newmills Corn and Flax Mills – (Dúchas) Open early-June to late-Sept, daily, 10am-6.30pm. Last admission 45min before closing. £2, £1 (child/student), £1.50 (senior citizen), £5 (family 2A+2C). Parking. ☎ 074 25115.

Fintown Railway – ♿ Operates May-Sept, daily, 11am-5pm. £2, £6 (family 2A+3C), £1 (child). Café. ☎ 075 46280.

Colmcille Heritage Centre – ♿ Open Easter and May to early-Oct, daily, 10.30am (1pm Sun) to 6.30pm; otherwise by appointment. £1.50, £1 (child). Guided tour (15min; Irish, English) available. Audio-guide available. Brochure. Audio-visual presentation (French, German, Irish). Parking. Tearoom. ☎ 074 37306, 37044.

Glebe Gallery – (Dúchas) (♿) Open Easter (Holy Saturday-Low Sunday) and late-May to late-Sept, daily except Fri, 11am-6.30pm. Last admission 1hr before closing. £3, £1.50 (child/student), £2.25 (senior citizen), £7.50 (family). Guided tour (35min) available. Parking. Tearoom (summer). Wheelchair access to ground floor and gallery only. ☎ 074 37071; Fax 074 37521

Glenveagh National Park – (Dúchas) (♿) Park and Visitor Centre: Open Easter week-end to early-Nov, daily, 10am-6.30pm; last admission 5pm. Castle: Guided tour (45min), same times as above. Park or castle £2, £1 (child/student), £1.50 (senior citizen), £5 (family). Audio-visual presentation (25min; French, German, Irish, Italian). Leaflet (Dutch, French, German, Irish, Italian, Spanish). Guided tour available. No photography in castle. Parking. Minibus (no charge) between Visitor Centre and Castle and gardens. Restaurant, cafeteria; tearoom in castle (Full season). Wheelchair access to Visitor Centre, gardens and ground floor of castle. ☎ 074 37090; Fax 074 37072.

Dunlewy Centre – Open mid-Apr to Nov, Mon-Sat, 10.30am-6pm, Sun, 11am-7pm. No charge. Guided tour of cottage, £3. Boat trip with commentary, £3. Craft shop. Restaurant. ☎ 075 31699; Fax 075 31968.

Raphoe Cathedral – Services: Sun, 8am, 12.15pm, 6pm; Wed, 10.30am; Saints' Days 8pm. ☎ 074 45226 (The Very Revd S White).

Seat of Power – ♿ Open daily, 9am (10am Sat; 11.30am Sun) to 5pm (10pm Fri-Sun). £3, reductions available. ☎ 074 41733; Fax 074 41228; www.infowing.ie/seatofpower

Cavanacor House – (♿) Open Easter-end Aug, Tues-Sun and bank hols, 12midday (2pm Sun) to 6pm. £2.50. Gallery: Open Tues-Sat, 12midday-6pm, no charge. Wheelchair access only to craft shop and tearoom. ☎/Fax 074 41143; joannaok7@hotmail. com; www.b.parsons.edu/~eokane/cavanacorgallery

DROGHEDA
🚌 Bus Station – ☎ 041 983 7070

Drogheda Museum – (♿) Open Mon-Sat, 10am-6pm, Sun, 2.30-5.30pm. £3, reductions available. Last tour (1hr) 1hr before closing. Walking tour of Drogheda available. Parking. Wheelchair access to ground floor only. ☎/Fax 041 983 3097; Fax 041 984 1599.

St Peter's Church (RC) – ♿ Open Jun-Aug, daily, 8.30am-9pm (7.30pm, Sat), Sep-Oct and Mar-May, daily, 8.30am-7.30pm; Nov-Feb, daily, 8.30am-6pm (7.30pm, Sat). Services: Sun 8am, 11am, midday; Sat, 6.15pm. ☎ 041 983 8537; Fax 041 984 1351; www.saintpetersdrogheda.ie

St Peter's Church (Anglican) – Open by arrangement. Services: Sun 8.30am, 11.45am. drogheda@armagh.anglican.org; www.drogheda.armagh.anglican.org

Excursion

Whiteriver Mills – Open Apr-Sep, daily, 10am (2pm Sun) to 6pm. £2, £1 (child). ☎ 041 685 1141.

DUBLIN
🛈 Dublin Tourism Centre, Suffolk Street
🛈 Baggot Street Bridge (Mon-Sat except bank hols)
🛈 Dublin Airport Arrivals Hall (daily)
🛈 Ferry Terminal, Dun Laoghaire (Mon-Sat)
🛈 The Square Shopping Centre, Tallaght – ☎ (Mon-Sat except bank hols)
🛈 ☎ 1859; 020 7493 3201

Dublin Bus City Tour – Operates May-Sept, daily, 9.30am-5pm, every 10min; 5-6.30pm, every 30min; Oct-Apr, daily, 9.30am-4.30pm, every 15min. No tour 17 Mar, 30 Oct, 25 Dec. Hop-on-hop-off circular tour (13 stops; min 1hr 15min) starting from 59 Upper O'Connell Street. £7, £3.50 (child). ☎ 01 873 4222; Fax 01 703 3031 (Dublin Bus).

Gray Line Bus Old Dublin Tour – Operates daily, Mar-Oct, 10am-5pm every 10-15min; Nov-Feb, 10am-4pm, every 30min. Hop-on-hop-off circular tour (9 stops; min 1hr) starting from 14 Upper O'Connell Street and including Merrion Square, Fitzwilliam Square and Phoenix Park. £850, £3 (child), £7.50 (concession); ticket valid all day. ☎ 01 605 7705 (Gray Line Tours); www.guidefriday.com

Guide Friday Bus Tour – Operates Mon-Fri, every 15min, Sat-Sun, every 10min (20-30min in winter) from 9.30am. Closed 21-27 Dec. Hop-on hop-off circular tour (20 stops; min 1hr 30min) starting from O'Connell Street. £8.50, £20 (family), £3 (child), £7.50 (student/senior); ticket valid all day. ☎ 01 676 5377 (Guide Friday (Ireland) Ltd), 01 605 7705 (Grayline); dublin@guidefriday.com; www.guidefriday.com

Bicycle Tours – Bike hire: £10 per day, £40 per week. Guided tour (3hr): Apr-Oct, daily, at 2pm; also Sat and Sun, 10am (Sat, 6am: must be booked in advance); arrive 15min before start time. £15, £12 (student), includes bike hire, insurance and guide. Book in advance by calling in person behind Kinlay House Hostel, Lord Edward Street (beside Christ Church Cathedral, or at Dublin Tourism Centre, Suffolk Street, or by phone or fax or email. Scenic route descriptions available. Rain gear, helmets and baby seats available. ☎ 01 679 0899; Fax 679 6504; dublinbiketours@connect.ie; www.connect.ie/dublinbiketours

Horse-Drawn Carriage Sightseeing Tour – Departs from St Stephen's Green (top of Grafton Street), in summer, daily; otherwise, weekends only or by appointment. 4/5 people per carriage. Long tour (1hr including Dublin Castle and the 2 cathedrals) £40 per carriage; medium tour (30min south of the river only) £20 per carriage; shorter ride £10 per carriage, shortest ride £5 per carriage. ☎ 01 453 4619. By appointment only; £40 per hour; ☎ 01 453 3333 (Francis McCabe).

Railway Preservation Society of Ireland – Steam train excursions throughout Ireland: mainly spring-autumn. Advance booking recommended. For details of times and fares apply to Railway Preservation Society of Ireland, Ashgrove House, Kill Avenue, Dun Laoghaire; 01 280 9147. Tickets on sale from Iarnrod Eireann at the Ticket Centre Lower Abbey Street, Dublin; at Pearse Station, Dublin; at Westland Row, Dublin.

Historical Walking Tours – Operate May-Sept, daily, at 11am, 3pm (also 12midday Sat-Sun); Oct-Apr, Fri-Sun, at 12midday. £6, reductions available. Special tours, weekly, June-Aug. Depart from Trinity College front gate. ☎ 01 878 0227; Fax 01 878 3787; tours@historicalinsights.ie; www.historicalinsights.ie

1916 Rebellion Walking Tour – Operates Apr to late-Sep, Tue-Sat, 11.30am, Sun, 12.30pm. £6. ☎ 01 676 2493; www.1916rising.com

Literary Tour – Operates daily at 7.30pm from The Duke pub, Duke Street.

Real Irish Pub Crawl – Operates July-Aug, Mon, Wed, Sat, 7pm, Sun, 12.30pm from O'Briens/Mercantile Bar, 28 Dame Street, Dublin 2. £6. ☎ 01 493 2676, 088 510 299, 088 212 2020.

National Concert Hall – (Dúchas) Open Mon-Sat, 10am-7pm (11pm concert evenings), Sun, 2hr before concert. £3 for concerts. Restaurant (10am-2.30pm and from 6pm on concert evenings). ☎ 01 475 1666; Fax 478 3797; info@nch.ie; www.nch.ie

Bank of Ireland Arts Centre – Box Office: Open Tue-Fri, 11am-4pm. £5. ☎ 01 671 1488.

Dublin Castle – (Dúchas) (♿) Guided tour (45min including State Apartments (official use permitting) and Undercroft) daily, 10am (2pm Sat-Sun and public holidays) to 5pm (4.50pm last admission). Closed Good Friday, 24-26 Dec. £3, £1 (child), £2 (reduction). Guided tour and Brochure (50p) (French, German, Italian, Spanish). Church of the Holy Trinity (entrance via Lower Yard): Open as above. Restaurant. Wheelchair access (except Undercroft). ☎ 01 677 7129; Fax 01 679 7831.

Chester Beatty Library (Dublin Castle) – Open Tues-Fri, 10am-5pm, Sat, 11am-5pm, Sun, 1pm-5pm. No charge. ☎ 01 4070 750; Fax 01 4070 760; info@cbl.ie; www.cbl.ie

Christchurch Cathedral – Open daily, 10am-5pm. Closed 26 Dec. Donation (£2). Self-guided tour with numbered leaflet (10 languages). ☎ 01 677 8099; Fax 01 679 8991; cccdub@indigo.ie; http://indigo.ie/~cccdub/

Dublinia – (♿) Open Apr-Sep, daily, 10am-5pm; Oct-Mar, daily, 11am (10am Sun and bank hols) to 4pm (4.30pm Sun and bank holidays). £3.95, £10 (family 2A+2C), £3 (concession). Audio-guide (5 languages). No wheelchair access to 17C tower or pedestrian bridge to cathedral (cross at street to reach Christchurch Cathedral). ☎ 01 679 4611; Fax 01 679 7116; info@dublinia.ie; www.dublinia.ie

St Patrick's Cathedral – ♿ Open Mon-Sat, 9am-6pm (Sat, 5pm Nov-Feb); Sun, 9am-11am, 12.45-3pm and 4.15-6pm (10-11am and 12.45-3pm Nov-Feb). Closed 25-26 Dec (except for services). Services: Sundays, 8.30am (Holy Eucharist), 11.15am (Sung Eucharist), 3.15pm (Choral Evensong); Mon-Fri, 8.30am (Holy Eucharist), 9.40am (Choral Matins (school term only), 5.35pm (Choral Evensong); no sung services on Wed in July-Aug; Sat, all year. £2.70, £6.50 (family 2A+2C), £2 (reduction). Leaflet (Dutch, French, German, Italian, Japanese, Spanish, Swedish, Irish). Parking. ☎ 01 453 9472 (Office), 475 4817 (Cathedral), 453 5312; Fax 01 454 6374; www.stpatrickscathedral.ie

Marsh's Library – (♿) Open Mon, Wed-Fri, 10am-12.45pm and 2-5pm; Sat, 10.30am-12.45pm. £2, £1 (concession). Brochure (15 languages). Guided tour (30min) by appointment. Access for the disabled (researchers only); telephone in advance. ☎ 01 454 3511; Fax 01 454 3511; marshlib@iol.ie; www.kst.dit.ie/marsh

Tailors' Hall – ♿ Open by appointment only. Bookings for functions to be made through Dublin Castle Conference Centre, Dublin 2. ☎ 01 679 3713; Fax 01 679 7831.

City Hall – Open Mon-Sat, 10am-5.15pm, Sun, 2pm-5pm. Closed 25 Dec. No charge. ☎ 01 672 2204; www.dublincorp.ie/cityhall

St Werburgh's Church – Open Mon-Fri, 10am-4pm by appointment. Services: Sun, 10am. Key available from 8 Castle Street. ☎ 01 478 3710.

St Audoen's Church (Ang) – (Dúchas) Admission times and charges available by telephone. Services: Sun, 10.15am. ☎ 01 661 3111 (Dœchas Head Office); Fax 01 661 6764.

Temple Bar Properties Office – ♿ Open Mon-Fri, 9am-5.30pm. ☎ 01 671 5717 (24hr Cultureline); 01 677 2255 (office); Fax 01 677 2525; info@temple-bar.ie; www.temple-bar.ie

Viking Adventure – ♿ Open Tues-Sat, 10am-4.30pm. £4.95, £13.50 (family 2A+4C), £2.95 (child), £3.95 (concession). Book and craft shop. ☎ 01 679 6040; Fax 01 679 6033; viking@dublintourism.ie

Trinity College Old Library – ♿ Open Mon-Sat, 9.30am-5pm, Sun and public hols (17 Mar, Good Fri, Easter Mon and Oct bank hol), midday-4.30pm (Sun, Jun-Sept, 9.30am-4.30pm). Closed 22 Dec-2 Jan. £4.50, £9 (family 2A+4C), £4 (concession), no charge (child under 12); joint ticket with Dublin Experience, £6, £13 (family), £5.50 (concession). ☎ 01 608 2320; www.tcd.ie/library

College Tour (including The Colonnades and the Book of Kells): Apr-Sep, daily, 10am-4pm (last tour), every 30min from the Front Square. £5.50; joint ticket with the Dublin Experience available.

Dublin Experience – Open late-May to Sept, daily, 10am-5pm (last show), every hour. Time 45min. £3, £6 (family); joint ticket with Old Library £6, £12 (family), £5.50 (reduction). Head sets (French, German, Italian). Refreshments. ☎ 01 608 1688.

Bank of Ireland and House of Lords – ♿ Open Tues-Fri, 10am-4pm. Closed public hols. £1.50, £1 (concession). ☎ 01 671 1488; Fax 01 670 7556.

Bewley's Oriental Café Museum – Open daily, 7.30am (8.30am Sun) to 9pm. Guided tour available in summer. Refreshments. ☎ 01 677 6761.

Powerscourt Centre – Open daily except Sun and bank hols, 9am-6pm. No charge.

Dublin Civic Museum – Open Tues-Sat, 10am-6pm, Sun, 11am-2pm. Closed Christmas, Easter and bank hols. No charge. Time 30min. ☎ 01 679 4260; Fax 01 6775 954.

St Ann's Church – Open Mon-Fri, 10am-4pm. Services: Sun 8am, 10.45am, 6.30pm; Mon-Fri, daily 12.45pm. Lunch-hour and evening concerts. Coffee Shop (midday-2.30pm). ☎ 01 676 7727.

National Museum (Kildare Street) – ♿ Open Tues-Sat, 10am (2pm Sun) to 5pm. Closed Good Friday, 25 Dec. No charge. Audio-visual presentation (18min; French, German, Irish). Guided tour (30min-45min) at frequent intervals; £1. Museum shop. Café. ☎ 01 6777 444; Fax 01 6777 828; www.heritageireland.ie

MUSEUMLINK shuttle service every 80min; £1 one way (National Museum Kildare Street – Natural History Museum Merrion Street – National Museum Collins Barracks).

Access: Buses 7, 7A, 8 (Burgh Quay); 10, 11, 13 (O'Connell Street).

National Gallery of Ireland – (Dúchas) ♿ Open Mon-Sat, 10am-5.30pm (8.30pm Thur), Sun, 2-5pm. Closed Good Friday, 24-26 Dec. No charge. Guided tour: Sat, 3pm, Sun, 2.15pm, 3pm, 4pm. Book shop. Restaurant. ☎ 01 661 5133; Fax 01 661 5372; artgall@eircom.ie; www.nationalgallery.ie

St Stephen's Church – Open Jun-Aug, as posted on church notice board. Services: Sun, 11am, Wed, 11.30am. ☎ 01 288 0663 (Vicarage).

Number Twenty Nine – Guided tour Tues-Sun, 10am (2pm Sun) to 5pm. Closed Good Fri, 2 weeks prior to Christmas. £2.50, £1 (reduction), no charge (child under 16). Audio-visual presentation (10min), followed by guided tour of exhibition. Brochure (French, German, Irish, Italian, Spanish). Tearoom. Gift shop. ☎ 01 702 6165; Fax 01 702 7796.

Natural History Museum – (♿) Open Tues-Sat, 10am (2pm Sun) to 5pm. No charge. Guided tour (30min-45min) at frequent intervals; £1. Wheelchair access to ground floor only. ☎ 01 677 7444; Fax 01 676 6116.

MUSEUMLINK shuttle service every 80min; £1 one way (Natural History Museum Merrion Street – National Museum Collins Barracks – National Museum Kildare Street).

Access: Buses 7, 7A, 8 (Burgh Quay).

Heraldic Museum – ♿ Open Mon-Fri, 10am-4.30pm, Sat, 10am-12.30pm. Closed public hols, 24 Dec-2 Jan. No charge. ☎ 01 603 0311; Fax 01 662 1062.

Parliament – Leinster House – Public gallery: Open during parliamentary sessions (Tue-Thur and sometimes Fri, by appointment). Closed Jan, Easter (2 weeks), mid-July to early-Oct and at Christmas. Cabinet Rooms: Guided tour by appointment, Jul, Sat. ☎ 01 668 9333 (Prime Minister's Office); 01 618 3296 (Captain of the Guard); info@oireachtas.irlgov.ie; www.irlgov.ie/oireachtas

Government Buildings – Guided tour (40min; Taoiseach's Office, Ceremonial Stairs, Cabinet Room) Sat, 10.30am-3.30pm. No charge; permit available same day from National Museum, 7-9 Merrion Row. ☎ 01 619 4116.webmaster@taoiseach.irlgov.ie

St Stephen's Green – (Dúchas) Open daily, 8am (10am Sun and bank hols) to sunset; 25 Dec, 10am-1pm. No charge. ☎ 01 475 7816.

Newman House – Open Jul-Aug, Tues-Sat, midday (2pm Sat) to 5pm; Sun, 11am-2pm; otherwise by appointment. £3, £2 (concession). Guided tour (40min) available. Leaflet (French, German, Italian, Spanish). ☎ 01 706 7422, 01 475 7255; Fax 01 706 7211.

University Church – ♿ Open daily. Services: Sat, 7pm; Sun 11am, midday, 5.30pm; other days, 10am, 1.05pm. Ramp for wheelchairs. ☎ 01 478 0616.

Iveagh Gardens – (Dúchas) Open daily, 8am (10am Sun) to 6pm (5pm Feb and Nov; 4pm Dec-Jan). No charge. ☎ 01 475 7816.

Irish Music Hall of Fame – Open daily, 10am-7pm (6pm last admission). £6. ☎ 01 878 3345; Fax 01 878 3225; www.irishmusichof.com

Garden of Remembrance – (Dúchas) (♿) Open daily, 11am (9.30am May-Sept) to 8pm (7pm Oct; 4pm Nov-Mar; 1pm 25 Dec). No charge. ☎ 01 661 3111 (Dœchas head office); 01 874 3074 (Garden).

Hugh Lane Municipal Gallery of Modern Art – ♿ Open Tues-Sun, 9.30am (11am Sun) to 6pm (5pm Fri-Sun). Closed Good Fri, at Christmas. No charge. Guided tour (40min) available, £10 charge (book in advance). Bookshop. Ramp. ☎ 01 874 1903; Fax 01 872 2182; info@hughlane.ie; www.hughlane.ie

Dublin Writers Museum – Open daily, 10am (11am Sun and public hols) to 5pm (6pm, Mon-Fri, June-Aug). £3.10, £1.45 (child), £2.60 (concession), £8.50 (family 2A+4C); combined ticket with James Joyce Tower or George Bernard Shaw Birthplace available. Audio-guide (French, German, Italian, Japanese, Spanish). Guided tour by appointment. Brochure (Dutch, French, German, Italian, Spanish, Japanese). Children's salon (Seomra na Nog). Restaurant; coffee shop. Bookshop. ☎ 01 872 2077; Fax 01 872 2231.

Rotunda Hospital Chapel – To visit apply in advance to the Matron's Office. ☎ 01 873 0700.

James Joyce Centre – Open daily, 9.30am (12.30pm Sun) to 5pm. £3, £6 (family), 75p (child), £2 (concession). Library. Café. ☎ 01 878 8547; Fax 01 878 8488; joycecen@iol.ie; www.jamesjoyce.ie

National Wax Museum – Open daily, 10am (12midday, Sun) to 5.30pm. £3, £2 (child), £2.50 (student). Coffee shop. ☎ 01 872 6340.

St Mary's Pro-Cathedral – Open 8.30am-6.30pm. Services: Sun, 8am (St Kevin's Oratory at rear of Pro-Cathedral), 10am, 11am (Sung Latin mass with Palestrina choir, except July-Aug), midday (Italian mass, St Kevin's Oratory), 12.30pm, 6.30pm; 1st Sun of month, 7pm (Spanish Mass, St Kevin's Oratory); Mon-Sat, 8.30am, 10am, 11am, 12.45pm, 5.45pm; Sat only, 6pm, except Aug (Vigil Mass for Sunday); 8pm (Vigil Mass for Young Adults, St Kevin's Oratory); 1st Fri of month only, 8pm (Irish Mass). Guide book. Leaflet. ☎ 01 874 5441; Fax 01 874 2406; www.procathedral.ie

Custom House – Open mid-Mar to Oct, daily, 10am (2pm Sat and Sun) to 12.30pm; Nov to mid-Mar, Wed-Fri, 10am -12.30pm, Sun, 2-5pm. £1, £3 (family 2A+2C). ☎ 01 8882 538.

St Michan's Church – (♿) Open Mar-Oct, Mon-Sat, 10am to 5pm (1pm Sat); Nov-Mar, Mon-Sat, 12.30-3.30pm. £2, £1 (child), £1.50 (concession). Guided tour including vaults (30-40min). Gift shop. Wheelchair access to church not vaults. ☎ 01 872 4154 (10am-1pm); Fax 01 878 2615; stmichan@iol.ie

Jameson Chimney Observation Tower – Open Mon-Sat, 10am-6pm, Sun, 11am-7pm. £5. ☎ 01 817 3838.

Old Jameson Distillery – ♿ Guided tour (1hr; French, German, Italian, Japanese, Spanish), 9.30am-5.30pm (last tour). Closed Good Fri, 25 Dec. £3.95, £1.50 (child), £3 (student/senior citizen). Gift shop. Restaurant; bar. ☎ 01 807 2355; Fax 807 2369.

Ceol – Open Mon-Sat, 10am-6pm, Sun, 11am-7pm. £5. 01 817 3820.

St Mary's Abbey – (Dúchas) Open mid-June to mid-Sept, Wed and Sun, 10am-5pm. Last admission 45min before closing. £1, 40p (child/student), 70p (senior citizen), £3 (family). Guided tour available. Access by stairs only. ☎ 01 872 1490.

National Museum (Collins Barracks) – Open Tues-Sat, 10am (2pm Sun) to 5pm. Guided tour (30min-45min) at frequent intervals; £1. Parking. Museum shop. Café. ☎ 01 677 7444; Fax 01 677 7828.

MUSEUMLINK shuttle service every 80min; £1 one way (National Museum Collins Barracks – National Museum Kildare Street – Natural History Museum Merrion Street).

Access: Buses 90 (Aston Quay), 25, 25A, 66, 67 (Middle Abbey Street).

Phoenix Park Visitor Centre – (Dúchas) ♿ Open June-Sept, daily, 10am-6pm; mid-Mar to May and Oct, daily, 9.30am to 5pm (5.30pm Apr-May); Nov to mid-Mar, Sat-Sun, 9.30am-4.30pm. Last admission 45min before closing. Closed 25-26 Dec. £2, £1 (child/student), £1.50 (senior citizen), £5 (family). Ashtown Castle: Guided tour (20min) only. Audio-visual presentation (21min). Nature Trails. Parking. Restaurant; coffee shop. ☎ 01 677 0095; Fax 01 820 5584.

President's Residence – Guided tour (1hr) Sat (except 24-26 Dec), 10.30am-4.30pm (3pm winter). No charge. Ticket available on the day from Phoenix Park Visitor Centre (☎ 01 677 0095). ☎ 01 670 9155.

Zoological Gardens – Open daily, 9.30am (10.30am Sun) to 6pm (5pm/sunset in winter). £6.30, £18.50 (family 2A+2C), £23.50 (family 2A+4C), £3.70 (child 3-16). Play areas. Refreshments. Shops. ☎ 01 677 1425; Fax 01 677 1660; info@dublinzoo. ie; www.dublinzoo.ie

Guinness Hopstore – ♿ Guided tour (1hr) daily, 9.30am to 5pm (last admission) (4.30pm, Sun and bank holidays) every 30min. Closed 1 Jan, Good Friday, St Stephens day, 25-26 Dec. £5, £1 (child), £4 (concession). ☎ 01 408 4800; Fax 01 408 4965; www.guinness.ie

Irish Museum of Modern Art – ♿ Open Tue-Sun, 10am (midday Sun and public hols) to 5.30pm. Closed Good Fri, 24-26 Dec. No charge. Guided tour: Wed and Fri, 2.30pm, Sun 12.15pm. Leaflets on the history of the building (Dutch, French, German, Irish, Italian, Spanish). Parking. Refreshments. Bookshop. ☎ 01 612 9900; Fax 01 612 9999; info@modernart.ie; www.modernart.ie

Royal Hospital Kilmainham – Closed until Autumn 2001. ☎ 01 612 9900; info@modernart.ie; www.modernart.ie

Kilmainham Gaol Museum – (♿) Guided tour (30min) Apr-Sept, daily, 9.30am-6pm (4.45pm last admission); Oct-Mar, Mon-Fri, 9.30am-5pm (4pm last admission), Sun, 10am-6pm (4.45pm last admission). Last tour 1hr before closing. Closed 24-26 Dec. £3.50, £1.50 (child/student), £2.50 (senior citizen), £8.60 (family). Audio-visual presentation (26min; French, German, Irish, Italian, Spanish). Parking. Restaurant. Ground floor of prison and exhibition accessible to wheelchairs. ☎ 01 453 5984; Fax 01 453 2037.

Drimnagh Castle – (♿) Guided tour Apr-Sep, Wed, Sat-Sun, 12midday-5pm; Oct-Mar, Sun, 2-5pm. Last tour 4.30pm. £2.50, £1 (child), £2 (senior citizen/student). Brochure (French, German, Italian). ☎ 01 450 2530; Fax 01 450 5401.

National Botanic Gardens – (Dúchas) Gardens: Open summer, daily, 9am (11am Sun) to 6pm; winter, daily (except 25 Dec), 10am (11am Sun) to 4.30pm. Glasshouses: Open Mon-Sat, 9am (10am winter) to 12.45pm and 2pm to 5.15pm (3.15pm Thurs, all year; 4.15pm winter; 5.45 Sat, summer), Sun, 2pm-5.45pm (4.15pm winter). Alpine houses: Open Mon-Fri, 10.45am-12.15pm and 2.15pm-3.15pm, Sun, 2pm-5.45pm, bank hols, 9am-12.45pm and 2-5.45pm. No charge. Guided tour (1hr) by appointment. Parking. Wheelchair available; 90% access (some steep gradients) for wheelchairs. ☎ 01 837 7596, 837 4388; Fax 01 836 0080.

GAA Museum – Open May-Sept, daily, 9.30am-5pm; Oct-Apr, Tues-Sun, 10am (midday Sun) to 5pm. £3, reductions available. ☎ 01 855 8176; Fax 01 855 8104; museum@gaa.ie

Marino Casino – (Dúchas) Guided tour May-Oct, daily, 10am-6pm (5pm, May and Oct); Feb-Apr and Nov, Sun and Thurs, midday-4pm. Last admission 45min before closing. Closed Dec and Jan. £2, £1 (child/student), £1.50 (senior citi-

Marino Casino, Dublin

Dúchas, Dublin

Howth Ferry to Ireland's Eye

zen), £5 (family). Parking. ☏ 01 833 1618. Access: From city centre by bus 20A, 20B, 27, 27B, 42; 123 Imp Bus from O'Connell Street; by DART – Clontarf Road Station.

North Bull Island – Open daily, 10.15am-1pm and 1.30-4pm (closed Fri afternoon). Audio-guide (French). Brochure (German, Spanish). Parking. ☏ 01 833 8341.

St Mary's Abbey – Key from Mrs O'Rourke, 13 Church Street, Howth.

Ireland's Eye Ferry from Howth – Operates daily (weather permitting), 11am-6pm (on demand), from East Pier, Howth Harbour. Return £5, £2.50 (child). ☏ 01 831 4200.

National Transport Museum – (♿) Open June-Sept, daily, 10am (2pm Sat) to 5.30pm; May and Oct, Sat-Sun and bank hols, 2-5.30pm; 26 Dec to 1 Jan, daily, 2-5.30pm. £1.60, 60p (concession), £4 (family 2A+5C). Parking. ☏ 01 848 0831.

Waterways Visitor Centre – (Dúchas) (♿) Open Jun–Sep, daily, 9.30am–5.30pm; Oct–May, Wed–Sun, 12.30–5.30pm. Last admission 45min before closing. Closed 1 Jan, 25-26 Dec. £2, £5 (family), £1 (child/student), £1.50 (senior citizen). Wheelchair access to ground floor only. ☏ 01 677 7510; Fax 01 677 7514; www.heritageireland.ie

Shaw Birthplace Museum – Open May-Oct, daily, 10am (11am Sun and public holidays)-1pm and 2pm-5pm. £2.70, £2.20 (concession), £1.40 (child), £7.95 (family 2A+4C); combined ticket with Dublin Writers Museum available. Audio-guide (30min; Dutch, French, German, Italian, Japanese, Spanish). Brochure (Dutch, French, German, Italian, Japanese, Spanish). Bookshop. ☏ 01 475 0854; Fax 01 872 2231.

Jewish Museum – Open May-Sept, Sun, Tues and Thur, 11am-3.30pm; Oct-Apr, Sun, 10.30am-2.30pm or by appointment. Time 1hr. Donation. ☏/Fax 01 490 1857 (answerphone).

Rathfarnham Castle – (Dúchas) (♿) Guided tour May-Oct, daily, 9.30am-5.30pm, Nov-Apr by appointment. Restoration in progress, phone in advance to confirm times (☏ 01 647 2466). Last tour 1hr before closing. £1.50, £4 (family), 60p (child/student), £1 (senior citizen). Leaflet (English only). Tea room (10am-5pm). ☏ 01 493 9461; out of season ☏ 01 661 3111 (Dœchas Head Office); info@heritageireland.ie; www.heritageireland.ie

Pearse Museum – (Dúchas) (♿) Park: Open daily, 10am-7pm (8pm Aug; 5.30pm Feb-Mar; 4.30pm Nov-Jan). Museum: Open daily, 10am-1pm and 2-5pm (5.30pm May-Aug; 4pm Nov-Jan). Last admission 45min before closing. Closed 25-26 Dec. No charge. Audio-visual presentation (20min). Guided tour (30min) by appointment. Open-air concerts (summer). Parking. Tearoom (summer, weekends ☏ 01 493 3053). Wheelchair access to ground floor only. ☏ 01 493 4208; Fax 01 493 6120.

Slide File, Dublin

National Maritime Museum of Ireland – (&) Open May-Sept, Tues-Sun; Apr and Oct, Sun, 1-5pm. £1.50, 80p (child), £4 (family). Wheelchair access to ground floor. ☎ 01 280 0969 (24hr).

James Joyce Museum – Open Apr-Oct, daily, 10am-1pm and 2-5pm (6pm Sun and public hols); Nov-Mar, by arrangement. £2.70, £7.95 (family 2A+4C), £2.20 (concession), £1.40 (child); combined ticket with Dublin Writers Museum available. Brochure (Danish, Dutch, French, German, Italian, Japanese, Spanish). ☎ 01 280 9265, 872 2077; Fax 01 280 9265; www.visitdublin.com/dliterary.htm

Dalkey Heritage Centre – Open Apr-Nov, Mon-Fri, 9.30am-5pm; Nov-Mar, Sat, Sun, public hols, 11am-5pm. £2.50, £8 (family 2A+3C), £1.50 (child), £2 (concession). ☎ 01 285 8366; 01 284 3141. diht@indigo.ie; www.dalkeyhomepage.ie

DUNDALK   🄸 Jocelyn Street – ☎ 042 933 5484

Historical Walking Tour – Operates Thur, 7pm. ☎ 087 288 1191, 042 932 8061 (Dundalk TIC); dundalktouristoffice@eircom.net; www.louthholidays.com

Louth County Museum – Open May-Sep, Mon-Sat, 10.30am-5.30pm, Sun and bank hols, 2pm-6pm. £3, reductions available. ☎ 042 932 7056/7; Fax 042 932 7058.

Excursions

Carlingford Heritage Centre – Open Mar-Oct, 9am-5pm, telephone for details. £1, reductions available. Video (12min). ☎ 042 937 3454; Fax 042 937 3882.

Carlingford Lough Cruise – Sea angling and cruising on Carlingford Lough on the MV Slieve Foy (35ft); licensed and insured; fast off-shore 105 turbo; fully equipped with latest electronics. ☎ 042 937 3239 (Peadar/Peter Elmore).

Carrickmacross Lace Gallery – Open mid-Apr to Oct, Mon-Tues and Thur-Fri, 9.30am-12.30pm and 1.30pm-5pm, ☎ 042 966 2506, 966 2088.

Patrick Kavanagh Centre – Open Mon-Fri, 10am (11am Oct-May) to 6pm (5pm Oct-May); Sat-Sun and public hols, 2pm-6pm (5pm May-Oct). Closed 25 Dec to 1 Jan. £2, reductions available. ☎/Fax 042 937 8560; infoatpkc@tinet.ie; www.patrickkavanaghcountry.com

E

ENNIS   🄸 Arthurs Row – ☎ 065 682 8366 (Mon-Fri; also Sat Apr-May+Oct; also Sun Jun-Sep)

Ennis Friary – (Dúchas) (&) Open late-May to late-Sep, daily, 9.30am-6.30pm (5.45pm last admission). £1, reductions available. Guided tour on request. Leaflet (French, German, Italian, Spanish). Parking. ☎ 065 682 9100.

Clare Museum – & Jun-Sep, daily, 9.30am-5.30pm; Oct-Mar, Mon-Sat, 9.30am-1pm and 2-5.30pm (closed Sat, Jan-Feb). Last admission 1hr before closing. Admission charge. ☎ 065 682 3382; Fax 065 684 2119; claremuseum@eircom.net

Excursions

Dromore Wood National Nature Reserve – (Dúchas) (&) Forest Park: Open daily. Information Centre: Open mid-Jun to mid-Sep, daily, 10am-6pm (5.15 last admission). No charge. Guidebook to two trails (20min and 40min) £1. ☎ 065 683 7166.

Dysert O'Dea Castle and Archeology Centre – Open May-Sep, daily, 10am-6pm. £3.50, reductions available. A/v presentation (English, German). Brochure (English only). Parking. Refreshments. ☎ 065 685 7401; 065 683 7722 (evenings and off season).

Clare Heritage Centre – & Open daily, 9.30am-5.30pm. Guided tour (30min) available. Brochure (French, German). Parking. Tearoom. ☎ 065 6837955; Fax 065 6837540; clareheritage@eircom.net; www.clareroots.net

Quin Franciscan Friary – (Dúchas) Open late-May to late-Sep, daily, 9.30am-6.30pm; also possibly Easter weekend. £1, reductions available. ☎ 01 647 2453.

Knappogue Castle – (&) Open Apr-Oct, daily, 9.30am-5.30pm (4.30pm last admission). Medieval banquets: Apr-Oct, daily, 5.30pm, 8.45pm. Castle £2.90, reductions available; banquet £32, reductions available. Parking. Wheelchair access to ground floor only. ☎ 061 368 103 (Castle), 061 361 511, 061 360 788 (Shannon Heritage); Fax 061 361 020.

Craggaunowen Centre – & Open mid-Apr to Oct, daily, 10am (9am mid-May to Aug) to 6pm (5pm last admission); telephone to check. £4.40, reductions available. Guided tour available. Brochure (French, German). Parking. Refreshments. ☎ 061 367 178, 061 367 178 (site); 061 360 788 (Shannon Heritage); Fax 061 361 020.

ENNISCORTHY

Enniscorthy Tour – Guided tour (30min/1hr; French) by appointment Jun-Sep, daily. Minimum 5 people. £2.50, reductions available. Departure from Castle Hill Craft, opposite the Castle. ☎ 054 36800; Fax 054 36628;

National 1798 Visitor Centre – ♿ Open daily, 9.30am (11am, Sun) to 5pm (last admission). £4, reductions available. A/v presentation (15min). Written guide (Dutch, French, German, Japanese, Spanish). Craft rooms. Tearooms. Parking. ☎ 054 37596; Fax 054 37198; 98com@iol.ie; www.wexford.ie

Wexford County Museum – (♿) Open Jun-Sep, Mon-Sat, 10am-6pm, Sun, 2pm-5.30pm; Oct-Nov and Feb-Mar, daily, 2pm-5.30pm; Dec-Jan, Sun 2pm-5pm. £3, reductions available. Guided tour (1hr) by appointment. Wheelchair access to ground floor. ☎/Fax 054 35926; wexmus@iol. ie

Carley's Bridge Potteries – Open Mon-Fri, 8.30am-5.45pm, Sat-Sun, 11am (2.30pm Sun) to 5pm. Closed bank hols. No charge. Guided tour (1hr): Mon-Fri. Showroom. Parking. One step at entrance. ☎ 054 33512, 33080; Fax 054 34360; jsutton@cbp.ie; www.cbp.ie

F

FINGAL

Malahide Castle – Open Apr-Oct, Mon-Sat, 10am-12.45pm and 2pm-5pm, Sun and public hols, 11am-12.45pm and 2pm-6pm; Nov-Mar, Mon-Fri, 10am-12.45pm and 2pm-5pm, Sat-Sun and public hols, 2-5pm. £3.15, reductions available; combined ticket with Fry Model Railway Museum or Newbridge House available. Audio-guide (Dutch, French, German, Italian, Finnish, Japanese, Spanish). Brochure (French, German, Italian, Japanese, Spanish). Parking. Restaurant, coffee shop; banquets on request. Craft shop. ☎ 01 846 2184, 846 2516; Fax 01 846 2537; malahidecastle@dublintourism.ie; www.visitdublin.com

Fry Model Railway – Open Apr-Sept, Mon-Thur and Sat, 10am-1pm and 2-5pm; Sun and public hols, 2pm-6pm; Oct-Mar, Sat-Sun and public hols, 2pm-5pm. £2.90, reductions available; combined ticket with Malahide Castle or Tara's Palace available. Parking. ☎ 01 846 3779; Fax 01 846 3723; fryrailway@dublintourism.ie; www.visitdublin.com

Tara's Palace – Open same times as Fry Model Railway (see above).

Newbridge House – Guided tour (45min) Apr-Sept Tues-Sat, 10am-1pm and 2-5pm; Sun and public hols, 2pm-6pm; Oct-Mar, Sat-Sun and public hols, 2-pm-5pm. House only £3, reductions available; farm only £1, reductions available; combined ticket with Malahide Castle £4.95, reductions available. Parking. Playground. Coffee shop. Gift shop. 01 843 6534; Fax 01 846 2537.

Ardgillan Castle – Open Jul-Aug, daily, 11am-6pm; Apr-Jun and Sep, Tues-Sun and public hols, 11am-6pm; Oct-Mar, Tues-Sun and public hols, 11am-4.30pm. Closed 23 Dec to 1 Jan. £3, reductions available. ☎ 01 849 2212; Fax 01 849 2786.

Skerries Mills – Open daily, 10.30am-6pm (4.30pm Oct-Mar). Closed 20 Dec to 1 Jan. ☎ 01 849 52008; Fax 01 849 5213.

Swords Castle – ♿ Open Mon, Wed, Thur-Fri, 10am-midday and 2pm-4pm (3pm Fri). No charge. ☎ 01 840 0891.

Lusk Heritage Centre – (Dúchas) Open mid-Jun to mid-Sep, Fri, 10am-5pm (4.15pm last admission). £1, reductions available. Guided tour by appointment (30min). Leaflet (French, German, Irish, Italian, Spanish). ☎ 01 843 7683.

G

GALWAY

Druid Theatre – ☎ 091 568 617 (Box office); 091 568 660 (Administration); Fax 091 563 109; info@druidtheatre.com; www.druidtheatre.com

Irish Theatre (Taibhdearc Na Gaillimhe) – ☎ 091 563 600 (box office); Fax 091 563 195.

St Nicholas Collegiate Church – Open 9am-4.30pm. Services: Sun, 8.30am, 11.30am, Wed, 10.30am. Brochure (Dutch, French, German, Italian, Japanese, Spanish). ☎ 091 564 648, 521 914 (rector), 091 588479 (bookings), 091 762012 /567985 (wardens).

Galway City Museum – Open Apr-Oct, daily, 10am-1pm and 2-5pm; Nov-Mar, Mon, Thur-Fri, 10am-1pm and 2pm-5pm. £1, reductions available. Guided tour (20min) by appointment. ✆/Fax 091 567 641.

Nora Barnacle House Museum – Open mid-May to mid-Sep, Mon-Sat, 10am-1pm and 2-5pm. £1. ✆ 091 564 743.

Bank of Ireland – Sword and Mace – Open Mon-Fri, 10am-4pm. Closed public hols. boi19eyresquare@bionet.ie

Excursions

Lough Corrib and River Cruises – ♿ Operate from Wood Quay, end-Apr to Oct, daily, at 12.30pm (Jul-Aug only), 2.30pm, 4.30pm. Time 90min. £6, reductions available. Commentary (various languages). Bar. ✆ 091 592 447 (Corrib Tours).

Aughnanure Castle – (Dúchas) Open Jun-Sep, daily, 9.30am-6.30pm (5.45pm last admission), £2, reductions available. Guided tour available. Parking. ✆ 091 552 214.

Glengowla Silver and Lead Mine – Guided tour Mar-Nov, daily, 9.30am-6.30pm, every 20min; Dec-Feb, most Sat-Sun. £3.75. ✆ 091 552 360, 552 021, Mobile 087 252 9850; www.iarecordings.org/mineg.html

GLENDALOUGH 🄸 ✆ 0404 45688 (Jun-Sep, Tue-Sun)

Glendalough Bus Service – Operates 11.30am, 6pm, from Dublin (west side of St Stephen's Green – in front of the Royal College of Surgeons) via Bray and Roundwood. Return £10.

Glendalough – (Dúchas) ♿ Site: Open daily. Visitor Centre: Open mid-Mar to mid-Oct, daily, 9.30am-6pm (6.30pm, Jun-Aug); late-Oct to mid-Mar, daily, 9.30am-5pm. Last admission 45min before closing. Closed 25-26 Dec. £2, reductions available. A/v presentation (French, German, Italian, if booked in advance). Guided tour (French, German, Italian, if booked in advance). Parking. Picnic area. ✆ 0404 45325, 45352.

K

KELLS

St Columba's Anglican Church – Open Jul-Aug, 10am-1pm and 2-5pm. Donation.

Excursions

St Kilian's Heritage Centre – ♿ Open Easter-Oct, Tues-Sun and bank hol Mon, 10am (2pm, Sat-Sun) to 6pm. £3, reductions available. Video (15min). Parking. Restaurant. Craft shop. ✆/Fax 046 42433.

Loughcrew Passage Graves – (Dúchas) Guided tour (1hr including 40min up and down) mid-June to mid-Sep, daily, 10am-6pm (5.15pm last admission to Cairn T; 5.30pm last time for returning key to Cairn L). £1, reductions available. Out of season, key available (£50 deposit) from Newgrange (✆ 041 982 4488; Fax 041 982 4798) or from Loughcrew Gardens (✆ 049 854 1356). ✆ 049 854 2009 (Loughcrew car park).

KENMARE 🄸 Kenmare Heritage Centre – ✆ 064 41233 (Apr-Oct, Mon-Sat; also Sun, Jul-Aug)
🄸 Glengarriff – ✆ 027 63084 (Jun-Sep, Mon-Sat)

Kenmare Heritage Centre – ♿ Open Easter-Sept, daily, 9.15am-1pm and 2pm-5.30pm. £2, reductions available. Audio-guide (French, German). ✆ 064 41233, 31633 (Heritage Centre).

Kenmare Lace and Design Centre – Open mid-Jun to Sep, Mon-Sat, 10am-5.30pm. No charge. Lace-making demonstrations: Good Fri to mid-Jun and Sep, 10.15am-5.30pm; in winter on request. ✆ 064 41491, 42636; Fax 064 42636.

Garinish Island Ferry (1) – Operates from Glengarriff July-Aug, daily, 9.30am (11am Sun) to 6.30pm (7pm Sun); Apr-June and Sept, daily, 10am (1pm Sun) to 6.30pm (7pm Sun); Mar and Oct, daily, 10am (1pm Sun) to 4.30pm (5pm Sun). Last landing 1hr before closing time. Time 10min usually including Seal Island. £2.50, reductions available. ✆ 027 63333, 63555 (Blue Pool Ferry); Fax 027 63149.

Garinish Island Ferry (2) – Operates from Glengarriff Mar-Oct, daily, £6, reductions available. ✆ 027 63116 (Harbour Queen Ferry), 087 234 5861 (mobile); Fax 027 63298.

Illnacullin, Garinish Island – (Dúchas) ♿ Open July-Aug, Mon-Sat, 9.30am-6.30pm, Sun, 11am-7pm; Apr-June and Sept, Mon-Sat, 10am-6.30pm, Sun, 1pm-7pm; Mar and Oct, Mon-Sat, 10am-4.30pm, Sun, 1pm-5pm. Last landing 1hr before closing time. £2.50, reductions available; separate charge for ferry. Self-guiding trails. Guide book (Irish, French, German, Italian, Spanish). Coffee shop. ✆ 027 63040; Fax 027 63149.

Glengarriff Bamboo Garden – ♿ Open Easter-Oct, daily, 10am-6pm (9pm Jun-Aug). £3, reductions available. Parking. Bamboo gift shop. ☎ 027 63570; Fax 027 63255; bambooparkltd@tinet.ie

Derreen Gardens, Lauragh – Open Apr-Sep, daily, 10am-6pm. Time approx 1hr. £3; garden map 20p. Parking. ☎ 064 83588.

Dursey Island Cable Car – ♿ Open Mon-Sat, 9am-10.30am and 2.30pm-4.30pm, Sun, 9am-10.15am and midday-1pm; return trip daily at 7pm. Return £2.50, reductions available. Parking (mainland terminal). ☎ 027 73017.

Bere Island Ferry – ♿ Operates (10min; weather permitting) in summer, 7 times daily; in winter, 5 times daily, (6 times Fri); Sun, reduced service. Return £15 (car + 2 passengers), return £4 (pedestrian). Parking. Refreshments. ☎ 027 75009 (Bere Island Ferry), 086 242 3140 (mobile); Fax 027 75000; biferry@indigo.ie

KILDARE
🄱 ☎ 045 522 696 (May-Sep)

Curragh Racecourse – Open Mar-Sep. For the Derby: £30 Reserved enclosure, £12 Grandstand; for Classic and group meetings: £10 all enclosures; other meetings £7 (Sat), £8 (Sun). ☎ 045 441 205; Fax 045 441 442.

Old Canal Hotel – Open Mon-Fri, 9am-5pm; Sat, Sun and public hols, 12.30-6pm. Heritage Centre. Art gallery. Restaurant. Canal barge trips, Apr-Sept: 1hr £3.50; 3hr (min 20 people) £8; 1hr (with tea and scones) £5; 1hr (with tea and sandwiches) £5.50; 3hr (with mulled wine, music and meal) £23. ☎/Fax 045 870 005; robertstown@tinet.ie or bargetour@ tinet.ie; www. kildare/community/ robertstown/devel/bartour.htm

Irish National Stud

Bord Fáilte, Dublin

Kildare Cathedral – Open Mon-Sat, 10am-1pm and 2pm-5pm, Sun, 2pm-5pm. Services: Sun, midday (Holy Communion). ☎ 045 441 654.

Irish National Stud and Irish Horse Museum – ♿ Open mid-Feb to mid-Nov, daily, 9.30am-6pm. Combined ticket with Japanese Gardens £6, reductions available. Brochure (10 languages). Parking. Refreshments. Gift/craft shop. ☎ 045 521 617, 522 963; Fax 045 522 964; stud@irish-national-stud.ie; www.irish-national-stud.ie

Japanese Gardens – ♿ Open same as Irish National Stud.

Peatland World – (♿) Open Mon-Fri, 9.30am-6pm, Sat-Sun, 2pm-6pm. £3.50, reductions available. Parking. Refreshments. ☎ 045 860 133; Fax 045 860 481.

KILKENNY
🄱 Shee Alms House, Rose Inn Street – ☎ 056 51500

Medieval Kilkenny Walking Tour – Operates from Kilkenny Tourist Office Mar-Oct, Mon-Sat, 6 times per day, Sun, 4 times; Nov-Feb, Tues-Sat, 3 times per day. £3, reductions available. ☎/Fax 056 65929 (Tynan Tours), 087 265 1745 (mobile).

Kilkenny Design Centre – ♿ Open Mon-Sat, 9am (10am Sun and bank hols, Jan-Mar) to 6pm. Restaurant: daily, 9am (10am Sun and bank hols) to 5pm. ☎ 056 22118; Fax 056 65905; info@kilkennydesigncentre.iol.ie; www.kilkennydesign.com

Mount Juliet – Advance booking required for sporting facilities. ☎ 056 73000; Fax 056 73019; info@mountjuliet.ie; www.mountjuliet.ie

Kilkenny Castle and Park – (Dúchas) (♿) Park: Open daily, 9am-8.30pm (6.30pm Apr & Sept, 5.30pm March & Oct, 4.30pm Feb & Nov, 4pm Jan & Dec). Closed 25 Dec. Castle: Guided tour only, Jun-Sep, daily, 10am-7pm; Apr-May, daily, 10.30am-5pm; Oct-Mar, daily except Mon, 10.30am (11am Sun) to 12.45pm and 2pm-5pm. Last admission 1hr before closing. Closed Good Friday and at Christmas. £3.50, reductions available. Film presentation. Butler Gallery of Contemporary Art (basement): Open as above. No charge. Tearoom (May-Sep). Wheelchair access to ground floor. ☎ 056 21450; Fax 056 63488; ☎ 056 61106 (Butler Gallery).

St Canice's Cathedral – ♿ Open Mon-Sat, 9am (10am Oct-Easter) to 1pm and 2pm-6pm (4pm Oct-Easter); Sun, 2pm-6pm (4pm Oct-Easter). Closed Wed and Holy Days, 10-11am; Good Friday, 25 Dec to 1 Jan. £1 donation per adult. Guided tour (30min). Leaflet (8 languages). Guide book. Gift shop. Round Tower: Open (weather permitting) Easter to mid-Sep; £1. ☎ 64971 (Cathedral), 056 21516 (Deanery); stcanicescathedral@eircom.net

Shee Alms House – Open Apr-Sep, Mon-Sat, 9am-6pm (7pm July-Aug); also May-Sept, Sun, 11am-1pm and 2-5pm; Oct, Mon-Sat, 9am-5pm; Nov-Mar, Mon-Fri, 9am-5pm. ☎ 056 51500; Fax 056 63955; info@southeasttourism.ie

Black Abbey – ♿ Open daily, 7.30am (8.30am Sat-Sun) to 7pm. No visiting during services. Donation. Brochure. ☎ 056 21279.

Rothe House – Open daily, 10.30am (1.30pm Sun) to 5.30pm. Closed Good Fri. £2, reductions available. A/v presentation. Guided tour (45min) available. Leaflet (French, German). ☎ 056 22893.

Tholsel – Open Mon-Fri, 9am-1pm and 2-5pm. No charge. ☎ 056 21076.

Ladywell Water Garden – Open daily, 10am-5pm (closed Sat-Sun, Jan-Feb). £1, reductions available. Coffee shop: Open Tues-Fri, 10am-5pm, Sun, midday-5.30pm. ☎ 056 24690.

Kilfane Glen and Waterfall – Open Jul-Aug, daily, 11am-6pm; Apr-Jun and Sep, Sun, 2-6pm. £4, reductions available. ☎ 056 24558; Fax 056 27491; susan@irishgardens.com; www.nicholasmosse.com

Jerpoint Abbey – (Dúchas) (♿) Open Jun to late-Sep, daily, 9.30am-6.30pm; Mar-May and mid-Sep to Nov, daily, 10am-5pm (4pm mid to end-Nov). £2, reductions available. Guided tour (45min) by appointment. Brochure (French, German, Spanish, Italian, Irish). Parking. ☎ 056 24623; Fax 056 54003.

Edmund Rice Centre – ♿ Open daily, 10am-1pm and 2-6pm (5pm Oct-Apr). Closed Good Fri, 25 Dec. No charge. Guided tour (approx 1hr) available. Parking. ☎ 056 25141.

Bród Tullaroan – Open Jun-Aug, Mon-Fri, 10am-5pm, Sun and public hols, 2-5pm; Easter-May and Sep-Nov, Sun, 2-5pm. £3, reductions available. ☎ 056 67107; reid@tinet.ie

Dunmore Cave – (Dúchas) Guided tour (40min) mid-Mar to Oct, daily, 10am-5pm (7pm mid-Jun to mid-Sep); Nov to mid-Mar, Sat-Sun + bank hols, 10am-5pm. May close for lunch. Last admission 45min before closing. Closed 25-26 Dec. £2, reductions available. Parking. No wheelchair access. ☎ 056 67726.

KILLALA
🅱 Ballina – ☎ 096 70848 (Apr-Sep, Mon-Sat)

St Patrick's Cathedral – Open during daylight hours. Services: Sun, 10.30am. ☎ 096 21654; 096 31384.

Excursions

Céide Fields Visitor Centre – (Dúchas) Open Jun-Sep, daily, 9.30am-6.30pm; mid-Mar to May and Oct-Nov, daily, 10am-5pm (4.30pm Nov); Dec to mid-Mar, telephone for details. Last admission 1hr before closing. Closed 25-26 Dec. £2.50, reductions available. A/v presentation (20min). Guided tour (45min) by appointment. Exhibition script (Dutch, French, German, Italian, Spanish). Parking. Tearoom. ☎ 096 43325; Fax 096 43261.

Belderrig Prehistoric Farm – (♿) Open Jun-Sep, 9.30am-6.30pm; mid-Mar to May and Oct-Nov, 10am-5pm (4.30pm Nov). £2.50, reductions available. A/v presentation (20min). Guide book and leaflets (French, German, Italian). Tearoom. Wheelchair access to Visitor Centre.

Cathedral of St Muredach – Open daily. Services: Mon-Fri, 8am, 10am; Sun, 8am, 9.30am, 11am, 12.30pm.

Waterpoint – Open daily, 10am (11am Sat-Sun) to 10pm (8pm Sat-Sun). Heated swimming pool; fun pool; water slide; activity room; adult health suite with steam room, jacuzzi and sauna. Snack bar. ☎ 096 36999; Fax 096 36988.

Seaweed Baths – Open May-Oct, daily, 10am-9pm (10pm Jul-Aug); Nov-Apr, Sat-Sun and bank hols, 10am-8pm. ☎ 096 36238; Fax 096 36895.

KILLALOE
🅱 Heritage Centre, The Bridge – ☎ 061 376 866 (May-Sep, daily)
🅱 Connolly street, Nenagh – ☎ 067 31610 (May to mid-Sep, Mon-Sat)

St Flannan's Cathedral – Open daily, during daylight hours. Guided visit to tower: only when shop is open, usually Easter-Sept, 11am-4.30pm. Cathedral, donation; tower and bells, £1. ☎/Fax 061 376 687.

Killaloe Heritage Centre – Open May-Sep, daily, 10am-6pm (5pm last admission). £1.70, reductions available. ☎ 061 361 511, 061 360 788 (Shannon Heritage); Fax 061 361 020.

Excursions

East Clare Heritage Centre – Open Jun-Oct, daily. A/v presentation (10min). Guided tour (French, German) by appointment. ☎ 061 921 351 (also information on boat trips from Mountshannon). eastclareheritage@eircom.net; http://homepage.eircom.net/~eastclareheritage

Holy Island Ferry from Mountshannon – Operates (weather permitting) from Mountshannon June to mid-Sep. £3 per person. ☎ 061 921 351.

Nenagh District Heritage Centre – Open May-Sep, Sun-Fri, 9.30am (2.30pm Sun) to 5pm; Oct-Apr, Mon-Fri, 9.30am-5pm. £2, reductions available. Guided tour (90min) by appointment. Brochure (French, German). Tipperary North Genealogical Centre: Open daily except bank holidays, 9.30am-5pm. ☎ 067 32633; ☎ 067 33850 (Genealogical Centre); Fax 067 33586.

KILLARNEY

🛈 Beech Road – ☎ 064 31633
🛈 Kerry County Airport, Farranfore – ☎ Freephone at Airport Terminal
🛈 Caherciveen RIC Barracks – ☎ 066 947 2589 (Jun-Sep, Mon-Sat)
🛈 Waterville – ☎ 066 947 4646 (Jun-Sep, Mon-Sat)

Lough Leane Boat Trips – Operate from Ross Castle (1hr; weather permitting) 5 times daily, on board Pride of the Lakes (☎/Fax 064 32638 Destination Killarney); 6 times daily on board Lily of Killarney (☎ 064 31068, 064 31251, 31567; Fax 064 34077 (Dero's Tours). £6, reductions available. Bus shuttle between Scott's Gardens and Ross Castle. ☎ 064 31068; Fax 064 35001 (Killarney Watercoach Cruises Ltd).

The Long Range, Killarney

Jaunting Car Trips – Operate from Killarney (south end of Main Street) and from Muckross Abbey and Muckross House. £6 (1hr round the lake); £24 (6mi/10km).

Gap of Dunloe – Operates Apr-Oct, daily (weather permitting), 10.30am-5pm (round tour (6-7hr) from Killarney by bus to Kate Kearney's Cottage, by pony or pony trap or on foot through the Gap to Lord Brandon's Cottage, by boat across the three lakes, by bus to Killarney). Bus and boat £13; pony £12; pony trap £10. ☎ 064 31633; Fax 064 34506 (Tourist Office); ☎ 064 30200; Fax 064 30201 (Gap of Dunloe Tours); ☎ 064 31052 (O'Connor); 064 31251, 31567; Fax 34077 (Deros Tours); ☎ 064 36666; Fax 36555 (Corcoran's).

Kerry Woollen Mills – ♿ Shop: Open Apr-Oct, daily except Sun, 9am-5pm; Nov-Mar, Mon-Fri, 9am-5pm. Parking. ☎ 064 44122; Fax 064 44556; sales@kerrywoollenmills.ie

St Mary's Cathedral – ♿ Open daily, 9am-9pm. If locked, apply to the Cathedral Office. No charge. Parking. ☎ 064 31014.

Museum of Irish Transport – Open Apr-Oct, daily, 10am-6pm. Time 1hr. £3, reductions available. Parking. ☎ 064 34677; Fax 064 31582.

St Mary's Church – Open daily, 10am-5pm.

Excursions

Killarney National Park – Open daily, 9am-5.30pm (7pm July-Aug). No charge. Muckross Information Centre: Open as for Muckross House (see below). Av presentation (20min). ☎ 064 31440.

Knockreer Demesne – Open daily. Tearoom at Deenagh Lodge. ☎ 064 36274.

Ross Castle – (Dúchas) (♿) Guided tour (40min) Easter-Oct, daily, 10am (9am Jun-Aug; 10am Easter-Apr) to 5pm (6.30pm Jun-Aug; 5pm Oct). Last admission 45min before closing. £3, reductions available. No photography. Parking. Wheelchair access to ground floor by appointment. ☎ 064 35851, 35852.

Muckross Friary – (Dúchas) Open mid-June to early-Sept, daily, 10am-5pm (4.15 last admission). No charge. Guided tours by appointment. ☎ 064 31440; Fax 064 33926.

Muckross House, Gardens and Farms – (Dúchas) ♿ House: Open daily, 9am-5.30pm (7pm July-Aug). Closed one week at Christmas. Farms: Open May-Sep, daily, 10am-7pm (6pm May); mid-Mar to Apr and Oct, Sat-Sun and bank hols, 2-6pm; last admission 1hr before closing. House and farms £6, reductions available; house or farms £4, reductions available. Leaflet (French, German, Italian, Spanish, Dutch). Parking. Licensed restaurant; picnic areas. Craft shop. ☎ 064 31440; Fax 064 33926; mucros@iol.ie

Kate Kearney's Cottage – ♿ Open daily, 9am-11.30pm (11pm Dec-Apr). No charge. Live entertainment, including Irish dancing: summer months, Wed, Fri-Sun. Restaurant (6.30-9.30pm); bar food (11am-8pm). Craft shop. Parking. ☎ 064 44146; Fax 064 44641.

Dunloe Castle Hotel Gardens – Open May-Sep, by appointment. Catalogue £1. ☎ 064 44111; Fax 064 44583; www.iol.ie/khl

Killorglin Puck Fair Exhibition – Open daily, midday-9pm. ☎ 066 61353 (Patrick Houlihan).

Valentia Island-Renard Point Car Ferry – Operates (5min shuttle service) Apr-Sep, daily, 8.15am (9am Sun) to 10pm. Car + passengers £3, return £4; pedestrian £2, return £3; cyclist £2, return £3. ☎ 066 9476141; Fax 066 9476377.

Skellig Experience – ♿ Open Apr-mid Nov, daily, 10am-6.30pm; Sept-Oct, Sat-Wed, 10am-6pm. Exhibition £3.50, reductions available. Skellig Islands Cruise available. Parking. Refreshments. Shop. ☎ 066 947 6306; Fax 066 947 76351.

Skellig Islands Ferry – Operate (weather permitting) by appointment. ☎ 066 947 3355 (Skellig Experience Centre). On Great Skellig, only very experienced climbers should continue above the monastery ruins to the cross carved near the summit.

Derrynane House and Historic Park – (Dúchas) (♿) Open May-Sept, Mon-Sat, 9am-6pm, Sun, 11am-7pm; Apr and Oct, Tues-Sun, 1pm-5pm; Nov-Mar, Sat-Sun, 1pm-5pm. Last admission 45min before closing. £2, reductions available. A/v presentation (25min). Guided tour (45min) by appointment. Parking. Coffee shop. Wheelchair access to ground floor. ☎ 066 947 5113; Fax 066 947 5432.

Church of the Transfiguration, Sneem – Open in summer, daily; in winter key available from café opposite. Services: Sun, 10am. ☎/Fax 064 41121; shawa@eircom.net

KILMALLOCK

Excursions

Lough Gur Interpretive Centre – ♿ Open May-Sep, daily, 10am-6pm (5.30pm last admission). £2.20, reductions available. Audio-guide. Parking. Refreshments. ☎ 061 385 186 (site); 061 361 511, 061 360 788 (Shannon Heritage); Fax 061 361 020.

Irish Dresden – Showroom: Open Mon-Fri, 9am-1pm and 2-5pm. Factory: Guided tour (20min) by appointment only Mon-Fri, 11.15am-midday and 3pm-4pm. ☎ 063 83030, 83236 (Irish Dresden Ltd, Dromcolliher, Co Limerick); Fax 063 83192.

De Valera Museum & Bruree Heritage Centre – ♿ Open daily, 10am (2pm Sat-Sun) to 5pm. £3, reductions available. A/v presentation (20min). Parking. Picnic area. ☎ 063 90530; 063 90900.

KILRUSH

🄱 Town Hall, The Square – ☎ 065 905 1577 (Jun-Sep, daily)
🄱 O'Connell Square, Kilkee – ☎ 065 905 6112 (Jun to early-Sep, daily)

Dolphin Watching on the Shannon – Operates from Kilrush Creek Marina (2hr approx; subject to demand and weather conditions) May-Sep. £9, reductions available. ☎/Fax 065 905 1327 (Griffins); www.shannondolphins.ie; shannondolphins@eircom.net

Dolphin Watching Cruise – Operates from Carrigaholt daily. £10, reductions available. Brochure. Accommodation available. ☎ 065 905 8156; 088 258 4711; dwatch@iol.ie; www.dolphinwatch.ie

Shannon Ferry (Killimer-Tarbert) – Visitor Centre: Open daily, 9am-9pm (7pm Oct-Mar). Free parking. Bureau de Change. Ferry operates (20min) daily (except 25 Dec) from Killimer (north bank), hourly on the hour, Apr-Sep, 7am (9am Sun) to 9pm; Oct-Mar, 7am (10am Sun) to 7pm; from Tarbert (south bank) hourly on the half hour, Apr-Sept, 7.30am (9.30am Sun) to 9.30pm; Oct-Mar, 7.30am (10.30am Sun) to 7.30pm. Capacity 44-60 vehicles. Car £9 (single), £13 (return); pedestrian £2 (single), £3 (return). ☎ 065 905 3124; Fax 065 905 3125 (Shannon Ferry Ltd); enquiries@shannonferries.com; www.shannonferries.com

Kilrush Heritage Centre – Open May-Sep, Mon-Sat and public hols, 10am-5.30pm; Sun, midday-4pm. £2, reductions available. ☎ 065 905 1047.

Vandeleur Walled Garden – Open summer, 10am-6pm (5.30pm last admission). Parking. Picnic sites. £1, reductions available. ☎ 065 905 1047.

Scattery Island Visitor Centre – (Dúchas) ♿ Open mid-June to mid-Sept, daily, 10.30am-1pm and 2-6.30pm (5.45pm last admission). Closed 25-26 Dec. No charge. Parking. ☎ 065 905 2144, 905 2139.

Scattery Island Ferry – Operates (15-20min; subject to tide and weather) from Kilrush Creek Marina Apr-Oct, daily; confirm timetable. 1-2hr on the island. Return £5, reductions available. ☎/Fax 065 905 1327 (Griffins); shannondolphins@eircom.net; shannondolphins@eircom.net

West Clare Railway – Open May-Sept, daily, 10am-6pm. Guided tour (30min), every 30min. £5, reductions available. Tea room, picnic area. Shop. ☎ 065 9051 284.

KINSALE

🛈 Pier Road – ☎ 021 477 2234
🛈 Ashe Street, Clonakilty – ☎ 023 33226 (May-Oct Mon-Sat; also Sun, Jul-Aug)

St Multose Church – Open Easter-Sep when possible, Mon-Sat, 10am-midday and 2-4pm. Donation. Guidebook. Services: Sun, 8am, 11.30am, Wed, midday (Eucharist). ☎ 021 772 220 (Rectory).

Kinsale Regional Museum – Open summer, Mon-Sat, 11am-1pm; winter, daily, 2pm (3pm Sun and public hols) to 5.30pm. Closed 25 Dec. £2, reductions available. Guided tour (20min). Brochure (French, German, Japanese, Spanish, Swedish). ☎ 021 772 044.

Desmond Castle – (Dúchas) Open mid-Apr to mid-June, Tues-Sun and bank hols, 10am-6pm; mid-June to early-Oct, daily, 10am-6pm. Last admission 45min before closing. £2, reductions available. Guided tour available on request. Brochure. Leaflet. Access by stone stairway. ☎ 021 774 855.

Charles Fort – (Dúchas) (♿) Open mid-Mar to Oct, daily, 10am-6pm; Nov to mid-Mar, Sat-Sun, 10am-5pm. Last admission 45min before closing. £2.50, reductions available. Guided tour (45min) available. Guide book (Irish, German, French, Spanish, Italian, Dutch). Parking. Tearoom. ☎ 021 772 263.

Lios Na gCon – Open summer, daily, 10am (11am Sat-Sun) to 5pm. £2, reductions available. Guided tours. Brochure. Leaflet. Parking. ☎ 023 33302 (9.15am-5pm), 023 33279 (after 6pm); Fax 023 34449.

West Cork Regional Museum – Open May-Oct, daily, 10.30am-5pm, Sun, 2.30pm-5.30pm. £1.50. Guided tour by appointment. Parking. ☎ 023 33115.

West Cork Model Railway Village – Open Feb-Oct, daily, 10am-5pm (6pm, summer). £3.50, reductions available. Parking. Tearoom. ☎/Fax 023 33224 (Clonakilty Enterprise Board Ltd, Town Hall, Kent Street, Clonakilty, Co Cork); Fax 023 34843; modelvillage@tinet.ie; www.clon.ie/mvillage.html

St Fachtna's Cathedral – (♿) Open daily. Services: Sun, 8am, 11.30am, Saints' Days and Holy Days, 11am. Leaflet (French, German). Bookshop: Sat, 2pm-5pm. Wheelchair access available on request. ☎ 023 48166.

KNOCK

🛈 ☎ 094 88193 (May-Sep, daily)
🛈 Knock Airport – ☎ 094 67247 (Jun-Sep, Mon-Sat)
🛈 Linenhall Street, Castlebar – ☎ 094 21207 (Apr-Aug, Mon-Sat)

Knock Folk Museum – ♿ Open May-Oct, daily, 10am-6pm (7pm July-Aug). £2.50, £1.50 (child/senior citizen), £9 (family). Guided tour (30min) by appointment. Brochure (English only). Guide Book (French). Parking. ☎ 094 88100; Fax 094 88295; info@knock-shrine.ie

Michael Davitt Memorial Museum – ♿ Open Mar-Oct, daily, 10am-6pm; otherwise by appointment. £2, reductions available. Parking.

Excursions

Foxford Woollen Mills Visitor Centre – Guided tour (1hr) daily, 10am (2pm Sun) to 6pm, every 20min. £3.75, reductions available. Guided tour (French, German, Italian, Spanish). Brochure (French, German, Italian, Spanish). Jewellery craft centre. Parking. Restaurant. Shop. Bureau de change. ☎ 094 56756; Fax 094 56794; foxfordwoollenmills@eircom.net

L

LIMERICK

🛈 Arthur's Quay – ☎ 061 317 522
🛈 Shannon Airport Arrivals Hall – ☎ 061 471 664

Limerick Walking Tours – Depart Mon-Fri, at 11am (historical tour) and 2.30pm (Angela's Ashes tour), Sat-Sun, by appointment; from St Mary's Action Centre, 44 Nicholas Street. £4. ☎/Fax 061 318 106; ☎ 061 327 108 (tour guide – Sat-Sun).

St Mary's Cathedral (Anglican) – Open summer, Mon-Sat, 9.30am-15pm; otherwise by appointment. Donation £1.50. Leaflet (French, German, Italian). ☎ 061 310 293; Fax 061 315 721.

Limerick Museum – ♿ Open Tues-Sat, 10am-1pm and 2.15-5pm. Closed public hols. No charge. Parking. ☎ 061 417 826; Fax 061 415 266.

King John's Castle – (♿) Open Jun-Aug, daily, 9am-6pm (5pm last admission); Apr-May and Sept-Oct, daily, 9.30am-5.30pm (4.30pm last admission). £4.40, reductions available. A/v presentation (20min). Audio-guide and brochure (French, German, Irish, Italian). Parking. Coffee shop. Wheelchair access to ground floor. ☎ 061 411 201 (Castle); 061 361 511, 061 360 788 (Shannon Heritage); Fax 061 361 020.

Old Bishop's Palace – Open Mon-Fri, 9am-5pm. ☎ 061 313 399 (Limerick Civic Trust); Fax 061 315 513.

Hunt Museum – ♿ Open Mon-Sat, 10am-5pm, Sun, 2-5pm. £4.20, reductions available. Guided tour (1hr; French, Italian, Spanish) by appointment. Visitor guide (French, Italian, Japanese, Spanish). Shop. Restaurant. ☎ 061 312 833; Fax 061 312 834; info@huntmuseum.com; www.ul.ie/~hunt

Georgian House and Garden – Open Mon-Fri, 10am-5pm, Sat-Sun, 2pm-4.30pm. £2, reductions available. ☎ 061 314 130; Fax 353 61 310 130.

St John's Cathedral (RC) – ♿ Open daily, 9am-6pm (8pm Sat-Sun). No charge. Brochure (French, German, Irish, Italian, Spanish). Guided tour available. Parking. ☎ 061 414 624; Fax 061 316 570; stjohnsparishlk@tinet.ie

Limerick City Gallery of Art – ♿ Open daily, 10am-6pm (1pm Sat, 7pm Thu). Closed 1 Jan and at Christmas. ☎ 061 310 633; Fax 061 311 345; lcgartzz@iol.ie; www.limerickcorp.ie

Excursions

Cratloe Woods House – (♿) Open June to mid-Sept, Mon-Sat, 2-6pm; otherwise by appointment. Guided tour. £3, reductions available. Tearoom. ☎ 061 327 028; Fax 327 031.

Bunratty Castle and Folk Park – ♿ Open June-Aug, daily, 9am-6.30pm (5.30pm last admission); Sept-May, daily, 9.30am-5.30pm; last admission to castle 4pm. Closed Good Fri, 24-26 Dec. £6.50, reductions available; Folk Park only £4.10 (after 4pm). Guided tour of castle available. Visitor map (Dutch, French, German, Irish, Italian, Japanese, Spanish). Brochure (French, German, Italian). Medieval banquets: daily, 5.30pm and 8.45pm; £32, reductions available. Traditional Irish night (Shannon céile): May-Oct, Mon-Fri, 7pm, Sat-Sun, 5.30pm and 8.45pm; £27, reductions available. Parking. Refreshments. ☎ 061 361 511, 061 360 788 (Shannon Heritage); Fax 061 361 020; reservations@shannon~dev.ie; www.shannonheritage.com

Glenstal Abbey Church – Open daily, 6.30am-9.30pm. ☎ 061 386 103; Fax 061 386 328; monks@glenstal.ie; www.glenstal.ie

LISMORE

🛈 Heritage Centre – ☎ 058 54975 (seasonal)

Lismore Castle Gardens – Open early Apr to mid-Oct, daily, 1.45-4.45pm. £3, reductions available. Leaflet (French). ☎ 058 54424; Fax 058 54896; lismoreestates@tinet.ie; www.lismorecastle.com

St Carthage's Cathedral (Anglican) – Open daily, 9am-6pm (4pm Oct-Mar). No charge. Information board (Dutch, French, German, Irish, Italian, Spanish, Swedish). Parking. ☎ 058 54137.

St Carthage's Church – Open daily, 9.30am-8pm (5pm winter). ☎ 058 54246.

Lismore Heritage Centre – Open Mar-Oct, daily, 9.30am-5.30pm, Nov-Feb, Mon-Fri, 9.30am-5.30pm. £3. A/v presentation (30min) and brochure (French, German, Italian). ☎ 058 54975; Fax 058 53009.

Excursion

Mount Melleray Abbey – Open 7.15am-8.30pm. ☎ 058 54404.

Lismore Castle

LONGFORD

🛈 Market Square – ☎ 043 46566 (May-Sep, Mon-Fri; also Sat, Jun-Sep)

St Mel's Cathedral (RC) – ♿ Open daily, 7.45am-8pm (9pm Sat, 6pm Sun). No charge. Parking. ☎ 043 46465.

St Mel's Diocesan Museum – Open Jun-Sep; telephone for details. ☎ 043 46465.

Excursions

Carrigglas Manor – ♿ Garden Museum: Open Jun-Aug, Mon-Tue, Fri, 10.30am-5pm, Sun, 2-6pm; May and Sep, Mon and Fri, 10.30am-3pm. House: Guided tour (45min; French, German, Italian): Jun-Aug, Mon-Tue and Fri, at 11am, midday, 2pm, 3pm, Sun at 2pm, 3pm, 4pm, 5pm; May and Sept, Mon and Fri, at 11am, midday, 2pm. Gardens and museum £2.50, reductions available; house £2.50 extra. Parking. Tearoom. Gift shop. ☎ 043 45165; Fax 043 41026; greenrock@tinet.ie

Ardagh Heritage Centre – Open daily, 9am-5pm. £2, reductions available. Video (15min). Restaurant. Craft shop. ☎ 043 75277; Fax 043 75278.

Corlea Trackway – (Dúchas) ♿ Guided tour Apr-Sep, daily, 10am-6pm (5.15pm last admission. £2.50, reductions available. A/v presentation (20min), displays. Parking. Tearoom; picnic area. ☎ 043 22386; 0905 74195 (Head Office for winter hours).

M

MALLOW

St James' Church – Open to visitors by appointment. Services: Sun, 11.30am. ☎ 022 21473 (Rector).

Excursions

Doneraile Wildlife Park – (Dúchas) (♿) Open mid-Apr to Oct, Mon-Sat, 8am (10am Sat) to 8.30pm, Sun and bank hols, 11am-7pm; Nov to mid-Apr, daily, 8am (10am Sat-Sun and bank hols) to 4.30pm. Closed 25-26 Dec. £1, reductions available. Parking. Picnic areas. Wheelchair access to pathways. ☎ 022 24244.

Annes Grove Gardens – Open mid-Mar to Sep, daily, 10am (1pm Sun) to 5pm (6pm Sun); otherwise by appointment. Time 45min. £3, reductions available. Leaflet and guided tour (French, German). Parking. Picnic area. ☎/Fax 022 26145.

MAYNOOTH

Maynooth College Visitor Centre – Open May-Sep, Mon-Fri, 11am-5pm, Sat-Sun, 2-6pm. No charge. Guided tour £3, reductions available. ☎ 01 708 3576; Fax 01 628 9063.

Excursions

Castletown House – (Dúchas) (♿) Restoration in progress. Guided tour Easter to Sept, daily, 10am (1pm Sat-Sun and public hols) to 6pm; Oct, Sun-Fri, 10am (1pm Sun and public hols) to 5pm; Nov, Sun, 1pm-5pm. Last admission 1hr before closing.

Slide File, Dublin

Wonderful Barn, Castletown

Closed Good Fri, Christmas/
New Year. £3, reductions avail-
able. No photography. Parking.
Coffee shop. ☎ 01 628 8252;
Fax 01 627 1811.

Steam Museum, Straffan –
(&) Open Jun-Aug, Tue-Sun
and bank hols, 2-6pm; Apr-
May and Sep, Sun and bank
hols, 2.30-5.30pm (last entry).
£3, reductions available; garden only £2. Parking. Tea-
house. Steam and Garden
shop. ☎ 01 627 3155; Fax
01 627 3477.

Coolcarrigan Gardens – Open
by appointment Apr-Aug. £3.
☎ 045 863 512,
01 834 1141.

MIDLETON
🛈 Jameson Heritage Centre –
☎ 021 461 3702 (Mar-Oct, daily)

Stephen Pearce Pottery – &
Stephen Pearce Gallery: Open
daily, 10am-6pm; closed 1 Jan
and 25-26 Dec. Pottery shop:
Open Mon-Fri, 8.30am-5pm
(4pm Fri); Sat, 10am-6pm,
Sun and bank hols, midday-6pm; closed 25-26 Dec. Workshop: Open Mon-Fri, 8.30am-
4.45pm (3.45pm Fri); closed Good Fri, bank hols and 2 weeks at Christmas. Café:
Open 10am-5pm. Parking. ☎ 021 4646 807; Fax 021 646 706; spearce@indigo.ie

Old Midleton Distillery – & Guided tour (60min) daily, 9am-6pm (4.30pm last tour);
otherwise by appointment. £3.95, reductions available. Guided tours. A/v presentation
(15min). Tutored whiskey tasting in the bar. Audio-guide, guided tour and brochure
(Dutch, French, German, Italian, Spanish). Parking. Restaurant. Gift shop. ☎ 021
613 594; Fax 021 613 642; dbyrne@idl.ie; www.irish-whiskey-trail.com

Excursions

Cloyne Cathedral – & Open May-Sep, daily, 10am-6pm; otherwise key available at
the cottage. Donation welcome. Guided tour by appointment. Service: Sun, midday.
Parking.

Barryscourt Castle – (Dúchas) Open May-Oct, daily, 10am-6pm; Oct-May, Fri-Wed,
11am-5pm; last admission 45min before closing. £1.50, reductions available. Parking. Tea shop. Craft shop. ☎ 021 882 218, 021 883 864.

MONAGHAN
🛈 Market House – ☎ 047 81122 (Apr-Oct, Mon-Sat)

St Macartan's Cathedral – & Open daily, 9am-6pm. No charge. Parking.
☎ 047 82300.

Monaghan County Museum – (&) Open Tue-Sat (except public hols), 11am-1pm and
2-5pm. No charge. ☎ 047 82928; Fax 047 71189; moncomuseum@tinet.ie

St Louis Convent Heritage Centre – Open Mon-Tue, Thur-Fri, 10am-midday and 2.30-
4.30pm, Sat-Sun, 2.30pm-4.30pm. £1. ☎ 047 83529.

Excursions

Rossmore Forest Park – Gates open daily. Parking £2. Picnic area. ☎ 047 81968.

Ulster Canal Stores – Open Jun-Sep, daily, 10am (2pm Sun) to 6pm. £1.50, reductions available. Lace exhibition and sales. Refreshments. Tourist Information Centre.
Cycle hire. ☎ 047 52125, 51718; Fax 047 51720; cloneslace@eircom.net;
clonesdevelopment@eircom.net; www.cluaincois.demon.co.uk

MULLINGAR
🛈 Market House – ☎ 044 48650

Mullingar Bronze and Pewter – Open Mon-Fri, 9.30am-6pm, Sat, 10am-5.30pm
(12.30pm Fri last tour). Parking. ☎ 044 44948, 43078, 48791.

Cathedral of Christ the King – & Open daily, 7.30am-9pm. Parking. ☎ 044 48338.

Mullingar Cathedral Museum – Open May-Sep, Thur, Sat-Sun, 3pm-4pm. £1. Parking. ☎ 044 48338.

Belvedere House and Gardens – Open daily, 10.30am-8pm (6.30pm, Sep-Oct; 4pm, Nov-Mar). £3.50, reductions available. Parking. Restaurant. Souvenir shop. ☎ 044 49060; Fax 044 49002; info@belvedere-house.ie; www.belvedere-house.ie

Tullynally Castle and Gardens – Gardens: Open May-Aug, daily, 2-6pm. Castle: Guided tour mid-June to end-July, daily, 2-6pm. Garden only £3; castle and gardens £4.50. Tearoom (daily, 2-6pm). ☎ 044 61159 or 61289; Fax 044 61856.

N

NEW ROSS

🚹 The Quay – ☎ 051 421 857 (May-Sep, Mon-Sat)

🚹 Hook Head Community Office – ☎ 051 397 502 (seasonal)

Galley Cruising Restaurants – Cruises from New Ross and Waterford Apr-Oct, daily, at 12.30pm (lunch; 2hr; £14); Apr-Sep, daily, at 5.30pm or 7pm (dinner; 2-3hr; £22-£26); Jun-Aug, at 3pm (afternoon tea; 2hr; £7). ☎ 051 421 723 (10am-7pm); Fax 051 421 950.

St Mary's Church – Services: Sun, 11.45am. ☎ 051 425 004.

Tholsel – Open by appointment Mon-Fri, 9am-5pm. ☎ 051 421 284 (New Ross Council).

Dunbrody Project – Open daily, 10am (midday Sat-Sun) to 5pm. £3, reductions available. ☎ 051 425 239; Fax 051 425 240.

Excursions

Duiske Abbey – Open daily, 8am-7.30pm. Mass: Mon-Fri, 10.30am (10am Jul-Aug), Sat, 11am, Sun, 8.30am, 11am, 7.30pm (vigil). The Abbey Centre: Mon-Fri, 10am-5pm; also Sat-Sun, June-Aug, 2-5pm.☎ 0503 24238.

Kennedy Arboretum – (Dúchas) ♿ Open daily, 10am-8pm (6.30pm Apr and Sep; 5pm Oct-Mar). Last admission 45min before closing. Closed Good Fri, 25 Dec. £2, reductions available. A/v presentation (15min). Guided tour (1hr 15min) by appointment. Self-guiding trails. Parking. Tearoom in summer (051 388 195); picnic area. ☎ 051 388 171; Fax 051 388 172.

Kennedy Homestead – Open May-Sep, 10am-5.30pm; Oct-Apr, by appointment. £2.50, reductions available. ☎ 051 388 264; Fax 051 388 761; info@kennedyhomestead.com; www.kennedyhomestead.com

Kilmokea Gardens – (♿) Open Mar-Nov, daily, 10am-5pm (6pm, gardens). £4 (including tea), no charge (accompanied child). Guided tour (1hr 30min) by appointment. Plants for sale. Teas and lunches in Georgian conservatory. ☎ 051 388 109; Fax 051 388 776; kilmokea@indigo.ie; www.kilmokea.com

Dunbrody Abbey – Open May-Sep, daily, 10am-6pm (7pm Jul-Aug). Abbey £1.50, reductions available; Maze £1.50, reductions available. ☎ 051 388 603 or 051 389 104 (after hours).

Ballyhack Castle – (Dúchas) Open Jun-Sep, daily, 10am-6.30pm (5.45pm last admission. £1, reductions available. Guided tours by appointment. Public parking nearby. Access by wooden steps. ☎ 051 389 468.

Duncannon Fort – (♿) Open June to mid-Sep, daily, 10am-5.30pm. £2, reductions available. Craft shop. Café. Guided tours available. ☎/Fax 051 389 454.

Tintern Abbey – ♿ Open daily, 9.30am-6.30pm. £1.50, reductions available. Guided tour available on request. ☎ 051 562 650.

Hook Lighthouse – Open Mar-Oct, daily, 9.30am-5.30pm. £3.50, reductions available. ☎ 051 397 055; Fax 051 397 056; thehook@eircom.net; www.thehook-wexford.com

P – R – S

PORTUMNA

Portumna Lifting Bridge – (Dúchas) Closed to road vehicles for 10-15min mid-Mar to early-Nov, Mon-Fri, 6 times daily, Sun, 4 times daily; early-Nov to mid-Mar, Mon-Fri, 3 times daily, Sun, twice daily.

Portumna Castle – (Dúchas) Open May-Jun, Tue-Sun, 10am-5pm; Jun to early-Oct, daily, 9.30am-6.30pm. Last admission 45min before closing. £1.50, reductions available. Guided tour. Parking. ☎ 0509 41658.

PORTUMNA

Clonfert Cathedral – Open May-Sep, daily, 9am-sunset. If locked, key available at the lodge. ☎/Fax 0509 51269; clonfert@clonfert-anglican.org

ROSCREA

Roscrea Heritage Centre (Castle and Damer House) – (Dúchas) Open Jun-Sep, daily, 9.30am-6.30pm (5.45pm last admission). £2.50, reductions available. Guided tour (45min) by appointment. Public parking nearby. Access to house by stone steps. ☎ 0505 21850.

RUSSBOROUGH

Russborough – Guided tour (including 5min film) Apr and Oct, Sun and bank hols, 10.30am-5.30pm; May-Sep, daily, 10.30am-5.30pm. Booklet (French, German, Italian, Spanish). Main rooms £4, reductions available. Restaurant. Shop. Craft workshops. Children's playground. ☎ 045 865 239; Fax 045 865 054.

SKIBBEREEN   🗐 North Street – ☎ 028 21766

West Cork Arts Centre – Open Mon-Sat, 10am-6pm. ☎ 028 22090; Fax 028 22084.

Baltimore-Sherkin Island Passenger Ferry – Operates (15min) from Baltimore Pier Jun-Sep, 8 times daily, 9am-8.30pm (7 times on Sun); Oct-May, 3 times daily, 10.30am-5.30pm; extra services at peak times. Return £5. ☎ 028 20125; 028 20218; www.sherkinisland.ie

Skull Harbour

Baltimore-Cape Clear Island Ferry – Operates daily (weather permitting); times available by telephone. Return £9, reductions available. ☎ 028 39135 (Capt O'Driscoll), 028 39159 (office); 028 20114; Fax 028 20442 (Booking Office); ccteo@iol.ie

Skull Ferry – Operates to Cape Clear Island (weather permitting) Jul-Aug, 3 times daily, 10am-5.30pm; May-Jun and Sep-Oct, daily, at 2.30pm. Operates to Sherkin Island and Baltimore Jul-Aug, 3 times daily, 10.30am-4.15pm. Return £9, reductions available. To Fastnet Rock Lighthouse twice weekly, at 7pm. ☎ 028 28278.

Baltimore-Skull Ferry – Operates Jun-Aug, daily: from Baltimore to Hare Island (15min) to Skull (35min) at 10am, 1.45pm and 4.40pm; from Skull to Hare Island (35min) to Baltimore (15min) at 11.30am, 3pm and 5.30pm. £6, reductions available. Approved by Bord Fáilte and Department of Marine. ☎ 028 39153, 087 268 0760 (mobile); Fax 028 39164 (Ciaran O'Driscoll, North Harbour, Cape Clear Island).

Excursions

Creagh Gardens – ♿ Open Mar-Oct, daily, 10am-6pm; otherwise by appointment. £3, reductions available. No dogs. Parking. ☎/Fax 028 22121.

The Liss Ard Foundation – (♿) Open May-Oct, Mon-Fri, 10am-6pm, Sat-Sun, mid-day-6pm; Nov-Mar, by arrangement. £3, reductions available. Parking. ☎ 028 22373; Fax 028 40187; lissardfoundation@eircom.net; www.lissard.com

St Barrahane's Church – Open daily. Services: in summer, Sun, 9.45am; in winter, first Sun of the month, 9am.

Schull Planetarium – (♿) Open Apr-May and Sep, Sun, 3-5pm (Starshow at 4pm); Jun, Tue and Sat, 3-5pm (Starshow at 4pm), Thur, 7-9pm (Starshow at 8pm); Jul-Aug, Tue-Sat, 2-5pm, Mon and Thur, 7-9pm (Starshows Tue and Sat at 4pm, Mon and Thur at 8pm; mid-July to mid-Aug, Wed-Fri, extra shows). Starshow: 45min. Star-show £3.50, reductions available. Parking. ☎ 028 28315, 28552; Fax 028 28467.

The Ewe Art Centre – (♿) Open May-Sep, daily, 10am-6pm. £2. Parking. ☎/Fax 028 35492; courses@theewe.com; www.theewe.com

Mizen Vision – Open mid Mar-May and Oct, daily, 10.30am-5pm; Jun-Sept, daily, 10am-6pm; Nov to mid-Mar, Sat-Sun, 11am-4pm. £3, reductions available. A/v presentations: Lighthouse-keeping (30min); Irish Lights (50min), Royal National Lifeboat Institution (RNLI) (35min). Parking. ☎ 028 35115 (summer only); otherwise ☎ 028 35591 or 35253; Fax 028 35603; mizenvision@eircom. net; www.westcorkweb.ie

SLIGO
🛈 Temple Street – ☎ 071 61201

Lough Gill Cruises – Wild Rose Water Bus: Operates mid-Jun to Sep, from Doorly Park (southeast of Sligo town centre) daily, at 2.30pm (3hr round tour of Lough Gill stopping at Parke's Castle) and 5.30pm (to Parke's Castle); from Parke's Castle (north-east corner of Lough Gill) daily, at 12.30pm (1hr to Innisfree), 1.30pm (to Doorly Park), 3.30pm (1hr to Innisfree), 4.30pm (to Sligo and back), 6.30pm (1hr to Innis-free); Fri, at 9pm (Irish music, bar); Apr, May, Oct, Sun only. Innisfree £5; Lough Gill £6. Refreshments. ☎ 071 64266; 0882 598 8869 (mobile).

Inishmurray Ferry – Boat trips (minimum 15 passengers) from Mullaghmore ☎ 071 66124 (Rodney Lomax), Brendan Merrifield ☎ 072 41874, 088 277 3874, and Rosses Point ☎ 071 42391 (Tommy McCallion).

Sligo Abbey – (Dúchas) Open early-Jun to Sep, daily, 9.30am-6.30pm (5.45pm last admission). £1.50, reductions available. Guided tour (45min) by appointment. Public parking nearby. Access by stone steps. ☎ 071 46406.

Model Arts and Niland Gallery – Open Tue-Sat, 10am-midday and 2-4.50pm (after-noons only, Oct-May). No charge. ☎ 071 41405; Fax 071 43694; modelart@iol.ie; www.iol.ie/~modelart/

Sligo County Museum – Open mid-Jun to mid-Sep, Mon-Sat, 10am-midday and 2-4.50pm; Apr-May and Oct-Dec, Tue-Sat, 2-4.50pm. No charge. ☎ 071 42212 (Museum); 071 47190 (Central Library); Fax 071 46798; sligolib@iol.ie

St John's Cathedral (Anglican) – Open Sun, 8am-midday; Mon-Sat, 10am-6pm (4pm winter) by prior arrangement. ☎ 071 62263 (The Dean, The Rectory, Strandhill Road, Sligo).

Cathedral of the Immaculate Conception (RC) – ♿ Open daily, 7am-9pm. No charge. Parking. ☎ 071 62670.

Carrowmore Megalithic Cemetery – (Dúchas) (♿) Site: Open daily. Visitor Centre: Open May-Oct, daily, 9.30am-6.30pm. £1.50, reductions available. A/v presentation (45min). Guided tour (45min) May-Sep. Parking. ☎ 071 61534.

Parke's Castle – (Dúchas) (♿) Open Apr-Oct, daily, 9.30am-6.30pm; early-Mar to end-Mar, daily, 10am-5pm. £2, reductions available. Guided tour (40min) by appoint-ment. A/v presentation (20min; French, German, Italian). Leaflet (French, German, Irish, Italian, Spanish). Tearoom. Wheelchair access to grounds. ☎ 071 64149.

Lissadell House – Guided tour (40min) Jun to mid-Sep, daily except Sun, 10.30am-1pm and 2-5pm (4.15 last admission). £3, reductions available. Parking. ☎/Fax 071 63150.

STROKESTOWN
🛈 Harrison Hall, Roscommon – ☎ 0903 26342 (May-Aug, Mon-Sat)

Strokestown Park Famine Museum – ♿ Open Apr-Oct, daily, 11am-5.30pm. Museum, house and garden £8.50; museum or house or garden £3.25. Leaflet (French, German). Restaurant. ☎ 078 33013; Fax 078 33712; info@strokestownpark.ie; www.strokestownpark.ie

Strokestown Park House – (♿) Guided tour (40min) Apr-Oct, daily, 11am-5.30pm. House only £3.25; house and museum £8.50. Leaflet (French, German). Restaurant. ☎ 078 33013; Fax 078 33712; info@strokestownpark.ie; www.strokestownpark.ie.

Roscommon County Heritage Centre – ♿ Open May-Sep, Tues-Sun, 2.30-4.30pm. Closed public hols. Donation. Parking. ☎ 078 33380; Fax 078 33398.

Excursions

Roscommon County Museum – ♿ Open Mon-Sat, 11am (10am mid-Sept to mid-May) to 3pm (5.30pm mid-Sept to mid-May). £1. Ramp. ☎ 0903 25613.

Clonalis House – (♿) Guided tour (45min) Jun to mid-Sep, Mon-Sat, 11am-5pm. £4, reductions available. Parking. Refreshments. Wheelchair access to ground floor. ☎/Fax 0907 20014; clonalis@iol.ie

Douglas Hyde Centre – ♿ Open May-Sep, Tues-Sun, 2-5pm (6pm Sat-Sun); possibly mornings also, telephone for details. Donation. Parking. Picnic area. ☎ 0907 70016.

T

TIPPERARY

Tipperary Excel Heritage Centre – Open daily, 9am-6pm. Closed Good Fri, 25 Dec to 2 Jan. £3.50, reductions available. Parking. Restaurant. Shop. ☎ 062 33466; Fax 062 31067; info@tipperary-excel.com; www.tipperary-excel.com

Old IRA Exhibition – Open daily, 10am-10pm (7pm in winter). Parking.

TRALEE

🅱 Ashe Hall – ☎ 066 712 1288
🅱 St John's Church, Listowel – ☎ 068 22590 (Jun-Sep, Mon-Sat)

Siamsa Tíre – National Folk Theatre of Ireland – ♿ Opening times according to performances, telephone for details. Closed Good Fri, 25-26 Dec. Gallery no charge; Theatre productions £12, reductions available. Refreshments. Audio loop. ☎ 066 712 3055; Fax 066 712 7276.

Aqua Dome – Open daily, 1pm (10am Jun-Aug) to 10pm. £5, Jun-Aug £6, reductions available. Parking. ☎ 066 712 8899 (Reception), 066 712 8755 (Administration), 066 712 9150 (24hr information); Fax 066 712 9130; www.discoverkerry.com/aquadome

Kerry – The Kingdom – ♿ Open mid-Mar to Oct, daily, 10am-6pm; Nov-Dec, daily, midday-5pm. Closed 24-27 Dec. £5.50, reductions available. Audio-guide (French, German). Commentary (Dutch, French, German, Irish, Italian, Japanese, Spanish). Museum brochure (Dutch, French, German, Italian, Spanish). Guided tour available. Parking. Craft shop. Café. ☎ 066 712 7777; Fax 066 712 7444; kcmuseum@indigo.ie.

Tralee-Blennerville Light Railway – ♿ Operates May to early-Oct, daily, 11am-5.30pm, on the hour from Ballyard Station in Tralee, on the half-hour from Blennerville. Closed Jun-Sep, second Sun and Mon for maintenance work. £3, reductions available. Audio-guide and brochure. Parking. Restaurant at Blennerville. ☎ 066 712 1064.

Excursions

Blennerville Windmill – ♿ Open Apr-Oct, daily, 10am-6pm. £3, reductions available. A/v presentation (8min). Brochure. Guided tour (30min) available. Parking. Restaurant. Craft centre. ☎ 066 712 1064.

Crag Cave – ♿ Guided tour (30min; French) mid-Mar to Nov, daily, 10am-6pm (6.30pm Jul-Aug). £4, reductions available. Brochure (Dutch, French, German, Italian, Spanish). Parking. Coffee shop. Craft shop. ☎ 066 714 1244; Fax 066 714 2352; cragcave@eircom.net; www.cragcave.com

Ardfert Cathedral – (Dúchas) (♿) Open May-Sep, daily, 9.30am-6.30pm (5.45pm last admission). £1.50, reductions available. Guided tour (45min) by appointment. Leaflet (French, German, Irish, Italian). Parking. Wheelchair access to exhibition area and viewing point. ☎ 066 713 4711.

Fenit Sea World – ♿ Open Mar-Sep, daily, 10am-6pm (9pm July-Aug); Oct-Dec, Sat-Sun. £4.50, reductions available. Parking. ☎/Fax 066 713 6544 or 066 712 1722 (Flatterys Travel Agency); www.fenitseaworld.com

Rattoo-North Kerry Museum – ♿ Open Apr-Sept, daily, 10am (2pm Sun) to 6pm. £2, reductions available. Guided tour available. ☎/Fax   066 713 1000.

St John's Theatre and Arts Centre – ♿ Open daily, 10am-6pm. Closed Good Fri; 23 Dec to 2 Jan. Monthly programme of theatre, music, dance, films, exhibitions and youth performance workshops. Parking. Refreshments. ☎ 068 22566; Fax 068 23485; www.local.ie

Tarbert Bridewell – Open Apr-Oct, daily, 10am-6pm. £3, reductions available. Guide books (French, German, Italian, Spanish). ☎ 068 36500; Fax 068 36500.

Tarbert House – Open May to mid-Aug, 10am-midday and 2-4pm. £2.50. ☎ 068 36198, 36500.

TRIM

ⓘ ☎ 046 37111 (May-Sep, Mon-Sat)

Trim Castle – Open mid-June to mid-Sept, daily, 10am-6pm (last admission, 5.15pm). Castle and guided tour of the keep £2.50, £6 (family), £1 (child/student). Castle only £1, £3 (family), 40p (child/student). Tour 45min. Leaflet/guide booklet. Parking. ☎ 046 38619; Fax 046 38618041 988 0300; Fax 041 982 3071.

TUAM

ⓘ ☎ 093 25486, 24463 (Jun-Aug, Mon-Sat)

St Mary's Cathedral – (♿) Opening times available by telephone. Services: Sun, Festivals and Holy Days, midday (Holy Communion). Guided tour: Jul-Aug. Ramp for wheelchairs on request. ☎ 093 25598 (Office), 092 46017 (Dean's residence), 093 24141 (Caretaker).

Cathedral of the Assumption – (♿) Open daily, 8.30am-9.30pm. Mass: Sun, 8.30am, 10am, 11.15am, 12.30pm, Mon-Fri, 9am, 10am, 7.30pm; Sat, 7.30pm. Ramp at the entrance. ☎ 093 24388.

Tuam Mill Museum – ♿ Open Jun-Sep, daily, 10am-6pm; Jul-Aug, guided tour available. A/v presentation. Parking. ☎ 093 24463, 24141.

TULLAMORE

ⓘ Tullamore Dew Heritage Centre – ☎ 0506 52617 (daily)

Tullamore Distillery Heritage Centre – ♿ Open May-Sep, Mon-Sat, 9am-6pm; Oct-Apr, Mon-Sat, 10am-5pm; all year, Sun, midday-5pm. Closed 25 Dec. £3.50, concessions available. Lift. Parking. ☎ 0506 25015; Fax 0506 25016; tullamoredhc@eircom.net; www.tullamore-dew.org

Excursion

Locke's Distillery Museum, Kilbeggan – (♿) Open Apr-Oct, daily, 9am-6pm; Nov-Mar, daily, 10am-4pm. Closed 23-30 Dec. £3.25, reductions available. Guided tour (French, German in summer). Self-guided tour (French, German, Italian, Spanish, Swedish). Parking. Restaurant/coffee shop. Very limited wheelchair access. ☎/Fax 0506 32134; www.iol.ie/wcmeathtc

W

WATERFORD

ⓘ The Granary, Merchants Quay – ☎ 051 875 823
ⓘ Waterford Crystal Visitor Centre – ☎ 051 358 397 (Mon-Sun)
ⓘ Tramore – ☎ 051 281 572 (Jun-Aug, Mon-Sat)

Garter Lane Arts Centre – ♿ Open Mon-Sat, 10am-6pm. No charge. Telephone for details of performances. ☎ 051 855 038; Fax 051 871 570; admin@garterlane.iol.ie

Walking Tours – Tour departs from Treasures at the Granary, Mar-Oct, daily, 11.45am, 1.45pm, and from Granville Hotel on the Quay, 15min later. £4. ☎ 051 873 711; Fax 051 850 645 (Jack Burtchaell).

Waterford Harbour Ferry (Passage East-Ballyhack) – Operates daily, 7am (9.30am Sun and public hols) to 10pm (8pm Oct-Mar). Closed 25-26 Dec. Capacity 30 cars. Return fare car £6.50; return fare pedestrian £1.50. ☎ 051 382 480, 382 488; Fax 051 382 598 (Passage East Ferry Co Ltd); passageferry@eircom.net; www.passageferry.com

Waterford Crystal – ♿ Visitor Centre: Open Apr-Oct, daily, 8.30am-6pm; Nov-Mar, Mon-Sat, 9am-5pm. Factory: Guided tour (2hr) Apr-Oct, daily, 8.30am-5pm; Nov-Mar, Mon-Fri, 9am-3.15pm. Showrooms: Mar-Oct, daily, 8.30am-6pm; Nov-Mar, daily, 9am-6pm; Jan-Feb, Mon-Fri, 9am-5pm. Admission charge. Brochure (major European languages). A/v presentation. Parking. Restaurant. ☎ 051 373 311; Fax 051 378 539.

Waterford Treasures at the Granary – ♿ Open daily, 10am-5pm (9.30am-9pm, Jun-Aug). £3; joint ticket with Reginald's Tower Museum £4; reductions available. Public parking nearby. ☎ 051 304 500; Fax 051 304 501; mail@waterfordtreasures.com; www.waterfordtreasures.com

Reginald's Tower Museum – (Dúchas) Open Easter-Oct, daily, 10am-5pm (9.30am-6.30pm, Jul-Aug). £1.50; jont ticket with Waterford Treasures £4; reductions available. Guided tour (45min) by appointment. Public parking nearby. ☎ 051 304 220.

City Hall – Open (functions permitting) Mon-Fri, 10am-5pm; telephone for details. No charge. Guided tours. ☎ 051 309 900 (Waterford Corporation); art@waterfordcorp.ie

Theatre Royal – Open for theatrical performances all year; details by telephone. Coffee shop. ☎ 051 874 402 (box office); theatreroyal@eircom.net; www.theatreroyalwaterford.com

French Church – (Dúchas) Access via Reginald's Tower Museum (see above).

Christchurch Cathedral – Audio performances: Jun-Aug, Mon-Sat, at 10.30am, 2.15pm, 3.30pm, 4pm, Sun, 2.30pm, 4pm; Apr-May and Sep-Oct, Mon-Fri, at 10.30am, 2.15pm, 4pm. Services: Sun, 8am, 10am, Wed, 10.30am. £2, reductions available. ☎/Fax 051 858 958; ☎ 086 818 3165 (mobile).

WATERFORD

Waterford Heritage Genealogical Service – Open Mon-Fri, 9am-5pm (1pm Fri).
☎ 051 876 123; Fax 051 850 645.

Chamber of Commerce – Open Mon-Fri, 9am-5pm. Leaflet (French). ☎ 051 872 639;
Fax 051 876 002; waterfordchamber@eircom.net

🛈 ☎ 098 25711
🛈 Newport – ☎ 098 41895 (Jun-Aug, Mon-Sat)
🛈 Achill – ☎ 098 45384 (Jun-Aug, Mon-Sat)
🛈 Cong – ☎ 092 46542 (Mar-Sep, Mon-Sat)

Clare Island Ferry (1) – Operates (20min) from Roonagh Quay Jul-Aug, 8 times daily;
Jun and Sep, 4 times daily; May, 3 times daily. Return £10, reductions available. The
Pirate Queen; capacity 96 passengers; sundeck; bar; video and commentary.
☎ 098 26307; Fax 098 28288 (Chris O'Grady, Clare Island Ferry and Clew Bay Cruises
Ltd). ☎ 087 241 3783 (mobile).

Westport House – Open Jul to late-Aug, daily, 11.30am (1.30pm Sat-Sun) to 5.30pm;
Jun and late-Aug to mid-Sep, daily, 2-5pm. Wildlife animal and bird park and leisure
attractions: Jul-Aug, same hours as above. Antique shop: Jun to mid-Sep, same hours
as above. House and attractions £12; house only £6; reductions available. Brochure
(French, German). Parking. Refreshments. ☎ 098 25430; Fax 098 25206.

Holy Trinity Church – Open Jul-Aug, daily. If locked, ask at the Rectory.

Clew Bay Heritage Centre – Open Apr-Oct, Mon-Fri, 10am-5pm, also July-Aug, Sun,
3-5pm. £2, reductions available. Parking.

Doo Lough, Co Mayo

Slide File, Dublin

Excursions

Louisburgh Folk and Heritage Centre – Open
Jun-Sep, daily, 11am-6pm;
Oct-May, by appointment.
£2.50, reductions available. Parking. Refreshments. ☎ 098 66341.

Ballintubber Abbey – Open
May-Sep, daily, 10.30am-
5pm. Donation. Guided tour
(1hr) available. Brochure.
Parking. Restaurant.
☎ 094 30934/30709; Fax
094 30018; btubabbey@
tinet.ie

Cong Abbey – (Dúchas)
Open sunrise-sunset; when
closed key available from
the caretaker, Michael
Collins, Abbey Street, Cong,
Co Mayo. ☎ 092 46068.

**Quiet Man Heritage
Centre** – Open Apr-Sep,
daily, 10am-6pm. £2.75,
£1 (child), £2.25 (senior).
Tours to The Quiet Man locations: daily, at 12midday,
2pm, 3pm. ☎ 092 46089;
Fax 092 46448.

Ashford Castle – Grounds and gardens, 9am-6pm. £4, £2 (child). ☎ 092 46003; Fax
092 46260; www.ashford.ie

Boat trip on Lough Corrib: daily (weather permitting). £10 per person (min 6).
☎ 092 46029.

🛈 Crescent Quay – ☎ 053 23111
🛈 Rosslare Kilrane – ☎ 053 33622

Wexford Festival Opera at the Theatre Royal – (♿) Mid Oct to early-Nov.
☎ 053 22400; Fax 053 24289 (Festival Office), 053 22144; Fax 053 47438 (Box
Office); info@wexopera.com; www.wexfordopera.com

Wexford Arts Centre – (♿) Open daily, 10am-6pm. Closed public hols. No charge for
exhibitions. Guided tour (15min) available. Restaurant. Disabled visitors must telephone
in advance. ☎ 053 23764; Fax 053 24544; wexfordartscentre@eircom.net

Franciscan Friary – (♿) Open Mon-Sat, 9.30am-1.30pm and 2.30pm-6pm. Closed
Sun and bank hols. Parking for the disabled; wheelchair access to church and friary.
☎ 053 22758; Fax 053 21499.

St Iberius' Church – Open daily, Mon-Sat, 10am-5pm. Donation £1. When closed, key available from The Rectory. Brochure (Dutch, French, German, Italian, Japanese, Spanish, Swedish). ☎ 053 43013; Fax 053 43013.

Westgate Heritage Centre – ♿ Opening times: check door.

Excursions

Wexford Wildfowl Reserve – (Dúchas) (♿) Open daily, 9am-6pm (10am-5pm, Oct to mid-Apr). Last admission 45min before closing. Closed 25 Dec. No charge. A/v presentation. Lectures. Guided tour on request. Bird watching. Resident warden. Parking. Picnic area. ☎ 053 23129; Fax 053 24785.

Tacumshane Windmill – (Dúchas) Key available from Gerry Meyler (pub next door).

Irish Agricultural Museum – (♿) Open Jun-Aug, Mon-Fri, 9am-5pm, Sat-Sun and bank hols, 11am-5pm; Apr-May and Sep to early-Nov, Mon-Fri, 9am-12.30pm and 1.30-5pm, Sat-Sun and bank hols, 2-5pm; early-Nov to Mar, Mon-Fri, 9am-12.30pm and 1.30-5pm. £3, reductions available. Parking. Refreshments (summer). Parking for the disabled; wheelchair access to ground floor. ☎ 053 42888 (weekdays); Fax 053 42213.

Boat Trips from Kilmore Quay – Operate Apr-Oct; groups only (max 12). Reef and wreck fishing. Environmental and sightseeing trips around Saltee Islands. ☎ 053 29704, 087 254 9111 (Dick Hayes).

Kilmore Quay Maritime Museum – Open Jun-Sep, daily, midday-6pm; Oct-May by appointment. £2, reductions available. Audio-guide (French, German). Guided tour available on request. Access by gangplank. ☎ 053 29655.

Irish National Heritage Park – ♿ Open Mar-Nov, daily, 9.30am-6.30pm (last admission according to time of year). £5, reductions available. Guided tour (French, German). A/v presentation (French, German, Spanish, Italian). Parking. Craft shop. Restaurant. ☎ 053 20733; Fax 053 20911; info@inhp.com; www.inhp.com

WICKLOW MOUNTAINS

🅑 Arklow – ☎ 0402 32484
🅑 Wicklow – ☎ 0404 69117

Wicklow Mountains National Park – (Dúchas) (♿) Information Point at Upper Lake, Glendalough: Open May-Aug, daily, 10am-6pm; Apr and Sept, Sat-Sun, 10am-6pm. Weekly guided walks: telephone for details. ☎ 0404 45425, 45338 (winter); Fax 0404 45306 (Sean Casey).

Poulaphouca Reservoir Waterbus – Operates May-Sep, daily, at 4pm from Blessington Lakes Leisure Centre; Mar-Apr and Oct-Dec, by appointment. Time 1hr. Capacity 78 seats. £6, reductions available. Advance booking advisable. Leaflet (Italian, French, Spanish). ☎ 045 865 092; Fax 045 865 024; blesflwf@tinet.ie

Clara Lara Fun Park – (♿) Open May-Aug, daily, 10.30am-6pm. £4.50 (some extra charges). Parking. Refreshments. ☎ 0404 46161.

Powerscourt Gardens – (♿) Open daily, 9.30am-5.30pm. Closed 25-26 Dec. Gardens and house exhibition: £6; house exhibition: £1.50; reductions available. Brochure (French, German, Italian, Spanish). Tree trail. Parking. Terrace café. Speciality shops. Garden Centre. Wheelchair access to part of the gardens. ☎ 01 204 6000; Fax 01 204 6900; gardens@powerscourt.ie; www.powerscourt.ie

Powerscourt Waterfall – (♿) Open Mar-Oct, daily, 9.30am-7pm; Nov-Feb, 10.30am-sunset. Closed 1 Jan, mid-Dec to 27 Dec. £2.50, reductions available. Nature trail. Play area for children. Parking. Refreshments. ☎ 01 204 6000; Fax 01 204 6900; gardens@powerscourt.ie; www.powerscourt.ie

Killruddery – (♿) Gardens: Open Apr-Sept, daily, 1-5pm. House: Open May-Jun and Sep, daily, 1-5pm. Garden £3; house and garden £4.50; reductions available. Parking. ☎/Fax 01 286 2777.

Avoca Handweavers – ♿ Kilmacanoge: Open daily, 9.30am-6pm (5.30pm winter). Parking. Restaurant. Café and Garden Terrace. ☎ 01 286 7466, 01 286 7482; Fax 01 286 2367, 01 276 0458.

Avoca Mill: Open daily, 9.30am-6pm (5.30pm winter). Guided tour of the weaving process. Parking. Tearoom. ☎ 0402 35105, 35284; Fax 0402 35446; info@avoca.ie; www.avoca.ie

Mount Usher Gardens – ♿ Open mid-Mar to end-Oct, daily, 10.30am-6pm. £4, reductions available. Guided tour (1hr) by appointment. Brochure (German). Parking. Tearoom. Craftshops. ☎/Fax 0404 40205; mount_usher.gardens@indigo.ie; www.mount-usher-gardens.com

Avondale – (♿) Park: Open daily. House: Open mid-Mar to Oct, daily, 11am-6pm (5pm last admission). Closed Good Fri. Grounds only £3 per car; House (extra) £3, reductions available. A/v presentation (25min). Leaflet (Danish, Dutch, French, German, Italian, Japanese). Guided tour available. Parking. Gift shop. Restaurant, coffee shop, picnic areas. ☎ 0404 46111; Fax 0404 46111.

Bray Heritage Centre – Open Mon-Sat, 10am-4pm (later in summer). Exhibition centre. Audioguide. ☎ 01 286 6796.

National Sea Life Centre – ♿ Open Apr-Sep, daily, 11am-5pm; less frequently in winter. £5.50, reductions available. ☎ 01 286 6939.

Wicklow Church – Open daily, 9.30am-sunset. Printed history on internal back wall.

Wicklow's Historic Goal – (♿) Open mid-Mar to Oct, daily, 10am-6pm (5pm Mar, Oct). Last admission 1hr before closing. £4.20, reductions available. Geneaology centre. Shop. Café. ☎ 0404 61599; Fax 0404 61612; wccgaol@eircom.net; www.wicklow.ie/gaol

Arklow Maritime Museum – Open Mon-Fri, 10am-1pm and 2-5pm; also Sat, May-Sep. £3, reductions available. Parking. ☎ 0402 32868; Fax 0402 32868.

Y

YOUGHAL

🅘 Heritage Centre – ☎ 024 92390 (May-Sep)
🅘 Ardmore Seafront car park – ☎ 024 94444 (seasonal)
🅘 Dungarvan – ☎ 058 41741 (all year)

Youghal Guided Walking Tour – Jun-Aug, Mon-Sat, at 11am and by appointment. £2.75. Time 90min; French. ☎ 024 20170, 92447; Fax 024 20170; youghal@eir com.ie; www.homepage.tinet.ie/~youghal

St Mary's Collegiate Church – Open mid-May to mid-Sep, daily, 9.30am-5.30pm. Brochure (Dutch, French, German, Italian). ☎ 024 92390; youghal@tinet.ie

Youghal Heritage Centre – Open Mon-Sat, 9.30am (10am Sat) to 1pm and 2pm-6pm (5.30pm winter). £1. Brochure. ☎ 024 20170, 92447; Fax 024 20170; youghal@ eircom.net

Excursion

Dungarvan Museum – Open Mon-Fri, 11am-1pm and 2-5pm. No charge. ☎ 058 45960.

NORTHERN IRELAND

A

ANTRIM
🛈 16 High Street – BT41 4AN – ☎ 028 9442 8331 – Fax 028 9448 7844

Clotworthy Arts Centre – Open Mon-Fri, 9.30am-9.30pm, Sat, 10am-5pm; also July and Aug only, Sun, 2pm-5pm. No charge.☎ 028 9442 8000.

Pogue's Entry – ♿ Open May-Sept, Thurs and Fri, 2-5pm, Sat, 10am-1pm and 2-5pm. No charge. Guided tour (15min). ☎ 028 9442 8996 (May-Sept). ☎ 028 9442 8000 (Clotworthy Arts Centre); Fax 028 9446 0360.

Antrim Castle Gardens – Open Mon-Fri, 9.30am-9pm, Sat-Sun, 10am (2pm Sun) to 5pm. No charge. ☎ 028 9442 8000 (Clotworthy Arts Centre); Fax 028 9446 0360.

Shane's Castle Grounds – Closed until further notice. ☎ 028 9442 8216; Fax 028 9446 8457.

Excursions

Patterson's Spade Mill – (NT) ♿ Open June-Aug, daily except Tues, 2-6pm; Apr, May and Sept, Sat-Sun and bank holiday Mon, 2-6pm; Good Friday-Easter Tuesday, 2-6pm. £3, reductions available. Ramps; wheelchairs available. ☎ 028 9443 3619.

Ballance House – (♿) Open Apr-Sept, Tues-Sun and bank holiday Monday, 11am (2pm Sat-Sun)-5pm. £2, 50p (child). Parking. Lunches and refreshments. Wheelchair access to ground floor only. ☎ 028 9264 8492; Fax 028 9264 8098.

Templetown Mausoleum – (NT) Open daily, during daylight hours. No charge. ☎ 028 9751 0721 (Regional Office).

Arthur Cottage – ♿ Open May-Sept, Mon-Sat, 10.30am-5pm (4pm Sat). £1.80, reductions available. Guided tour (30min). Craft demonstrations: June-Aug, Tues, Fri, Sat, at 1.30pm. Parking. ☎ 028 2588 0781 (May-Sept), 028 2566 0300; Fax 028 2566 0400; devel.leisure@ballymena.gov.uk; www.ballymena.gov.uk

Glens of ANTRIM
🛈 Narrow Gauge Road, Larne – BT40 1XB – ☎ 028 2826 0088 – Fax 028 2826 0660
🛈 7 Mary Street, Ballycastle – BT54 6QH – ☎ 028 2076 2024 – Fax 028 2076 2515

Larne Lough Ferry (Larne-Island Magee) – Operates (weather permitting) daily, 7.30am-5.30pm (5pm Sat-Sun), every hour; more frequently early mornings and late afternoons. Single 60p, 30p (child). ☎ 028 2827 4085.

Carnfunnock Country Park – Open Easter-Sept, daily, 10am-6pm (8pm July-Aug). Maze: no charge Jul-Aug. Crazy ball, putting and 9-hole golf course: prices by telephone. Parking. Miniature railway. ☎ 028 2827 0541; ☎/Fax 028 2826 0088 (Larne TIC).

Glenariff Forest Park – ♿ Open daily, 10am-sunset. Car £3; coach £20; pedestrians £1.50, reductions available. Parking. Restaurant; picnic area. ☎ 028 2175 8232; Fax 028 2175 8828.

Holy Trinity Church – Open daily, 9am (8.30am Sun) to sunset. If closed, try next door (Sexton's house). ☎ 028 2076 2024 (Ballycastle TIC).

Carrick-a-Rede Rope Bridge – (NT) Open (except in high winds) Apr–Sep, daily, 10am–6pm (8pm July–Aug). Guided tour by appointment. Tea room; information point. Parking £3. ☎ 028 2073 1582 (NT Visitor Services Manager).

Rathlin Island-Ballycastle Ferry – *Operates (weather permitting) June-Sept, daily, from Ballycastle (45min) at 9.30am, 11.30am, 4pm, 6pm; from Rathlin at 8.30am, 10.30am, 3pm, 5pm; Oct-May, telephone for details. Return £7.80, reductions available.* ☎ 028 2076 9299.

Glenariff Falls, Co Antrim

In case of bad weather, overnight accommodation available on the island at Rathlin Guesthouse (☎ 028 2076 3917) and at The Manor House (☎ 028 2076 3964).

Rathlin Island by Minibus – Operates approximately Apr-Aug, daily from the harbour. West Lighthouse bird sanctuary return £4, £2 (child); Rue Point return £2.50, £1 (child). ☎ 028 7026 3909; Fax 028 7026 3988 (Augustin McCurdy).

ARMAGH   🛈 40 English Street – BT61 7BA – ☎ 028 3752 1800 – Fax 028 3752 8329

St Patrick's Anglican Cathedral – ♿ Open daily, 9.30am-5pm (4pm Sun and winter). No charge. Guided tour (20min) available (charge). Leaflet (French, German etc). Parking. St Patrick's Day (17 Mar) pilgrimage to Hill of Patrick. ☎ 028 3752 3142; Fax 028 3752 4177.

St Patrick's Roman Catholic Cathedral – Open daily, 10.30am-5pm. Services: Sun, 9am, 10.30am, 12midday. No charge. Guided tour by appointment with the Sacristan. Parking. ☎ 028 3752 2638.

Royal Irish Fusiliers Museum – Open Mon-Fri and bank hols, 10am-12.30pm and 1.30-4pm. £2, £1 (concession). Guided tour (30min). ☎ 028 3752 2911.

Armagh County Museum – ♿ Open Mon-Fri, 10am-5pm, Sat, 10am-1pm and 2-5pm. Closed 12-13 July, 25-26 Dec. No charge. ☎ 028 3752 3070; Fax 028 3752 2631.

Palace Stables Heritage Centre and Primate's Chapel – ♿ Open July-Aug, Mon-Sat, 10am-5.30pm, Sun, 1-6pm; Sept-June, Mon-Sat, 10am-5pm, Sun, 2-5pm. Closed at Christmas. Guided tour (90min). £3.50, reductions available. Sensory gardens. Adventure playground. Parking. Licensed restaurant. Parking for the disabled. ☎ 028 3752 9629; Fax 028 3752 9630; stables@armagh.gov.uk; www.armagh.gov.uk

St Patrick's Trian – Open Mon-Sat 10am-5pm (5.30pm, July-Aug), Sun 2-5pm (1-6pm, July-Aug). Time 1hr 15min. Closed 25-26 Dec. £3.75, reductions available. ☎ 028 3752 1801; Fax 028 3751 0180; acdc@iol.ie; www.armagh.gov.uk

Armagh Planetarium – ♿ Open daily 10am (1.15pm, Sat-Sun) to 4.45pm. Closed Good Fri, 12 July, 24-27 Dec. Show (45min) at 2pm, 3pm, 4pm. £3.75, reductions available; exhibition only £1. Exhibition (1hr). Astropark (20min walk). ☎ 028 3752 3689; Fax 028 3752 6187; www.armagh-planetarium.co.uk

Observatory not open to the public; www.star.arm.ac.uk

Armagh Robinson Public Library – Open Mon–Fri, 10am–1pm and 2–4pm. Closed public hols. No charge. Guided tour (charge). Parking. ☎ 028 3752 3142; Fax 028 3752 4177; armroblib@aol.com

Excursions

The Argory – (NT) (♿) Open June–Aug, daily except Tues, 2pm (1pm public holidays)–6pm; Apr–May and Sept, Sat–Sun and public holidays, 2pm (1pm public holidays)-6pm; Good Friday-Easter Tuesday, 2-6pm. Last admission 45min before closing. £3, reductions available. Guided tour (1hr). Parking £1.50. Tearoom; picnic area. Wheelchair available; wheelchair access to ground floor, walks, tearoom. ☎ 028 8778 4753; Fax 028 8778 9598.

Armagh Observatory

Slide File, Dublin

Ardress House – (NT) (&) House: Open June-Aug, daily except Tues, 2-6pm; May and Sept, Sat-Sun and public holidays, 2-6pm; Apr, Sat-Sun, 2-6pm; Good Friday-Easter Tuesday, 2-6pm. Farmyard: Open as above. House and Farmyard: £2.70, reductions available. Farm only: £2.40. Guided tour (30min). Parking. Picnic area. Wheelchair access to ground floor, part of farmyard and picnic area. ✆/Fax 028 3885 1236; vagest@smtp.ntrust.org.uk

Orange Order Museum – Open Mon-Sat, 10.30am-5.30pm; apply at 52 Main Street, Loughgall. ✆ 028 3889 1524 (Caretaker).

Tayto Potato Crisp Factory – Guided tour by appointment only (1hr 30min; max 60 people) Mon-Thur, at 10.30am, 1.30pm, Fri, at 10.30am. Closed Easter, 12-13 July, Christmas week. No charge. Brochure (French, German). Parking. ✆ 028 3884 0249, ext 256/248; Fax 028 3884 0085.

Gosford Forest Park – & Open daily, 10am-sunset. £1.50, reductions available; £3 (car). Guided tour (2hr) by appointment. Parking. Café, barbecue area. Pony trekking. ✆ 028 3755 2169 (Forest Ranger), 028 3755 1277.

Navan Fort Visitor Centre – & Site: Open daily. Visitor Centre: Open daily (except 1 week at Christmas) 10am (11am Sat, 12midday Sun) to 5pm. Last tour 90min before closing. £3.95, reductions available. Guided tour of site (30min) by appointment. Interactive exhibition. Parking. Restaurant. ✆ 028 3752 5550; Fax 028 3752 2323; navan@enterprise.net; www.navan.com

B

BANGOR   🛈 34 Quay Street – BT20 5ED – ✆ 028 9127 0069 – Fax 028 9127 4466

Bangor Bay Cruise – Operates from Bangor seafront July-Aug, daily, 2pm; May-June and Sept-Oct, Sat-Sun, 2pm. Time 20-30min. Also bird watching, angling and longer pleasure cruises. £2, £1 (child). ✆ 028 9145 5321 (Bangor Harbour Boats).

Belfast Lough Cruises – Operate from Donaghadee (weather permitting) June-Sept, daily. Time 2-3hr. Fishging tackle provided. Licensed. ✆ 028 9188 3403 (Nelson's Boats), 0378 893 920.

Copeland Islands-Donaghadee Ferry – Operates July-Aug, daily; May-Oct, by appointment. ✆ 028 9188 3403 (Nelson's Boats); 0378 893 920 (boat).

Bangor Abbey – Open Mon, Wed, Fri, 10am-12midday; apply to the Parish office beside church; otherwise by appointment. ✆ 028 9145 1087.

North Down Heritage Centre – & Open Tues-Sun and bank hol Mon, 10.30am (2pm Sun) to 5.30pm (4.30pm Sep-Jun). No charge. Guided tour (45min) by appointment. Leaflet (French, German, Spanish). Parking. Refreshments. ✆ 028 9127 1200; Fax 028 9127 1370; bangor_heritage_centre@yahoo.com; www.north_down. gov.uk/heritage/

Excursions

Crawfordsburn Country Park – & Open daily, 9am-8pm (4.45pm Oct-Easter). Visitor Centre: Open Mon-Fri, 10am-5pm; Sat-Sun, 10am-6pm (5pm Oct-Easter). Closed one week at Christmas. Grey Point Fort: Open Easter-Oct, daily except Tues, 2-5pm; Oct-Easter, Sun, 2-5pm. Parking. Restaurant. Braille leaflet and audiotape. ✆ 028 9185 3621; Fax 028 9185 2580.

Ulster Folk and Transport Museum – & Open July-Aug, daily, 10.30am (midday Sun)-6pm; Apr-June and Sept, Mon-Fri, 9.30am-5pm, Sat, 10.30am-6pm, Sun, midday-6pm; Oct-Mar, Mon-Fri, 9.30am-4pm, Sat-Sun, 12.30-4.30pm. Time 4-5hr. £4, reductions available. Brochure (French, German, Italian, Japanese, Spanish). Parking. Refreshments. ✆ 028 9042 8428; Fax 028 9042 8728.

Somme Heritage Centre – Open Jul-Aug, daily, 10am (noon Sat-Sun) to 5pm; Apr-Jun and Sept, Sat-Thur, 10am (noon Sat-Sun) to 4pm. £3.75, reductions available. Parking. ✆ 028 9182 3202; www.irishsoldier.org

Ballycopeland Windmill – (HM) Open Apr-Sept, Tue-Sun and bank hol Mon, 10am (2pm Sun) to 7pm. £1, reductions available. ✆ 028 9186 1413 (windmill); 028 9023 5000 (Historic Monuments).

BELFAST   🛈 St Anne's Court, 59 North Street – BT1 1NB –
          ✆ 028 9024 6609 – Fax 028 9031 2424
     🛈 Belfast International Airport – BT29 4AB – ✆ 028 9442 2888 – Fax 028 9445 2084
          🛈 Belfast City Airport – BT3 9JH – ✆ 028 9045 7745 – Fax 028 9045 9198

Citybus Tours – Operate (subject to demand) from Castle Place, end May-early Sept: Belfast City Tour (3hr) Mon-Sat at 1.30pm; £9, reductions available; Belfast Living History tour (2hr 30min) Tues, Thur and Sun at 1pm; £9, reductions available; Lagan Experience (2hr 30min) Wed, 1pm; £10; City Hopper Tour (55min) Tues-Sat, 10am-

4pm, hourly; £5, reductions available. Commentary. Refreshments. ☎ 028 9045 8484 (tours), 9024 6485 (gen enquiries); Fax 028 9064 1629; feedback@translink.co.uk; www.translink.co.uk

Ulster Museum – ♿ Open daily, 10am (1pm Sat, 2pm Sun) to 5pm. Closed New Year, Christmas. No charge. Café. Shop. ☎ 028 9038 3000; www.ulstermuseum.org.uk

Botanic Gardens – Open daily, 7.30am-sunset. Palm House and Tropical Ravine: Open daily, 10am-12midday and 1-4pm (5pm Apr-Sept). No charge. Guided tour for a fee by appointment on ☎ 028 9032 0202 (Reg Maxwell). Parking. ☎ 028 9032 4902; maxwells@belfastcity.gov.uk; www.parks.belfastcity.gov.uk

Belfast City Hall – ♿ Guided tour (1hr) June-Sept, Mon-Fri at 10.30am, 11.30am and 2.30pm, Sat at 2.30pm; Oct-May, Mon-Sat at 2.30pm. No charge. Brochure (French, German). Closed 1 Jan, 3 Jan, 17 Mar, Easter Mon and Tue, May Day and late Spring bank hol, 12-13 July, late summer bank hol, 25-26 Dec. No charge. ☎ 028 9027 0456, 028 9032 0202 ext 2346, 028 9027 0405 (minicom).

Linen Hall Library – Open Mon-Sat, 9.30am-5.30pm (4pm Sat). Closed public hols. No charge. Guided tour (20min) by appointment. Refreshments. ☎ 028 9032 1707; Fax 028 9043 8586; info@linenhall.com

St Anne's Cathedral (Anglican) – (♿) Open Mon-Sat, 9am-5pm; Sun, 9.30am-4.30pm. Guided tour: 10am-4pm. No charge. Leaflet (French, German, Italian, Spanish). Choral Services: Sun, 11am and 3.30pm, Tues, 5.15pm. ☎ 028 9032 8332; Fax 028 9023 8855; belfast.cathedral@dial.pipex.com

Crown Liquor Saloon – (NT) ♿ Open Mon-Sat, 11.30am-midnight, Sun, 12.30-10pm. Closed 12-13 July, 25-26 Dec. No charge. Full bar and snack lunches. ☎ 028 9024 9476.

Sinclair Seamen's Church – Open Sun, 11am-1pm and 6.30-8.30pm; also Mar-Oct, Wed, 2-4pm. ☎ 028 9077 2429 (Mrs Carole Davis).

St Malachy's Church – Open daily, 8am-5.30pm approx; otherwise by appointment. Mass: 8am (Mass), 1pm, 5pm. ☎ 028 9032 1713; 028 9023 3241 (Caretaker).

Oval Church – (♿) Open Sun, Wed, 10.30am-12.30pm; otherwise by appointment. Musical recital: July-Aug, Wed at 1.15pm. ☎ 028 9084 3592 (Minister), 028 9042 2639; Fax 028 9059 4070.

Lagan Lookout – ♿ Open Apr-Sept, daily, 11am (12noon Sat, 2pm Sun) to 5pm; Oct-Mar, Tues-Sun, 11am (1pm Sat, 2pm Sun) to 3.30pm (4.30pm Sat-Sun). £1.50, 75p (child), £4 (family). ☎ 028 9031 5444; Fax 028 9031 1955.

Presbyterian Historical Society Museum (Church House) – ♿ Open Mon-Tue and Thur-Fri, 10am-12.30pm, Wed, 1pm-3.30pm. Closed public holidays. No charge. ☎ 028 9032 2284.

Royal Ulster Rifles Museum – Open Mon-Fri, 10am-4pm (3pm Fri). Closed public hols. Guided tour (30min). ☎ 028 9023 2086; rurmuseum@yahoo.co.uk; www.members.tripod.co.uk/rurmuseum/museum

Excursions

Zoological Gardens – ♿ Open daily, 10am-5pm (3.30pm Oct-Mar). Closed 25 Dec. Time 2-3hr. £5.50, reductions available; reduced rate in winter. Leaflet (French, German, Italian, Spanish). Parking. Café. ☎ 028 9077 6277; Fax 028 9037 0578.

Belfast Castle and Gardens – ♿ Open (functions permitting) daily, 9am-10pm (6pm Sun). Closed 25-26 Dec. No charge. Lift. ☎ 028 9077 6925.

Stormont – Grounds: Open daily during daylight hours.

Glencairn People's Museum – ♿ Open daily, 10am (1pm Sun) to 4pm. No charge. Restaurant. ☎ 028 9071 5599.

C

CARRICKFERGUS

🚹 Heritage Plaza, Antrim Street – BT38 7DG – ☎ 028 9336 6455 – Fax 028 9335 0350

Carrickfergus Castle – (HM) ♿ Open Apr-Sept, Mon-Sat, 10am-6pm, Sun, 2pm (12pm June-Aug) to 6pm; Oct-Mar, Tue-Sun and hol Mon, 10am (2pm Sun) to 4pm. Last admission 30min before closing. Closed 25-26 Dec. £2.70, reductions available; joint ticket with Knight Ride £4.85, reductions available. Guided tour by appointment. Brochure (French, German, Italian, Spanish). Parking. ☎ 028 9335 1273; Fax 028 9336 5190.

St Nicholas Church – ☎ 028 9336 3244 (The Vicarage).

Knight Ride – ♿ Open daily, 10am (midday Sun) to 6pm (5pm Oct-Mar). £2.70, reductions available; joint ticket with Carrickfergus Castle £4.85, reductions available. Leaflet (French, German, Spanish, Italian). ☎ 028 9336 6455; Fax 028 9335 0350; touristinfo@carrickfergus.org; www.carrickfergus.org

Excursions

Andrew Jackson and US Rangers Centres – Open Apr-May and Oct, Mon-Fri, 10am-1pm and 2-4pm, Sat-Sun, 2-4pm; June-Sept, Mon-Fri, 10am-1pm and 2-6pm, Sat-Sun, 2-6pm. £1.20, 60p (concession). Parking. ☎ 028 9336 6455 (Tourist Information Centre).

Railway Preservation Society of Ireland – Steam trains and historic carriages: Open all year, Sat-Sun, 10am-5pm; mid-June to Aug, Sun, 2-5pm. Steam train excursions throughout Ireland: mainly Spring-Autumn. Advance booking recommended. Parking. Details of times and fares available from Tourist Information Centres in Belfast, Carrickfergus, Bangor and Lisburn; from the Railway Preservation Society of Ireland, Whitehead Excursion Station, Castleview Road, Whitehead BT38 9NA (send sae). ☎/Fax 028 9335 3567 (recorded message when unattended).

CASTLE COOLE

Castle Coole – (NT) (♿) Grounds: Open to pedestrians during daylight hours. House: Open June-Aug, daily except Thur, 1-6pm; Apr, May and Sept, Sat-Sun and public holidays, 1-6pm; Good Friday-Easter Tues, 2-6pm. Last admission 45min before closing. £3, reductions available. Guided tour (45min). Parking. Tearoom; picnic area. Gift shop. ☎ 028 6632 2690; Fax 028 6632 5665; ncasco@smtp.ntrust.org.uk

D – E

DOWNPATRICK   🅱 74 Market Street – BT30 6LZ – ☎ 028 4461 2233 – Fax 028 4461 2350

Down Cathedral – ♿ Open Mon-Fri and public hols, 9.15am-5pm; Sat-Sun, 2-5pm. Closed Good Friday, 25-26 Dec. Donation. Guided tour available. Brochure (French, German, Italian). Parking. Bookshop. ☎ 028 4461 4922; Fax 028 4461 4456; www.cathedral.down.anglican.org

Down County Museum – (♿) Open Jun-Aug, daily, 10am (2pm Sat-Sun) to 5pm; Sep-May, Tue-Sat, 10am (2pm Sat-Sun) to 5pm. No charge. Guided tour (1hr) by prior arrangement. Brochure (French, German, Spanish). ☎ 028 4461 5218.

Excursions

St Patrick's Memorial Church – Open daily, 8am-sunset. Service: Sun, 10am. ☎ 028 4461 3101.

Jordan's Castle – (HM) Open Apr-Sept, daily except Mon, 10am (2pm Sun) to 6pm. 75p, reductions available.

Seaforde Garden – Open Easter-Sept, Mon-Sat, 10am-5pm, Sun, 1-6pm. Admission charge. Parking. ☎ 028 4481 1225.

DUNGANNON   🅱 Ballygawley Road, Killymaddy Centre (off A 4) – BT70 1TF – ☎ 028 8776 7259 – Fax 028 8776 7911

Tyrone Crystal – ♿ Guided tour (45min) Mon-Fri, 9.30am-3pm. £2, no charge (senior citizen/child under 12). Factory Shop and coffeeshop: Open Mon-Sat, 9am-5pm. Parking. Wheelchair available. ☎ 028 8772 5335; Fax 028 8772 6260; tyrcrystal@aol.com; www.tyronecrystal.com

Heritage World – ♿ Open Mon-Thur, 9am-1pm and 2-5pm, Fri, 9am-1pm. Genealogical consultation fee £10 minimum. Ramp. ☎ 028 8767 039; Fax 028 8767 663.

Excursions

Cornmill Heritage Centre – ♿ Open Mon-Fri 10am-4pm, Sat-Sun by appointment. Last admission 1hr before closing time. £1.50, reductions available. Parking. Lift. ☎ 028 8774 8532; Fax 028 8774 8695.

Donaghmore Heritage Centre – Open Mon-Fri, 9am-5pm. ☎ 028 8776 7039.

Parkanaur Forest Park – ♿ Open daily, 8am-sunset. No charge. Deer enclosure. Wildfowl pond. Guided tour (1hr) by appointment. Parking. ☎ 028 8775 9311.

Simpson Grant Homestead – ♿ Open Easter-end Sept, Tues-Sat, midday-5pm, Sun, 2-6pm. Time 1hr. £1.50, 75p (concession). Guided tour on request. Parking. Refreshments. ☎ 028 8555 7133.

Clogher Cathedral (St Marcatan) – Open by prior arrangement only. Guided tour on request. ☎ 028 8554 8288 (Mr Jack Johnston, Ratory, Clogher). ☎ 028 8554 8946 (Mr W Taggart, 35 Main Street, Clogher). ☎ 028 8554 8235 (The Very Revd R Moore, The Deanery, Augher Road, Clogher).

ENNISKILLEN 🖥 Wellington Road – BT74 7EF – ☎ 028 6632 3110 – Fax 028 6632 5511

Lough Erne Waterbus Cruises – Operates from Round "O" Jetty (Brook Park, Belleek Road (A 46), Enniskillen) July-Aug, daily at 10.30am, 2.15pm, 4.15pm, also Tues, Thur and Sun at 7.15pm evening cruise to Bellanaleck; May-June, Sun and public holidays at 2.30pm; Sept, Tues, Sat and Sun at 2.30pm. Time 1hr 45min (stopping for 30min at Devenish Island). £6, reductions available. MV Kestrel, all weather vessel (covered deck); capacity 56; refreshments, bar. ☎ 028 6632 2882 (Erne Tours Ltd); Fax 028 6638 7954.

Upper Lough Erne Cruises – For times and prices contact Share Holiday Village, Lisnakea. ☎ 028 6772 2122; Fax 028 6772 1893; share@dnet.co.uk; www.sharevillage.org

Day Boats – Enniskillen ☎ 028 6632 2882, Fax 028 6638 7954 (Erne Tours Ltd, Round 'O' Jetty, Brook Park, Belleek Road); Killadeas ☎ 028 6862 8100 (Manor House Marine); 028 6862 1557 (B Ternan, The Beeches, Killadeas); Kesh ☎ 028 6863 2328, 028 6632 2666 (G Keown, Erinona Boats, Boa Island Bridge); Belleek ☎ 028 6865 8181 (Belleek Angling Centre, The Thatch, Main Street); Newtownbutler ☎ 028 6773 8118 (Crom Estate); Teemore ☎ 028 6774 8893 (Shannon-Erne Country Cottages & Cruisers).

Enniskillen Castle – (&) Open July-Aug, Tues-Fri and bank holiday Mon, 10am-5pm, other Mon and Sat-Sun, 2-5pm; May, June and Sept, Tues-Fri and bank holiday Mon, 10am-5pm, other Mon and Sat, 2-5pm; Oct-Apr, Tues-Fri and bank holiday Mon, 10am-5pm, other Mon, 2-5pm. Subject to variation at New Year and Christmas. Guide and information (French, German, Spanish, Italian). £2, reductions available. Parking. Lift. ☎ 028 6632 5000; Fax 028 6632 7342; castle@fermanagh.gov.uk

Regimental Museum of the Royal Inniskilling Fusiliers – (&) Open bank hols, 10am-5pm; May-Sept, Tue-Fri, 10am-5pm, Mon and Sat (also Sun, July-Aug), 2pm-5pm; Oct, Tue-Fri, 10am-5pm, Mon, 2pm-5pm. ☎ 028 6632 3142.

Cole's Monument – Open mid-May to mid-Sept, daily, 11am-1pm and 2-6pm. 70p, 30p (child). Brochure (French, German).

Excursions

Florence Court – (NT) Grounds: Open daily, 10am-7pm/sunset. Closed 25 Dec. Parking £2. House: (&) Guided tour (45min) Good Fri to Easter Tue, daily, 1-6pm; June-Aug, daily except Tue, 1-6pm; Apr-May and Sep, Sat-Sun and bank hols, 1-6pm. Last tour 45min before closing. £3, reductions available. Parking. Restaurant. Tearoom; picnic area. Wheelchair access to ground floor and garden. ☎ 028 6634 8249; Fax 028 6634 8873; ufcest@smtp.ntrust.org.uk

Florence Court Forest Park – For walkers: Open at all hours. For cars: Open daily except 25 Dec, 10am-7pm (4pm, Oct-Mar). £2.50 (per car) during busy periods. Parking. ☎ 028 6634 8497.

Marble Arch Caves and Nature Reserve – Forest Nature Reserve: Open daily. Caves: Guided tour (1hr 15min) Easter-Sept, daily, 10am-4.30pm (last tour; 5pm July-Aug). £6, reductions available. Audio-visual presentation (20min). Tour translations in French, German, Spanish and Italian. Advance booking recommended (from 9am). Tour may be curtailed by heavy rain. Stout shoes and warm clothes advisable. Parking. Refreshments. Caves unsuitable for wheelchairs (unless reached via upper car park: telephone for details). ☎ 028 6634 8855; Fax 028 6634 8928; mac@fermanagh.gov.uk; www.fermanagh-online.com/tourism

Devenish Island Ferry – Open Apr-Sept, daily, at 10am, 1pm, 3pm, 5pm; also bank hol Mon (closed following Tues. Access by ferry (capacity 26) from Trory Point. £2.25, reductions available. Guided tour (90min) available. Parking. ☎ 028 9023 5000.

Devenish Island – Open daily except Mon, 10am (2pm Sun) to 7pm. £2.25, reductions available.

Castle Archdale Country Park – Open daily. Visitor Centre: Open July-Aug, daily except Mon, 11am-7pm; Sep-Jun, by arrangement. No charge. Parking. ☎ 028 6862 1588; Fax 028 6862 1375.

White Island Ferry – Operates from Castle Archdale Marina (weather permitting) Easter-Aug: Apr-Jun Sun only 2-6pm; July-Aug daily 11am-6pm; every hour on the hour; check with the Marina at Castle Archdale. £3, £2 (child/senior citizen). Maximum 12 passengers. Guided tour available. Parking. ☎ 028 6862 1333.

White Island – Open Jun-Sep, daily except Mon, 10am (2pm Sun) to 7pm. £2.25, £1.20 (child/senior citizen).

Janus Figure, Co Fermanagh

Castle Caldwell Forest Park – &. Open daily. No charge. Parking. Café (summer).

Belleek Pottery – Pottery: Guided tour (30min), Mon-Fri, every 30min (3.30pm, Fri, last tour). £2.50. Audio-guide (French, German, Italian). Brochure (French, German, Italian). Visitor Centre: Open Jul-Aug, daily, 9am (10am Sat, 11am Sun) to 8pm (6pm Sat-Sun); Mar-Jun and Sep-Oct, daily, 9am (10am Sat, 2pm Sun) to 6pm (5.30pm Mon-Sat in Oct); Nov-Feb, Mon-Fri, 9am-5.30pm. Museum. Showroom. Parking. Restaurant. ☎ 028 6865 8501; Fax 028 6865 8625.

ExplorErne – &. Open Good Fri to Sept, daily, 10.30am-6pm. Exhibitions £1, reductions available. Parking. ☎ 028 6865 8866; Fax 028 6865 8833.

Tully Castle – (HM) Open Apr-Sep, daily, 10am-6pm. £1, 50p (concession). ☎ 028 9054 3037.

Lough Navar Forest Park – Open daily, sunrise-sunset. £2.50 (car), £1.50 (motorcycle), £5 (minibus) during busy periods. Parking. Picnic area; fishing. ☎ 028 6864 1256; Fax 028 6864 1743.

Crom Estate – (NT) &. Visitor Centre: Open Apr-Sept, daily, 10am (midday Sun) to 6pm. £3 by car or boat. Guided walks by arrangement. Guide book (English only). Parking. Tearoom. Gift shop. ☎ 028 6773 8174; ☎/Fax 028 6773 8118.

G – L

GIANT'S CAUSEWAY

🔲 44 Causeway Road, Bushmills – BT57 8FU –
☎ 028 2073 1855 – Fax 028 2073 2537

Giant's Causeway and Bus Shuttle – (NT) (&.) Open daily. Bus shuttle to Causeway (15min): &. Operates during the season every 15min. Return: £1, 60p (senior citizen). Minibus with hoist. Visitor Centre (owned by Moyle District Council): Open all year, daily, 10am-7pm (6pm June; 5pm Mar-May and Sept-Oct; 4.30pm Jan-Feb and Nov-Dec). Audio-visual presentation (12min; French, German, Italian, Spanish); £1, reductions available. Guided tour of Causeway by appointment. Parking (not owned by NT) £3. Craft and souvenir shops. Tearoom. Visitor Centre ☎ 028 2073 1855; Fax 028 2073 2537; NT shop/tearoom ☎ 028 2073 2972; NT office ☎ 028 2073 1159, 028 2073 1582, 028 2073 2143; Fax 028 2073 2962.

LISBURN

🔲 Irish Linen Centre and Lisburn Museum – BT49 0HA –
☎ 028 9266 0038 – Fax 028 9260 7889

🔲 The Courthouse, Hillsborough – ☎ 028 9268 9717 – Fax 028 9268 9016

The Irish Linen Tour – Operates June-Sept, certain Wed; details by telephone. £10, £9 (concession). Full-day tour includes McConvilles in Dromore, a traditional flax frame and water-powered scutching mill (demonstration of scutching), the Linen Centre in Lisburn; two local factories (Ferguson's Irish Linen, Ewart Lidell); lunch not included in price; booking essential. ☎ 028 4062 3322; Fax 028 4062 3114 (Banbridge TIC).

Irish Linen Centre and Lisburn Museum – &. Open Mon-Sat, 9.30am-5.30pm. Last admission 1hr before closing. No charge. Time 2hr. Leaflet (French, German). Audio exhibition commentary available on request. Speciality linen and crafts shop. Coffee shop. Tourist Information Centre. Loop system. ☎ 028 9266 3377; Fax 028 9267 2624.

LISBURN

Christchurch Cathedral – Services: Sun, 11am, 6.30pm; also second and fourth Sun in the month, 9.30am. Key available from the Sexton's House in the church grounds. ☎ 028 9260 2400 (Office), 028 9266 2865 (Rectory).

Hillsborough Court House – (HM) Open Mon-Sat, 9am-5.30pm, July-Aug, Sun, 2-6pm. No charge. ☎ 028 9054 3037.

Hillsborough Fort – (HM) Open Apr-Sept, Tues-Sat and hol Mon, 10am (2pm Sun) to 7pm. No charge. Parking. ☎ 028 9268 3285.

Rowallane Gardens – (NT) ♿ Open Apr-Oct, daily, 10.30am (2pm, Sat-Sun) to 6pm; Nov to end-Mar, Mon-Fri, 10.30am-5pm. Closed 1 Jan, 25-26 Dec. Time 2hr. £2.50, reductions available; winter £1.40. Parking. Tearoom. Wheelchair available. ☎ 028 9751 0131.

Hilden Brewery Centre – Open daily, 10am-5pm. Guided tour of brewery (40min), daily, at 11.30am and 2.30pm. £4.50, £4.20 (concession), includes tasting. Audio-visual display. Tap Room restaurant. Parking. ☎ 028 9266 3863.

Drumbeg Church – Open daily, 8am-5pm.

Malone House – ♿ Open Mon-Sat, 9am-4.30pm. Closed 25 Dec. No charge. Parking. Restaurant. ☎ 028 9068 1246; Fax 028 9068 2197.

LONDONDERRY

🏠 44 Foyle Street – BT48 6AT – ☎ 028 7126 7284 – Fax 028 7137 7992; info@derryvisitor.com

City Walls and Gates – (♿) Accessible daily. No charge. Information panels. Guided walking tours available. Access for wheelchairs except at the Bishop's Gate. ☎ 028 7126 7284 (Tourist Information Centre); info@derryvisitor.com; www.derryvisitor.com

St Columb's Cathedral (Anglican) – Open summer, Mon-Sat, 9am-5pm; winter, 9am-1pm and 2-4pm. £1. Audio-visual presentation: The History and Role of the Cathedral; The Siege of Derry in 1689. Brochure (French, German, Italian, Spanish). ☎ 028 7126 7313; dean@derry.anglican.org

Tower Museum – Open July-Aug, daily, 10am (2pm Sun) to 5pm; June, Tues-Sat and bank holiday Mon, 10am-5pm. Last admission 4.30pm. £4, £1.50 (concession), £8 (family). ☎ 028 7137 2411; Fax 028 7137 7633; tower.museum@derrycity.gov.uk

Fifth Province – ♿ Open Mon-Fri. Show: at 11.30am and 2.30pm. £3, £1 (child/reduction). Public parking. ☎ 028 7137 3177.

Long Tower Church – Open Mon-Sat, 7.30am-9pm; Sun, 8am-6.30pm.

Guildhall – ♿ Open Mon-Fri, 9am-5pm, except bank hol Mon. No charge. ☎ 028 7137 7335; Fax 028 7137 7964.

Harbour Museum – Open Mon-Fri, 10am-1pm and 2-4.30pm. No charge. ☎ 028 7137 7331; Fax 028 7137 7633.

St Eugene's Cathedral (RC) – Open Mon-Sat, 7.30am (8.30am Sat) to 9pm; Sun, 6.30am-7pm. ☎ 028 7126 2894, 7126 5712; Fax 028 7137 7494; steugenesderry@uk.online.uk

Foyle Valley Railway Centre – ♿ Telephone for times. Train excursion £2.50, reductions available. Free parking. Refreshments. ☎ 028 7126 5234.

Workhouse Museum – Open Mon-Thur, 10am-4pm (Sat, 4.30pm); closed Fri. No charge. ☎ 028 7131 8328.

M

MOUNT STEWART

Mount Stewart House, Gardens and Temple – (NT) ♿ House: Open May-Sept, daily except Tue, 1-6pm; Apr and Oct, Sat-Sun, 1-6pm; Good Fri-Low Sund, 1-6pm. Guided tour (45min). Gardens: Open Apr-Sept, daily, 11am-6pm; Oct, Sat-Sun, 11am-6pm; Mar, Sun, 2-5pm and 17 Mar (St Patrick's Day). Temple of the winds: Open Apr-Oct, Sat-Sun, 2-5pm. Guided tour (15min) available. House, gardens and temple £3.50, reductions available; temple £1. Parking. Tearoom. Shop. Wheelchairs and powered buggy, sympathetic hearing scheme. ☎ 028 4278 8387, 8487; Fax 028 4278 8569; umsest@smtp.ntrust.org.uk

MOURNE MOUNTAINS

🏠 1014 The Promenade, Newcastle – BT33 0AA – ☎ 028 4372 2222 – Fax 028 4372 2400 🏠 6 Newcastle Street, Kilkeel – ☎ 028 4176 2525 – Fax 028 4176 9947

Mourne Countryside Centre – Open Mon-Fri, 9am-5pm; also June-Sept, Sat-Sun, 9am-5pm via adjoining offices of Mourne Heritage Trust. Brochure. Programme of hill walks. ☎ 028 4372 4059; Fax 028 4372 6493; mht@mourne.co.uk

Mount Stewart Gardens

Our Lady of the Assumption Church (RC) – Open daily, 8am-8pm.

Murlough National Nature Reserve – (NT) Open daily, sunrise–sunset. Information Centre: Open (weather permitting) June–Aug and first weekend of Sept, daily, 10am–5pm. Parking £2 (car). ☎ 028 4375 1467, 4372 4362; Fax 028 4375 1467; umnnrw@smtp.ntrust.org.uk

Dundrum Castle – (HM) Open Apr-Sept, daily except Mon, 10am (2pm Sun) to 7pm. 75p, 40p (child/senior citizen). Guided tour (30min). Parking. ☎ 028 9054 3037 (Historic Monuments, Belfast).

Tollymore Forest Park – ♿ Open daily, 10am-sunset. £2, reductions available, £3.80 (car). Guided tour by appointment. Parking. Café; picnic areas. Fishing. ☎ 028 4372 2428.

Castlewellan Forest Park – ♿ Open daily, 10am-sunset. £3.80 (car). Guided tour by appointment. Parking. Café; barbecue site. Fishing. ☎ 028 4377 8664; Fax 028 4377 1762.

Brontë Centre – Drumballyroney Church and School House – (♿) Open Mar-Sep, Tue-Fri, 11am-5pm, Sat-Sun, 2-6pm. £2, reductions available. Guide book (French, German). Parking. Picnic sites. Wheelchair access to church and school. ☎ 028 4063 1152.

Mourne Mountains

Silent Valley Reservoir – ♿ Open daily, 10am-6.30pm (4pm Oct-Apr). £3 (car). Information Centre: Open as above. No charge. Parking. Bus Shuttle between car park and Ben Crom Reservoir: July-Aug, daily; May-June and Sept, Sat-Sun; £1.20, 90p (reduction). Refreshments (summer). ☎ 0845 744 0088.

Annalong Marine Park and Cornmill – (♿) Open Feb-Nov, Wed-Sun, 11am-5pm. £1.30, reductions available. Parking. Wheelchair access to Marine Park only. ☎ 028 4376 8736.

Greencastle – (HM) Open Apr-Sep, daily except Mon, 10am (2pm Sun) to 6pm. 75p, reductions available. Parking. ☎ 028 9054 3037.

Narrow Water Castle – (HM) Open Apr-Sept, daily except Mon, 10am (2pm Sun) to 6pm. 75p, reductions available. Parking. ☎ 028 4271 1491 (castle); ☎ 028 9054 3037 (Historic Monuments).

N

Lough NEAGH

Lough Neagh Boat Trip – Operates (weather permitting) Sat-Sun, every 30min; Mon-Fri from Kinnego Marina (south shore) to Lough Neagh Discovery Centre (30min). Fares from £4, reductions available. Capacity 12. ☎ 028 3832 7573.

Lough Neagh Fishing – Permits available from Fisheries Conservancy Board, 1 Mahon Road, Portadown. Open Mon-Fri, 9am-1pm and 2pm-5pm. Licence for game and coarse fishing £21 per annum, £10 for 8 days, £4 for 1 day. Licence for coarse fishing (rod and line) £8 per annum, £4 for 8 days, less for 3 days. ☎ 028 3833 4666; Fax 028 3833 8912. tfearon@fcbni.force9.co.uk

Lower Bann Fishing – Permits available from Bann System Ltd, 54 Castleroe Road, Coleraine, BT51 3RL. Max fee £200 per day. ☎ 028 7034 4796; Fax 028 7035 6527; ed@irishsociety.freeserve.co.uk; www.bannsystem.infm.ulst.ac.uk

Lough Neagh Discovery Centre Oxford Island – ♿ Open Apr-Sep, daily, 10am-7pm; Oct-Mar, Wed-Sun, 10am-5pm. £2, reductions available. Bird-watching hides. Exhibition guide sheet (French, German, Spanish). Parking. Café. ☎ 028 3832 2205; oxford.island@craigavon.gov.uk; www.craigavon.gov.uk/discovery.htm

Peatlands Park – ♿ Park: Open daily (except 25 Dec), 9am-9pm/sunset. Visitor Centre: Open June-Aug, daily, 2pm-6pm; also Easter-Sept, Sat-Sun and public holidays, 2pm-6pm. Narrow-gauge railway: Open as for Visitor Centre. Guided tour by appointment. Parking. Picnic area. Tearoom. ☎ 028 3885 1102; Fax 028 3885 1821.

Kinturk Cultural Centre – ♿ Open Jun-Sep, Mon-Fri, 10am-8pm, Sat-Sun, 11am-6pm; Oct-May, daily except Sat, 11am (12.30pm Sun) to 6pm. £1.50, reductions available. Audio-visual presentation. Lough Neagh Exhibition. Guided walks and boat trips. Parking. Licensed restaurant. ☎ 028 8673 6512.

Bellaghy Bawn – (HM) Open June-Sept, Mon-Sat, 10am (12midday Sat) to 5pm, Sun, 2pm-6pm. Oct-Mar, Mon-Fri, 10am-5pm. ☎ 028 7938 6812; Fax 028 7938 6556.

Larrybann, Co Antrim

Slide File: Dublin

NEWRY

Newry Cathedral – Open daily, 8am-6pm. ☎ 028 3026 2586; Fax 028 3026 7505.

Newry Museum – (&) Open Mon-Fri, 10.30am-4.30pm. No charge. Café. Wheelchair access to Arts Centre but not museum. ☎ 028 3026 6232.

Excursions

Slieve Gullion Forest Park – Open Easter-Sept, daily, from 8am. £2.50 (car). ☎ 028 4173 8284, 028 3084 8226; Fax 028 4173 9413.

Cardinal O'Fiaich Centre (Aras An Chairdineil) – Open Sun-Sat, 10am (2pm Sun) to 5pm (6pm (bank hols), Sat by appointment only. £2.50, reductions available. Restaurant. Souvenir shop. ☎ 028 3086 8757; info@ofiaichcentre_cullyhanna.co.uk; www.bluescreensolutions.co.uk/hugh

P

PORTRUSH

🛈 Dunluce Centre, Sandhill Drive – BT56 8BT –
☎ 028 7082 3333 – Fax 028 7082 2256
🛈 Railway Road, Coleraine – ☎ 028 7034 4723 – Fax 028 7035 1756

Causeway Coast Open-top Bus – Operates (weather permitting, otherwise normal single-decker bus is used) July-Aug, Mon-Sun (check at bus depot for 12-13 July); from Coleraine, at 9.10am, 11.30am, 1.50pm, 4pm, 6.15pm; from Giant's Causeway, at 10.20am, 12.40pm, 2.55pm, 5.10pm, 6.55pm. Journey may be broken at Portstewart, Portrush, Portballintrae, Bushmills. North Region Bus Timetable (Service 177) available from Ulster bus depots and TICs. Return £3.60; single £2. ☎ 028 7034 3334.

Dunluce Centre – (&) Open East and Jul-Aug, daily, 10am-7pm; Apr-June and Sep, daily, midday-5pm (6pm, Sat-Sun, June); Mar and Oct, Sat-Sun, midday-5pm. £5, reductions available. Parking. Café. ☎ 028 7082 4444; Fax 028 7082 2256; dayout@dunlucecentre.freeserve.co.uk; www.touristnetuk.com/ni/dunluce

Countryside Centre – Open June-Aug, daily except Tues, 10am-6pm; Sept, telephone for opening times. No charge. Parking. ☎ 028 7082 3600; www.nics.gov.uk/ehs/

Dunluce Castle – (HM) Open Apr-Sep, daily except Mon, 10am (12pm Sun, Jun-Aug; 2pm Sun, Apr-May and Sept) to 6pm; Oct-Mar, Tue-Sun and hol Mon, 10am (2pm Sun) to 4pm. Last admission 30min before closing. £1.50, reductions available. Audio-guide in foreign languages £1. Parking.

Bushmills Distillery – (&) Guided tour (1hr) Apr-Oct, Mon-Sat, 9.30am-5.30pm, Sun, midday-5.30pm (4pm last tour); Nov-Mar, Mon-Fri, at 10.30am, 11.30am, 1.30pm, 2.30pm, 3.30pm. £3.50, reductions available. Parking. Wheelchair access to Visitor Centre, shops, restaurant. ☎ 028 2073 1521; Fax 028 2073 1339; www.irish-whiskey-trail.com

Benvarden House – Open Jun-Aug, Tue-Sun and bank hol Mon, 1.30pm-5pm. No dogs. £2.50, reductions available. ☎ 028 2074 1331.

Leslie Hill Open Farm – (&) Open Easter-May, Sun and bank hols, 2-6pm; Jun, Sat-Sun, 2-6pm; Jul-Aug, Mon-Sat, 11am-6pm; Sep, Sun, 2-6pm. £2.90, reductions available. Tearoom. Shop. ☎ 028 2766 6803.

Hezlett House – (NT) (&) Guided tour (40min; max 15 people) Jun-Aug, daily except Tue, 12-5pm; Apr-May and Sep, Sat-Sun and public hols, 12-5pm; Good Fri-Easter Tue, daily, 12-5pm. Last tour 30min before closing. £1.80, reductions available. Parking. Wheelchair access to ground floor. ☎/Fax 028 7084 8567.

Downhill Castle – (NT) Grounds: daily, sunrise-sunset. Mussenden Temple: Open Jul-Aug, daily, midday-6pm; Apr-Jun and Sep, Sat-Sun and public hols, midday-6pm; Good Fri to Easter Tue, midday-6pm. No charge. Parking. Picnics welcome. ☎ 028 7084 8728.

S

SPERRIN MOUNTAINS

🛈 The Burnavon, Burn Road, Cookstown – BT80 8TA –
☎ 028 8676 6727 – Fax 028 8676 5853
🛈 Council Offices, 7 Connell Street, Limavady – BT49 0HA – ☎ 028 7776 0307 – Fax 028 7772 2010
🛈 1 Market Street, Omagh – BT78 1EE – ☎ 028 8224 7831 – Fax 028 8224 0774
🛈 Abercorn Square, Strabane – BT82 8AE – ☎ 028 7188 3735 – Fax 028 7138 2264 (seasonal)

Sperrin Heritage Centre – Open Apr-Oct, Mon-Sat, 11.30am-6pm, Sun 2pm-7pm. Last admission 45min before closing. £2.15, reductions available. Audio-guide (French, German). Parking. Refreshments. ☎ 028 8164 8142.

Springhill – (NT) (♿) Open Jul-Aug, daily except Thur, 2-6pm; Apr-Jun and Sep, Sat-Sun and public hols, 2-6pm; Good Fri to Easter Tue, daily, 2-6pm. £2.75, reductions available. Parking. Refreshments. Wheelchair access to ground floor; sympathetic hearing scheme. ☎/Fax 028 8674 8210.

Wellbrook Beetling Mill – (NT) Open Jul-Aug, daily except Tue, 2-6pm; Apr-Jun and Sep, Sat-Sun and public hols, 2-6pm; Good Fri to Easter Tue, daily, 2-6pm. £2, reductions available. Guided tour (30min). Leaflet (French, German). Parking. ☎ 028 8675 1715; Fax 028 8675 1735.

Drum Manor Forest Park – ♿ *Open daily, 8am-10pm (4.30pm winter). £1, £2.50 (car). Guided tour by appointment. Parking. Refreshments. Caravan and camping site.* ☎ *028 8775 9311.*

Ulster Plantation Centre, Draperstown – Open Easter-Sept, Mon-Sat, 10am-5pm, Sun, 1-5pm; Oct-Easter, Mon-Fri, 10am-5pm. ☎ 028 7962 7800; Fax 028 7962 7732; info@theflightoftheearlsexperience; www.theflightoftheearlsexperience

Ulster-American Folk Park – ♿ Open Easter to late-Sep, Mon-Sat, 10.30am-6pm, Sun and public hols, 11am-6.30pm; Oct-Easter, Mon-Fri, 10.30am-5pm. Last admission 90min before closing. £4, reductions available. Brochure (French, German). Parking. Café; picnic area. ☎ 028 8224 3292; Fax 028 8224 2241; uafp@iol.ie; www.folkpark.com

Ulster History Park – ♿ Open Apr-Sept, daily, 10am-5.30pm (6.30pm Jul-Aug); Oct-Mar, Mon-Fri, 10am-5pm. Last admission 1hr before closing. £3.75. Guided tour (2hr). Brochure (French, German, Spanish). Parking. Refreshments; picnic area; cafeteria. ☎ 028 8164 8188; Fax 028 8164 8011; www.omagh.gov.uk/historypark.htm.

Gortin Glen Forest Park – Open daily, 10am-sunset. £2.50 (car). Guided tour (1hr) by appointment. Parking. Play area for children. Picnic areas; barbecue by arrangement. Campsite £1.70 per person/night. ☎ 028 8164 8217; Fax 028 8164 8070.

Gray's Printing Press – (NT) ♿ Open Apr-Sep, Tues-Sat, 2-5pm. Closed bank hols. £2, reductions available. Audio-visual presentation. Guided tour (1hr) by arrangement. ☎ 028 7188 4094.

Wilson Ancestral Home – Open daily, 1-6pm; ring the bell and wait.

Roe Valley Country Park – Open daily. Visitor Centre: Open summer, daily, 10am-8pm; winter, Mon-Fri, 10am-5pm. Guided tours organized by the environmental educator (☎ 028 7167 532). ☎ 028 7772 2074.

Dungiven Priory – (HM) Open daily. No charge. ☎ 028 9054 3037.

Maghera Old Church – (HM) Key from the Recreation Centre (reception) in St Lurach's Road, east of Bank Square. ☎ 028 9054 3037

STRANGFORD LOUGH

🄸 31 Regent Street, Newtownards – ☎ 028 9182 6846 – Fax 028 9182 6681
🄸 The Stables, Castle Street, Portaferry – ☎ 028 4272 9882 – Fax 028 4272 9822

Castle Ward Opera Festival – Information from ☎ 028 66 1090.

Strangford Narrows Car Ferry – Operates daily (except 25 Dec), every 30min. From Strangford (on the hour and half-hour) Mon-Fri, 7.30am-10.30pm, Sat, 8am-11pm, Sun, 9.30am-10.30pm. From Portaferry (15min past and 15min to the hour) Mon-Fri, 7.45am-10.45pm, Sat, 8.15am-11.15pm, Sun, 9.45am-10.45pm. Car £4.20; passenger 85p, 45p (child); motorcycle £2.70. ☎ 028 4488 1637; Fax 028 4488 1249.

Strangford Tower House – (HM) Key from the house opposite. ☎ 028 9054 3037.

Kilclief Castle – (HM) Open Apr-Sep, Tue-Sun, 10am (2pm Sun) to 6pm. 75p, 40p (concession). ☎ 028 9054 3037.

Castle Ward – (NT) ♿ House: Guided tour (1hr) Jun-Aug, daily except Thur, 1-6pm; Apr (from Easter), May and Sep-Oct, Sat-Sun and bank hols, 1-6pm; Good Fri to Low Sun, 1-6pm. £2.60, reductions available. Estate and Grounds: Open daily, during daylight hours. Car £3.50; £1.75 (out of season). Strangford Lough Wildlife Centre: Open as house, 1pm-5pm (6pm Sat-Sun). Adventure playground. Parking. Tearoom. ☎ 028 4488 1204.

Quoile Countryside Centre – ♿ Open Apr-Sept, daily, 11am-5pm; Oct-Mar, Sat-Sun, 1-5pm. Closed 1 Jan, 25-26 Dec. No charge. Parking. Wheelchair access to new birdhide. ☎ 028 4461 5520; Fax 028 4461 3280.

Inch Abbey – (HM) Open Apr-Sep, daily except Mon, 10am (2pm Sun) to 7pm; Oct-Mar, Sat, 10am-1.30pm. £1, 50p (concession). Parking. ☎ 028 9054 3037.

Lightship Ballydorn, Strangford Lough

Delamont Country Park – Open daily, 9am-sunset. Adventure playground. Look-out tower. Orienteering. Boat trips. Pony trekking routes. Plant sales. Parking. Tea room; picnic area. Gift shop. ☎/Fax 028 4482 8333 (Park Warden).

Nendrum Monastery – (HM) Open Apr-Sept, daily except Mon, 10am (2pm Sun) to 7pm. 75p, 40p (concession). Parking. ☎ 028 9054 3037.

Wildfowl and Wetlands Centre (Castle Espie) – ♿ Open Mar-Oct, Mon-Sat, 10.30am-5pm, Sun, 11.30am-6pm; Nov-Feb, Mon-Fri, 11.30am-4.15pm, Sat, 11.30am-4.30pm, Sun, 11.30am-5pm. Closed 24-25 Dec. £3.50, reduction available. Bird-hides. Education centre. Parking. Coffee room. ☎ 028 9187 4146; Fax 028 9187 3857.

Scrabo Country Park and Tower – (♿) Country park: Open daily. Scrabo Tower: Open Easter and Jun-Sep, daily except Fri, 10.30am-6pm. No charge. Parking. ☎ 028 9181 1491; Fax 028 9182 0695 (Warden).

Grey Abbey – (HM) Open Apr-Sep, Tue-Sat, 10am-7pm; Oct-Mar, Sat-Sun, 10am (2pm Sun) to 4pm. £1, reductions available. Guided tour (30min). Parking. ☎ 028 4278 8585 (Supervisor), 028 9054 3037 (Historic Monuments, Belfast).

Exploris – Portaferry Aquarium – ♿ Open daily, 10am (11am Sat, 1pm Sun) to 6pm (5pm Sep-Mar). £3.95, reductions available. Visitor map and guide (French, German, Spanish). Parking. Café. Gift shop. Ramp; lifts. ☎ 028 4272 8062; Fax 028 4272 8396.

Index

A

434